THE ESSAY CONNECTION

THE ESSAY CONNECTION

Readings for Writers

TENTH EDITION

Lynn Z. Bloom
The University of Connecticut

WADSWORTH
CENGAGE Learning·

Australia • Brazil • Japan • Korea • Mexico • Singapore • Spain • United Kingdom • United States

WADSWORTH
CENGAGE Learning·

The Essay Connection,
Tenth Edition
Lynn Z. Bloom

Senior Publisher: Lyn Uhl

Publisher: Monica Eckman

Acquiring Sponsoring Editor: Kate Derrick

Development Editor: Kathy Sands Boehmer

Assistant Editor: Cat Salerno

Editorial Assistant: Abbie Rickard

Media Editor: Cara Douglass-Graff

Marketing Manager: Melissa Holt

Marketing Coordinator: Brittany Blais

Marketing Communications Manager: Linda Yip

Print Buyer: Betsy Donaghey

Manufacturing Manager: Marcia Locke

Rights Acquisitions Specialist: Jessica Elias

Cover Designer: Nicole Sage Steiner

Cover Image: www.agefotostock.com

Art and Cover Direction, Production Management, and Composition: PreMediaGlobal

Library of Congress Control Number: 2011938977

ISBN-13: 978-0-8400-3007-8

ISBN-10: 0-8400-3007-X

Wadsworth
20 Channel Center St.
Boston, MA 02210
USA

Cengage Learning is a leading provider of customized learning solutions with office locations around the globe, including Singapore, the United Kingdom, Australia, Mexico, Brazil and Japan. Locate your local office at **international.cengage.com/region**

Cengage Learning products are represented in Canada by Nelson Education, Ltd.

For your course and learning solutions, visit **www.cengage.com**.

Purchase any of our products at your local college store or at our preferred online store **www.cengagebrain.com**.

Instructors: Please visit **login.cengage.com** and log in to access instructor-specific resources.

Printed in the United States of America
1 2 3 4 5 6 7 15 14 13 12 11

Brief Contents

Contents

✦ Student author

PART III *CLARIFYING IDEAS* 226

6. Description 226

12. Human Rights and World Peace: Universal Declaration of Human Rights, and Nobel Peace Prize Speeches   568

Topical Table of Contents

IDENTITY

✦   Student writings.

GROWING UP/FAMILIES/HERITAGE

WORK AND PLAY

TURNIING POINTS/WATERSHED EXPERIENCES

NATURAL WORLD/ECOLOGY

SCIENCE AND TECHNOLOGY

ETHICS/HUMAN RIGHTS

EDUCATION

LANGUAGE, DIGITAL MEDIA, LITERATURE, THE ARTS

HUMOR AND SATIRE

CREATIVE WRITING/GRAPHIC ESSAYS

Graphic Essays/Graphic Argument

Creative Nonfiction

Fiction

Poetry

Preface: Transforming a Textbook for a Transformed World

Like the symbolic bridge on the cover of this book, *The Essay Connection* attempts to span the distance between reading and writing and bring the two activities closer together. To read, to write is to be human, to find the voice, the power, and the authority to communicate. As we become immersed in a new century, the importance of communication—clear, elegant, to the point—has never been more important.

"Writing," observes Toni Morrison, "is discovery; it's talking deep within myself." In *The Essay Connection*, the voices in this conversation are many and varied—professional writers, experts in a variety of fields, and students with their own abilities and experiences, side by side. Their good writing is good reading in itself, provocative, elegant, engaging, sometimes incendiary. This writing is also a stimulus to critical thinking, ethical reflection, social and political analysis, humorous commentary—and decision-making, on how to live in the present and make meaningful contributions to life in the ever-changing yet uncertain future. These are among the many possibilities when students write essays of their own. This Tenth Edition is designed not only to keep up with major changes but also to anticipate them.

What's Familiar, What's New

In the spirit of renovating an elegant building, the changes made to this edition of *The Essay Connection* retain the fundamental character of its distinguished architecture while bringing the work fully into the present.

Reading Images

Photographs, illustrations, cartoons, and other graphics often travel in the company of words, and so they do in highly significant ways in the revised *Essay Connection*, holding up their share of the dialogue. This edition features more—and more diverse—visual elements than ever before, with more photographs accompanying individual essays, more visual arguments, and a full color insert on ecological issues.

Graphic Essays, Cartoons, and Op-art   Graphic essays are demanding and often more complicated than they appear to be at first glance. They tell a story, make a point—or more stories with more points— sometimes with no words at all, as in the cartoon narratives of Lynda Barry's "Common Scents," Art Spiegelman's "Mein Kampf," and Roz Chast's "An Excerpt from Men Are from Belgium, Women Are from New Brunswick."

Some clusters of graphic works are chosen to reflect and refract on one another, forming a visual commentary in juxtaposition. Thus the cluster "Reading Icons" incorporates a photograph of sculptor Auguste Rodin's famous statue, the massive "Thinker," bent and brooding, with Mike Peters's good-natured cartoon sequence of three alternatives, "The Nail Biter," "The Thumb Sucker," and "The Nose Picker"—its meaning, and humor, dependent on the viewer's knowledge of the original. Istvan Banyai's "Inflation" makes its argument through and about bodies. In this cartoon Banyai equates ballooning inflation, in this case, in the cost of postage with increasing obesity: something will eventually explode. "The Road to Success" (1913) is a visual allegory graphically representing a mountain of impediments, such as Lack of Preparation, undermined by the River of Failure. The Right System provides the path and ultimately the railroad route through True Knowledge to the pinnacle of Success. Other cartoon sequences in juxtaposition offer ethical critiques: Open's op-art depiction of worsening constraints on air travel ("We've eliminated all cargo compartments . . ."), and Garry Trudeau's satire on student partying, now starting "on Wednesday night."

Photographs As Arguments, As Advocacy   The diverse photographs in the Tenth Edition range from the historical (the escort of black children to a newly integrated school during the Civil Rights era) to the timeless (school children posing for a class photo) to the contemporary (a firefighter drinking from a hydrant in front of the collapsing World Trade Center; beachgoers sunbathing near a makeshift memorial to the Iraq War dead). All of the pictures in *The Essay Connection* can be interpreted literally but also gain meaning from their contexts. Thus Dorothea Lange's haunting photograph of the beautiful "Migrant Mother" surrounded by her children echoes scores of classical iconic

Madonna-and-child paintings, transmuted into the harsh 1930s Depression era. Although questions and commentary accompany each image, readers are encouraged to bring their own understanding to the stories they tell.

Color Photo Essay The eight color photographs in the photo essay, *The Environment: Save It or Lose It*, illustrate the worldwide significance of ecological issues. The Grand Tetons reflected in a pristine lake look stunningly beautiful, as does an illuminated globe photographed from outer space, until we realize that its brightness comes from lights in heavily populated areas such as the one epitomized in the photograph of "Seven Million Londoners" at Oxford Circus. The insert shows that the term **ecology** itself is no longer value-free. For the other photographs illuminate the detrimental effects of contemporary civilization on the environment: adjacent sections of Haiti and the Dominican Republic, brown versus green; overcrowding at Yellowstone National Park that requires buffalo to cross the road, halting a line of tourists' cars; a mountain of wrecked cars—what will become of them? What, in fact, will become of Earth itself, as the glaciers melt, the Amazon burns? These photographs ask the questions; international cooperation (or the lack thereof) will furnish the answers.

Other Readings

The readings in the Tenth Edition of *The Essay Connection* are a lively, varied, timely, and provocative blend of favorite essays, modern and contemporary works, and new selections by a wide range of writers in a wide range of genres, including creative nonfiction and poetry. The first two chapters discuss the phenomena which have become progressively more interrelated as the current generation of digital natives reaches college. Section One, "On Communication—Writing and Social Media" in the first chapter addresses "The Writing Process" itself: "Reading, Motivation, Warmup, Vision, Re-vision." Chapter 2, new to the Tenth Edition, focuses on "Social Media—Thinking, Reading, Writing in an Electronic Era," because in the twenty-first century social media are intimately intertwined with the writing process. Chapters 3–10 are organized according to familiar rhetorical principles: *narration, process analysis, cause and effect, description, definition, comparison and contrast,* and *argument* (which is covered in two separate chapters, dealing first with deductive and inductive arguments and then with emotional and ethical appeals). The concluding chapters, 11 and 12, are mini-casebooks, brief collections of thematically related essays on *"Identity" and "Human Rights and World Peace."*

New and Familiar Authors   Among the essays new to this edition of *The Essay Connection* are those by Nicholas Carr, Brian Doyle, Barbara Ehrenreich, Scott McCloud and Toni Morrison, as well as the United Nations *Universal Declaration of Human Rights*. Significant representations of women, cultures, and writers who address issues of class, race, ethnicity, and disability have been retained; new are considerations of social media, identity, the environment, and health. Many favorite essays have been retained from the previous edition. Although humorous works by authors such as Sherman Alexie, Mark Twain, Ntozake Shange, and David Sedaris signal the book's upbeat tone, as well as by cartoonists such as Lynda Barry, Roz Chast, Ji Li, and Art Spiegelman, they do not diminish the seriousness of the book's essential concerns or its underlying ethical stance.

Creative Nonfiction   The label *creative nonfiction* makes explicit in this edition of *The Essay Connection* what real writers have known all along, that many writers use the techniques of fiction to tell true stories. As two distinguished pieces, student Amanda N. Cagle's "On the Banks of the Bogue Chitto" and Meredith Hall's "Killing Chickens" reveal, these techniques include a narrator or narrative voice, plot, characters, dialogue, and setting. Other autobiographical essays use these techniques to provide social commentary and critique with a human face, a human voice—Frederick Douglass's "Resurrection," Scott Russell Sanders's "Under the Influence: Paying the Price of My Father's Booze," and Dr. Martin Luther King, Jr.'s "Letter from Birmingham Jail."

Fiction   There are two works of fiction in this edition of *The Essay Connection*. Tim O'Brien's "How to Tell a True War Story" is a chapter of his Vietnam War novel *The Things They Carried*, and Jonathan Safran Foer's "Here we Aren't, So Quickly." Readers believe that the creative nonfiction works by Cagle and Hall are true because the authors say so, even though these works read like stories. Fiction writers send the same signals: they use character, plot, dialogue, settings, and symbols to explore multiple themes in works we are not expected to regard as literally true. Yet even while O'Brien is giving us advice on "How to

Tell a True War Story," he is pointing out the ambiguity of the truth, the blurred line between fact and fiction, which concurrently compels our belief—and calls it into question. Foer's photo-montage technique, juxtaposing short clips of a couple's life history from adolescence through courtship, marriage, parenthood to an indefinite middle age, is more clearly fictive; reading at a normal pace offers a fast combination of images that combine to show "Here We Aren't, So Quickly." Foer lets his readers fill in the blanks.

Poetry   The five poems in this new edition of *The Essay Connection* provide powerful, condensed, forthright commentary on the rhetorical theme of the chapters they begin, and on the topics discussed in the essays they accompany. All are by distinguished contemporary writers: Mary Oliver's "August," about a happy immersion in summer's bounty; V. Penelope Pelizzon's "Clever and Poor," the story of her parents' deceptive courtship, in which cleverness conceals poverty; Janice Mirikitani's satiric "Recipe" for anglo "Round Eyes"; Marilyn Nelson's "Friends in the Klan," from a biographical series on George Washington Carver.

Mini-Casebooks   Chapter 11 addresses "Identity": international, national, and individual. Who we are, as individuals, students, members of families, ethnicities, citizens of a particular place and of the world, comprises an identity that is ever changing as the world's values, priorities, and very survival are in flux. Chapter 12, on "Human Rights and World Peace," is composed of the "United Nations Universal Declaration of Human Rights" and excerpts from Nobel Peace Prize acceptance speeches by men and women of global distinction who form an international spectrum of the brave, the bold, the morally beautiful. Their talks, like their works, are beacons of faith, hope, goodwill, and moral courage. Intended to provoke discussion and debate on substantial issues, the essays in these chapters reflect not only on one another, but also on many other essays throughout this book and on the illustrations as well, including those that comprise the color photo essay.

Student Authors   Twelve distinguished essays and one creative nonfiction piece (Amanda N. Cagle's "On the Banks of the Bogue Chitto,") are by students. Although all the works were written when the students were enrolled in American universities, the students themselves come from all over the United States and the world at large. They discuss a variety of compelling subjects: growing up (Scott Allison) and coming to terms with oneself and one's values (Matt Nocton). Some are comically self-deprecating (Jason Verge); others present serious interpretations of abilities and disabilities earned in war (Sheryl Kennedy), or through being either overweight (Meaghan Roy-O'Reilly), or skeletal (Ryan O'Connell). Essays by Ning Yu, Megan McGuire, and Zara Rix address other issues of identity—with intertwined themes of ethnicity, religion, class—political, social and economic, in ways that provide increased understanding of one's heritage and one's family members. Cabell Hankinson Gathman and Tim Stobierski explore the advantages, liabilities and complication of digital technology; while Matthew Allen analyzes apparent objectivity in scientific writing. All provide examples of excellent writing that other students will find meaningful as models in form, technique, and substance.

Support for Critical Thinking, Reading, and Writing

The essays are placed in a context of materials designed to encourage reading, critical thinking, and good writing. The following materials reinforce *The Essay Connection's* pervasive emphasis on the process(es) of writing.

- **Topical Clusters.** Many readings are clustered thematically within the chapters to encourage dialogue and debate among authors, and among student readers and writers. For example, Chapter 6, "Description," introduces the joys of eating in Mark Twain's "Uncle John's Farm," followed by reflections on nutrition in Marion Nestle's interpretive analysis, "Eating Made Simple" (the good, the bad, the problematic food groups) and Michael Pollan's "The Meal," an indictment of fast food, reinforced by Kim Warp's cartoon, "Rising Sea Levels—an Alternative Theory." Two essays in Chapter 8, "Comparison and Contrast," further complicate issues of eating and body size, Suzanne Britt's "That Lean and Hungry Look" (she extols "a hot fudge sundae for easing tension") and student Meagan McGuire's "Wake Up Call," where the children in her family forage for the food their mother has neglected to provide. Chapter 10, "Appealing to Emotions and Ethics," addresses issues of identity—individual, ethnic, racial—in Janice Mirikitani's poem, "Recipe" for Western "Round Eyes"; Abraham Lincoln's "Gettysburg Address"; and Jonathan Swift's "Modest Proposal."

That identity is intertwined with human rights and the very survival of individuals, climates, and nations is reinforced as these essays are juxtaposed with Peter Singer's "The Singer Solution to World Poverty" and Edward Hoagland's "Children Are Diamonds." Other topics, reiterated and refracted in various chapters, include ecology, civil and human rights, war and peace, and—ever and always—how to read, write, and think with clarity, elegance, honesty.

- **Blended Essay Types.** It is essential to remember that because these are real essays by real writers, who use whatever writing techniques suit their purpose, there are very few "pure" types: they illustrate not only the rhetorical mode that is the focus of the chapter, but others as well. For instance, Scott Russell Sanders's "Under the Influence: Paying the Price of My Father's Booze," in the *cause and effect* chapter, also incorporates *descriptions* of his alcoholic father's behavior, an *explanation* and *analysis* of "the family secret," an analysis of the *causes and effects* of his father's problem on his own life. "Under the Influence" also presents a powerful argument against drinking, both implied (as in the portrait of Sanders's father, himself under the influence and his problematic influence on his wife and children) and overt (as in facts and figures "In the United States alone, some ten or fifteen million people share his ailment...." That most essays are a mixture of types and techniques is reflected in the *Mixed Modes* category the study questions. Throughout the book, *Mixed Modes* should serve as a realistic reminder of the nature and the complexity of the works at hand.
- **Tables of Contents.** The main Table of Contents reflects the book's organization, by types of writing. The Topical Table of Contents offers an alternative organization by subject to provide numerous other possibilities for discussion and writing.
- **Chapter introductions.** These define the particular type of writing in the chapter and identify its purposes (descriptions, process analysis, etc.), uses, and typical forms. They also discuss the rhetorical strategies authors typically use in that type of writing (for instance, how to structure an argument to engage a hostile audience), illustrated with reference to essays in the chapter, summarized in a concluding checklist.
- **Author biographies.** These capsule biographies are intended to transform the writers from names into real people, focusing on how, why, and what the authors write.

- **Study questions.** These follow the essays and are intended to encourage thoughtful discussion and writing about *Content,* rhetorical *Strategies/Structures/Language,* and larger concerns. These are addressed by a series of writing and discussion prompts: "Journal Writing"; "Dialogues," which call attention to similar themes or literary devices in the essay just read and one or more others; "Mixed Modes," which help students consider the diverse rhetorical concepts embedded in a single essay; and "Second Look," which put the focus on how the photographs, cartoons, and other visual elements in the book relate to the text selections and encourage students to analyze them as they would a written text.
- **Suggestions for Writing.** Each set of study questions ends with *Suggestions for Writing* pertinent to a given work. Most chapters end with a longer list of *Additional Topics for Writing* that encourage dialogue and debate about essays related in theme, technique, or mode. Often these incorporate **multiple strategies for writing in a given mode** and ways to avoid potential pitfalls.

Companion Website for *The Essay Connection,* 10th Edition
www.login.cengage.com for instructors
www.cengagebrown.com for students
The Essay Connection's companion website offers additional resources for writing and research, including author web links; visual literacy activities; an annotated student essay; interactive flashcard of glossary terms; and practice quizzes that test reading comprehension. Instructors are also able to access an online Instructor's Resource Manual and sample syllabi.

Infotrac® College Edition with InfoMarks™
PAC ISBN-10: 0534558534 | ISBN-13: 9780534558536
InfoTrac® College Edition, an online research and learning center, offers over 20 million full-text articles from nearly 6000 scholarly and popular periodicals. The articles cover a broad spectrum of disciplines and topics—ideal for every type of researcher.
www.cengage.com/infotrac (Access code/card is required.)

Enhanced InSite for Composition
2-semester IAC: 0495898910 PAC: 0195898929
1-semester IAC: 1111679444 PAC: 1111679452

This online writing and research tool includes electronic peer review, an originality checker, an assignment library, help with common grammar and writing errors, and access to InfoTrac® College Edition. Portfolio management gives you the ability to grade papers, run originality reports, and offer feedback in an easy-to-use online course management system. Using InSite's peer review feature, students can easily review and respond to their classmates' work. Other features include fully integrated discussion boards, streamlined assignment creation, and more. Visit www.cengage.com/insite to view a demonstration.

Turnitin® Originality Checker
PAC (1-semester) ISBN-10: 1413030181 | ISBN-13: 9781413030181
PAC (2-semester) 978-1-4130-3019-8

This proven online plagiarism-prevention software promotes fairness in the classroom by helping students learn to correctly cite sources and allowing instructors to check for originality before reading and grading papers. Visit www.cengage.com/turnitin for more information. (Access code/card required.)

WebTutor Toolbox
Backboard PAC: 978-0-534-27489-4 IAC: 978-0-534-27491-7
Webct PAC: 978-0-534-27488-7 IAC: 978-0-534-27490-0

Acknowledgments

The Essay Connection has, in various ways, been in the making for the past forty years, and I am particularly indebted to the candid commentaries of multitudes of writing teachers and students over the years whose preferences and perplexities have so significantly influenced both the shape and emphasis of this volume, and the process-oriented style of teaching that it reflects.

I am also indebted to the reviewers who contributed to the development of the Tenth Edition of *The Essay Connections*:

Yvonne Bruce, John Carroll University; LeJeanne Raymond, Richard Bland College; Jean Roberts, Old Dominion University; Tony Spicer, Eastern Michigan University; and Amy Towne, Florida Gulf Coast University.

Scott Allison, University of Connecticut writing intern, contributed significantly to every aspect of this Tenth Edition, from its initial outline through countless revisions and rewrites. In addition, as a student reader he vetted every selection, new and retained; and he is the author of an exemplary student essay, "Picturesque." His work built on the previous editions prepared with the help of superb research assistants, Sarah Appleton, Kathrine Aydelott, Matthew Simpson, Valerie M. Smith, Laura Tharp, Ning Yu, and Denise M. Lovett, who also prepared the Instructor's Guide.

Cengage Learning staff: Lyn Uhl, Publisher; Kate Derrick, Sponsoring Editor; Kathy Sands-Boehmer, Development Editor. All have aided the creation of this edition with goodwill, good humor, and good sense.

When the first edition of *The Essay Connection* was in process, my sons, Laird and Bard, contributors to that volume, were in high school. Over the intervening years they've earned doctorates (in biology and computer science), have married inspiring women, Sara (a U.S. attorney) and Vicki (a food scientist), and parented joyous children, Paul, Beth, and Rhys. An ever-active participant in the protracted process of making *The Essay Connection* more friendly to readers has been my writer-friendly husband, Martin Bloom, social psychologist, professor, world traveler, fellow author, and most recently, artist. He has provided a retentive memory for titles and key words that I've called out from an adjacent lane during our daily lap swims, the collage du jour, homemade apple pies at bedtime, and all the comforts in between. My whole family keeps me cheerful; every day is a gift.

Lynn Z. Bloom

University of Connecticut

THE ESSAY
CONNECTION

The Writing Process: Reading, Motivation, Warmup, Vision, Re-Vision

Warmup: Getting Started

To expect some people to learn to write by showing them a published essay or book is like expecting novice bakers to learn to make a wedding cake from looking at the completed confection, resplendent with icing and decorations. Indeed, the completed product in each case offers a model of what the finished work of art should look like—in concept, organization, shape, and style. Careful examination of the text exposes the intricacies of the finished sentences, paragraphs, logic, illustrative examples, and nuances of style. The text likewise provides cues about the context (intellectual, political, aesthetic . . .) in which it originated, its purpose, and its intended audience. But no matter how hard you look, it's almost impossible to detect in a completed, professionally polished work much about the process by which it was composed—the numerous visions and revisions of ideas and expression; the effort, frustration, even exhilaration; whether the author was composing in bed, at a desk, or at a computer terminal. Blood, sweat, and tears don't belong on the printed page any more than they belong in the gymnast's flawless public performance on the balance beam. The audience wants not to agonize over the production but to enjoy the result.

Becoming a Writer

For better and for worse, computers and other manifestations of electronic technology influence the ways we think, read, and write as we will see in Chapter 2, "Social Media—Thinking, Reading, Writing in

An Electronic Era". For college students, writing provides innumerable opportunities both for processing what you're already been exposed to and escaping from it. You can help yourself focus if you shut out the distractions—other people's words arriving by screen, headphones, or music, and colors and images moving in and through your peripheral vision.

As you start to work, urges Stephen King in "A door . . . you are willing to shut", find a private writing space, keeping people and other distractions out and yourself in. "The closed door is your way of telling the world and yourself that you mean business; you have made a serious commitment to write. . . ." King suggests you settle on a "daily writing goal" and get to work.

For many people, the most difficult part of writing is getting started. It's hard to begin if you don't know what to write about. Sometimes people make lists to generate and sort out ideas.

You may end up writing a piece—preferably short—composed entirely of lists. Even if you simply go somewhere and take notes on what you see, once you've organized them into categories that make logical or artistic sense, you've got the start—if not the finish—of a paper.

Writers' Notebooks

Keeping a writer's diary or notebook, whether you do it with pencil, pen, computer, or even cell phone, can be a good way to get started—and even to keep going. Writing regularly—and better yet, at a designated time of the day or week, can give you a lot to think about while you're writing, and a lot to expand on later. You could keep an account of what you do every day (6:30–7:30, swimming laps, shower; 7:30–8:15, breakfast—toasted English muffin, orange juice, raspberry yogurt . . .), but if your life is routine, that might get monotonous.

A provocative and potentially useful writer's notebook might contain any or all of the following types of writing, and more:

- Reactions to one's reading
- Provocative quotations—invented, read, or overheard; appealing figures of speech; dialogue, dialect
- Lists—including sights, sounds, scents
- Memorable details—of clothing, animals, objects, settings, phenomena, processes
- Personal aspirations, fears, joy, anger
- Sketches of people, either intrinsically interesting or engaged in intriguing activities, whether novel or familiar
- Analyses of friendships, family relationships
- Commentary on notable events, current or past, national or more immediate
- Possibilities for adventure, exploration, conflict
- Jokes, anecdotes, and humorous situations, characters, comic mannerisms, punch lines, provocative settings

You'll need to put enough explanatory details in your notebook to remind yourself three weeks—or three years—later what something meant when you wrote it down. In a writer's notebook you can be most candid, most off guard, for there you are writing primarily for yourself. You're also writing for yourself when you are freewriting—writing rapidly, with or without a particular subject, without editing, while you're in the process of generating ideas. As you freewrite you can free-associate, thinking of connections among like and unlike things or ideas, exploring their implications. Anything goes into the notebook, but not everything stays in later drafts if you decide to turn some of your most focused discussion into an essay. If you get into the habit of writing regularly on paper, you may find that you are also hearing the "voices in your head" that professional writers often experience. As humorist James Thurber explained to an interviewer, "I never quite know when I'm not writing. Sometimes my wife comes up to me at a party and says, 'Dammit, Thurber, stop writing.' Or my daughter will look up from the dinner table and ask, 'Is he sick?' 'No,' my wife says, 'he's writing something.'"

Playing around with words and ideas in a notebook or in your head can also lead to an entire essay: a narrative, character sketch, reminiscence, discussion of how to do it, an argument, review, or some other form suitable for an extended piece of writing.

No matter what you write about, rereading a notebook entry or a freewriting can provide some material to start with. Ask yourself, "What do I want to write about?" "What makes me particularly happy—or angry?" Don't write about something that seems bland. If it doesn't appeal to you, it will not attract your readers either. As you write you will almost automatically be using description, narration, comparison and contrast, and other rhetorical techniques to express yourself, even if you don't attach labels to them.

Re-Vision and Revision

The pun is intentional. *Re-vision* and *revision* both mean, literally, "to see again." Writers have a passionate commitment to their work. Because they are fully invested in their writing, mind, heart, and spirit, they care enough about it to be willing to rewrite again and again and again until they get it right—in subject and substance, structure and style.

Of course, this example is meant to inspire you, as well, to be willing "to see again." When you take a second, careful look at what you wrote as a freewriting or a first draft, chances are you'll decide to change it. If and when you do, you're approaching the process that most professional writers use—and your own work will be one step closer to professional. As playwright Neil Simon says, "Rewriting is when writing really gets to be fun. . . . In baseball you only get three swings and you're out. In rewriting, you get almost as many swings as you want and you know, sooner or later, you'll hit the ball."

Some people think that revision means correcting the spelling and punctuation of a first—and only—draft. Writers who care about their work know that such changes, though necessary, are editorial matters remote from the heart of real revising. For to revise is to rewrite and rewrite again, though not in the spirit that Calvin tells Hobbes in the cartoon, making bad writing incomprehensible. Novelist Toni Morrison affirms, "The best part of all, the absolutely most delicious part, is finishing it and then doing it over. . . . I rewrite a lot, over and over again, so that it looks like I never did. I try to make it look like I never touched it, and that takes a lot of time and a lot of sweat." In "Strangers" (7–10) Morrison explores the process by which we make meaning, how we interpret "strangers," strange people, phenomena. We fear that strangers will "Disturb. Betray. Prove they are not like us" (¶ 4). But when we look more closely we realize that "there are no strangers. There are only versions of ourselves, many of which we have not embraced, most of which we wish to protect ourselves from." But the reader's job, the writer's job, is to "romance those strangers back into our own mirrors," to make and keep them human.

When you rewrite, you are doing what computer language identifies as *insert, delete, cut and paste* (reorganize), and *edit*. The concept of "draft" may have become elusive for people writing on a computer; one part of a given document may have been revised extensively, other parts may be in various stages of development, while still others have yet to be written. For simplicity's sake, we'll use the term *draft* throughout *The Essay Connection* to refer to one particular version of a given essay (whether the writer considers it finished or not), as opposed to other versions of that same document. Even if you're only making a grocery list, you might add and subtract material, or change the organization. If your original list identified the items in the order they occurred to you, as lists often do, you could regroup them according to your route through the supermarket by categories of similar items: produce, staples, meat, dairy products, providing extra details when necessary—"a pound of Milagro super-hot green chilies" and "a half gallon of Death by Chocolate ice cream."

Some writers compose essentially in their minds. They work through their first drafts in their heads, over and over, before putting much—if anything—down on paper. As Joyce Carol Oates says, "If you are a writer, you locate yourself behind a wall of silence and no matter what you are doing, driving a car or walking or doing housework . . . you can still be writing." There is a lot of revising going on, but it's mostly mental. What appears on the paper the first time is what stays on the paper, with occasional minor changes. This writing process appears to work best with short pieces that can easily be held in the mind—a poem, a writing with a fixed and conventional format (such as a lab report), a short essay with a single central point, a narrative in which each point in the sequence reminds the writer of what comes next, logically, chronologically, psychologically. If you write that way, then what we say about revising on paper should apply to your mental revising, as well.

Other writers use a first draft, and sometimes a second, and a third, and more, to enable themselves to think on paper. Novelist E. M. Forster observed, "How do I know what I think until I see what I say?" How you wrote the first draft may provide cues about what will need special attention when you revise. If you use a first draft to generate ideas, in revising you'll want to prune and shape to arrive at a precise subject and focus, and an organization that reinforces your emphasis. Or your first draft may be a sketch, little more than an outline in paragraph form, just to get down the basic ideas. In revising, you'd aim to flesh out this bare-bones discussion by elaborating on these essential points, supplying illustrations, or consulting references that you didn't want to look up the first time around. On the other hand, you may typically write a great deal more than you need, just to be sure of capturing random and stray ideas that may prove useful. Your revising of such an ample draft might consist, in part, of deleting irrelevant ideas and redundant illustrations.

Donald M. Murray suggests a three-stage revision process that you might find helpful in general, whether or not you've settled on your own particular style of revising:

1. A quick first reading "to make sure that there is a single dominant meaning" and enough information to support that meaning.
2. A second quick reading, only slightly slower than the first, to focus on the overall structure and pace.
3. A third reading, "slow, careful, line-by-line editing of the text . . . here the reader cuts, adds, and reorders, paragraph by paragraph, sentence by sentence, word by word" (*Write to Learn*, Fort Worth, TX: Harcourt, 1993, 167).

First you look at the forest, then at the shape and pattern of the individual trees, then close up, at the branches and leaves. Although this may sound slow and cumbersome, if you try it, you'll find that it's actually faster and easier than trying to catch everything in one laborious reading, alternating between panoramic views and close-ups.

John Trimble, in *Writing with Style* (Englewood Cliffs, N.J.: Prentice Hall, 1975), offers a number of suggestions for writing in a very readable style that work equally well for first drafts as well as for revision. Trimble's cardinal principles are these: (1) Write as if your reader is a "companionable friend" who appreciates straightforwardness and has a sense of humor. (2) Write as if you were "talking to that friend," but had enough time to express your thoughts in a concise and interesting manner. He also suggests that if you have written three long sentences in a row, make the fourth sentence short. Even very short. Use contractions. Reinforce abstract discussions with "graphic illustrations, analogies, apt quotations, and concrete details." To achieve continuity, he advises, make sure each sentence is connected with those preceding and following it. And, most important, "Read your prose aloud. *Always* read your prose aloud. If it sounds as if it's come out of a machine or a social scientist's report . . . spare your reader and rewrite it."

Ernest Hemingway has said that he "rewrote the ending of *A Farewell to Arms*, the last page of it, thirty-nine times before I was satisfied"— which means a great deal of rewriting, even if you don't think he kept exact count.

"Was there some technical problem?" asked an interviewer. "What had you stumped?"

"Getting the words right," said Hemingway.

This is the essence of revision.

With look and thought you will end up with, as Brian Doyle illustrates, "The Greatest"—in this case "Nature Essay Ever." Wow! (25–27)

Strategies for Revising

1. Does my draft have a *thesis*, a focal point? Does the thesis cover the entire essay, and convey my attitude toward the subject?
2. Does my draft contain sufficient *information and evidence* to support that meaning? Is the writing developed sufficiently, or do I need to provide additional information, steps in an argument, illustrations, or analysis of what I've already said?
3. Who is my intended *audience*? Will they understand what I've said? Do I need to supply any background information? Will I meet my readers as friends, antagonists, or on neutral ground? How will this relationship determine what I say, the order in which I say it, and the language I use?
4. Do the *form* and *structure* of my writing suit the subject? (For instance, would a commentary on fast-food restaurants be more effective in an essay or description, comparison and contrast, analysis, some combination of the three—or as a narrative or satire?) Does the *proportioning* reinforce my emphasis (in other words, do the most important points get the most space)? Or do I need to expand some aspects and condense others?
5. Is the writing recognizably mine in *style*, *voice*, and *point of view*? Is the body of my prose like that of an experienced runner: tight and taut, vigorous, self-contained, and supple? Do I like what I've said? If not, am I willing to change it?

READING IMAGES

TONI MORRISON

Toni Morrison (born in 1931 in Lorain, Ohio), was educated at Howard University (BA, 1953) and Cornell, where she wrote a much-quoted 1955 Master's thesis on suicide in the works of Virginia Woolf and William Faulkner. After teaching at Texas Southern (1955-57) and Howard (1957-64) universities, she began an eighteen year editorial career at Random House while developing a parallel career as a distinguished novelist. She currently holds an endowed humanities professorship at Princeton. Critic Trudier Harris says, "If the last two decades of the twentieth century could be called the age of African-American women writers, then Toni Morrison can be credited with creating the yardstick by which others are measured . . . as author, critic, lecturer, teacher, and public servant." In subject matter, intensity, and innovation, her literary stature is comparable to that of James Joyce or William Faulkner, and as disturbing of readers' comfort zones.

Morrison's debut novel, *The Bluest Eye* (1970), was a harbinger of her courageous, unflinching treatment of racism and sexism, technically and stylistically sophisticated. In this work, black eleven-year-old Pecola believes that blue eyes, the epitome of whiteness, will make her beautiful and popular. Instead, she is rejected by everyone. Her father rapes and impregnates her; insanity is her tragic refuge. Morrison's novels *Sula* (1973), *Song of Solomon* (1977), *Tar Baby* (1981) were bestsellers. *Beloved* (1987) won national and international awards, including the Pulitzer Prize. *Beloved*, the story of a runaway slave who kills one of her children, the title character (and tries to kill her other three) in order to keep them from slavery, is a complicated interweaving of the themes of slavery, flight, guilt, love, motherhood, heritage, history, and redemption. For these and *Jazz* (1992) Morrison was awarded the Nobel Prize in Literature in 1993.

"Strangers" is Morrison's introduction to Robert Bergman's collection of photographs, *A Kind of Rapture* (1998). Here she reaffirms her understanding—exemplified in *Beloved*—that "there are no strangers. There are only versions of ourselves, many of which we have not embraced, most of which we wish to protect ourselves from. For the stranger is not foreign, she is random, not alien but remembered . . ."

Strangers

I AM IN THIS river place—newly mine—walking in the yard when I see   1
a woman sitting on the seawall at the edge of a neighbor's garden. A homemade fishing pole arcs into the water some twenty feet from her

hand. A feeling of welcome washes over me. I walk toward her, right up to the fence that separates my place from the neighbor's, and notice with pleasure the clothes she wears: men's shoes, a man's hat, a well-worn colorless sweater over a long black dress. The woman turns her head and greets me with an easy smile and a "How you doing?" She tells me her name (Mother Something) and we talk for some time—fifteen minutes or so—about fish recipes and weather and children. When I ask her if she lives there, she answers no. She lives in a nearby village, but the owner of the house lets her come to this spot any time she wants to fish, and she comes every week, sometimes several days in a row when the perch or catfish are running and even if they aren't because she likes eel, too, and they are always there. She is witty and full of the wisdom that older women always seem to have a lock on. When we part, it is with understanding that she will be there the next day or very soon after and we will visit again. I imagine more conversations with her. I will invite her into my house for coffee, for tales, for laughter. She reminds me of someone, something. I imagine a friendship, casual, effortless, delightful.

2   She is not there the next day. She is not there the following days, either, And I look for her every morning. The summer passes, and I have not seen her at all. Finally, I approach the neighbor to ask about her and am bewildered to learn that the neighbor does not know who or what I am talking about. No old woman fished from her wall—ever—and none had permission to do so. I decide that the fisherwoman fibbed about the permission and took advantage of the neighbor's frequent absences to poach. The fact of the neighbor's presence is proof that the fisherwoman would not be there. During the months following, I ask lots of people if they know Mother Something. No one, not even people who have lived in nearby villages for seventy years, has ever heard of her.

3   I feel cheated, puzzled, but also amused, and wonder off and on if I have dreamed her. In any case, I tell myself, it was an encounter of no value other than anecdotal. Still. Little by little, annoyance then bitterness takes the place of my original bewilderment. A certain view from my windows is now devoid of her, reminding me every morning of her deceit and my disappointment. What was she doing in that neighborhood, anyway? She didn't drive, had to walk four miles if indeed she lived where she said she did. How could she be missed on the road in that hat, those awful shoes? I try to understand the intensity of my chagrin, and why I am missing a woman I spoke to for fifteen minutes. I get nowhere except for the stingy explanation that she had come into my space (next to it, anyway—at the property line, at the edge, just at the fence, where the most interesting things always happen), and had implied promises of female camaraderie, of opportunities for me to be generous, of protection and protecting. Now she is gone, taking with her my good opinion of myself, which, of course, is unforgivable.

4   Isn't that the kind of thing that we fear strangers will do? Disturb. Betray. Prove they are not like us. That is why it is so hard to know

what to do with them. The love that prophets have urged us to offer the stranger is the same that Jean-Paul Sartre[1] could reveal as the very mendacity of Hell. The signal line of "No Exit," *"L'enfer, c'est les autres,"* raises the possibility that "other people" are responsible for turning a personal world into a public hell. In the admonition of a prophet and the sly warning of an artist, strangers as well as the beloved are understood to tempt our gaze, to slide away or to stake claims. Religious prophets caution against the slide, the looking away; Sartre warns against love as possession.

The resources available to us for benign access to each other, for vaulting the mere blue air that separates us, are few but powerful: language, image, and experience, which may involve both, one, or neither of the first two. Language (saying, listening, reading) can encourage, even mandate, surrender, the breach of distances among us, whether they are continental or on the same pillow, whether they are distances of culture or the distinctions and indistinctions of age or gender, whether they are the consequences of social invention or biology. Image increasingly rules the realm of shaping, sometimes becoming, often contaminating, knowledge. Provoking language or eclipsing it, an image can determine not only what we know and feel but also what we believe is worth knowing about what we feel.

These two godlings, language and image, feed and form experience. My instant embrace of an outrageously dressed fisherwoman was due in part to an image on which my representation of her was based. I immediately sentimentalized and appropriated her. I owned her or wanted to (and I suspect she glimpsed it). I had forgotten the power of embedded images and stylish language to seduce, reveal, control. Forgot, too, their capacity to help us pursue the human project—which is to remain human and to block the dehumanization of others.

But something unforeseen has entered into this admittedly oversimplified menu of our resources. Far from our original expectations of increased intimacy and broader knowledge, routine media presentations deploy images and language that narrow our view of what humans look like (or ought to look like) and what in fact we are like. Succumbing to the perversions of media can blur vision, resisting them can do the same. I was clearly and aggressively resisting such influences in my encounter with the fisherwoman. Art as well as the market can be complicit in the sequestering of form from formula, of nature from artifice, of humanity from commodity. Art gesturing toward representation has, in some exalted quarters, become literally beneath contempt. The concept of what it is to be human has altered, and the word *truth* needs quotation marks around it so that its absence (its elusiveness) is stronger than its presence.

---

[1]French existentialist philosopher and playwright (1905–1980) from *No Exit* (1944) may be translated as "Hell is other people."

8   Why would we want to know a stranger when it is easier to estrange another? Why would we want to close the distance when we can close the gate? Appeals in arts and religion for comity in the Common Wealth are faint.

9   It took some time for me to understand my unreasonable claims on that fisherwoman. To understand that I was longing for and missing some aspect of myself, and that there are no strangers. There are only versions of ourselves, many of which we have not embraced, most of which we wish to protect ourselves from. For the stranger is not foreign, she is random, not alien but remembered; and it is the randomness of the encounter with our already known—although unacknowledged—selves that summons a ripple of alarm. That makes us reject the figure and the emotions it provokes—especially when these emotions are profound. It is also what makes us want to own, govern, administrate the Other. To romance her, if we can, back into our own mirrors. In either instance (of alarm or false reverence), we deny her personhood, the specific individuality we insist upon for ourselves.

10   Robert Bergman's radiant portraits of strangers provoked this meditation. Occasionally, there arises an event or a moment that one knows immediately will forever mark a place in the history of artistic endeavor. Bergman's portraits represent such a moment, such an event. In all its burnished majesty his gallery refuses us unearned solace, and one by one by one the photographs unveil *us,* asserting a beauty, a kind of rapture, that is as close as can be to a master template of the singularity, the community, the unextinguishable sacredness of the human race.

Content

1. What is the significance of Morrison's title, "Strangers"?

2. "Provoking language or eclipsing it, an image can determine not only what we know and feel but also what we believe is worth knowing about what we feel" (¶ 5). Pick an image you love. Why is this so important to you? Why do you love it? What language do you use to talk about it? Does your reaction to this image validate Morrison's observation?

3. Morrison says "language and image feed and form experience" (¶ 6). Explain. In what ways do your own responses to a particular image influence your later experiences of this phenomenon?

4. Why is the image of the fisherwoman (¶ 1) so important to Morrison? Does it matter whether or not the woman really existed? Morrison says she "sentimentalized and appropriated" the "outrageously dressed fisherwoman" to her own purposes. "I owned her" (¶ 6). In what ways did she do this? Is it ethically wrong to impose our own interpretations on people we don't know?

5. Morrison argues against letting the media "blur" the viewer's vision by "deploy[ing] images and language that narrow our view of what humans look like (or ought to look like)." How can viewers—of images, photographs,

media–maintain sufficient independence of mind and vision to avoid falling for the cliches and conventions of media stereotypes?

Strategies/Structures/Language

6. In what ways does Morrison use the "outrageously dressed fisherwoman" as a symbol? Identify several interpretations of this symbol.

7. Words attempt to translate visual symbols into language. With what advantages? Drawbacks?

For Writing

8. *Journal writing.* Find two or three intriguing images of people whom you don't know and paste them into your notebook. What about these images fascinates you? Invent a background, a history, for each person. What clues are you using to make your case? How much of these stories are projections on your part? If you later learn of the identities of these people, how closely does the reality conform to your imaginative version?

9. *Dialogue.* Compare your discussion of Morrison's "Strangers" with the analysis of icons by Rodin, Peters, and D'Angelo, that follows (pp. 12–13)

10. *Second look.* To the extent that we know ourselves, we recognize and respect our uniqueness. How can we, as viewers, readers, and writers allow to others–images, people we see, the "specific individuality we insist upon for ourselves" (¶ 9).

READING ICONS

RODIN, *The Thinker*

Auguste Rodin made the original cast of his iconic sculpture, "The Thinker," in 1880. It was cast as a large bronze in 1902. During his lifetime Rodin authorized the production of as many casts of each of his sculptures as the market would bear, in various sizes; there were, for instance, 319 casts of "The Kiss." Thus, if you have seen one you have not seen them all, although since 1956 French law has limited the production of casts to twelve of each sculpture. The small bronze depicted here is owned by the Iris and Gerald B. Cantor Foundation, which since 1945 has collected, lent, and sold some 750 of Rodin's works to museums and universities. Does the ubiquity of this sculpture detract from its significance? Would you prefer to think of any given work of art as unique, even though many reproductions of beloved works are available?

MIKE PETERS, *Mother Goose and Grimm*

To be famous is to provoke imitation and satire, even if the original object, work, or person is beloved. Even if viewers don't have a photograph of Rodin's original "The Thinker" at hand, the cartoonist, Mike Peters, is counting on them to recognize the model for his spinoffs. Does the fact that we're expected to laugh at the cartoon affect the way we view the original? Why or why not? Does the juxtaposition of the sculpture and the cartoon create a resonance of the way we read each work that wouldn't exist if we read each in isolation?

MIKE D'ANGELO, *Do-It-Yourself Emoticons*

Obvious	More Nuanced	Sophisticated, Subtle
;-) wink	O+ female	~:-) baby
:-(sad	O-> male	,,-,,/"> dog
:-< really sad	8-I nerd	**,,-,,/"> French poodle
:-I bored	*:-I thinking	:-I:-I deja vu
:-\ undecided	:-# don't tell anyone	(::O::) bandaid; offering help
}{ face to face	:-$ embarrassed	=):-)= Uncle Sam

The potential for passion lies in your very fingertips as they tippy-tap over your computer keys. We've all used some of those naked icons of emotion—the smiley face :-)*, the laugh* :-D*, and others such as those identified in the "Obvious" column above. Advanced communicators may have tried "More Nuanced" versions in the middle column, or perhaps* ^5 *(high five) or* : ^D *("Great!", or "I like it"). With a little practice, you too can create your own emoticons, as seen in the "Sophisticated, Subtle" column. Once you've seen "dog" and "French poodle," you could move on to* ~~,,----,,/"> *(skunk); to get a snake, you might have to tilt the screen. If you've laid down* I**-------I *(bed and pillow), you can put someone in it:* I**O-/-----/I.

Content

1. Rodin's figure *The Thinker* has become an iconic symbol of intellectual activity. Why is Peters's rendering of other, less cerebral but equally solitary activities humorous? Can you translate the visual joke into words? In what ways do the figures' facial expressions contribute to the viewer's understanding of the joke?

2. *The Thinker* suggests that thinking is a physical activity separate from writing. How do Peters's labels contribute to the humor of the image? Wouldn't the activity of each sculpture be obvious without the label? What is the significance of the position of each figure's head and the expression on each figure's face?

3. The sculptor is not dressed as Rodin, an early twentieth-century sculptor, might have been. What image of the sculptor does the cartoon convey? What does the cartoonist's rendering of the artist and the museum's representative suggest about the cartoonist's image of himself? What does the cartoon suggest about our culture's perception of thinking and of art?

4. How does emoticon, a form of graphic art that transforms text into images, fill in the gaps in textual electronic communications? Why might the adult reader find emoticon a foreign concept?

Strategies/Structures/Language

5. Describe the process of reading a cartoon. What information do you need to bring to Peters's cartoon to understand its humor?

6. To learn to read and write a series of emoticon symbols would be like learning another language. Is this practical? Why use emoticon? Under what circumstances? Are emoticon symbols here to stay?

7. What is the point of the increasing complexity of the emoticon symbols? How does D'Angelo's arrangement of the symbols ask the reader to participate in the construction of meaning?

For Writing

8. *Journal Writing.* Find a cartoon or a short comic strip, perhaps on the Internet, that you find particularly interesting. What information does the cartoon or comic ask you to contribute in order to understand it? How does language help the image create meaning for the viewer? What the image and the language leave unstated? Compare the cartoon or comic strip you have chosen with Kim Warp's "Rising Sea Levels—An Alternative Theory" (266). What knowledge does each image ask you to supply? How does Warp's rendering of her characters add to the humor of the cartoon? Alternatively, compare your cartoon or comic strip to Lynda Barry's "Common Scents." How do Barry's characters' physiognomy, physique, and speech expand and develop the narrator's commentary?

9. *Dialogues.* In "Reading the Comics" (132–34), Scott McCloud illustrates how the artist and the reader collaborate as "partners in crime" to provide "closure" on the characters depicted in action. They thereby cooperate in interpreting the character's "inner life," "visual distinction," and "expressive traits" that McCloud elaborates on throughout his work. How does the viewer deduce these qualities of the artist and the museum representative in Peters's Mother Goose and Grimm cartoon (12)?

ELIE WIESEL

Elie Wiesel (1928–), a survivor of the Holocaust, explains, "For me, literature abolishes the gap between [childhood and death]. . . . Auschwitz marks the decisive, ultimate turning point . . . of the human adventure. Nothing will ever again be as it was. Thousands and thousands of deaths weigh upon every word. How speak of redemption after Treblinka? and how speak of anything else?" As a survivor, he became a writer in order to become a witness: "I believed that, having survived by chance . . . I knew the story had to be told. Not to transmit an experience is to betray it." Wiesel has developed a literary style that reflects the distilled experience of concentration camps, in which "a sentence is worth a page, a word is worth a sentence. The unspoken weighs heavier than the spoken. . . . Say only the essential—say only what no other would say . . . a style sharp, hard, strong, in a word, pared. . . . Speak as a witness on the stand speaks. With no indulgence to others or oneself."

In May 1944, when he was fifteen, Wiesel was forcibly removed from his native town of Sighet, Hungary ("which no longer exists," he says, "except in the memory of those it expelled"), to the first of several concentration camps. Although six million Jews died in the camps, including members of his family, Wiesel was liberated from Buchenwald in April 1945 and sent to Paris, where he studied philosophy. For twenty years he worked as a journalist for Jewish newspapers, but the turning point in his career as a writer came in 1954 when he met novelist François Mauriac, who urged him to speak on behalf of the children in concentration camps. This encouraged Wiesel (who has lived in New York since 1956) to write some forty books of fiction, nonfiction, poetry, and drama, starting in 1958 with *Night*, which opens, "In the beginning was faith, confidence, illusion." He published his memoirs *All the Rivers Run to the Sea* in 1995, and *And the Sea Is Never Full* in 1999. Wiesel, true citizen of the world, named Jewish "Humanitarian of the Century," received the Nobel Peace Prize in 1986 for his efforts epitomized in "Why I Write: Making No Become Yes," originally published in the *New York Times Book Review*, April 14, 1986.

Why I Write: Making No Become Yes

W hy do I write? 1

Perhaps in order not to go mad. Or, on the contrary, to touch the 2 bottom of madness. Like Samuel Beckett, the survivor expresses himself "en désepoir de cause"—out of desperation.

Speaking of the solitude of the survivor, the great Yiddish and Hebrew 3 poet and thinker Aaron Zeitlin addresses those—his father, his brother, his friends—who have died and left him: "You have abandoned me," he says to them. "You are together, without me. I am here. Alone. And I make words."

So do I, just like him. I also say words, write words, reluctantly. 4

There are easier occupations, far more pleasant ones. But for the sur- 5 vivor, writing is not a profession, but an occupation, a duty. Camus calls it "an honor." As he puts it: "I entered literature through worship." Other writers have said they did so through anger, through love. Speaking for myself, I would say—through silence.

It was by seeking, by probing silence that I began to discover the per- 6 ils and power of the word. I never intended to be a philosopher, or a theologian. The only role I sought was that of witness. I believed that, having survived by chance, I was duty-bound to give meaning to my survival, to justify each moment of my life. I knew the story had to be told. Not to transmit an experience is to betray it. This is what Jewish tradition teaches us.

© Brian Steidle

The United States Holocaust Memorial Museum provides ongoing exhibits of "man's inhumanity to man" wherever, whenever it occurs in the world. These exhibits serve as witnesses to genocide through photographs, sound and text, background information, and suggestions about how people worldwide can help the living victims, and "help the dead vanquish death," as Wiesel explains. Brian Steidle's photograph from the exhibit "In Darfur my camera was not nearly enough," shows the beginning of the burning of the village of Um Zeifa, Darfur, Sudan in 2004, after being looted and attacked by the Janjaweed. This government-supported militia, along with Sudanese government soldiers, has waged ethnic war— murdering tens of thousands of African ethnic groups, raping thousands of women, and driving over 1.5 million civilians from their homes, torching their villages and looting their property. What is the point, the hope, the expectation of exposing audiences in America—including yourselves as students—to such pictures?

But how to do this? "When Israel is in exile, so is the word," says the Zohar. The word has deserted the meaning it was intended to convey—impossible to make them coincide. The displacement, the shift, is irrevocable.

7   This was never more true than right after the upheaval. We all knew that we could never, never say what had to be said, that we could never express in words, coherent, intelligible words, our experience of madness on an absolute scale. The walk through flaming night, the silence before and after the selection, the monotonous praying of the condemned, the Kaddish of the dying, the fear and hunger of the sick, the shame and suffering, the haunted eyes, the demented stares. I thought that I would never be able to speak of them. All words seemed inadequate, worn, foolish, lifeless, whereas I wanted them to be searing.

Where was I to discover a fresh vocabulary, a primeval language? The 8
language of night was not human, it was primitive, almost animal—hoarse
shouting, screams, muffled moaning, savage howling, the sound of beating.
A brute strikes out wildly, a body falls. An officer raises his arm and a whole
community walks toward a common grave. A soldier shrugs his shoulders,
and a thousand families are torn apart, to be reunited only by death. This was
the concentration camp language. It negated all other language and took its
place. Rather than a link, it became a wall. Could it be surmounted? Could
the reader be brought to the other side? I knew the answer was negative, and
yet I knew that "no" had to become "yes." It was the last wish of the dead.

The fear of forgetting remains the main obsession of all those who 9
have passed through the universe of the damned. The enemy counted on
people's incredulity and forgetfulness. How could one foil this plot? And
if memory grew hollow, empty of substance, what would happen to all we
had accumulated along the way? Remember, said the father to his son, and
the son to his friend. Gather the names, the faces, the tears. We had all taken
an oath: "If, by some miracle, I emerge alive, I will devote my life to testify-
ing on behalf of those whose shadow will fall on mine forever and ever."

That is why I write certain things rather than others—to remain 10
faithful.

Of course, there are times of doubt for the survivor, times when one 11
gives in to weakness, or longs for comfort. I hear a voice within me telling
me to stop mourning the past. I too want to sing of love and of its magic.
I too want to celebrate the sun, and the dawn that heralds the sun. I would
like to shout, and shout loudly: "Listen, listen well! I too am capable of victory, do you hear? I too am open to laughter and joy! I want to stride, head
high, my face unguarded, without having to point to the ashes over there
on the horizon, without having to tamper with facts to hide their tragic ugliness. For a man born blind, God himself is blind, but look, I see, I am not
blind." One feels like shouting this, but the shout changes to a murmur.
One must make a choice; one must remain faithful. A big word, I know.
Nevertheless, I use it, it suits me. Having written the things I have written,
I feel I can afford no longer to play with words. If I say that the writer in
me wants to remain loyal, it is because it is true. This sentiment moves all
survivors; they owe nothing to anyone, but everything to the dead.

I owe them my roots and my memory. I am duty-bound to serve 12
as their emissary, transmitting the history of their disappearance, even if
it disturbs, even if it brings pain. Not to do so would be to betray them,
and thus myself. And since I am incapable of communicating their cry by
shouting, I simply look at them. I see them and I write.

While writing, I question them as I question myself. I believe I have 13
said it before, elsewhere. I write to understand as much as to be understood. Will I succeed one day? Wherever one starts, one reaches darkness.
God? He remains the God of darkness. Man? The source of darkness. The
killers' derision, their victims' tears, the onlookers' indifference, their

complicity and complacency—the divine role in all that I do not understand. A million children massacred—I shall never understand.

14   Jewish children—they haunt my writings. I see them again and again. I shall always see them. Hounded, humiliated, bent like the old men who surround them as though to protect them, unable to do so. They are thirsty, the children, and there is no one to give them water. They are hungry, but there is no one to give them a crust of bread. They are afraid, and there is no one to reassure them.

15   They walk in the middle of the road, like vagabonds. They are on the way to the station, and they will never return. In sealed cars, without air or food, they travel toward another world. They guess where they are going, they know it, and they keep silent. Tense, thoughtful, they listen to the wind, the call of death in the distance.

16   All these children, these old people, I see them. I never stop seeing them. I belong to them.

17   But they, to whom do they belong?

18   People tend to think that a murderer weakens when facing a child. The child reawakens the killer's lost humanity. The killer can no longer kill the child before him, the child inside him.

19   But with us it happened differently. Our Jewish children had no effect upon the killers. Nor upon the world. Nor upon God.

20   I think of them, I think of their childhood. Their childhood is a small Jewish town, and this town is no more. They frighten me; they reflect an image of myself, one that I pursue and run from at the same time—the image of a Jewish adolescent who knew no fear, except the fear of God, whose faith was whole, comforting, and not marked by anxiety.

21   No, I do not understand. And if I write, it is to warn the reader that he will not understand either. "You will not understand, you will never understand," were the words heard everywhere during the reign of night. I can only echo them. You, who never lived under a sky of blood, will never know what it was like. Even if you read all the books ever written, even if you listen to all the testimonies ever given, you will remain on this side of the wall, you will view the agony and death of a people from afar, through the screen of a memory that is not your own.

22   An admission of impotence and guilt? I do not know. All I know is that Treblinka and Auschwitz cannot be told. And yet I have tried. God knows I have tried.

23   Have I attempted too much or not enough? Among some twenty-five volumes, only three or four penetrate the phantasmagoric realm of the dead. In my other books, through my other books, I have tried to follow other roads. For it is dangerous to linger among the dead, they hold on to you and you run the risk of speaking only to them. And so I have forced myself to turn away from them and study other periods, explore other destinies and teach other tales—the Bible and the Talmud, Hasidism and its fervor, the shtetl and its songs, Jerusalem and its echoes,

the Russian Jews and their anguish, their awakening, their courage. At times, it has seemed to me that I was speaking of other things with the sole purpose of keeping the essential—the personal experience—unspoken. At times I have wondered: And what if I was wrong? Perhaps I should not have heeded my own advice and stayed in my own world with the dead.

But then, I have not forgotten the dead. They have their rightful 24 place even in the works about the Hasidic capitals Ruzhany and Korets, and Jerusalem. Even in my biblical and Midrashic tales, I pursue their presence, mute and motionless. The presence of the dead then beckons in such tangible ways that it affects even the most removed characters. Thus they appear on Mount Moriah, where Abraham is about to sacrifice his son, a burnt offering to their common God. They appear on Mount Nebo, where Moses enters solitude and death. They appear in Hasidic and Talmudic legends in which victims forever need defending against forces that would crush them. Technically, so to speak, they are of course elsewhere, in time and space, but on a deeper, truer plane, the dead are part of every story, of every scene.

"But what is the connection?" you will ask. Believe me, there is one. 25 After Auschwitz everything brings us back to Auschwitz. When I speak of Abraham, Isaac and Jacob, when I invoke Rabbi Yohanan ben Zakkai and Rabbi Akiba, it is the better to understand them in the light of Auschwitz. As for the Maggid of Mezeritch and his disciples, it is in order to encounter the followers of their followers that I reconstruct their spellbound, spellbinding universe. I like to imagine them alive, exuberant, celebrating life and hope. Their happiness is as necessary to me as it was once to themselves.

And yet—how did they manage to keep their faith intact? How did 26 they manage to sing as they went to meet the Angel of Death? I know Hasidim who never vacillated—I respect their strength. I know others who chose rebellion, protest, rage—I respect their courage. For there comes a time when only those who do not believe in God will not cry out to him in wrath and anguish.

Do not judge either group. Even the heroes perished as martyrs, 27 even the martyrs died as heroes. Who would dare oppose knives to prayers? The faith of some matters as much as the strength of others. It is not ours to judge, it is only ours to tell the tale.

But where is one to begin? Whom is one to include? One meets a 28 Hasid in all my novels. And a child. And an old man. And a beggar. And a madman. They are all part of my inner landscape. The reason why? Pursued and persecuted by the killers, I offer them shelter. The enemy wanted to create a society purged of their presence, and I have brought some of them back. The world denied them, repudiated them, so I let them live at least within the feverish dreams of my characters.

It is for them that I write, and yet the survivor may experience re- 29 morse. He has tried to bear witness; it was all in vain.

30   After the liberation, we had illusions. We were convinced that a new world would be built upon the ruins of Europe. A new civilization would see the light. No more wars, no more hate, no more intolerance, no fanaticism. And all this because the witnesses would speak. And speak they did, to no avail.

31   They will continue, for they cannot do otherwise. When man, in his grief, falls silent, Goethe says, then God gives him the strength to sing his sorrows. From that moment on, he may no longer choose not to sing, whether his song is heard or not. What matters is to struggle against silence with words, or through another form of silence. What matters is to gather a smile here and there, a tear here and there, a word here and there, and thus justify the faith placed in you, a long time ago, by so many victims.

32   Why do I write? To wrench those victims from oblivion. To help the dead vanquish death.

(Translated from the French by Rosette C. Lamont)

Content

1. Wiesel says, "The only role I sought [as a writer] was that of witness" (¶ 6). What does he mean by "witness"? Find examples of this role throughout the essay.

2. What does Wiesel mean by "not to transmit an experience is to betray it" (¶ 6)? What experience does his writing transmit? Why is this important to Wiesel? To humanity? Does "Why I Write" fulfill Wiesel's commitment to "make no become yes" (¶ 8)? Explain.

Strategies/Structures/Language

3. Identify some of Wiesel's major ethical appeals in this essay. Does he want to move his readers to action as well as to thought?

4. Why would Wiesel use paradoxes in an effort to explain and clarify? Explain the meaning of the following paradoxes:

   a. "No, I do not understand. And if I write, it is to warn the reader that he will not understand either" (¶ 21).
   b. I write "to help the dead vanquish death" (¶ 32).

5. For what audience does Wiesel want to explain "Why I Write"? What understanding of Judaism does Wiesel expect his readers to have? Of World War II? Of the operation of concentration camps? Why does he expect his reasons to matter to these readers, whether or not they have extensive knowledge of any of them?

6. Does Wiesel's style here fulfill his goals of a style that is "sharp, hard, strong, pared"? Why is such a style appropriate to the subject?

7. Explain the meaning of "concentration camp language" (¶ 8). Why did it negate all other language and take its place (¶ 8)?

For Writing

8. ***Journal Writing.*** Make a list of reasons to write. Which reasons appeal to you the most? Why? Is the form of writing (electronic, pen, or pencil) important to you? Do you find certain occasions more conducive to writing? What sources of inspiration do you find most powerful?

9. ***Dialogues.*** Elie Wiesel's motive for writing comes from a sense of duty; of witnessing the Holocaust "to give meaning to my survival" (¶ 6). Why do you write when you are not required to do so in school? How do these motives differ? Does the quality of the writing depend on the writer's motives? Is all writing in a sense personal? Is all writing in a sense moral?

10. Consider Wiesel's descriptions of Jewish children's experience of persecution and impending death during the Holocaust (¶s 14–20). Compare Wiesel's choice of descriptive language with Suzanne Britt's in "That Lean and Hungry Look" and with Martin Luther King, Jr.'s description of the social condition of African Americans in "Letter from Birmingham Jail" (399–413). How does each author use specific language to generalize about the condition of a group of people? How does each author's choice of language shape the reader's perception of that group?

11. ***Second Look.*** How might the scope and arrangement of Brian Steidle's photograph in this essay illustrate Wiesel's question, "Have I attempted too much or not enough?" (¶ 23)?

12. What experiences, in your view, are so powerful that they must not be forgotten? Do such experiences require what Wiesel calls "a fresh vocabulary" (¶ 8)? Do you find that language is inadequate to the task of conveying a particularly painful or joyful experience? How might you supplement word choice to allow a reader to understand a particularly significant experience?

STEPHEN KING

"People want to be scared," says Stephen King (born 1947, a.k.a. Richard Bachman and John Swithen), but "beneath its fangs and fright wig," horror fiction is quite conservative, for readers understand that "the evildoers will almost certainly be punished." After working as a janitor, mill hand, and laundry laborer, King graduated from the University of Maine (BA, 1970) and taught high school English briefly while writing his enormously popular first novel, *Carrie* (1974). This inaugurated a career-long series of bestsellers, including *The Shining* (1977), *From a Buick 8* (2002), *Lisey's Story* (2006), and *Under the Dome* (2009) as well as short stories, film, and video scripts characterized by a mix of horror, fantasy, science fiction, and humor. In June 1999 he was hit by a car while taking his habitual walk along a Maine highway. During his long recuperation from serious injuries he wrote *On Writing: A Memoir of the Craft* (2000), in which "A door . . . you are willing to shut" appears.

"Once I start to work on a project," explains King, "I don't stop and I don't slow down. . . . I write every day, workaholic dweeb or not. That includes Christmas, the Fourth [of July], and my birthday." Not working, he says, "is the real work. When I'm writing, it's all the playground, and the worst three hours I ever spent there were still pretty damn good." The work starts, he says, by finding "a door . . . you are willing to shut," avoiding distractions such as telephones and video games. "Put your desk in the corner, and every time you sit down there to write, remind yourself of why it isn't in the middle of the room. Life isn't a support-system for art. It's the other way around."

"A door . . . you are willing to shut"

1   You can read anywhere, almost, but when it comes to writing, library carrels, park benches, and rented flats should be courts of last resort—Truman Capote said he did his best work in motel rooms, but he is an exception; most of us do our best in a place of our own. Until you get one, you'll find your new resolution to write a lot hard to take seriously.

2   Your writing room doesn't have to sport a Playboy Philosophy decor, and you don't need an Early American rolltop desk in which to house your writing implements. I wrote my first two published novels, *Carrie* and *'Salem's Lot*, in the laundry room of a doublewide trailer, pounding away on my wife's portable Olivetti typewriter and balancing a child's desk on my thighs; John Cheever reputedly wrote in the basement of his Park Avenue apartment building, near the furnace. The space can be humble (probably *should* be, as I think I have already suggested), and it really needs only one thing: a door which you are willing to shut. The closed door is your way of telling the world and yourself that you mean business; you have made a serious commitment to write and intend to walk the walk as well as talk the talk.

3   By the time you step into your new writing space and close the door, you should have settled on a daily writing goal. As with physical exercise, it would be best to set this goal low at first, to avoid discouragement. I suggest a thousand words a day, and because I'm feeling magnanimous, I'll also suggest that you can take one day a week off, at least to begin with. No more; you'll lose the urgency and immediacy of your story if you do. With that goal set, resolve to yourself that the door stays closed until that goal is met. Get busy putting those thousand words on paper

or on a floppy disk. In an early interview (this was to promote *Carrie*, I think), a radio talk-show host asked me how I wrote. My reply—"One word at a time"—seemingly left him without a reply. I think he was trying to decide whether or not I was joking. I wasn't. In the end, it's always that simple. Whether it's a vignette of a single page or an epic trilogy like *The Lord of the Rings*, the work is always accomplished one word at a time. The door closes the rest of the world out; it also serves to close you in and keep you focused on the job at hand.

If possible, there should be no telephone in your writing room, certainly no TV or videogames for you to fool around with. If there's a window, draw the curtains or pull down the shades unless it looks out at a blank wall. For any writer, but for the beginning writer in particular, it's wise to eliminate every possible distraction. If you continue to write, you will begin to filter out these distractions naturally, but at the start it's best to try and take care of them before you write. I work to loud music—hard-rock stuff like AC/DC, Guns 'n Roses, and Metallica have always been particular favorites—but for me the music is just another way of shutting the door. It surrounds me, keeps the mundane world out. When you write, you want to get rid of the world, do you not? Of course you do. When you're writing, you're creating your own worlds. 4

I think we're actually talking about creative sleep. Like your bedroom, your writing room should be private, a place where you go to dream. Your schedule—in at about the same time every day, out when your thousand words are on paper or disk—exists in order to habituate yourself, to make yourself ready to dream just as you make yourself ready to sleep by going to bed at roughly the same time each night and following the same ritual as you go. In both writing and sleeping, we learn to be physically still at the same time we are encouraging our minds to unlock from the humdrum rational thinking of our daytime lives. And as your mind and body grow accustomed to a certain amount of sleep each night—six hours, seven, maybe the recommended eight—so can you train your waking mind to sleep creatively and work out the vividly imagined waking dreams which are successful works of fiction. 5

But you need the room, you need the door, and you need the determination to shut the door. You need a concrete goal, as well. The longer you keep to these basics, the easier the act of writing will become. Don't wait for the muse. As I've said, he's a hardheaded guy who's not susceptible to a lot of creative fluttering. This isn't the Ouija board or the spirit-world we're talking about here, but just another job like laying pipe or driving long-haul trucks. Your job is to make sure the muse knows where you're going to be every day from nine 'til noon or seven 'til three. If he does know, I assure you that sooner or later he'll start showing up, chomping his cigar and making his magic. 6

Content

1. Why are "the basics" King identifies—"the room," "the door," "the determination to shut the door," and "a concrete goal"—so important for writing? In your own experience, is each of equal importance? Do you share King's preference for writing with the shades drawn to "loud music—hard-rock stuff"? What is your ideal writing environment? How can you or do you control it?

2. King characterizes the act of "creating your own worlds" as "creative sleep" (¶s 3–4). Does King's view of writing pertain to nonfiction writing? How might you apply his advice to autobiographical writing or a paper on an academic subject?

Strategies/Structures/Language

3. Advice givers often preach. And readers often resent being preached at. King delivers his advice very emphatically. Is he preaching? If he doesn't offend you, will you take his advice?

4. King alludes to the muse of creativity—traditionally considered a beautiful woman playing alluring music—as a male, "chomping his cigar and making his magic" (¶ 6). Why does King choose such a macho muse instead of a more traditional figure? How does this muse relate to King's writing—his subjects and his style?

5. "A door which you are willing to shut" (¶ 2) works on both the literal and metaphorical levels. Explain why this is a good way to get double mileage out of your language.

For Writing

6. *Journal Writing.* Take King's advice and find a private writing space to which you can retreat daily. Write one page (around 250 words) a day for a full week. As the week goes on, try changing some of the features in your environment (write at different times of the day or night, let people or pets in or keep them out, turn the music or TV on or off) and record the effect of each of these changes.

7. *Dialogues.* King emphasizes that discipline ("you need the determination to shut the door" [¶ 6]) is a prerequisite for writing successfully: "make sure the muse knows where you are going to be" (¶ 6). In contrast, Toni Morrison emphasizes the importance of finding the stories behind images, transforming "Strangers" (pp. 7–10) into people familiar to us. How does each writer's definition of the work of getting ideas suggest their motives for writing? If you have read any of King's fiction, discuss how he might have applied his reading of literature generally, of science fiction in particular, and perhaps knowledge he has acquired through reading other types of texts to the work of creating his fictional worlds.

8. *Mixed Modes.* Write an essay that describes the process of how you learned the basics of some activity that you now know how to do well. What did you have to learn first? How did you then build on that skill or knowledge? Where did you go astray? How did you finally achieve the desired result? Do you see any analogies between the process you describe and that of writing? Does writing about the process you have described clarify how you learned from your successes and failures?

BRIAN DOYLE

Brian Doyle is an award-winning essayist and editor of the University of Portland's *Portland Magazine*. He has published work in the *Atlantic Monthly, Orion, Harper's,* and the *Best American Essays* anthologies (1998, 1999, 2003, and 2005). His collections of creative nonfiction include *Saints Passionate and Peculiar* (2002), *Leaping: Revelations and Epiphanies* (2003), and *The Grail: A Year of Ambling and Shambling Through an Oregon Vineyard in Pursuit of the Best Pinot Noir Wine in the Whole Wide World* (2006). His first volume of poems, *Epiphanies and Elegies: Very Short Stories* was published in 2007. "The Greatest Nature Essay Ever," first published in *Orion* (2008) explains in five engaging paragraphs how and why nature essays work, to make "you think, *Man, this is why I read nature essays, to be startled and moved like that, wow.*"

The Greatest Nature Essay Ever

. . . would begin with an image so startling and lovely and wondrous that you   1
would stop riffling through the rest of the mail, take your jacket off, sit down
at the table, adjust your spectacles, tell the dog to lie *down,* tell the kids to make

Dougal Waters/Photodisc/Jupiter Images

---

their *own* sandwiches for heavenssake, that's why god gave you *hands,* and read straight through the piece, marveling that you had indeed seen or smelled or heard *exactly* that, but never quite articulated it that way, or seen or heard it articulated that way, and you think, *man, this is why I read nature essays, to be startled and moved like that, wow.*

2   The next two paragraphs would smoothly and gently move you into a story, seemingly a small story, a light tale, easily accessed, something personal but not self-indulgent or self-absorbed on the writer's part, just sort of a cheerful nutty everyday story maybe starring an elk or a mink or a child, but then there would suddenly be a sharp sentence where the dagger enters your heart and the essay spins on a dime like a skater, and you are plunged into waaay deeper water, you didn't see it coming at all, and you actually shiver, your whole body shimmers, and much later, maybe when you are in bed with someone you love and you are trying to evade his or her icy feet, you think, *my god, stories do have roaring power, stories are the most crucial and necessary food, how come we never hardly say that out loud?*

3   The next three paragraphs then walk inexorably toward a line of explosive Conclusions on the horizon like inky alps. Probably the sentences get shorter, more staccato. Terser. Blunter. Shards of sentences. But there's no opinion or commentary, just one line fitting into another, each one making plain inarguable sense, a goat or even a senator could easily understand the sentences and their implications, and there's no shouting, no persuasion, no eloquent pirouetting, no pronouncements and accusations, no sermons or homilies, just calm clean clear statements one after another, fitting together like people holding hands.

4   Then an odd paragraph, this is a most unusual and peculiar essay, for right here where you would normally expect those alpine Conclusions, some Advice, some Stern Instructions & Directions, there's only the quiet murmur of the writer tiptoeing back to the story he or she was telling you in the second and third paragraphs. The story slips back into view gently, a little shy, holding its hat, nothing melodramatic, in fact it offers a few gnomic questions without answers, and then it gently slides away off the page and off the stage, it almost evanesces or dissolves, and it's only later after you have read the essay three times with mounting amazement that you see quite how the writer managed the stagecraft there, but that's the stuff of another essay for another time.

5   And finally the last paragraph. It turns out that the perfect nature essay is quite short, it's a lean taut thing, an arrow and not a cannon, and here at the end there's a flash of humor, and a hint or tone or subtext of sadness, a touch of rue, you can't quite put your finger on it but it's there, a dark thread in the fabric, and there's also a shot of espresso hope, hope against all odds and sense, but rivetingly there's no call to arms, no clarion brassy trumpet blast, no website to which you are directed, no hint that you, yes you, should be ashamed of how much water you use or the car you drive or the fact that you just turned the thermostat up to seventy, or that you actually have not voted in the past two elections despite what you told the kids and the goat. Nor is there a rimshot ending, a bang, a last twist of the dagger. Oddly, sweetly,

the essay just ends with a feeling eerily like a warm hand brushed against your cheek, and you sit there, near tears, smiling, and then you stand up. Changed.

Content

1. What's a nature essay about?
2. Why should a nature essay "begin with an image . . . startling and lovely and wondrous" (¶ 1)?
3. Why incorporate true stories into essays? What sorts of stories could a nature essay tell? Are these stories special, or different from those in other types of essays?
4. Why does a nature essay avoid giving "Conclusions, some Advice, some Stern Instructions & Directions" (¶ 4)?

Strategies/Structures/Language

5. What is the structure of Doyle's essay? Does this reflect his precepts about what "the greatest nature essay *ever*" should be like?
6. What is the effect of Doyle's equation of goats with senators to explain how an essay's sentences work: "each one making plain inarguable sense, a goat or even a senator could easily understand the sentences and their implications" (¶ 3)?
7. Doyle follows this with a string of five negatives ("no shouting . . .") before employing the ultimate, positive simile, "calm clean clear statements one after another, fitting together like people holding hands" (¶ 3). Likewise, he personifies the nature essay in (¶ 4), "a little shy, holding its hat." What is the effect of describing the way the nature essay works in human terms, rather than in naturalistic images?
8. Doyle's style is poetic. Explain why, using examples from this essay as well as from actual poetry, if you wish (consider, for instance, Robert Frost's "Stopping by Woods on a Snowy Evening").

For Writing

9. *Journal writing.* Keep a nature notebook for five days, in which you record precise observations about the natural world as you experience it. Try to write at different times of day/night when you are in a variety of moods to see what influence these have on the nature of your observations, and on your style.
10. *Mixed modes.* Apply Doyle's precepts to an analysis of some of the other nature essays in this book, such as Michael Pollan's "The Meal" (247–54) and Matt Nocton's "Harvest of Gold, Harvest of Shame" (271–76).
11. Using Doyle's analysis as a guide, write your own five or six paragraph version of "The Greatest Nature Essay *Ever*." Incorporate a good story or two.

RACHEL TOOR

Rachel Toor (born 1962 in Pennsylvania) wrote *Admissions Confidential: An Insider's Account of the Elite College Selection Process* (2001) after working in the Office of Undergraduate Admissions at Duke University. She is also the author of *The Pig and I: How I Learned to Love Men (Almost) as Much as I Love My Pets* (2005) and *Personal Record: A Love Affair with Running* (2008). Toor writes a monthly column in *The Chronicle of Higher Education* and is a Senior Writer for *Running Times* magazine. She is Assistant Professor of Creative Writing at the Inland Northwest Center for Writers in Spokane, Washington, the graduate writing program of Eastern Washington University. "Which One of These Essay Questions Is the Real Thing?" first appeared in *The Chronicle of Higher Education* (2007). Toor's mock admissions essays capture the spontaneity of personal writing, even as they are carefully crafted to convey the (often unintended) irony, humor, self-embellishment, and flashes of candor that the college admissions process can elicit from applicants.

Which of These Essay Questions Is the Real Thing?

Please tell us what you do in your free time.
(No more than 500 words.)

1   When I was 12 years old, I got the international record for my age group for the marathon. After that I moved up to running longer races, and regularly compete in 100-milers. I run eight miles before school (I get up at 3 a.m.) and on some days do 12 to 15 miles after school. I am a member of the Future Farmers of America and a nationally ranked cheese taster. I go to Dairy Products contests and Agriscience Fairs at the local, regional, state, and national levels. In order to fully appreciate the process of making cheeses, I have purchased a cow, a goat, and a sheep.

2   I work part time as an auto mechanic. Mostly I rebuild engines and program automobile computer equipment. When I saw the photos on the wall at Pete's (where I work), I began thinking of earning extra money that I need through modeling. Now I do runway shows for Victoria's Secret and Frederick's of Hollywood.

3   At school this year, I am taking eight AP classes, and because I have maxed out the math and science curriculum, I am auditing classes in topology, geophysics, and nonlinear dynamics at our community college.

The Chronicle of Higher Education, April 27, 2007. Copyright © 2007 by Rachel Toor. Reprinted by permission of the author.

I have written a play that will be produced at the local rep company, and my self-titled debut CD will be released next fall.

I am president of the National Honor Society, the Speech and Debate   4
Club, the Pro-Life Club, the Gay/Straight Alliance, and the Unwed Mothers on Crack Club. I am treasurer of Key Club, Habitat for Humanity, Teens for a Drug-Free America, and the Legalize Cannabis Club. I participate in French Club, Latin Club, Multicultural Club, the Aryan Youth Nation, Kids on Prozac, the Anime Society, Parent Management Group, and the Knitting Bee.

I am captain of the field-hockey, soccer, and bingo teams. I am a   5
cheerleader for boys' water polo, and occasionally I join the Polar Bear Club for a dip.

I attend meetings of NYLC, AIME, SADD, FBLA, ASB, JROTC, JSA,   6
YCC, FCA, Al-Anon, and BYOB.

I go to Chinese school and Hebrew school, and participate in our   7
church youth group.

I am certified as a PADI scuba diver and am currently licensed to fly   8
a plane, give manicures, and do Reiki massage therapy.

I have more than 30,000 friends on MySpace.   9

Please forgive me, but I do not understand the question.   10

What is the most important social problem currently facing society?

The most important social problem currently facing society is home-   11
lessness. There are more homeless people today than ever before in history! Many people do not have homes and are living on the street, and this is not a good thing. Something must be done about homelessness!

Every day on my way to soccer practice, I see homeless people.   12
They've got grocery carts they steal and use to carry their crud around. They use cardboard boxes like blankets. Sometimes they write crazy stuff on the boxes, like "Out of Work Vet." I mean, if you're a vet, there are plenty of sick animals that could use your services. Get a job! Other people do.

When I had to do my court-ordered community service, I got sent   13
to work in the homeless shelter. These people smelled bad! It's like they didn't know the first thing about personal hygiene. I was wearing a nice pair of Abercrombie khakis and an Izod shirt and they called me "rich boy"! My Beemer is two years old!

In conclusion, homelessness is a big problem.   14

If you were a vegetable, which vegetable would you be?

If I were a member of the vegetable kingdom, I would be an artichoke.   15
First, I am unique. I am not like the cookie-cutter cucumbers, all   16
long and cylindrical and boring. I am not one of those oddly formed root vegetables—you know the way sweet potatoes can go all twisted and

weird, with fat middles and pointy ends? I am unique, but not weird. I have more substance than the leafy greens, more heft than an herb. No anorexic carrot am I. I am neither miniature, like a brussels sprout, nor overgrown, like a squash. I don't have the flashiness of eggplant, nor the dirtiness of a potato.

17   It is true, my edges are sharp. (It's not easy being green.) On the outside I can be incisive to the point of drawing blood, especially if you rub me the wrong way. I'm not shiny and polished, but rather a bit gruff and gritty. But that tough, sturdy, complex protective covering is there for one reason.

18   My outer shell is a coat of armor. While some people may find me off-putting and different, when you peel away the many layers and get to know me, you realize that at the core, I am all heart, soft and fuzzy.

19   I am an artichoke. Not your average vegetable, but one that stands out from the crowded produce shelf.

Please tell us why you want to attend Fancy Pants University.

20   Fancy Pants University is an excellent school, with excellent teachers and excellent students. Fancy Pants University has a beautiful campus, with nice buildings and big trees and very green grass. The food at Fancy Pants is delicious and nutritious. The sports teams always win and the parties are always fun. Everyone I met while visiting was friendly and welcoming. My tour guide was extremely intelligent *and* hot. I have wanted to go to Fancy Pants since before I could talk. Everyone I know who went there is really, really smart and got really well educated. I like that the classes are smaller than at State U., and that there is an honor code and a club for left-handed origamists as well as a support group for perfectionists. Plus my parents say I need to be able to get a high-paying job after college, and they think the Fancy Pants name will help. Those are some of the many reasons I really want to attend Different Name University.

Content

1. To what extent should students write candid application essays? In what ways should they tailor their essays to particular schools?

2. What do Toor's mock answers to essay questions suggest about student admission essays? How is your perception of these essays influenced by knowing that the writer is not a student, but faculty?

3. Does Toor expect students, college faculty and administrators, or parents to read this piece? What does publication in the *Chronicle of Higher Education* imply about the intended audience? How might a student's reactions to this differ from an admissions officer's or a parent's?

Strategies/Structures/Language

4. Toor's humor employs hyperbole (exaggeration), irony (an expression contrary to intended meaning), and pleonasm (superfluous words). Find an example of each and explain why the effect is humorous.

5. How close are any of these essays to the real thing? If an applicant can write a skilful parody, should they take this risk in submitting an actual application? Explain.

For Writing

6. **Journal Writing.** What expectations of college governed your own college application? Compare your expectations of college with your experience of it thus far. Have your experiences changed your view of the value of a college education?

7. Do these satirical treatments of the college application essay suggest that the process should be reformed? If so, in what ways? Would a change in the application process help students choose a more appropriate institution? How does the application process shape student expectations of what college will be like as well as their actual experience of college? In what respects have your early college experiences fulfilled or disappointed your expectations?

Social Media— Thinking, Reading, Writing in an Electronic Era

College age readers are the first generation of Americans to have grown up in a multimedia era in which sounds and images are available nonstop, day and night, night and day. *Generation M2: Media in the Lives of 8-to-18-Year Olds*, a Kaiser Family Foundation Study by Victoria Robert, Ulla Foehr, and Donald Roberts, reported in 2010 that children spend an average of more than seven and a half hours per day, seven days a week, on recreational use of media—outside of school assignments: "The TV shows they watch, video games they play, songs they listen to, books they read and websites they visit are an enormous part of their lives, offering a constant stream of messages about families, peers, relationships, gender roles, sex, violence, food, values, clothes and an abundance of other topics too long to list" (1).

Consider the type of electronic devices that are ever at the ready, whether you are awake or asleep. Is your cell phone on and near at hand—even in your hand—while you're in class? In bed? Are you wired to an umbilical, the iPod, while you're walking—on city streets, around campus, with or without friends nearby? Can you exercise—bike, run, even swim—without the comforting insulation of surround sound? How many electronic devices are on in your dorm room or workspace at any given time—computer, iPad, cellphone, iPod, ebook, TV—and how many applications are open and running concurrently? How many times in twenty-four hours do you consult these devices? What would you miss most if you didn't have it? Student E. Cabell Hankison Gathman's "Cell Phones" (61–66) offers a dual love-affair–with her cell phone and a lover who conducts significant aspects of an on-again off-again relationship by–you guessed it–cellphone.

How often do you look at Facebook—and what do you look at? What sites do you consult on the Internet? Why? Do you play electronic games? Do you interrupt the work–or play–you should be concentrating on with Internet diversions and distractions? When you look up one site are you drawn to another, and another, and yet another that leads you farther and farther into the deep woods of distraction? Do you lose sleep, exercise in these electronic pursuits? How often do you eat while in their presence? When you are face-to-face with friends, do you keep these electronic devices on? Do you find yourself mentally in another realm, wishing that you could text them instead so you could follow other electronic trails? How often do you notice people sitting together, over a meal, perhaps, or on a train or subway, but ignoring the human presence while texting or chatting with another on a cellphone?

It is clear that these media have innumerable advantages. The essay by Tim Berners-Lee, inventor of the World Wide Web, "Long Live the Web: A Call for Continued Open Standards and Neutrality" (429–38), reminds us of the ubiquity of the Web, honoring the "profound concept" and "egalitarian principles" "that any person could share information with anyone else, anywhere." The Web, says Berners-Lee, is "vital to democracy," and as long as information remains free to all users, everyone can take advantage of the ease of doing research and indeed of finding virtually anything in the world, anywhere in the world.

It is also clear that social media are highly competitive, in constant flux, and insatiably ravenous. As Ben Sisario observes in "Turning the Grammys Into an Interactive Event" in but one analysis of social media that could be multiplied daily by thousands:

> In the age of social media, the audience's reactions to a live event can have instantaneous effect, guided as much by what happens on screen as by what other fans are saying about it online. . . . Amazon . . . attracted customers by sending sales links on Twitter for all the [Super Bowl's] music, whether heard on commercials or live in the stadium.
>
> The trick with social media, though, is that the faucet must always be on, and the stream must remain compelling within a discourse that changes by the second. It can be easy to find things to say when big stars crowd the Grammy stage for special performances . . . But what about the other 364 days of the year? . . . "We build this enormous machine, and it needs to be fed constantly." . . . [So the academy uses social media to promote numerous smaller] industry and educational gatherings throughout the year, [such as a] "Social Media Rock Stars Summit" [involving musicians] "as well as executives from Facebook, pandora and Foursquare."
>
> "All old media will be encroached on and hurt by new media," Mr. Garland [a social media tracking executive] said. But, if you look at where the vulnerabilities are, they have everything to do with traditional media being non-participatory and not time sensitive" (*New York Times* 2-11-11C 1, 17).

In "Tinfoil Underwear" (193–98) James Fallows addresses the issue of Internet privacy and commercial capture of data, for use, misuse, and abuse. Most people, he contends, forget that "Nearly every interaction in today's digital life is traceable," permanent, and can be employed to the user's detriment (¶ 8). Thus every call one makes from a cell phone, and all "E-mail messages, Web search requests, music-download orders, and all other signals sent from a computer," "every query you send to Google" is warehoused, forever, because "firms from Google and Yahoo to Amazon, eBay, and Expedia . . . are all in an endless struggle to entice more people to spend more time on their sites, so they can sell more advertising" (¶ 9–14).

Users beware—not only for commercial reasons, but social ones. The devices that connect people with the wide, wide world including the military on duty with their families at home, present a paradox different from the one Tim Stobierski discusses in his essay, "A Paradox" (66–68), a paradox unanticipated by the authors of the essays in this chapter. Text messages can start and sustain revolutions of national and international consequence, as is evidenced by the ability of ordinary citizens to communicate and organize protests and rebellions that foment major political changes in Egypt, Bahrain, Yemen, and Iran, among other restive countries. The response of the Egyptian government, a five-day Internet blackout that severed Internet connections for twenty million of its citizens online, in a significant but ultimately futile act of self-preservation, is a testament to the Internet's enormous power. That other countries—China, Cuba, Syria—have on occasion censored Facebook and other social networking services is a further indication of both the promise and the threat of social media.

Despite such potent interconnectedness, social media also insulate their users from the vast universe in which we live. Growing up surrounded by sounds—from iPods, computers, and cell phones—may erect an electronic wall between the listener and the rest of the world, including other sounds, natural and human. Confronting electronic screens—of computers, televisions, even automobile GPSs day in and night out—imposes other people's configurations of reality on one's own view of the world, just as an orientation to books and newspapers did for earlier generations. Sherry Turkle, an MIT professor whose observations on "How Computers Change the Way We Think," the first essay in this chapter (37–43), is "fascinated by how technology changes the self." Among the changes are today's dramatically different conceptions of privacy, authentic selves, "powerful ideas" versus PowerPoint—which "encourages presentation, not conversation"—and the deleterious effects of rapid word processing on thinking.

Turkle's newest book, *Alone Together: Why We Expect More From Technology and Less From Each Other* (2011) is the third book in her trilogy on the evolving relationships of humans to digital technology. Her research does not yield uniformly positive analysis: robots that "want to be buddies" implicitly promise "an emotional connection they can never deliver." Information overload and the effects of social networks can be overwhelming, she says. Her field research, hundreds of interviews with "children, teenagers, adults, and the elderly encountering the latest tech gadgets" leads her to somber conclusions. "[M]any of us are already a little too cozy with our machines—the smartphones and laptops we turn to for distraction and comfort so often that we can forget how to sit quietly with our own thoughts. In that way . . . science fiction has become reality: [sic] We are already cyborgs, reliant on digital devices in ways that many of us could not have imagined just a few years ago." *Alone Together* concludes, "'We talk about 'spending' hours on e-mail, but we, too, are being spent. We have invented inspiring and enhancing technologies, and yet we have allowed them to diminish us." "Put down the BlackBerry"—she admonishes—"you're forgetting how to just *be*" (Jeffrey R. Young, "Programmed for Love," *Chronicle Review* 21 Jan. 2011, B9).

Nicholas Carr, in "Is Google Making Us Stupid? What the Internet is Doing to Our Brains," (45–54) addresses similar problems: The "easy assumption" of Google's computer scientists that "we'd all be better off if our brains were supplemented, or even replaced, by an artificial intelligence is unsettling. It suggests a belief that intelligence is the output of a mechanical process, a series of discrete steps that can be isolated, measured, and optimized," leaving little space for "the fuzziness of contemplation," the insights of ambiguity (¶ 28). In addition, the Internet has profoundly changed the way he reads because of its continuous opportunities for diversions and distractions through online "searching and surfing"; he has trouble in concentrating "after two or three pages. I get fidgety, lose the thread, begin looking for something else to do. The deep reading that used to come naturally has become a struggle" (¶ 1–2)—for Carr, and by implication, everyone else "searching and surfing" the Web.

In a comparable vein, William Deresiewicz in "Faux Friendship" (56–60) offers a critique of "the social networking sites of the new century—Friendster, MySpace, both launched in 2003, and Facebook in 2004." The friendship circle that is their "premise-and promise," expands "to engulf the whole of the social world, and in so doing, [it has] destroyed both its own nature and that of the individual friendship itself." "There they are," claim the social networks, "my friends, all in the same place. Except, of course, they're not in the same place, or, rather, they're not my friends. They're simulacra of my friends, little dehydrated packets of images and information, no more my friends than a set of baseball cards is the New York Mets" (¶ 2). The restricted message space of Facebook and Twitter manipulates images and truncates communication; instead of accommodating dialogue, and long, intimate "three-hour conversations," posting information is the substitute, "like pornography, a slick, impersonal exhibition" (¶ 10). Echoing Turkle, he concludes, "We have given our hearts to machines, and now we are turning into machines" (¶ 11). Student Tim Stobierski, in "The Paradox" (66–68) puts it this way. Social media provide a myriad of opportunities for communicating via cellphone, texting, and Facebook—so much so that "we have forgotten how to talk to one another. We have forgotten the etiquette of conversation. We are no longer comfortable speaking, opening ourselves up." But to live fully—he concludes—is to be vulnerable, to open up to meaningful human communication. Live—as both an adjective and a verb, a designation and an admonition.

Readers of this section are welcome to defend the benefits of social media, which indeed none of us except perhaps hermits would be willing to forgo. Yet the essays in this section are written by people, professionals, and students alike, who are open-minded, evenhanded. They are not urging us to throw the babies out with the bathwater; even if we wanted to do so, it would be difficult to survive without them in contemporary American culture. But they are unanimous in recommending a balance between the mediated e-communication of multitaskers, instant and distracting, and—if you will—naked interaction, real-life face-to-face conversations in real time, slow time, with the cell phone and iPod turned off.

SHERRY TURKLE

Sherry Turkle is a clinical psychologist and sociology professor at Massachusetts Institute of Technology. She was born in 1948 in New York City, and was educated at Harvard (BA, 1970; PhD, 1976). Her research and writing focus on the cultural and psychological implications of computer technology. She looks at "computers as carriers of culture, as objects that give rise to new metaphors, to new relationships between people and machines, between different people, and most significantly between people and their ways of thinking about themselves." Her books include *The Second Self: Computers and the Human Spirit* (1984), *Life on the Screen: Identity in the Age of the Internet* (1995), *Simulation and Its Contents* (2009) is followed by *Alone Together* which focused on how creating alter egos in virtual worlds helped people create and shape their identities. In addition to identities as "Turkle the social scientist," the author, and the professor, she adds others: "the cyberspace explorer, the woman who might log on as a man, or as another woman, or as, simply, ST" (from "Who Am We?"). "How Computers Change the Way We Think" was originally published in the *Chronicle of Higher Education* on January 30, 2004.

How Computers Change the Way We Think

The tools we use to think change the ways in which we think. The invention of written language brought about a radical shift in how we process, organize, store, and transmit representations of the world. Although writing remains our primary information technology, today when we think about the impact of technology on our habits of mind, we think primarily of the computer.

My first encounters with how computers change the way we think came soon after I joined the faculty at the Massachusetts Institute of Technology in the late 1970s, at the end of the era of the slide rule and the beginning of the era of the personal computer. At a lunch for new faculty members, several senior professors in engineering complained that the transition from slide rules to calculators had affected their students' ability to deal with issues of scale. When students used slide rules, they had to insert decimal points themselves. The professors insisted that that required students to maintain a mental sense of scale, whereas those who relied

SHERRY TURKLE, "How Computers Change the Way We Think," CHRONICLE OF HIGHER EDUCATION 30, January 2004. Reprinted by permission of the author.

on calculators made frequent errors in orders of magnitude. Additionally, the students with calculators had lost their ability to do "back of the envelope" calculations, and with that, an intuitive feel for the material.

3   That same semester, I taught a course in the history of psychology. There, I experienced the impact of computational objects on students' ideas about their emotional lives. My class had read Freud's essay on slips of the tongue, with its famous first example: The chairman of a parliamentary session opens a meeting by declaring it closed. The students discussed how Freud interpreted such errors as revealing a person's mixed emotions. A computer-science major disagreed with Freud's approach. The mind, she argued, is a computer. And in a computational dictionary—like we have in the human mind—"closed" and "open" are designated by the same symbol, separated by a sign for opposition. "Closed" equals "minus open." To substitute "closed" for "open" does not require the notion of ambivalence or conflict.

4   "When the chairman made that substitution," she declared, "a bit was dropped; a minus sign was lost. There was a power surge. No problem."

5   The young woman turned a Freudian slip into an information-processing error. An explanation in terms of meaning had become an explanation in terms of mechanism.

6   Such encounters turned me to the study of both the instrumental and the subjective sides of the nascent computer culture. As an ethnographer and psychologist, I began to study not only what the computer was doing *for* us, but what it was doing *to* us, including how it was changing the way we see ourselves, our sense of human identity.

7   In the 1980s, I surveyed the psychological effects of computational objects in everyday life—largely the unintended side effects of people's tendency to project thoughts and feelings onto their machines. In the 20 years since, computational objects have become more explicitly designed to have emotional and cognitive effects. And those "effects by design" will become even stronger in the decade to come. Machines are being designed to serve explicitly as companions, pets, and tutors. And they are introduced in school settings for the youngest children.

8   Today, starting in elementary school, students use e-mail, word processing, computer simulations, virtual communities, and PowerPoint software. In the process, they are absorbing more than the content of what appears on their screens. They are learning new ways to think about what it means to know and understand.

9   What follows is a short and certainly not comprehensive list of areas where I see information technology encouraging changes in thinking. There can be no simple way of cataloging whether any particular change is good or bad. That is contested terrain. At every step we have to ask, as educators and citizens, whether current technology is leading

us in directions that serve our human purposes. Such questions are not technical; they are social, moral, and political. For me, addressing that subjective side of computation is one of the more significant challenges for the next decade of information technology in higher education. Technology does not determine change, but it encourages us to take certain directions. If we make those directions clear, we can more easily exert human choice.

Thinking about privacy

Today's college students are habituated to a world of online blogging, instant messaging, and Web browsing that leaves electronic traces. Yet they have had little experience with the right to privacy. Unlike past generations of Americans, who grew up with the notion that the privacy of their mail was sacrosanct, our children are accustomed to electronic surveillance as part of their daily lives. 10

I have colleagues who feel that the increased incursions on privacy have put the topic more in the news, and that this is a positive change. But middle-school and high-school students tend to be willing to provide personal information online with no safeguards, and college students seem uninterested in violations of privacy and in increased governmental and commercial surveillance. Professors find that students do not understand that in a democracy, privacy is a right, not merely a privilege. In 10 years, ideas about the relationship of privacy and government will require even more active pedagogy. (One might also hope that increased education about the kinds of silent surveillance that technology makes possible may inspire more active political engagement with the issue.) 11

Avatars or a self?

Chat rooms, role-playing games, and other technological venues offer us many different contexts for presenting ourselves online. Those possibilities are particularly important for adolescents because they offer what Erik Erikson described as a moratorium, a time out or safe space for the personal experimentation that is so crucial for adolescent development. Our dangerous world—with crime, terrorism, drugs, and AIDS—offers little in the way of safe spaces. Online worlds can provide valuable spaces for identity play. 12

But some people who gain fluency in expressing multiple aspects for self may find it harder to develop authentic selves. Some children who write narratives for their screen avatars may grow up with too little experience of how to share their real feelings with other people. For those who are lonely yet afraid of intimacy, information technology has made it possible to have the illusion of companionship without the demands of friendship. 13

From powerful ideas to PowerPoint

14   In the 1970s and early 1980s, some educators wanted to make programming part of the regular curriculum for K–12 education. They argued that because information technology carries ideas, it might as well carry the most powerful ideas that computer science has to offer. It is ironic that in most elementary schools today, the ideas being carried by information technology are not ideas from computer science like procedural thinking, but more likely to be those embedded in productivity tools like Power-Point presentation software.

15   PowerPoint does more than provide a way of transmitting content. It carries its own way of thinking, its own aesthetic—which not surprisingly shows up in the aesthetic of college freshmen. In that aesthetic, presentation becomes its own powerful idea.

16   To be sure, the software cannot be blamed for lower intellectual standards. Misuse of the former is as much a symptom as a cause of the latter. Indeed, the culture in which our children are raised is increasingly a culture of presentation, a corporate culture in which appearance is often more important than reality. In contemporary political discourse, the bar has also been lowered. Use of rhetorical devices at the expense of cogent argument regularly goes without notice. But it is precisely because standards of intellectual rigor outside the educational sphere have fallen that educators

Larry Williams/keepsake/Corbis

"Read" the picture as an illustration of Angier's "Why Men Don't Last" (353–56). How can you tell he's angry? Would you interpret the picture the same way if the figure were a woman rather than a man? Or if the figure looked more like a college student than a career person?

must attend to how we use, and when we introduce, software that has been designed to simplify the organization and processing of information.

In "The Cognitive Style of PowerPoint" (Graphics Press, 2003),   17 Edward R. Tufte suggests that PowerPoint equates bulleting with clear thinking. It does not teach students to begin a discussion or construct a narrative. It encourages presentation, not conversation. Of course, in the hands of a master teacher, a PowerPoint presentation with few words and powerful images can serve as the jumping-off point for a brilliant lecture. But in the hands of elementary-school students, often introduced to PowerPoint in the third grade, and often infatuated with its swooshing sounds, animated icons, and flashing text, a slide show is more likely to close down debate than open it up.

Developed to serve the needs of the corporate boardroom, the   18 software is designed to convey absolute authority. Teachers used to tell students that clear exposition depended on clear outlining, but presentation software has fetishized the outline at the expense of the content.

Narrative, the exposition of content, takes time. PowerPoint, like so   19 much in the computer culture, speeds up the pace.

Word processing vs. thinking

The catalog for the Vermont Country Store advertises a manual type-   20 writer, which the advertising copy says "moves at a pace that allows time to compose your thoughts." As many of us know, it is possible to manipulate text on a computer screen and see how it looks faster than we can think about what the words mean.

Word processing has its own complex psychology. From a peda-   21 gogical point of view, it can make dedicated students into better writers because it allows them to revise text, rearrange paragraphs, and experiment with the tone and shape of an essay. Few professional writers would part with their computers; some claim that they simply cannot think without their hands on the keyboard. Yet the ability to quickly fill the page, to see it before you can think it, can make bad writers even worse.

A seventh grader once told me that the typewriter she found in her   22 mother's attic is "cool because you have to type each letter by itself. You have to know what you are doing in advance or it comes out a mess." The idea of thinking ahead has become exotic.

Taking things at interface value

We expect software to be easy to use, and we assume that we don't have   23 to know how a computer works. In the early 1980s, most computer users who spoke of transparency meant that, as with any other machine, you could "open the hood" and poke around. But only a few years later,

Macintosh users began to use the term when they talked about seeing their documents and programs represented by attractive and easy-to-interpret icons. They were referring to an ability to make things work without needing to go below the screen surface. Paradoxically, it was the screen's opacity that permitted that kind of transparency. Today, when people say that something is transparent, they mean that they can see how to make it work, not that they know how it works. In other words, transparency means epistemic opacity.

24   The people who built or bought the first generation of personal computers understood them down to the bits and bytes. The next generation of operation systems were more complex, but they still invited that old-time reductive understanding. Contemporary information technology encourages different habits of mind. Today's college students are already used to taking things at (inter) face value; their successors in 2014 will be even less accustomed to probing below the surface.

Simulation and its discontents

25   Some thinkers argue that the new opacity is empowering, enabling anyone to use the most sophisticated technological tools and to experiment with simulation in complex and creative ways. But it is also true that our tools carry the message that they are beyond our understanding. It is possible that in daily life, epistemic opacity can lead to passivity.

26   I first became aware of that possibility in the early 1990s, when the first generation of complex simulation games were introduced and immediately became popular for home as well as school use. SimLife teaches the principles of evolution by getting children involved in the development of complex ecosystems; in that sense it is an extraordinary learning tool. During one session in which I played SimLife with Tim, a 13-year-old, the screen before us flashed a message: "Your orgot is being eaten up." "What's an orgot?" I asked. Tim didn't know. "I just ignore that," he said confidently. "You don't need to know that kind of stuff to play."

27   For me, that story serves as a cautionary tale. Computer simulations enable their users to think about complex phenomena as dynamic, evolving systems. But they also accustom us to manipulating systems whose core assumptions we may not understand and that may not be true.

28   We live in a culture of simulation. Our games, our economic and political systems, and the ways architects design buildings, chemists envisage molecules, and surgeons perform operations all use simulation technology. In 10 years the degree to which simulations are embedded in every area of life will have increased exponentially. We need to develop a new form of media literacy: readership skills for the culture of simulation.

29   We come to written text with habits of readership based on centuries of civilization. At the very least, we have learned to begin with the journalist's traditional questions: who, what, when, where, why, and how. Who

wrote these words, what is their message, why were they written, and how are they situated in time and place, politically and socially? A central project for higher education during the next 10 years should be creating programs in information-technology literacy, with the goal of teaching students to interrogate simulations in much the same spirit, challenging their built-in assumptions.

Despite the ever-increasing complexity of software, most computer 30 environments put users in worlds based on constrained choices. In other words, immersion in programmed worlds puts us in reassuring environments where the rules are clear. For example, when you play a video game, you often go through a series of frightening situations that you escape by mastering the rules—you experience life as a reassuring dichotomy of scary and safe. Children grow up in a culture of video games, action films, fantasy epics, and computer programs that all rely on that familiar scenario of almost losing but then regaining total mastery: There is danger. It is mastered. A still-more-powerful monster appears. It is subdued. Scary. Safe.

Yet in the real world, we have never had a greater need to work our way 31 out of binary assumptions. In the decade ahead, we need to rebuild the culture around information technology. In that new socio-technical culture, assumptions about the nature of mastery would be less absolute. The new culture would make it easier, not more difficult, to consider life in shades of gray, to see moral dilemmas in terms other than a battle between Good and Evil. For never has our world been more complex, hybridized, and global. Never have we so needed to have many contradictory thoughts and feelings at the same time. Our tools must help us accomplish that, not fight against us.

Information technology is identity technology. Embedding it in a 32 culture that supports democracy, freedom of expression, tolerance, diversity, and complexity of opinion is one of the next decade's greatest challenges. We cannot afford to fail.

When I first began studying the computer culture, a small breed of 33 highly trained technologists thought of themselves as "computer people." That is no longer the case. If we take the computer as a carrier of a way of knowing, a way of seeing the world and our place in it, we are all computer people now.

Content

1. What new technologies does Turkle claim are changing the way people think? Have you experienced the changes in thought patterns that she describes, such as the tendency of PowerPoint presentations to "close down debate" (¶ 17) or of word processing to "make bad writers even worse" (¶ 21)?

2. Is there any technology or program that Turkle should add to her list, based on your experience? What mind-altering computing experiences have you had that she doesn't mention?

3. At the end of the article, Turkle asserts that current computing habits and software may undermine "democracy, freedom of expression, tolerance, diversity, and complexity of opinion" (¶ 32). Look over the article again to determine the precise reasons she gives to support these conclusions. Which arguments do you find to be the most convincing? Why?

4. Do you ever intentionally try to get away from technology, or have you ever had to be away from the Internet or the computer for an extended period of time? Did you notice any changes in your thinking process or attitudes as a result? Explain what happened and whether the experience was positive or negative.

Strategies/Structures/Language

5. One of the main strategies Turkle uses is the past/present contrast, such as the idea that the typewriter allowed people to put more thought into their writing (¶ 22). What other examples can you find of Turkle comparing current technology to past technology? To what extent are these comparisons effective at persuading the reader to accept her conclusions?

For Writing

6. With a group of classmates, determine how much experience each person has with the technologies that Turkle mentions. For example, how many of your colleagues have experience with PowerPoint? How many participate in chat rooms, role-playing games, simulation games, or use a screen avatar? Discuss with the group whether any of these technologies may be changing or shaping your basic thought processes, and write a collaborative paper reporting on and analyzing your findings.

7. Can you think of some solutions to the issues that Turkle raises in her article? To what extent can we lessen computer technology's negative impact on our thinking? Is the solution technological, or would it help to educate the public about the dangers Turkle outlines? Write a paper explaining how some, or all, of the issues Turkle discusses could be resolved.

8. Can you think of any computing technology that might help humans to *improve* their thought processes? Invent a program or online service that could help enhance mental functioning or perhaps enhance the democratic process, freedom of expression, or tolerance. Write a proposal persuading readers to support your effort to make your invention available to the public, stressing the way it will improve the way we think.

9. *Dialogues.* Turkle raises privacy issues (¶s 10–11) that James Fallows, also discusses in "Tinfoil Underwear" (192–98). Do you agree that today's students are, as Turkle argues, "uninterested in violations of privacy" (¶ 11)? Which aspects of Fallows's and discussions seem most relevant to students today? Which of these aspects might "inspire more active political engagement," as Turkle hopes (¶ 11)?

NICHOLAS CARR

Nicholas Carr (born 1959) earned a B.A. from Dartmouth and an M.A. from Harvard. Carr has written on technology for numerous publications, including the *Guardian*, the *New York Times Magazine, Wired*, and *Die Zeit*. Since 2005 in his blog, Rough Type, he has explored the impact of information technologies on individuals, business, and society. This focus is mirrored in his books, *Does IT matter?* (2004) and *The Shallows: What the Internet Is Doing to Our Brains* (2010). Similarly, in *The Big Switch: Rewiring the World from Edison to Google* (2008), he demonstrates how and why "[T]he interplay of technological and economic forces rarely produces the results we at first expect . . . [T]he economic forces that the World Wide Computer is unleashing . . . the replacement of skilled as well as unskilled workers with software, the global trade in knowledge work, and the ability of companies to aggregate volunteer labor and harvest its economic value—we're left with a prospect that is far from Utopian. The erosion of a middle class may well accelerate, as the divide widens between a relatively small group of extraordinarily wealthy people—the digital elite—and a very large set of people who face eroding fortunes and a persistent struggle to make ends meet. In the YouTube economy, everyone is free to play, but only a few reap the rewards."

"Is Google Making Us Stupid?" originally published in *Atlantic* (2008), argues that "media are not just passive channels of information. They supply the stuff of thought, but they also shape the process of thought. And what the Net seems to be doing is chipping away my capacity for concentration and contemplation. My mind now expects to take in information the way the Net distributes it: in a swiftly moving stream of particles." The essay was included in *The Best American Science and Nature Writing, The Best Technology Writing*, and *The Best Spiritual Writing*.

Is Google Making us Stupid? What the Internet Is Doing to Our Brains

"Dave, stop. Stop, will you? Stop, Dave. Will you stop, Dave?" So the supercomputer HAL pleads with the implacable astronaut Dave Bowman in a famous and weirdly poignant scene toward the end of Stanley Kubrick's 2001: *Space Odyssey*. Bowman, having nearly been sent to a deep-space death by the malfunctioning machine, is calmly coldly disconnecting the memory circuits that control its artificial brain. "Dave, my mind is going," HAL says, forlornly. "I can feel it. I can feel it." 1

I can feel it, too. Over the past few years I've had an uncomfortable sense that someone, or something, has been tinkering with my brain, remapping the neural circuitry, reprogramming the memory. My mind isn't 2

Nicholas Carr, "Is Google Making Us Stupid? What the Internet is Doing to Our Brains" Atlantic July/August 2008 56–60, 62–63. Reprinted by permission of the author.

going—so far as I can tell—but it's changing. I'm not thinking the way I used to think. I can feel it most strongly when I'm reading. Immersing myself in a book or a lengthy article used to be easy. My mind would get caught up in the narrative or the turns of the argument, and I'd spend hours strolling through long stretches of prose. That's rarely the case anymore. Now my concentration often starts to drift after two or three pages. I get fidgety, lose the thread, begin looking for something else to do. I feel as if I'm always dragging my wayward brain back to the text. The deep reading that used to come naturally has become a struggle.

3   I think I know what's going on. For more than a decade now, I've been spending a lot of time online, searching and surfing and sometimes adding to the great databases of the Internet. The Web has been a godsend to me as a writer. Research that once required days in the stacks or periodical rooms of libraries can now be done in minutes. A few Google searches, some quick clicks on hyperlinks, and I've got the telltale fact or pithy quote I was after. Even when I'm not working, I'm as likely as not to be foraging in the Web's info-thickets—reading and writing e-mails, scanning headlines and blog posts, watching videos and listening to podcasts, or just tripping from link to link to link. (Unlike footnotes, to which they're sometimes likened, hyperlinks don't merely point to related works; they propel you toward them.)

4   For me, as for others, the Net is becoming a universal medium, the conduit for most of the information that flows through my eyes and ears and into my mind. The advantages of having immediate access to such an incredibly rich store of information are many, and they've been widely described and duly applauded. "The perfect recall of silicon memory," *Wired's* Clive Thompson has written, "can be an enormous boon to thinking." But that boon comes at a price. As the media theorist Marshall McLuhan pointed out in the 1960s, media are not just passive channels of information. They supply the stuff of thought, but they also shape the process of thought. And what the Net seems to be doing is chipping away my capacity for concentration and contemplation. My mind now expects to take in information the way the Net distributes it: in a swiftly moving stream of particles. Once I was a scuba diver in the sea of words. Now I zip along the surface like a guy on a Jet Ski.

5   I'm not the only one. When I mention my troubles with reading to friends and acquaintances—literary types, most of them—many say they're having similar experiences. The more they use the Web, the more they have to fight to stay focused on long pieces of writing. Some of the bloggers I follow have also begun mentioning the phenomenon. Scott Karp, who writes a blog about online media, recently confessed that he has stopped reading books altogether. "I was a lit major in college, and used to be [a] voracious book reader," he wrote. "What happened" He speculates on the answer: "What if I do all my reading on the web not so much because the way I read has changed, i.e. I'm just seeking convenience, but because the way I THINK has changed?"

Bruce Friedman, who blogs regularly about the use of computers 6
in medicine, also has described how the Internet has altered his mental
habits. "I now have almost totally lost the ability to read and absorb a
longish article on the web or in print," he wrote earlier this year. A pa-
thologist who has long been on the faculty of the University of Michigan Medical School, Friedman elaborated on his comment in a telephone
conversation with me. His thinking, he said, has taken on a "staccato"
quality, reflecting the way he quickly scans short passages of text from
many sources online. "I can't read *War and Peace* anymore," he admitted.
"I've lost the ability to do that. Even a blog post of more than three or four
paragraphs is too much to absorb. I skim it."

Anecdotes alone don't prove much. And we still await the long- 7
term neurological and psychological experiments that will provide a
definitive picture of how Internet use affects cognition. But a recently
published study of online research habits, conducted by scholars from
University College London, suggests that we may well be in the midst
of a sea change in the way we read and think. As part of the five-year research program, the scholars examined computer logs documenting the
behavior of visitors to two popular research sites, one operated by the
British Library and one by a U.K. educational consortium, that provide
access to journal articles, e-books, and other sources of written information. They found that people using the sites exhibited "a form of skim-
ming activity," hopping from one source to another and rarely returning
to any source they'd already visited. They typically read no more than
one or two pages of an article or book before they would "bounce" out to
another site. Sometimes they'd save a long article, but there's no evidence
that they ever went back and actually read it. The authors of the study
report:

> It is clear that users are not reading online in the traditional sense;
> indeed there are signs that new forms of "reading" are emerging as
> users "power browse" horizontally through titles, contents pages
> and abstracts going for quick wins. It almost seems that they go
> online to avoid reading in the traditional sense.

Thanks to the ubiquity of text on the Internet, not to mention the 8
popularity of text-messaging on cell phones, we may well be reading more
today than we did in the 1970s or 1980s, when television was our medium
of choice. But it's a different kind of reading, and behind it lies a different kind of thinking—perhaps even a new sense of the self. "We are not
only *what* we read," says Maryanne Wolf, a developmental psychologist at
Tufts University and the author of *Proust and the Squid: The Story and Science of the Reading Brain*. "We are *how* we read." Wolf worries that the style
of reading promoted by the Net, a style that puts "efficiency" and "immediacy" above all else, may be weakening our capacity for the kind of deep

reading that emerged when an earlier technology, the printing press, made long and complex works of prose commonplace. When we read online, she says, we tend to become "mere decoders of information." Our ability to interpret text, to make the rich mental connections that form when we read deeply and without distraction, remains largely disengaged.

9   Reading, explains Wolf, is not an instinctive skill for human beings. It's not etched into our genes the way speech is. We have to teach our minds how to translate the symbolic characters we see into the language we understand. And the media or other technologies we use in learning and practicing the craft of reading play an important part in shaping the neural circuits inside our brains. Experiments demonstrate that readers of ideograms, such as the Chinese, develop a mental circuitry for reading that is very different from the circuitry found in those of us whose written language employs an alphabet. The variations extend across many regions of the brain, including those that govern such essential cognitive functions as memory and the interpretation of visual and auditory stimuli. We can expect as well that the circuits woven by our use of the Net will be different from those woven by our reading of books and other printed works.

10   Sometime in 1882, Friedrich Nietzsche bought a typewriter—a Malling-Hansen Writing Ball, to be precise. His vision was failing, and keeping his eyes focused on a page had become exhausting and painful, often bringing on crushing headaches. He had been forced to curtail his writing, and he feared that he would soon have to give it up. The typewriter rescued him, at least for a time. Once he had mastered touch-typing, he was able to write with his eyes closed, using only the tips of his fingers. Words could once again flow from his mind to the page.

11   But the machine had a subtler effect on his work. One of Nietzsche's friends, a composer, noticed a change in the style of his writing. His already terse prose had become even tighter, more telegraphic. "Perhaps you will through this instrument even take to a new idiom," the friend wrote in a letter, noting that, in his own work, his "'thoughts' in music and language often depend on the quality of pen and paper."

12   "You are right," Nietzsche replied, "our writing equipment takes part in the forming of our thoughts." Under the sway of the machine, writes the German media scholar Friedrich A. Kittler, Nietzsche's prose "changed from arguments to aphorisms, from thoughts to puns, from rhetoric to telegram style."

13   The human brain is almost infinitely malleable. People used to think that our mental meshwork, the dense connections formed among the 100 billion or so neurons inside our skulls, was largely fixed by the time we reached adulthood. But brain researchers have discovered that that's not the case. James Olds, a professor of neuroscience who directs the

Krasnow Institute for Advanced Study at George Mason University, says that even the adult mind "is very plastic." Nerve cells routinely break old connections and form new ones. "The brain," according to Olds, "has the ability to reprogram itself on the fly, altering the way it functions."

As we use what the sociologist Daniel Bell has called our "intellectual technologies"—the tools that extend our mental rather than our physical capacities—we inevitably begin to take on the qualities of those technologies. The mechanical clock, which came into common use in the 14th century, provides a compelling example. In *Technics and Civilization,* the historian and cultural critic Lewis Mumford described how the clock "disassociated time from human events and helped create the belief in an independent world of mathematically measurable sequences." The "abstract framework of divided time" became "the point of reference for both action and thought." 14

The clock's methodical ticking helped bring into being the scientific mind and the scientific man. But it also took something away. As the late MIT computer scientist Joseph Weizenbaum observed in his 1976 book, *Computer Power and Human Reason: From Judgment to Calculation,* the conception of the world that emerged from the widespread use of timekeeping instruments "remains an impoverished version of the older one, for it rests on a rejection of those direct experiences that formed the basis for, and indeed constituted, the old reality." In deciding when to eat, to work, to sleep, to rise, we stopped listening to our senses and started obeying the clock. 15

The process of adapting to new intellectual technologies is reflected in the changing metaphors we use to explain ourselves to ourselves. When the mechanical clock arrived, people began thinking of their brains as operating "like clockwork." Today, in the age of software, we have come to think of them as operating "like computers." But the changes, neuroscience tells us, go much deeper than metaphor. Thanks to our brain's plasticity, the adaptation occurs also at a biological level. 16

The Internet promises to have particularly far-reaching effects on cognition. In a paper published in 1936, the British mathematician Alan Turing proved that a digital computer, which at the time existed only as a theoretical machine, could be programmed to perform the function of any other information-processing device. And that's what we're seeing today. The Internet, an immeasurably powerful computing system, is subsuming most of our other intellectual technologies. It's becoming our map and our clock, our printing press and our typewriter, our calculator and our telephone, and our radio and TV. 17

When the Net absorbs a medium, that medium is re-created in the Net's image. It injects the medium's content with hyperlinks, blinking ads, and other digital gewgaws, and it surrounds the content with the content of all the other media it has absorbed. A new e-mail message, for instance, may announce its arrival as we're glancing over the latest 18 headlines at a newspaper's site. The result is to scatter our attention and diffuse our concentration.

19   The Net's influence doesn't end at the edges of a computer screen, either. As people's minds become attuned to the crazy quilt of Internet media, traditional media have to adapt to the audience's new expectations. Television programs add text crawls and pop-up ads, and magazines and newspapers shorten their articles, introduce capsule summaries, and crowd their pages with easy-to-browse info-snippets. When, in March of this year, *The New York Times* decided to devote the second and third pages of every edition to article abstracts, its design director, Tom Bodkin, explained that the "shortcuts" would give harried readers a quick "taste" of the day's news, sparing them the "less efficient" method of actually turning the pages and reading the articles. Old media have little choice but to play by the new-media rules.

20   Never has a communications system played so many roles in our lives—or exerted such broad influence over our thoughts—as the Internet does today. Yet, for all that's been written about the Net, there's been little consideration of how, exactly, it's reprogramming us. The Net's intellectual ethic remains obscure.

21   About the same time that Nietzsche started using his typewriter, an earnest young man named Frederick Winslow Taylor carried a stopwatch into the Midvale Steel plant in Philadelphia and began a historic series of experiments aimed at improving the efficiency of the plant's machinists. With the approval of Midvale's owners, he recruited a group of factory hands, set them to work on various metalworking machines, and recorded and timed their every movement as well as the operations of the machines. By breaking down every job into a sequence of small, discrete steps and then testing different ways of performing each one, Taylor created a set of precise instructions—an "algorithm," we might say today—for how each worker should work. Midvale's employees grumbled about the strict new regime, claiming that it turned them into little more than automatons, but the factory's productivity soared.

22   More than a hundred years after the invention of the steam engine, the Industrial Revolution had at last found its philosophy and its philosopher. Taylor's tight industrial choreography—his "system," as he liked to call it—was embraced by manufacturers throughout the country and, in time, around the world. Seeking maximum speed, maximum efficiency, and maximum output, factory owners used time-and-motion studies to organize their work and configure the jobs of their workers. The goal, as Taylor defined it in his celebrated 1911 treatise, *The Principles of Scientific Management*, was to identify and adopt, for every job, the "one best method" of work and thereby to effect "the gradual substitution of science for rule of thumb throughout the mechanic arts." Once his system was applied to all acts of manual labor, Taylor assured his followers, it would bring about a restructuring not only of industry but of society, creating a

Utopia of perfect efficiency. "In the past the man has been first," he declared; "in the future the system must be first."

Taylor's system is still very much with us; it remains the ethic of 23
industrial manufacturing. And now, thanks to the growing power that
computer engineers and software coders wield over our intellectual lives,
Taylor's ethic is beginning to govern the realm of the mind as well. The
Internet is a machine designed for the efficient and automated collection, transmission, and manipulation of information, and its legions of
programmers are intent on finding the "one best method"—the perfect
algorithm—to carry out every mental movement of what we've come to
describe as "knowledge work."

Google's headquarters, in Mountain View, California—the Googleplex—is 24
the Internet's high church, and the religion practiced inside its walls is
Taylorism. Google, says its chief executive, Eric Schmidt, is "a company
that's founded around the science of measurement," and it is striving to
"systematize everything" it does. Drawing on the terabytes of behavioral
data it collects through its search engine and other sites, it carries
out thousands of experiments a day, according to the *Harvard Business
Review,* and it uses the results to refine the algorithms that increasingly
control how people find information and extract meaning from it. What
Taylor did for the work of the hand, Google is doing for the work of
the mind.

The company has declared that its mission is "to organize the world's 25
information and make it universally accessible and useful." It seeks to
develop "the perfect search engine," which it defines as something that
"understands exactly what you mean and gives you back exactly what
you want." In Google's view, information is a kind of commodity, a utilitarian resource that can be mined and processed with industrial efficiency.
The more pieces of information we can "access" and the faster we can extract their gist, the more productive we become as thinkers.

Where does it end? Sergey Brin and Larry Page, the gifted young 26
men who founded Google while pursuing doctoral degrees in computer
science at Stanford, speak frequently of their desire to turn their search
engine into an artificial intelligence, a HAL-like machine that might be
connected directly to our brains. "The ultimate search engine is something
as smart as people—or smarter," Page said in a speech a few years back.
"For us, working on search is a way to work on artificial intelligence." In
a 2004 interview with *Newsweek*, Brin said, "Certainly if you had all the
world's information directly attached to your brain, or an artificial brain
that was smarter than your brain, you'd be better off." Last year, Page
told a convention of scientists that Google is "really trying to build artificial intelligence and to do it on a large scale."

Such an ambition is a natural one, even an admirable one, for a pair 27
of math whizzes with vast quantities of cash at their disposal and a small

army of computer scientists in their employ. A fundamentally scientific enterprise, Google is motivated by a desire to use technology, in Eric Schmidt's words, "to solve problems that have never been solved before," and artificial intelligence is the hardest problem out there. Why wouldn't Brin and Page want to be the ones to crack it?

28   Still, their easy assumption that we'd all "be better off" if our brains were supplemented, or even replaced, by an artificial intelligence is unsettling. It suggests a belief that intelligence is the output of a mechanical process, a series of discrete steps that can be isolated, measured, and optimized. In Google's world, the world we enter when we go online, there's little place for the fuzziness of contemplation. Ambiguity is not an opening for insight but a bug to be fixed. The human brain is just an outdated computer that needs a faster processor and a bigger hard drive.

29   The idea that our minds should operate as high-speed data-processing machines is not only built into the workings of the Internet, it is the network's reigning business model as well. The faster we surf across the Web—the more links we click and pages we view—the more opportunities Google and other companies gain to collect information about us and to feed us advertisements. Most of the proprietors of the commercial Internet have a financial stake in collecting the crumbs of data we leave behind as we flit from link to link—the more crumbs, the better. The last thing these companies want is to encourage leisurely reading or slow, concentrated thought. It's in their economic interest to drive us to distraction.

30   Maybe I'm just a worrywart. Just as there's a tendency to glorify technological progress, there's a countertendency to expect the worst of every new tool or machine. In Plato's *Phaedrus*, Socrates bemoaned the development of writing. He feared that, as people came to rely on the written word as a substitute for the knowledge they used to carry inside their heads, they would, in the words of one of the dialogue's characters, "cease to exercise their memory and become forgetful." And because they would be able to "receive a quantity of information without proper instruction," they would "be thought very knowledgeable when they are for the most part quite ignorant." They would be "filled with the conceit of wisdom instead of real wisdom." Socrates wasn't wrong—the new technology did often have the effects he feared—but he was shortsighted. He couldn't foresee the many ways that writing and reading would serve to spread information, spur fresh ideas, and expand human knowledge (if not wisdom).

31   The arrival of Gutenberg's printing press, in the 15th century, set off another round of teeth gnashing. The Italian humanist Hieronimo Squarciafico worried that the easy availability of books would lead to intellectual laziness, making men "less studious" and weakening their minds. Others argued that cheaply printed books and broadsheets would

undermine religious authority, demean the work of scholars and scribes, and spread sedition and debauchery. As New York University professor Clay Shirky notes, "Most of the arguments made against the printing press were correct, even prescient." But, again, the doomsayers were unable to imagine the myriad blessings that the printed word would deliver.

So, yes, you should be skeptical of my skepticism. Perhaps those   32
who dismiss critics of the Internet as Luddites or nostalgists will be proved correct, and from our hyperactive, data-stoked minds will spring a golden age of intellectual discovery and universal wisdom. Then again, the Net isn't the alphabet, and although it may replace the printing press, it produces something altogether different. The kind of deep reading that a sequence of printed pages promotes is valuable not just for the knowledge we acquire from the author's words but for the intellectual vibrations those words set off within our own minds. In the quiet spaces opened up by the sustained, undistracted reading of a book, or by any other act of contemplation, for that matter, we make our own associations, draw our own inferences and analogies, foster our own ideas. Deep reading, as Maryanne Wolf argues, is indistinguishable from deep thinking.

If we lose those quiet spaces, or fill them up with "content," we will   33
sacrifice something important not only in our selves but in our culture. In a recent essay, the playwright Richard Foreman eloquently described what's at stake:

> I come from a tradition of Western culture, in which the ideal (my ideal) was the complex, dense and "cathedral-like" structure of the highly educated and articulate personality—a man or woman who carried inside themselves a personally constructed and unique version of the entire heritage of the West. [But now] I see within us all (myself included) the replacement of complex inner density with a new kind of self—evolving under the pressure of information overload and the technology of the "instantly available."

As we are drained of our "inner repertoire of dense cultural inheritance,"   34
Foreman concluded, we risk turning into "'pancake people—spread wide and thin as we connect with that vast network of information accessed by the mere touch of a button."

I'm haunted by that scene in *2001*. What makes it so poignant, and   35
so weird, is the computer's emotional response to the disassembly of its mind: its despair as one circuit after another goes dark, its childlike pleading with the astronaut—"I can feel it. I can feel it. I'm afraid"—and its final reversion to what can only be called a state of innocence. HAL's outpouring of feeling contrasts with the emotionlessness that characterizes the human figures in the film, who go about their business with an almost robotic efficiency. Their thoughts and actions feel scripted, as if they're following the steps of an algorithm. In the world of 2001, people have

become so machinelike that the most human character turns out to be a machine. That's the essence of Kubrick's dark prophecy: as we come to rely on computers to mediate our understand ing of the world, it is our own intelligence that flattens into artificial intelligence.

Content

1. Assuming that you have grown up with ready access to the Internet and to cell phones, are you reading the way Carr does, "Once I was a scuba diver in the sea of words. Now I zip along the surface like a guy on a Jet Ski" (¶ 4)? Is Carr right? Or is he overstating the case. Analyze the way the Internet works to encourage superficial reading.

2. Carr speculates that because there are so many texts on the Internet, "not to mention the popularity of text-messaging on cell phones, we may be reading more today than we did in the 1970s or 1980s . . . But it's a different kind of reading, and behind it lies a different kind of thinking" (¶ 8). What differences in reading and thinking does Carr identify? Do the positive features of reading online (such as accessing millions of documents) outweigh the losses, such as detachment from the process of making "the rich mental connections that form when we read deeply and without distraction (¶ 8)?

3. Carr explains that "The Internet is a machine designed for the efficient and automated collection, transmission, and manipulation of information" (¶ 21). Is this how you think of the Internet? Apply Carr's analysis to a particular type of information; is he accurate? In what ways does your use of the Internet reflect these functions?

4. Carr claims that "The idea that our minds should operate as high-speed data-processing machines is not only built into the workings of the Internet, it is the network's reigning business model as well" (¶ 29). Is he accurate? Does Turkle's analysis in "How Computers Change the Way We Think" (37–43) corroborate Carr's views? Complicate them?

Strategies/Structures/Language

5. Is Carr's essay written in a style to make it easy for readers to speed read, as if they were reading it on the Internet? In your answer, consider its overall structure, argument, major points, sentence length and variety, and vocabulary.

For Writing

6. *Journal writing.* Choose something to read on the Internet, say an article from *The New York Times* online edition. As you read it, identify all the distractions that occur while you're reading—electronic (hyperlinks, blinking ads, music and other sounds, and other digital gewgaws) (¶ 18), in the context where you're reading (say, your room), and otherwise (your mind wandering). What is the effect of these distractions on your ability to understand, remember, interpret, and retain the information in the article? How many of these distractions are related to social media? What would be the optimum conditions for you to read in-depth and to remember what you've read? With other students, construct some guidelines for effective exam study.

7. **Mixed modes.** Working in a group of three, provide individual answers to the following questions and then compare your results. Under what circumstances, if any, do you—or would you—dive deeply into "the sea of words" (¶ 4). Analyze your own reading habits. Do you read everything the same way or do you have different styles of reading for hardcopy vs online texts, school materials vs news vs recreational reading. Do you voluntarily read material that isn't online? If so, what do you read, and for what purposes? Do you enjoy reading? If so, what materials? If not, why not? Write a brief report that interprets and explains your findings.

8. Write an essay, based on your own experience, that either affirms Carr's conclusion, accepts it with modification, or calls it into question: "The kind of deep reading that a sequence of printed pages promotes is valuable not just for the knowledge we acquire from the author's words but for the intellectual vibrations those words set off within our own minds. In the quiet spaces opened up by the sustained, undistracted reading of a book . . . we make our own associations, draw our own inferences and analogies, foster our own ideas" (¶ 32).

Edward Koren/The New Yorker/Cartoon Bank

(A crowd disperses outside a church; their eyes glued to handheld devices. A sign next to them reads "United Church of OMG.")

WILLIAM DERESIEWICZ

William Deresiewicz (born 1964) is a literary critic whose work has appeared in *The Nation, The American Scholar*, the *London Review of Books*, and *The New York Times*. From 1998 to 2008 Deresiewicz was an English professor at Yale University, where he published *Jane Austen and the Romantic Poets* (2004). In 2009, he was nominated for the National Magazine Award for his reviews and criticism, sometimes controversial, often informal. For instance, in "You Talkin' to Me?" *(New York Times Book Review,* Jan. 9, 2005) he claims, ". . . there is no such thing as Correct English, and there never has been."

Deresiewicz's essay, "Faux Friendship," originally published in *The Chronicle of Higher Education* in 2009—and written in correct English— begins with the statement, "We live at a time when friendship has become both all and nothing at all." He discusses modern relationships and how they have been affected, created, and destroyed by "our brave new mediated world." Social networking sites, he explains, are "just the latest stages of a long attenuation" of the nature and intensity of friendship that has occurred in our increasingly high-tech era.

Faux Friendship

1   We live at a time when friendship has become both all and nothing at all. . . . What, in our brave new mediated world, is friendship becoming? The Facebook phenomenon, so sudden and forceful a distortion of social space, needs little elaboration. Having been relegated to our screens, are our friendships now anything more than a form of distraction? When they've shrunk to the size of a wall post, do they retain any content? If we have 768 "friends," in what sense do we have any? Facebook isn't the whole of contemporary friendship, but it sure looks a lot like its future. Yet Facebook—and MySpace, and Twitter, and whatever we're stampeding for next—are just the latest stages of a long attenuation. They've accelerated the fragmentation of consciousness, but they didn't initiate it. They have reified the idea of universal friendship, but they didn't invent it. In retrospect, it seems inevitable that once we decided to become friends with everyone, we would forget how to be friends with anyone. We may pride ourselves today on our aptitude for friendship—friends, after all, are the only people we have left—but it's not clear that we still even know what it means. . . .

2   With the social-networking sites of the new century—Friendster and MySpace were launched in 2003, Facebook in 2004—the friendship circle has expanded to engulf the whole of the social world, and in so doing, destroyed both its own nature and that of the individual friendship itself.

Chronicle of Higher Education 6 Dec. 2009. Used by permission of the author.

Facebook's very premise—and promise—is that it makes our friendship circles visible. There they are, my friends, all in the same place. Except, of course, they're not in the same place, or, rather, they're not my friends. They're simulacra of my friends, little dehydrated packets of images and information, no more my friends than a set of baseball cards is the New York Mets.

I remember realizing a few years ago that most of the members of 3 what I thought of as my "circle" didn't actually know one another. One I'd met in graduate school, another at a job, one in Boston, another in Brooklyn, one lived in Minneapolis now, another in Israel, so that I was ultimately able to enumerate some 14 people, none of whom had ever met any of the others. To imagine that they added up to a circle, an embracing and encircling structure, was a belief, I realized, that violated the laws of feeling as well as geometry. They were a set of points, and I was wandering somewhere among them. Facebook seduces us, however, into exactly that illusion, inviting us to believe that by assembling a list, we have conjured a group. Visual juxtaposition creates the mirage of emotional proximity. "It's like they're all having a conversation," a woman I know once said about her Facebook page, full of posts and comments from friends and friends of friends. "Except they're not."

Friendship is devolving, in other words, from a relationship to a 4 feeling—from something people share to something each of us hugs privately to ourselves in the loneliness of our electronic caves, rearranging the tokens of connection like a lonely child playing with dolls. The same path was long ago trodden by community. As the traditional face-to-face community disappeared, we held on to what we had lost— the closeness, the rootedness—by clinging to the word, no matter how much we had to water down its meaning. Now we speak of the Jewish "community" and the medical "community" and the "community" of readers, even though none of them actually is one. What we have, instead of community, is, if we're lucky, a "sense" of community—the feeling without the structure; a private emotion, not a collective experience. And now friendship, which arose to its present importance as a replacement for community, is going the same way. We have "friends," just as we belong to "communities." Scanning my Facebook page gives me, precisely, a "sense" of connection. Not an actual connection, just a sense.

What purpose do all those wall posts and status updates serve? 5 On the first beautiful weekend of spring this year, a friend posted this update from Central Park: "[So-and-so] is in the Park with the rest of the City." The first question that comes to mind is, if you're enjoying a beautiful day in the park, why don't you give your iPhone a rest? But the more important one is, why did you need to tell us that? We have always shared our little private observations and moments of feeling—it's part of what friendship's about, part of the way we remain present in one another's lives—but things are different now. Until a few years ago, you could share your thoughts with only one friend at a time (on the phone, say), or maybe with a small group, later, in person. And when you did, you were talking to specific people, and you tailored what you said, and how you said it, to who they were—their interests, their personalities, most of all, your degree of mutual intimacy. "Reach out and touch someone" meant someone in particular, someone you were actually thinking about. It meant having a conversation. Now we're just broadcasting our stream of consciousness, live from Central Park, to all 500 of our friends at once, hoping that someone, anyone, will confirm our existence by answering back. We haven't just stopped talking to our friends as individuals, at such moments, we have stopped thinking of them as individuals. We have turned them into an indiscriminate mass, a kind of audience or faceless public. We address ourselves not to a circle, but to a cloud. . . .

6   Perhaps I need to surrender the idea that the value of friendship lies precisely in the space of privacy it creates: not the secrets that two people exchange so much as the unique and inviolate world they build up between them, the spider web of shared discovery they spin out, slowly and carefully, together. There's something faintly obscene about performing that intimacy in front of everyone you know, as if its real purpose were to show what a deep person you are. Are we really so hungry for validation? So desperate to prove we have friends?

7   But surely Facebook has its benefits. Long-lost friends can reconnect, far-flung ones can stay in touch. I wonder, though. Having recently moved across the country, I thought that Facebook would help me feel connected to the friends I'd left behind. But now I find the opposite is true. Reading about the mundane details of their lives, a steady stream of trivia and ephemera, leaves me feeling both empty and unpleasantly full, as if I had just binged on junk food, and precisely because it reminds me of the real sustenance, the real knowledge, we exchange by e-mail or phone or face-to-face. And the whole theatrical quality of the business, the sense that my friends are doing their best to impersonate themselves, only makes it worse. The person I read about, I cannot help feeling, is not quite the person I know. . . .

8   Finally, the new social-networking Web sites have falsified our understanding of intimacy itself, and with it, our understanding of ourselves. The absurd idea, bruited about in the media, that a MySpace profile or "25 Random Things About Me" can tell us more about someone than even a good friend might be aware of is based on desiccated notions about what knowing another person means: First, that intimacy is confessional—an idea both peculiarly American and peculiarly young, perhaps because both types of people tend to travel among strangers, and so believe in the instant disgorging of the self as the quickest route to familiarity. Second, that identity is reducible to information: the name of your cat, your favorite Beatle, the stupid thing you did in seventh grade. Third, that it is reducible, in particular, to the kind of information that social-networking

Web sites are most interested in eliciting, consumer preferences. Forget that we're all conducting market research on ourselves. Far worse is that Facebook amplifies our longstanding tendency to see ourselves ("I'm a Skin Bracer man!") in just those terms. We wear T-shirts that proclaim our brand loyalty, pique ourselves on owning a Mac, and now put up lists of our favorite songs. "15 movies in 15 minutes. Rule: Don't take too long to think about it."

So information replaces experience, as it has throughout our culture. 9
But when I think about my friends, what makes them who they are, and why I love them, it is not the names of their siblings that come to mind, or their fear of spiders. It is their qualities of character. This one's emotional generosity, that one's moral seriousness, the dark humor of a third. Yet even those are just descriptions, and no more specify the individuals uniquely than to say that one has red hair, another is tall. To understand what they really look like, you would have to see a picture. And to understand who they really are, you would have to hear about the things they've done. Character, revealed through action: the two eternal elements of narrative. In order to know people, you have to listen to their stories.

But that is precisely what the Facebook page does not leave room 10
for, or 500 friends, time for. Literally does not leave room for. E-mail, with its rapid-fire etiquette and scrolling format, already trimmed the letter down to a certain acceptable maximum, perhaps a thousand words. Now, with Facebook, the box is shrinking even more, leaving perhaps a third of that length as the conventional limit for a message, far less for a comment. (And we all know the deal on Twitter.) The 10-page missive has gone the way of the buggy whip, soon to be followed, it seems, by the three-hour conversation. Each evolved as a space for telling stories, an act that cannot usefully be accomplished in much less. Posting information is like pornography, a slick, impersonal exhibition. Exchanging stories is like making love: probing, questing, questioning, caressing. It is mutual. It is intimate. It takes patience, devotion, sensitivity, subtlety, skill—and it teaches them all, too.

They call them social-networking sites for a reason. Networking once 11
meant something specific: climbing the jungle gym of professional contacts in order to advance your career. The truth is that Hume and Smith were not completely right. Commercial society did not eliminate the self-interested aspects of making friends and influencing people, it just changed the way we went about it. Now, in the age of the entrepreneurial self, even our closest relationships are being pressed onto this template. A recent book on the sociology of modern science describes a networking event at a West Coast university: "There do not seem to be any singletons—disconsolately lurking at the margins—nor do dyads appear, except fleetingly." No solitude, no friendship, no space for refusal—the exact contemporary paradigm. At the same time, the author assures us, "face time" is valued in this "community" as a "high-bandwidth interaction," offering

"unusual capacity for interruption, repair, feedback and learning." Actual human contact, rendered "unusual" and weighed by the values of a systems engineer. We have given our hearts to machines, and now we are turning into machines. The face of friendship in the new century.

Content

1. Deresiewicz argues that "It seems inevitable that once we decided to become friends with everyone [on Facebook and other social networks] we would forget how to be friends with anyone" (¶ 1). What evidence does he use to support this claim?

2. What does Deresiewicz mean by my alleged social network "friends" are "simulacra of my friends, little dehydrated packets of images and information, no more my friends than a set of baseball cards is the New York Mets" (¶ 2).

3. What has caused today's youth, as well as their elders, to substitute the appearance of friendship for friendship itself? Deresiewicz says, "Reading about the mundane details of their lives, a steady stream of trivia and ephemera, leaves me feeling both empty and unpleasantly full, as if I had just binged on junk food. . . ." (¶ 7) How can a person recognize true friendship in comparison with "faux friendship"?

4. The existence of true friendship implies ethic and ethos. What are its components? What is the ethos of social network "friendship"? What is the appropriate conduct of Facebook "friends"?

5. What is a "friendship circle" (¶ 2)? Is it just a list of names that the creator of a Facebook page has assembled? How does this differ from a true community?

Strategies/Structures/Language

6. Deresiewicz frequently employs metaphors: "Friendship," says Deresiewicz, is "devolving . . . from a relationship to a feeling–from something people share to something each of us hugs privately to ourselves in the loneliness of our electronic caves, rearranging the tokens of connection like a lonely child playing with dolls." Metaphors imply analogous connections between objects, states of mind, or other conditions that might initially seem very different. If they're effective, they provide an intensified understanding of the topic at hand. In the "friendship" metaphor quoted here, and in other metaphors you find in this essay, identify the implied connections and explain whether these metaphors give you a newer, sharper understanding of the subject.

For Writing

7. **Journal.** Examine your own Facebook profile construction. What images, text have you put on this? What kind of character, personality are you trying to convey? For what audience?

8. Do you consider this audience your "friends"? Do you know any or all of these people? How well? In what ways? Do you ever spend extended time in person with any of them? If so, under what circumstances? If not, why not? Could you, would you call on any of them for help in an emergency? Aid on an exam? Solace in time of grief? Or are these superficial, social friends only available for limited contact in pleasant social situations, if that?

9. **Dialogue.** Are social media making us socially stupid? Do you agree, with Nicholas Carr, that "Google is Making Us Stupid" (45–54)? Is our stupidity the same in both cases?

10. With a classmate, preferably a "friend," write a definition of true friendship. Use this to analyze the quality of three significant friendships in your life. Are these depicted accurately on Facebook, or do you know and interact with these friends in other ways?

E. CABELL HANKINSON GATHMAN

Gathman, born in Tucson, Arizona in 1981, earned a MS in sociology from the University of Wisconsin-Madison in 2005, where she is currently pursuing her PhD. Her research interests focus on the uses of multiple Internet technologies to develop and maintain relationships–social networking sites, virtual worlds, blogs, and chats. For additional information, on her "uncombable" "Atomic Pink" hair, tattoos, body piercings, medical history, and cats, consult Gathman's blog and website.

"Cell Phones," originally published in Sherry Turkle's *The Inner History of Devices* (2008), details Gathman's dependence on cell phones; her first one, as a nineteen-year-old student in Japan in 2000 was "pearlescent pink," with ring-tones keyed to her callers. She spent long, often anxious hours using the cell to transcend—and maintain—insulation, isolation, self-esteem. One love affair, conducted by cell, threatened to undermine all of the cell's positive benefits until she changed phones—and voilá, "My new RAZR is a part of me that is freshly born, unscarred."

Cell Phones

I **went to Japan** in the Year of the Dragon, a terrified bleached blonde foreigner, because my heart was broken. I wanted to be alone, but it was in Tokyo in 2000 that I got my first cell phone. I don't remember how popular cell phones were in the United States at that time.   1

In high school, a few of my classmates had owned pagers, although we mostly associated them with drug dealing. During my college years no one in my family had a cell phone nor did my freshman or sophomore year dorm mates. As a female exchange student, however, I was housed in the Tokyo YWCA whose rooms did not have landlines. There was a single shared phone in the first floor corridor, across from the caretaker's apartment. Talking on it transported me to my imaginings of a 1950s'   2

Turkle, Sherry, ed., The Inner History of Devices, pp. 41–48, © 2008 Massachusetts Institute of Technology, by permission of The MIT Press.

dormitory—it seemed a lot like prison. Receiving calls on the YMCA phone was even worse than attempting to make them, so the first thing resident students recommended to newcomers was that we get *keitai denwa*—cell phones—*keitai* for short.

3   I was nineteen years old, which made me a minor under Japanese law, unable to sign the *keitai* contract. Olga from Uzbekistan pretended to be my older sister and signed on my behalf. My choice of phone models was restricted by my near-total illiteracy in Japanese; I needed something bilingual, and I also wanted something pink. Fortunately I was in Japan, where even bilingual phones came in pink—and not just pink, but a softly gleaming pearlescent shade, the keys smooth and jewel-like, marked with *hiragana* and Roman alphabetic characters beside the larger numerals. It wasn't long before I'd plastered the back of it with a sparkling translucent sticker of Hello Kitty wearing a scorpion costume, denoting my Western zodiac sign. When I came back from Hiroshima, it was with the dangling addition of a souvenir *keitai* charm from Miyajima Island, a metal maple leaf in brilliant neons.

4   It wasn't an international cell phone really, but it was possible to purchase international calling cards for it. It let me talk to my parents and to friends. I had a laptop but no Internet at the YWCA, and it was a semester before I figured out that I could get an Ethernet cable and connect my laptop on campus instead of waiting for the horrible slow machines at the student computer lab to become available. I mostly called people very late at night while drunk, which meant that it was usually about nine o'clock in the morning in Missouri, the place I was calling. My parents were pretty much the only ones willing to pay to call me, so if I wanted to talk to my friends, I had to call them. Looking back, I can see that this might have depressed me, but at the time it suited me fine. I had run off to Japan because it was the only place far enough away that seemed safe; I took comfort in controlling with whom I was in contact.

5   Alone in Japan I was safe from my relational ineptitude. In Missouri, there was a guy whose neediness had smothered me and a girl who made me wonder if I would ever find someone interesting who was also non-toxic. The only time I received a call from someone outside of my family, it was a mutual friend who phoned to tell me that the needy guy and the toxic girl had moved in together. She said she thought I would "want to know." It took me three intensive Harajuku shopping trips and an all-day visit to Tokyo Disney to recover from that phone call. After that, I preferred the radio silence. It was a soothing necessity. Sometimes, for a moment, I would think I saw someone on the street I didn't want to see, but of course it was never she—always some slightly-off doppelganger, redrawn Japanese. And she didn't call.

6   I text messaged in Japan more than I ever have since. It was much cheaper than on American plans, and as my Japanese improved, the phonetic *kana* and pictographic *kanji* allowed me to communicate

exponentially more meaning within the character limit for a single message than I ever could in English, even with the use of chat argot. Texting gave me something to do on the train, speeding through the city, never idle. In Tokyo, a world in itself, my glittering fairyland of the future, the *keitai* was an easy way to find my fellow students on the spur of the moment, colliding like lonely atoms in coffee shops and among the English language paperback racks at Kinokuniya. Throughout my travels on that colossal neon grid, the *keitai* was my talisman.

I brought it back to the United States even though it didn't work here—J-Phone, unlike its competitor DoCoMo, had no agreement with any U.S. mobile carriers. I tucked it into a drawer with its charger, and every now and then I took it out and stroked its plastic skin, switched it on and tried to remember the world that was and the blonde girl who had moved through it, carrying this *keitai*. Tokyo sat trapped inside it: the ring tone that I'd so painstakingly programmed, the old text messages, many of them in *kanji* and *hiragana*, exchanged with the people I knew there. Unlike email, those messages could be accessed only through the single handset onto which they had been downloaded. Unlike ruby slippers, the *keitai* could never really take me back, and it could never be integrated into my American life. Like my year in Japan, it just didn't fit. I came back from Tokyo feeling in some ways as if I'd never left Missouri at all—I was different, everything was different, but somehow no one realized that the world had shifted. Like Lucy coming out of the wardrobe in *The Chronicles of Narnia*, no one even noticed I'd been gone. My *keitai* held the voices of Japan; it was useless to try to make it talk to Americans. That interval of my life was simply past, and no one remembered it but me. If I hadn't had the phone, it might not have ever happened at all.

American cell phones were ugly and squat. I knew more people who carried them, but the landline in my dorm room was free of charge and at Truman State University in Kirksville, Missouri, where everyone I knew spent most of their time around the first-floor dorm lounge anyway, a cell seemed kind of pointless. There were no trains in Kirksville, no massive bookstores where you could lose your friends between the second floor and the fourth. I didn't need a cell phone there, and if I couldn't get a shiny pink one, then I didn't *want* one, either.

It was only two years later, when I graduated and picked up for Wisconsin, that I thought a cell phone seemed "worth it," and even then, only for practical reasons. It was the unlimited off-peak minutes that did it, the prospect of being able to make free calls on nights and weekends to people I was leaving behind. That cell phone was a very basic, navy blue Nokia, and our relationship was purely business. I carried it in my bag. It made me reachable in a strange place. I had cable Internet, and the only calls I ever got on my landline were for someone named Earl, who seemed to have run afoul of various authorities. No one believed me when I said he didn't live there anymore. I got the landline disconnected.

10   A couple of years after that, I switched networks and got a new Audiovox flip phone. Being able to keep my old phone number was a big deal, and the companies did everything they could to make it easy—no notifications of a changed number to be made, no relationships to be reaffirmed or discarded with the switch. I had to transfer my Nokia contact list to the new handset myself, but it seemed worth it. The new model felt like the future. It was silver, not pink, but that was still an improvement over the matte navy blue of the plastic brick I'd been carrying around. And the Audiovox had a camera. I was very, very upset when, during the first month I owned the phone, I dropped it and scratched its casing. It still worked, but I couldn't shake the feeling that a luminous future had been marred.

11   It was some time before I discovered the vast selection of ring tones that I could download for the Audiovox. I quickly amassed quite the collection—"Girls Just Wanna Have Fun" announced my sisters; when my academic adviser called, the phone played "Sympathy for the Devil." My default was usually the theme song from *Buffy the Vampire Slayer*, a peppy number that worked well when translated into polyphonic midi format and announced to anyone in earshot that here was a fellow *Buffy* viewer, if they cared.

12   I became involved with a man, an unavailable one this time—needy in his own way, but hardly willing to touch my shoulder in public. I can't really blame my cell phone, but in my heart of hearts I know it enabled our inappropriate connection. We rarely spoke in public—certainly nothing personal, no touching, nothing to betray us. He called me in the middle of the night, when we were both alone. Sometimes when I was trying to fight my way back to myself, to preserve some pride, I tried to get the cell phone to help me: the phone could be turned off, set to silent, shoved into a drawer across the apartment. Perhaps he was doing the same thing or just cared less. He didn't always answer his phone when I called— maybe half the time. But I got nervous if my cell phone was more than a yard away, afraid I might somehow miss his call, despite more than once having been woken from a relatively sound sleep by a ring tone from another room. I slept with the Audiovox at arm's reach, the volume cranked to maximum, waiting for the ring tone I'd set to herald his calls. Our song. He heard it once, when he had to call my phone to wake me up from a nap *so* that I would let him into my apartment—of course I was sleeping with it at my side. He commented on it later, how he heard it on the other side of the door, our song signaling his presence. Our song, rendered polyphonic, my way of having him inside my Audiovox.

13   Sometimes I went to the Verizon Web site just to look at the call log for my account, as if the number of minutes we'd spoken in the past week could be plugged into a formula that would yield n, where *n = how much he loves me*. Once when he was angry he didn't call me for a week. I spent hours with my phone burning a lonely, desperate hole in my pajama pocket. We communicated more by email and chat than by phone, actually, but the phone calls always meant more to me; they

remain relatively unspoiled in memory. He called me to whisper in my ear; he called me when I had to fly home to my dying grandmother. I saved voice mail for as long as Verizon would allow, calling back at the end of the twenty-one-day default period just to preserve them.

When he broke up with me, it wasn't by phone. He waited until I was once again in a foreign land, California, this time, away from everyone I knew, and then he broke up with me via instant messenger. We didn't speak for four months. Finally, he wanted to talk to me, but he didn't want to see me, and once again the cell phone was how he made me—how he made us—invisible. I thought at the time that he was afraid of me, that the phone was protecting him from me, but really it wasn't much different from the way the phone had always protected him—kept me secret, made me safe. Or maybe, because it was so easy to feel that I could be hidden inside his phone and inside his computer—never mind the data trail—he never had to confront whether the reality of what we had was really as bad as he thought it was. If he kept me in the invisible cracks of machines, he could have some part of me without facing me or his fears.   14

I took his number off my phone within hours after he'd broken it off. I had too much pride to leave myself easy access to his voice mail. I knew he'd never have the courage to pick up my calls. I didn't want to leave my own pathetic data trail. My grandmother died that same week, but I kept her number. There was still something that felt like a connection I didn't want to delete. I still have her number in my address book. His number, on the other hand, I wish I'd never known it at all. Yet I couldn't bring myself to delete his ring tone. Whenever I cycled through my store of tones, to change my default or set a tone for a particular contact, there it was, playing automatically as soon as I reached it on the list. Every time I heard it, it shocked me for a moment with instinctive pleasure, the sense that we shared something, that he wanted to talk to me, before it filtered through the present and I remembered that he hadn't even called to say he wasn't going to call anymore. I would skip past it as quickly as possible, but I always knew it was coming and didn't get rid of it. I came to think of this with a certain sense of humor: just my little tendency toward techno-mediated, psychic self-mutilation.   15

And then, last month, I got a new phone, an upgrade from Verizon. I consulted with my blog readership about which model to choose, first narrowing the field to two choices because of their superior built-in cameras, music-playing capabilities, and availability in pink. There were so many conflicting opinions that I finally had to go by instinct, choosing the model that seemed to have the more intuitive interface: the Motorola RAZR V3m. Its pink wasn't as vibrant as I would have liked, but there was a wide range of snap-on cases available for it, and I was able to find one in a pink and black zebra-skin pattern that seemed to be just right for me. I have also spent a lot of money on its ring tones. These are extravagant gifts to this phone and no other—unlike telephone contacts, Verizon will not let me transfer ring tones phone-to-phone. So, my dead   16 grandmother's telephone number is in my new phone, transferred with the rest of my telephone contacts. My dead relationship's ring tone is not.

17   And it's not just his ring tone that's gone. He belongs to another artifact. It sometimes feels as though the year of my life I spent in that ill-advised love affair was poured into the now-obsolete Audiovox. Like a gift that still possesses something of the soul of the giver, the phone itself had come to be haunted by the voice that spoke so often through it. I gave back everything he had given me, but I couldn't get him out of my phone. I used to get tattooed when love went wrong, remaking my body into one that had never known the touch of my former partner. Now I have a new phone into which I have never spoken too soon or not wisely enough. Now I have a phone from which I have never failed to hear the words I wanted. My new RAZR is a part of a me that is freshly born, unscarred.

18   And I carry it everywhere. I frequently speak on it as I move through public places—I find that it provides insulation against panhandling and unwelcome advances. It's difficult, after all, to engage someone in conversation when they are already talking to somebody else. If I can't get a signal, I don't go as far as my friends who will pretend to talk to a dead phone; I just play Tetris instead. The blonde girl with her pearlescent pink *keitai* will never walk the streets of Tokyo again, but now there's a pink-haired woman with a pink zebra-skin RAZR that trills "Heartbreak Beat" for default calls in Boston.

TIMOTHY STOBIERSKI

Timothy Stobierski was born in 1989 in Ansonia, Connecticut. He earned his BA in English with a concentration in creative writing from the University of Connecticut in 2011, after a brief stint as a science student. Despite the change in discipline, much of his writing maintains elements of the scientific method: exploring the causes, effects, and correlations between ideas, actions, and outcomes.

"The Paradox," written in the style of a newspaper op-ed, explores the effects of the text-messaging revolution on today's society. The short piece examines the psychology behind a contradictory realization, the fact that "as we become more integrated, the gulf between individuals is growing instead of shrinking."

The Paradox

1   I grew up in a time and family before cell-phones, meaning that I grew up in a time and family before text messaging. When I needed to talk to somebody I would do just that: I would call them from a landline and

I would actually *talk* to them. It was either that or wait until I was face to face with the person.

In my junior year of high school I got my first cell-phone. I probably   2
sent my first text message on that very same day, to try it out. Today, at least ninety-five percent of my communication is conducted via text. The only people I actually speak to over the phone: my bank or any other administrative service, wrong-numbers, and my mother.

The obvious reason for this is that it's easy. It's easier to type out a   3
brief message and just send it to the other person than it is to talk to them: you convey the information and you don't get stuck in a conversation that you don't want to take part in. There's no time commitment, and you can text from anywhere, at anytime—at work, at church, at school. The truly skilled amongst us can even text with their phone in their pocket. They could probably get away with texting in a courtroom, as a judge sentenced them to two years for texting while driving. "OMG! Can't believe it. 2 yrs??!"

But while the reasons are obvious, the effects are less so. I'm not   4
talking about the effects that get all of the media attention–texting while driving, sexting, bullying via text, or cheating on exams by text. I'm talking about the psychological and cultural effects that go unnoticed.

Texting has caused our society to become more interconnected than   5
it has ever been before in history, while distancing us from each other at the same time. We are forever at the fingertips of the people we know; we can instantly be reached no matter where we are or what we are doing. And in a sense this is a good thing. Texting increases productivity, the flow of information. In an emergency, it can be the most effective way of alerting the masses. But at the same time it has the effect of sterilizing human contact.

To speak to someone over the phone is to make yourself vulnerable.   6
On one level there is the fact that you are actually in a sort of contact with the other person: you hear and feel their voice in your ear, and that can be an intimate interaction. You are allowing them in. On another level is the fact that you are giving up some control over the situation when you talk to someone on the phone. In a phone conversation there is the danger of awkward silence. There is the danger that you cannot precisely control what you are going to say in response to someone. There is the danger that an important message might get muddled by emotion.

By text, you can plan out your response. You can precisely word   7
the message you want to convey. And that's the only thing the person can see: your words. They cannot hear your tone, the slight crack in your voice when you get excited. They can't hear the worry when you're giving bad news. "Mom had a heart attack" is so much easier to convey by text than it is by telephone call. And that is perhaps the biggest allure in text-messaging. It's clean-cut. It's simply a conveyance of information.

8   I know people my own age who have been fired from jobs or who have turned jobs down because of their reluctance to answer telephones. I know people who openly flirt by text but don't know how to interact with one another when they are face to face. I know two separate couples that have broken up by text. I have myself ignored phone calls only to text the person, "What do you want?"

9   This isn't just an issue concerning text messaging. Facebook allows us to keep tabs on people that we may not have actually spoken to in years, even decades. Twitter makes us keen on even the most intimate moments of each other's day to day lives. Emails get sent from one cubicle to another right next door when all it would take is two seconds to stand up and peer over the wall that divides them. Some university professors across the country have even begun allowing students to text in their answers because students are more comfortable with the anonymity of texting than they are with raising their hands and speaking their answers out loud.

10   All of these technologies have served a role in this paradox whereby, as we become more integrated, the gulf between individuals is growing instead of shrinking. We are distancing ourselves from each other at the same time we are exposing ourselves to each other. It isn't a matter of cell phone vs. computer, or of Facebook vs. Twitter. It's a matter of human interaction vs. the cold hard coding of technology.

11   The big question here is: when hearing another person's voice coming out of the receiver of a telephone is too intimate to bear, what does this say about our society and where we are going?

12   Simply put, it says that we have forgotten how to talk to one another. We have forgotten the etiquette of conversation. We are no longer comfortable speaking, opening ourselves up. We don't want to give up control. We don't want to make ourselves vulnerable.

13   The problem there is that that's life. If you're not willing to open up, then you're not really living.

Content

1. Gathman and Stobierski each discuss their relationship to cell phones. Both authors text incessantly; what purposes does the texting serve?

2. Stobierski talks only to his mother by phone; why? Gathman also holds actual conversations on her cell. With whom? Under what circumstances? She gets "nervous if my cell phone was more than a yard away" (¶ 12) and spends "hours with my phone burning a lonely, desperate hole in my pajama pocket" (¶ 13). Is she addicted to the phone itself, or to the elusive boyfriend who might or might not call? Or to both? Is such addiction a natural phenomenon of contemporary life? What does Stobierski think?

3. Gathman's boyfriend breaks up by "instant messenger" (¶ 14). Do you know anyone who has had this experience? Does the remoteness of this form of break up

dehumanize the relationship: "If he kept me in the invisible cracks of machines, he could have some part of me without facing me or his fears" (¶ 14)? Do texting and instant messaging downplay interpersonal sensitivity? Lead to cruel if not unethical behavior? Amplify.

4. Stobierski observes that "Texting has caused our society to become more interconnected than it has ever been before in history, while distancing us from each other at the same time" (¶ 5). Amplify these remarks. Have you yourself experienced this paradox? Does this apply to Gathman's romantic relationship?

Strategies/Structures/Language

5. Gathman's essay is an autobiographical narrative; Stobierski's is an op-ed piece. Identify the features that characterize the genre of each piece. For what audience is each intended?

6. Gathman gives her cell phones personalities, through their brand names, colors, and ring tones. She began this as a nineteen-year-old; is this anthropomorphization of an inanimate object typical of a teenager? Would mature adults be likely to do this? Explain.

7. Think of other material objects that are considered reflections of the owner's/user's personality—clothing, houses, cars. Are there any conspicuous differences between cell phones as metaphors (or avatars) of their users, and other material objects?

For Writing

8. *Journal.* Keep a message log for 24 hours, noting every text message you send and receive, the respondent, and the time. *Quantitative analysis:* Then, tally the results. Is this a typical day?

Qualitative analysis. How many of these messages were "necessary"? What other reasons do you have for messaging? Do you feel, as Stobierski says, uncomfortable at actually speaking aloud? Do you use your cell as a substitute for speech, as a supplement, or both? Do you ever turn off the cell? Under what circumstances? When it's off, do you wish it were on?

9. *Dialogues.* What points do Stobierski and Gathman agree on concerning cell use? Are there any points of disagreement?

10. *Second Look.* If Google is making us stupid, as Carr argues, is texting making us even stupider, obsessively dependent on the continuous exchange of trivial messages?

As you answer this question, analyze your own texting behavior and compare yours with that of a partner. Write up your findings, and use these as the basis for writing "A survival guide to texting." What principles will it cover?

11. Has the ease and frequency of writing short text messages interfered with, even curtailed, your desire, if not ability, to write longer pieces that are serious, thoughtful, analytic, reflective–the kind that are required in college? Write a thoughtful, reflective essay on this topic, as an analogue to Carr's views on reading.

Narration

Western culture is embedded in narrative: what happened then, and then, and after that, with causation and consequences strung together like beads along a timeline necklace. Analyses of processes (Chapter 4), cause-and-effect relationships (Chapter 5), some descriptions (Chapter 6), and many arguments (Chapters 9 and 10) are based on narrative, stated directly or implied. Research proposals in the social, physical, and natural sciences, in medicine and business, require narrative interpretations: if we do this, we expect these events or phenomena to follow and to yield the following results.

Most commonly, we think of narration as telling a story, true or invented, or containing some mixture of each. Narration is a particularly attractive mode of writing, and ours is a storytelling culture. It is as old as Indian legends, Br'er Rabbit, Grimm's fairy tales, and the stories of Edgar Allan Poe. It is as new as speakers' warm-up jokes ("A funny thing happened on my way to . . .") and anecdotal leads to otherwise impersonal news stories. Narration can be as profound as the story of a life, the chronicle of a discovery, the history of a nation, or the account of one single, intense moment. Consider how Don DeLillo begins a brief story:

> Ash was spattering the windows, Karen was half dressed, grabbing the kids and trying to put on some clothes and talking with her husband and scooping things to take out to the corridor, and they looked at her, twin girls, as if she had fourteen heads.
>
> They stayed in the corridor for a while, thinking there might be secondary explosions. They waited, and began to feel safer, and went back to the apartment.
>
> At the next impact, Marc knew in the sheerest second before the shock wave broadsided their building that it was a second plane, impossible, striking the second tower. Their building was two blocks away, and he'd thought the first crash was an accident.

This excerpt from DeLillo's essay "In the Ruins of the Future" (*Harper's*, December 2001, 33) contains the major elements of a narrative.

1. *Characters:* Karen, Marc (whom we later learn is DeLillo's nephew), their twin daughters, and unidentified antagonists who are crashing planes into the World Trade Center
2. *Setting:* an apartment two blocks away from the World Trade Center
3. *Conflict:* terrorists versus New York's peaceful civilian population
4. *Plot*—beginning to unfold: Will this family survive? Will more attacks occur? What will be the consequences?
5. *Motives:* although the attackers' motives are murky, the victims' are clear—safety for themselves and their children
6. *Point of view:* a third-person account by an omniscient narrator who understands what the characters are thinking

It is unnecessary to specify the date, indelibly engraved on the minds of the readers as well as the participants. Only *dialogue* is missing but actions and eloquent silence say what is necessary. All these features make the incident or any vivid narrative a particularly easy form of writing for readers to remember. As this narration reveals, a narrative does *not* necessarily have to be a personal essay.

Narratives can be whole novels, stories, creative nonfiction essays, poems, or segments of other types of writings. They can be as long and as complicated as Charles Dickens's novels or an account of the events leading up to 9/11 and its aftermath, including the war in Iraq and a host of unforeseen consequences see Sheryl Kennedy's "About Suffering" (498–503). Or they can be short and to the point, as in V. Penelope Pelizzon's elliptical interpretation of her parents' courtship in "Clever and Poor" (285–86). This evocative poem (yes, poems can and do tell stories) offers revealing, snapshot-like glimpses of two people [*characters*], both clever and heartbreakingly poor—the woman "here off the Yugoslav train" [*setting*], arriving to meet the "newspaper-man who liked her in the picture." The primary *purpose* of the meeting is matrimony. But the woman's expectations of escaping poverty, the immediate *motivation* for her journey, are immediately undercut by "what is poor is what she sees" in the dispiriting station [*setting*] at which she arrives, with its cracked clock and girls selling "candle grease"—a poor offering indeed, reflected, perhaps literally, in the poverty of her husband-to-be, "his shined shoes tied with twine." How the *plot* will unfold is implied by the clever deceptions already accomplished by the cape "hiding her waist" as her presumably out-of-wedlock baby is "left with the nuns" and the valiant attempts of each of the characters to hide their poverty—a condition evident to the sympathetic narrator [*point of view*], the daughter who wrote the poem, and the readers, as well.

A narrative need not be fictional, as the above examples and the essays in this section indicate. When you're writing a narrative based on real people and actual incidents, you shape the material to emphasize the *point of view, sequence of action* (a chase, an exploration), a *theme* (greed, pleasure), a *particular relationship between characters* (love, antagonism), or the *personalities of the people involved* (vigorous, passive). This shaping—supplying information or other specific details where necessary, deleting trivial or irrelevant material—is essential in transforming skeletal notes or diary entries into three-dimensional configurations.

A narrative can *exist for its own sake*, as does "Clever and Poor." As sixteenth-century poet and courtier Sir Philip Sidney observed, such writing can attract "children from play and old men from the chimney corner." Through a narrative you can also *illustrate or explore a personality or an idea*, as in the photograph of the slave's scarred back on p. 88, a silent but articulate protest.

In "The Inheritance of Tools" (135–42), Scott Russell Sanders uses a comparable narrative technique to interpret the character of his father. As Sanders's essay becomes a tribute to his father, and to the extended family of which his father was a member, Sanders describes his legacy, the carpenters' tools ("the hammer [that] had belonged to him, and to his father before him") and the knowledge of how to use them, transmitted through years of patient teaching and an insistence on high-quality work, "making sure before I drove the first nail that every line was square and true." This type of description consists of stories embedded within stories: how Sanders's father taught him to use the hammer (¶s 6, 9), the saw (¶s 10, 12), the square (¶s 14–16). Still more stories incorporate the current use to which Sanders puts this knowledge (he Is building a bedroom in the basement), the incident of the gerbil escaping behind the new bedroom wall (¶s 17, 22), learning of his father's death (¶s 26, 28)—all embedded in the matrix of the stories of four generations of the Sanders family.

If you wish to write a personal narrative you can *present a whole or partial biography or autobiography*, as does Frederick Douglass in "Resurrection" (86–91), an excerpt from his *Life and Times* that recounts a single narrative incident in the life of a slave. Here Douglass tells the story of how he defied—in a two-hour fistfight—a Simon Legree—like overseer who had determined to break his spirit through repeated beatings. This, explains Douglass, was "the turning-point in my career as a slave. . . . It recalled the departed self-confidence, and inspired me again with a determination to be free. . . . It was a glorious resurrection, from the tomb of slavery, to the heaven of freedom." The photograph on p. 88 corroborates Douglass's story with a story of its own.

Through narration you can *impart information* or *an account of historical events*, from either an impartial or—more likely—an engaged eyewitness point of view. The resulting narrative is always an interpretation, whether of an individual, a group, or a historical or contemporary event. Jason Verge's "The Habs" (105–109) presents a comical account of his lifelong love for his favorite hockey team, the Montreal Canadiens, as well as a facetious self-portrait: "If you had to give up either me or hockey, which would you choose?'" asks his girlfriend. If she has to ask, we know the answer. Self-mockery is a convincing stance for any sports fan to adopt, since not everyone reading the narrative is guaranteed to love the home team—whatever that team may be—as much as the author does. Verge writes to entertain readers, partly at his own expense.

At other times, the narrative point of view can be satiric and highly critical of causes, unfolding events, outcomes, or all three. Sherman Alexie's satiric "What Sacagawea Means to Me" (83–85) is a critical commentary on white America's appropriation and exploitation of the historical Sacagawea, transformed into an icon ("our mother") in the process. Alexie tells only fragments of Sacagawea's story—that she accompanied Lewis and Clark on their "immigrant" expedition to spread the colonizing virus amongst the Indians; that she carried her first child, baby "Jean-Baptiste," with her on the journey; that she "died of some mysterious illness when she was only in her twenties." Sacagawea's biography—whether actual or imaginative, literal or symbolic—is composed of many contradictions embedded in the question "Why wouldn't she ask her brother and her tribe to take revenge against the men who had enslaved her?" Indeed, they are asked by the narrator, a Native American who himself is "a contradiction; I am Sacagawea."

Art Spiegelman's "Mein Kampf (My Struggle)" (93–95), with its embedded story of the Nazi death camps of the Holocaust, signals satire in its very title—also the title of Adolf Hitler's autobiography. In a mere sixteen cartoon panels we are invited to "read" the author's multigenerational life story and to interpret this through the split perspective of his critical eyes and our own. Thus we understand the Cave of Memory to be full of the memories identified by the signs on the labeled doors—"repressed memories," memories erotic and neurotic, intrauterine memories and childhood memories. His childhood memories are augmented by two photographs: one of Spiegelman as a child in a Cisco Kid outfit and one of his small son, Dashiell, in a Superman costume—both prepared to hold their own, if not to conquer their own corners of the world. The antihero cartoonist renders his life, the memories of his parents who "survived Auschwitz," and the image of his own child to comment on the need for struggle and survival against evil.

Fables, parables, and other *morality* or *cautionary tales* are as old as Aesop, as familiar as the Old and New Testaments of the Bible, as contemporary as Anne Fadiman's "Under Water" (100–104), a cautionary tale whose sunny beginning belies its complex moral undertow, which the narrator does not fully acknowledge until the passage of slow time for reflection, twenty-seven years after she was eighteen and "wanted to hurry through life as fast as I could." Although Fadiman focuses on telling the story and what it means to her, she expects the readers to apply to their own lives the moral understanding gained from reading about her experience of pleasure transformed, over time, to shame. The photograph on p. 101 captures the event, but does it convey the spirit and tone of Fadiman's essay?

Must a story have a happy ending? This is guaranteed only in some versions of some fairy tales, and then only after great suffering. Douglass's victory over the vicious slave overseer, Covey, strengthened him to defy other oppressors and eventually to escape to freedom, where he found life difficult as well. Fadiman survives her teenage companion's death by drowning, but lives for years with the guilt. Although the desperately hopeful couple in Pelizzon's poem may marry, their beginning does not augur well for their future.

To write a narrative you can ask, What do I want to demonstrate? Through what characters, performing what actions or thinking what thoughts? In what setting and time frame? From what point of view do I want to tell the tale? Do I want to use a first-person involved narrator who may also be a character in the story, as are the narrators of all the essays in this section? Or would a third-person narrator be more effective, either on the scene or depending on the reports of other people, as in the account of terrorism quoted on 70? An easy way to remember these questions is to ask yourself:

1. *Who* participated?
2. *What* happened?
3. *Why* did this event/these phenomena happen?
4. *When* did it (or they) happen?
5. *Where* did it (or they) happen?
6. *How* did it (or they) happen? Under what circumstances?
7. Was the outcome expected, unexpected? With what consequences, actual or potential?

Narratives have as many purposes, as many plots, as many characters as there are people to write them. You have but to examine your life, your thoughts, your experiences, to find an unwritten library of narratives yet to tell. Therein lie a thousand tales. Or a thousand and one. . . .

Strategies for Writing: Narration

1. You will need to consider, "What is the purpose of my narrative?" Am I telling the tale for its own sake, or am I using it to make a larger point?
2. For what audience am I writing this? What will they have experienced or be able to understand, and what will I need to explain? How do I want my audience to react?
3. What is the focus, the conflict of my narrative? How will it begin? Gain momentum and develop to a climax? End? What emphasis will I give each part, or separate scenes or incidents within each part?
4. Will I write from a first- or third-person point of view? Will I be a major character in my narrative? As a participant or as an observer? Or both, if my present self is observing my past self?
5. What is my attitude toward my material? What tone do I want to use? Will it be consistent throughout, or will it change during the course of events?

TIM O'BRIEN

Tim O'Brien's "striking sequence of stories," *The Things They Carried* (1990), is told by a character named—surprise!—Tim O'Brien. Says this narrator, "In June of 1968, a month after graduating from Macalester College (in Minnesota, where the author grew up), I was drafted to fight a war I hated. I was twenty-one years old." O'Brien the author (born 1947) first came to public notice with the anecdotal *If I Die in a Combat Zone, Box Me Up and Ship Me Home* (1973), followed by a number of other novels including *Northern Lights* (1975), *In the Lake of the Woods* (1994), and *Tomcat in Love* (1998). *Going after Cacciato* (1978) won the National Book Award. His most recent novel, *July, July* (2002), is a tale of disillusioned baby boomers—with the Vietnam War hovering in the background "like some unfinished business from the past." In response to an interviewer's query, "What can you teach people, just for having been in a war?" O'Brien said, "By 'teach,' I mean provide insight, philosophy . . . and that means reading and hard thought. I didn't intend *If I Die* to stand as a profound statement, and it's not. Teaching is one thing and telling stories is another. I wanted to use stories to alert readers to the complexity and ambiguity of a set of moral issues—but without preaching a moral lesson." O'Brien teaches in Texas State University, San Marcos every other year.

Like all meaningful war fiction, *The Things They Carried* puts a human face on the faceless abstraction of war. It is the single book that many say gets closest to the truth of the Vietnam War. Indeed, although "How to Tell a True War Story" is the seventh chapter of a work that is nominally fiction, what O'Brien says about writing the truth is dead accurate, and it applies to all sorts of creative nonfiction and personal essays, as well as to fiction.

- "A true war story is never moral. It does not instruct, nor encourage virtue, nor suggest models of proper human behavior, nor restrain men from doing the things men have always done. If a story seems moral, do not believe it." (¶ 8)
- "You can tell a true war story if it embarrasses you. If you don't care for obscenity, you don't care for the truth. . . . " (¶ 9)
- "In any [true] war story . . . it's difficult to separate what happened from what seemed to happen. What seems to happen becomes its own happening and has to be told that way. The angles of vision are skewed." (¶ 18)
- "You can tell a true war story by the questions you ask. Somebody tells a story, let's say, and afterward you ask, 'Is it true?' and if the answer matters, you've got your answer." (¶ 51)
- "[Yet] absolute occurrence is irrelevant. A thing may happen and be a total lie; another thing may not happen and be truer than the truth." (¶ 55)
- "In war you lose your sense of the definite, hence your sense of the truth itself, and therefore it's safe to say that in a true war story nothing is ever absolutely true." (¶ 47)

- "It comes down to gut instinct. A true war story, if truly told, makes the stomach believe." (¶ 24)
- "Often in a true war story there is not even a point, or else that point doesn't hit you until twenty years later, in your sleep. . . ." (¶ 48)
- "In the end, of course, a true war story is never about war. It's about sunlight. . . . It's about love and memory. It's about sorrow. It's about sisters who never write back and people who never listen." (¶ 64)

How to Tell a True War Story

1   This is true.

2   I had a buddy in Vietnam. His name was Bob Kiley, but everybody called him Rat.

3   A friend of his gets killed, so about a week later Rat sits down and writes a letter to the guy's sister. Rat tells her what a great brother she had, how together the guy was, a number one pal and comrade. A real soldier's soldier, Rat says. Then he tells a few stories to make the point, how her brother would always volunteer for stuff nobody else would volunteer for in a million years, dangerous stuff, like doing recon or going out on these really badass night patrols. Stainless steel balls, Rat tells her. The guy was a little crazy, for sure, but crazy in a good way, a real daredevil, because he liked the challenge of it, he liked testing himself, just man against gook. A great, great guy, Rat says.

4   Anyway, it's a terrific letter, very personal and touching. Rat almost bawls writing it. He gets all teary telling about the good times they had together, how her brother made the war seem almost fun, always raising hell and lighting up villes and bringing smoke to bear every which way. A great sense of humor, too. Like the time at this river when he went fishing with a whole damn crate of hand grenades. Probably the funniest thing in world history, Rat says, all that gore, about twenty zillion dead gook fish. Her brother, he had the right attitude. He knew how to have a good time. On Halloween, this real hot spooky night, the dude paints up his body all different colors and puts on this weird mask and hikes over to a ville and goes trick-or-treating almost stark naked, just boots and balls and an M-16. A tremendous human being, Rat says. Pretty nutso sometimes, but you could trust him with your life.

5   And then the letter gets very sad and serious. Rat pours his heart out. He says he loved the guy. He says the guy was his best friend in the world. They were like soul mates, he says, like twins or something, they had a whole lot in common. He tells the guy's sister he'll look her up when the war's over.

6   So what happens?

Rat mails the letter. He waits two months. The dumb cooze never   7
writes back.

A true war story is never moral. It does not instruct, nor encourage vir-   8
tue, nor suggest models of proper human behavior, nor restrain men
from doing the things men have always done. If a story seems moral, do
not believe it. If at the end of a war story you feel uplifted, or if you feel
that some small bit of rectitude has been salvaged from the larger waste,
then you have been made the victim of a very old and terrible lie. There
is no rectitude whatsoever. There is no virtue. As a first rule of thumb,
therefore, you can tell a true war story by its absolute and uncompromising allegiance to obscenity and evil. Listen to Rat Kiley. Cooze, he says.
He does not say bitch. He certainly does not say woman, or girl. He says
cooze. Then he spits and stares. He's nineteen years old—it's too much
for him—so he looks at you with those big sad gentle killer eyes and says
cooze, because his friend is dead, and because it's so incredibly sad and
true: she never wrote back.

You can tell a true war story if it embarrasses you. If you don't   9
care for obscenity, you don't care for the truth; if you don't care for the
truth, watch how you vote. Send guys to war, they come home talking
dirty.

Listen to Rat: "Jesus Christ, man, I write this beautiful f***in' letter,   10
I slave over it, and what happens? The dumb cooze never writes back."

The dead guy's name was Curt Lemon. What happened was, we crossed   11
a muddy river and marched west into the mountains, and on the third
day we took a break along a trail junction in deep jungle. Right away,
Lemon and Rat Kiley started goofing. They didn't understand about
the spookiness. They were kids; they just didn't know. A nature hike,
they thought, not even a war, so they went off into the shade of some
giant trees—quadruple canopy, no sunlight at all—and they were giggling and calling each other yellow mother and playing a silly game
they'd invented. The game involved smoke grenades, which were
harmless unless you did stupid things, and what they did was pull out
the pin and stand a few feet apart and play catch under the shade of
those huge trees. Whoever chickened out was a yellow mother. And if
nobody chickened out, the grenade would make a light popping sound
and they'd be covered with smoke and they'd laugh and dance around
and then do it again.

It's all exactly true.   12

It happened, to *me*, nearly twenty years ago, and I still remem-   13
ber that trail junction and those giant trees and a soft dripping sound
somewhere beyond the trees. I remember the smell of moss. Up in the
canopy there were tiny white blossoms, but no sunlight at all, and I
remember the shadows spreading out under the trees where Curt Lemon
and Rat Kiley were playing catch with smoke grenades. Mitchell Sanders

sat flipping his yo-yo. Norman Bowker and Kiowa and Dave Jensen were dozing, or half dozing, and all around us were those ragged green mountains.

14   Except for the laughter things were quiet.

15   At one point, I remember, Mitchell Sanders turned and looked at me, not quite nodding, as if to warn me about something, as if he already *knew*, then after a while he rolled up his yo-yo and moved away.

16   It's hard to tell you what happened next.

17   They were just goofing. There was a noise, I suppose, which must've been the detonator, so I glanced behind me and watched Lemon step from the shade into bright sunlight. His face was suddenly brown and shining. A handsome kid, really. Sharp gray eyes, lean and narrow-waisted, and when he died it was almost beautiful, the way the sunlight came around him and lifted him up and sucked him high into a tree full of moss and vines and white blossoms.

18   In any war story, but especially a true one, it's difficult to separate what happened from what seemed to happen. What seems to happen becomes its own happening and has to be told that way. The angles of vision are skewed. When a booby trap explodes, you close your eyes and duck and float outside yourself. When a guy dies, like Curt Lemon, you look away and then look back for a moment and then look away again. The pictures get jumbled; you tend to miss a lot. And then afterward, when you go to tell about it, there is always that surreal seemingness, which makes the story seem untrue, but which in fact represents the hard and exact truth as it *seemed*.

19   In many cases a true war story cannot be believed. If you believe it, be skeptical. It's a question of credibility. Often the crazy stuff is true and the normal stuff is necessary to make you believe the truly incredible craziness.

20   In other cases you can't even tell a true war story. Sometimes it's just beyond telling. . . .

21   In a true war story, if there's a moral at all, it's like the thread that makes the cloth. You can't extract the meaning without unraveling the deeper meaning. And in the end, really, there's nothing much to say about a true war story, except maybe "Oh."

22   True war stories do not generalize. They do not indulge in abstraction or analysis.

23   For example: War is hell. As a moral declaration the old truism seems perfectly true, and yet because it abstracts, because it generalizes, I can't believe it with my stomach. Nothing turns inside.

24   It comes down to gut instinct. A true war story, if truly told, makes the stomach believe.

This one does it for me. I've told it before—many times, many versions—but here's what actually happened. 25

We crossed that river and marched west into the mountains. On the third day, Curt Lemon stepped on a booby-trapped 105 round. He was playing catch with Rat Kiley, laughing, and then he was dead. The trees were thick; it took nearly an hour to cut an LZ for the dustoff. 26

Later, higher in the mountains, we came across a baby VC water buffalo. What it was doing there I don't know—no farms or paddies—but we chased it down and got a rope around it and led it along to a deserted village where we set up for the night. After supper Rat Kiley went over and stroked its nose. 27

He opened up a can of C rations, pork and beans, but the baby buffalo wasn't interested. 28

Rat shrugged. 29

He stepped back and shot it through the right front knee. The animal did not make a sound. It went down hard, then got up again, and Rat took careful aim and shot off an ear. He shot it in the hindquarters and in the little hump at its back. He shot it twice in the flanks. It wasn't to kill; it was to hurt. He put the rifle muzzle up against the mouth and shot the mouth away. Nobody said much. The whole platoon stood there watching, feeling all kinds of things, but there wasn't a great deal of pity for the baby water buffalo. Curt Lemon was dead. Rat Kiley had lost his best friend in the world. Later in the week he would write a long personal letter to the guy's sister, who would not write back, but for now it was a question of pain. He shot off the tail. He shot away chunks of meat below the ribs. All around us there was the smell of smoke and filth and deep greenery, and the evening was humid and very hot. Rat went to automatic. He shot randomly, almost casually, quick little spurts in the belly and butt. Then he reloaded, squatted down, and shot it in the left front knee. Again the animal fell hard and tried to get up, but this time it couldn't quite make it. It wobbled and went down sideways. Rat shot it in the nose. He bent forward and whispered something, as if talking to a pet, then he shot it in the throat. All the while the baby buffalo was silent, or almost silent, just a light bubbling sound where the nose had been. It lay very still. Nothing moved except the eyes, which were enormous, the pupils shiny black and dumb. 30

Rat Kiley was crying. He tried to say something, but then cradled his rifle and went off by himself. 31

The rest of us stood in a ragged circle around the baby buffalo. For a time no one spoke. We had witnessed something essential, something brand-new and profound, a piece of the world so startling there was not yet a name for it. 32

Somebody kicked the baby buffalo. 33

It was still alive, though just barely, just in the eyes. 34

"Amazing," Dave Jensen said. "My whole life, I never seen anything like it." 35

36   "Never?"

37   "Not hardly. Not once."

38   Kiowa and Mitchell Sanders picked up the baby buffalo. They hauled it across the open square, hoisted it up, and dumped it in the village well.

39   Afterward, we sat waiting for Rat to get himself together.

40   "Amazing," Dave Jensen kept saying. "A new wrinkle. I never seen it before."

41   Mitchell Sanders took out his yo-yo. "Well, that's Nam," he said. "Garden of Evil. Over here, man, every sin's real fresh and original."

42 How do you generalize?

43   War is hell, but that's not the half of it, because war is also mystery and terror and adventure and courage and discovery and holiness and pity and despair and longing and love. War is nasty; war is fun. War is thrilling; war is drudgery. War makes you a man; war makes you dead.

44   The truths are contradictory. It can be argued, for instance, that war is grotesque. But in truth war is also beauty. For all its horror, you can't help but gape at the awful majesty of combat. You stare out at tracer rounds unwinding through the dark like brilliant red ribbons. You crouch in ambush as a cool, impassive moon rises over the nighttime paddies. You admire the fluid symmetries of troops on the move, the harmonies of sound and shape and proportion, the great sheets of metal-fire streaming down from a gunship, the illumination rounds, the white phosphorus, the purply orange glow of napalm, the rocket's red glare. It's not pretty, exactly. It's astonishing. It fills the eye. It commands you. You hate it, yes, but your eyes do not. Like a killer forest fire, like cancer under a microscope, any battle or bombing raid or artillery barrage has the aesthetic purity of absolute moral indifference—a powerful, implacable beauty—and a true war story will tell the truth about this, though the truth is ugly.

45   To generalize about war is like generalizing about peace. Almost everything is true. Almost nothing is true. At its core, perhaps, war is just another name for death, and yet any soldier will tell you, if he tells the truth, that proximity to death brings with it a corresponding proximity to life. After a firefight, there is always the immense pleasure of aliveness. The trees are alive. The grass, the soil—everything. All around you things are purely living, and you among them, and the aliveness makes you tremble. You feel an intense, out-of-the-skin awareness of your living self—your truest self, the human being you want to be and then become by the force of wanting it. In the midst of evil you want to be a good man. You want decency. You want justice and courtesy and human concord, things you never knew you wanted. There is a kind of largeness to it, a kind of godliness. Though it's odd, you're never more alive than when you're almost dead. You recognize what's valuable. Freshly, as if for the first time, you love what's best in yourself and in the world, all that might be lost. At the hour of dusk you sit at your foxhole and look out on a wide river turning pinkish red, and at the

mountains beyond, and although in the morning you must cross the river and go into the mountains and do terrible things and maybe die, even so, you find yourself studying the fine colors on the river, you feel wonder and awe at the setting of the sun, and you are filled with a hard, aching love for how the world could be and always should be, but now is not.

Mitchell Sanders was right. For the common soldier, at least, war has the feel—the spiritual texture—of a great ghostly fog, thick and permanent. There is no clarity. Everything swirls. The old rules are no longer binding, the old truths no longer true. Right spills over into wrong. Order blends into chaos, love into hate, ugliness into beauty, law into anarchy, civility into savagery. The vapors suck you in. You can't tell where you are, or why you're there, and the only certainty is overwhelming ambiguity. 46

In war you lose your sense of the definite, hence your sense of truth itself, and therefore it's safe to say that in a true war story nothing is ever absolutely true. 47

Often in a true war story there is not even a point, or else the point doesn't hit you until twenty years later, in your sleep, and you wake up and shake your wife and start telling the story to her, except when you get to the end you've forgotten the point again. And then for a long time you lie there watching the story happen in your head. You listen to your wife's breathing. The war's over. You close your eyes. You smile and think, Christ, what's the *point*? 48

This one wakes me up. 49

In the mountains that day, I watched Lemon turn sideways. He laughed and said something to Rat Kiley. Then he took a peculiar half step, moving from shade into bright sunlight, and the booby-trapped 105 round blew him into a tree. The parts were just hanging there, so Dave Jensen and I were ordered to shinny up and peel him off. I remember the white bone of an arm. I remember pieces of skin and something wet and yellow that must've been the intestines. The gore was horrible, and stays with me. But what wakes me up twenty years later is Dave Jensen singing "Lemon Tree" as we threw down the parts. 50

You can tell a true war story by the questions you ask. Somebody tells a story, let's say, and afterward you ask, "Is it true?" and if the answer matters, you've got your answer. 51

For example, we've all heard this one. Four guys go down a trail. A grenade sails out. One guy jumps on it and takes the blast and saves his three buddies. 52

Is it true? 53

The answer matters. 54

You'd feel cheated if it never happened. Without the grounding reality, it's just a trite bit of puffery, pure Hollywood, untrue in the way all such stores are untrue. Yet even if it did happen—and maybe it did, anything's possible—even then you know it can't be true, because a true war story does not depend upon that kind of truth. Absolute occurrence 55 is irrelevant. A thing may happen and be a total lie; another thing may not happen and be truer than the truth. For example: Four guys go down a trail. A grenade sails out. One guy jumps on it and takes the blast, but it's a killer grenade and everybody dies anyway. Before they die, though, one of the dead guy says, "The f*** you do *that* for?" and the jumper says, "Story of my life, man," and the other guy starts to smile but he's dead.

56   That's a true story that never happened.

57 Twenty years later, I can still see the sunlight on Lemon's face. I can see him turning, looking back at Rat Kiley, then he laughed and took that curious half step from shade into sunlight, his face suddenly brown and shining, and when his foot touched down, in that instant, he must've thought it was the sunlight that was killing him. It was not the sunlight. It was a rigged 105 round. But if I could ever get the story right, how the sun seemed to gather around him and pick him up and lift him high into a tree, if I could somehow recreate the fatal whiteness of that light, the quick glare, the obvious cause and effect, then you would believe the last thing Curt Lemon believed, which for him must've been the final truth.

58 Now and then, when I tell this story, someone will come up to me afterward and say she liked it. It's always a woman. Usually it's an older woman of kindly temperament and humane politics. She'll explain that as a rule she hates war stories; she can't understand why people want to wallow in all the blood and gore. But this one she liked. The poor baby buffalo, it made her sad. Sometimes, even, there are little tears. What I should do, she'll say, is put it all behind me. Find new stories to tell.

59   I won't say it but I'll think it.

60   I'll picture Rat Kiley's face, his grief, and I'll think, *You dumb cooze.*

61   Because she wasn't listening.

62   It *wasn't* a war story. It was a *love* story.

63   But you can't say that. All you can do is tell it one more time, patiently, adding and subtracting, making up a few things to get at the real truth. No Mitchell Sanders, you tell her. No Lemon, no Rat Kiley. No trail junction. No baby buffalo. No vines or moss or white blossoms. Beginning to end, you tell her, it's all made up. Every goddamn detail—the mountains and the river and especially that poor dumb baby buffalo. None of it happened. *None* of it. And even if it did happen, it didn't happen in the mountains, it happened in this little village on the Batangan Peninsula, and it was raining like crazy, and one night a guy named Stink Harris woke up screaming with a leech on his tongue. You can tell a true war story if you just keep on telling it.

64   And in the end, of course, a true war story is never about war. It's about sunlight. It's about the special way that dawn spreads out on a river when you know you must cross the river and march into the mountains and do things you are afraid to do. It's about love and memory. It's about sorrow. It's about sisters who never write back and people who never listen.

SHERMAN ALEXIE

Sherman Alexie (born 1966) is a Spokane/Coeur d'Alene Indian who grew up on the Spokane Indian Reservation in Wellpinit, Washington. By the time he earned his BA from the University of Washington (1995)— prognostic of his literary future—he had already published five volumes of poetry, a collection of short stories, and a novel, *Reservation Blues*. Indeed, the novel's title is the motif for much of Alexie's writing. His works include the films *Smoke Signals* (1998) and *The Business of Fancydancing* (2002), collections of stories such as *Ten Little Indians* (2003), and the novels *The Low Ranger* and *Tonto Fistfight in Heaven* (1994), *Indian Killer* (1996), and *The Absolutely True Diary of a Part-Time Indian*, the latter of which won the 2007 National Book Award for Young People's Literature. His latest novel is *War Dances* (2009) All present Alexie's characteristically ironic, humorous interpretations of three profound central questions: "What does it mean to live as an Indian in this time? As an Indian man? On an Indian reservation?" Alexie's Indians, laid-back, casual, comic, often drunk, are waging war on two fronts. They battle as colonized people must on reservations—against alcoholism, poverty, and cultural destruction; they can never be treated fairly—anywhere. They also battle the stereotyping of Indians, not only in the popular media (as in the iconic figures of Tonto and Sacagawea), but also in the "Mother Earth Father Sky" clichés promoted in the works of other Indians, such as N. Scott Momaday. Along with the publication of numerous books (sixteen to date, and counting) have come a host of awards.

Alexie says, "I think humor is the most effective political tool out there, because people will listen to anything if they're laughing. . . . There's nothing worse than earnest emotion and I never want to be earnest. I always want to be on the edge of offending somebody. . . . Humor is really just about questioning the status quo." "What Sacagawea Means to Me," first published in *Time* (June 30, 2002) offers a critique of the mythic, white version of the Lewis and Clark expedition, a "multicultural, trigenerational, bigendered, animal-friendly" exploration, through a counterinterpretation of their faithful companion and guide Sacagawea, the American Eve.

What Sacagawea Means to Me

In the future, every U.S. citizen will get to be Sacagawea for fifteen minutes. For the low price of admission, every American, regardless of race, religion, gender, and age, will climb through the portal into Sacagawea's Shoshone Indian brain. In the multicultural theme park called Sacagawea Land, you will be kidnapped as a child by the Hidatsa tribe and sold to Toussaint Charbonneau, the French-Canadian trader who will take you   1 as one of his wives and father two of your children. Your first child, Jean-Baptiste, will be only a few months old as you carry him during your long journey with Lewis and Clark. The two captains will lead the adventure, fighting rivers, animals, weather, and diseases for thousands of miles, and you will march right beside them. But you, the aboriginal multitasker, will also breastfeed. And at the end of your Sacagawea journey, you will be shown the exit and given a souvenir T-shirt that reads, IF THE U.S. IS EDEN, THEN SACAGAWEA IS EVE.

2   Sacagawea is our mother. She is the first gene pair of the American DNA. In the beginning, she was the word, and the word was possibility. I revel in the wondrous possibilities of Sacagawea. It is good to be joyous in the presence of her spirit, because I hope she had moments of joy in what must have been a grueling life. This much is true: Sacagawea died of some mysterious illness when she was only in her twenties. Most illnesses were mysterious in the nineteenth century, but I suspect that Sacagawea's indigenous immune system was defenseless against an immigrant virus. Perhaps Lewis and Clark infected Sacagawea. If that is true, then certain postcolonial historians would argue that she was murdered not by germs but by colonists who carried those germs. I don't know much about the science of disease and immunities, but I know enough poetry to recognize that individual human beings are invaded and colonized by foreign bodies, just as individual civilizations are invaded and colonized by foreign bodies. In that sense, colonization might be a natural process, tragic and violent to be sure, but predictable and ordinary as well, and possibly necessary for the advance, however constructive and destructive, of all civilizations.

3   After all, Lewis and Clark's story has never been just the triumphant tale of two white men, no matter what the white historians might need to believe. Sacagawea was not the primary hero of this story either, no matter what the Native American historians and I might want to believe. The story of Lewis and Clark is also the story of the approximately forty-five nameless and faceless first- and second-generation European Americans who joined the journey, then left or completed it, often without monetary or historical compensation. Considering the time and place, I imagine those forty-five were illiterate, low-skilled laborers subject to managerial whims and nineteenth-century downsizing. And it is most certainly the story of the black slave York, who also cast votes during this allegedly democratic adventure. It's even the story of Seaman, the domesticated Newfoundland dog who must have been a welcome and friendly presence and who survived the risk of becoming supper during one lean time or another. The Lewis and Clark Expedition was exactly the kind of multicultural, trigenerational, bigendered, animal-friendly, government-supported, partly French-Canadian project that should rightly be celebrated by liberals and castigated by conservatives.

4   In the end, I wonder if colonization might somehow be magical. After all, Miles Davis is the direct descendant of slaves and slave owners.

Hank Williams is the direct descendant of poor whites and poorer Indians. In 1876 Emily Dickinson was writing her poems in an Amherst attic while Crazy Horse was killing Custer on the banks of the Little Big Horn. I remain stunned by these contradictions, by the successive generations of social, political, and artistic mutations that can be so beautiful and painful. How did we get from there to here? This country somehow gave life to Maria Tallchief and Ted Bundy, to Geronimo and Joe McCarthy, to Nathan Bedford Forrest and Toni Morrison, to the Declaration of Independence and Executive Order No. 1066, to Cesar Chavez and Richard Nixon, to theme parks and national parks, to smallpox and the vaccine for smallpox.

As a Native American, I want to hate this country and its contra-   5
dictions. I want to believe that Sacagawea hated this country and its contradictions. But this country exists, in whole and in part, because Sacagawea helped Lewis and Clark. In the land that came to be called Idaho, she acted as diplomat between her long-lost brother and the Lewis and Clark party. Why wouldn't she ask her brother and her tribe to take revenge against the men who had enslaved her? Sacagawea is a contradiction. Here in Seattle, I exist, in whole and in part, because a half-white man named James Cox fell in love with a Spokane Indian woman named Etta Adams and gave birth to my mother. I am a contradiction; I am Sacagawea.

Content

1. Alexie's short piece depends on readers to understand a host of common cultural references: Sacagawea as a cultural and historical figure; Lewis and Clark and the purpose(s) and nature of their expedition; other members of the expedition (including the Newfoundland dog); and all of the people and events referred to in ¶ 4: Miles Davis, Hank Williams, Emily Dickinson, Crazy Horse, and Custer. Do you recognize most of them? If you don't can you still understand Alexie's general point and the means by which he is making it? Or is he too allusive? Explain.

2. Identify and amplify from your own knowledge of history the various roles in American history that Alexie attributes to Sacagawea whether she actually played them or not: Indian icon who helped Lewis and Clark on their expedition (a fact so well-known that Alexie does not fully articulate it in this essay); child kidnap victim; wife of a French-Canadian trader; mother of infant Jean-Baptiste, who accompanied her on the journey. He also calls her the mother of our nation, an undeserving victim of "immigrant" viruses, diplomat between her "long-lost brother and the Lewis and Clark party," a "contradiction" who lives on in subsequent Indian generations. Do you disagree with any of his interpretations? If so, explain why.

3. Why does Alexie say "Sacagawea was not the primary hero of [the Lewis and Clark story], no matter what the Native American historians and I might want to believe" (¶ 3). Who is the hero, if not Lewis and Clark or Sacagawea?

Strategies/Structures/Language

4. Why does Alexie set up Sacagawea's brain as a "multicultural theme park called Sacagawea Land," into which readers go for a "low price of admission" to allegedly recreate the Indian's experiences? What are readers expected to learn as a consequence of all the roles they'll play therein (see question 1)?

5. At what point in the essay do you recognize that Alexie is being sarcastic? Why did he title the piece "What Sacagawea Means to Me"?

For Writing

6. Write a short "true" story of some historical event—particularly one involving oppression of other groups or cultures—that you thought you understood but that a new rendering (perhaps as a new story rather than just a collection of facts) or new information reveals a new concept to you and to your readers. How much information will you have to supply? How much can you expect your readers to understand? If you can write with a partner who represents the other culture you're examining, so much the better.

7. *Journal Writing.* Choose a particular theme park and describe how it both represents and fails to represent American history, society, or culture. What myths about America does this theme park employ and promote? Do these myths necessarily mask contemporary social problems or realities?

8. *Dialogues.* Compare Alexie's view of American culture as the product of "successive generations of social, political, and artistic mutations that can be so beautiful and painful" (¶ 4) with Hogan's commentary on the relation of the physical terrain to the human spirit. Alexie refers to colonization as a "tragic and violent . . . , but [also] predictable and ordinary" process (¶ 2). How does Hogan illustrate American history? After reading both Alexie and Hogan, do you believe that a cultural heritage can survive invasive colonization and assimilation? What reasons do Alexie and Hogan provide, or allude to, in support of the idea that ethnic groups should preserve their history and culture?

9. *Mixed Modes.* Alexie redefines—implicitly or explicitly—concepts such as colonization, heroism, culture, and even the notion of story itself. How do these concepts support his conclusion that "I am Sacagawea" (¶ 5)? Does his definition of American culture as inherently contradictory suggest integration or conflict?

10. *Second Look.* In what ways does the photograph in this essay, of Franz Boas and George Hunt holding a backdrop behind a Kwakiutl woman, capture the essence of "What Sacagawea Means to Me"? How can this late-nineteenth-century photograph enrich our understanding of Alexie's essay?

FREDERICK DOUGLASS

Frederick Douglass (1817–1895) was born a slave in Talbot County, Maryland. Unlike many slaves, he learned to read, and the power of this accomplishment—coupled with an iron physique and the will to match—enabled him to escape to New York in 1838. For the next twenty-five years he toured the country as a powerful spokesperson for the abolitionist movement, serving as an adviser to Harriet Beecher Stowe, author of *Uncle Tom's Cabin*, and to President Lincoln, among others. After the war he campaigned for civil rights for African Americans and women. In 1890 his political significance was acknowledged in his appointment as minister to Haiti.

Slave narratives, written or dictated by the hundreds in the nineteenth century, provided memorable accounts of the physical, geographical, and psychological movement from captivity to freedom. Douglass's autobiography, an abolitionist document like many other slave narratives, is exceptional in its forthright language and absence of stereotyping of either white or black people; his people are multidimensional. Crisis points, and the insights and opportunities they provide, are natural topics for personal narratives. This episode, taken from the first version (of four) of *The Narrative of the Life of Frederick Douglass, an American Slave* (1845), explains the incident that was "the turning point in my career as a slave," for it enabled him to make the transformation from slave to independent human being.

Resurrection

I have already intimated that my condition was much worse, during the first six months of my stay at Mr. Covey's, than in the last six. The circumstances leading to the change in Mr. Covey's course toward me form an epoch in my humble history. You have seen how a man was made a slave; you shall see how a slave was made a man. On one of the hottest days of the month of August, 1833, Bill Smith, William Hughes, a slave named Eli, and myself, were engaged in fanning wheat. Hughes was clearing the fanned wheat from before the fan. Eli was turning, Smith was feeding, and I was carrying wheat to the fan. The work was simple, requiring strength rather than intellect; yet, to one entirely unused to such work, it came very hard. About three o'clock of that day, I broke down; my strength failed me; I was seized with a violent aching of the head, attended with extreme dizziness; I trembled in every limb. Finding what was coming, I nerved myself up, feeling it would never do to stop work. I stood as long as I could stagger to the hopper with grain. When I could stand no longer, I fell, and felt as if held down by an immense weight. The fan of course stopped; every one had his own work to do; and no one could do the work of the other, and have his own go on at the same time. 1

Mr. Covey was at the house, about one hundred yards from the treading-yard where we were fanning. On hearing the fan stop, he left immediately, and came to the spot where we were. He hastily inquired what the matter was. Bill answered that I was sick, and there was no one to bring wheat to the fan. I had by this time crawled away under the side of 2

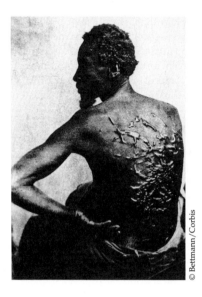

Interpret the pattern on the slave's back. What stories does this tell? Is there any ambiguity or uncertainty about their meaning? Do you need to know that this is a photograph of a slave to be able to understand the picture? Does it matter whether this picture was taken in the United States or somewhere else? (See also the discussion in Second Look, following this essay.)

© Bettmann/Corbis

the post and rail-fence by which the yard was enclosed, hoping to find re-lief by getting out of the sun. He then asked where I was. He was told by one of the hands. He came to the spot, and, after looking at me awhile, asked me what was the matter. I told him as well as I could, for I scarce had strength to speak. He then gave me a savage kick in the side, and told me to get up. I tried to do so, but fell back in the attempt. He gave me an-other kick, and again told me to rise. I again tried, and succeeded in gain-ing my feet; but, stooping to get the tub with which I was feeding the fan, I again staggered and fell. While down in this situation, Mr. Covey took up the hickory slat with which Hughes had been striking off the half-bushel measure, and with it gave me a heavy blow upon the head, mak-ing a large wound, and the blood ran freely; and with this again told me to get up. I made no effort to comply, having now made up my mind to let him do his worst. In a short time after receiving this blow, my head grew better. Mr. Covey had now left me to my fate. At this moment I resolved, for the first time, to go to my master, enter a complaint, and ask his protec-tion. In order to do this, I must that afternoon walk seven miles; and this, under the circumstances, was truly a severe undertaking. I was exceed-ingly feeble; made so as much by the kicks and blows which I received, as by the severe fit of sickness to which I had been subjected. I, however, watched my chance, while Covey was looking in an opposite direction, and started for St. Michael's. I succeeded in getting a considerable dis-tance on my way to the woods, when Covey discovered me, and called after me to come back, threatening what he would do if I did not come. I disregarded both his calls and his threats, and made my way to the woods as fast as my feeble state would allow; and thinking I might be overhauled by him if I kept to the road, I walked through the woods, keeping far enough from the road to avoid detection, and near enough to prevent losing my way. I had not gone far before my little strength again failed me. I could go no farther. I fell down, and lay for a considerable time. The blood was yet oozing from the wound on my head. For a time I thought I should bleed to death; and think now that I should have done so, but that the blood so matted my hair as to stop the wound. After lying there about three quarters of an hour, I nerved myself up again, and started on my way, through bogs and briers, barefooted and bareheaded, tearing my feet sometimes at nearly every step; and after a journey of about seven miles, occupying some five hours to perform it, I arrived at master's store. I then presented an appearance enough to affect any but a heart of iron. From the crown of my head to my feet, I was covered with blood. My hair was all clotted with dust and blood; my shirt was stiff with blood. My legs and feet were torn in sundry places with briers and thorns, and were also covered in blood. I suppose I looked like a man who had escaped a den of wild beasts, and barely escaped them. In this state I appeared before my master, humbly entreating him to interpose his authority for my protection. I told him all the circumstances as well as I could, and it seemed, as I spoke, at times to affect him. He would then walk the floor, and seek to justify Covey by saying he expected I deserved it. He asked me what I wanted. I told him, to let me get a new home; that as sure as I lived with Mr. Covey again, I should live with but to die with him; that Covey would surely kill me; he was in a fair way for it. Master Thomas ridiculed the idea that there was any danger of Mr. Covey's killing me, and said that he knew Mr. Covey, that he was a good man, and that he could not think of taking me from him; that, should he do so, he would lose the whole year's wages; that I belonged to Mr. Covey for one year, and that I must go back to him, come what might; and that I must not trouble him with any more stories, or that he would himself *get hold of me*. After threatening me thus, he gave me a very large dose of salts, telling me that I might remain in St. Michael's that night, (it being quite late,) but that I must be off back to Mr. Covey's early in the morning; and that if I did not, he would *get hold of me*, which meant that he would whip me. I remained all night, and, according to his orders, I started off to Covey's in the morning, (Saturday morning), wearied in body and broken in spirit. I got no supper that night, or breakfast that morning. I reached Covey's about nine o'clock; and just as I was getting over the fence that divided Mrs. Kemp's fields from ours, out ran Covey with his cowskin, to give me another whipping. Before he could reach me, I succeeded in getting to the cornfield; and as the corn was very high, it afforded me the means of hiding. He seemed very angry, and searched for me a long time. My behavior was altogether unaccountable. He finally gave up the chase, thinking, I suppose, that I must come home for something to eat; he would give himself no further trouble in looking for me. I spent that day mostly in the woods, having the alternative before me—to go home and be whipped to death, or stay in the woods and be starved to death. That night, I fell in with Sandy Jenkins, a slave with whom I was somewhat acquainted. Sandy had a free wife who lived about four miles from Mr. Covey's; and it being Saturday, he was on his way to see her. I told him my circumstances, and he very kindly invited me to go home with him. I went home with him, and talked this whole matter over, and got his advice as to what course it was best for me to pursue. I found Sandy an old adviser. He told me, with great solemnity, I must go back to Covey; but that before I went, I must go with him into another part of the woods, where there was a certain *root*, which, if I would take some of it with me, carrying it *always on my right side*, would render it impossible for Mr. Covey, or any other white man, to whip me. He said he had carried it for years; and since he had done so, he had never received a blow, and never expected to while he carried it. I at first rejected the idea, that the simple carrying of a root in my pocket would have any such effect as he had said, and was not disposed to take it; but Sandy impressed the necessity with much earnestness, telling me it could do no harm, if it did no good. To please him, I at length took the root, and, according to his direction, carried it upon my right side. This was Sunday morning. I immediately started for home; and upon entering the yard gate, out came Mr. Covey on his way to meeting. He spoke to me very kindly, bade me drive the pigs from a lot near by, and passed on towards the church. Now, this singular conduct of Mr. Covey really made me begin to think that there was something in the *root* which Sandy had given me; and had it been on any other day than Sunday, I could have attributed the conduct to no other cause than the influence of that root; and as it was, I was half inclined to think the *root* to be something more than I at first had taken it to be. All went well till Monday morning. On this morning, the virtue of the *root* was fully tested. Long before daylight, I was called to go and rub, curry, and feed, the horses. I obeyed, and was glad to obey. But whilst thus engaged, whilst in the act of throwing down some blades from the loft, Mr. Covey entered the stable with a long rope; and just as I was half out of the loft, he caught hold of my legs, and was about tying me. As soon as I found what he was up to, I gave a sudden spring, and as I did so, he holding to my legs, I was brought sprawling on the stable floor. Mr. Covey seemed now to think he had me, and could do what he pleased; but at this moment—from whence came the spirit I don't know—I resolved to fight; and, suiting my action to the resolution, I seized Covey hard by the throat; and as I did so, I rose. He held on to me, and I to him. My resistance was so entirely unexpected, that Covey seemed taken all aback. He trembled like a leaf. This gave me assurance, and I held him uneasy, causing the blood to run where I touched him with the ends of my fingers. Mr. Covey soon called out to Hughes for help. Hughes came, and while Covey held me, attempted to tie my right hand. While he was in the act of doing so, I watched my chance, and gave him a heavy kick close under the ribs. This kick fairly sickened Hughes, so that he left me in the hands of Mr. Covey. This kick had the effect of not only weakening Hughes, but Covey also. When he saw Hughes bending over with pain, his courage quailed. He asked me if I meant to persist in my resistance. I told him I did, come what might; that he had used me like a brute for six months, and that I was determined to be used so no longer. With that, he strove to drag me to a stick that was lying just out of the stable door. He meant to knock me down. But just as he was leaning over to get the stick, I seized him with both hands by his collar, and brought him by a sudden snatch to the ground. By this time, Bill came. Covey called upon him for assistance. Bill wanted to know what he could do. Covey said, "Take hold of him, take hold of him!" Bill said his master hired him out to work, and not to help whip me; so he left Covey and myself to fight our own battle out. We were at it for nearly two hours. Covey at length let me go, puffing and blowing at a great rate, saying that if I had not resisted, he would not have whipped me half so much. The truth was, that he had not whipped me at all. I considered him as getting entirely the worst end of the bargain; for he had drawn no blood from me, but I had from him. The whole six months afterwards, that I spent with Mr. Covey, he never laid the weight of his finger upon me in anger. He would occasionally say, he didn't want to get hold of me again. "No," thought I, "you need not; for you will come off worse than you did before."

This battle with Mr. Covey was the turning-point in my career as a slave. It rekindled the few expiring embers of freedom, and revived within me a sense of my own manhood. It recalled the departed self-confidence, and inspired me again with a determination to be free. The gratification afforded by the triumph was a full compensation for whatever else might follow, even death itself. He only can understand the deep satisfaction which I experienced, who has himself repelled by force the bloody arm of slavery. I felt as I never felt before. It was a glorious resurrection, from the tomb of slavery, to the heaven of freedom. My long-crushed spirit rose, cowardice departed, bold defiance took its place; and I now resolved that, however long I might remain a slave in form, the day had passed forever when I could be a slave in fact. I did not hesitate to let it be known of me, that the white man who expected to succeed in whipping, must also succeed in killing me.   3

Content

1. Twelve years after he successfully defied Mr. Covey, Douglass identified this incident as "the turning-point in my career as a slave" (¶ 3). Why? Would Douglass have been able to recognize its significance at the time or only in retrospect?

2. Would slave owners have been likely to read Douglass's autobiography? Why or why not? Would Douglass's emphasis have been likely to change for an audience of Northern post–Civil War blacks? Southern antebellum whites? What,

if anything, does Douglass expect his audience—mostly white Northerners—to do about slavery, as a consequence of having read his narrative?

Strategies/Structures/Language

3. Douglass's account begins with Friday afternoon and ends with Monday morning, but some events receive considerable emphasis while others are scarcely mentioned. Which ones does he focus on? Why?

4. Why is paragraph 2 so long? Should it have been divided into shorter units, or is the longer unit preferable? Justify your answer.

5. Douglass provides considerable details about his appearance after his first beating by Covey (¶ 2), but scarcely any about the appearance of either Covey or Master Thomas. Why?

6. How sophisticated is Douglass's level of diction? Is it appropriate for the narrative he tells? How is this related to his self-characterization?

For Writing

7. Write a narrative in which you recount and explain the significance of an event in which you participated that provided you with an important change of status in the eyes of others. Provide enough specific details so readers unfamiliar with either you or the situation can experience it as you did.

8. **Dialogues.** Tim O'Brien (75–82) writes that a "true war story is never moral . . . If at the end of a war story you feel uplifted, or if you feel that some small bit of rectitude has been salvaged from a larger waste, then you have been made the victim of a very old and terrible lie" (¶ 8). Is Douglass's "battle with Mr. Covey" (¶ 3) a war story? Does Douglass's narrative of moral and physical victory over his condition conceal some aspects of the "larger waste" of slavery? What aspects of Douglass's autobiography (88–89) support the idea that his narrative conceals some aspects of slavery in order to highlight other aspects?

9. Douglass's narrative uses Christian imagery to describe his battle with Covey, while Martin Luther King, Jr. appeals to the Christian ethics of his audience. Why does each writer pursue his particular strategy?

10. **Mixed Modes.** The sentence "You have seen how a man was made a slave; you shall see how a slave was made a man" (¶ 1) is an example of *metabasis*, a statement that summarizes what has been said and tells the reader what will follow. It is also an *antithesis*, or the juxtaposition of contrasting ideas, since it contrasts the state of slavery with the state of manhood, and a *chiasmus*, because the paired concepts in the first part of the sentence ("a man was made a slave") are reversed in the second part. How do these multiple functions—summary and preparation, contrast, and reversal—set the pattern and theme for the narrative of Douglass's battle with Covey? What does this statement suggest about Douglass's characterization of freedom and humanity?

11. **Second Look.** Douglass was concerned in his autobiography with illustrating the evils of slavery while excluding specific details of his escape to the North in order to protect those who had helped him. How does the photograph in this essay, particularly the anonymity of the scarred man and the plain background, articulate a similar concern? What kind of judgment does the photograph seem to

ask of the viewer? How does the response the photograph appears to elicit differ from Douglass's appeal to his audience?

ART SPIEGELMAN

Art Spiegelman's innovative work *Maus, A Survivor's Tale* (two volumes: 1986 and 1992), a classic of Holocaust literature, is a sequentially illustrated narrative of genocide, survival, and family history. The idea of depicting Jews as mice and Nazis as persecutory cats came to Spiegelman when his college film professor compared cartoon cat-and-mouse chases to racist film stereotypes. Born to Holocaust survivors in Stockholm, Sweden (1948), Spiegelman grew up in Queens, New York City, in a neighborhood with many Jewish families. Influenced by popular cartoons and *Mad Magazine*, he made drawings for his junior high school newspaper, attended the famous public High School of Art and Design, and made it through three years at Harpur College in upstate New York before personal and family crises intervened. Spiegelman suffered a nervous breakdown and shortly afterward his mother committed suicide, partly out of depression after the loss of her brother in a car accident. In 1971 Spiegelman moved to San Francisco, where he joined the dynamic underground comic book scene and taught at the San Francisco Academy of Art. Returning to New York (1975), Spiegelman married, taught at the School of Visual Arts, and began researching *Maus* by journeying to Auschwitz in 1978 and again in 1986. Spiegelman received the Pulitzer prize in 1992. His recent work includes *In the Shadow of No Towers* (2004), about the September 11 attacks—seen from his perspective as a downtown New Yorker—and the geopolitical aftermath.

"Mein Kampf and B. A Nose! (2009), selections from his sketch books. (My Struggle)," taken from the *New York Times Magazine* (1996), ironically bears the same title as Adolf Hitler's autobiography and manifesto of Nazi ideology. Spiegelman's struggle, however, concerns his artistic vision—specifically, how to find a new topic when a "5,000-pound mouse" is breathing down his neck.

Mein Kampf (My Struggle)

"Mein Kampf (My Struggle)" by Art Spiegelman, first published in The New York Times Magazine, May 12, 1996. Copyright © 1996 by Art Spiegelman, reprinted with permission of The Wylie Agency LLC.

Content

1. As "Mein Kampf" begins, we learn that Spiegelman's previous artistic creation, *Maus*, is overpowering and intimidating him; the rest of the narrative unfolds from that premise. What other problems is Spiegelman facing, and how does he attempt to solve them?

2. What is the message of the last few panels, in which the artist's son appears? What is resolved by the ending, or in what way is the reader perhaps left hanging? Explain why this ending is either effective or ineffective.

Strategies/Structures/Language

3. For some readers, comics are mainly associated with humor; yet in "Mein Kampf" Spiegelman uses the comic book form to handle serious themes such as his troubled past, his artistic self-doubts, and his lack of appropriate memories. In what ways do his comic book techniques especially reinforce his themes?

4. What is the irony in Spiegelman showing himself being chased by a gigantic mouse, given what you know about his two-volume series *Maus* (see the headnote for information)? What are some of the other ways that "Mein Kampf" uses visual or verbal humor? For what purposes?

5. How does Spiegelman use line, texture, frame-to-frame pacing, and approach to the human figure to create a visual narrative? For example, is it appropriate to set the action in the "murky caverns" of his memory? In what other ways do the visuals support the topics and themes of "Mein Kampf"?

6. For many readers, comics—or "sequential art"—have an instant attraction. Why do you suppose this is so? What are your favorite comic strips or works of sequential art, and why do you enjoy them?

For Writing

7. If you had the talents of a comic strip artist, what story would you tell? Would you base your work on your life experience, or would you create fiction and fantasy? What characters would you create? What color themes and visual effects would you use? (See Scott McCloud, "Reading the Comics," in Chapter 4.) Explore ideas for a work of sequential art, including a description of your topic, characters, and a sample story or episode. What are your artistic and literary goals, and how would the piece achieve them?

8. **Dialogues.** Compare the reasons Spiegelman includes his son in "Mein Kampf" with the roles Lynda Barry gives to her grandmother and husband in "Common Scents" (Chapter 7). How do these characters act as observers of American culture? What information do they provide the reader about the narrator? Do you see a parallel between the conflicts Barry and Spiegelman describe?

9. **Mixed Modes.** Write a panel-by-panel analysis of *how* "Mein Kampf" works as a narrative. What does the progression from one part of the sequence to the next tell you, aside from the information you get in the dialogue balloons? (See questions 3, 4, and 5 for ideas.) Consider details, such as the labels on the doors of Spiegelman's memories, as well as larger factors, such as his movements and facial expressions. Or compare Spiegelman's "Mein Kampf" with Lynda Barry's "Common Scents" (Chapter 7).

LINDA HOGAN

Linda Hogan (born in 1947 in Denver, Colorado) is a Chickasaw writer, essayist, playwright, environmental theorist, social and political commentator, and activist. Her poetry has been collected in *Calling Myself Home*

(1978), *Eclipse* (1983), *Seeing Through the Sun* (1985), *Book of Medicines* (1993), *People of the Whale* (2008), and *The Inner Journey Views from Native Traditions* (2009). She has also published a memoir (*The Woman Who Watches over the World: A Native Memoir*, 2001), essays (*Dwellings*, 1995), novels (*Mean Spirit*, 1990; *Solar Storms*, 1995, and *Power*, 1998), and short stories ("Aunt Moon's Young Man," in *The Best American Short Stories*, 1989). Her work voices her concerns with racism, poverty, ethno-history, eco-feminism, and spiritual environmentalism. Notable for her use of allegory and myth to explore humanity's—and especially women's—relationship to nature, Hogan locates spirituality in the natural world. Hogan has won multiple literary awards and edited anthologies on nature and spirituality. She currently teaches at the University of Colorado at Boulder.

Waking

Last night thunder and lightning opened the world. Hail beat down on earth, drumming the roof. I watched the round layers of ice bounce off the ground. This morning I wake early to the sound of the young horse running, to the voices of magpies teaching their young to fly, the wings fluttering as they jump only from branch to branch, the parents hovering, urging, flying away, calling the young ones to them. A woodpecker hammers at a hole in the dead tree.   1

From the swaddling comfort of bed, I look out to watch such joy. It is a new morning and beautiful and I rise with the beauty to a morning knowing more of my past has slipped away and that this night of storms, this morning of beauty may also disappear, so I write it down.   2

Time. I have lost it, and I think of my ancestors who tied knots in ropes to keep track of it, or other tribes who painted events and each year revealed them, telling the stories.   3

Daily something is lost from me. It began with an accident I don't remember, an impact to my head, a woman finding my body in the road. I do remember hearing once, as if in a very far distance, the sound of sirens, entrancing like the ones in the *Odyssey* calling me to an island and I surrendered and went to that island where I still live, never going back home, never returning to the same journey and at night there is the unraveling of memory that takes place and parts of my past disappear. Yet I am happy. I think, I have forgotten last month and it should matter, but it doesn't.   4

I remain on that island without intending it, but I am conscious. I can recall many things: what I read, that I bought pillowcases. But not what someone said or a movie I saw. We laugh. I can see reruns and think they are new. And the shadows of words sometimes only float past. I try to recall them. I say, It is the thing with a handle. It is the thing that cleans the floor.   5

LINDA HOGAN, "Waking" from BEST AMERICAN SPIRITUAL WRITING 2006. Ed Philip Zaleski. Houghton Mifflin, 2006, pp. 149–151 Reprinted by permission of Linda Hogan.

6   But I know there are rooms of jade. From the hospital bed there was a great traveling and I was awake in other worlds. Not dreams, nothing even similar to dreams, but a new kind of waking. I traveled. I described to my daughter and friend in great detail the jade carvings in China. I saw the carved jade and silk embroideries of another world. There were pale animals, beautifully polished, a horse, great detail in the carvings of a wall made of jade, entire vignettes of life carved by some artist of the past, a woman sitting and playing an instrument, trees trimmed to some notion of perfection. Jade, the stone of heaven, once carried from the White Jade River by camels. There were also the fabrics, silks and brocades with embroidery, some with gold stitches. I traveled maps with no roads, no towns, no named waters. The world was China, I suppose, and I was a child digging through earth to the other side and succeeding, through soil, stone, magma, through the darkness of unconsciousness to another kind of waking and seeing.

7   At the same time, others traveled toward me, passing through the walls. In the room with me were ancestors I hadn't seen, far ones, from before the Trail of Tears of Chickasaws to Oklahoma, a woman dressed in lavender and wearing a turban as our women did in the past. I wonder if she was my own blood. I remember my father's own recent awakening in bed before his death to the old ones, our people. He said the names of the grandmothers, some I'd never heard, as he looked up at them smiling, and then he introduced me, placing me in my line at the bottom of our world, the present, in my own place as a woman, a grandmother.

8   But for me, I was going to live, and live with memory loss. Important events vanished from my memory. Some didn't. It was random. I forgot neighbors' faces. I remembered some small detail of a poem. Rumi: *Break the wine glass and go toward the glassblower's breath*. The names of the wildflowers in bloom around my house would be gone. What I told someone I told again and again. What I asked, I repeated. Words were gone. I searched for them, coming up with things similar until someone guessed.

9   No one has ever seen an atom yet they believe it is there. No one has ever understood how the brain works. Who could think that love might be electrical, or that consciousness could be chemical? The brain is an organ. The mind is a transient. But the body, I find, is not the husk for the soul. It is knowing. It is consciousness. For a time I was a divine traveler through no will of my own, far beyond my world and its limits. It was a virginal state. While I slept, a restless spirit woke to travel another reality, another realm or layer of existence. But my body, even without words, knows this world, every morning the first morning. I watch the light move, lengthen. Daily there is beauty. The wildflowers still exist, even nameless. They know their own names and those are beyond human knowing. Ask me the name of the month and I could say October when it is June, but there is bread and butter. Pleasure. I listen to the thunder, look at the dew in

the flowers. There is joy even in such vulnerability, such fragility. There is even happiness.

Awakening isn't always to a state of enlightenment. It isn't always a sudden change in consciousness. I can't say I know what it is. I can't say I understand the boundary, the skin, between the worlds we may journey or where I now live. Stirrings there I feel, but don't know. 10

Unconscious, a richness was there. Perhaps it is because I was missing. This is what is said about the self. That when you are given up, a whole cosmos opens. I remember Lakota Wallace Black Elk once saying about the space program, that we have always traveled through the universe. 11

I was a sleeper for three weeks and sometimes still. And yet something grows in it, something wakes. Something else owns this mind, this awakening, and it is a mystery, as if the soul lives larger than the human knows or thinks. Morning after morning has been my world, the sunrise always beautiful, everything newly seen. I am afraid to miss any of it. 12

It is an infant life, too soon to tell what it will become but I trust it is a sacred beginning like all beginnings. Sometimes you drink from an empty bowl thinking it is full and it is. Sometimes you open your empty palm and receive. The world is always fresh. Sometimes there is morning with birds and the sound of a running horse and you are awake. 13

Content

1. How does the narrator's loss of memory and time change her perceptions of her immediate surroundings? How does this loss paradoxically enhance her experience of the immediate present?

2. Identify and describe the various states of consciousness the narrator experiences. How does memory loss seem to give her access to these states? What imagery does the narrator use to describe these experiences?

3. "Waking" employs several *antitheses* (contrasting ideas) to describe the narrator's experience, including present/past, body/mind, awake/asleep, empty/full, and self/cosmos. How does Hogan's use of names and her inability to remember names break down these distinctions? What is the significance of the narrator's use of the two meanings of the word *siren* (¶ 4)?

Strategies/Structures/Language

4. Why does the narrator begin and end her essay with images of nature and new life? How does the pattern of the text reflect its theme?

5. How does Hogan's use of visual imagery, such as "knots in ropes" to keep track of time (¶ 3), "the unraveling of memory" at night (¶ 4), and "maps with no roads, no towns, no named waters" (¶ 6) illustrate how she now perceives immediate experience (see question 2)?

6. The narrator's use of contrasting ideas (see question 3) leads to a paradox: memory loss brings knowledge. How do her allusions to the Greek poet Homer,

Native American history and historical figures, and the mystic poet Rumi contribute to the idea that knowing is a process of the unconscious?

For Writing

7. *Journal Writing.* Describe the conscious and unconscious elements of an experience in which you struggled to understand something, such as an emotionally charged event or an intellectual problem. How did your unconscious processes, perhaps while you dreamed or were immersed in some absorbing activity such as running or hiking, help you come to terms with the event or solve the problem?

8. *Dialogues.* Both Hogan and Brian Doyle employ images of nature to explore the human spirit. How does each writer characterize the human relationship to nature?

9. *Second Look.* "Waking" emphasizes the experience of the active consciousness while the body is at rest. Choose a photograph from *The Essay Connection* that seems to convey the same paradoxical sense of movement and stasis. Using your chosen photograph, explain Hogan's idea that the resting body "is knowing" and not simply "the husk for the soul" (¶ 9).

ANNE FADIMAN

Anne Fadiman was born (in 1953) to bookish parents, the noted writer/ editor Clifton Fadiman and writer Annalee Fadiman. After graduating from Harvard (BA, 1975), Fadiman worked as an editor and staff writer for *Life* magazine, then as a columnist for *Civilization*, the now-defunct magazine of the Library of Congress. From 1998 to 2004 she was editor of the *American Scholar*, Phi Beta Kappa's national magazine, which published distinguished essays, including her award-winning commentary on "Mail," a learned romp that moves wittily from stagecoach delivery to e-mail. Her first book, *The Spirit Catches You and You Fall Down: A Hmong Child, Her American Doctors, and the Collision of Two Cultures* (1997), won a National Book Critics Circle Award for general nonfiction. She has published two collections of essays, *Ex Libris: Confessions of a Common Reader* (1998) and *At Large and At Small* (2007). Since 2005, Fadiman has been writer-in-residence at Yale.

"Under Water" is the account of a happy summer wilderness expedition that turned into a tragedy. Fadiman is full of regret prompted by her inability not only to rescue her fellow student, but by her unworthy— though thoroughly human—thoughts during the futile rescue and ever since: "I find myself wanting to backferry, to hover midstream, suspended. I might then avoid many things: harsh words, foolish decisions, moments of inattention, regrets that wash over me, like water."

Under Water

W hen I was eighteen, I was a student on a month-long wilderness   1
program in western Wyoming. On the third day, we went canoeing
on the Green River, a tributary of the Colorado that begins in the glaciers
of the Wind River Range and flows south across the sagebrush plains.
Swollen by warm-weather runoff from an unusually deep snowpack,
the Green was higher and swifter that month—June of 1972—than it had
been in forty years. A river at flood stage can have strange currents. There
is not enough room in the channel for the water to move downstream in
an orderly way, so it collides with itself and forms whirlpools and boils
and souse holes. Our instructors decided to stick to their itinerary nevertheless, but they put in at a relatively easy section of the Green, one that
the flood had merely upgraded, in the international system of white-wa-
ter classification, from Class I to Class II. There are six levels of difficulty,
and Class II was not an unreasonable challenge for novice paddlers.

The Green River did not seem dangerous to me. It seemed   2
magnificently unobstructed. Impediments to progress—the rocks and

*What has happened in this picture? What is about to happen? With what consequences?
How does Fadiman's story in "Under Water" influence the ways you "read" this
picture? Would you "read" it differently if you saw it as an ad for a wilderness travel
company? An adventure film?*

stranded trees that under normal conditions would protrude above the surface—were mostly submerged. The river carried our aluminum canoe high and lightly, like a child on a broad pair of shoulders. We could rest our paddles on the gunwales and let the water do our work. The sun was bright and hot. Every few minutes, I dipped my bandanna in the river, draped it over my head, and let an ounce or two of melted glacier run down my neck.

3   I was in the bow of the third canoe. We rounded a bend and saw, fifty feet ahead, a standing wave in the wake of a large black boulder. The students in the lead canoe were backferrying, slipping crabwise across the current by angling their boat diagonally and stroking backward. Backferrying allows paddlers to hover midstream and carefully plan their course instead of surrendering to the water's pace. But if they lean upstream—a natural inclination, for few people choose to lean toward the difficulties that lie ahead—the current can overflow the lowered gunwale and flip the boat. And that is what happened to the lead canoe.

4   I wasn't worried when I saw it go over. Knowing that we might capsize in the fast water, our instructors had arranged to have our gear trucked to our next campsite. The packs were all safe. The water was little more than waist-deep, and the paddlers were both wearing life jackets. They would be fine. One was already scrambling onto the right-hand bank.

5   But where was the second paddler? Gary, a local boy from Rawlins, a year or two younger than I, seemed to be hung up on something. He was standing at a strange angle in the middle of the river, just downstream from the boulder. Gary was the only student on the course who had not brought sneakers, and one of his mountaineering boots had become wedged between two rocks. The other canoes would come around the bend in a moment, and the instructors would pluck him out.

6   But they didn't come. The second canoe pulled over to the bank and ours followed. Thirty seconds passed, maybe a minute. Then we saw the standing wave bend Gary's body forward at the waist, push his face underwater, stretch his arms in front of him, and slip his orange life jacket off his shoulders. The life jacket lingered for a moment at his wrists before it floated downstream, its long white straps twisting in the current. His shirtless torso was pale and undulating, and it changed shape as hills and valleys of water flowed over him, altering the curve of the liquid lens through which we watched him. I thought, He looks like the flayed skin of St. Bartholomew in the Sistine Chapel. As soon as I had the thought, I knew that it was dishonorable. To think about anything outside the moment, outside Gary, was a crime of inattention. I swallowed a small, sour piece of self-knowledge: I was the sort of person who, instead of weeping or shouting or praying during a crisis, thought about something from a textbook (H. W. Janson's *History of Art*, page 360).

Once the flayed man had come, I could not stop the stream of im- 7
ages: Gary looked like a piece of seaweed, Gary looked like a waving
handkerchief, Gary looked like a hula dancer. Each simile was a way to
avoid thinking about what Gary was, a drowning boy. To remember these
things is dishonorable, too, for I have long since forgotten Gary's last
name and the color of his hair and the sound of his voice.

I do not remember a single word that anyone said. Somehow, we 8
got into one of the canoes, all five of us, and tried to ferry the twenty feet
or so to the middle of the river. The current was so strong, and we were
so incompetent, that we never got close. Then we tried it on foot, linking arms to form a chain. The water was so cold that it stung. And it was
noisy—not the roar and crash of white water but a groan, a terrible bass
grumble, from the stones that were rolling and leaping down the riverbed. When we got close to Gary, we couldn't see him; all we could see
was the reflection of the sky. A couple of times, groping blindly, one of
us touched him, but he was as slippery as soap. Then our knees buckled
and our elbows unlocked, and we rolled downstream, like the stones. The
river's rocky load, moving invisibly beneath its smooth surface, pounded
and scraped us. Eventually, the current heaved us, blue-lipped and panting, onto the bank. In that other world above the water, the only sounds
were the buzzing of bees and flies. Our wet sneakers kicked up red dust.
The air smelled of sage and rabbitbrush and sunbaked earth.

We tried again and again, back and forth between the worlds. Wet, 9
dry, cold, hot, turbulent, still.

At first, I assumed that we would save him. He would lie on the 10
bank and the sun would warm him while we administered mouth-to-
mouth resuscitation. If we couldn't get him out, we would hold him upright in the river; and maybe he could still breathe. But the Green River
was flowing at nearly three thousand cubic feet—about ninety tons—per
second. At that rate, water can wrap a canoe around a boulder like tinfoil.
Water can uproot a tree. Water can squeeze the air out of a boy's lungs,
undo knots, drag off a life jacket, lever a boot so tightly into the riverbed
that even if we had had ropes—the ropes that were in the packs that were
in the trucks—we could never have budged him.

We kept going in, not because we had any hope of rescuing Gary after 11
the first ten minutes, but because we had to save face. It would have been
humiliating if the instructors came around the bend and found us sitting
in the sagebrush, a docile row of five with no hypothermia and no skinned
knees. Eventually, they did come. The boats had been delayed because one
had nearly capsized, and the instructors had made the other students stop
and practice backferrying until they learned not to lean upstream. Even
though Gary had already drowned, the instructors did all the same things
we had done, more competently but no more effectively, because they, too,
would have been humiliated if they hadn't skinned their knees. Men in wet
suits, belayed with ropes, pried the body out the next morning.

12   When I was eighteen, I wanted to hurry through life as fast as I could. Twenty-seven years have passed, and my life now seems too fast. I find myself wanting to backferry, to hover midstream, suspended. I might then avoid many things: harsh words, foolish decisions, moments of inattention, regrets that wash over me, like water.

Content

1. From what point of view does Anne Fadiman narrate the events that take place in "Under Water"? In what ways does Fadiman as author prepare her readers to interpret Fadiman as a character in this tale? How does she want the readers to react to the circumstances she describes and to the others on this trip, including the instructors?

2. Anne Fadiman's statement "The Green River did not seem dangerous to me. . . . Impediments to progress—the rocks and stranded trees that under normal conditions would protrude above the surface—were mostly submerged" (¶ 2) is meant to be read literally. Why can we also say it possesses another level of meaning that transcends the literal?

Strategies/Structures/Language

3. Fadiman's tale unfolds chronologically, although she speaks in the present, merely remembering the past. How and why does she foreshadow the events that will occur with statements such as "Class II was not an unreasonable challenge for novice paddlers" (¶ 1)? At what point in the story is a reader likely to become aware of the inevitable outcome toward which the narrative is moving? Why not simply begin with the drowning of the young man?

4. Does Fadiman's tale contain all the major components of a narrative: characters, conflict, motives, plot, setting, point of view, and dialogue? Find examples from the text to illustrate which features are there. Since "Under Water" looks and reads like a short story, how do you know it's true?

5. Fadiman uses some extremely vivid description—for example, "Then we saw the standing wave bend Gary's body forward at the waist, push his face underwater, stretch his arms in front of him, and slip his orange life jacket off his shoulders" (¶ 6). What effect is such graphic representation likely to have on her readers?

For Writing

6. *Journal Writing.* Describe an incident you either witnessed or participated in that involved a serious error of judgment. This can be anything from a car accident to rejecting, insulting, discriminating against, or otherwise mistreating someone, to a benign event that turned serious and ugly. Explore how the story might be told from the point of view of another person involved in the incident. How does the shift in perspective change your implicit or explicit judgments of those involved?

7. *Dialogues.* Fadiman describes the students' and the instructors' hopeless efforts to rescue a drowned boy as saving face, and so suggests that others' perceptions play a major role in shaping our behavior. How does Peter Singer's

"The Singer Solution to World Poverty" (481–87) or Bill McKibben's "Designer Genes" (515–25) suggest that human behavior can and should be shaped? How does each author express our ethical obligations to one another? In what situations is peer pressure appropriate and effective in promoting ethical behavior?

8. **Mixed Modes.** In the last paragraph, Fadiman's narrative becomes an analogy for her own life. Find the metaphors in the narrative that prepare the reader for this final paragraph. How do these metaphors and the structure of the essay serve Fadiman's larger purpose?

9. **Second Look.** Fadiman's essay describes several contrasts that incorporate the ideas of "wet, dry, cold, hot, turbulent, still" (¶ 9), as well as the contrast between her desire "to hurry through life" and then "wanting to backferry" (¶ 12). How does the photograph in this essay capture these contrasts?

10. Write a true story in which the setting, preferably a natural one, plays a major role in relation to the human participants. This role may be benign or malevolent, active or passive, but it should be important and the humans should be constantly aware of this role. Because you will need to pay close attention to the specific details of the setting, it should be a place you either know well or can revisit.

JASON VERGE

A Canadian who was born in Ottawa (1982) and grew up in Montreal, Jason Verge's first language was French. His earliest passion was for the Montreal Jason Canadiens, "The Habs," whose example encouraged him to play hockey as an adolescent. Then he "did what any die-hard hockey fan would do after graduating high school": he decided to attend college in Hawaii, where because of the time difference, he had to watch the games live at 9 a.m. Transferring to Marymount University, he completed his BA in English in 2005. Verge says he is "currently putting the finishing touches" on his first novel. Although he once owned a recording company, he decided he was not suited for the business world when he "accepted an 8-bit Nintendo in lieu of cash payment." He has now returned to writing.

He says of "The Habs," "my friends were tired of hearing me talk incessantly about hockey, so I decided to get it down on paper. It's a love letter to the sport and to the team, for the Habs are inextricably linked with the identities of myself and my family. I wanted the piece to be humorous without losing its honesty."

The Habs

Game seven: the deciding game of the Stanley Cup finals. I was six, captured in old home movies running and screaming "By the power of Greyskull!" at the top of my lungs. It was the only phrase I knew how to say in English, learned from episodes of *He-man.* Earlier that night, my family had been embroiled in a heated political argument, as was the custom when we got together. Watching the Montreal Canadiens play hockey was the only viable reason to put political arguments on hiatus, and so we had. With the game on, the light conflict in the air turned to a deep sense of unity. My grandfather—usually a calm man—cheered like a rabid child during the games. For the length of three periods, all worries went away; there were no financial worries, there were no disagreements. The only thing that seemed to matter in the entire universe was the Montreal Canadiens, or "the Habs," as we called them. The Habs were in our blood.

2   Calling the team "Habs" started in the 1920s as a joke. The Canadiens logo has an "H" in the center of the "C," which initially stood for "Hockey" in "Club de hockey Canadien." Tex Rickard, an Anglophone from the Toronto Maple Leafs, asked a Montreal coach what it stood for, and the coach said "Habitants" to mess with him. ("Club de hockey Canadien" was plastered everywhere when Tex asked.) Somehow, the name stuck. The story is mostly ignored these days because it's completely inexplicable—to most people—why the guy lied and said "Habitants" instead of the plain truth. A Montreal fan, however, instantly knows why the coach lied: because the team and the city's culture are inextricably linked and because no Toronto Maple Leafs Fan is deserving of a straight answer.

3   The Island of Montreal in Quebec is an oddity of sorts; the population is bilingual, whereas the rest of Quebec is devoutly French. Quebec has always been the proverbial stepchild of Canada; they have a different culture than the rest of Canada and never quite fit in. Quebec is a province divided between those who wish to secede from Canada (the devout French) and those who wish to remain a part of the country. Referendums occur where they actually vote on this issue; the last decided by 1 percent to stay. Whereas Americans determined divisive issues through a bloody civil war, Canadians prefer to vote incessantly on something until people lose their passion. It's too cold outside to fight. The votes from Montreal always swing the decision toward staying a part of the country. Somewhere down the line, the Habs became intertwined with the political debate. Habs fans are loyal to Canada. When the Habs played the Quebec Nordiques, people would come out in full force, the Habs fans being loyalists and the Nordiques fans being separatists. A win on the ice was a political victory of sorts, a justification for a person's given side of the political debate. Not only is hockey a way of life in Canada, it's also used to make important political decisions. (A little known fact: Canada entered World War I because the Habs won the night the decision was made.)

4   I was too big for the team jerseys when I started playing hockey in a league. The jerseys they handed out were made for the typical twelve-year-old, and I was anything but. I was already well over six feet by that

time. I tried to stuff myself into the assigned jersey and ended up looking like a giant marshmallow. Instead, they let me wear my bright red Canadiens jersey. I'd imagine myself playing for the Habs, my family proudly watching me on TV (I'd reserve my tickets to the game for groupies).

Since the leagues were organized by age, I ended up playing with people I towered over. Years later, my dad would tell me that a lot of the parents were upset that a kid my height was allowed to play in the league. My dad tells me that that kind of made him proud. I was a goaltender, so it's not as if my physical play was a big factor—though I'm pretty sure I still hold the record for most penalty minutes by a goaltender. I wasn't a mean kid; in fact, most of the penalty minutes were justified. The only female player in the league was on my team, and I didn't take too kindly to watching her get roughed up. I was a big brother to her; if someone hurt her, I'd politely snatch their legs with my stick and trip them. It was nothing personal; it was all part of the game. Yep, I was a true gentleman. 5

Jacques Plante was the goalie for the Habs in the sixties. He was the first goalie to wear a mask during play, but only after years of pucks hitting him in the face. He had a reputation of being fearless on the ice and a true gentleman off it. In one game a puck hit him in the face and tore it open; he went back to the trainers, received over thirty stitches near his eye, and was back on the ice the next period. He didn't complain to anyone. The cut was so bad that the swelling and blood almost completely blinded him, yet the tough bastard continued to play despite not being able to see. The coach eventually figured out that Plante couldn't see; when the coach asked him why he didn't say something, Plante said he didn't want to bother anyone. Jacques Plante was a true gentleman. 6

I did what any die-hard hockey fan would do after graduating high school: I decided to attend university in Hawaii. Apparently I was too busy thinking about doing homework on a beach to think of the ramifications it would have on my hockey viewing. Fortunately, I brought a few hockey videos, which I rationed with more intensity than the people in the movie *Alive* rationed peanuts. 7

However, my roommate from France was able to get a constant flow of soccer on the TV, feeding his addiction. His happiness made me sick. The soccer players, with the little shin guards and floppy hair, made me sick. Soccer was the bizzaro hockey; soccer blazed at the equivalent speed of a physics lecture. I began to lose my mind. 8

Luckily, salvation came in the form of the occasional game on ESPN 43. Since Hawaii had a six-hour time difference, it meant watching hockey at an ungodly early hour, or watching the replay. Since I enjoyed the consumption of beer during a game, I opted for the replay. Getting drunk at noon didn't quite appeal to me. I was so excited for that first game that I shook. The puck dropped and a giant grin appeared on my face. Not two minutes into the first period, the sports ticker on the bottom of the screen revealed the final score of the very game I was watching. I'm 9 pretty sure I snapped something internally. I wanted the world to feel my wrath; I wanted to stand outside the movie theater and tell everyone how their movie would end.

10   Two weeks later, I would get my second chance. I slapped duct tape across the bottom of the screen so I wouldn't be able to see the ticker. During intermission, the nice people at ESPN told me the final score of the game once again. I screamed in such agony that Janine, a girl across the hall, came to see what was wrong. She got my mind off of the game with tales of her sexual exploits. I told her that I was a writer, and she responded by letting me read her diary. Based on what I read, I vowed never to touch Janine.

11   When my third attempt came around, I was emaciated and pale, despite the Hawaiian sun. Hadn't shaved. I was all set to turn off the TV when intermission began. I made it to the second period, and then I heard a knock on the door. It was Janine. I decided her tales of sexual exploits could wait: "Go away!" I yelled.

12   "What's wrong?"

13   "I'm not talking to anyone until the game's over."

14   "Your door's locked."

15   "Go away."

16   "Let me in, I saw the score and they lost."

17   From that point on, I disliked Janine. I began to wonder if I could get televised hockey in the mountains of Tibet. I also vowed to watch the next game live at—cringe—nine in the morning.

18   It took college to make me realize how counterproductive getting drunk at nine in the morning is. You'd think they'd cover it in high school, in health class or something. I found a friend who shared my enthusiasm for the sport, at least, so he claimed. I had a sneaking suspicion all he really wanted was an excuse to drink at nine in the morning. Through that experience, I learned that beer is not a proper substitute for milk in cereal (foams too much when you chew). Tuition put to good use.

19   After the first two meetings of the nine A.M. drinkers club, we disbanded. I was content simply watching hockey. The whole experience made me grateful for every minute of hockey I'd get to see.

20   Maurice "The Rocket" Richard played for the Habs back around the time my father was a kid. I see a twinkle in my dad's eye when he says Richard's name—I get the same twinkle these days. "The Rocket" was a quiet, humble man. In a way, I like to think of myself as having the same demeanor. On the ice, Richard became the most clutch player of all time. He received a concussion in a deciding playoff game against the Leafs one year and had to be carried off—he wobbled back on and scored the game-winning goal. When the reporters asked him about it later, he had no recollection. The following year, against the same team, he was evicted from the game and suspended for fighting back. After the announcer reported his fate, riots started. Police flooded the Montreal forum. The riots

leaked out onto the street; the city shut down. Richard stood quiet despite the passion of his fans; he always felt weird talking about himself to the press. Despite his taciturn demeanor, he became a deity in Montreal. At his funeral, a decade ago, decades after he stopped playing, two hundred thousand people showed up.

I watched all but three of the eighty-two regular season Montreal games last year. My girlfriend at the time asked me, "If you had to give up either me or hockey, which would you choose?" I may be a man, but I'm not stupid. I told her I'd give up hockey. Then I told her never to ask me that question again—ever. After years of philosophy and ethics courses, I still have yet to encounter a bigger dilemma. After she left the room, I rubbed my jersey on my face and assured it that I would never give it up.

I have spent so many years devoted to my Habs that it has become a religion to me. I've spent a small fortune on a piece of cardboard with a Habs player on it. I've missed a final because it clashed with a playoff game. How could I not love a sport that combines the gracefulness of ice skating and the brutality of football? It is a paradox; it is beautiful yet violent. I am a Canadian; I come from a culture where aggressions are played out on the ice and not off it. Hockey is the opiate of my people.

I call my dad during intermissions to talk about the game, much as he'd call his dad when he was younger. I once told my mom that I wanted my ashes dumped in the arena the Canadiens play in. She didn't like the idea.

(Update: Due to arbitration, the 2004 hockey season was officially canceled until further notice. The author is currently seeking out a local mental institution that will willingly let him pretend it is 1993, the last year the Canadiens won the Stanley Cup.)

Content

1. If you're an American reader, what do you find in "The Habs" that makes it distinctively Canadian? (If possible, discuss your views with a Canadian reader.) At the editor's suggestion, Verge added paragraph 2, explaining the origin of the term "the Habs." Would you have understood the meaning of the term without this explanation?

2. Are rabid hockey fans any different from enthusiasts of any other sport?

3. If Verge is such a proud Canadian citizen and "die-hard" Habs fan, why would he choose to go to college in Hawaii? Are his reasons self-evident, or don't they matter?

Strategies/Structures/Language

4. Why is this piece funny? Do readers need to know much—or anything—about hockey to appreciate the humor?

5. Like many comic writers, Verge characterizes himself in a variety of self-deprecations. Identify some. Are readers expected to take him at his word—that is, is he an utterly reliable narrator? Why or why not?

For Writing

6. Write an essay explaining your lifelong love for an activity (such as reading, cooking, driving, painting, playing or listening to music, shopping), an individual (running, fishing, boating) or team sport, or participation in a worthy cause whose purpose is to benefit others rather than yourself. At the outset, try writing comic and serious versions of the same subject until you find a mode and vocabulary that does justice to both the topic and your attitude toward it. Try out alternative versions on a reader to see how he or she reacts.

7. *Journal Writing.* Do you identify with a particular sport or team? What does your appreciation of that sport or team say about your political beliefs, background, or cultural identity? Explore the ways in which that identification liberates or restricts you in your personal development—or both.

8. *Dialogues.* O'Brien, Alexie, Spiegelman, Fadiman, and Verge use satire and irony to make their points—all of which are critical of either the author, the subject, or both. What clues do these authors provide to tell readers to read these figuratively, rather than literally?

9. *Mixed Modes.* Team sports often function as a metaphor for life. What other activities (e.g., creative, individual, or noncompetitive) allow people to express their desires, aggressions, and fears? Compare the kinds of ideals these activities encourage with those that team sports promote.

Additional Topics for Writing
Narration

(For strategies for writing narration, see p. 74.)

Multiple Strategies for Writing: Narration

In writing on any of the narrative topics below, you you'll find it useful to draw on a variety of strategies to help tell your story.

You may choose to write your narrative using elements of *creative nonfiction*, and thus to tell the story through:

- A *narrator* in the role of a storyteller or a character or both
- *Dialogue*
- A *time sequence*, either in chronological order or with flashbacks or flash-for-wards, which, in combination, will provide a *plot*, with beginning, middle, and end
- *Setting(s)*
- *Symbolism*, through characters, objects, events
- An *implied*—rather than an overt—point or argument

Through the preceding techniques, or in a more conventional essay form, narratives can employ:

- *Character sketches: who* was involved
- *Illustrations* and *examples: what* happened and *when*
- *Process analysis: how* it happened
- *Cause* and *effect: why* it happened, with *what consequences*

Feel free to experiment, to use what works and discard what doesn't—but save the rejects in a separate file; you may be able to use them somewhere else.

1. Write two versions of the earliest experience you can remember that involved some fright, danger, discovery, or excitement. Write the first version as the experience appeared to you at the time it happened. Then, write another version interpreting how the experience appears to you now.

2. Write a narrative of an experience you had that taught you a difficult lesson. (See Fadiman, "Under Water" (100–04); Yu, "Red and Black, or One English Major's Beginning" (161–71); and Nocton, "Harvest of Gold, Harvest of Shame" (271–76)) You can either make explicit the point of the lesson or imply it through your reactions to the experience.

3. Sometimes a meaningful incident or significant relationship with someone can help us to mature, easily or painfully. Tell the story of such an incident or relationship in your own life or in the life of someone you know well. Douglass addresses this in "Resurrection" (86–91), Cagle in "On the Banks of the Bogue Chitto" (231–35), Sanders in "The Inheritance of Tools" (135–42) and "Under the Influence: Paying the Price of My Father's Booze" (180–91), and McGuire in "Wake Up Call" (376–82).

4. Have you ever witnessed an event important to history, sports, science, or some other field of endeavor? If so, tell the story either as an eyewitness or from

the point of view of someone looking back on it and more aware now of its true meaning.

5. If you have ever been to a place that is particularly significant to you, narrate an incident to show its significance through specified details. (See Fadiman, "Under Water" (100–04); Twain, "Uncle John's Farm" (238–45))

6. Have you ever worshipped someone as a hero or heroine or modeled yourself after someone? Or have you ever been treated as someone's particular favorite (or nemesis)? Tell the story of this special relationship you have (or had) with a parent or grandparent, brother or sister, friend or antagonist, spouse, employer, teacher. Through narrating one or two typical incidents to convey its essence, show why this relationship has been beneficial, harmful, or otherwise significant to you. Control your language carefully to control the mood and tone.

7. If you have had a "watershed experience"—made an important discovery, survived a major traumatic event, such as an automobile accident, a natural disaster, a flood, or a family breakup; met a person who has changed your life—that has changed your life or your thinking about life significantly, narrate the experience and analyze its effects, short- or long-term. You will need to explain or imply enough of what you were like beforehand so readers can recognize the effects of the experience. (See Wiesel, "Why I Write"; Douglass, "Resurrection"; or O'Reilly, "Balancing Act" 14–20, 86–91, 219–23).

8. Explain what it is like to be a typical student or employee (on an assembly line, in a restaurant or store, or elsewhere) through an account of "A Day in the Life of . . ." If you find that life to be boring or demeaning, your narrative might be an implied protest or an argument for change. (See Barry, "Common Scents" 318–28; Nocton, "Harvest of Shame" (271–76)).

9. Write a fairy tale or fable, a story with a moral, or some other cautionary tale. Make it suitable for children (but don't talk down to them) or for people of your own age. (See Doyle, "The Greatest Nature Essay Ever" (25–27); Spiegelman, "Mein Kampf (My Struggle)" (93–95) and Gawande, "On Washing Hands" (152–59)).

10. Write a pseudo-diary, an imaginary account of how you would lead a day in your life if all your wishes were fulfilled—or if all your worst fears were realized.

11. Imagine that you're telling a major news event of the day (or of your lifetime) to someone fifty years from now. What details will you have to include and explain to make sure your reader understands it? (See O'Brien, "How to Tell a True War Story" (75–82)).

12. Using your own experiences or those of someone you know well, write an essay showing the truth or falsity of an adage about human nature, such as:

a. Quitters never win. Or do they?
b. Try hard and you'll succeed. Or will you?
c. It doesn't matter whether you win or lose, it's how you play the game.
d. Absence makes the heart grow fonder, or Out of sight, out of mind.

Process Analysis

Analysis involves dividing something into its component parts and explaining what they are, on the assumption that it is easier to consider and to understand the subject in smaller segments than in a large, complicated whole (See introductions to chapters 5, Cause and Effect, and 8, Comparison and Contrast). To analyze the human body, you could divide it into systems—skeletal, circulatory, respiratory, digestive, neurological—before identifying and defining the components of each. Of the digestive system, for instance, you would discuss the mouth, pharynx, esophagus, stomach, and large and small intestines. Scott McCloud's "Reading the Comics" (132–34), illustrates, in two brief but densely packed pages, how cartoonists in their readers in a two-way process of making meaning.

You can analyze a process in the same way, focusing on *how* rather than *what*, that will lead to a particular consequence, product, or result. Meredith Hall's true story, "Killing Chickens" (118–21), briefly narrates the events that led to the breakup of her marriage (her husband's affair with her best friend) embedded in the dual processes of killing chickens to make room for the incoming brood of new chicks and celebrating a birthday. Both are metaphorical activities frought with doom and disaster as they refract on a marriage in the process of shattering to pieces.

A *directive process analysis* identifies the steps in how to make or do something: how to sail a catamaran; how to get to Kuala Lumpur; how to make brownies; how to prevent the spread of germs (see Atul Gawande "On Washing Hands" 152–59). The Introduction to Chapter 1, for instance, explains the general processes embedded in reading and writing essays, poetry, stories, and creative nonfiction. One of the differences between an art and a science is that in the arts even those who follow a similar process will end up with qualitatively different results. For example, an accomplished singer's or writer's style is so markedly different from that of any other singer or writer that the individual performer is immediately recognized.

An *informative process analysis* can identify the stages by which something is created or formed, or how something is done. In "Hooked from the First Cigarette" (122–31), Joseph DiFranza explains the evidence for his hypothesis that "limited exposure to nicotine—as little as one cigarette—can change the brain, modifying its neurons in a way that stimulates the craving to smoke" using considerations of cause and effect incorporated with an analysis of the process by which the first cigarette leads to addiction. DiFranza's controversial research contradicts conventional claims that "people smoke primarily for pleasure," becoming psychologically and physically dependent on nicotine only as it builds up in their blood as they smoke more and more heavily.

A process analysis can incorporate an explanation and appreciation of a way of life, as implied in the photograph of the Mennonite carpenter (137), taken in 1999 but in many respects timeless.

Atul Gawande's "On Washing Hands" (152–59) critiques the customary processes by which hospitals try to maintain sanitary standards. He offers an alternative process, embedding in it an analysis of how difficult it is to change the culture of a hospital, with its ever changing personnel and patients, ever on the move; and even more difficult, how hard it is for the staff to be ever vigilant in washing their hands after every contact with a non-sanitary substance—"Our 70 percent compliance just wasn't good enough" (¶ 12), even 99 percent compliance isn't really good enough, for even a single slip can taint the process, and possibly contaminate the vulnerable patients, as Gawande knows all too well. This essay may also be read as an analysis of cause and effect (see p. 175).

An analysis can also incorporate a critique of a process, sometimes as a way to advocate an alternative, as Scott Russell Sanders does in showing the deleterious effects of alcoholism on alcoholics' families in "Under the Influence: Paying the Price of My Father's Booze" (180–91). Matt Nocton's "Harvest of Gold, Harvest of Shame" (271–76) provides both an overt explanation of a process—how tobacco is harvested—and an implied critique of the exploitation of the migrant workers who do the backbreaking labor. Each worker must "must tie [a burlap sack] around his waist as a source of protection against the dirt and rocks that he will be dragging himself through for the next eight hours."

A process analysis can also embed a critique political, ethical, or both. Barbara Ehrenreich's "Serving in Florida" (143–51) analyzes the process by which managers maintain control over restaurant servers ("Managers can sit–for hours at a time if they want–but it's their job to see that no one else ever does, even when there's nothing to do, and this is why, for servers, slow times can be as exhausting as rushes. You start dragging out each little chore . . . " ¶ 2). They hold meetings to harangue the workers about petty rules; they invent more petty rules to harass the employees; they police the employees like bad cops–there are no good cops (¶ 3–4). But, even worse than the dubious ethics of the way such restaurant managers function is the fact that the workers are not paid a living wage, which Ehrenreich documents with a list of specific examples (a couple "paying $170 a week for a one-person trailer") (¶ 6), a process of economic ruin from which the hapless workers can never escape.

Ning Yu's "Red and Black, or One English Major's Beginning" (161–71) is an explanation of how he learned English from two sources: his father, a sophisticated professor of Chinese language and literature, and the anti-intellectual members of the People's Liberation Army, who expelled (and imprisoned) the intellectuals and took over the schools. Ning analyzes how the Reds taught: by lecturing and having the middle school pupils memorize verbal "hand grenades"—"Drop your guns! Down with U.S. Imperialism!"—which they didn't understand. Here Ning criticizes the teachers, the process, and the results: "books were dangerous," and ignorance prevailed. In contrast, Dr. Yu does it right, beginning with the alphabet, then on to the basics of grammar, and then the reading of short sentences and learning vocabulary, to provide his son with an adequate foundation for genuine reading and understanding—a particularly important heritage while Dr. Yu is imprisoned.

The following suggestions for writing an essay of process analysis are in themselves—you guessed it—a process analysis.

To write about a process, for whatever audience, you first have to *make sure you understand it yourself*. If it is a process you can perform, such as parallel parking or hitting a good tennis forehand, try it out before you begin to write, and note the steps and possible variations from start to finish.

Early on you will need to *identify the purpose or function of the process and its likely outcome:* "How to lose twenty pounds in ten weeks." Then the steps or stages in the process occur in a given sequence; it is helpful to *list them in their logical or natural order* and to *provide time markers* so your readers will know what comes first, second, and thereafter. "First, have a physical exam. Next, work out a sensible diet, under medical supervision. Then . . ."

If the process involves many simultaneous operations, for clarity you may need to *classify all aspects of the process and discuss each one separately*, as you might in explaining the photograph of what the Chinese boy is doing in order to learn to read and write his native language (165). For instance, since playing the violin requires bowing with the right hand and fingering with the left, it makes sense to consider each by itself. After you have done this, however, be sure to *indicate how all of the separate elements of the process fit together*. To play the violin successfully, the right hand does indeed have to know what the left hand is doing. If the process you are discussing is cyclic or circular—as in the life cycle of a plant, or the water cycle, involving evaporation, condensation, and precipitation—start with whatever seems to you most logical or most familiar to your readers.

If you are using specialized or technical language, *define your terms* unless you are writing for an audience of experts. You will also need to *identify specialized equipment* and *be explicit about whatever techniques and measurements your readers need to know*. For example, an essay on how to throw a pot would need to tell a reader who had never potted what the proper consistency of the clay should be before one begins to wedge it or how to tell when all the air bubbles have been wedged out. But how complicated should an explanation be? The more your reader knows about your subject, the more sophisticated your analysis can be, with less emphasis, if any, on the basics. How thin can the pot's walls be without collapsing? Does the type of clay (white, red, with or without grog) make any difference? The reverse is true if you are writing for novices—keep it simple to start with.

If subprocesses are involved in the larger process, you can either *explain these where they would logically come in the sequence* or *consider them in footnotes or an appendix.* You do not want to sidetrack your reader from the main thrust. For instance, if you were to explain the process of Prank Day, an annual ritual at Cal Tech, you might begin with the time by which all seniors have to be out of their residence halls for the day: 8 a.m. You might then follow a typical prank from beginning to end: the selection of a senior's parked car to disassemble; the transportation of its parts to the victim's dorm room; the reassembling of the vehicle; the victim's consternation when he encounters it in his room with the motor running. If the focus is on the process of playing the prank, you probably would not want to give directions on how to disassemble and reassemble the car; to do so would require a hefty manual. But you might want to supplement your discussion with helpful hints on how to pay (or avoid paying) for the damage.

After you have finished your essay, if it explains how to perform a process, ask a friend, preferably one who is unfamiliar with the subject, to try it out. (Even people who know how to tie shoelaces can get all tangled up in murky directions.) She can tell you what is unclear, what needs to be explained more fully—and even point out where you are belaboring the obvious. Ask your reader to tell you how well she understands what you have said. If, by the end, she is still asking you what the fundamental concept is, you will know you have got to run the paper through your typewriter or computer once again.

Process analysis can serve as a vehicle for explaining personal relationships. For example, an analysis of the sequential process of performing some activity can serve as the framework for explaining a complicated relationship among the people involved in performing the same process or an analogous one. In such essays the relationship among the participants or the character of the person performing the process is more important than the process itself; whether or not the explanation is sufficient to enable the readers to actually perform the process is beside the point.

Scott Russell Sanders's "The Inheritance of Tools" (135–42) is typical of such writing. Although his father is showing Sanders, as a young child, how to pound nails and saw, the information is not sufficient in the text, even for such a simple process, to provide clear directions of how to do it. The real point of Sanders's commentary is not instructions in how to use tools, but in the relationship between the tender father and his admiring son.

Writing parodies of processes, particularly those that are complicated, mysterious, or done badly—may be the ideal revenge of the novice learner or the person obsessed with or defeated by a process. Parodies such as these may include a critique of the process, a satire of the novice or victim (often the author), or both.

Strategies for Writing: Process Analysis

1. Is the purpose of my essay to provide directions—a step-by-step explanation of how to do or make something? Or is the essay's purpose informative—to explain how something happens or works? Do I know my subject well enough to explain it clearly and accurately?

2. If I am providing directions, how much does my audience already know about performing the process? Should I start with definitions of basic terms ("sauté," "dado") and explanations of subprocesses, or can I focus on the main process at hand? Should I simplify the process for a naive audience, or are my readers sophisticated enough to understand its complexities? Likewise, if I am providing an informative explanation, where will I start? How complicated will my explanation become? The assumed expertise of my audience will help determine my answers.

3. Have I presented the process in logical or chronological sequence (first, second, third . . .)? Have I furnished an overview so that my readers will have the outcome (or desired results) and major aspects of the process in mind before they immerse themselves in the particulars of the individual steps?

4. Does my language fit both the subject, however general or technical, and the audience? Do I use technical terms when necessary? Which of these do I need to define or explain for my intended readers?

5. What tone will I use in my essay? A serious or matter-of-fact tone will indicate that I am treating my subject "straight." An ironic, exaggerated, or understated tone will indicate that I am treating it humorously.

MEREDITH HALL

Meredith Hall was born in 1949 and grew up in New Hampshire. She quit college at eighteen, but was compelled by divorce to return at age forty; she was the only full-time, nontraditional student at Bowdoin College. This experience ("a time when my great intellectual hungers were fed") changed her life and launched her career as a teacher and writer. Her award-winning essays have been published in many journals and anthologies including *Creative Nonfiction, Southern Review,* and *The New York Times.* In 2005, she received the Gift of Freedom Award, a two-year writing grant from A Room of Her Own Foundation. Her memoir, *Without a Map,* was published in 2007. She teaches in the MFA program at the University of New Hampshire, and lives on the coast of Maine.

Of "Killing Chickens," Hall says, "The image of the soft, dusty light in the chicken coop and my little hens laid out one by one has come to embody for me the difficulties of our family breakup. Love and violence tangle in this essay. My children were unaware of what I was doing outside, of my first desperate efforts to take charge of my new life. Inside the house, they had already started their own young reckoning. That it was such a beautiful spring day, so full of promise, and my birthday, plays in my memory against the finality and trauma of the deaths and the impending divorce."

As you read this piece of creative nonfiction—a true story and so labeled—compare this with the fictional short stories you have read—or Jonathan Safran Foer's "Here We Aren't So Quickly" (340–44) What, if any, aspects of "Killing Chickens" itself—events, characters, dialogue, setting, details of everyday life—tell you this is a true story rather than a work of fiction? Or does your understanding that this is a true story arise from the fact that the author identifies it as truth rather than fiction? Suppose Hall had called it "fiction." Would you have read it any differently?

Killing Chickens

1   I tucked her wings tight against her heaving body, crouched over her, and covered her flailing head with my gloved hand. Holding her neck hard against the floor of the coop, I took a breath, set something deep and hard inside my heart, and twisted her head. I heard her neck break with a crackle. Still she fought me, struggling to be free of my weight, my gloved hands, my need to kill her. Her shiny black beak opened and closed, opened and closely silently, as she gasped for air. I didn't know this would happen. I was undone by the flapping, the dust rising and choking me, the disbelieving little eye turned up to mine. I held her beak closed, covering that eye. Still she pushed, her reptile legs bracing against mine, her warmth, her heart beating fast with mine. I turned her head on her floppy

MEREDITH HALL, "Killing Chickens," CREATIVE NONFICTION #18 INTIMATE DETAILS, 2001. Reprinted with permission.

neck again, and again, corkscrewing her breathing tube, struggling to end the gasping. The eye, turned around and around, blinked and studied me. The early spring sun flowed onto us through a silver stream of dust, like a stage light, while we fought each other. I lifted my head and saw that the other birds were eating still, pecking their way around us for stray bits of corn. This one, this twisted and broken lump of gleaming black feathers, clawed hard at the floor, like a big stretch, and then deflated like a pierced ball. I waited, holding her tiny beak and broken neck with all my might.

I was killing chickens. It was my 38th birthday. My best friend, 2 Ashley, had chosen that morning to tell me that my husband had slept with her a year before. I had absorbed the rumors and suspicions about other women for 10 years, but this one, I knew, was going to break us. When I roared upstairs and confronted John, he told me to go fuck myself, ran downstairs and jumped into the truck. Our sons, Sam and Ben, were making a surprise for me at the table; they stood behind me silently in the kitchen door while John gunned the truck out of the yard. "It's okay, guys," I said. "Mum and Dad just had a fight. You better go finish my surprise before I come peeking."

I carried Bertie's warm, limp body outside and laid her on the grass. 3 Back inside the coop, I stalked my hens and came up with Tippy-Toes. I gathered her frantic wings and crouched over her. John was supposed to kill off our beautiful but tired old hens, no longer laying, last month to make way for the new chicks that were arriving tomorrow. But he was never around, and the job had not been done. I didn't know how to do this. But I was going to do it myself. This was just a little thing in all the things I was going to have to learn to do alone.

I had five more to go. Tippy-Toes tried to shriek behind my glove. 4 I clamped my hand over her beak and gave her head a hard twist. I felt her body break deep inside my own chest.

Two down. I felt powerful, capable. I could handle whatever came 5 to me.

But I needed a rest. I was tired, exhausted, with a heavy, muffled 6 weight settling inside. "I'm coming in," I called in a false, singsong voice from the kitchen door. "Better hide my surprise." Ten and 7, the boys knew something was up, something bigger than the moody, dark days John brought home, bigger than the days-long silent treatment John imposed on me if I asked too many questions about where he had been and why. Sam and Ben were working quietly in the kitchen, not giggling and jostling the way they usually did. Their downy blond heads touched as they leaned over their projects. I felt a crush of sadness, of defeat. We were exploding into smithereens on this pretty March day, and we all knew it.

"I have to make a cake!" I sang from the doorway. "When are you 7 guys going to be done in there?"

"Wait! Wait!" they squealed. It was an empty protest, their cheer as 8 hollow as mine.

9   Our old house smelled good, of wood and the pancakes the three of us had eaten this morning, in that other world of hope and tight determination before Ashley's phone call. We lived on a ridge high over the mouth of the Damariscotta River on the coast of Maine. From our beds, we could all see out over Pemaquid Point, over Monhegan Island, over the ocean to the edge of the Old World. The rising sun burst into our sleep each morning. At night, before bed, we lay on my bed together—three of us—naming Orion and Leo and the Pleiades in whispers. Monhegan's distant light swept the walls of our rooms all night at 36-second intervals. Our little house creaked in the wind during February storms. Now spring had come, and the world had shifted.

10   "Help me make my cake," I said to the boys. They dragged their chairs to the counter.

11   "Mum, will Dad be home for your birthday tonight?" Sam asked. Both boys were so contained, so taut, so helpless. They leaned against me, quiet.

12   Guilt and fear tugged me like an undertow. I started to cry.

13   "I don't know, my loves. I think this is a really big one."

14   Bertie and Tippy-Toes lay side by side on the brown grass, their eyes open, necks bent. I closed the coop door behind me and lunged for the next hen.

15   "It's all right," I said softly. "It's all right. Everything's going to be all right. Shhh, Silly, shh." I crouched over her. Silly was the boys' favorite because she let them carry her around the yard. I hoped they would forget her when the box of peeping balls of fluff arrived tomorrow.

16   "It's okay, Silly," I said quietly, wrapping my gloved fingers around her hard little head. she was panting, her eyes wild, frantic, betrayed. I covered them with my fingers and twisted her neck hard. Her black wings, iridescent in the dusty sunlight, beat against my legs. I held her close to me while she scrabbled against my strong hands. I started to cry again.

17   When I went back up to the house, Bertie and Tippy-Toes and Silly and Mother Mabel lay on the grass outside the coop.

18   Benjamin came into the kitchen and leaned against my legs. "What are we going to do?" he asked.

19   "About what, Sweetheart?" I hoped he was not asking me about tomorrow. Or the next day.

20   "Nothing," he said, drifting off to play with Sam upstairs.

21   We frosted the cake blue, Ben's favorite color, and put it on the table next to their presents for me, wrapped in wallpaper. I wanted to call someone, to call my mother or my sister. Yesterday I would have called Ashley, my best friend, who had listened to me cry and rail about John again and again. Instead, I brought in three loads of wood and put them in the box John had left empty.

"Sam, will you lay up a fire for tonight? And Ben, go down to the   22
cellar and get a bunch of kindling wood."

Like serious little men, my children did what I asked.   23

"What are we going to make for my birthday supper?"   24

"I thought we were going to Uncle Stephen's and Aunt Ashley's"   25
Sam said.

"Know what?" I said. "Know what I want to do? Let's just stay here   26
and have our own private little party. Just us."

I felt marooned with my children. I sat at the table, watching while   27
they did their chores, then headed back out to finish mine.

Minnie Hen was next. She let me catch her and kill her without   28
much fight. I laid her next to the others in the cold grass.

Itty-Bit was last. She was my favorite. The others had chewed off her   29
toes, one by one, when she was a chick. I had made a separate box for her, a
separate feeder, separate roost, and smeared antibiotic ointment four times
a day on the weeping stubs. She survived, and ate from my hand after
that. She had grown to be fierce with the other hens, never letting them too
close to her, able to slip in, grab the best morsels and flee before they could
peck her. I had come to admire her very much, my tough little biddie.

She cowered in the corner, alone. I sat next to her, and she let me pull   30
her up into my lap. I stroked her feathers smooth, stroke after stroke. Her
comb was pale and shriveled, a sign of her age. I knew she hadn't laid an
egg for months. She was shaking. I held her warmth against me, cooing
to her, "It's all right, Itty-Bit. Everything's going to be all right. Don't be
scared." My anger at John centered like a tornado on having to kill this
hen. "You stupid, selfish son of a bitch," I said. I got up, crying again,
holding Itty-Bit tight to me. I laid her gently on the floor and crouched
over her. The sun filled the coop with thick light.

That night, after eating spaghetti and making a wish and blowing   31
out 38 candles and opening presents made by Sam and Benjamin—a mail
holder made from wood slats, a sculpture of 2-by-4s and shells; after baths
and reading stories in bed and our sweet, in-the-dark, whispered good
nights; after saying "I don't know what is going to happen" to my scared
children; after banking the fire and turning off the lights, I sat on the porch
in the cold, trying to imagine what had to happen next. I could see the
outline of the coop against the dark, milky sky. I touched my fingers, my
hands, so familiar to me. Tonight they felt like someone else's. I wrapped
my arms around myself—thin, tired—and wished it were yesterday.

Tomorrow morning, I thought, I have to turn over the garden and   32
go to the dump. Tomorrow morning, I have to call a lawyer. I have to figure out what to say to Sam and Benjamin. I have to put Ben's sculpture on
the mantel and put some mail in Sam's holder on the desk. I have to clean
out the coop and spread fresh shavings.

JOSEPH R. DIFRANZA

Joseph R. DiFranza (born in 1954 in Revere, Massachusetts) is a family physician and professor in the Department of Family Medicine and Community Health at the University of Massachusetts Medical School in Worcester, where he received his MD (1981). DiFranza serves on the board of the Tobacco Control Resource Center, which implements tobacco control projects in the interests of public health. He has published extensively on nicotine dependence; the effects of tobacco advertising; smoking among children, adolescents, and young adults; the effectiveness of laws banning tobacco sales to children; and maternal smoking and tobacco-related complications in pregnancy. In "Hooked from the First Cigarette," originally published in *Scientific American* (2008), DiFranza combines empirical observations of his patients' struggles with smoking with his own and colleagues' research to describe the development of a new theory of nicotine dependence, "that as little as one cigarette" can cause nicotine addiction. In combining his experiences as a family physician with the work of developing hypotheses and testing them, DiFranza links theoretical research with its applications, the prevention and cure of nicotine addiction.

Hooked from the First Cigarette

1   While I was training to become a family doctor, I learned the conventional wisdom about nicotine addiction. Physicians have long believed that people smoke primarily for pleasure and become psychologically dependent on that pleasure. Tolerance to the effects of nicotine prompts more frequent smoking; when the habit reaches a critical frequency—about five cigarettes per day—and nicotine is constantly present in the blood, physical dependence may begin, usually after thousands of cigarettes and years of smoking. Within hours of the last cigarette, the addicted smoker experiences the symptoms of nicotine withdrawal: restlessness, irritability, inability to concentrate, and so on. According to this understanding, those who smoke fewer than five cigarettes per day are not addicted.

2   I was armed with this knowledge when I encountered the proverbial patient who had not read the textbook. During a routine physical, an adolescent girl told me she was unable to quit smoking despite having started only two months before. I thought this patient must be an outlier, a rare exception to the rule that addiction takes years to develop. But my curiosity was piqued, so I went to the local high school to interview students about their

smoking. There a 14-year-old girl told me that she had made two serious attempts to quit, failing both times. This was eyeopening because she had smoked only a few cigarettes a week for two months. When she described her withdrawal symptoms, her story sounded like the lament of one of my two-pack-a-day patients. The rapid onset of these symptoms in the absence of daily smoking contradicted most of what I thought I knew about nicotine addiction. And when I tracked that received wisdom back to its source, I found that everything I had learned was just a poor educated guess.

With funding from the National Cancer Institute and the National Institute on Drug Abuse (NIDA), I have spent the past decade exploring how nicotine addiction develops in novice smokers. I now know that the model of addiction described in the opening paragraph is fiction. My research supports a new hypothesis asserting that limited exposure to nicotine—as little as one cigarette—can change the brain, modifying its neurons in a way that stimulates the craving to smoke. This understanding, if proved correct, may someday provide researchers with promising avenues for developing new drugs and other therapies that could help people kick the habit.

A Loss of Autonomy

When I started this investigation in 1997 with my colleagues at the University of Massachusetts Medical School in Worcester, our first challenge was to develop a reliable tool to detect the first symptoms of addiction as they emerged. In my view, the defining feature of addiction is the loss of autonomy, when the smoker finds that quitting cigarettes requires an effort or involves discomfort. To detect this loss, I devised the Hooked on Nicotine Checklist (HONC); an answer of "yes" to any of the questions on the list indicates that addiction has begun [*see box on p. 127*]. Now in use in 13 languages, the HONC is the most thoroughly validated measure of nicotine addiction. (And the checklist could easily be adapted to the study of other drugs.)

We administered the HONC to hundreds of adolescents repeatedly over three years. It turned out that the rapid onset of addiction was quite common. The month after the first cigarette was by far the most likely time for addiction to begin; any of the HONC symptoms, including cravings for cigarettes and failed attempts at quitting, could appear within the first weeks of smoking. On average, the adolescents were smoking only two cigarettes a week when the first symptoms appeared. The data shattered the conventional wisdom and provided a wealth of insight into how addiction starts. But when I presented these findings in February 2000 and proclaimed that some youths had symptoms of addiction after smoking just one or two cigarettes, I was widely regarded as the professor who had not read his textbook correctly.

Many laypeople told me that they knew from experience that I was on the right track. But if any scientists believed me, they were not willing to

QUICK ADDICTION

Researchers have proposed a new theory to explain how withdrawal symptoms can develop so quickly in novice smokers. Although this model is controversial, it may some-day lead to a better understanding of cigarette addiction.

A HEALTHY BALANCE
In nonsmokers, the brain's systems for generating and inhibiting cravings are in balance. The craving-generation system triggers appetitive behavior (such as eating), and the craving-inhibition system stops the behavior when the individual is satiated (at the end of the meal).

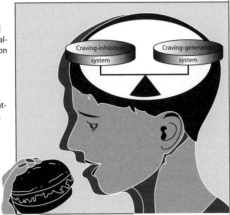

THE FIRST CIGARETTE
Nicotine stimulates the craving-inhibition system until its activity far exceeds that of the craving-generation system. The brain attempts to restore its balance by rapidly developing adaptations that boost the activity of the craving-generation system. (These changes are called withdrawal-related adaptations.)

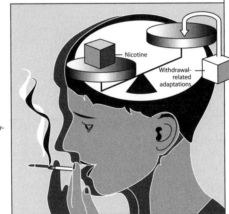

WITHDRAWAL
Once the effects of nicotine wear off, the craving-inhibition system is no longer stimulated and returns to a lower level of activity. But the craving-generation system, enhanced by the withdrawal-related adaptations, now throws the brain off-balance again, producing an intense desire for the one thing that can inhibit, the craving—another cigarette.

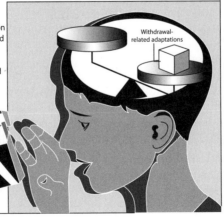

Artwork: Lisa Apfelbacher. Reprinted with permission.

risk their reputations by admitting it publicly. Skepticism was widespread. How could addiction start so quickly? How could withdrawal symptoms be present in smokers who do not maintain constant blood levels of nicotine?

Vindication has come with time as teams of investigators led by Jennifer O'Loughlin of McGill University, Denise Kandel of Columbia University and Robert Scragg of the University of Auckland in New Zealand replicated all of my discoveries. A dozen studies have now established that nicotine withdrawal is common among novice smokers. Of those who experience symptoms of addiction, 10 percent do so within two days of their first cigarette and 25 to 35 percent do so within a month. In a very large study of New Zealand youths, 25 percent had symptoms after smoking one to four cigarettes. And the early appearance of HONC symptoms increased the odds that the youths would progress to daily smoking by nearly 200-fold.

These results raise the question of how the nicotine from a single cigarette could alter the brain enough to trigger the onset of addiction. Earlier research with laboratory animals has found that chronic high-dose exposure to nicotine—the equivalent of one to three packs a day—stimulates an increase in the number of neuron receptors that have a high affinity for nicotine. Autopsies of human smokers reveal 50 to 100 percent increases in the brain's frontal lobe, hippocampus and cerebellum.

I persuaded Theodore Slotkin of Duke University to determine the minimum nicotine exposure needed to provoke this so-called up-regulation of receptors. On consecutive days his team administered small amounts of nicotine (equivalent to one to two cigarettes) to rats and found up-regulation in the hippocampus—which is involved in long-term memory—by the second day. Subsequently, Arthur Brody and his colleagues at the University of California, Los Angeles, discovered that the nicotine from one cigarette was sufficient to occupy 88 percent of the brain's nicotinic receptors. Although the role of receptor up-regulation in addiction is unknown, these studies make it physiologically plausible that adolescents could have withdrawal symptoms just two days after their first cigarette.

According to addiction researchers, withdrawal symptoms result from drug-induced homeostatic adaptations—the body's attempts to keep its functions and chemicals in balance. For example, certain addictive drugs increase the production of neurotransmitters—chemicals that transmit signals among neurons—and in response the body develops adaptations that inhibit these chemicals. When the user stops taking the drug, however, the inhibition becomes excessive and withdrawal symptoms appear. We know that these withdrawal-related adaptations could develop rapidly after the first cigarette, because other addictive drugs such as morphine produce similar changes very quickly. But most longtime smokers find they can forgo cigarettes for only an hour or two before craving another, whereas novice smokers can go weeks without lighting up. Amazingly, in the early stages of addiction a single cigarette can suppress withdrawal symptoms for weeks, even though the nicotine is gone from the body within a day.

A Nicotine Glossary

Nicotine withdrawal: A cluster of symptoms that include craving, restlessness, nervousness, irritability, difficulty concentrating and difficulty sleeping.

Latency to withdrawal: The symptom-free interval between the last cigarette and the onset of withdrawal symptoms. It can shrink from weeks to minutes over many years of tobacco use.

Dependence-related tolerance: The mechanism that causes the latency to withdrawal to shrink gradually over time.

Abstinence-related adaptations: A mechanism that mimics the action of nicotine by inhibiting craving. It develops in ex-smokers to counter the enduring effects of dependence-related tolerance.

11   The explanation for this remarkable fact is that the consequences of flooding the brain with nicotine linger long after the event itself. Nicotine triggers brain circuits involving biochemical compounds such as acetylcholine, dopamine, GABA, glutamate, noradrenaline, opioid peptides and serotonin. In rats, a single dose of nicotine increases noradrenaline synthesis in the hippocampus for at least one month, and nicotine's effects on certain neurological and cognitive functions also persist for weeks. Although it is not known if any of these phenomena are related to withdrawal, they establish that the impact of nicotine far outlasts its presence in the brain.

12   The symptom-free interval between the last cigarette and the onset of withdrawal is called the latency to withdrawal (LTW). For novice smokers the LTW is long, and a cigarette every few weeks keeps withdrawal in check. With repeated use, however, tolerance develops and the impact of each cigarette diminishes; the LTW shortens, and cigarettes must be spaced at ever closer intervals to stave off withdrawal. This phenomenon of diminishing LTW is called dependence-related tolerance. Compared with the withdrawal-related adaptations that may appear overnight, dependence-related tolerance typically develops at a glacial pace. It may take years for the LTW to shrink enough to require someone to smoke five cigarettes a day. In reality, then, withdrawal symptoms are the cause of long-term heavy use, not the other way around as we had previously thought.

Time for a New Theory

13   I had always been skeptical of the notion that smokers were addicted to the pleasure of smoking, because some of my most addicted patients hated the habit. If the conventional thinking were correct, shouldn't the

most addicted smokers enjoy it the most? Eric Moolchan of the NIDA demonstrated that although adolescents showed increasing levels of addiction over time, they reported decreasing pleasure from smoking. A new theory was needed to explain these discoveries.

While struggling to understand the rapid onset of nicotine addiction, 14 a paradox occurred to me. The only action of nicotine that is obvious to the casual observer is that it provides a temporary suppression of craving for itself, yet only people previously exposed to nicotine crave it. How can one drug both create craving and suppress it? I began to speculate that the direct immediate action of nicotine is to suppress craving and that this action could become magnified to an extreme because subsequent doses of nicotine provoke greater responses than the first dose. (This phenomenon, common to all addictive drugs, is known as sensitization.) The brain might then quickly develop withdrawal-related adaptations to counter the action of nicotine, thereby restoring the homeostatic balance. But when the action of nicotine wore off, these adaptations would stimulate craving for another cigarette.

Under this sensitization-homeostasis theory, nicotine is addictive not 15 because it produces pleasure but simply because it suppresses craving. Because nicotine stimulates neurons, I envisioned it activating the nerve cells in a craving-inhibition system in the brain. Activation of this hypothesized system would then suppress the activity in a complementary system for generating cravings. The natural role of the craving-generation system would be to receive sensory cues (such as sights and smells), compare them with memories of rewarding objects (such as food), and produce craving to

The Hooked on Nicotine Checklist

Researchers use the following questions to determine whether adolescent smokers are addicted. An answer of "yes" to any one of the questions indicates that addiction has begun:

1. Have you ever tried to quit smoking, but couldn't?
2. Do you smoke now because it is really hard to quit?
3. Have you ever felt like you were addicted to tobacco?
4. Do you ever have strong cravings to smoke?
5. Have you ever felt like you really needed a cigarette?
6. Is it hard to keep from smoking in places where you are not supposed to, like school?

When you tried to stop smoking (or, when you haven't used tobacco for a while):

7. Did you find it hard to concentrate because you couldn't smoke?
8. Did you feel more irritable because you couldn't smoke?
9. Did you feel a strong need or urge to smoke?
10. Did you feel nervous, restless or anxious because you couldn't smoke?

motivate and direct appetitive behavior (such as eating). The role of the craving-inhibition system would be to signal satisfaction so that the animal would stop the appetitive behavior when it became appropriate to do so.

16   Because the body would try to keep these two systems in balance, the nicotine-induced suppression of the craving-generation system would trigger the development of withdrawal-related adaptations that would boost the system's activity. During the withdrawal period, when the inhibitory effect of nicotine has worn off, the craving-generation system would be left in a state of excitement that would result in the excessive desire for another cigarette [*see box on 126*]. These shifts in brain activity would come about through rapid changes in the configurations of neuron receptors, which would explain why adolscents could start to crave cigarettes after smoking just once.

17   The first support for this model has come from the many functional magnetic resonance imaging (fMRI) studies of humans showing that cue-induced craving for nicotine, alcohol, cocaine, opiates and chocolate increases metabolic activity in the anterior cingulate gyrus and other frontal-lobe areas of the brain. This finding suggests the existence of a craving-generation system. And Hyun-Kook Lim and his colleagues at the Korea College of Medicine recently found evidence that nicotine suppresses this system. The researchers demonstrated that prior administration of the drug can block the pattern of regional brain activation that accompanies cue-induced craving in humans.

18   The sensitization-homeostasis model can also explain dependence-related tolerance. Repeated suppression of activity in the craving-generation system triggers another homeostatic adaptation that stimulates craving by shortening the duration of nicotine's inhibitory effects. As mentioned earlier, tolerance develops much more slowly than the withdrawal-related adaptations, but once it emerges tolerance becomes firmly entrenched. Although it usually takes two years or more before adolescents need to smoke five cigarettes a day, I noticed that when my patients quit smoking and then relapsed, it took them only a few days to return to their old frequency, even after a lengthy abstinence.

19   Along with Robert Wellman of Fitchburg State College, I investigated this phenomenon in a study that asked 2,000 smokers how much they smoked before quitting, how long they had remained abstinent and how much they smoked immediately after relapsing. Smokers who relapsed after an abstinence of three months resumed smoking at about 40 percent of their previous rate, indicating that their LTW had lengthened. We believe the craving-free interval between cigarettes increases because the withdrawal-related adaptations disappear during the first few weeks of abstinence. With the resumption of smoking, however, the withdrawal-related adaptations quickly redevelop, and over the next few weeks relapsed smokers find they must smoke just as often as they used to.

We also discovered, however, that abstinences greater than three months had almost no additional impact on the length of the LTW. Even after years of abstinence, smoking resumed at about 40 percent of the prior rate, typically six or seven cigarettes a day. This finding suggests that increases in tolerance are permanent; a relapsing smoker will never get as much suppression of craving from a single cigarette as a novice smoker will. In other words, the brain of a smoker is never restored to its original state. [20]

But if dependence-related tolerance stimulates the craving-generation system and never completely goes away, why don't former smokers continue hungering for cigarettes forever? Our research subjects could not tell us why their craving for nicotine eventually lessened, so I looked at what the sensitization-homeostasis theory would predict. I reasoned that former smokers must develop abstinence-related adaptations that mimic the action of nicotine, inhibiting the craving-generation system and restoring homeostasis. Smoking cessation would not result in a quiet return to normal brain function; rather it would trigger a dynamic period of neuroplasticity during which new adaptations would appear in the former smoker's brain. Because of these adaptations, the ex-smoker's brain would resemble neither that of the smoker nor of the nonsmoker. [21]

To test this prediction, Slotkin and his colleagues examined the brains of rats before nicotine exposure, during exposure, during withdrawal and long after withdrawal. They found clear-cut evidence of changes in the functioning of neurons in the brain's cortex that employ acetylcholine and serotonin to transmit signals—changes that appeared only after the acute withdrawal period. As predicted, the brains of the "ex-smoker" rats showed unique adaptations that were not present in the "smokers" or "nonsmokers." And at the College of Medicine at the Catholic University of Korea, HeeJin Lim and colleagues found evidence of brain remodeling in humans who quit smoking by studying brain-derived neurotrophic factor, a stimulant of neuroplasticity. Levels of this factor in ex-smokers tripled after two months of abstinence. [22]

Thus, abstinence-related adaptations seem to counter the tolerance-related adaptations by inhibiting the craving-generation system so that it eventually stops compelling the former smoker to light up. Smoking cues in the environment might still provoke craving, however, and if the long-abstinent smoker were to surrender to an urge to smoke just once, nicotine would again produce a profound suppression of activity in the craving-generation system. The abstinence-related adaptations would then make a bad situation worse. Because these adaptations mimic the effect of nicotine, they would need to be removed to restore homeostasis; when the effect of nicotine wears off, the tolerance-related adaptations would be left unopposed in stimulating the craving-generation system. Struck with a strong craving, the relapsing smoker would need to puff six or seven cigarettes a day to keep it under control. [23]

New Hope for Smokers

24   This model of addiction by no means represents the prevailing opinion. In my view, addiction is an accident of physiology. Because so many careers have been built on the assumption that the roots of addiction lie in psychology rather than physiology, I did not expect my ideas to receive a warm welcome.

25   Whether or not the sensitization-homeostasis theory is correct, it is clear that the nicotine from the first cigarette is sufficient to trigger a remodeling of the brain. Although some may argue about what criteria should be used to render a proper diagnosis of addiction, it is now well established that adolescents have many symptoms of addiction very soon after they smoke their first cigarette. This finding underlines the importance of bolstering government funding for antismoking campaigns, which has fallen in recent years.

26   To fully test my theory, which has been simplified here, researchers need a reliable method to detect sensitization in humans. I have worked with Jean A. King and her colleagues at the Center for Comparative NeuroImaging to demonstrate nicotine sensitization in rats using fMRI. Images comparing brain responses to the first dose of nicotine and to the fifth dose given four days later illustrate the dramatic changes in brain function in areas such as the anterior cingulate gyrus and hippocampus. We have just received funding from the NIDA to use fMRI to visualize sensitization in smokers, with future plans to determine which brain regions are involved in the craving-inhibition and craving-generation systems.

27   Our long-term goal is to identify drugs that can manipulate these systems to treat or cure addiction. Although nicotine-replacement therapies

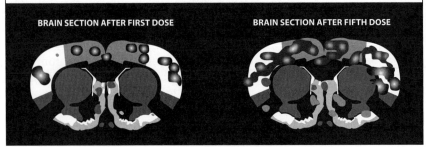

NICOTINE ON THE BRAIN

Recent studies have confirmed that nicotine evokes rapid changes in brain physiology. The author and Jean A. King of the Center for Comparative NeuroImaging at the University of Massachusetts Medical School used functional magnetic resonance imaging (fMRI) to measure levels of metabolic activity in the brains of rats given a dose of nicotine on five consecutive days. The response to the first dose was relatively limited, but brain activity was much more intense and widespread after the fifth dose. These findings indicate that the brain quickly becomes sensitized to nicotine, enabling addiction to appear after just a few doses.

BRAIN SECTION AFTER FIRST DOSE   BRAIN SECTION AFTER FIFTH DOSE

Images reprinted courtesy of UMASS Medical School.

may double the success rate for smoking cessation, failed attempts still far outnumber the successes. The sensitization-homeostasis theory suggests that what is needed is a therapy that will suppress craving without stimulating compensatory responses that only make the craving worse in the long run. A better understanding of the addiction process may help researchers develop new treatments that can safely liberate smokers from nicotine's deadly pull.

Content

1. How did DiFranza's hypothesis that "limited exposure to nicotine—as little as one cigarette—can change the brain, modifying its neurons in a way that stimulates the craving to smoke" (¶ 3) challenge "conventional wisdom about nicotine addiction" (¶ 1)? What evidence does DiFranza provide that supports his hypothesis that a single cigarette can trigger the onset of addiction (¶s 8–11)?

2. How does diminishing "latency to withdrawal (LTW)," or "dependence-related tolerance," explain why withdrawal symptoms are the cause of, rather than the effect of, long-term, heavy smoking (¶ 12)?

3. What is "sensitization" (¶ 14)? How does this add to the concept of dependence-related tolerance in explaining the brain's craving for tobacco (¶ 15–18)? What evidence suggests that "the brain of a smoker is never restored to its original state" (¶ 20)?

4. What are "abstinence-related adaptations" (¶ 21)? How does the sensitization-homeostasis model explain why quitting smoking reduces the brain's craving for tobacco (¶ 22–23)?

Strategies/Structures/Language

5. DiFranza uses several examples of how his empirical observations about patients who smoke have led him to question conventional wisdom about smoking and conduct research (¶s 2, 6, 10, 13, 18). How do his observations help him explain and help the reader understand the complex research on the brain he describes?

6. DiFranza characterizes smoking as an addiction with a physiological basis and concludes that "the nicotine from the first cigarette is sufficient to trigger a remodeling of the brain" (¶ 25). Why does he then add that "some may argue about what criteria should be used to render a proper diagnosis of addiction" (¶ 25)? Is the evidence that links this remodeling with addiction tentative? For example, which studies does DiFranza cite that suggest that the susceptibility to addiction varies among individuals?

For Writing

7. *Journal Writing.* DiFranza has spoken out against the tobacco industry for marketing cigarettes to children, in particular against R. J. R. Nabisco's cartoon character Joe Camel. In "Why Men Don't Last" (Chapter 8), Natalie Angier alludes to the impact of advertisements on behavior: "the Marlboro Man who never even gasps for breath" portrays "the image of the dispassionate, resilient,

action-oriented male" (¶ 20). Is the association of smoking with strength and fearlessness, or stylishness and sophistication, changing? Do you see a future in which smoking is obsolete? What would it take to convince children and teens not to smoke?

8. ***Dialogues.*** In "Under the Influence: Paying the Price of My Father's Booze" (Chapter 5), Scott Russell Sanders describes his family's understanding of his father's alcoholism as "a moral weakness, a sin" (¶ 25) and yet his fear of becoming an alcoholic is rooted in his understanding of addiction as a physiological problem: he sips "warily," listening "for the turning of a key in my brain" (¶ 55). Does DiFranza's research suggest that views of addiction are likely to change? How does he suggest that society deals with addictive behaviors?

9. If you are a smoker, use your own experiences—with smoking and with trying to quit—as the basis for writing a reply to DiFranza in which you either corroborate or refute his research.

10. If you are not a smoker, why not? Write a paper based on your own experiences, offering guidelines to prevent teenagers from starting to smoke.

SCOTT McCLOUD

Scott McCloud (born in Boston in 1960) decided at the age of fifteen to become a professional comic book artist. He created the superhero story series *Zot!* (1984–1991) and is the author of *Understanding Comics* (2000), and *Making Comics: Storytelling Secrets of Comics, Manga and Graphic Novels* (2006). McCloud's focus on the art form of comics, from theory to mechanics, aims to challenge the cultural barrier between high and low culture. McCloud won the Quill Award in 2007 in the Graphic Novel category. His work has been translated into more than fifteen languages.

In "Reading the Comics" (from *Understanding Comics*) McCloud explains the process of how artist and reader collaborate to provide "closure" that makes comics readable. He combines accessible, practical language with graphics to show as much as to tell. At the same time, he represents the process as fluid, leaving room for the magic, individuality, and discovery of the artist's work.

THE CLOSURE OF *ELECTRONIC* MEDIA IS *CONTINUOUS,* LARGELY *INVOLUNTARY* AND *VIRTUALLY IMPERCEPTIBLE.*

BUT CLOSURE IN *COMICS* IS *FAR* FROM CONTINUOUS AND *ANYTHING* BUT *INVOLUNTARY!*

NOW YOU *DIE!!*

NO! NO!

EEYAA!!

EVERY ACT COMMITTED TO PAPER BY THE COMICS ARTIST IS *AIDED* AND *ABETTED* BY A *SILENT ACCOMPLICE.*

AN *EQUAL PARTNER IN CRIME* KNOWN AS *THE READER.*

I MAY HAVE DRAWN AN *AXE* BEING *RAISED* IN THIS EXAMPLE, BUT I'M NOT THE ONE WHO LET IT *DROP* OR DECIDED HOW *HARD* THE BLOW, OR *WHO* SCREAMED, OR *WHY.*

NOW YOU *DIE!!*

NO! NO!

EEYAA!!

THAT, DEAR READER, WAS *YOUR SPECIAL CRIME,* EACH OF YOU COMMITTING IT IN YOUR OWN *STYLE.*

ALL OF YOU *PARTICIPATED* IN THE MURDER. ALL OF YOU *HELD THE AXE* AND *CHOSE YOUR SPOT.*

Content

1. Read the words and images in McCloud's first three panels to explain how he arrives at an explanation of the way comics work in the fourth, "Comics **is** closure." In this case, a process becomes a definition.

2. In what ways do panels 5-9 extend the process and the definition, as readers are required to participate in making meaning and attaining closure?

Strategies/Structures/Language

3. "Read" other photographs in *The Essay Connection* [such as—Martin Luther King and Civil Rights (399) and "Migrant Mother" (483)] to provide an interpretation of each that satisfies your understanding of what is represented. Do the accompanying commentaries corroborate your interpretations, or complicate them? Did your reading provide satisfying "closure"? Or not?

For Writing

4. Make a collection of several photographs, drawings, cartoons and other illustrations that address the same issue or theme. Then write an interpretive essay in which you make connections among them. How do you know whether or not your interpretation is "right"? Does it matter?

SCOTT RUSSELL SANDERS

Scott Russell Sanders (born 1945) grew up in Ohio, earned a PhD in English from Cambridge University in 1971, and has taught ever since at Indiana University. His books include fiction, a biography of Audubon, and several essay collections. Among them, *In Limestone Country* (1985), *Staying Put* (1993), *Writing from the Center* (1995), and *Hunting for Hope* (1998) focus on living and writing in the Midwest. In his most recent books, *A Private History of Awe* (2006) and *A Conservationist Manifesto* (2009), Sanders pursues his concerns with spirituality, nature, social justice, and community. "My writing . . . is bound together by a web of questions" concerning "the ways in which human beings come to terms with the practical problems of living on a small planet, in nature . . . and families and towns. . . ."

The elegiac "The Inheritance of Tools" appeared in the award-winning *The Paradise of Bombs* (1987), personal essays mainly about the American culture of violence. This essay reveals Sanders's concerns, as a writer and as a son, husband, and father, with the inheritance of skills and values through the generations. Here narration is explanation. Sanders shows how tools become not just extensions of the hand and brain, but of the human heart, as the knowledge of how to use and care for them is transmitted from grandfather to father to son to grandchildren.

The Inheritance of Tools

1   At just about the hour when my father died, soon after dawn one February morning when ice coated the windows like cataracts, I banged my thumb with a hammer. Naturally I swore at the hammer, the reckless thing, and in the moment of swearing I thought of what my father would say: "If you'd try hitting the nail it would go in a whole lot faster. Don't you know your thumb's not as hard as that hammer?" We both were doing carpentry that day, but far apart. He was building cupboards at my brother's place in Oklahoma; I was at home in Indiana, putting up a wall in the basement to make a bedroom for my daughter. By the time my mother called with news of his death—the long distance wires whittling her voice until it seemed too thin to bear the weight of what she had to say—my thumb was swollen. A week or so later a white scar in the shape of a crescent moon began to show above the cuticle and month by month it rose across the pink sky of my thumbnail. It took the better part of a year for the scar to disappear, and every time I noticed it I thought of my father.

2   The hammer had belonged to him, and to his father before him. The three of us have used it to build houses and barns and chicken coops, to upholster chairs and crack walnuts, to make doll furniture and bookshelves and jewelry boxes. The head is scratched and pockmarked, like an old plowshare that has been working rocky fields, and it gives off the sort of dull sheen you see on fast creek water in the shade. It is a finishing hammer, about the weight of a bread loaf, too light, really, for framing walls, too heavy for cabinet work, with a curved claw for pulling nails, a rounded head for pounding, a fluted neck for looks, and a hickory handle for strength.

3   The present handle is my third one, bought from a lumberyard in Tennessee, down the road from where my brother and I were helping my father build his retirement house. I broke the previous one by trying to pull sixteen-penny nails out of floor joists—a foolish thing to do with a finishing hammer, as my father pointed out. "You ever hear of a crowbar?" he said. No telling how many handles he and my grandfather had gone through before me. My grandfather used to cut down hickory trees on his farm, saw them into slabs, cure the planks in his hayloft, and carve handles with a drawknife. The grain in hickory is crooked and knotty, and therefore tough, hard to split, like the grain in the two men who owned this hammer before me.

4   After proposing marriage to a neighbor girl, my grandfather used this hammer to build a house for his bride on a stretch of river bottom in northern Mississippi. The lumber for the place, like the hickory for the handle, was cut on his own land. By the day of the wedding he had not quite finished the house, and so right after the ceremony he took his wife

home and put her to work. My grandmother had worn her Sunday dress for the wedding, with a fringe of lace tacked on around the hem in honor of the occasion. She removed this lace and folded it away before going out to help my grandfather nail siding on the house. "There she was in her good dress," he told me some fifty-odd years after that wedding day, "holding up them long pieces of clapboard while I hammered, and together we got the place covered up before dark." As the family grew to four, six, eight, and eventually thirteen, my grandfather used this hammer to enlarge his house room by room, like a chambered nautilus expanding its shell.

By and by the hammer was passed along to my father. One day 5 he was up on the roof of our pony barn nailing shingles with it, when I stepped out the kitchen door to call him for supper. Before I could yell, something about the sight of him straddling the spine of that roof and

Bojan Brecelj/Encyclopedia/Corbis

Despite the United States' diverse population—composed of significant numbers of Asians, Hispanics, African Americans, and others from around the world— Americans tend to regard with suspicion people from religious groups that are not mainstream, particularly if their clothing or hair styles are distinctive and separatist. What values and qualities emanate from the picture of the Mennonite carpenter above, taken by Bojan Brecelj? What is the man doing? With what tools? In what room are they? What is its condition? Do you assume the people in this picture are father and daughter? Why? Are they healthy? Clean? At ease? What distinctive clothing are they wearing? Why? Do you find them attractive? How does this photograph comment on Sanders's "The Inheritance of Tools"? What is the heritage of the little girl in this picture?

swinging the hammer caught my eye and made me hold my tongue. I was five or six years old, and the world's commonplaces were still news to me. He would pull a nail from the pouch at his waist, bring the hammer down, and a moment later the *thunk* of the blow would reach my ears. And that is what had stopped me in my tracks and stilled my tongue, that momentary gap between seeing and hearing the blow. Instead of yelling from the kitchen door, I ran to the barn and climbed two rungs up the ladder—as far as I was allowed to go—and spoke quietly to my father. On our walk to the house he explained that sound takes time to make its way through air. Suddenly the world seemed larger, the air more dense, if sound could be held back like any ordinary traveler.

6   By the time I started using this hammer, at about the age when I discovered the speed of sound, it already contained houses and mysteries for me. The smooth handle was one my grandfather had made. In those days I needed both hands to swing it. My father would start a nail in a scrap of wood, and I would pound away until I bent it over.

7   "Looks like you got ahold of some of those rubber nails," he would tell me. "Here, let me see if I can find you some stiff ones." And he would rummage in a drawer until he came up with a fistful of more cooperative nails. "Look at the head," he would tell me. "Don't look at your hands, don't look at the hammer. Just look at the head of that nail and pretty soon you'll learn to hit it square."

8   Pretty soon I did learn. While he worked in the garage cutting dovetail joints for a drawer or skinning a deer or tuning an engine, I would hammer nails. I made innocent blocks of wood look like porcupines. He did not talk much in the midst of his tools, but he kept up a nearly ceaseless humming, slipping in and out of a dozen tunes in an afternoon, often running back over the same stretch of melody again and again, as if searching for a way out. When the humming did cease, I knew he was faced with a task requiring great delicacy or concentration, and I took care not to distract him.

9   He kept scraps of wood in a cardboard box—the ends of two-by-fours, slabs of shelving and plywood, odd pieces of molding—and everything in it was fair game. I nailed scraps together to fashion what I called boats or houses, but the results usually bore only faint resemblance to the visions I carried in my head. I would hold up these constructions to show my father, and he would turn them over in his hands admiringly, speculating about what they might be. My cobbled-together guitars might have been alien spaceships, my barns might have been models of Aztec temples, each wooden contraption might have been anything but what I had set out to make.

10   Now and again I would feel the need to have a chunk of wood shaped or shortened before I riddled it with nails, and I would clamp it in a vise and scrape at it with a handsaw. My father would let me lacerate the board until my arm gave out, and then he would wrap his hand around

mine and help me finish the cut, showing me how to use my thumb to guide the blade, how to pull back on the saw to keep it from binding, how to let my shoulder do the work.

"Don't force it," he would say, "just drag it easy and give the teeth a 11 chance to bite."

As the saw teeth bit down, the wood released its smell, each kind 12 with its own fragrance, oak or walnut or cherry or pine—usually pine because it was the softest, easiest for a child to work. No matter how weathered and gray the board, no matter how warped and cracked, inside there was this smell waiting, as of something freshly baked. I gathered every smidgen of sawdust and stored it away in coffee cans, which I kept in a drawer of the workbench. When I did not feel like hammering nails, I would dump my sawdust on the concrete floor of the garage and landscape it into highways and farms and towns, running miniature cars and trucks along miniature roads. Looming as huge as a colossus, my father worked over and around me, now and again bending down to inspect my work, careful not to trample my creations. It was a landscape that smelled dizzyingly of wood. Even after a bath my skin would carry the smell, and so would my father's hair, when he lifted me for a bedtime hug.

I tell these things not only from memory but also from recent observa- 13 tion, because my own son now turns blocks of wood into nailed porcupines, dumps cans full of sawdust at my feet and sculpts highways on the floor. He learns how to swing a hammer from the elbow instead of the wrist, how to lay his thumb beside the blade to guide a saw, how to tap a chisel with a wooden mallet, how to mark a hole with an awl before starting a drill bit. My daughter did the same before him, and even now, on the brink of teenage aloofness, she will occasionally drag out my box of wood scraps and carpenter something. So I have seen my apprenticeship to wood and tools reenacted in each of my children, as my father saw his own apprenticeship renewed in me.

The saw I use belonged to him, as did my level and both of my 14 squares, and all four tools had belonged to his father. The blade of the saw is the bluish color of gun barrels, and the maple handle, dark from the sweat of hands, is inscribed with curving leaf designs. The level is a shaft of walnut two feet long, edged with brass and pierced by three round windows in which air bubbles float in oil-filled tubes of glass. The middle window serves for testing if a surface is horizontal, the others for testing if a surface is plumb or vertical. My grandfather used to carry this level on the gun rack behind the seat in his pickup, and when I rode with him I would turn around to watch the bubbles dance. The larger of the two squares is called a framing square, a flat steel elbow, so beat up and tarnished you can barely make out the rows of numbers that show how to figure the cuts on rafters. The smaller one is called a try square, for marking right angles, with a blued steel blade for the shank and a brass-faced block of cherry for the head.

15   I was taught early on that a saw is not to be used apart from a square: "If you're going to cut a piece of wood," my father insisted, "you owe it to the tree to cut it straight."

16   Long before studying geometry, I learned there is a mystical virtue in right angles. There is an unspoken morality in seeking the level and the plumb. A house will stand, a table will bear weight, the sides of a box will hold together, only if the joints are square and the members upright. When the bubble is lined up between two marks etched in the glass tube of a level, you have aligned yourself with the forces that hold the universe together. When you miter the corners of a picture frame each angle must be exactly forty-five degrees, as they are in the perfect triangles of Pythagoras, not a degree more or less. Otherwise the frame will hang crookedly, as if ashamed of itself and of its maker. No matter if the joints you are cutting do not show. Even if you are butting two pieces of wood together inside a cabinet, where no one except a wrecking crew will ever see them, you must take pains to ensure that the ends are square and the studs are plumb.

17   I took pains over the wall I was building on the day my father died. Not long after that wall was finished—paneled with tongue-and-groove boards of yellow pine, the nail holes filled with putty and the wood all stained and sealed—I came close to wrecking it one afternoon when my daughter ran howling up the stairs to announce that her gerbils had escaped from their cage and were hiding in my brand new wall. She could hear them scratching and squeaking behind her bed. Impossible! I said. How on earth could they get inside my drum-tight wall? Through the heating vent, she answered. I went downstairs, pressed my ear to the honey-colored wood, and heard the *scritch scritch* of tiny feet.

18   "What can we do?" my daughter wailed. "They'll starve to death, they'll die of thirst, they'll suffocate."

19   "Hold on," I soothed. "I'll think of something."

20   While I thought and she fretted, the radio on her bedside table delivered us the headlines: Several thousand people had died in a city in India from a poisonous cloud that had leaked overnight from a chemical plant. A nuclear-powered submarine had been launched. Rioting continued in South Africa. An airplane had been hijacked in the Mediterranean. Authorities calculated that several thousand homeless people slept on the streets within sight of the Washington Monument. I felt my usual helplessness in the face of all these calamities. But here was my daughter, weeping because her gerbils were holed up in a wall. This calamity I could handle.

21   "Don't worry," I told her. "We'll set food and water by the heating vent and lure them out. And if that doesn't do the trick, I'll tear the wall apart until we find them."

22   She stopped crying and gazed at me. "You'd really tear it apart? Just for my gerbils? The *wall?*" Astonishment slowed her down only for a second, however, before she ran to the workbench and began tugging at

drawers, saying, "Let's see, what'll we need? Crowbar. Hammer. Chisels. I hope we don't have to use them—but just in case."

We didn't need the wrecking tools. I never had to assault my hand- 23 some wall, because the gerbils eventually came out to nibble at a dish of popcorn. But for several hours I studied the tongue-and-groove skin I had nailed up on the day of my father's death, considering where to begin prying. There were no gaps in that wall, no crooked joints.

I had botched a great many pieces of wood before I mastered the 24 right angle with a saw, botched even more before I learned to miter a joint. The knowledge of these things resides in my hands and eyes and the webwork of muscles, not in the tools. There are machines for sale— powered miter boxes and radial-arm saws, for instance—that will enable any casual soul to cut proper angles in boards. The skill is invested in the gadget instead of the person who uses it, and this is what distinguishes a machine from a tool. If I had to earn my keep by making furniture or building houses, I suppose I would buy powered saws and pneumatic nailers; the need for speed would drive me to it. But since I carpenter only for my own pleasure or to help neighbors or to remake the house around the ears of my family, I stick with hand tools. Most of the ones I own were given to me by my father, who also taught me how to wield them. The tools in my workbench are a double inheritance, for each hammer and level and saw is wrapped in a cloud of knowing.

All of these tools are a pleasure to look at and to hold. Merchants 25 would never paste NEW NEW NEW! signs on them in stores. Their designs are old because they work, because they serve their purpose well. Like folk songs and aphorisms and the grainy bits of language, these tools have been pared down to essentials. I look at my claw hammer, the distillation of a hundred generations of carpenters, and consider that it holds up well beside those other classics—Greek vases, Gregorian chants, *Don Quixote*, barbed fish hooks, candles, spoons. Knowledge of hammering stretches back to the earliest humans who squatted beside fires, chipping flints. Anthropologists have a lovely name for those unworked rocks that served as the earliest hammers. "Dawn stones," they are called. Their only qualification for the work, aside from hardness, is that they fit the hand. Our ancestors used them for grinding corn, tapping awls, smashing bones. From dawn stones to this claw hammer is a great leap in time, but no great distance in design or imagination.

On that iced-over February morning when I smashed my thumb with the 26 hammer, I was down in the basement framing the wall that my daughter's gerbils would later hide in. I was thinking of my father, as I always did whenever I built anything, thinking how he would have gone about the work, hearing in memory what he would have said about the wisdom of hitting the nail instead of my thumb. I had the studs and plates nailed together all square and trim, and was lifting the wall into place when the phone rang upstairs. My wife answered, and in a moment she came to the basement door and called down softly to me. The stillness in her voice made me drop the framed wall and hurry upstairs. She told me my father was dead. Then I heard the details over the phone from my mother. Building a set of cupboards for my brother in Oklahoma, he had knocked off work early the previous afternoon because of cramps in his stomach. Early this morning, on his way into the kitchen of my brother's trailer, maybe going for a glass of water, so early that no one else was awake, he slumped down on the linoleum and his heart quit.

27   For several hours I paced around inside my house, upstairs and down, in and out of every room, looking for the right door to open and knowing there was no such door. My wife and children followed me and wrapped me in arms and backed away again, circling and staring as if I were on fire. Where was the door, the door, the door? I kept wondering. My smashed thumb turned purple and throbbed, making me furious. I wanted to cut it off and rush outside and scrape away at the snow and hack a hole in the frozen earth and bury the shameful thing.

28   I went down into the basement, opened a drawer in my workbench, and stared at the ranks of chisels and knives. Oiled and sharp, as my father would have kept them, they gleamed at me like teeth. I took up a clasp knife, pried out the longest blade, and tested the edge on the hair of my forearm. A tuft came away cleanly, and I saw my father testing the sharpness of tools on his own skin, the blades of axes and knives and gouges and hoes, saw the red hair shaved off in patches from his arms and the backs of his hands. "That will cut bear," he would say. He never cut a bear with his blades, now my blades, but he cut deer, dirt, wood. I closed the knife and put it away. Then I took up the hammer and went back to work on my daughter's wall, snugging the bottom plate against a chalk line on the floor, shimming the top plate against the joists overhead, plumbing the studs with my level, making sure before I drove the first nail that every line was square and true.

Content

1. Sanders characterizes his father, and grandfather, and himself by showing how they used tools and transmitted this knowledge to their children. What characteristics do they have in common? Why does he omit any differences they might have, focusing on their similarities?

2. Sanders distinguishes between a machine and a tool, saying "The skill is invested in the gadget instead of the person who uses it" (¶ 24). Why does he favor tools over machines? Do you agree with his definition? With his preference?

Strategies/Structures/Language

3. What is the point of this essay? Why does Sanders begin and end with the relation between banging his thumb with a hammer and his father's death?

4. Why does Sanders include the vignette of his daughter and her gerbils, which escaped inside the "drum-tight wall" he had just built (¶s 17–23)? Would he really have wrecked the wall to get the gerbils out?

5. For what audience is Sanders writing? Does it matter whether or not his readers know how to use tools?

6. Show, through specific examples, how Sanders's language and quotations of his father's advice fits his subject, tools, and the people who use them. Consider phrases such as "ice coated the windows like cataracts" (¶ 1) and "making sure before I drove the first nail that every line was square and true" (¶ 28).

For Writing

7. Sanders defines the "inheritance" of tools as, "So I have seen my apprenticeship to wood and tools reenacted in each of my children, as my father saw his own apprenticeship renewed in me" (¶ 13). Tell the story of your own apprenticeship with a tool or collection of tools (kitchen utensils, art supplies, a sewing machine, computer, skis, or other equipment). The explanation of your increasing skill in learning to use it should be intertwined with your relationship with the person who taught you how to use it (not necessarily a family member) and the manner of the teaching—and of the learning.

8. ***Journal Writing.*** Identify an important skill or specific knowledge (which differs from learning to use a tool as in question 7) that you have learned from your parents or grandparents. How do you use this inheritance? What are some of the tangible ways people inherit values from older generations?

9. ***Dialogues.*** Sanders's father is the central figure in two essays in *The Essay Connection*, "The Inheritance of Tools" and "Under the Influence: Paying the Price of My Father's Booze" (180–91). Each uses a series of stories, narratives, to characterize this significant figure in Sanders's life, yet the father of "Inheritance" is a very different character from the father of "Under the Influence." Write an essay in which you compare and contrast Sanders's portraits of his father to show the different ways of presenting the same person.

10. ***Mixed Modes.*** Write a description of someone you know well, or of a public figure you know a great deal about, using two or more significant stories that illustrate the contradictory sides of the same person.

11. ***Second Look.*** How does the photograph here illustrate a particular relationship between the man, his tools, and his workplace? Does the inclusion of the child influence your interpretation of the photograph? How does the photograph suggest movement? What does the arrangement of the two figures, window, wall of tools, and the object being crafted suggest about its focus?

BARBARA EHRENREICH

Barbara Ehrenreich (b.1941), a social critic, grew up in Butte, Montana, in a working-class family. Ehrenreich earned a doctorate in biology from Rockefeller University (1968) and began writing soon after, bringing a decidedly liberal viewpoint to modern political and social issues. Her twenty books include *Fear of Falling: The Inner Life of the Middle Class* (1989), *The Worst Years of Our Lives: Irrelevant Notes on a Decade of Greed* (1990), *Bait and Switch* (2005), and *Bright-sided: How Relentless Promotion of Positive Thinking Has Undermined America* (2009)–a critique of the "happiness movement" inspired, in part, by her anger over society's demands that women experiencing breast cancer (herself included) should be relentlessly positive and cheerful, hugging those pink teddy bears.

In her most famous book, *Nickel and Dimed: On (Not) Getting By in America* (2001), Ehrenreich reports from the perspective of a minimally-skilled worker, impoverished, underpaid, and exploited. To research for the book, she moved to different parts of the United States and lived only on the income she could make working as a housecleaner, a nursing home aide, a Wal-Mart sales clerk and, in the excerpt below, as a server in a series of Florida restaurants. From her experience she learned that "one job is not enough; you need at least two if you intend to live indoors."

Serving in Florida

1   I could drift along like this, in some dreamy proletarian idyll, except for two things. One is management. If I have kept this subject to the margins so far it is because I still flinch to think that I spent all those weeks under the surveillance of men (and later women) whose job it was to monitor my behavior for signs of sloth, theft, drug abuse, or worse. Not that managers and especially "assistant managers" in low-wage settings like this are exactly the class enemy. Mostly, in the restaurant business, they are former cooks still capable of pinch-hitting in the kitchen, just as in hotels they are likely to be former clerks, and paid a salary of only about $400 a week. But everyone knows they have crossed over to the other side, which is, crudely put, corporate as opposed to human. Cooks want to prepare tasty meals, servers want to serve them graciously, but managers are there for only one reason—to make sure that money is made for some theoretical entity, the corporation, which exists far away in Chicago or New York, if a corporation can be said to have a physical existence at all. Reflecting on her career, Gail tells me ruefully that she swore, years ago, never to work for a corporation again. "They don't cut you no slack. You give and you give and they take."

2   Managers can sit—for hours at a time if they want—but it's their job to see that no one else ever does, even when there's nothing to do, and this is why, for servers, slow times can be as exhausting as rushes. You start dragging out each little chore because if the manager on duty catches you in an idle moment he will give you something far nastier to do. So I wipe, I clean, I consolidate catsup bottles and recheck the cheesecake

supply, even tour the tables to make sure the customer evaluation forms are all standing perkily in their places—wondering all the time how many calories I burn in these strictly theatrical exercises. In desperation, I even take the desserts out of their glass display case and freshen them up with whipped cream and bright new maraschino cherries; anything to look busy. When, on a particularly dead afternoon, Stu finds me glancing at a *USA Today* a customer has left behind, he assigns me to vacuum the entire floor with the broken vacuum cleaner, which has a handle only two feet long, and the only way to do that without incurring orthopedic damage is to proceed from spot to spot on your knees.

On my first Friday at Hearthside there is a "mandatory meeting   3 for all restaurant employees," which I attend, eager for insight into our overall marketing strategy and the niche (your basic Ohio cuisine with a tropical twist?) we aim to inhabit. But there is no "we" at this meeting. Phillip, our top manager except for an occasional "consultant" sent out by corporate headquarters, opens it with a sneer: "The break room—it's disgusting. Butts in the ashtrays, newspapers lying around, crumbs." This windowless little room, which also houses the time clock for the entire hotel, is where we stash our bags and civilian clothes and take our half-hour meal breaks. But a break room is not a right, he tells us, it can be taken away. We should also know that the lockers in the break room and whatever is in them can be searched at any time. Then comes gossip; there has been gossip; gossip (which seems to mean employees talking among themselves) must stop. Off-duty employees are henceforth barred from eating at the restaurant, because "other servers gather around them and gossip." When Phillip has exhausted his agenda of rebukes, Joan complains about the condition of the ladies' room and I throw in my two bits about the vacuum cleaner. But I don't see any backup coming from my fellow servers, each of whom has slipped into her own personal funk; Gail, my role model, stares sorrowfully at a point six inches from her nose. The meeting ends when Andy, one of the cooks, gets up, muttering about breaking up his day off for this almighty bullshit.

Just four days later we are suddenly summoned into the kitchen at   4 3:30 P.M., even though there are live tables on the floor. We all—about ten of us—stand around Phillip, who announces grimly that there has been a report of some "drug activity" on the night shift and that, as a result, we are now to be a "drug-free" workplace, meaning that all new hires will be tested and possibly also current employees on a random basis. I am glad that this part of the kitchen is so dark because I find myself blushing as hard as if I had been caught taking up in the ladies' room myself: I haven't been treated this way—lined up in the corridor, threatened with locker searches, peppered with carelessly aimed accusations—since at least junior high school. Back on the floor, Joan cracks, "Next they'll be telling us we can't have *sex* on the job." When I ask Stu what happened to inspire the crackdown, he just mutters about "management decisions"

and takes the opportunity to upbraid Gail and me for being too generous with the rolls. From now on there's to be only one per customer and
it goes out with the dinner, not with the salad. He's also been riding the
cooks, prompting Andy to come out of the kitchen and observe—with the
serenity of a man whose customary implement is a butcher knife—that
"Stu has a death wish today."

5   Later in the evening, the gossip crystallizes around the theory that
Stu is himself the drug culprit, that he uses the restaurant phone to order
up marijuana and sends one of the late servers out to fetch it for him. The
server was caught and she may have ratted out Stu, at least enough to cast
some suspicion on him, thus accounting for his pissy behavior. Who knows?
Personally, I'm ready to believe anything bad about Stu, who serves no evident function and presumes too much on our common ethnicity, sidling up
to me one night to engage in a little nativism directed at the Haitian immigrants: "I feel like I'm the foreigner here. They're taking over the country."
Still later that evening, the drug in question escalates to crack. Lionel, the
busboy, entertains us for the rest of the shift by standing just behind Stu's
back and sucking deliriously on an imaginary joint or maybe a pipe.

6   The other problem, in addition to the less-than-nurturing
management style, is that this job shows no sign of being financially
viable. You might imagine, from a comfortable distance, that people who
live, year in and year out, on $6 to $10 an hour have discovered some
survival stratagems unknown to the middle class. But no. It's not hard to
get my coworkers talking about their living situations, because housing,
in almost every case, is the principal source of disruption in their lives,
the first thing they fill you in on when they arrive for their shifts. After a
week, I have compiled the following survey:

> Gail is sharing a room in a well-known downtown flophouse for
> $250 a week. Her roommate, a male friend, has begun hitting on
> her, driving her nuts, but the rent would be impossible alone.
>
> Claude, the Haitian cook, is desperate to get out of the two-
> room apartment he shares with his girlfriend and two other,
> unrelated people. As far as I can determine, the other Haitian men
> live in similarly crowded situations.
>
> Annette, a twenty-year-old server who is six months pregnant
> and abandoned by her boyfriend, lives with her mother, a postal clerk.
>
> Marianne, who is a breakfast server, and her boyfriend are
> paying $170 a week for a one-person trailer.
>
> Billy, who at $10 an hour is the wealthiest of us, lives in the
> trailer he owns, paying only the $400-a-month lot fee.
>
> The other white cook, Andy, lives on his dry-docked boat,
> which, as far as I can tell from his loving descriptions, can't be
> more than twenty feet long. He offers to take me out on it once it's
> repaired, but the offer comes with inquiries as to my marital status,
> so I do not follow up on it.

Tina, another server, and her husband are paying $60 a night for a room in the Days Inn. This is because they have no car and the Days Inn is in walking distance of the Hearthside. When Marianne is tossed out of her trailer for subletting (which is against trailer park rules), she leaves her boyfriend and moves in with Tina and her husband.

Joan, who had fooled me with her numerous and tasteful outfits (hostesses wear their own clothes), lives in a van parked behind a shopping center at night and showers in Tina's motel room. The clothes are from thrift shops.[1]

It strikes me, in my middle-class solipsism, that there is gross im-   7
providence in some of these arrangements. When Gail and I are wrapping silverware in napkins—the only task for which we are permitted to sit— she tells me she is thinking of escaping from her roommate by moving into the Days Inn herself. I am astounded: how she can even think of paying $40 to $60 a day? But if I was afraid of sounding like a social worker, I have come out just sounding *like* a fool. She squints at me in disbelief: "And where am I supposed to get a month's rent and a month's deposit for an apartment?" I'd been feeling pretty smug about my $500 efficiency, but of course it was made possible only by the $1,300 had allotted myself for start-up costs when I began my low-wage life: $1,000 for the first month's rent and deposit, $100 for initial groceries and cash in my pocket, $200 stuffed away for emergencies. In poverty, as in certain propositions in physics, starting conditions are everything.

There are no secret economies that nourish the poor; on the contrary,   8
there are a host of special costs. If you can't put up the two months' rent you need to secure an apartment, you end up paying through the nose for a room by the week. If you have only a room, with a hot plate at best, you can't save by cooking up huge lentil stews that can be frozen for the week ahead. You eat fast food or the hot dogs and Styrofoam cups of soup that can be microwaved in a convenience store. If you have no money for health insurance—and the Hearthside's niggardly plan kicks in only after three months—you go without routine care or prescription drugs and end up paying the price. Gail, for example, was doing fine, healthwise anyway, until she ran out of money for estrogen pills. She is supposed to be on the company health plan by now, but they claim to have lost her application form and to be beginning the paperwork all over again. So she spends $9 a pop for pills to control the migraines she wouldn't have, she insists, if her estrogen supplements were covered. Similarly, Marianne's boyfriend lost his job as a roofer because he missed so much time after getting a cut on his foot for which he couldn't afford the prescribed antibiotic.

---

[1] I could find no statistics on the number of employed people living in cars or vans, but according to a 1997 report of the" National Coalition for the Homeless, "Myths and Facts about Homelessness," nearly one-fifth of all homeless people (in twenty-nine cities across the nation) are employed in full- or part-time jobs.

9   My own situation, when I sit down to assess it after two weeks of work, would not be much better if this were my actual life. The seductive thing about waitressing is that you don't have to wait for payday to feel a few bills in your pocket, and my tips usually cover meals and gas, plus something left over to stuff into the kitchen drawer I use as a bank. But as the tourist business slows in the summer heat, I sometimes leave work with only $20 in tips (the gross is higher, but servers share about 15 percent of their tips with the busboys and bartenders). With wages included, this amounts to about the minimum wage of $5.15 an hour. The sum in the drawer is piling up but at the present rate of accumulation will be more than $100 short of my rent when the end of the month comes around. Nor can I see any expenses to cut. True, I haven't gone the lentil stew route yet, but that's because I don't have a large cooking pot, potholders, or a ladle to stir with (which would cost a total of about $30 at Kmart, somewhat less at a thrift store), not to mention onions, carrots, and the indispensable bay leaf. I do make my lunch almost every day—usually some slow-burning, high-protein combo like frozen chicken patties with melted cheese on top and canned pinto beans on the side. Dinner is at the Hearthside, which offers its employees a choice of BLT, fish sandwich, or hamburger for only $2. The burger lasts longest, especially if it's heaped with gut-puckering jalapenos, but by midnight my stomach is growling again.

10   So unless I want to start using my car as a residence, I have to find a second or an alternative job. I call all the hotels I'd filled out housekeeping applications at weeks ago—the Hyatt, Holiday Inn, Econo Lodge, Ho Jo's, Best Western, plus a half dozen locally run guest houses. Nothing. Then I start making the rounds again, wasting whole mornings waiting for some assistant manager to show up, even dipping into places so creepy that the front-desk clerk greets you from behind bullet-proof glass and sells pints of liquor over the counter. But either someone has exposed my real-life housekeeping habits—which are, shall we say, mellow—or I am at the wrong end of some infallible ethnic equation: most, but by no means all, of the working housekeepers I see on my job searches are African Americans, Spanish-speaking, or refugees from the Central European post-Communist world, while servers are almost invariably white and monolingually English-speaking. When I finally get a positive response, I have been identified once again as server material. Jerry's—again, not the real name—which is part of a well-known national chain and physically attached here to another budget hotel, is ready to use me at once. The prospect is both exciting and terrifying because, with about the same number of tables and counter seats, Jerry's attracts three or four times the volume of customers as the gloomy old Hearthside.

11   Picture a fat person's hell, and I don't mean a place with no food. Instead there is everything you might eat if eating had no bodily consequences—the cheese fries, the chicken-fried steaks, the fudge-laden desserts—only here every bite must be paid for, one way or another, in

human discomfort. The kitchen is a cavern, a stomach leading to the lower intestine that is the garbage and dishwashing area, from which issue bizarre smells combining the edible and the offal: creamy carrion, pizza barf, and that unique and enigmatic Jerry's scent, citrus fart. The floor is slick with spills, forcing us to walk through the kitchen with tiny steps, like Susan McDougal in leg irons. Sinks everywhere are clogged with scraps of lettuce, decomposing lemon wedges, water-logged toast crusts. Put your hand down on any counter and you risk being stuck to it by the film of ancient syrup spills, and this is unfortunate because hands are utensils here, used for scooping up lettuce onto the salad plates, lifting out pie slices, and even moving hash browns from one plate to another. The regulation poster in the single unisex rest room admonishes us to wash our hands thoroughly, and even offers instructions for doing so, but there is always some vital substance missing—soap, paper towels, toilet paper—and I never found all three at once. You learn to stuff your pockets with napkins before going in there, and too bad about the customers, who must eat, although they don't realize it, almost literally out of our hands.

The break room summarizes the whole situation: there is none, be-   12
cause there are no breaks at Jerry's. For six to eight hours in a row, you never sit except to pee. Actually, there are three folding chairs at a table immediately adjacent to the bathroom, but hardly anyone ever sits in this, the very rectum of the gastro-architectural system. Rather, the function of the peri-toilet area is to house the ashtrays in which servers and dishwashers leave their cigarettes burning at all tunes, like votive candles, so they don't have to waste time lighting up again when they dash back here for a puff. Almost everyone smokes as if their pulmonary well-being depended on it—the multinational melange of cooks; the dishwashers, who are all Czechs here; the servers, who are American natives—creating an atmosphere in which oxygen is only an occasional pollutant. My first morning at Jerry's, when the hypoglycemic shakes set in, I complain to one of my fellow servers that I don't understand how she can go so long without food. "Well, I don't understand how *you* can go so long without a cigarette," she responds in a tone of reproach. Because work is what you do for others; smoking is what you do for yourself. I don't know why the antismoking crusaders have never grasped the element of defiant self-nurturance that makes the habit so endearing to its victims—as if, in the American workplace, the only thing people have to call their own is the tumors they are nourishing and the spare moments they devote to feeding them.

Now, the Industrial Revolution is not an easy transition, espe-   13
cially, in my experience, when you have to zip through it in just a couple of days. I have gone from craft work straight into the factory, from the air-conditioned morgue of the Hearthside directly into the flames. Customers arrive in human waves, sometimes disgorged fifty at a time

from their tour buses, peckish and whiny. Instead of two "girls" on the floor at once, there can be as many as six of us running around in our brilliant pink-and-orange Hawaiian shirts. Conversations, either with customers or with fellow employees, seldom last more than twenty seconds at a time. On my first day, in fact, I am hurt by my sister servers' coldness. My mentor for the day is a supremely competent, emotionally uninflected twenty-three-year-old, and the others, who gossip a little among themselves about the real reason someone is out sick today and the size of the bail bond someone else has had to pay, ignore me completely. On my second day, I find out why. "Well, it's good to see *you* again," one of them says in greeting. "Hardly anyone comes back after the first day." I feel powerfully vindicated—a survivor—but it would take a long time, probably months, before I could hope to be accepted into this sorority.

14   I start out with the beautiful, heroic idea of handling the two jobs at once, and for two days I almost do it: working the breakfast/lunch shift at Jerry's from 8:00 till 2:00, arriving at the Hearthside a few minutes late, at 2:10, and attempting to hold out until 10:00. In the few minutes I have between jobs, I pick up a spicy chicken sandwich at the Wendy's drive-through window, gobble it down in the car, and change from khaki slacks to black, from Hawaiian to rust-colored polo. There is a problem, though. When, during the 3:00–4:00 o'clock dead time, I finally sit down to wrap silver, my flesh seems to bond to the seat. I try to refuel with a purloined cup of clam chowder, as I've seen Gail and Joan do dozens of times, but Stu catches me and hisses "No *eating*." although there's not a customer around to be offended by the sight of food making 'contact with a server's lips. So I tell Gail I'm going to quit, and she hugs me and says she might just follow me to Jerry's herself.

15   But the chances of this are minuscule. She has left the flophouse and her annoying roommate and is back to living in her truck. But, guess what, she reports to me excitedly later that evening, Phillip has given her permission to park overnight in the hotel parking lot, as long as she keeps out of sight, and the parking lot should be totally safe since it's patrolled by a hotel security guard! With the Hearthside offering benefits like that, how could anyone think of leaving? This must be Phillip's theory, anyway. He accepts my resignation with a shrug, his main concern being that I return my two polo shirts and aprons.

16   Gail would have triumphed at Jerry's, I'm sure, but for me it's a crash course in exhaustion management. Years ago, the kindly fry cook who trained me to waitress at a Los Angeles truck stop used to say: Never make an unnecessary trip; if you don't have to walk fast, walk slow; if you don't have to walk, stand. But at Jerry's the effort of distinguishing necessary from unnecessary and urgent from whenever would itself be too much of an energy drain. The only thing to do is to treat each shift as a one-time-only emergency: you've got fifty starving

people out there, lying scattered on the battlefield, so get out there and feed them! Forget that you will have to do this again tomorrow, forget that you will have to be alert enough to dodge the drunks on the drive home tonight—just burn, burn, burn! Ideally, at some point you enter what servers call a "rhythm" and psychologists term a "flow state," where signals pass from the sense organs directly to the muscles, bypassing the cerebral cortex, and a Zen-like emptiness sets in. I'm on a 2:00–10:00 P.M. shift now, and a male server from the morning shift tells me about the time he "pulled a triple"—three shifts in a row, all the way around the clock—and then got off and had a drink and met this girl, and maybe he shouldn't tell me this, but they had sex right then and there and it was like *beautiful.*

Content

1. Based on your knowledge of the world of work, does Ehrenreich accurately reflect the difference between managers and workers when she says, "Cooks want to prepare tasty meals, servers want to serve them graciously, but managers are there for only one reason—to make sure that money is made for some theoretical entity, the corporation" (¶ 1)?

2. Is a manager's job in a restaurant much different from other managerial jobs you're familiar with? What fundamental differences exist between managerial jobs, even poorly paid ones, and minimum-wage jobs?

3. Based on information that Ehrenreich provides, who are the working poor? Why don't their minimum wage jobs provide enough income to provide adequate food, clothing, shelter, and medical care? What social and economic supports are necessary to ensure not only survival, but a healthful quality of life for people with low incomes?

4. Ehrenreich's analysis of the work life of a typical food server is juxtaposed with her own expectations of life and work as an educated middle-class professional. Compare and contrast these two life styles. If the author—and her readers—were not actually educated and middle-class, would the server's life seem as difficult and unacceptable as Ehrenreich presents it?

Strategies/Structures/Language

5. Explain how Ehrenreich uses a process analysis—a detailed anatomization of what she has to do when she works as a waitress—to make an argument about the lives of people, particularly women, who work at minimum wage jobs. Does such a life have any advantages?

6. Ehrenreich uses anatomical metaphors to interpret the kitchen and bathroom areas of "Jerry's" restaurant: "The kitchen is a cavern, a stomach leading to the lower intestine that is the garbage and dishwashing areas, from which issue bizarre smells combining the edible and the offal . . . Jerry's scent, citrus fart" (¶ 11). Does this metaphor of the restaurant as the entrails of the human body also serve as a commentary on the status of the people who work there, and of the work that they do? Explain your answer.

For Writing

7. *Journal Writing.* Although in our democratic society we may claim that all honest work has merit, in what ways do our actual values dispute this claim? Isn't one major reason for earning a college degree to provide insulation against minimum wage, unskilled labor jobs?

8. *Dialogues.* Does Ehrenreich make too grim and biased a case against manual labor? Compare "Serving in Florida" with the interpretations of working with one's hands presented by Sanders in "The Inheritance of Tools" (135–42), and Nocton in "Harvest of Gold, Harvest of Shame" (271–76).

9. Using evidence from "Serving in Florida" and other analyses of minimum wage jobs, including Ehrenreich's *Nickled and Dimed*, write an argument making the case that it is preferable to be on welfare that to work at a minimum wage job, or vice-versa.

10. What, in your view, are the characteristics of an ideal job? In your answer, write a critique of both minimum wage jobs and welfare, and present a concrete plan for earning a living wage. Your argument can take into account the current histories of middle class people who have been laid off, or recent college graduates who cannot find a job—the *New York Times*, available online, is unfortunately full of such stories, as well as jobs you have had, good and bad.

ATUL GAWANDE

Atul Gawande (born in 1965 in Brooklyn) earned an MA in politics, philosophy, and economics from Oxford in 1989. From Harvard Medical School he earned an MD in 1995 and a Master's in Public Health in 1999. He holds a joint appointment at both schools, in surgery and in health policy, and is a surgeon at Brigham and Women's Hospital in Boston and a staff writer for *The New Yorker*. His collection of essays, *Complications: A Surgeon's Notes on an Imperfect Science* (2002), performs "exploratory surgery on medicine itself, laying bare a science not in its idealized form but as it actually is— complicated, perplexing, profoundly human." Gawande takes readers into dramatic territory, the operating room, "where science is ambiguous, information is limited, the stakes are high, yet decisions must be made."

"On Washing Hands" first appeared in the *New England Journal of Medicine* in 2004 and is reprinted in his *Better: A Surgeon's Notes on Performance* (2007). He completed the trilogy with The *Checklist Manifesto: How to Get Things Right* (2009). Gawande shows in this essay that hand-washing is far from a simple matter of policy; it is as complex to prescribe as it is critical to the lives of patients. Gawande shows how the work of preventing infection must overcome deeply ingrained habits and professional demands on health care workers, and he draws on the history of infectious disease to illustrate how cultural beliefs, personal antagonism, and professional competition play a crucial role in the advancement of medical knowledge.

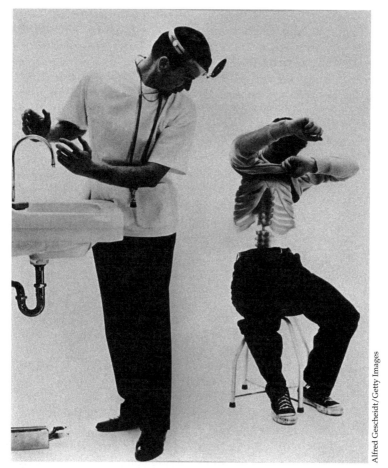

Alfred Gescheidt/Getty Images

What is going on in this photograph? What is missing?

On Washing Hands

One ordinary December day, I took a tour of my hospital with Deborah Yokoe, an infectious disease specialist, and Susan Marino, a microbiologist. They work in our hospital's infection-control unit. Their full-time job, and that of three others in the unit, is to stop the spread of infection in the hospital. This is not flashy work, and they are not flashy people. Yokoe is forty-five years old, gentle voiced, and dimpled. She wears sneakers at work. Marino is in her fifties and reserved by nature. But they have coped with influenza epidemics, Legionnaires' disease, fatal bacterial meningitis, and, just a few months before, a case that, according to the patient's brain-biopsy results, might have been Creutzfeld-Jakob disease—a nightmare, not only because it is incurable and fatal but also because the infectious agent that causes it, known as a prion, cannot be killed by usual heat-sterilization procedures. By the time the results came back, the neurosurgeon's brain-biopsy instruments might have transferred the disease to other patients, but infection-control team members tracked the instruments down in time and had them chemically sterilized. Yokoe and Marino have seen measles, the plague, and rabbit fever (which is caused by a bacterium that is extraordinarily contagious in hospital laboratories and feared as a bioterrorist weapon). They once instigated a nationwide recall of frozen strawberries, having traced a hepatitis A outbreak to a batch served at an ice cream social. Recently at large in the hospital, they told me, have been a rotavirus, a Norwalk virus, several strains of *Pseudomonas* bacteria, a superresistant *Klebsiella*, and the ubiquitous scourges of modern hospitals—resistant *Staphylococcus aureus* and *Enterococcus faecalis*, which are a frequent cause of pneumonias, wound infections, and bloodstream infections.

2   Each year, according to the U.S. Centers for Disease Control, two million Americans acquire an infection while they are in the hospital. Ninety thousand die of that infection. The hardest part of the infection-control team's job, Yokoe says, is not coping with the variety of contagions they encounter or the panic that sometimes occurs among patients and staff. Instead, their greatest difficulty is getting clinicians like me to do the one thing that consistently halts the spread of infections: wash our hands.

3   There isn't much they haven't tried. Walking about the surgical floors where I admit my patients, Yokoe and Marino showed me the admonishing signs they have posted, the sinks they have repositioned, the new ones they have installed. They have made some sinks automated. They have bought special five-thousand-dollar "precaution carts" that store everything for washing up, gloving, and gowning in one ergonomic, portable, and aesthetically pleasing package. They have given away free movie tickets to the hospital units with the best compliance. They have issued hygiene report cards. Yet still, we have not mended our ways. Our hospital's statistics show what studies everywhere else have shown—that we doctors and nurses wash our hands one-third to one-half as often as we are supposed to. Having shaken hands with a sniffling patient, pulled a sticky dressing off someone's wound, pressed a stethoscope against a sweating chest, most of us do little more than wipe our hands on our white coats and move on—to see the next patient, to scribble a note in the chart, to grab some lunch.

4   This is, embarassingly, nothing new. In 1847, at the age of twenty-eight, the Viennese obstetrician Ignaz Semmelweis famously deduced that, by not washing their hands consistently or well enough, doctors were themselves to blame for childbed fever. Childbed fever, also known

as puerperal fever, was the leading cause of maternal death in childbirth in the era before antibiotics (and before the recognition that germs are the agents of infectious disease). It is a bacterial infection—most commonly caused by *Streptococcus*, the same bacteria that causes strep throat—that ascends through the vagina to the uterus after childbirth. Out of three thousand mothers who delivered babies at the hospital where Semmelweis worked, six hundred or more died of the disease each year—a horrifying 20 percent maternal death rate. Of mothers delivering at home, only 1 percent died. Semmelweis concluded that doctors themselves were carrying the disease between patients, and he mandated that every doctor and nurse on his ward scrub with a nail brush and chlorine between patients. The puerperal death rate immediately fell to 1 percent—incontrovertible proof, it would seem, that he was right. Yet elsewhere, doctors' practices did not change. Some colleagues were even offended by his claims; it was impossible to them that doctors could be killing their patients. Far from being hailed, Semmelweis was ultimately dismissed from his job.

Semmelweis's story has come down to us as Exhibit A in the case for the obstinacy and blindness of physicians. But the story was more complicated. The trouble was partly that nineteenth-century physicians faced multiple, seemingly equally powerful explanations for puerperal fever. There was, for example, a strong belief that miasmas of the air in hospitals were the cause. And Semmelweis strangely refused to either publish an explanation of the logic behind his theory or prove it with a convincing experiment in animals. Instead, he took the calls for proof as a personal insult and attacked his detractors viciously.

"You, Herr Professor, have been a partner in this massacre," he wrote to one University of Vienna obstetrician who questioned his theory. To a colleague in Wurzburg he wrote, "Should you, Herr Hofrath, without having disproved my doctrine, continue to teach your pupils [against it], I declare before God and the world that you are a murderer and the 'History of Childbed Fever' would not be unjust to you if it memorialized you as a medical Nero." His own staff turned against him. In Pest, where he relocated after losing his post in Vienna, he would stand next to the sink and berate anyone who forgot to scrub his or her hands. People began to purposely evade, sometimes even sabotage, his hand-washing regimen. Semmelweis was a genius, but he was also a lunatic, and that made him a failed genius. It was another twenty years before Joseph Lister offered his clearer, more persuasive, and more respectful plea for antisepsis in surgery in the British medical journal *Lancet*.

One hundred and forty years of doctors' plagues later, however, you have to wonder whether what's needed to stop them is precisely a lunatic. Consider what Yokoe and Marino are up against. No part of human skin is spared from bacteria. Bacterial counts on the hands range from five thousand to five million colony-forming units per square centimeter.

The hair, underarms, and groin harbor greater concentrations. On the hands, deep skin crevices trap 10 to 20 percent of the flora, making removal difficult, even with scrubbing, and sterilization impossible. The worst place is under the fingernails. Hence the recent CDC guidelines requiring hospital personnel to keep their nails trimmed to less than a quarter of an inch and to remove artificial nails.

8   Plain soaps do, at best, a middling job of disinfecting. Their detergents remove loose dirt and grime, but fifteen seconds of washing reduces bacterial counts by only about an order of magnitude. Semmelweis recognized that ordinary soap was not enough and used a chlorine solution to achieve disinfection. Today's antibacterial soaps contain chemicals such as chlorhexidine to disrupt microbial membranes and proteins. Even with the right soap, however, proper hand washing requires a strict procedure. First, you must remove your watch, rings, and other jewelry (which are notorious for trapping bacteria). Next, you wet your hands in warm tap water. Dispense the soap and lather all surfaces, including the lower one-third of the arms, for the full duration recommended by the manufacturer (usually fifteen to thirty seconds). Rinse off for thirty full seconds. Dry completely with a clean, disposable towel. Then use the towel to turn the tap off. Repeat after any new contact with a patient.

9   Almost no one adheres to this procedure. It seems impossible. On morning rounds, our residents check in on twenty patients in an hour. The nurses in our intensive care units typically have a similar number of contacts with patients requiring hand washing in between. Even if you get the whole cleansing process down to a minute per patient, that's still a third of staff time spent just washing hands. Such frequent hand washing can also irritate the skin, which can produce a dermatitis, which itself increases bacterial counts.

10   Less irritating than soap, alcohol rinses and gels have been in use in Europe for almost two decades but for some reason only recently caught on in the United States. They take far less time to use—only about fifteen seconds or so to rub a gel over the hands and fingers and let it air-dry. Dispensers can be put at the bedside more easily than a sink. And at alcohol concentrations of 50 to 95 percent, they are more effective at killing organisms, too. (Interestingly, pure alcohol is not as effective—at least some water is required to denature microbial proteins.)

11   Still, it took Yokoe over a year to get our staff to accept the 60 percent alcohol gel we have recently adopted. Its introduction was first blocked because of the staff's fears that it would produce noxious building air. (It didn't.) Next came worries that, despite evidence to the contrary, it would be more irritating to the skin. So a product with aloe was brought in. People complained about the smell. So the aloe was taken out. Then some of the nursing staff refused to use the gel after rumors spread that it would reduce fertility. The rumors died only after the infection-control

unit circulated evidence that the alcohol is not systemically absorbed and a hospital fertility specialist endorsed the use of the gel.

With the gel finally in wide use, the compliance rates for proper 12 hand hygiene improved substantially: from around 40 percent to 70 percent. But—and this is the troubling finding—hospital infection rates did not drop one iota. Our 70 percent compliance just wasn't good enough. If 30 percent of the time people didn't wash their hands, that still left plenty of opportunity to keep transmitting infections. Indeed, the rates of resistant *Staphylococcus* and *Enterococcus* infections continued to rise. Yokoe receives the daily tabulations. I checked with her one day not long ago, and sixty-three of our seven hundred hospital patients were colonized or infected with MRSA (the shorthand for methicillin-resistant *Staphylococcus aureus*) and another twenty-two had acquired VRE (vancomycin-resistant *Enterococcus*)—unfortunately, typical rates of infection for American hospitals.

Rising infection rates from superresistant bacteria have become the 13 norm around the world. The first outbreak of VRE did not occur until 1988, when a renal dialysis unit in England became infested. By 1990, the bacteria had been carried abroad, and four in one thousand American ICU patients had become infected. By 1997, a stunning 23 percent of ICU patients were infected. When the virus for SARS—severe acute respiratory syndrome—appeared in China in 2003 and spread within weeks to almost ten thousand people in two dozen countries across the world (10 percent of whom were killed), the primary vector for transmission was the hands of health care workers. What will happen if (or rather, when) an even more dangerous organism appears—avian flu, say, or a new, more virulent bacteria? "It will be a disaster," Yokoe says.

Anything short of a Semmelweis-like obsession with hand washing 14 has begun to seem inadequate. . . .

We always hope for the easy fix: the one simple change that will 15 erase a problem in a stroke. But few things in life work this way. Instead, success requires making a hundred small steps go right—one after the other, no slipups, no goofs, everyone pitching in. We are used to thinking of doctoring as a solitary, intellectual task. But making medicine go right is less often like making a difficult diagnosis than like making sure everyone washes their hands.

It is striking to consider how different the history of the operating 16 room after Lister has been from that of the hospital floor after Semmelweis. In the operating room, no one pretends that even 90 percent compliance with scrubbing is good enough. If a single doctor or nurse fails to wash up before coming to the operating table, we are horrified—and certainly not shocked if the patient develops an infection a few days later. Since Lister we have gone even further in our expectations. We now make sure to use sterile gloves and gowns, masks over our mouths, caps over our hair. We apply antiseptics to the patient's skin and lay down sterile drapes. We put our instruments through steam heat sterilizers or, if any are too delicate to tolerate the autoclave, through chemical sterilizers. We have reinvented almost every detail of the operating room for the sake of antisepsis. We have gone so far as to add an extra person to the team, known as the circulating nurse, whose central job is, essentially, to keep the team antiseptic. Every time an unanticipated instrument is needed for a patient, the team can't stand around waiting for one member to break scrub, pull the thing off a shelf, wash up, and return. So the circulator was invented. Circulators get the extra sponges and instruments, handle the telephone calls, do the paperwork, get help when it's needed. And every time they do, they're not just making the case go more smoothly. They are keeping the patient uninfected. By their very existence, they make sterility a priority in every case.

17   Stopping the epidemics spreading in our hospitals is not a problem of ignorance—of not having the know-how about what to do. It is a problem of compliance—a failure of an individual to apply that know-how correctly. But achieving compliance is hard. Why, after 140 years, the meticulousness of the operating room has not spread beyond its double doors is a mystery. But the people who are most careful in the surgical theater are frequently the very ones who are least careful on the hospital ward. I know because I have realized I am one of them. I generally try to be as scrupulous about washing my hands when I am outside the operating room as I am inside. And I do pretty well, if I say so myself. But then I blow it. It happens almost every day. I walk into a patient's hospital room, and I'm thinking about what I have to tell him concerning his operation, or about his family, who might be standing there looking worried, or about the funny little joke a resident just told me, and I completely forget about getting a squirt of that gel into my palms, no matter how many laminated reminder signs have been hung on the walls. Sometimes I do remember, but before I can find the dispenser, the patient puts his hand out in greeting and I think it too strange not to go ahead and take it. On occasion I even think, Screw it—I'm late, I have to get a move on, and what difference does it really make what I do this one time?

18   A few years ago, Paul O'Neill, the former secretary of the Treasury and CEO of the aluminum giant Alcoa, agreed to take over as head of a regional health care initiative in Pittsburgh, Pennsylvania. And he made solving the problem of hospital infections one of his top priorities. To show it could be solved, he arranged for a young industrial engineer named Peter Perreiah to be put on a single forty-bed surgical unit at a Pittsburgh veterans hospital. When he met with the unit's staff, a doctor who worked on the project told me, "Peter didn't ask, 'Why don't you wash your hands?' He asked, 'Why can't you?'" By far the most common answer was time. So, as an engineer, he went about fixing the things that burned up the staff's time. He came up with a just-in-time supply system that kept not only gowns and gloves at the bedside but also gauze and

tape and other things the staff needed, so they didn't have to go back and forth out of the room to search for them. Rather than make everyone clean their stethoscopes, notorious carriers of infection, between patients, he arranged for each patient room to have a designated stethoscope on the wall. He helped make dozens of simplifying changes that reduced both the opportunities for spread of infection and the difficulties of staying clean. He made each hospital room work more like an operating room, in other words. He also arranged for a nasal culture to be taken from every patient upon admission, whether the patient seemed infected or not. That way the staff knew which patients carried resistant bacteria and could preemptively use more stringent precautions for them—"search-and-destroy" the strategy is sometimes called. Infection rates for MRSA—the hospital contagion responsible for more deaths than any other—fell almost 90 percent, from four to six infections per month to about that many in an entire year. . . .

At one point during my tour with Yokoe and Marino, we walked 19 through a regular hospital unit. And I finally began to see the ward the way they do. Flowing in and out of the patients' rooms were physical therapists, patient care assistants, nurses, nutritionists, residents, students. Some were good about washing. Some were not. Yokoe pointed out that three of the eight rooms had bright yellow precaution signs because of patients inside with MRSA or VRE. Only then did I realize we were on the floor of one of my own patients. One of those signs hung on his door.

He was sixty-two years old and had been in the hospital for almost 20 three weeks. He had arrived in shock from another hospital, where an operation had gone awry. I performed an emergency splenectomy for him and then had to go back in again when the bleeding still didn't stop. He had an open abdominal wound and could not eat. He had to receive his nutrition intravenously. He was recovering, though. Three days after admission, he was out of the intensive care unit. Initial surveillance cultures were completely negative for resistant organisms. New cultures ten days after admission, however, came back positive for both MRSA and VRE. A few days after that, he developed fevers up to 102 degrees. His blood pressure began dropping. His heart rate climbed. He was septic. His central line—his lifeline for nutrition—had become infected, and we had to take it out.

Until that moment, when I stood there looking at the sign on his 21 door, it had not occurred to me that I might have given him that infection. But the truth is I may have. One of us certainly did.

Content

1. Why, according to Gawande, do bacteria spread so easily (¶s 1, 7–8)?
2. Why do hospital workers resist efforts to improve hygiene? Why are operating room standards so much better and more strictly enforced than elsewhere in the hospital?

3. How does the story of Ignac Semmelweis's campaign to promote hand-washing (¶s 4–6) help explain the contemporary problem of ensuring that health-care workers thoroughly and regularly wash their hands?

4. What might be some of the difficulties in implementing the protocol for pre-venting the spread of infection developed by Peter Perreiah (¶ 18)? Would his system reduce the need for frequent hand-washing?

Strategies/Structures/Language

5. How does Gawande's explanation of the process of a typical day in his life as a surgeon help the reader understand the problem of compliance with hygiene protocol (¶ 17)?

6. Why does Gawande begin and end his essay with the two members of his hospital's infection-control unit? Why does he end with the analysis of his own patient (¶s 20–22)?

For Writing

7. ***Journal Writing.*** Gawande explains some of the fears, prejudices, and habits that have hindered the regular use of alcohol gel among hospital staff. Why, in your opinion, are many individuals reluctant to follow expert advice? Have you or some-one you know followed expert advice that turned out, in retrospect, to be right (or wrong)? What were the consequences of following or not following that advice?

8. ***Mixed Modes.*** Gawande observes that while thorough hand-washing or the use of alcohol gel is the single most important way to stop the spread of infection, campaigns to improve hygiene compliance often fail to check infections. Compare the steps followed in a hospital operating room to keep it antiseptic (¶ 16) with the system Perreiah developed (¶ 18) to reduce infections outside the operating room. How do they differ? Are the two protocols complementary?

9. ***Second Look.*** How might the image in this essay illustrate Gawande's sur-prise at discovering that one of the patients in the hospital with an infection was his own (¶s 20–22)? What potential sites of infection does this photograph in-clude? What does the photograph suggest about the doctor-patient relationship?

10. Research the history of particular and significant medical advancements such as the development of vaccines or anesthesia; therapies to treat mental health problems such as addiction or war-related disorders; knowledge of pre-ventive care such as nutrition; or the emergence of a professional specialty such as nursing. What role did particular scientists or other historical figures play in the diffusion and application of this knowledge? Did "the obstinacy and blindess" (¶ 5) of a group of individuals hinder the spread of this advance? Did the advance require people to change their behavior?

11. Gawande argues that although every year "two million Americans ac-quire an infection while they are in the hospital," the hardest task of a hospital infection-control team is "getting clinicians like me to do the one thing that con-sistently halts the spread of infections: wash our hands" (¶ 2). How can the public ensure that health care providers develop effective public health policies—and enforce them—such as reducing infections through hygiene protocol? Write an es-say that addresses a public health concern and the role of health care providers or other institutions such as schools [see Joseph DiFranza's "Hooked from the First

Cigarette," (122–31), or Marion Nestle's "Eating Made Simple" (255–62)], and offer suggestions for how to resolve the problem. Write a letter either to your representative in the state legislature or Congress in which you analyze the problem and propose an action plan. Send a copy to the editor of your local newspaper.

NING YU

Ning Yu was born in 1955 in Beijing, People's Republic of China, and came to the United States in 1986 for graduate study. He earned a PhD in English from the University of Connecticut in 1993 and is now a professor of English and Chinese literature at Western Washington University, at work on a translation of 301 Chinese nature poems.

Ning Yu recounts some of the significant events of his youth in the following prize-winning essay. When he was in fourth grade, his school was closed down as a consequence of the "Great Proletarian Cultural Revolution," which overturned the existing social order. The intellectual class (the "blacks," in Yu's classification scheme) to which Yu's family belonged because his father was a professor of Chinese language and literature, were replaced on their jobs by members of the People's Liberation Army, "the reds," whose status—as we can see from Ning Yu's teachers—was determined by their political loyalty rather than their academic training. So Ning Yu learned one kind of English at school, the rote memorization of political slogans: "Down with the Soviet Neo-Czarists!" He explains that the Cultural Revolution stifled originality of language, as well as of thought. "Consequently," he says, "I used the clichés deliberately to create a realistic atmosphere for my story, and also ironically to attack the decade of clichés."

Ning Yu learned another kind of English, the rich, imaginative language of high-culture literature, from his father. On the verge of his fourth imprisonment as an intellectual (and therefore by definition subversive), Dr. Yu taught his teenage son the alphabet and some basic grammar. He gave his son a copy of Jane Austen's *Pride and Prejudice* and an old English-Chinese dictionary and told him to translate the novel—which Ning Yu "struggled through from cover to cover" during the nineteen months of his father's incarceration. Ning Yu's essay makes clear the relations among politics, social class, and education under the Maoist regime.

Red and Black, or One English Major's Beginning

I have always told my friends that my first English teacher was my father. That is the truth, but not the whole truth. It was a freezing morning more than twenty years ago, we, some fifty-odd boys and girls, were   1 shivering in a poorly heated classroom when the door was pushed open and in came a gust of wind and Comrade Chang Hong-gen, our young teacher. Wrapped in an elegant army overcoat, Comrade Chang strode in front of the blackboard and began to address us in outrageous gibberish. His gestures, his facial expressions, and his loud voice unmistakably communicated that he was lecturing us as a People's Liberation Army captain would address his soldiers before a battle—in revolutionary war movies, that is. Of course we didn't understand a word of the speech until he translated it into Chinese later:

> Comrades, red-guards, and revolutionary pupils:
>
> The Great Revolutionary Teacher Marx teaches us: "A foreign language is an important weapon in the struggle of human life." Our Great Leader, Great Teacher, Great Supreme-Commander, and Great Helmsman, Chairman Mao, has also taught us that it is not too difficult to learn a foreign language. "Nothing in the world is too difficult if you are willing to tackle it with the same spirit in which we conquered this mountain."
>
> Now, as you know, the Soviet Social Imperialists and the U.S. Imperialists have agreed on a venomous scheme to enslave China. For years the U.S. Imperialists have brought war and disaster to Vietnam; and you must have heard that the Soviet troops invaded our Jewel Island in Heilongjiang Province last month. Their evil purpose is obvious—to invade China, the Soviets from the north and the Americans from the south through Vietnam.
>
> We are not afraid of them, because we have the leadership of Chairman Mao, the invincible Mao Zedong Thought, and seven hundred million people. But we need to be prepared. As intellectual youth, you must not only prepare to sacrifice your lives for the Party and the Motherland, but also learn to stir up our people's patriotic zeal and to shatter the morale of the enemy troops. To encourage our own people, you must study Chairman Mao's works very hard and learn your lessons well with your teacher of Chinese; to crush the enemy, you must learn your English lessons well with me.

2   Then Comrade Chang paused, his face red and sweat beading on the tip of his nose. Though nonplussed, we could see that he was genuinely excited, but we were not sure whether his excitement was induced by "patriotic zeal" or the pleasure of hearing grandiose sounds issued from his own lips. For my part, I suspected that verbal intoxication caused his excitement. Scanning the classroom, he seemed to bask in our admiration rather than to urge us to sacrifice our lives for the Party. He then translated the speech into Chinese and gave us another dose of eloquence:

From now on, you are not pupils anymore, but soldiers—young, intellectual soldiers fighting at a special front. Neither is each English word you learn a mere word anymore. Each new word is a bullet shot at the enemy's chest, and each sentence a hand grenade.

Comrade Chang was from a "red" family. His name *hong* means red in Chinese, and *gen* means root, so literally, he was "Chang of Red Root." Students said that his father was a major in the People's Liberation Army, and his grandfather a general, and that both the father and the grandfather had "contributed a great deal to the Party, the Motherland, and the Chinese working people." When the "Great Proletarian Cultural Revolution" started, Mr. Chang had just graduated from the Beijing Foreign Languages Institute, a prestigious university in the capital where some thirty languages were taught to people "of red roots." Red youngsters were trained there to serve in the Foreign Ministry, mostly in Chinese embassies and consulates in foreign countries. We understood that Comrade Chang would work only for a token period in our ghetto middle school. At the time, the Foreign Ministry was too busy with the Cultural Revolution to hire new translators, but as soon as the "Movement" was over and everything back to normal, Comrade Chang, we knew, would leave us and begin his diplomatic career.

In the late 1960s the Revolution defined "intellectual" as "subversive." So my father, a university professor educated in a British missionary school in Tianjin, was regarded as a "black" element, an enemy of the people. In 1967, our family was driven out of our university faculty apartment, and I found myself in a ghetto middle school, an undeserving pupil of the red expert Comrade Chang.

In a shabby and ill-heated schoolroom I began my first English lesson, not "from the very beginning" by studying the alphabet, but with some powerful "hand grenades":

> Give up; no harm!
> Drop your guns!
> Down with the Soviet Neo-Czarists!
> Down with U.S. Imperialism!
> Long live Chairman Mao!
> We wish Chairman Mao a long, long life!
> Victory belongs to our people!

These sentences turned out to be almost more difficult and more dangerous to handle than real grenades, for soon the words became mixed up in our heads. So much so that not a few "revolutionary pupils" reconstructed the slogans to the hearty satisfactions of themselves but to the horror of Comrade Chang:

> Long live the Soviet Neo-Czarists!
> Victory belongs to your guns!

Upon hearing this, Comrade Chang turned pale and shouted at us, "You idiots! Had you uttered anything like that in Chinese, young as you are, you could have been thrown into jail for years. Probably me too! Now you follow me closely: Long live Chairman Mao!"

7   "Long live Chairman Mao!" we shouted back.

8   "Long live Chairman Mao!"

9   "Long live Chairman Mao!"

10   "Down with the Soviet Neo-Czarists!"

11   "Down with the Soviet Neo-Czarists!"

12   Comrade Chang decided that those two sentences were enough for idiots to learn in one lesson, and he told us to forget the other sentences for the moment. Then he wrote the two sentences on the chalkboard and asked us to copy them in our English exercise books. Alas, how could anybody in our school know what that was!

13   I wrote the two sentences on my left palm and avoided putting my left hand in my pocket or mitten for the rest of the day. I also remembered what Comrade Chang said about being thrown into jail, for as the son of a "black, stinking bourgeois intellectual," I grasped the truth in his warning. The two English sentences were a long series of meaningless, unutterable sounds. Comrade Chang had the power to impose some Chinese meaning on my mind. So, before I forgot or confused the sounds, I invented a makeshift transliteration in Chinese for the phonetically difficult and politically dangerous parts of the sentences. I put the Chinese words *qui, mian*, and *mao* (cut, noodle, hair) under "Chairman Mao," and *niu za sui* (beef organ meat) under "Neo-Czarists." "Down with" were bad words applied to the enemies; "long live" were good words reserved for the great leader. These were easy to remember. So I went home with a sense of security, thinking the device helped me distinguish the Great Leader from the enemy.

14   The next morning, Comrade "Red Roots" asked us to try our weapons before the blackboard. Nobody volunteered. Then Comrade Chang began calling us by name. My friend "Calf" was the first to stand up. He did not remember anything. He didn't try to learn the words, and he told me to "forget it" when I was trying to memorize the weird sounds. In fact, none of my classmates remembered the sentences.

15   My fellow pupils were all "red" theoretically. But they were not Comrade Chang's type of red. Their parents were coolies, candy-peddlers, or bricklayers. Poor and illiterate. Before the 1949 revolution, these people led miserable lives. Even the revolution didn't improve their lives much, and parents preferred their children to do chores at home rather than fool around with books, especially after the "Great Proletarian Cultural Revolution" started in 1966. Books were dangerous. Those who read books often ran into trouble for having ideas the Party didn't want them to have. "Look at the intellectuals," they said. "They suffer even more than us illiterates." They also knew that their children could not become

What does it mean to become literate? Are there significant differences in this process among cultures, nationalities? Compare your own experience of learning to read and write English or another language with the processes of language learning that Ning Yu describes in this essay.

"red experts" like Comrade Chang, because they themselves were working people who didn't contribute to the Party, the Motherland—or to the liberation of the working people themselves.

Thus my friends didn't waste time in remembering nonsense. Still Comrade Chang's questions had to be answered. Since I was the only one in class not from a red family, my opinion was always the last asked, if asked at all. I stood up when Comrade Chang called my name. I had forgotten the English sounds too, for I took Calf's advice. But before I repeated the apology already repeated fifty times by my friends, I glanced at my left palm and inspiration lit up my mind. "Long live *qie mian mao!* Down with *niu za sui!*" My friends stared, and Comrade Chang glared at me. He couldn't believe his ears. "Say that again." I did. This time my classmates burst into a roar of laughter. "Cut noodle hair! Beef organ meat!" they shouted again and again.

"Shut up!" Comrade Chang yelled, trembling with anger and pointing at me with his right index finger. "What do you mean by 'cut noodle hair'? That insults our great leader Chairman Mao." Hearing that, the class suddenly became silent. The sons and daughters of the "Chinese working people" knew how serious an accusation that could be. But Calf stood up and said: "Comrade Teacher, it is truly a bad thing that Ning Yu should associate Chairman Mao with such nonsense as 'cut noodle hair.' But he didn't mean any harm. He was trying to throw a hand grenade at the enemy. He also called the Soviets 'beef organ meat.' He said one bad thing (not enough respect for Chairman Mao) but then said a good thing (condemning the Soviets). One take away one is zero. So he didn't really do anything wrong, right?"

18   Again the room shook with laughter.

19   Now Comrade Chang flew into a rage and began to lecture us about how class enemies often say good things to cover up evil intentions. Calf, Chang said, was a red boy and should draw a line between himself and me, the black boy. He also threatened to report my "evil words" to the revolutionary committee of the middle school. He said that in the "urgent state of war" what I said could not be forgiven or overlooked. He told me to examine my mind and conduct severe self-criticism before being punished. "The great proletarian dictatorship," he said, "is all-powerful. All good will be rewarded and all evil punished when the right time comes." He left the classroom in anger without giving us any new hand grenades.

20   I felt ruined. Destroyed. Undone. I could feel icy steel handcuffs closing around my wrists. I could hear the revolutionary slogans that the mobs would shout at me when I was dragged off by the iron hand of the Proletarian Dictatorship. My legs almost failed me on my way home.

21   Calf knew better. "You have nothing to worry about, Third Ass."

22   I am the third child in my family, and it is a tradition of old Beijing to call a boy by number. So usually my family called me Thirdy. But in my ghetto, when the kids wanted to be really friendly, they added the word "ass" to your number or name. This address upset me when I first moved into the neighborhood. I was never comfortable with that affix during the years I lived there, but at that moment I appreciated Calf's kindness in using that affix. Words are empty shells. It's the feeling that people attach to a word that counts.

23   "I'll be crushed like a rotten egg by the iron fist of the Great Proletarian Dictatorship," I said.

24   "No way. Red Rooty is not going to tell on you. Don't you know he was more scared than you? He was responsible. How could you say such things if he had not taught you? You get it? You relax. *Qie mian mao!* You know, you really sounded like Rooty." Calf grinned.

25   Although Calf's wisdom helped me to "get it," relax I could not. My legs were as stiff as sticks and my heart beat against my chest so hard that I could hardly breathe. For many years I had tried to get rid of my "blackness" by hard work and good manners. But I could not succeed. No matter how hard I tried I could not change the fact that I was not "red." The Party denied the existence of intermediate colors. If you were not red, logically you could only be black. What Chang said proved what I guessed. But, when cornered, even a rabbit may bite. Comrade Chang, I silently imagined, if I have to be crushed, you can forget about your diplomatic

career. I created a drama in which Comrade Chang, the red root, and I, the black root, were crushed into such fine powder that one could hardly tell the red from the black. All one could see was a dark, devilish purple.

The next morning, I went to school with a faltering heart, expecting to be called out of the classroom and cuffed. Nothing happened. Comrade Chang seemed to have forgotten my transgression and gave us three handfuls of new "bullets." He slowed down too, placing more emphasis on pronunciation. He cast the "bullets" into hand grenades only after he was sure that we could shoot the "bullets" with certainty.

Nothing happened to me that day, or the next day, or the week after. Calf was right. As weeks passed, my dislike of Chang dwindled and I began to feel something akin to gratitude to him. Before learning his English tongue twisters, we only recited Chairman Mao's thirty-six poems. We did that for so long that I memorized the annotations together with the text. I also memorized how many copies were produced for the first, the second, and the third printing. I was bored, and Teacher Chang's tongue twisters brought me relief. Granted they were only old slogans in new sounds. But the mere sounds and the new way of recording the sounds challenged me. Still, as an old Chinese saying goes, good luck never lasts long.

Forty hand grenades were as many as the Party thought proper for us to hold. Before I mastered the fortieth tongue twister—"Revolutionary committees are fine"—our "fine" revolutionary committee ordered Comrade Chang to stop English lessons and to make us dig holes for air raid shelters. Comrade Chang approached this new task with just as much "patriotic zeal" as he taught English. In truth he seemed content to let our "bullets" and "hand grenades" rust in the bottom of the holes we dug. But I was not willing to let my only fun slip away easily. When digging the holes I repeated the forty slogans silently. I even said them at home in bed. One night I uttered a sentence as I climbed onto my top bunk. Reading in the bottom bunk, my father heard me and was surprised. He asked where I had learned the words. Then for the first time I told him about Comrade Chang's English lessons.

Now it may seem strange for a middle school boy not to turn to his family during a "political crisis." But at that time, it was not strange at all. By then my mother, my sister, and my brother had already been sent to the countryside in two different remote provinces. Getting help from them was almost impossible, for they had enough pressing problems themselves. Help from my father was even more impractical: he was already "an enemy of the people," and therefore whatever he said or did for me could only complicate my problems rather than resolve them. So I kept him in the dark. Since we had only each other in the huge city of eight million people, we shared many things, but not political problems.

Our home in the working class neighborhood was a single seventeen-square-meter room. Kitchen, bathroom, sitting room, study, bedroom, all

26

27

28

29

30

in one. There was no ceiling, so we could see the black beams and rafters when we lay in bed. The floor was a damp and sticky dirt, which defied attempts at sweeping and mopping. The walls were yellow and were as damp as the dirt floor. To partition the room was out of the question. Actually my parents had sold their king-sized bed and our single beds, and bought two bunk beds in their stead. My mother and sister each occupied a top bunk, my father slept in one bottom bunk, and my brother and I shared the other. Red Guards had confiscated and burned almost all of my father's Chinese books, but miraculously they left his English books intact. The English books were stuffed under the beds on the dirt floor. We lived in this manner for more than a year till the family members were scattered all over China, first my siblings to a province in the northwest, and then my mother to southern China. They were a thousand miles from us and fifteen hundred miles from each other. After they left, I moved to the top bunk over my father, and we piled the books on the other bed. Thanks to the hard covers, only the bottom two layers of the books had begun to mold.

31   That evening, after hearing me murmuring in English, my father gestured for me to sit down on his bunk. He asked me whether I knew any sentences other than the one he had heard. I jumped at the opportunity to go through the inventory of my English arsenal. After listening to my forty slogans my father said: "You have a very good English teacher. He has an excellent pronunciation, standard Oxford pronunciation. But the sentences are not likely to be found in any books written by native English speakers. Did he teach you how to read?"

32   "I can read all those sentences if you write them out."

33   "If *I* write them? But can't *you* write them by yourself?"

34   "No."

35   "Did he teach you grammar?"

36   "No."

37   "Did he teach you the alphabet?"

38   "No."

39   My father looked amused. Slowly he shook his head, and then asked: "Can you recognize the words, the separate words, when they appear in different contexts?"

40   "I think so, but I'm not sure."

41   He re-opened the book that he was reading and turned to the first page and pointed with his index finger at the first word in the first sentence, signaling me to identify it.

42   I shook my head.

43   He moved the finger to the next word. I didn't know that either. Nor did I know the third word, the shortest word in the line, the word made up of a single letter. My father traced the whole sentence slowly, hoping that I could identify some words. I recognized the bullet "in" and at once threw a hand grenade at him: "Beloved Chairman Mao,

you are the red sun *in* our hearts." Encouraged, my father moved his finger back to the second word in the sentence. This time I looked at the word more closely but couldn't recognize it. "It's an 'is,' " he said. "You know 'are' but not 'is'! The third word in this sentence is an 'a'. It means 'one.' " It is the first letter in the alphabet and you don't know that either! What a teacher! A well-trained one too!" He then cleared his throat and read the whole sentence aloud: "It is a truth universally acknowledged, that a man in possession of a good fortune, must be in want of a wife."

The sounds he uttered reminded me of Chang's opening speech, but they flowed out of my father's mouth smoothly. Without bothering about the meaning of the sentence, I asked my father to repeat it several times because I liked the rhythm. Pleased with my curiosity, my father began to explain the grammatical structure of the sentence. His task turned out to be much harder than he expected, for he had to explain terms such as "subject," "object," "nouns," "verbs" and "adjectives." To help me understand the structure of the English sentence, he had to teach me Chinese grammar first. He realized that the Great Proletarian Culture Revolution had made his youngest son literally illiterate, in Chinese as well as English.

That night, our English lessons started. He taught me the letters A through F. By the end of the week, I had learned my alphabet. Afterward he taught the basics of grammar, sometimes using my hand grenades to illustrate the rules. He also taught me the international phonetic symbols and the way to use a dictionary. For reading materials, he excerpted simple passages from whatever books were available. Some were short paragraphs while others just sentences. We started our lessons at a manageable pace, but after a couple of months, for reasons he didn't tell me till the very last, he speeded up the pace considerably. The new words that I had to memorize increased from twenty words per day to fifty. To meet the challenge, I wrote the new words on small, thin slips of paper and hid them in the little red book of Chairman Mao, so that I could memorize them during the political study hours at school. In hole-digging afternoons I recited the sentences and sometimes even little paragraphs—aloud when I was sure that Chang was not around.

Before the sounds and shapes of English words became less elusive, before I could confidently study by myself, my father told me that I would have to continue on my own. He was going to join the "Mao Zedong Thought Study Group" at his university. In those years, "Mao Zedong Thought Study Group" was a broad term that could refer to many things. Used in reference to my father and people like him, it had only one meaning: a euphemism for imprisonment. He had been imprisoned once when my mother and siblings were still in Bejing. Now it had come again. I asked, "Are you detained or arrested?" "I don't know," he said. "It's just a Study Group." "Oh," I said, feeling the weight of the words. Legally, detention couldn't be any longer than fifteen days; arrest had to be followed by a conviction and a sentence, which also had a definite term. "Just a Study Group" could be a week or a lifetime. I was left on my own in a city of eight million people, my English lessons indefinitely postponed. What was worse, some people never returned alive from "Study Groups."

47   "When are you joining them?"

48   "Tomorrow."

49   I pretended to be "man" enough not to cry, but my father's eyes were wet when he made me promise to finish *Pride and Prejudice* by the time he came back.

50   After he left for the "Study Group," bedding roll on his shoulder, I took my first careful look at the book he had thrust into my hands. It was a small book with dark green cloth covers and gilt designs and letters on its spine. I lifted the front cover; the frontispiece had a flowery design and a woman figure on the upper right corner. Floating in the middle of the flowery design and as a mother, holding a baby, she held an armful of herbs, two apples or peaches, and a scroll. Her head tilted slightly toward her right, to an opened scroll intertwined with the flowers on the other side of the page. On the unrolled scroll, there were some words. I was thrilled to find that I could understand all the words in the top two lines with no difficulty except the last word: EVERYMAN, / I WILL GO WITH THEE. . . .

51   Two months after father entered the "Study Group," I stopped going to his university for my monthly allowance. The Party secretary of the bursar's office wore me out by telling me that my father and I didn't deserve to be fed by "working people." "Your father has never done any positive work," meaning the twenty years my father taught at the university undermined rather than contributed to socialist ideology. To avoid starvation, I picked up horse droppings in the streets and sold them to the farming communes in the suburb. Between the little cash savings my father left me and what I earned by selling dung, I managed an independent life. Meanwhile, I didn't forget my promise to my father. When I saw him again nineteen months later, I boasted of having thumbed his dictionary to shreds and struggled through Austen's novel from cover to cover. I hadn't understood the story, but I had learned many words.

52   My father was not surprised to find that I took pleasure in drudgery. He knew that looking up English words in a dictionary and wrestling with an almost incomprehensible text could be an exciting challenge. It provided an intellectual relief for a teenager living at a time when the entire country read nothing but Chairman Mao's works. "Don't worry whether you are red or black," my father said. "Just be yourself. Just be an ordinary everyman. Keep up with your good work,

and when you learn English well enough, you'll be sure of a guide 'in your most need.'"

Content

1. An essay of dividing its subject often draws rigid boundaries between its categories so that they are mutually exclusive. Is that true in Ning Yu's essay? Are the "reds" in total opposition to the "blacks"? If there is any overlap or intermingling among these groups, where does it occur (see, for instance, ¶ 15)? Explain your answer.

2. What sorts of comparisons can Ning Yu count on his American readers to make between his childhood, schooling, living conditions, and their own? What sorts of information does he need to supply each time he introduces an unfamiliar concept? Has he done this successfully?

3. For what reasons—political, cultural, ethical—can Ning Yu expect Western readers to be sympathetic to the plight of himself and his father? Illustrate your answer with specific examples.

Strategies/Structures/Language

4. Much of the humor in this essay depends on the students' failure to understand the English slogans their equally uncomprehending teachers oblige them to memorize. Find some examples. What would strike English-speaking readers as funny, but not the pupils?

5. Have you ever been given a "label"—based on your race, social class, gender, political or religious affiliation, place of residence (street or area, city or town, state)? If so, what was (or is) that label? How accurate are its connotations? Are they favorable, unfavorable, or a mixture? Does the label stereotype or limit the ways people are expected to react to it? Did (or do) you feel comfortable with that label?

For Writing

6. Have you or anyone you know well ever experienced persecution or harassment—intellectual, political, economic, racial, religious, or for other reasons? If so, write a paper explaining the causes, effects, and resolution (if any) of the problem. If it is extremely complex, select one or two aspects to concentrate on in your paper. Can you count on your audience to be sympathetic to your point of view? If not, what will you need to do to win them to your side?

7. *Journal Writing.* Have the values of your home ever clashed with those promoted in your school or in another environment (such as a club) away from home? Did you feel torn between loyalties? Alternatively, have you, like Yu's friend Calf, helped a friend through such a conflict? Explore how conflicts between family culture and society outside the home can be both difficult and foster personal growth.

8. *Mixed Modes.* Because Comrade Chang's students have not been taught the English alphabet or grammar, the "hand grenades" he has them memorize (¶ 5)

do not "crush the enemy" (¶ 1), but, ironically, ricochet back and frighten him. Can you find other examples of irony in Yu's narrative?

9. ***Second Look.*** Does Yu's experience of learning English suggest that there are significant differences in the process of becoming literate among cultures and nationalities? Consider how the photograph in this essay conveys the process of learning to read and write and compare it with your own experience.

10. If you or someone you know has learned English (or another language) well enough to speak and read it fluently, write a brief "Literacy Autobiography" explaining the essence and the highlights of the process.

Additional Topics for Writing
Process Analysis

(For strategies for writing process analysis, see p. 117.)

Multiple Strategies for Writing: Process Analysis

In writing on any of the process analysis topics below, you can choose among a variety of strategies to help explain a process and interpret its consequences:

- *Definitions, explanations* of terms, equipment involved in the process
- A *narrative* of how the process proceeds, from start to finish
- *Illustrations* and *examples*: to show what happens, and in what sequence
- *Diagrams, drawings, flow charts, graphs:* to clarify and explain
- *Cause* and *effect*: to show why the process is justified or recommended, with what anticipated consequences
- *Comparison* and *contrast*, between your recommendation and alternative ways of achieving the same or a similar result
- Consideration of *short-term* and *long-term consequences* of a particular process

1. Write an essay in which you provide directions on how to perform a process—how to do or make something at which you are particularly skilled. In addition to the essential steps, you may wish to explain your own special technique or strategy that makes your method unique or better. Some possible subjects (which may be narrowed or adapted as you and your instructor wish) are these:

a. How to get a good job, permanent or summer
b. How to live meaningfully in a post 9/11 world (See Chapter 12, "Human Rights and World Peace.")
c. How to contribute to a "green" world, as an individual or member of a larger group (see photo insert)
d. How to scuba dive, hang-glide, rappel, jog, lift weights, train for a marathon or triathlon
e. How to do good for others, short term or long term
f. How to be happy
g. How to stay healthy, become stronger, gain or lose weight, stop smoking (see DiFranza, 122–31) or drinking (see Sanders, 135–42)
h. How to build a library of books, music, DVDs
i. How to shop at a garage sale or secondhand store
j. How to repair your own car, bicycle, computer, or other machine
k. How to live cheaply (but enjoyably)
l. How to study for a test—in general or in a specific subject
m. How to administer first aid for choking, drowning, burns, or some other medical emergency
n. How to get rich
o. Anything else you know that others might want to learn

2. Write an informative essay in which you explain how one of the following occurs or works. Although you should pick a subject you know something about, you may need to supplement your information by consulting outside sources.

a. How I made a major decision (to be—or not to be—a member of a particular profession, to practice a particular religion or lifestyle . . .)
b. How a computer (or amplifier, piano, microwave oven, or other machine) works
c. How to save energy through using a "green" product, such as a bicycle (specify kind), hybrid car, solar heating, and show how the device works
d. How a professional develops skill in his or her chosen field—that is, how one becomes a skilled electrical engineer, geologist, chef, tennis coach, surgeon . . . ; pick a field in which you are interested
e. How birds fly (or learn to fly), or some other process in the natural world
f. How a system of the body (circulatory, digestive, respiratory, skeletal, neurological) works
g. How the earth (or the solar system) was formed
h. How the scientific method (or a particular variation of it) functions in a particular field
i. How a well-run business (pick one of your choice—manufacturing, restaurant, clothing or hardware store, television repair service . . .) functions
j. How a specific area of our federal government (or your particular local or state government legislative, executive, judicial) came into existence, or has changed over time
k. How a system or process has gone wrong (may be satiric or humorous)
l. How a particular drug or other medicine was developed and/or how it works, including its benefits and hazards
m. How a great idea (on the nature of love, justice, truth, beauty . . .) found acceptance in a particular religion, culture, or smaller group
n. How a particular culture (ethnic, regional, tribal, religious) or subculture (preppies, yuppies, pacifists, punk rockers, motorcycle gangs . . .) developed, rose, and/or declined in a larger or smaller group

3. Write a humorous paper explaining a process of the kind identified below. You will need to provide a serious analysis of the method you propose, even though the subject itself is intended to be amusing. (See Verge's "The Habs" (105–09)).

a. How to make or do anything badly or inelegantly, without expertise or ability
b. How to be popular
c. How to survive in college
d. How to survive a broken love affair
e. How to be a model babysitter/son/daughter/student/employee/lover/spouse/parent
f. How to become a celebrity
g. Any of the topics in Writing Suggestions 1 or 2 above
h. How a process can go dreadfully wrong

Cause and Effect

Writers often explore the relationships between cause and effect. Sometimes they simply list the causes (or the consequences), and then either assume the consequences (or the causes) are obvious or let the readers draw their own conclusions. This is a common strategy of short poetry. Mary Oliver's "August" (179), for example, cites many natural causes that in combination create this perfect day of acceptance of nature and acceptance of self, epitomized in "this happy tongue."

Or they can probe more intensively, asking, "*Why* did something happen?" or "*What* are its consequences?" or both. Why did the United States develop as a democracy rather than as some other form of government? What have the effects of this form of government been on its population? Or you, as a writer, may choose to examine a chain reaction in which, like a Rube Goldberg cartoon device, Cause *A* produces Effect *B*, which in turn causes *C*, which produces Effect *D*: Peer pressure (Cause *A*) causes young men to drink to excess (Effect *B*), which causes them to drive unsafely (Cause *C*, a corollary of Effect *B*) and results in high accident rates in unmarried males under age twenty-five (Effect *D*).

Process analysis can also deal with events or phenomena in sequence, focusing on the *how* rather than the *why*. To analyze the process of drinking and driving would be to explain, as an accident report might, how Al C. O'Hall became intoxicated (he drank seventeen beers and a bourbon chaser in two hours at the Dun Inn) and how he then roared off at 120 miles an hour, lost control of his lightweight sports car on a curve, and plowed into an oncoming sedan.

Two conditions have to be met to prove a given cause:

B cannot occur without *A*.
Whenever *A* occurs, *B* must also occur.

Thus a biologist who observed, repeatedly, that photosynthesis *(B)* occurred in green plants whenever a light source *(A)* was present and that it only occurred under this condition could infer that light causes photosynthesis. This would be the immediate cause. The more *remote* or *ultimate cause* might be the source of the light if it were natural (the sun). Artificial light (electricity) would have a yet more remote cause, such as water or nuclear power.

But don't be misled by a coincidental time sequence. Just because *A* preceded *B* in time doesn't necessarily mean that *A* caused *B*. Although it may appear to rain every time you wash your car, the car wash doesn't cause the rain. To blame the car wash would be an example of the *post hoc, ergo propter hoc* fallacy (Latin for "after this, therefore because of this").

Indeed, in cause-and-effect papers ultimate causes may be of greater significance than immediate ones, especially when you're considering social, political, or psychological causes rather than exclusively physical phenomena. Looking for possible causes from multiple perspectives is a good way to develop ideas to write about. It's also a sure way to avoid oversimplification, attributing a single cause to an effect that results from several. Scott Russell Sanders's analysis of his father in "Under the Influence: Paying the Price of My Father's Booze" (180–91) presents an *argument*—as well as an *explanation*—and uses *comparison and contrast* to illustrate *cause and effect*. Sanders uses the single case of his father's alcoholism and its numerous, devastating effects on his family to serve as an analysis of alcoholism in general: the secret drinking, the unsafe driving, the weaving walk, his mother's accusations, his father's rage, the children cowering in fear, the fights, the sneakiness, and the unseemly behavior. Sanders's reaction to his father's drinking, as a child who blames himself as the cause of his father's horrifying behavior, may also be generalized to describe the impact of parental drinking on many children of alcoholics: "I lie there [in bed] hating him, loving him, fearing him, knowing I have failed him. I tell myself he drinks to ease the ache . . . I must have caused by disappointing him somehow, a murderous ache I should be able to relieve by doing all my chores, earning A's in school. . . . He would not . . . drink himself to death, if only I were perfect." Readers can be counted on to recognize that Sanders's childhood explanation is inaccurate and inadequate even as they acknowledge the devastating impact of the father's alcoholism on the entire family—his articulate son in particular.

The essays in this section treat cause and effect in a variety of ways. Because causes and effects are invariably intertwined, writers usually acknowledge the causes even when they're emphasizing the effects, and vice versa.

Two of the essays in this section—as well as others (see, for instance, Sanders, "The Inheritance of Tools" [135–42] and Yu, "Red and Black, or One English Major's Beginning" [161–71])—deal with the causes and effects of education, formal and informal, on the students involved, and with the consequences of that education—or lack of it—not only to the individual, but to society.

Two student essays, Ryan O'Connell's "Standing Order" (215–18) and Meaghan Roy-O'Reilly's "Balancing Act" (219–23) deal with eating disorders which occurred when Ryan was in high school; Meaghan's began when she was even younger. Although they are concerned with the causes, both focus more on the effects and the processes (in Ryan's case, quick and dramatic; in Meaghan's case, much more gradual) by which these were treated–and ultimately, resolved successfully.

In "Tinfoil Underwear" (192–98), James Fallows explains how computer users can try to protect their secrets, including the "evidence we leave behind when we browse, shop, communicate, and amuse ourselves on the Internet," using measures ranging from "tools of disguise" such as encryption software, to avoiding sending e-mails "they would not want to see broadly forwarded," to passing laws that would create a "privacy firewall." All—except the most extreme measure, "doing absolutely nothing"—involve a host of other processes, which have a multiplier effect of consequences, some predictable, others surprising.

Sanders's account of alcoholism is personal and biographical, not medical. Atul Gawande's "On Washing Hands" (152–59), discussed in the previous chapter as an example of process analysis, may also be interpreted for its treatment of cause and effect. He brings a down-to-earth, personal, humane perspective to a medical subject so commonplace that it is often overlooked. Although Semmelweis had to argue 150 years ago that less-than-sterile hands caused infection, today it is no longer necessary to prove this obvious causal connection. Nevertheless, the fact that every year two million Americans become afflicted with hospital-induced infections and ninety thousand die is a shocking reminder of how cause and effect are neglected. How easy, how all-too-human it is for medical personnel, in hurrying from one sick person to another, to forget to wash their hands after greeting and treating patients, opening doors, and otherwise contaminating their hands (or gloves)—and more. Gawande also shows how it is possible for hospitals to keep the necessary sanitizing equipment close at hand in patients' rooms as well as in the sterile high-stakes territory of the operating room, the only place where thorough sanitation is maintained with consistent vigilance.

The cause-and-effect process Gawande explains seems simple in comparison with the complex issues involved in the causes and the consequences of global warming. In "The Physical Science behind Climate Change" (199–211), members of the 2007 Intergovernmental Panel on Climate Change—Collins, Colman, Haywood, Manning, and Mote—"place the probability that global warming has been caused by human activities at greater than 90 percent" (in contrast with a 66 percent probability reported in 2001). They contend that rapid increases in "the atmospheric concentrations of carbon dioxide, methane and nitrous oxide" in the past two hundred (but particularly the past twenty) years have been caused mostly by humans (aerosols, ozone, aircraft contrails), and explain why in considerable detail. They also discuss "The Consequences of Ongoing Warming" (208), which include rising temperatures and changes in precipitation as well as the consequences of these phenomena—"the state of the ocean and the cryosphere (sea ice, the great ice sheets in Greenland and Antarctica, glaciers, snow, frozen ground, and ice on lakes and rivers)" and numerous additional consequences worldwide, as indicated by the diagram and extensive captions. In "Our Moral Footprint" (211–14), Vaclav Havel, Czech president (1993–2003) and playwright, reinforces the scientists' evidence with a humanistic plea for moral responsibility: "Technological measures and regulations are important, but equally important is support for education, ecological training and ethics—a consciousness of the commonality of all living beings and an emphasis on shared responsibility." Failure to do this won't destroy the planet, he says, but it may destroy the human race.

A paper of cause-and-effect analysis requires you, as a thoughtful and careful writer, to know your subject well enough to avoid oversimplification and to shore up your analysis with specific, convincing details. You won't be expected to explain all the causes or effects of a particular phenomenon; that might be impossible for most humans, even the experts. But you can do a sufficiently thorough job with your chosen segment of the subject to satisfy yourself and help your readers to see it your way. Maybe they'll even come to agree with your interpretation. Why? Because. . . .

Strategies for Writing: Cause and Effect

1. What is the purpose of my cause-and-effect paper? Will I be focusing on the cause(s) of something, or its effect(s), short- or long-term? Will I be using cause and effect to explain a process? Analyze a situation? Present a prediction or an argument?
2. How much does my audience know about my subject? Will I have to explain some portions of the cause-and-effect relationship in more detail than others to compensate for their lack of knowledge? Or do they have sufficient background so I can focus primarily on new information or interpretations?
3. Is the cause-and-effect relationship I'm writing about valid? Or might there be other possible causes (or effects) that I'm overlooking? If I'm emphasizing causes, how far back do I want to go? If I'm focusing on effects, how many do I wish to discuss, and with how many examples?
4. Will I be using narration, description, definition, process analysis, argument, or other strategies in my explanation or analysis of cause(s) and effect(s)?
5. How technical or nontechnical will my language be? Will I need to qualify any of my claims or conclusions with "probably," or "in most cases," or other admissions that what I'm saying is not absolutely certain? What will my tone be—explanatory, persuasive, argumentative, humorous?

MARY OLIVER

Born in Cleveland, Ohio (1935), Mary Oliver attended both Ohio State University and Vassar College. In her first book of poems, *No Voyage, and Other Poems* (1963), the influence of moderns such as Edna St. Vincent Millay, William Carlos Williams, and James Wright was clearly evident, but her distinctive style and vision emerged in *Twelve Moons* (1979); *American Primitive* (1983), which won the Pulitzer Prize; *Dream Work* (1986); *House of Light* (1990); and *New and Selected Poems* (1992), which won a National Book Award. Oliver's main poetic interest is the natural world—its landscapes and especially its wealth of living things. Yet, as she explained to the *Bloomsbury Review*, she employs nature "in an emblematic way" to explore "the human condition." Oliver shares her advice to aspiring poets in *Rules for the Dance: A Handbook for Writing and Reading Metrical Verse* (1998). Recent volumes of poetry and essays include *The Leaf and the Cloud* (2000), *Owls and other Fantasies* (2003), *Three* (2005), *Thirst: Poems* (2006), and *Our World* (2007).

　　In "August," from *American Primitive*, late-summer ripeness draws the poet into the brambles, compelling the reader to follow. There is a sense of rapture and realization ("there is this happy tongue"), yet the reader is left with unresolved mysteries. If, amidst the blackberries, her body "accepts what it is," what is her body, then, and what relation does it bear to the undertone of dark and black images that haunts this poem?

August

When the blackberries hang
swollen in the woods, in the brambles
nobody owns, I spend

all day among the high
branches, reaching
my ripped arms, thinking

of nothing, cramming
the black honey of summer
into my mouth; all day my body

accepts what it is. In the dark
creeks that run by there is
this thick paw of my life darting among

the black bells, the leaves; there is
this happy tongue.

SCOTT RUSSELL SANDERS

"Under the Influence," from *Secrets of the Universe* (1991), is full of examples that describe the effects of alcoholism—on the alcoholic father, on
his wife, alternately distressed and defiant, and on his children, cowering
with guilt and fear. Sanders uses especially the example of himself, the
eldest son, who felt responsible for his father's drinking, guilty because
he couldn't get him to stop, and obligated to atone for his father's sins
through his own perfection and accomplishment. Although at the age of
forty-four Sanders knows that his father was "consumed by disease rather
than by disappointment," he writes to understand "the corrosive mixture
of helplessness, responsibility, and shame that I learned to feel as the son
of an alcoholic." Through the specific example of his family's behavior,
Sanders illustrates the general problem of alcoholism that afflicts some "ten
or fifteen million people." He expects his readers to generalize and to learn
from his understanding.

Under the Influence: Paying the Price of My Father's Booze

1   My father drank. He drank as a gut-punched boxer gasps for breath,
as a starving dog gobbles food—compulsively, secretly, in pain and
trembling. I use the past tense not because he ever quit drinking but because he quit living. That is how the story ends for my father, age sixty-
four, heart bursting, body cooling, slumped and forsaken on the linoleum
of my brother's trailer. The story continues for my brother, my sister, my
mother, and me, and will continue as long as memory holds.

2   In the perennial present of memory, I slip into the garage or barn to
see my father tipping back the flat green bottles of wine, the brown cyl-
inders of whiskey, the cans of beer disguised in paper bags. His Adam's
apple bobs, the liquid gurgles, he wipes the sandy-haired back of a hand
over his lips, and then, his bloodshot gaze bumping into me, he stashes
the bottle or can inside his jacket, under the workbench, between two
bales of hay, and we both pretend the moment has not occurred.

3   "What's up, buddy?" he says, thick-tongued and edgy.

4   "Sky's up," I answer, playing along.

5   "And don't forget prices," he grumbles. "Prices are always up. And
taxes."

6   In memory, his white 1951 Pontiac with the stripes down the hood and
the Indian head on the snout lurches to a stop in the driveway; or it is the

1956 Ford station wagon, or the 1963 Rambler shaped like a toad, or the sleek 1969 Bonneville that will do 120 miles per hour on straightaways; or it is the robin's-egg-blue pickup, new in 1980, battered in 1981, the year of his death. He climbs out, grinning dangerously, unsteady on his legs, and we children interrupt our game of catch, our building of snow forts, our picking of plums, to watch in silence as he weaves past us into the house, where he drops into his overstuffed chair and falls asleep. Shaking her head, our mother stubs out a cigarette he has left smoldering in the ashtray. All evening, until our bedtimes, we tiptoe past him, as past a snoring dragon. Then we curl fearfully in our sheets, listening. Eventually he wakes with a grunt, Mother slings accusations at him, he snarls back, she yells, he growls, their voices clashing. Before long, she retreats to their bedroom, sobbing—not from the blows of fists, for he never strikes her, but from the force of his words.

Left alone, our father prowls the house, thumping into furniture, rummaging in the kitchen, slamming doors, turning the pages of the newspaper with a savage crackle, muttering back at the late-night drivel from television. The roof might fly off, the walls might buckle from the pressure of his rage. Whatever my brother and sister and mother may be thinking on their own rumpled pillows, I lie there hating him, loving him, fearing him, knowing I have failed him. I tell myself he drinks to ease the ache that gnaws at his belly, an ache I must have caused by disappointing him somehow, a murderous ache I should be able to relieve by doing all my chores, earning A's in school, winning baseball games, fixing the broken washer and the burst pipes, bringing in the money to fill his empty wallet. He would not hide the green bottles in his toolbox, would not sneak off to the barn with a lump under his coat, would not fall asleep in the daylight, would not roar and fume, would not drink himself to death, if only I were perfect. 7

I am forty-four, and I know full well now that my father was an alcoholic, a man consumed by disease rather than by disappointment. What had seemed to me a private grief is in fact, of course, a public scourge. In the United States alone, some ten or fifteen million people share his ailment, and behind the doors they slam in fury or disgrace, countless other children tremble. I comfort myself with such knowledge, holding it against the throb of memory like an ice pack against a bruise. Other people have keener sources of grief: poverty, racism, rape, war. I do not wish to compete to determine who has suffered most. I am only trying to understand the corrosive mixture of helplessness, responsibility, and shame that I learned to feel as the son of an alcoholic. I realize now that I did not cause my father's illness, nor could I have cured it. Yet for all this grownup knowledge, I am still ten years old, my own son's age, and as that boy I struggle in guilt and confusion to save my father from pain. 8

Consider a few of our synonyms for *drunk*: tipsy, tight, pickled, soused, and plowed; stoned and stewed, lubricated and inebriated, juiced and sluiced; three sheets to the wind, in your cups, out of your mind, under 9 the table; lit up, tanked up, wiped out; besotted, blotto, bombed, and buzzed; plastered, polluted, putrefied; loaded or looped, boozy, woozy, fuddled, or smashed; crocked and shit-faced, corked and pissed, snockered and sloshed.

10   It is a mostly humorous lexicon, as the lore that deals with drunks—in jokes and cartoons, in plays, films and television skits—is largely comic. Aunt Matilda nips elderberry wine from the sideboard and burps politely during supper. Uncle Fred slouches to the table glassy-eyed, wearing a lampshade for a hat and murmuring, "Candy is dandy, but liquor is quicker." Inspired by cocktails, Mrs. Somebody recounts the events of her day in a fuzzy dialect, while Mr. Somebody nibbles her ear and croons a bawdy song. On the sofa with Boyfriend, Daughter Somebody giggles, licking gin from her lips, and loosens the bows in her hair. Junior knocks back some brews with his chums at the Leopard Lounge and stumbles home to the wrong house, wonders foggily why he cannot locate his pajamas, and crawls naked into bed with the ugliest girl in school. The family dog slurps from a neglected martini and wobbles to the nursery, where he vomits in Baby's shoe.

11   It is all great fun. But if in the audience you notice a few laughing faces turn grim when the drunk lurches onstage, don't be surprised, for these are the children of alcoholics. Over the grinning mask of Dionysus, the leering face of Bacchus, these children cannot help seeing the bloated features of their own parents. Instead of laughing, they wince, they mourn. Instead of celebrating the drunk as one freed from constraints, they pity him as one enslaved. They refuse to believe *in vino veritas*, having seen their befuddled parents skid away from truth toward folly and oblivion. And so these children bite their lips until the lush staggers into the wings.

12   My father, when drunk, was neither funny nor honest; he was pathetic, frightening, deceitful. There seemed to be a leak in him somewhere, and he poured in booze to keep from draining dry. Like a torture victim who refuses to squeal, he would never admit that he had touched a drop, not even in his last year, when he seemed to be dissolving in alcohol before our very eyes. I never knew him to lie about anything, ever, except about this one ruinous fact. Drowsy, clumsy, unable to fix a bicycle tire, balance a grocery sack, or walk across a room, he was stripped of his true self by drink. In a matter of minutes, the contents of a bottle could transform a brave man into a coward, a buddy into a bully, a gifted athlete and skilled carpenter and shrewd businessman into a bumbler. No dictionary of synonyms for *drunk* would soften the anguish of watching our prince turn into a frog.

13   Father's drinking became the family secret. While growing up, we children never breathed a word of it beyond the four walls of our house. To this day, my brother and sister rarely mention it, and then only when I press them. I did not confess the ugly, bewildering fact to my wife until his wavering and slurred speech forced me to. Recently, on the seventh anniversary of my father's death, I asked my mother if she ever spoke of

his drinking to friends. "No, no, never," she replied hastily. "I couldn't bear for anyone to know."

The secret bores under the skin, gets in the blood, into the bone, and stays there. Long after you have supposedly been cured of malaria, the fever can flare up, the tremors can shake you. So it is with the fevers of shame. You swallow the bitter quinine of knowledge, and you learn to feel pity and compassion toward the drinker. Yet the shame lingers and, because of it, anger.

For a long stretch of my childhood we lived on a military reservation in Ohio, an arsenal where bombs were stored underground in bunkers and vintage airplanes burst into flames and unstable artillery shells boomed nightly at the dump. We had the feeling, as children, that we played within a minefield, where a heedless footfall could trigger an explosion. When Father was drinking, the house, too, became a minefield. The least bump could set off either parent.

The more he drank, the more obsessed Mother became with stopping him. She hunted for bottles, counted the cash in his wallet, sniffed at his breath. Without meaning to snoop, we children blundered left and right into damning evidence. On afternoons when he came home from work sober, we flung ourselves at him for hugs and felt against our ribs the telltale lump in his coat. In the barn we tumbled on the hay and heard beneath our sneakers the crunch of broken glass. We tugged open a drawer in his workbench, looking for screwdrivers or crescent wrenches, and spied a gleaming six-pack among the tools. Playing tag, we darted around the house just in time to see him sway on the rear stoop and heave a finished bottle into the woods. In his good-night kiss we smelled the cloying sweetness of Clorets, the mints he chewed to camouflage his dragon's breath.

I can summon up that kiss right now by recalling Theodore Roethke's lines about his own father:

> *The whiskey on your breath*
> Could make a small boy dizzy;
> But I hung on like death:
> Such waltzing was not easy.

Such waltzing was hard, terribly hard, for with a boy's scrawny arms I was trying to hold my tipsy father upright.

For years, the chief source of those incriminating bottles and cans was a grimy store a mile from us, a cinderblock place called Sly's, with two gas pumps outside and a mangy dog asleep in the window. Inside, on rusty metal shelves or in wheezing coolers, you could find pop and Popsicles, cigarettes, potato chips, canned soup, raunchy postcards, fishing gear, Twinkies, wine, and beer. When Father drove anywhere on errands, Mother would send us along as guards, warning us not to let him out of our sight. And so with one or more of us on board, Father would cruise up to Sly's, pump a dollar's worth of gas or plump the tires with air, and then, telling us to wait in the car, he would head for the doorway.

19   Dutiful and panicky, we cried, "Let us go with you!"

20   "No," he answered. "I'll be back in two shakes."

21   "Please!"

22   "No!" he roared. "Don't you budge or I'll jerk a knot in your tails!"

23   So we stayed put, kicking the seats, while he ducked inside. Often, when he had parked the car at a careless angle, we gazed in through the window and saw Mr. Sly fetching down from the shelf behind the cash register two green pints of Gallo wine. Father swigged one of them right there at the counter, stuffed the other in his pocket, and then out he came, a bulge in his coat, a flustered look on his reddened face.

24   Because the mom and pop who ran the dump were neighbors of ours, living just down the tar-blistered road, I hated them all the more for poisoning my father. I wanted to sneak in their store and smash the bottles and set fire to the place. I also hated the Gallo brothers, Ernest and Julio, whose jovial faces beamed from the labels of their wine, labels I would find, torn and curled, when I burned the trash. I noted the Gallo brothers' address in California and studied the road atlas to see how far that was from Ohio, because I meant to go out there and tell Ernest and Julio what they were doing to my father, and then, if they showed no mercy, I would kill them.

25   While growing up on the back roads and in the country schools and cramped Methodist churches of Ohio and Tennessee, I never heard the word *alcoholic*, never happened across it in books or magazines. In the nearby towns, there were no addiction-treatment programs, no community mental-health centers, no Alcoholics Anonymous chapters, no therapists. Left alone with our grievous secret, we had no way of understanding Father's drinking except as an act of will, a deliberate folly or cruelty, a moral weakness, a sin. He drank because he chose to, pure and simple. Why our father, so playful and competent and kind when sober, would choose to ruin himself and punish his family we could not fathom.

26   Our neighborhood was high on the Bible, and the Bible was hard on drunkards. "Woe to those who are heroes at drinking wine and valiant men in mixing strong drink," wrote Isaiah. "The priest and the prophet reel with strong drink, they are confused with wine, they err in vision, they stumble in giving judgment. For all tables are full of vomit, no place is without filthiness." We children had seen those fouled tables at the local truck stop where the notorious boozers hung out, our father occasionally among them. "Wine and new wine take away the understanding," declared the prophet Hosea. We had also seen evidence of that in our father, who could multiply seven-digit numbers in his head when sober but when drunk could not help us with fourth-grade math. Proverbs

warned: "Do not look at wine when it is red, when it sparkles in the cup and goes down smoothly. At the last it bites like a serpent and stings like an adder. Your eyes will see strange things, and your mind utter perverse things." Woe, woe.

Dismayingly often, these biblical drunkards stirred up trouble for 27 their own kids. Noah made fresh wine after the flood, drank too much of it, fell asleep without any clothes on, and was glimpsed in the buff by his son Ham, whom Noah promptly cursed. In one passage—it was so shocking we had to read it under our blankets with flashlights—the patriarch Lot fell down drunk and slept with his daughters. The sins of the fathers set their children's teeth on edge.

Our ministers were fond of quoting St. Paul's pronouncement that 28 drunkards would not inherit the kingdom of God. These grave preachers assured us that the wine referred to in the Last Supper was in fact grape juice. Bible and sermons and hymns combined to give us the impression that Moses should have brought down from the mountain another stone tablet, bearing the Eleventh Commandment: Thou shalt not drink.

The scariest and most illuminating Bible story apropos of drunkards 29 was the one about the lunatic and the swine. We knew it by heart: When Jesus climbed out of his boat one day, this lunatic came charging up from the graveyard, stark naked and filthy, frothing at the mouth, so violent that he broke the strongest chains. Nobody would go near him. Night and day for years, this madman had been wailing among the tombs and bruising himself with stones. Jesus took one look at him and said, "Come out of the man, you unclean spirits!" for he could see that the lunatic was possessed by demons. Meanwhile, some hogs were conveniently rooting nearby. "If we have to come out," begged the demons, "at least let us go into those swine." Jesus agreed, the unclean spirits entered the hogs, and the hogs raced straight off a cliff and plunged into a lake. Hearing the story in Sunday school, my friends thought mainly of the pigs. (How big a splash did they make? Who paid for the lost pork?) But I thought of the redeemed lunatic, who bathed himself and put on clothes and calmly sat at the feet of Jesus, restored—so the Bible said—to "his right mind."

When drunk, our father was clearly in his wrong mind. He became 30 a stranger, as fearful to us as any graveyard lunatic, not quite frothing at the mouth but fierce enough, quick-tempered, explosive; or else he grew maudlin and weepy, which frightened us nearly as much. In my boyhood despair, I reasoned that maybe he wasn't to blame for turning into an ogre: Maybe, like the lunatic, he was possessed by demons.

If my father was indeed possessed, who would exorcise him? If he 31 was a sinner, who would save him? If he was ill, who would cure him? If he suffered, who would ease his pain? Not ministers or doctors, for we could not bring ourselves to confide in them; not the neighbors, for we pretended they had never seen him drunk; not Mother, who fussed and pleaded but could not budge him; not my brother and sister, who were only kids. That left me. It did not matter that I, too, was only a child, and a bewildered one at that. I could not excuse myself.

32   On first reading a description of delirium tremens—in a book on alcoholism I smuggled from a university library—I thought immediately of the frothing lunatic and the frenzied swine. When I read stories or watched films about grisly metamorphoses—Dr. Jekyll and Mr. Hyde, the mild husband changing into a werewolf, the kindly neighbor inhabited by a brutal alien—I could not help but see my own father's mutation from sober to drunk. Even today, knowing better, I am attracted by the demonic theory of drink, for when I recall my father's transformation, the emergence of his ugly second self, I find it easy to believe in being possessed by unclean spirits. We never knew which version of Father would come home from work, the true or the tainted, nor could we guess how far down the slope toward cruelty he would slide.

33   How far a man *could* slide we gauged by observing our backroad neighbors—the out-of-work miners who had dragged their families to our corner of Ohio from the desolate hollows of Appalachia, the tight-fisted farmers, the surly mechanics, the balked and broken men. There was, for example, whiskey-soaked Mr. Jenkins, who beat his wife and kids so hard we could hear their screams from the road. There was Mr. Lavo the wino, who fell asleep smoking time and again, until one

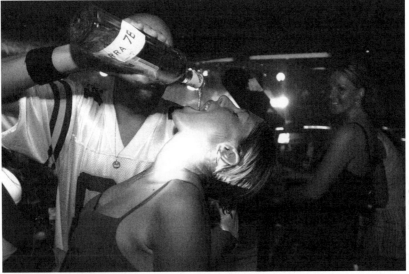

AP Images/Victor R. Caivano

What are the conspicuous features of this photograph? Where does the light fall? Why is the young woman allowing the man to pour liquor into her open mouth instead of drinking it herself? What does the onlooker's smile indicate?

night his disgusted wife bundled up the children and went outside and left him in his easy chair to burn; he awoke on his own, staggered out coughing into the yard, and pounded her flat while the children looked on and the shack turned to ash. There was the truck driver, Mr. Sampson, who tripped over his son's tricycle one night while drunk and got mad, jumped into his semi, and drove away, shifting through the dozen gears, and never came back. We saw the bruised children of these fathers clump onto our school bus, we saw the abandoned children huddle in the pews at church, we saw the stunned and battered mothers begging for help at our doors.

Our own father never beat us, and I don't think he beat Mother, 34 but he threatened often. The Old Testament Yahweh was not more terrible in His rage. Eyes blazing, voice booming, Father would pull out his belt and swear to give us a whipping, but he never followed through, never needed to, because we could imagine it so vividly. He shoved us, pawed us with the back of his hand, not to injure, just to clear a space. I can see him grabbing Mother by the hair as she cowers on a chair during a nightly quarrel. He twists her neck back until she gapes up at him, and then he lifts over her skull a glass quart bottle of milk, and milk spilling down his forearm, and he yells at her, "Say just one more word, one goddamn word, and I'll shut you up!" I fear she will prick him with her sharp tongue, but she is terrified into silence, and so am I, and the leaking bottle quivers in the air, and milk seeps through the red hair of my father's uplifted arm, and the entire scene is there to this moment, the head jerked back, the club raised.

When the drink made him weepy, Father would pack, kiss each 35 of us children on the head, and announce from the front door that he was moving out. "Where to?" we demanded, fearful each time that he would leave for good, as Mr. Sampson had roared away for good in his diesel truck. "Someplace where I won't get hounded every minute," Father would answer, his jaw quivering. He stabbed a look at Mother, who might say, "Don't run into the ditch before you get there," or "Good riddance," and then he would slink away. Mother watched him go with arms crossed over her chest, her face closed like the lid on a box of snakes. We children bawled. Where could he go? To the truck stop, that den of iniquity? To one of those dark, ratty flophouses in town? Would he wind up sleeping under a railroad bridge or on a park bench or in a cardboard box, mummied in rags like the bums we had seen on our trips to Cleveland and Chicago? We bawled and bawled, wondering if he would ever come back.

He always did come back, a day or a week later, but each time there 36 was a sliver less of him.

In Kafka's *Metamorphosis*, which opens famously with Gregor Samsa waking up from uneasy dreams to find himself transformed into an insect, 37

Gregor's family keep reassuring themselves that things will be just fine again "when he comes back to us." Each time alcohol transformed our father we held out the same hope, that he would really and truly come back to us, our authentic father, the tender and playful and competent man, and then all things would be fine. We had grounds for such hope. After his tearful departures and chapfallen returns, he would sometimes go weeks, even months, without drinking. Those were glad times. Every day without the furtive glint of bottles, every meal without a fight, every bedtime without sobs encouraged us to believe that such bliss might go on forever.

38   Mother was fooled by such a hope all during the forty-odd years she knew Greeley Ray Sanders. Soon after she met him in a Chicago delicatessen on the eve of World War II and fell for his butter-melting Mississippi drawl and his wavy red hair, she learned that he drank heavily. But then so did a lot of men. She would soon coax or scold him into breaking the nasty habit. She would point out to him how ugly and foolish it was, this bleary drinking, and then he would quit. He refused to quit during their engagement, however, still refused during the first years of marriage, refused until my older sister came along. The shock of fatherhood sobered him, and he remained sober through my birth at the end of the war and right on through until we moved in 1951 to the Ohio arsenal. The arsenal had more than its share of alcoholics, drug addicts, and other varieties of escape artists. There I turned six and started school and woke into a child's flickering awareness, just in time to see my father begin sneaking swigs in the garage.

39   He sobered up again for most of a year at the height of the Korean War, to celebrate the birth of my brother. But aside from that dry spell, his only breaks from drinking before I graduated from high school were just long enough to raise and then dash our hopes. Then during the fall of my senior year—the time of the Cuban Missile Crisis, when it seemed that the nightly explosions at the munitions dump and the nightly rages in our household might spread to engulf the globe—Father collapsed. His liver, kidneys, and heart all conked out. The doctors saved him, but only by a hair. He stayed in the hospital for weeks, going through a withdrawal so terrible that Mother would not let us visit him. If he wanted to kill himself, the doctors solemnly warned him, all he had to do was hit the bottle again. One binge would finish him.

40   Father must have believed them, for he stayed dry the next fifteen years. It was an answer to prayer, Mother said, it was a miracle. I believe it was a reflex of fear, which he sustained over the years through courage and pride. He knew a man could die from drink, for his brother Roscoe had. We children never laid eyes on doomed Uncle Roscoe, but in the stories Mother told us he became a fairy-tale figure, like a boy who took the wrong turn in the woods and was gobbled up by the wolf.

The fifteen-year dry spell came to an end with Father's retirement   41
in the spring of 1978. Like many men, he gave up his identity along with
his job. One day he was a boss at the factory, with a brass plate on his
door and a reputation to uphold; the next day he was a nobody at home.
He and Mother were leaving Ontario, the last of the many places to
which his job had carried them, and they were moving to a new house in
Mississippi, his childhood stomping ground. As a boy in Mississippi, Father sold Coca-Cola during dances while the moonshiners peddled their
brew in the parking lot; as a young blade, he fought in bars and in the
ring, winning a state Golden Gloves championship; he gambled at poker,
hunted pheasant, raced motorcycles and cars, played semiprofessional
baseball, and, along with all his buddies—in the Black Cat Saloon, behind
the cotton gin, in the woods—he drank hard. It was a perilous youth to
dream of recovering.

After his final day of work, Mother drove on ahead with a car full of   42
begonias and violets, while Father stayed behind to oversee the packing.
When the van was loaded, the sweaty movers broke open a six-pack and
offered him a beer.

"Let's drink to retirement!" they crowed. "Let's drink to freedom! to   43
fishing! hunting! loafing! Let's drink to a guy who's going home!"

At least I imagine some such words, for that is all I can do, imagine,   44
and I see Father's hand trembling in midair as he thinks about the fifteen
sober years and about the doctors' warning, and he tells himself, *God-
damnit, I am a free man,* and *Why can't a free man drink one beer after a lifetime
of hard work?* and I see his arm reaching, his fingers closing, the can tilting to his lips. I even supply a label for the beer, a swaggering brand that
promises on television to deliver the essence of life. I watch the amber
liquid pour down his throat, the alcohol steal into his blood, the key turn
in his brain.

Soon after my parents moved back to Father's treacherous stomping   45
ground, my wife and I visited them in Mississippi with our four-year-old
daughter. Mother had been too distraught to warn me about the return
of the demons. So when I climbed out of the car that bright July morning
and saw my father napping in the hammock, I felt uneasy, and when he
lurched upright and blinked his bloodshot eyes and greeted us in a syr-
upy voice, I was hurled back into childhood.

"What's the matter with Papaw?" our daughter asked.   46

"Nothing," I said. "Nothing!"   47

Like a child again, I pretended not to see him in his stupor, and be-   48
hind my phony smile I grieved. On that visit and on the few that remained
before his death, once again I found bottles in the workbench, bottles in
the woods. Again his hands shook too much for him to run a saw, to make
his precious miniature furniture, to drive straight down back roads. Again
he wound up in the ditch, in the hospital, in jail, in the treatment center.

Again he shouted and wept. Again he lied. "I never touched a drop," he swore. "Your mother's making it up."

49   I no longer fancied I could reason with the men whose names I found on the bottles—Jim Beam, Jack Daniel's—but I was able now to recall the cold statistics about alcoholism: ten million victims, fifteen million, twenty. And yet, in spite of my age, I reacted in the same blind way as I had in childhood, by vainly seeking to erase through my efforts whatever drove him to drink. I worked on their place twelve and sixteen hours a day, in the swelter of Mississippi summers, digging ditches, running electrical wires, planting trees, mowing grass, building sheds, as though what nagged at him was some list of chores, as though by taking his worries upon my shoulders I could redeem him. I was flung back into boyhood, acting as though my father would not drink himself to death if only I were perfect.

50   I failed of perfection; he succeeded in dying. To the end, he considered himself not sick but sinful. "Do you want to kill yourself?" I asked him. "Why not?" he answered. "Why the hell not? What's there to save?" To the end, he would not speak about his feelings, would not or could not give a name to the beast that was devouring him.

51   In silence, he went rushing off to the cliff. Unlike the biblical swine, however, he left behind a few of the demons to haunt his children. Life with him and the loss of him twisted us into shapes that will be familiar to other sons and daughters of alcoholics. My brother became a rebel, my sister retreated into shyness, I played the stalwart and dutiful son who would hold the family together. If my father was unstable, I would be a rock. If he squandered money on drink, I would pinch every penny. If he wept when drunk—and only when drunk—I would not let myself weep at all. If he roared at the Little League umpire for calling my pitches balls, I would throw nothing but strikes. Watching him flounder and rage, I came to dread the loss of control. I would go through life without making anyone mad. I vowed never to put in my mouth or veins any chemical that would banish my everyday self. I would never make a scene, never lash out at the ones I loved, never hurt a soul. Through hard work, relentless work, I would achieve something dazzling—in the classroom, on the basketball court, in the science lab, in the pages of books—and my achievement would distract the world's eyes from his humiliation. I would become a worthy sacrifice, and the smoke of my burning would please God.

52   It is far easier to recognize these twists in my character than to undo them. Work has become an addiction for me, as drink was an addiction for my father. Knowing this, my daughter gave me a placard for the wall: WORKAHOLIC. The labor is endless and futile, for I can no more redeem myself through work than I could redeem my father. I still panic in the face of other people's anger, because his drunken temper was so terrible. I shrink from causing sadness or disappointment even to strangers, as though I were still concealing the family shame. I still notice every twitch

of emotion in those faces around me, having learned as a child to read the weather in faces, and I blame myself for their least pang of unhappiness or anger. In certain moods I blame myself for everything. Guilt burns like acid in my veins.

I am moved to write these pages now because my own son, at the age of ten, is taking on himself the griefs of the world, and in particular the griefs of his father. He tells me that when I am gripped by sadness, he feels responsible; he feels there must be something he can do to spring me from depression, to fix my life and that crushing sense of responsibility is exactly what I felt at the age of ten in the face of my father's drinking. My son wonders if I, too, am possessed. I write, therefore, to drag into the light what eats at me—the fear, the guilt, the shame—so that my own children may be spared. 53

I still shy away from nightclubs, from bars, from parties where the solvent is alcohol. My friends puzzle over this, but it is no more peculiar than for a man to shy away from the lions' den after seeing his father torn apart. I took my own first drink at the age of twenty-one, half a glass of burgundy. I knew the odds of my becoming an alcoholic were four times higher than for the children of nonalcoholic fathers. So I sipped warily. 54

I still do—once a week, perhaps, a glass of wine, a can of beer, nothing stronger, nothing more. I listen for the turning of a key in my brain. 55

Content

1. This essay abounds in examples of alcoholism. Which examples are the most memorable? Are these also the most painful? The most powerful? Explain why.

2. Sanders says that in spite of all his "grown-up knowledge" of alcoholism, "I am still ten years old, my own son's age" (¶ 8) as he writes this essay. What does he mean by this? What kind of a character is Sanders in this essay? What kind of a character is his father? Is there any resemblance between father and son?

Strategies/Structures/Language

3. Is Sanders writing for alcoholic readers? Their families? People unfamiliar with the symptoms of alcoholism? Or is he writing mostly for himself, to try to come to terms with the effects of his father's alcoholism on him then and now?

4. Each section of this essay (¶s 1–8, 9–14, 15–24, 25–31, 32–36, 37–44, 45–52, 53–55) focuses on a different sort of example. What are they, and why are they arranged in this particular order?

5. Why does Sanders wait until late in the essay (¶ 39) to discuss his father's sobriety, and then devote only three paragraphs to a state that lasted fifteen years?

6. What is the tone of this essay? How does Sanders, one of the victims of alcoholism as both a child and an adult, avoid being full of self-pity? Is he angry at his father? How can you tell?

For Writing

7. *Journal Writing.* "Father's drinking became the family secret," says Sanders (¶ 13). Every family has significant secrets. Explain one of your family secrets, illustrating its effects on various family members, particularly on yourself. If you wish to keep the secret, don't show your essay to anyone; the point of writing this is to help yourself understand or come to terms with the matter.

8. Sanders depicts the impact of his father's alcoholism on the family as a personal perspective on a social problem. Define an economic, political, ecological, social, or personal problem (unemployment, waste disposal, AIDS, hunger, housing, racism, or another subject of your choice) so your readers can understand it from an unusual perspective—your own or that of your sources. Illustrate its causes, effects, or implications with several significant examples—perhaps those of a perpetrator or victim.

9. *Dialogues.* In "The Inheritance of Tools" (Chapter 4), Sanders describes how his father shows him how to use force constructively. Compare the images Sanders uses to convey the idea of construction with those he uses in "Under the Influence" to convey the idea of deterioration.

10. *Mixed Modes.* How does Sanders's use of biblical passages that refer to drunkenness (¶s 26–28) illustrate the family's understanding of alcoholism as "an act of will" (¶ 25)? How does the story about Jesus driving the demons from the lunatic (¶ 29) help the reader understand "the fear, the guilt, the shame" the narrator has endured for so long (¶ 53)?

11. *Second Look.* Interpret the photograph in this essay with respect to your own experience of drinking or that of your friends. Collaborate with someone whose experiences are different from yours. What generalizations or conclusions can you draw?

JAMES FALLOWS

James Fallows (born in 1949 in Redlands, California) earned a BA at Harvard and studied economics at Oxford as a Rhodes Scholar (1970–72). His first book, *National Defense*, won the American Book Award in 1981. He is also the author of *Breaking the News: How the Media Undermine American Democracy* (1996), *Blind into Baghdad: America's War in Iraq* (2006) and **Postcards from Tomorrow Square: Reports from China** (2009). An article he wrote in response to the 9/11 attacks, "The Fifty-first State?," won the National Magazine Award. He is also a software designer and instrument-rated pilot. Since 1979 he has served in various editorial capacities at *The Atlantic Monthly*, where he currently writes a technology column, including "Tinfoil Underwear," reprinted here from the March 2006 issue. Here, Fallows describes the way businesses compile personal information on computer users, the difficulties facing users who want to protect that information, and the choices that will increasingly face our online society.

Tinfoil Underwear

How concerned, really, should ordinary computer users be about the evidence we leave behind when we browse, shop, communicate, and amuse ourselves on the Internet? Early this year, as controversy built over the government's warrantless surveillance of telephone and computer messages, I asked a number of technology experts whether they were worried about their own privacy, and what steps, if any, they would recommend to the nonexpert computing public. I found strong agreement among them about the scale and nature of the problem, and a surprising emphasis on the need and the right way to deal with it.

The main thing the experts said they know, and the public probably doesn't, is how completely modern life has shifted to an "on-the-record" basis. You can drop a letter in a mailbox without a return address and still expect to have it delivered. But that is about the only form of untraceable communication left. Most people understand this change to some degree. As long ago as the mid-1980s, a major twist in the plot of Scott Turow's *Presumed Innocent* involved computerized logs of calls made and received. Today a novel could be based on the details preserved in a single credit-card statement.

What most of us might not grasp is just how many activities can now be logged and stored. "To a large extent, we've willingly sacrificed our privacy for the conveniences of the Internet age," says Richard Forno, principal consultant with the information security firm KRvW Associates. OnStar and similar services keep track of locations from which customers make calls. This can be a lifesaver in an emergency, but it also creates a record. Amazon and other online retailers can refine their sense of what we're looking for by analyzing permanent records of past purchases. We avoid the nuisance of reregistering each time we visit favorite sites, notably newspaper sites, by permitting (even if inadvertently) our computers to store "cookies," the small files that are created by the site we've visited and identify us when we return.

"There are three big categories" of possible intrusions into people's online privacy, according to Kevin Bankston, a lawyer with the Electronic Frontier Foundation, or EFF, in San Francisco. These are "what you store on your own computer, what other people are storing about you, and what's actually being captured or overheard in real time, by surveillance."

The first problem—cookies, old files, unfortunate browsing histories, and other potentially compromising data left on a machine—is the easiest for users to control. Nicole Wong, an associate general counsel at

Google, made me burst out laughing with her preposterously wholesome illustration of how awkward situations might arise. "Suppose a husband was shopping online for his wife's birthday present, and he didn't want to spoil the surprise by having her see the sites he had visited—" (When I interjected "Come on!" she replied, "I've been interviewed before.") For instance, Internet Explorer, Firefox, and other major browsers can be set up not to retain cookies, temporary files, or histories of sites visited. This solves the problem, of course, only for family members or others who might want to peruse the contents of your hard drive.

6   Most people I spoke with said that the third problem—the highly publicized threat of eavesdropping by a Big Brotherish state—might bother them as a policy matter, but was not an active personal worry. EFF's Kevin Bankston pointed out that users could go far toward protecting themselves by encrypting their communications with powerful, relatively easily installed utilities like PGP ("Pretty Good Privacy"), a program that sells for $99 and up at pgp.com, and GPG, an open-source counterpart available for free at gnupg.org. "We don't know the [National Security Agency]'s code-breaking capabilities," Bankston said, "but [any sort of encryption] would certainly slow them down."

7   It was the second category—the inexorable pileup of information on a variety of Web sites—that all of the experts identified as the major long-term threat to a user's privacy. "Data is being collected that was never collected before, that should not be collected now, and that cannot be protected in the long run," says Marc Rotenberg, executive director of the Electronic Privacy Information Center, a civil-liberties advocacy group based in Washington. The technical developments that make this possible cannot easily be undone, but the business policies could be.

8   Nearly every interaction in today's digital life is traceable. Cell-phone calls are of course routed to and from particular handsets—actually, to unique Subscriber Identity Modules, or SIM cards, inside the handset, each associated with a particular customer. E-mail messages, Web search requests, music-download orders, and all other signals sent from a computer are marked with the "IP address," or Internet Protocol address, of the machine that sent them. This is a number something like "192.165.1.204" that identifies your particular computer amid the vastness of the Internet. IP addresses differ from phone numbers in many ways: some are permanently assigned to a given machine, some are reassigned session by session, some are shared on local networks. But in the end, their function is similar. They let other people reach you, and tell others who is trying to reach them.

9   Every query you send to Google contains both the terms you're looking for and the IP address of your machine. Every site you visit can register the fact that someone from your IP address was there. (You can delete the cookies placed by ViolentOverthrowOfTheGovernment.org on your machine; you can't do anything about the site's own logs.) Every

time you choose a story to read on an online news site the story you read, and your IP address, can be recorded in the site's log. Every blog posting or comment, every email sent even under a fictitious account name, every item bid on through eBay or bought from an online merchant, every request for a map to be downloaded or a picture viewed—they all carry an IP address.

Like a phone number, an IP address is merely digits, without a 10 person's name attached. But the connection between IP addresses and real people is almost as close as with telephone accounts. Anyone who pays for home Internet service, whether cable, DSL, or humble dial-up, has been assigned an IP address by a company that also knows the customer's name. Most for-pay WiFi hot spots also require customers to create accounts with a real name and billing address. You can still go online without revealing your identity, if you're willing to live like a fugitive: paying cash to use Internet cafés, sticking strictly to free, public WiFi spots, libraries, or schools. But for most people this is a chore.

The main privacy concerns about IP addresses stem from one busi- 11 ness decision: the companies that collect and own the information traceable to them have decided to retain it more or less forever.

Why would Google, which receives hundreds of millions of search 12 requests per day, warehouse every one of them, with IP address attached? Because it can. Disk storage has become essentially free. Also it wants to, because for Google and most other online firms, real-world transaction data is the most precious form of market intelligence. Nicole Wong, of Google, gave me the standard reasons why this ever-expanding hoard of data is best for the company and for its users as well. It may be retained to help firms investigate and remedy "click fraud," or invalid clicks on advertisements, in which it matters (for reasons not worth going into here) how many requests come from each unique address. It helps show the "geolocation" of all requests, "which lets us address a number of issues at a geographic level, such as where there might be too much latency [slowness in Google's response to a query], for example, in Africa."

The real reason, for firms from Google and Yahoo to Amazon, eBay, 13 and Expedia, is that they are all in an endless struggle to entice more people to spend more time on their sites, so they can sell more advertising. This whole effort, they believe, depends crucially on their ability to "personalize" their services. "The information about you is gold, and it's used for ever more perfect marketing to you," Kevin Bankston told me. "Nothing will change that unless there is a law to force them to stop."

For users, "the fear is Panopticon," says Lawrence Lessig, of Stan- 14 ford Law School, referring to the unseen but all-seeing observer in a prison watchtower once proposed by Jeremy Bentham. "The critical point to recognize is that there simply is no such thing as anonymity on the Internet. That is not because of its technical architecture. It is because of the business model of these companies, which depends on gathering and storing as much data about the customer as you possibly can."

15   What's the potential harm? Every person I spoke with gave an example. A few were political, but most concerned the drawbacks of life in which everyone is on the record, all the time. A spouse in a divorce case might ask for Web-browsing histories to show the other spouse's peccadilloes or peculiar interests. Vetting applicants for jobs—or nominees for official positions—could become even more intrusive than it is already, and even less forgiving of adventure or eccentricity, in an extension of today's "just Google him" effect.

16   No one suggests that an online firm will deliberately disgorge everything it knows about you. Technically, Google could list every IP address that has ever launched a search for "underaged hotties" or "how to make a bomb." Commercially, that would be suicide. Since the Googles and Yahoos need users' trust in order to keep getting data, they, like banks or credit-card companies, have a strong incentive to compete on trustworthiness. But the long-run fear is that as unprecedented amounts of personal information pile up, all of it linked by IP addresses, more will ultimately be used.

17   So what are we supposed to do about it? The answers I got covered a very wide range, with one area of consensus that made me think differently about how hard individual users should—or should not—try to protect their own secrets.

18   At one extreme is the approach that Richard Forno describes as "wearing tinfoil underwear." Marvelous tools of disguise exist, starting with encryption software for e-mail. Perhaps the most powerful one, called Tor, can be found at the Electronic Frontier Foundation Web site, tor.eff.org. Originally funded by the Navy, the system effectively conceals a user's IP address by bouncing every Web query among routers around the world, making it harder to trace back to its origin. Tor is free but somewhat tricky to install (I have succeeded, but it took time), and it slows Web response time noticeably. I would use it only if I were working on a project I really wanted to keep under cover.

19   There are other, more modest protective measures. Politicians and CEOs should think twice about doing anything they wouldn't want to see on the front page of a newspaper. Everyone else should think twice before sending e-mail they would not want to see broadly forwarded. (I get and send more e-mail than ever for routine business, but stick to the phone or meetings for anything sensitive.) To keep your computer from piling up data you'd rather not have it store, you can configure your Web browser to reject all cookies, or to ask you before it accepts any. (In IE, you find this via Tools/Internet Settings/Privacy. In Firefox, via Tools/Options/Privacy/Cookies.) Doing without cookies means not being able to use some sites or services at all, for instance Gmail, plus manually logging into other sites every single time. A more moderate step is to have the browser accept cookies but purge them whenever you close the browser.

On the other extreme is the approach Lawrence Lessig takes. "I don't   20
do anything" about privacy, he says. "I think there is no way to hide. I just
live life thinking everything is in the open." Esther Dyson, of CNET, says
something similar. "The short answer is: Nothing," she replied by e-mail
when I asked what concealing steps she takes. "For a while I tried flag-
ging every cookie I got, just for fun, but I let them all go through anyway,
so eventually I stopped."

Mitchell Kapor, the founder of Lotus, who now directs the Open   21
Source Applications Foundation, does take a few protective measures.
When using an Internet café, he doesn't log on to PayPal, his credit-card
account, or any other site that involves his finances, just in case some
keystroke-capture program has been installed. He wasn't comfortable
using Gmail as one of his personal e-mail accounts until he grilled Google
officials and determined that they "took privacy and security seriously
when they store mail." Kapor said that what changed his mind was
evidence that Google understands how important a reputation for guarding privacy is to the company's prospects. "They do take steps," he told
me, "to make sure that Google employees don't just satisfy their curiosity
by looking at people's e-mail, as well as making sure that if you delete the
account, they clobber all copies everywhere, including the backups."

Between these alternatives—the hypercautious approach of encod-   22
ing all e-mail and the fatalistic belief that Big Brother will see everything
anyway—lay the surprise in what I heard from these informants. This
was the idea that legislation—the intrusion of the stodgy old pre-digital
government—offers modern computer users their best hope.

"When your choices are the tinfoil or doing nothing, that's not   23
right," Lessig says. "I would rather think about how we could actually
increase privacy without giving up the versatility of the Internet."

For instance, a future law might require Google and other companies to   24
strip specific IP addresses from records of searching or browsing activity that they intended to store for more than a brief period. This would
be a balancing act similar to the creation of the "do-not-call" list for tele-
marketers. It would preserve the legitimate commercial value of aggregate data about Internet use, while protecting individuals if the records
were dredged up in legal proceedings—or simply lost, stolen, or exposed
through negligence or incompetence. TiVo already applies such a policy.
It keeps records of aggregate viewing patterns, which is how it knows
that the Janet Jackson breast exposure, from the 2004 Super Bowl, is the
most replayed event in TiVo history—but it removes all evidence of which
specific customers have viewed or replayed which shows.

Nicole Wong unsurprisingly rejects the idea of controls on her own com-   25
pany. But she also suggests that the real privacy firewall, or at least wall,
will be built through legislation, rather than ever warier behavior by

individual users or more restraint by companies. "I don't think that the fix for user privacy is companies providing less service," she told me. "At the systemic level, the solution is to limit what personal data the government can ask for"—and by extension to limit what information banks, potential employers, divorcing spouses, and other potential snoops can find out.

26   "This is a big, macro public-policy issue about the design of our infrastructure," Marc Rotenberg, of EPIC, says. "It involves payment systems, communications networks, identification, transportation toll design. It's not something that will be solved by 'privacy survivalism'— anonymizers, dark glasses, people paying for everything in cash. Collective problems require collective solutions."

27   I feel worse than I did when I started this project, because I've realized how fully exposed my whole life is. I feel better when I think that companies could be required to purge data every so often, or to store data in a way that makes it hard to link one person's name and IP address to the details of what he or she has done online. Then I remember that Congress would need to concentrate long enough to enact this change in a thoughtful, far-reaching way with minimal glitches, and I really start worrying.

Content

1. Why, according to Fallows, should individuals be concerned about privacy on the Internet? What types of information about an individual can others access? Which type of traceable information poses the greatest threat to privacy?

2. With the technology Fallows describes, what can Internet users do to protect their privacy?

3. Why do businesses collect and store transaction data from the Internet? How does data collection help users? How else might data collection be utilized?

4. Why might legislation be needed to protect users' privacy? According to Fallows, how might such legislation work? What are the alternatives to government regulation of data on the Internet?

Strategies/Structures/Language

5. Fallows elicits the reader's interest in his thesis by beginning his essay with a question: "How concerned, really, should ordinary computer users be about the evidence we leave behind when we browse, shop, communicate, and amuse ourselves on the Internet?" (¶ 1). Is this effective? How does his inclusion of the word "really" modify the meaning of the question?

6. Fallows uses his interview with Nicole Wong of Google three times in his article. How does each of these instances, including his quotes of Wong, support his argument?

For Writing

7. *Journal Writing.* Does the idea that there is no anonymity on the Internet and that your email, searches, downloads, and other activities are logged and stored worry you? Or, do you take the position that "there is no way to hide" (¶ 20)?

8. *Dialogues.* Sherry Turkle, in "How Computers Change the Way We Think" (Chapter 2), argues that contemporary college students are not interested in electronic surveillance and violations of privacy (¶ 10–11). Do you agree with Turkle that our society should promote "information-technology literacy" (¶ 29)? Is such literacy necessary in order to have a public debate on government regulations on data collection and storage?

9. *Mixed Modes.* Why does Fallows include in this article his own process of investigation of the privacy issues involved in data collection? Identify when he uses himself as a source that supports his argument, such as when he claims to have installed encryption software for email (¶ 18). Explain how this strategy engages the reader and effectively illustrates the dangers and difficulties the Internet presents to users. Why does Fallows end his article on a skeptical note?

10. If you (or someone you know well) have ever experienced identity theft or theft of credit card numbers or other personal information, describe your experiences. What, if anything, could have been done to prevent this? Are there measures that can be taken to prevent such theft in the future?

11. Present your conclusions for question 10 in a ten-step list, "How to Avoid Identity Theft." Discuss these with a partner to make sure they are clear and, presumably, efficient and effective.

CLIMATE CHANGE

WILLIAM COLLINS, ROBERT COLMAN, JAMES HAYWOOD, MARTIN R. MANNING, AND PHILIP MOTE

These authors were members of Working Group I of the Inter-governmental Panel on Climate Change (IPCC), which in 2007 presented the "fourth in a series of assessments of the state of knowledge" on climate change, "written and reviewed by hundreds of scientists worldwide." William Collins is a professor in the Department of Earth and Planetary Science at the University of California, Berkeley, and a senior scientist at Lawrence Berkeley National Laboratory and the National Center for Atmospheric Research in Boulder, Colorado. Robert Colman is a senior research scientist in the Climate Dynamics Group at the Australian Bureau of Meteorology Research Center in Melbourne. James Haywood is the manager of aerosol research in the Observational Based Research Group and the Chemistry, Climate, and Ecosystem Group at the Met Office in Exeter, England. Martin R. Manning is director of the IPCC WG I Support Unit at the National Oceanic and Atmospheric Administration Earth System Research Laboratory in Boulder, Colorado. Philip Mote is the climatologist of the state of Washington, and a research scientist in the Climate Impacts Group at the University of Washington.

These scientists coauthored both the longer report identified above and the analysis of "The Physical Science behind Climate Change," reprinted here from *Scientific American* (2007). They address critical issues relating to the fundamental question, "Are human activities primarily responsible for observed climate changes or might these be the result of some other cause?" and the implications of the fact that there is a 90% probability that humans are causing the problems.

The Physical Science behind Climate Change

1   For a scientist studying climate change, "eureka" moments are unusually rare. Instead progress is generally made by a painstaking piecing together of evidence from every new temperature measurement, satellite sounding or climate-model experiment. Data get checked and rechecked, ideas tested over and over again. Do the observations fit the predicted changes? Could there be some alternative explanation? Good climate scientists, like all good scientists, want to ensure that the highest standards of proof apply to everything they discover.

2   And the evidence of change *has* mounted as climate records have grown longer, as our understanding of the climate system has improved and as climate models have become ever more reliable. Over the past 20 years, evidence that humans are affecting the climate has accumulated inexorably, and with it has come ever greater certainty across the scientific community in the reality of recent climate change and the potential for much greater change in the future. This increased certainty is starkly reflected in the latest report of the Intergovernmental Panel on Climate Change (IPCC), the fourth in a series of assessments of the state of knowledge on the topic, written and reviewed by hundreds of scientists worldwide.

3   The panel released a condensed version of the first part of the report, on the physical science basis of climate change, in February. Called the "Summary for Policymakers," it delivered to policymakers and ordinary people alike an unambiguous message: scientists are more confident than ever that humans have interfered with the climate and that further human-induced climate change is on the way. Although the report finds that some of these further changes are now inevitable, its analysis also confirms that the future, particularly in the longer term, remains largely in our hands—the magnitude of expected change depends on what humans choose to do about greenhouse gas emissions.

Jargon Buster

RADIATIVE FORCING . . . is the change in the energy balance of the earth from preindustrial times to the present.

LONG-LIVED GREENHOUSE GASES include carbon dioxide, methane, nitrous oxide and halocarbons. The observed increases in these gases are the result of human activity.

OZONE is a gas that occurs both in the earth's upper atmosphere and at ground level. At ground level ozone is an air pollutant. In the upper atmosphere, an ozone layer protects life on the earth from the sun's harmful ultraviolet rays.

SURFACE ALBEDO is the reflectivity of the earth's surface: a lighter surface, such as snow cover, reflects more solar radiation than a darker surface does.

AEROSOLS are airborne particles that come from both natural (dust storms, forest fires, volcanic eruptions) and man-made sources, such as the burning of fossil fuels.

CONTRAILS, or vapor trails, are condensation trails and artificial clouds made by the exhaust of aircraft engines.

TROPOSPHERE is the layer of the atmosphere close to the earth. It rises from sea level up to about 12 kilometers (7.5 miles).

STRATOSPHERE lies just above the troposphere and extends upward about 50 kilometers.

The physical science assessment focuses on four topics: drivers of 4 climate change, changes observed in the climate system, understanding cause-and-effect relationships, and projection of future changes. Important advances in research into all these areas have occurred since the IPCC assessment in 2001. In the pages that follow, we lay out the key findings that document the extent of change and that point to the unavoidable conclusion that human activity is driving it.

Drivers of Climate Change

Atmospheric concentrations of many gases—primarily carbon dioxide, 5 methane, nitrous oxide and halocarbons (gases once used widely as refrigerants and spray propellants)—have increased because of human activities. Such gases trap thermal energy (heat) within the atmosphere by means of the well-known greenhouse effect, leading to global warming. The atmospheric concentrations of carbon dioxide, methane and nitrous oxide remained roughly stable for nearly 10,000 years, before the abrupt and rapidly accelerating increases of the past 200 years [*see right illustrations in box on page 202*].

Growth rates for concentrations of carbon dioxide have been faster in the past 10 years than over any 10-year period since continuous atmospheric monitoring began in the 1950s, with concentrations now roughly 35 percent above preindustrial levels (which can be determined from air bubbles trapped in ice cores). Methane levels are roughly two and a half times preindustrial levels, and nitrous oxide levels are around 20 percent higher.

6   How can we be sure that humans are responsible for these increases? Some greenhouse gases (most of the halocarbons, for example) have no natural source. For other gases, two important observations demonstrate human influence. First, the geographic differences in concentrations reveal that sources occur predominantly over land in the more heavily populated Northern Hemisphere. Second, analysis of isotopes, which can distinguish among sources of emissions, demonstrates that the majority of the increase in carbon dioxide comes from combustion of fossil fuels (coal, oil and natural gas). Methane and nitrous oxide increase derive from agricultural practices and the burning of fossil fuels.

7   Climate scientists use a concept called radiative forcing to quantify the effect of these increased concentrations on climate. Radiative forcing is the change that is caused in the global energy balance of the earth relative to preindustrial times. (Forcing is usually expressed as watts per square meter.) A positive forcing induces warming; a negative forcing induces cooling. We can determine the radiative forcing associated with

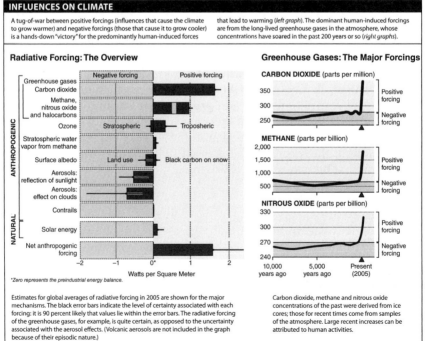

INFLUENCES ON CLIMATE

A tug-of-war between positive forcings (influences that cause the climate to grow warmer) and negative forcings (those that cause it to grow cooler) is a hands-down "victory" for the predominantly human-induced forces that lead to warming (*left graph*). The dominant human-induced forcings are from the long-lived greenhouse gases in the atmosphere, whose concentrations have soared in the past 200 years or so (*right graphs*).

Radiative Forcing: The Overview

*Zero represents the preindustrial energy balance.

Watts per Square Meter

Greenhouse Gases: The Major Forcings

CARBON DIOXIDE (parts per million)

METHANE (parts per billion)

NITROUS OXIDE (parts per billion)

Estimates for global averages of radiative forcing in 2005 are shown for the major mechanisms. The black error bars indicate the level of certainty associated with each forcing: it is 90 percent likely that values lie within the error bars. The radiative forcing of the greenhouse gases, for example, is quite certain, as opposed to the uncertainty associated with the aerosol effects. (Volcanic aerosols are not included in the graph because of their episodic nature.)

Carbon dioxide, methane and nitrous oxide concentrations of the past were derived from ice cores; those for recent times come from samples of the atmosphere. Large recent increases can be attributed to human activities.

Daniela Naomi Molnar

the long-lived greenhouse gases fairly precisely, because we know their atmospheric concentrations, their spatial distribution and the physics of their interaction with radiation.

Climate change is not driven just by increased greenhouse gas concentrations; other mechanisms—both natural and human-induced—also play a part. Natural drivers include changes in solar activity and large volcanic eruptions. The report identifies several additional significant human-induced forcing mechanisms—microscopic particles called aerosols, stratospheric and tropospheric ozone, surface albedo (reflectivity) and aircraft contrails—although the influences of these mechanisms are much less certain than those of greenhouse gases [*see left illustrations in box on page 202*]. 8

Investigators are least certain of the climatic influence of something called the aerosol cloud albedo effect, in which aerosols from human origins interact with clouds in complex ways and make the clouds brighter, reflecting sunlight back to space. Another source of uncertainty comes from the direct effect of aerosols from human origins: How much do they reflect and absorb sunlight directly as particles? Overall these aerosol effects promote cooling that could offset the warming effect of long-lived greenhouse gases to some extent. But by how much? Could it overwhelm the warming? Among the advances achieved since the 2001 IPCC report is that scientists have quantified the uncertainties associated with each individual forcing mechanism through a combination of many modeling and observational studies. Consequently, we can now confidently estimate the total human-induced component. Our best estimate is some 10 times larger than the best estimate of the natural radiative forcing caused by changes in solar activity. 9

This increased certainty of a net positive radiative forcing fits well with the observational evidence of warming discussed next. These forcings can be visualized as a tug-of-war, with positive forcings pulling the earth to a warmer climate and negative ones pulling it to a cooler state. The result is a no contest; we know the strength of the competitors better than ever before. The earth is being pulled to a warmer climate and will be pulled increasingly in this direction as the "anchorman" of greenhouse warming continues to grow stronger and stronger. 10

Observed Climate Changes

The many new or improved observational data sets that became available in time for the 2007 IPCC report allowed a more comprehensive assessment of changes than was possible in earlier reports. Observational records indicate that 11 of the past 12 years are the warmest since reliable records began around 1850. The odds of such warm years happening in sequence purely by chance are exceedingly small. Changes in three important quantities—global temperature, sea level and snow cover in the Northern Hemisphere [*see box on 206*]—all show evidence of warming, although the details vary. The previous IPCC assessment reported a warming trend of 11

0.6 ± 0.2 degree Celsius over the period 1901 to 2000. Because of the strong recent warming, the updated trend over 1906 to 2005 is now 0.74 ± 0.18 degree C. Note that the 1956 to 2005 trend alone is 0.65 ± 0.15 degree C, emphasizing that the majority of 20th-century warming occurred in the past 50 years. The climate, of course, continues to vary around the increased averages, and extremes have changed consistently with these averages—frost days and cold days and nights have become less common, while heat waves and warm days and nights have become more common.

12   The properties of the climate system include not just familiar concepts of averages of temperature, precipitation, and so on but also the state of the ocean and the cryosphere (sea ice, the great ice sheets in Greenland and Antarctica, glaciers, snow, frozen ground, and ice on lakes and rivers). Complex interactions among different parts of the climate system are a fundamental part of climate change—for example, reduction in sea ice increases the absorption of heat by the ocean and the heat flow between the ocean and the atmosphere, which can also affect cloudiness and precipitation.

13   A large number of additional observations are broadly consistent with the observed warming and reflect a flow of heat from the atmosphere into other components of the climate system. Spring snow cover, which decreases in concert with rising spring temperatures in northern midlatitudes, dropped abruptly around 1988 and has remained low since. This drop is of concern because snow cover is important to soil moisture and water resources in many regions.

14   In the ocean, we clearly see warming trends, which decrease with depth, as expected. These changes indicate that the ocean has absorbed more than 80 percent of the heat added to the climate system: this heating is a major contributor to sea-level rise. Sea level rises because water expands as it is warmed and because water from melting glaciers and ice sheets is added to the oceans. Since 1993 satellite observations have permitted more precise calculations of global sea-level rise, now estimated to be 3.1 ± 0.7 millimeters per year over the period 1993 to 2003. Some previous decades displayed similarly fast rates, and longer satellite records will be needed to determine unambiguously whether sea-level rise is accelerating. Substantial reductions in the extent of Arctic sea ice since 1978 (2.7 ± 0.6 percent per decade in the annual average, 7.4 ± 2.4 percent per decade for summer), increases in permafrost temperatures and reductions in glacial extent globally and in Greenland and Antarctic ice sheets have also been observed in recent decades. Unfortunately, many of these quantities were not well monitored until recent decades, so the starting points of their records vary.

15   Hydrological changes are broadly consistent with warming as well. Water vapor is the strongest greenhouse gas; unlike other greenhouse gases, it is controlled principally by temperature. It has generally increased since at least the 1980s. Precipitation is very variable locally but has increased in several large regions of the world, including eastern North and South America, northern Europe, and northern and central

Asia. Drying has been observed in the Sahel, the Mediterranean, southern Africa and parts of southern Asia. Ocean salinity can act as a massive rain gauge. Near-surface waters of the oceans have generally freshened in middle and high latitudes, while they have become saltier in lower latitudes, consistent with changes in large-scale patterns of precipitation.

Reconstructions of past climate—paleoclimate—from tree rings and   16
other proxies provide important additional insights into the workings of the climate system with and without human influence. They indicate that the warmth of the past half a century is unusual in at least the previous 1,300 years. The warmest period between A.D. 700 and 1950 was probably A.D. 950 to 1100, which was several tenths of a degree C cooler than the average temperature since 1980.

Attribution of Observed Changes

Although confidence is high both that human activities have caused a pos-   17
itive radiative forcing and that the climate has actually changed, can we confidently link the two? This is the question of attribution: Are human activities primarily responsible for observed climate changes, or is it possible they result from some other cause, such as some natural forcing or simply spontaneous variability within the climate system? The 2001 IPCC report concluded it was *likely* (more than 66 percent probable) that most of the warming since the mid-20th century was attributable to humans. The 2007 report goes significantly further, upping this to *very likely* (more than 90 percent probable).

The source of the extra confidence comes from a multitude of   18
separate advances. For a start, observational records are now roughly five years longer, and the global temperature increase over this period has been largely consistent with IPCC projections of greenhouse gas–driven warming made in previous reports dating back to 1990. In addition, changes in more aspects of the climate have been considered, such as those in atmospheric circulation or in temperatures within the ocean. Such changes paint a consistent and now broadened picture of human intervention. Climate models, which are central to attribution studies, have also improved and are able to represent the current climate and that of the recent past with considerable fidelity. Finally, some important apparent inconsistencies noted in the observational record have been largely resolved since the last report.

The most important of these was an apparent mismatch between   19
the instrumental surface temperature record (which showed significant warming over recent decades, consistent with a human impact) and the balloon and satellite atmospheric records (which showed little of the expected warming). Several new studies of the satellite and balloon data have now largely resolved this discrepancy—with consistent warming found at the surface and in the atmosphere.

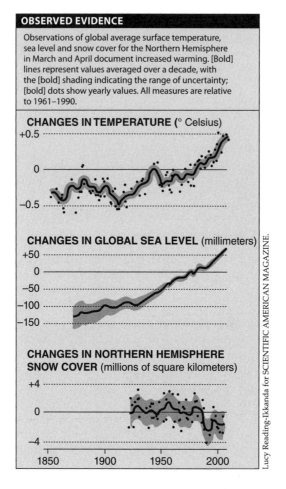

OBSERVED EVIDENCE

Observations of global average surface temperature, sea level and snow cover for the Northern Hemisphere in March and April document increased warming. [Bold] lines represent values averaged over a decade, with the [bold] shading indicating the range of uncertainty; [bold] dots show yearly values. All measures are relative to 1961–1990.

CHANGES IN TEMPERATURE (° Celsius)

CHANGES IN GLOBAL SEA LEVEL (millimeters)

CHANGES IN NORTHERN HEMISPHERE SNOW COVER (millions of square kilometers)

Lucy Reading-Ikkanda for SCIENTIFIC AMERICAN MAGAZINE.

20   An experiment with the real world that duplicated the climate of the 20th century with constant (rather than increasing) greenhouse gases would be the ideal way to test for the cause of climate change, but such an experiment is of course impossible. So scientists do the next best thing: they simulate the past with climate models.

21   Two important advances since the last IPCC assessment have increased confidence in the use of models for both attribution and projection of climate changes. The first is the development of a comprehensive, closely coordinated ensemble of simulations from 18 modeling groups around the world for the historical and future evolution of the earth's climate. Using many models helps to quantify the effects of uncertainties in various climate processes on the range of model simulations. Although some processes are well understood and well represented by physical equations (the flow of the atmosphere and ocean or the propagation of sunlight and heat, for example), some of the most critical components of the climate system are less well understood, such as clouds, ocean

eddies and transpiration by vegetation. Modelers approximate these components using simplified representations called parameterizations. The principal reason to develop a multimodel ensemble for the IPCC assessments is to understand how this lack of certainty affects attribution and prediction of climate change. The ensemble for the latest assessment is unprecedented in the number of models and experiments performed.

The second advance is the incorporation of more realistic representations of climate processes in the models. These processes include the behavior of atmospheric aerosols, the dynamics (movement) of sea ice, and the exchange of water and energy between the land and the atmosphere. More models now include the major types of aerosols and the interactions between aerosols and clouds. [22]

When scientists use climate models for attribution studies, they first run simulations with estimates of only "natural" climate influences over the past 100 years, such as changes in solar output and major volcanic eruptions. They then run models that include human-induced increases in greenhouse gases and aerosols. The results of such experiments are striking. Models using only natural forcings are unable to explain the observed global warming since the mid-20th century, whereas they can do so when they include anthropogenic factors in addition to natural ones. Large-scale *patterns* of temperature change are also most consistent between models and observations when all forcings are included. [23]

Two patterns provide a fingerprint of human influence. The first is greater warming over land than ocean and greater warming at the surface of the sea than in the deeper layers. This pattern is consistent with greenhouse gas–induced warming by the overlying atmosphere: the ocean warms more slowly because of its large thermal inertia. The warming also indicates that a large amount of heat is being taken up by the ocean, demonstrating that the planet's energy budget has been pushed out of balance. A second pattern of change is that while the troposphere (the lower region of the atmosphere) has warmed, the stratosphere, just above it, has cooled. If solar changes provided the dominant forcing, warming would be expected in both atmospheric layers. The observed contrast, however, is just that expected from the combination of greenhouse gas increases and stratospheric ozone decreases. This collective evidence, when subjected to careful statistical analyses, provides much of the basis for the increased confidence that human influences are behind the observed global warming. Suggestions that cosmic rays could affect clouds, and thereby climate, have been based on correlations using limited records; they have generally not stood up when tested with additional data, and their physical mechanisms remain speculative. [24]

What about at smaller scales? As spatial and temporal scales decrease, attribution of climate change becomes more difficult. This problem arises because natural small-scale temperature variations are less "averaged out" and thus more readily mask the change signal. Nevertheless, continued warming means the signal is emerging on smaller scales. The report has [25]

FACING OUR FUTURE . . .

The Consequences of Ongoing Warming

Global warming is real and, as Working Group I of the IPCC stated in its January–February 2007 report, "very likely" to be largely the result of human activities for at least the past half a century. But is that warming significant enough to pose real problems? That determination fell to Working Group II, a similarly international assembly of scientists who focused on the vulnerability of natural and human environments to climate change.

In the April 2007 summary of its findings, Working Group II concluded that human-induced warming over the past three and a half decades has indeed had a discernible influence on many physical and biological systems. Observational evidence from all continents and most oceans shows that many natural systems are being affected by regional climate changes, particularly temperature increases. The ground in permafrost regions is becoming increasingly unstable, rock avalanches in mountainous areas are more frequent, trees are coming into leaf earlier, and some animals and plants are moving to higher latitudes or elevations.

Looking to the future, the group also projected that ongoing shifts in climate would affect the health and welfare of millions of people around the world. The severity of the effects would depend on precisely how much warming occurred. Among the most probable consequences:

- More frequent heat waves, droughts, fires, coastal flooding and storms will raise the toll of deaths, injuries and related diseases.
- Some infectious diseases, such as malaria, will spread to new regions.
- High concentrations of ground-level ozone will exacerbate heart and respiratory ailments.
- By the 2080s, rising sea levels will flood the homes and property of millions of people, especially in the large deltas

of Asia and Africa and on small islands.

The harm from these changes will be most severe for impoverished communities. The poor are generally more dependent on climate-sensitive resources such as local water and food, and by definition their adaptive capacities are economically limited.

The effects of global warming would not be universally bad, particularly for the next few decades. For example, whereas higher temperatures would hurt the growth of important cereals in equatorial nations fairly quickly, they would for a time raise productivity on farms in mid- to high-latitude countries, such as the U.S. But once the temperature increase exceeded three degrees Celsius (5.4 degrees Fahrenheit), agricultural declines would set in even there, barring widespread adaptive changes.

What Needs to be Done

The human race can respond to climate change in two ways: adaptation and mitigation. Adaptation means learning how to survive and prosper in a warmer world. Mitigation means limiting the extent of future warming by reducing the net release of greenhouse gases to the atmosphere. Given that rising temperatures are already encroaching on us and that an unstopped increase would be overwhelming, a strong combination of both adaptation and mitigation will be essential. Unfortunately, disagreements over the feasibility, costs and necessity of mitigation have notoriously bogged down global responses to date.

To project mitigation strategies for the looming problems—and their costs—Working Group III of the IPCC considered various estimates of economic expansion, population growth and fossil-fuel use for its 2007 report. The six resulting scenarios predict atmospheric concentrations of carbon dioxide equivalents (that is, greenhouse gases and aerosols equivalent to carbon dioxide) ranging from 445 parts per million to 1,130 ppm, with corresponding increases in temperatures from 2.0 to as much as 6.1 degrees C (approximately 3.6 to 11 degrees F) over preindustrial levels. To keep the temperature increase to the lowest of those projections, the group estimates that the world must stabilize atmospheric greenhouse gases at 445 ppm by 2015. (Current concentrations are approaching 400 ppm.) The scientists believe that any higher temperatures might trigger severe flooding in some places and severe drought in others, wipe out species and cause economic havoc.

The group's report looks in detail at the most promising technologies and policies for holding the

Central and South America
- Gradual replacement of tropical forest by savanna in eastern Amazonia
- Replacement of semiarid vegetation by arid-land vegetation
- Species extinctions in many tropical areas
- Reduced water availability
- Loss of arable land in drier areas
- Decreased yields of some important crops
- Reduced livestock productivity

gases at 445 ppm. It emphasizes the importance of improving energy efficiency in buildings and vehicles, shifting to renewable energy sources and saving forests as "carbon sinks." Policies include setting a target for global emissions, emissions trading schemes, caps, taxes and incentives.

But the IPCC scientists made their assessment before a study published online this past April in the *Proceedings of the National Academy of Sciences USA* reported that worldwide carbon dioxide emissions between 2000 and 2004 increased at three times the rate of the 1990s—from 1.1 to 3.2 percent a year. In other words, the actual global emissions since 2000 grew faster than those projected in the highest of the scenarios developed by the IPCC. That research indicates that the situation is more dire than even the bleak IPCC assessment forecasts.

The Regional Picture

The lists here indicate just some of the disturbing effects, beyond those enumerated in the discussion at the left, that Working Group II foresees in various parts of the world over the coming century. The group made most of these predictions with high or very high confidence. Find more details at www.ucar.edu/news/features/climatechange/regionalimpacts.jsp and at the IPCC Web site (www.ipcc.ch).

North America
- In the western mountains, decreased snowpack, more winter flooding and reduced summer flows
- An extended period of high fire risk and large increases in area burned
- Increased intensity, duration and number of heat waves in cities historically prone to them
- In coastal areas, increased stress on people and property as climate interacts with development and pollution

Europe
- Increased risk of inland flash floods
- In the south, more health-threatening heat waves and wildfires, reduced water availability and hydropower potential, endangered crop production and reduced summer tourism
- In the central and eastern areas, more health-threatening heat waves and peatland fires and reduced summer rainfall and forest productivity
- In the north, negative impacts eventually outweigh such initial benefits as reduced heating demand and increased crop yields and forest growth

Asia
- Increased flooding, rock avalanches and water resource disruptions as Himalayan glaciers melt
- Ongoing risk of hunger in several developing regions because of crop productivity declines combined with rapid population growth and urbanization

Australia and New Zealand
- Intensified water security problems in southern and eastern Australia and parts of New Zealand by 2030
- Further loss of biodiversity in ecologically rich sites by 2020
- Increased storm severity and frequency in several places

Small islands
- Threats to vital infrastructure, settlements and facilities because of sea-level rise
- Reduced water resources in many places by midcentury
- Beach erosion, coral bleaching and other deteriorating coastal conditions, leading to harmed fisheries and reduced value as tourist destinations
- Invasion by nonnative species, especially on mid- and high-latitude islands

Polar regions
- Thinning and shrinking of glaciers and ice sheets
- Changes in the extent of Arctic sea ice and permafrost
- Deeper seasonal thawing of permafrost

Africa
- Decreased water availability by 2020 for 75 million to 250 million people
- Loss of arable land, reduced growing seasons and reduced yields in some areas
- Decreased fish stocks in large lakes

Daniela Naomi Molnar

found that human activity is likely to have influenced temperature significantly down to the continental scale for all continents except Antarctica.

26   Human influence is discernible also in some extreme events such as unusually hot and cold nights and the incidence of heat waves. This does not mean, of course, that individual extreme events (such as the 2003 European heat wave) can be said to be simply "caused" by human-induced climate change—usually such events are complex, with many causes. But it does mean that human activities have, more likely than not, affected the *chances* of such events occurring.

Projections of Future Changes

27 How will climate change over the 21st century? This critical question is addressed using simulations from climate models based on projections of future emissions of greenhouse gases and aerosols. The simulations suggest that, for greenhouse gas emissions at or above current rates, changes in climate will very likely be larger than the changes already observed during the 20th century. Even if emissions were immediately reduced enough to stabilize greenhouse gas concentrations at current levels, climate change would continue for centuries. This inertia in the climate results from a combination of factors. They include the heat capacity of the world's oceans and the millennial timescales needed for the circulation to mix heat and carbon dioxide throughout the deep ocean and thereby come into equilibrium with the new conditions.

28   To be more specific, the models project that over the next 20 years, for a range of plausible emissions, the global temperature will increase at an average rate of about 0.2 degree C per decade, close to the observed rate over the past 30 years. About half of this near-term warming represents a "commitment" to future climate change arising from the inertia of the climate system response to current atmospheric concentrations of greenhouse gases.

29   The long-term warming over the 21st century, however, is strongly influenced by the future rate of emissions, and the projections cover a wide variety of scenarios, ranging from very rapid to more modest economic growth and from more to less dependence on fossil fuels. The best estimates of the increase in global temperatures range from 1.8 to 4.0 degrees C for the various emission scenarios, with higher emissions leading to higher temperatures. As for regional impacts, projections indicate with more confidence than ever before that these will mirror the *patterns* of change observed over the past 50 years (greater warming over land than ocean, for example) but that the *size* of the changes will be larger than they have been so far.

30   The simulations also suggest that the removal of excess carbon dioxide from the atmosphere by natural processes on land and in the ocean will become less efficient as the planet warms. This change leads to a higher percentage of emitted carbon dioxide remaining in the atmosphere, which then further accelerates global warming. This is an important positive feedback on the carbon cycle (the exchange of carbon compounds

throughout the climate system). Although models agree that carbon-cycle changes represent a positive feedback, the range of their responses remains very large, depending, among other things, on poorly understood changes in vegetation or soil uptake of carbon as the climate warms. Such processes are an important topic of ongoing research.

The models also predict that climate change will affect the physical and chemical characteristics of the ocean. The estimates of the rise in sea level during the 21st century range from about 30 to 40 centimeters, again depending on emissions. More than 60 percent of this rise is caused by the thermal expansion of the ocean. Yet these model-based estimates do not include the possible acceleration of recently observed increases in ice loss from the Greenland and Antarctic ice sheets. Although scientific understanding of such effects is very limited, they could add an additional 10 to 20 centimeters to sea-level rises, and the possibility of significantly larger rises cannot be excluded. The chemistry of the ocean is also affected, as the increased concentrations of atmospheric carbon dioxide will cause the ocean to become more acidic. 31

Some of the largest changes are predicted for polar regions. These include significant increases in high-latitude land temperatures and in the depth of thawing in permafrost regions and sharp reductions in the extent of summer sea ice in the Arctic basin. Lower latitudes will likely experience more heat waves, heavier precipitation, and stronger (but perhaps less frequent) hurricanes and typhoons. The extent to which hurricanes and typhoons may strengthen is uncertain and is a subject of much new research. 32

Some important uncertainties remain, of course. For example, the precise way in which clouds will respond as temperatures increase is a critical factor governing the overall size of the projected warming. The complexity of clouds, however, means that their response has been frustratingly difficult to pin down, and, again, much research remains to be done in this area. 33

We are now living in an era in which both humans and nature affect the future evolution of the earth and its inhabitants. Unfortunately, the crystal ball provided by our climate models becomes cloudier for predictions out beyond a century or so. Our limited knowledge of the response of both natural systems and human society to the growing impacts of climate change compounds our uncertainty. One result of global warming is certain, however. Plants, animals and humans will be living with the consequences of climate change for at least the next thousand years. 34

VACLAV HAVEL

Vaclav Havel (born in 1936 in Prague) is a writer, dramatist, politician, and human rights activist. He was repeatedly arrested and imprisoned in the 1970s and 1980s for speaking out against the Communist regime, including for his leading role in promoting the human rights manifesto Charter 77. Havel was elected President of Czechoslovakia in 1989 after the fall of the communist government in what has become known as the "Velvet Revolution." In 1993, he became the first President of the Czech Republic. He was reelected in 1998 and served until 2003. He is currently the chair of the International Council of the Human Rights Foundation. Havel has received multiple honorary doctorates, prizes, and awards, including the Gandhi Peace Prize in 2003 and the Presidential Medal of Freedom in 2008. In addition to plays and collections of poetry, he has written numerous books and articles on human rights, globalization, and Czech and European culture, history, and politics, including a political memoir, *To the Castle and Back* (2007). In "Our Moral Footprint," first published in the *New York Times* in 2007, Havel appeals to readers to recognize the moral imperative of preserving the planet and argues that humanity should transcend its contemporary economic, cultural, and political conflicts and develop "a consciousness of the commonality of all living beings."

Our Moral Footprint

1   Over the past few years the questions have been asked ever more forcefully whether global climate changes occur in natural cycles or not, to what degree we humans contribute to them, what threats stem from them and what can be done to prevent them. Scientific studies demonstrate that any changes in temperature and energy cycles on a planetary scale could mean danger for all people on all continents.

2   It is also obvious from published research that human activity is a cause of change; we just don't know how big its contribution is. Is it necessary to know that to the last percentage point, though? By waiting for incontrovertible precision, aren't we simply wasting time when we could be taking measures that are relatively painless compared to those we would have to adopt after further delays?

3   Maybe we should start considering our sojourn on earth as a loan. There can be no doubt that for the past hundred years at least, Europe and the United States have been running up a debt, and now other parts of the world are following their example. Nature is issuing warnings that we must not only stop the debt from growing but start to pay it back. There is little point in asking whether we have borrowed too much or what would happen if we postponed the repayments. Anyone with a mortgage or a bank loan can easily imagine the answer.

4   The effects of possible climate changes are hard to estimate. Our planet has never been in a state of balance from which it could deviate through human or other influence and then, in time, return to its

original state. The climate is not like a pendulum that will return to its original position after a certain period. It has evolved turbulently over billions of years into a gigantic complex of networks, and of networks within networks, where everything is interlinked in diverse ways.

Its structures will never return to precisely the same state they were   5
in 50 or 5,000 years ago. They will only change into a new state, which, so long as the change is slight, need not mean any threat to life.

Larger changes, however, could have unforeseeable effects within   6
the global ecosystem. In that case, we would have to ask ourselves whether human life would be possible. Because so much uncertainty still reigns, a great deal of humility and circumspection is called for.

We can't endlessly fool ourselves that nothing is wrong and that we   7
can go on cheerfully pursuing our wasteful lifestyles, ignoring the climate threats and postponing a solution. Maybe there will be no major catastrophe in the coming years or decades. Who knows? But that doesn't relieve us of responsibility toward future generations.

I don't agree with those whose reaction is to warn against restricting   8
civil freedoms. Were the forecasts of certain climatologists to come true, our freedoms would be tantamount to those of someone hanging from a 20th-story parapet.

Whenever I reflect on the problems of today's world, whether they con-   9
cern the economy, society, culture, security, ecology or civilization in general, I always end up confronting the moral question: what action is responsible or acceptable? The moral order, our conscience and human rights—these are the most important issues at the beginning of the third millennium.

We must return again and again to the roots of human existence and   10
consider our prospects in centuries to come. We must analyze everything open-mindedly, soberly, unideologically and unobsessively, and project our knowledge into practical policies. Maybe it is no longer a matter of simply promoting energy-saving technologies, but chiefly of introducing ecologically clean technologies, of diversifying resources and of not relying on just one invention as a panacea.

I'm skeptical that a problem as complex as climate change can be   11
solved by any single branch of science. Technological measures and regulations are important, but equally important is support for education, ecological training and ethics—a consciousness of the commonality of all living beings and an emphasis on shared responsibility.

Either we will achieve an awareness of our place in the living and   12
life-giving organism of our planet, or we will face the threat that our evolutionary journey may be set back thousands or even millions of years. That is why we must see this issue as a challenge to behave responsibly and not as a harbinger of the end of the world.

The end of the world has been anticipated many times and has   13
never come, of course. And it won't come this time either. We need not fear for our planet. It was here before us and most likely will be here after us. But that doesn't mean that the human race is not at serious risk. As a

result of our endeavors and our irresponsibility our climate might leave no place for us. If we drag our feet, the scope for decision-making—and hence for our individual freedom—could be considerably reduced.

Content

1. What evidence do the authors of "The Physical Science behind Climate Change" offer that human activities are responsible for the increase in greenhouse gases (¶s 5–6)? What natural mechanisms contribute to climate change (¶ 8)? What is a "net positive radiative forcing" and what factors contribute to it (¶s 9–10)?

2. What quantities and properties of our climate system do Collins et al. consider in their discussion of observational data (¶s 11–15)? How does this data indicate that our climate is changing?

3. Why did the IPCC 2007 report draw a stronger link between human activities and observed climate changes than its previous report ("The Physical Science Behind Climate Change," ¶s 17–26)? What did Working Group II of the IPCC add to those findings ("The Consequences of Ongoing Warming")?

4. How is our climate likely to change over the next century ("The Physical Science behind Climate Change," ¶s 27–32)? What are the consequences of those changes ("The Consequences of Ongoing Warming")? Why do scientists believe that future changes in climate will be larger than those the earth has seen in the past?

5. Why does Vaclav Havel ("Our Moral Footprint") believe that environmental policies should not depend on determining the extent to which human activity is driving global climate change? What kinds of policies does Havel suggest to accommodate this perspective?

Strategies/Structures/Language

6. Collins and his coauthors prepare the reader for a detailed discussion of scientific evidence for climate change by arguing that scientific progress "is generally made by a painstaking piecing together of evidence" (¶ 1). Find other examples of stylistic devices that prepare or guide the reader through their analysis. These devices might include asking a question that the text then answers, summarizing information already provided in order to build on that information, and using metaphors and examples.

7. Why does Havel compare the human relationship to the earth with a loan (¶ 3)? How does Havel's description of our planet (¶s 4–6) support his argument that we must "achieve an awareness of our place in the living and life-giving organism of our planet" (¶ 12)?

For Writing

8. **Journal Writing.** Havel says that since so much about our planet's climate is uncertain, "a great deal of humility and circumspection is called for" (¶ 6). Do you agree? How might our society learn to acquire "a consciousness of the commonality of all living beings" (¶ 11)?

9. **Dialogues.** Select one of the problems of managing the earth's natural resources (other than global warming) that is identified in the color photo insert and explain its connection and contribution to the problem of global warming and climate change. What kinds of adaptation and mitigation strategies would address the problem? Discuss what the consequences of inaction in addressing this problem are likely to be and which regions of the world are likely to be hardest hit. What aspects of this problem suggest that international cooperation is necessary to adapt to a warmer future and mitigate its consequences?

10. **Mixed Modes.** Choose one or more of the effects of global warming that Working Group II of the IPCC foresees in the coming century as described in "The Regional Picture" on (209). Research the issue(s) in a particular region and propose a combination of adaptation and mitigation strategies that are available in that region. Explain why your proposed solution is the best of the possible strategies.

"What does this cartoon illustrate about the relationship between cause and effect? Be careful what you wish for."

RYAN O'CONNELL

Ryan O'Connell was born in Connecticut in 1988. He earned a BA in English and a BS in elementary education (2011) at the University of Connecticut, and is pursuing a career in teaching. He has also worked as a blacksmith.

He explains why and how he wrote "Standing Order": "In the fall of 2003 I received a lead role in my high school's quadrennial musical. A freshman at the time, I pressured myself to excel onstage to make an impression on my peers. With such self-pressure, however, came the need for control. I began to diet and exercise for my role, began to harness my weight. In a matter of months I lost fifty pounds—too much, too fast. I was diagnosed with anorexia nervosa, an eating disorder that sometimes accompanies the "perfection" I had intended to achieve."

"The following essay describes my first night as a patient at Boston Children's Hospital, soon after the musical had ended. I wrote it to the essentials, omitting (most noticeably) quotation marks to replicate the severity of the disease as it manifests itself to its host. Anorexia being a disorder that most often affects women, this piece strives to represent the illness as it appears to a young man."

Standing Order

1   The wheelchair did it. For three months I had managed to shirk reality, from physicians to outpatient programs, but when I stepped from the van in front of Boston Children's Hospital, reality took my shoulder and made me sit.

2   I can walk, I said.

3   No, you can't, the orderly replied. You're too sick.

4   This wasn't sick. Sick was when you coughed. I feel fine, I said.

5   You're not fine, she explained. You lost a lot of weight. Your heart's at thirty bpm. It should be seventy.

6   I'm not dead, I said.

7   You will be, if you don't sit awhile.

8   Her last word offered some relief. This isn't permanent, I thought. They want you to play the game, so play. I can stand up to use the bathroom. They can't tell your bowels not to move. The bathroom will be your standing zone, your gym. Toilets make great spotters for curl-ups.

9   This is how an eating disorder speaks to you. Anorexia in particular finds the workout in everything. I was not bulimic, bathroom notions aside. My parents worked for the food I ate—it would do them nothing to serve it to porcelain. Even then I thought it odd that a shred of nobility could endure the throes of this selfish illness, but that is what the disease does, crossing tendrils with your former self and burping some honor. It will find comfort in hospital bathrooms.

10   Will my room even have a John? It has to, I thought. They treat other sicknesses here. Some of them demand quick relief.

11   The orderly wheeled me into an examination room. Strip to your underwear, she said.

12   I removed my socks last. Hospital floor tiles are cold to bear while you fumble a shirt, and in my emaciated state there was no foot muscle left for insulation. I climbed onto the table, lay down. I straightened my back. The body paper ripped beneath me. We need a new ream anyway, the orderly said, opening the closet.

13   I imagined wrapping myself in the torn length like takeout. Maybe someone would eat me in my manila frame. A chicken nugget. Without ketchup. Without honey mustard or sweet and sour sauce. Sorry, the hospital ran out. This is how an eating disorder speaks to you.

14   The nurse came to do an electrocardiogram. She had trouble with my body hair. It was falling out now, tuft by tuft, but that did not keep it from resisting the metal leads. She produced a razor, shaved squares on each of my limbs, applied conducting gel like seed in the bare white plots. I lay back, stared at the ceiling.

15   Unclench your fists, the nurse said.

I had not even realized I was doing it. Before the hospital I would 16
sometimes stand at my bed for an hour or more before it crossed my mind
to get in and sleep.

This should only take a minute. She turned a knob. The click of the 17
machine.

I don't mind the cold, I said. 18

You'll warm up. How long has it been since your last meal? 19

I ate a granola bar last night. 20

Have you had any water since then? 21

I had a glass of water, too. 22

The rest of the minute was silent. I did not want to talk. Even that 23
could be exhausting. It had been a long time since I had eaten brainy fats.

A beep. Printer noise. 24

Twenty-seven beats per minute, the nurse remarked. You'll be here 25
awhile. At Boston, I mean. She took a pair of glasses from her pocket.

I know. 26

I'd feel better if you had some water. 27

No, thanks. 28

She studied the spreadsheet until the orderly came back. She would 29
not leave me in the room alone. A urine bottle swayed from the arm of my
wheelchair. There would be no bathroom gym, no walking. They would
make me pass from bed, run the deep yellows through software.

I will not drink anything, I thought. I can save myself the degrada- 30
tion of that bottle. Thirst exchanged for the illusion of dignity. This is how
an eating disorder speaks to you. I was fifteen.

My parents were not ghosts in all this. They were there to admit 31
me, there to admit to themselves that it was not possible to care for me
anymore. They stood beside me at the EKG, walked with the orderly as
she wheeled me to my room. For all its conceit the eating disorder never
pushed them out of sight, but that was about all it dared forfeit.

My father once handed me a bottle of Gatorade. Have a drink, he 32
said. You need the electrolytes.

I said nothing. I did not drink. 33

Ryan, please, he said. 34

I can't. 35

We looped like this a few times. He gave up. 36

Even then I knew my father was worried, but it was my only 37
thought. He left the bottle on my bedstead. I put it in a drawer.

That first night in the hospital my parents bought me dinner. We ate 38
in my room. The intravenous swayed in its saddlebag. We had pineapple
and pita chips. Flavors exhumed. Like laundry you neglect to wash, but it
is your stench and that makes it okay.

The guilt came an hour later. It came for the slightest things. I had 39
just eaten a normal dinner.

My heart's racing, I said. 40

41   My mother clicked the nurse button.

42   It's not racing, my father replied. It's coming up to speed.

43   It's racing.

44   You're orthostatic. The right speed feels faster than what you're used to.

45   I shouldn't have eaten that.

46   To the disease anything is a binge. It ascends from the otherlands and reminds you that nutrition makes you think. Pineapple and pita chips, the heralds of memory. I did not want to think about the past, about what preceded my hospitalization, but the calories were already churning and for that, the disease said, I was Lot's wife.

47   The nurse came.

48   My heart's racing, I said.

49   She checked my monitor. It's faster, she replied. The right kind of faster.

50   I feel bloated.

51   Do you have to use the bathroom?

52   I had not swallowed a drop at dinner. Yet even this achievement, I realized, could not absolve the water in pineapple. My bladder had shrunk in the past few months. A cup of fruit was enough to fill it.

53   If you do, I'll have to ask your parents to leave, she added.

54   There was a John across the room, door ajar. From above the sink a dim light shone down, lacing the walls with the wax glow of a confessional. I wondered how far my IV could stretch.

55   I can't use the bathroom?

56   We'd like you to use the bottle.

57   I'll have to stand.

58   You're on bed rest. Lean over the mattress.

59   The nurse handed me the bottle, drew the curtain.

60   In the ninth grade I was offered a lead role in my high school's spring show. I got it in my head that a lead needed a jaw line. I went to the gym, did without dessert. That was January. By March my skin started to turn yellow. I stopped sweating. On doctor's orders I wore a heart monitor under my shirt, the tangle of cords like chicken wire down my chest.

61   The bottle cap unscrews, the nurse called. Let me know when you're done.

62   I lifted the gurney, leaned over the side of the bed.

63   I had been onstage two weeks before. I still wanted to be there, I supposed. If only to exploit my liberty to stand.

64   This is how an eating disorder speaks beside your right mind. It wasn't often that we thought the same things. When it happened it felt wrong for all the right reasons. A moment of solidarity, then confusion as the disease scraped for a reason to disagree with its host, keep its balance.

65   The monitor clicked and sounded a change in bpm. The bottle filled.

66   Footsteps. The nurse. You okay in there?

67   I turned but could not see the screen from where I lay. The tone did nothing to indicate the direction my heart had chosen to swing. The bottle filled. I'm here, I said.

MEAGHAN ROY-O'REILLY

Meaghan Roy-O'Reilly was born in 1990 and grew in up rural northeastern Connecticut. She is currently an undergraduate student at the University of Connecticut studying Molecular and Cell Biology. Though she began her undergraduate career as an English major, she realized rather quickly that she preferred fluffy bestsellers to great works of literature and that despite her passion for writing, she could never think of anything interesting to say. This early-mid-life crisis prompted her to switch to a scientific major, which proved to be a crash-course in reading, comprehending and critiquing dry scientific literature regarding the immune systems of both mice and men.

In the fall of her junior year, she began to learn about the genre of scientific non-fiction. She writes, "Humankind has amassed a terrific wealth of scientific information, but as the knowledge base grows, so does the intellectual gap between the scientific community and the general public. Creative science writing represents a venue for showcasing important scientific discoveries without condescending to the reader and may be particularly useful in matters of public health."

"Balancing Act" is one of the more personal essays she has written; it is a marriage of her personal and scientific knowledge regarding food and disordered eating.

Balancing Act

I've always had an addictive personality. I read books until bindings 1 crack and covers rip; I listen to songs on endless loop until I know every note, every nuance. Gazes don't linger long enough, kisses are cut too short. No matter what, I'm left wanting more: more love, more praise, more time. More food.

The main room of the gym is endless, row after row of sleek black equip- 2 *ment ready and primed to test its users. On three walls, mirrors run from floor to ceiling; everyone in the room is running straight towards their own reflection. The fourth and final wall is one all-encompassing window that faces the parking lot, so the world can watch the patrons watch themselves.*

I'm six years old. Despite my love of food, I am a tiny little thing. 3 My family tells me I eat like a bird, and since birds actually eat up to one half of their body weight a day, this is a relatively accurate assessment. I savor every bite, a good Italian child; food is comfort, and home.

The gym population is overwhelmingly female; not surprising, given that 4 *this gym is famed for its wealth of cardio equipment, the best exercise for weight loss. Everywhere you look, there are girls in t-shirts and candy colored shorts, their hair pulled back and fixed perfectly in place with thin plastic headbands. Long, tan legs in cute sneakers pound against the treadmill belts, but it's hard to tell exactly what these girls are chasing. Or what might be chasing them.*

I'm in elementary school now and at first, so social and outgoing, 5 pushy and flirtatious. I play soccer, I play basketball and I don't pay any mind to the calories in my granola bar or the size tag on my jeans. But I'm not so tiny anymore; I'm taller and heavier than any of my friends. No one ever mentions it, but is that judgment in their eyes? Disgust? I'm starting to get nervous about eating around people, so I fast until I get home. As soon as I get inside my house, before I take off my shoes, put down my backpack, before I have time to think, I find myself sitting on the kitchen floor in front of the cabinets. Somehow, there's an empty bread bag in my lap and a box of cake mix in my hands. It tastes awful, saccharine and goes down like sawdust but I keep eating until I don't feel empty.

6   *There is a scale at the gym, in the women's locker room. It's a serious scale, with sliding bars and weights just like the one at the doctor's office. I step on, so very carefully. The first weight measures in increments of fifty pounds; as I slide it over the correct slot, it locks in place with a dull thud. Holding my breath, I slide the second weight along the bar, silently hoping as it measures my worth down to the ounce.*

7   I need to go to the doctor's for a physical. I've done everything I can to delay it, but to no avail; I soon find myself trapped in an exam room with a well meaning nurse and my mother. To my surprise, I don't feel anything at all as the nurse whispers the ugliest of numbers— ("*two-hundred pounds*"). I maintain icy neutrality as my mom covers her mouth in shock. I am Switzerland, remote and impartial, as the doctor explains to me the error of my ways while the pretty nurse tries to give me her sad, all-knowing smile. I'm ten years old.

8   *The gym is a cold place. They keep it a brisk sixty degrees most of the time. The patrons enter wearing long pants and sweatshirts, layers that maybe slowly shed during the course of the workout. One high school student on the treadmill is running at least seven miles an hour, has been for the last twenty minutes, yet he's still dressed as if he were headed into a blizzard. It looks like torture; his cheeks bloom red and I can hear his heavy breath from across the room. Yet over the course of an hour, he can probably sweat off at least three pounds of water. He's a competitive high school wrestler with a meet later this afternoon and he knows that if he can endure sixty minutes of exercise underneath all that fabric, he'll have a good chance of making weight.*

9.   I'm dying. I turn the fact over in my mind as I lay in bed, my tongue thick and swollen with salt and chocolate. Not today, or next year but eventually this is going to kill me. I'm a freshman in high school; I am smart enough to know the definitions of the words my doctors have been whispering behind my back for years: diabetes, hypertension. Heart failure. My parents have tried everything; exercise and health food, crying and pleading. I want to make them happy, I do, but I become someone else when the emptiness takes over. An animal that creeps to the kitchen and devours forbidden things while everyone else sleeps, a frightening creature that no one can control. People have asked me for years what inspired me to lose weight. It's an easy answer, but they're always sorry they asked. Pure and simple—it was fear.

10   *As soon as you exit the gym and step outside, the realities of the outside world hit you. There's a Chinese restaurant next door, sweet and savory tendrils*

of temptation weaving their way through the cold air of the parking lot. I pause, rapt, watching people smile and talk, raising forks full of sticky rice, thick orange sauce and fragrant vegetables to their open mouths. The envy rises so quickly in my chest that for a second, it's hard to breathe. I covet every mouthful.

I'm about two months into my first low carb diet. As promised to   11 me by Cosmopolitan magazine, the results have been nothing short of miraculous. I lose ten pounds in the first two weeks alone. My parents, my friends and even my teachers have noticed but they're too polite to come out and ask if I've lost weight, so they say things like "You look great. Did you do something different to you hair?" My heart soars at each and every compliment, every appreciative glance. I'm addicted.

During a class at the gym, one of the trainers explains the danger of low   12 *carb diets. For the first few weeks, you eliminate them almost completely, eating only vegetables, fats and protein. Weight loss can reach astronomical rates. People eagerly follow this fad diet without questioning the mechanism behind this seemingly miraculous phenomenon, which is really quite simple; your body interprets this lack of carbohydrates as starvation. When you eat carbohydrates, insulin is released in order to help you absorb nutrients. Even if you're eating enough, if you don't eat bread or fruit or pasta, you don't release any insulin. Your body begins burning fat in a wild attempt to sustain you. You start producing ketone bodies from your fat stores, which you need to nourish your brain in the absence of carbohydrate intake. Acetone, one of the ketone bodies, is exhaled in your breath. People on severely restricted low carb diets actually smell sweet, like fruit or nail-polish remover. The mechanics of a low carb diet actually mirror exactly the effects of a well-known disease: Type 1 Diabetes.*

Over the next few months, the rate of weight loss slows and slows   13 until it finally stops altogether. My parents and doctors are thrilled; I've dropped from morbidly obese to merely "overweight", but I'm not satisfied. I want more. So in secret, I begin my own extreme low carb diet, refusing to add back in fruits and whole grains like the diet advises. By springtime of my sophomore year, I've lost fifty pounds in total. Sometimes I get dizzy lifting my backpack in the morning, but I'm finally the right dress size. And then one day, I fail an exam and fight with my best friend. I come home and there's a pizza in the refrigerator. I'm ashamed, I'm angry. I'm empty. I sit down on the cold linoleum and pull the stiff pizza box into my lap. I take small bites, one after another. The cheese is cold, like glue and there are tears running down my cheeks but I'm too tired to care anymore.

Rapid weight loss comes with a price, the trainer says. If you starve your-   14 *self, your body will throw up any defense it can to keep you going. It will degrade your muscle into glucose to fuel your brain. It will lower your body temperature, your energy levels, all in an effort to keep you alive. So by the time you go off the diet, your body has become hyper-efficient. It's lowered the amount of calories you need to function. You break the diet and all of the sudden, you're heavier than you've ever been.*

In half the time it took to lose the weight, I've gained it all back. It's   15 junior year and I'm looking for a homecoming dress at Macy'. I try to slide the largest size they have up over my hips and it gets stuck. I can't count how many times I've dissolved in tears like this inside a dressing room, sinking to the floor in a sea of crinoline, hand over my mouth so no one can hear. I look at my reflection in the mirror, both fascinated and horrified by what I see. In this moment, for the first time in living memory, I stop feeling sorry for myself.

16   *The first time I walked into the gym, I was scared stiff. Surrounded by college boys who could bench-press their own weight and soccer moms who could contort themselves into pretzels, I felt so out of place. I could barely touch my own toes, or walk up a flight of stairs without having to catch my breath.*

17   I'm a freshman in college and I'm agonizing over what to wear. I've bought clothes to fit my new medium-sized frame, but they look all wrong. The stylish skinny jeans and oversized sweater make me look odd and lumpy. Later on in the day, the jeans start to cut into my stomach and I feel swollen and defeated. I come home and yank them off, contemplating eating the leftover cookies my mom brought home from work. Sometimes I eat the cookies and sometimes I throw them in the trash, but either way I inevitably find myself at the gym a few hours later, lifting weights or jogging on the treadmill; slow and self-conscious, but steady.

18   *I thought that maybe if I bought some high-tech exercise clothing, working out would be easier. But all the spandex and lycra in the world weren't going to make running that first mile, or doing that first set of pushups any easier. In fact, those stretchy shiny fabrics made things all the worse—after a week of catching glimpses of my lumps and bumps in those damn gym mirrors, I gave up and started wearing my dad's athletic shorts.*

19   It's the end of sophomore year, finals week. According to my doctor, my BMI is dead-on average; I've reached my goal. Part of me wants to continue losing weight; it whispers that another five or ten pounds lost would give me grace and poise and killer legs. I still can't wear the skinny jeans or clinging sweater dresses; I've learned to appreciate the empire waist and the retro flare. I've developed a grudging appreciation for gym; if you squint, you can almost see my biceps and I can run a mile without stopping, although I prefer to do so only if something large and angry is chasing me. The panic of the school-day used to make it hard for me to sleep, but nothing feels better than crawling into bed, muscles aching with lactic acid and passing out before my head can hit the pillow.

20   *Four times a week, I drag myself out of bed at ridiculous hours and through those shiny glass doors to lift weights, to run. And for those few slow, sweaty hours, I finally feel a connection my body. There is such peace to be found hidden in the muscle of your legs, the strength of your arms. Fat doesn't trap me or define me anymore; its only job is to provide me with the power to fight for the things that really matter.*

21   I still have trouble knowing when enough is enough. There still aren't enough cookies, or snow days or kisses to satisfy me. I still weigh myself too often and gaze longingly at food I know I shouldn't have. To be honest, sometimes I still find myself sitting in front of the kitchen cabinets,

searching and searching for something to fill me up. But I've found a tenuous sort of balance, precious and fragile and now that I possess it, I don't want to give it up. After all, I've always had an addictive personality.

Content

1. Both essays explain the process of how an eating disorder develops and can be treated. What similarities exist between these disorders and their treatment? What differences?

2. Eating disorders are often private, secret, and shameful. Why have the authors written these essays? Provide several reasons for each. What are their attitudes toward their disorders? Do these change over the course of time they are dealing with the disorder?

3. What should students expect to derive from reading these essays? Could an essay on an eating disorder be dangerous for vulnerable readers to encounter? Could they provoke dangerous behavior? Could they provide cautionary tales and thus serve as good, therapeutic examples?

Strategies/Structures/Language

4. Each essay is an autobiographical narrative. Could each be considered a case history, as well? These essays are written in language accessible to general readers; should the authors have included any clinical language or medical information? Why or why not?

5. What is the tone of each essay? What attitude does each author have toward his or her eating disorder? Does this change throughout the course of its cause and treatment?

6. How do the authors want their readers to react to them as characters in these essays? As sufferers from eating disorders? As people whose eating disorders are under control at the time they wrote the essays? (What clues does O'Connell provide to let readers know that he will recover?)

. 7. What is the significance of the title of each essay? Of the repetition of key phrases, such as O'Connell's "This is how an eating disorder speaks to you" (¶ 9).

8. Suppose that one or both eating disorders had not been resolved, but was ongoing, resistant to treatment or improvement. Would it then have been suitable to include in a textbook such as *The Essay Connection*? Or must a true illness story have a satisfying resolution to be appropriate reading for students?

For writing

9. *Dialogues*. Not all problems, medical or otherwise, have satisfactory resolutions. As Ehrenreich illustrates in "Serving in Florida" (143–51), people who work at minimum wage jobs are likely to remain at depressed economic levels, no matter how hard they work. Or, even when a solution is available, as Gawande illustrates in "On Washing Hands" (152–59), people don't always act on it. Select a problem, present a solution, and propose a process by which it could be implemented.

10. Or pick a problem, propose several solutions, and argue in favor of one.

11. Write a case history of a problem that you've experienced and either resolved or not. Analyze the reasons for your success, or failure (if any–some problems may be too complicated to expect an easy resolution).

Additional Topics for Writing Cause and Effect

(For strategies for writing cause and effect, see 178.)

Multiple Strategies for Writing: Cause and Effect

In writing on any of the cause-and-effect topics below, you can employ assorted strategies to help explain either the causes or the effects, and to interpret their consequences:

- *Definitions, explanations* of terms, equipment involved in the process
- *Illustrations* and *examples*: to show what happens, and in what sequence
- *Diagrams, drawings, flow charts, graphs* to clarify and explain
- *Logical sequence of interrelated steps or ideas*
- Consideration of *short-term* and *long-term consequences* of a particular effect—literal, material, psychological, emotional, economic, ethical, ecological, political, or other
- Examination of whether there is a *confusion* or *lack of clarity* between cause and effect; sometimes effects are mistaken for causes, and vice versa, or the wrong people or phenomena are credited with or blamed for a particular cause or effect

1. Write an essay, adapted to an audience of your choice, explaining either the causes or the effects of one of the following:

a. Substance abuse by teenagers, young adults, or another group (see Sanders, "Under the Influence . . ." (180–91)

b. America's 50 percent divorce rate (see Hall, "Killing Chickens" 118–21; McGuire, "Wake Up Call" (376–82)

c. Genetic engineering (see McKibben, "Designer Genes" (515–25)

d. Teenage pregnancy or smoking (see DiFranza "Hooked from the First Cigarette" (122–31)

e. The popularity of a given television show, movie or rock star, film, book, or type of book (such as romance, Gothic, Western)

f. Current taste in clothing, food, cars, architecture, interior decoration

g. The Civil War; the Great Depression; World War II; the Vietnam War; the attack on the World Trade Center; or another historical event—such as the war in Iraq, Afghanistan, Darfur, Bosnia, or elsewhere

h. The popularity of a particular spectator or active sport

i. Your personality or temperament

j. Success in college or in business

k. Finding or losing one's religious faith

l. Racial, sexual, or religious discrimination

m. An increasingly higher proportion of working women (or mothers of young children)

n. Illiteracy

o. The American Dream that "if you work hard you're bound to succeed"

p. The actual or potential consequences of nuclear leaks, meltdowns, global warming, or natural disaster (see Collins et al., "The Physical Science behind Climate Change" (199–211)

q. Vanishing animal or plant species; or the depletion of natural resources

r. The effects of outsourcing

s. Decrease in the number of people in training for skilled labor—electricians, plumbers, carpenters, tool and die makers, and others

t. A sudden change in personal status (from being a high school student to being a college freshman; from living at home to living away from home; from being dependent to being self-supporting; from being single to being married; from being childless to being a parent; from being married to widowed . . .)

2. Write a seemingly objective account of a social phenomenon or some other aspect of human behavior of which you actually disapprove, either because the form and context seem at variance, or because the phenomenon itself seems to you wrong, or to cause unanticipated problems, such as Anne Fadiman illustrates in "Under Water" (100–104), and Bill McKibben analyzes in "Designer Genes" (515–25). You can justify your opinion (and convince your readers) through your choice of details and selection of a revealing incident or several vignettes. Ethical issues are suitable for a serious essay that examines the consequences of a process or set of beliefs, such as those Peter Singer addresses in "The Singer Solution to World Poverty" (481–87). Social and cultural phenomena are particularly suitable subjects for a comic essay—the causes or consequences of nerd or geek or yuppie or twenty-something behaviors—ways of spending money and leisure time and foolish, trivial, or wasteful things to spend it on.

Description

When you describe a person, place, thing, experience, or phenomenon, you want your readers to understand it as you do and to experience its sounds, tastes, smells, or textures, both physical and emotional. You want to put your readers there—where you are, where your subject is—and enable them to see it through your eyes, interpret it through your understanding. Because you can't include everything, the details you select, the information you impart, will determine your emphasis, so pick the information that matters most to your point of view. You may decide to focus on only the big picture, the outline, the bare essentials, as do Kim Warp in "Rising Sea Levels—An Alternative Theory" (266) and Istvan Banyai in "Inflation" (311)—both convey considerable meaning in their cartoons by using minimal details. Or you may choose a closer perspective, concentrating on the small, revealing details as does Mark Twain in "Uncle John's Farm" (238–45), with its thickly sensuous descriptions of nature's bounty rendered through his childhood consciousness.

Your description can *exist for its own sake*, though in fact, few do. Most descriptions function in more than one way, for more than one purpose. A description, perhaps accompanied by a photograph or diagram, can exist *to show*—no surprise—*what something looks like or how it works*. Thus Linda Villarosa's "How Much of the Body Is Replaceable?" (235–37) simply presents the evidence to demonstrate that "from the top of the head to the tips of the toes, nearly every part of the body can be replaced. . . ." The accompanying diagram identifies the nature of the many replacement options—hair, brain, eyes, skin, heart, blood vessels, joints—with captions that explain the nature of the replacement and some of the research in progress. Issues of medical ethics, longevity, cost and allocation of medical time and resources, rationing, theology, and psychology—all of which would involve interpretation and might affect whether the replacements would actually be used—are off the table in this presentation.

Or *a description can serve as an argument*, with or without words. For instance, compare Villarosa's diagram with the two other graphic renderings of the human body in this chapter. Cartoonist Kim Warp's "Rising Sea Levels—An Alternative Theory" (266) makes its point about obesity by simply showing fat people happily eating while partially immersed in a rising body of water. In a comparable vein, Istvan Banyai's "Inflation" (311) needs no words to demonstrate—and implicitly argue against—astonishing inflation of both prices and the human body. His line drawings of the expanding figure on postage stamps from 1929–2050, with prices inflating from 3¢ to 1,000,000¢ during this time, say it all.

A description can also entertain. Such descriptions can be inviting, welcoming. Mark Twain serves up nostalgia as he invites readers to visit "Uncle John's Farm" (238–45), with its appeal to the senses, for an abundance of sensory details are often the mainstay of description. Thus Twain evokes *sound* ("I know the crackling sound [a ripe watermelon] makes when the carving knife enters its end"); *smell* ("I can call back . . . [from] the deep woods, the earthy smells"); *touch* ("how snug and cozy one felt, under the blankets [on stormy nights]"); *taste* ("I know the taste of the watermelon which has been honestly come by, and I know the taste of the watermelon which has been acquired by art"); and *sight* ("I can see the white and black children grouped on the hearth, with the firelight playing on their faces and the shadows flickering upon the walls"). Twain calls on all our senses to take us to his beloved farm—and to love it as he does.

Indeed, most descriptions of places, like descriptions of people, phenomena, processes, and other subjects, are strongly influenced by the observer's aims, experiences, and values. Thus in much nontechnical writing the descriptions you provide are bound to be subjective, intended both to guide and influence your readers to see the topic your way rather than theirs. As a writer you can't afford to leave critical spaces blank; you must provide direction to influence your readers' interpretations. We have heard, to the point of cliché, that one picture is worth a thousand words, yet very often pictures need some words to expand and focus the interpretation to which the picture invites us. This is true not only of the cartoon on 266 for which we could come up with a variety of captions, but for all the pictures and diagrams throughout *The Essay Connection*, including Linda Villarosa's schematic diagram of replaceable parts of the body (235–37). Although the diagram shows us what parts are replaceable, we need written explanations to flesh out the figure.

Other *descriptions tell stories*, of people or places, re-creating the *emotional sense* of a person, place, or experience. Amanda Cagle's stunning creative nonfiction interpretation of her family's heritage and life "On the Banks of the Bogue Chitto" (231–35) views her Jena Choctaw family "through the dim and unreal morning shadows" in the Louisiana bayou where she was born and raised, where her free-spirited father taught her to shoot panthers with a bow and arrow. She describes her father in sensory language, "*listening* to the murmur of earthworms beneath his feet, *tasting* the first tomatoes, *watching* the swirls and ripples on the Bogue Chitto" [emphasis supplied]. Yet when her father "tried to conform to an employer's schedule, the rhythm of his own life always got in the way," and Cagle's description becomes an indictment of the white culture that has caused her teenage brother's unexplained suicide and her father's subsequent grief, breakdown, and entrapment in a dull, demeaning job as a mail carrier.

David Sedaris, in "Make That a Double" (267–69) presents a comical description of the illogical gender assignment in the French language, a straightforward binary classification scheme. In fact, as Sedaris correctly understands, a noun is indeed either masculine or feminine—and its gender "affects both its articles and its adjectives." The comic complication is one of logic—that if something is feminine or masculine in real life, its grammatical gender, or "sexual assignment," will logically correspond to that reality. Not so, as Sedaris discovers, "*Vagina* is masculine . . . while the word *masculinity* is feminine." His solution to the problem hinges on another classification system, singular and plural, for "the plural article does not reflect gender" and is consequently "the same for both the masculine and the feminine." That this requires him to buy two of everything, creating still other problems, seems a small price to pay for solving the grammatical dilemma. Sedaris multiplies examples in a hilarious description of utter illogic that can count on the readers' common sense to make its point.

Michael Pollan's "The Meal" (247–54) describes in entertaining and explicit detail "the meal at the end of the industrial food chain . . . prepared by McDonald's and eaten in a moving car." To demonstrate that "well-designed fast food has a fragrance and flavor all its own," Pollan analyzes the "generic fast-food flavor" and composition of McNuggets, chicken pieces processed with thirteen corn-related products—which he lists and explains—and "several completely synthetic ingredients, quasiedible substances that . . . come from . . . a petroleum refinery or chemical plant." Along with "leavening agents" and antioxidants are "'anti-foaming agents' like dimethylpolysiloxene"—a probable carcinogen and an established cause of mutations, tumors, and reproductive problems; "it's also flammable." Pollan's lively description becomes an argument with every added nugget of information, an indictment of the destructive agricultural and manufacturing processes that transform potentially nutritious food into "a signifier of comfort food." "The more you concentrate on how it tastes, the less like anything it tastes."

In "Eating Made Simple" (255–62), Marion Nestle's nutrition research enables her to describe and interpret a mountain of conflicting diet advice on such topics as calories, meat, fish and heart disease, and sodas and obesity. Sound dietary principles remain constant, she says: "eat less; move more; eat fruits, vegetables and whole grains; and avoid too much junk food." Nestle explains nutritional issues involved in each and why the research—often on a single nutrient sponsored by industries that have an economic stake in the outcome—is confusing and contradictory. In a characteristic section, "Are Organics Healthier?" she identifies a typical fundamental conflict using a list (characteristic of description). The U.S. Department of Agriculture forbids producers of "Certified Organic Foods" from using "synthetic pesticides, herbicides, fertilizers, genetically modified seeds, irradiation or fertilizers derived from sewage sludge." Nevertheless, because the USDA's "principal mandate is to promote conventional agriculture"—which uses everything on this list—the USDA refuses to say that organic foods are either safer or more nutritious. Though common sense would agree with these claims, supportive research is costly and scarce. In honesty, Nestle concludes that even if further research confirms that organic foods are more nutritious, "all fruits and vegetables contain certain useful nutrients, albeit in different combinations and concentrations," and that the main reason to buy organics is not for their presumed health benefits, but because "they are far less likely to damage the environment." Both Pollan and Nestle present a great deal of information in describing their subject and explaining the problems inherent in defining good nutrition; both analyze the information and imply—to the extent that their evidence allows them to do so—potential solutions to the problems they identify, but with the caution characteristic of good scientists and careful journalists. Although their presentations are balanced, in conclusion they tip the balance through selective details, flat-out assertion, tone, or a combination of these.

The point of Matt Nocton's careful description in "Harvest of Gold, Harvest of Shame" (271–76) is clear throughout because of his prevailing tone and choice of language. Tone, the prevailing mood of the essay, like a tone of voice, conveys your attitude toward your subject and toward the evidence you present in support of your point. It is clear from the tone of all the essays in this chapter—indeed, all the essays in the entire *Essay Connection*—that the authors care deeply about their subjects. Nocton reports in a relatively objective tone on his personal experience with an aspect of farming—in this case, the harvesting of tobacco by a business that employs migrant and contract laborers, racial and ethnic minorities overseen by white bosses. Keeping himself out of the essay, he does not say in the essay that as a teenager, after two days on the job he was promoted to "bentkeeper" over the heads of minority employees with far more experience. Nevertheless, Nocton's concern for the workers and anger over their exploitation is apparent in the way he recounts the harvesting process, detail by detail, dirty, dusty, hot, and humiliating: each worker "must tie [a burlap sack] around his waist as a source of protection against the dirt and rocks that he will be dragging himself through for the next eight hours." Nocton's essay, like the creative nonfiction narratives by Amanda Cagle ("On the Banks of the Bogue Chitto" 231–35) and Meredith Hall ("Killing Chickens" 118–21) illustrate that these days, in nonfiction, anyway, unless it's satire, readers generally prefer understatement to overkill. There are always exceptions; the superabundance of good things at Twain's "Uncle John's Farm" (238–45) illustrates our—perhaps occasional—preference for overindulgence epitomized in Mae West's observation that "Too much of a good thing is—absolutely splendid." As the authors and illustrators in this chapter show us, there is a world of difference in descriptions, a compelling, complex world to explore. Whether we want the pictures wide-angled or narrow, distant or close up, sharply focused or fuzzy, is up to us—and our readers.

Strategies for Writing: Description

1. What is my main purpose in writing this descriptive essay? To present and interpret factual information about the subject? To re-create its essence as I have experienced it, or the person, as I have known him or her? To form the basis for a story, a cause-and-effect sequence, or an argument—overt or implied? What mixture of objective information and subjective impressions will best fit my purpose?

2. If my audience is completely unfamiliar with the subject, how much and what kinds of basic information will I have to provide so they can understand what I'm talking about? (Can I assume that they've seen lakes, but not necessarily Lake Tahoe, the subject of my paper? Or that they know other grandmothers, but not mine, about whom I'm writing?) If my readers are familiar with the subject, in what ways can I describe it so they'll discover new aspects of it?

3. What particular characteristics of my subject do I wish to emphasize? Will I use in this description details revealed by the senses—sight, sound, taste, smell, touch? Any other sort of information, such as a person's characteristic behavior, gestures, ways of speaking or moving or dressing, values, companions, possessions, occupation, residence, style of spending money, beliefs, hopes, vulnerabilities? Nonsensory details will be particularly necessary in describing an abstraction, such as somebody's temperament or state of mind.

4. How will I organize my description? From the most dominant to the least dominant details? From the most to the least familiar aspects (or vice versa)? According to what an observer is likely to notice first, second . . . last? Or according to some other pattern?

5. Will I use much general language, or will my description be highly specific throughout? Do I want to evoke a clear, distinct image of the subject? Or a mood—nostalgic, thoughtful, happy, sad, or otherwise?

AMANDA N. CAGLE

Amanda N. Cagle was born in Louisiana in 1979. She earned a BA in French (2000) and an MA in English (2001) at Mississippi State University, and a PhD in English at the University of Connecticut (2006) with a dissertation on American Indian women's poetry. She has taught at the Louisiana School for Math, Science, and the Arts. Cagle's essays and poetry have appeared in *Ontario Review, Louisiana Review*, and *Revista Atenea*.

"On the Banks of the Bogue Chitto" won the Aetna Creative Nonfiction Award at the University of Connecticut and appeared in the Spring 2005 issue of the *Ontario Review*. The Bogue Chitto, which means "Big Creek" in Choctaw, winds through southern Louisiana and Mississippi.

On the Banks of the Bogue Chitto

I was born on the banks of the Bogue Chitto. It was no accident. My mother   1
wasn't caught miles from a hospital when she found herself in labor. She and my father purposefully walked from our plank-walled shotgun house into those woods and down to that bank. His arms supported her, and hers fitted over her taut belly like an insect's wings. It was early morning, and the light seemed false, my father used to say, like lamplight. Hung together in the gray were crows that fell lightly on the pines like a covering of ash. Even in January, the green kudzu vines curled tightly around the black bones of the cypress and the willow oak. My mother had already given birth to two children on the banks of the Bogue Chitto, and my father's mother, and her mothers, and many mothers before them had come to the same place.

This river is all the truth I've ever needed. It's where most of my family   2
was born, where we were named, where we've found our food, where two of us have since chosen to die. It's where I've gone when the world's seemed too much. In this river, my grandmother proved herself to be the greatest catfish grabber in history by pulling an eighty-three-pound flathead to the banks. It's where my father was taught by his father to be a warrior. Where he taught me. I remember him standing on the bank beside me while I peered through the thickets and the dark roots of the forest floor to the slightest shift of shade and light. I stepped a few paces forward sure the very silence of the earth would follow me. I gently notched my arrow, pulled the bow taut, released the narrow shaft, and watched the panther's paw break into red blossoms.

When I think of my father, I like to remember times like these.   3
I like to imagine that he is still the greatest of all the Jena Choctaw warriors. For many years, my brother Jason and I were convinced he was. When the Arrow Trucking Company would not let my father off work for

AMANDA CAGLE, "On the Banks of the Bogue Chitto" from THE ONTARIO REVIEW, Spring 2005 reprinted by permission of the author.

Jason's seventh birthday, he came ripping through our pasture at 5:00 in the morning with the big rig and its goods in tow. My father, Jason and I spent the morning picking Satsumas and the afternoon sitting on the banks of the Bogue Chitto chewing sugar cane which was heavy with the scent of hay and syrup.

4   That night, Jason and I slept in the cab of the 18-wheeler. We were not afraid that someone would steal up on us in the night to enter this mighty truck parked in our field. We knew our father would find a way to make things okay. Maybe the owner would come with a gun, and our father would tell a joke so funny that the man would laugh, pat him on the back and forget all about his truck. Maybe our father would hear the man coming and speed off into the night before he even arrived.

5   Of course, my father was fired from this job, as he would be from many others. He was not a very good employee. He wasn't good at making money or keeping it. He couldn't stand to be indoors, and as much as he tried to conform to an employer's schedule, the rhythm of his own life always got in the way. No job could hold him. When the needle-tooth garmade ripples in the river, my father forgot about work and headed out on the pirogue. When the cornfields stretched skyward and the watermelons grew too heavy for the vines, he could be found not at work but in the fields.

6   Somehow, I always expected him to be out there. When I was a child, I used to love to search for him through the dim and unreal morning shadows. He would be listening to the murmur of earthworms beneath his feet, tasting the first tomatoes, watching the swirls and ripples on the Bogue Chitto. These were his greatest moments. These were the times when he allowed himself to be free of the world. The water of the Bogue Chitto opened itself up to him, and he spent every day trapping and fishing along her banks.

7   I never thought nor hoped that there would come a time when the world owned him, when the water of the Bogue Chitto no longer flowed through him like a vein. But that time came when the state threatened to seize our land after my father had failed to come up with the money for the property taxes. He had lived on those thirty-three acres all of his life. The land had belonged to his father, his grandfather, and many fathers before them. He had tried to borrow money and to sell rebuilt car engines, but he couldn't get enough.

8   After the state assessed my father's land, they sent a social worker to assess his children. Jason, two cousins, and I ran into the woods when the social worker arrived. We watched the house from the tree line, unsure of what we were watching for. All I could picture was the man running after us with a giant net, scooping us up, and throwing us into his car.

9   Before long, we decided to head for the safety of our clubhouse, hidden deep in the tangled woods. Here we kept the bones we hunted and found like treasure. Most of them were from a neighbor's herd. The big bones came from sick cows that wandered off and starved or lay down between close trees and died. We had femurs, long and polished by the heat to a metallic whiteness. There were crescent ribs thin and pale as the

This mangrove swamp, with Spanish moss dripping from the branches, presents striking images of trees ethereal and eerie. Where is this located? Where is the shore? What's under the water? What time of day is it? What's the temperature? The humidity level? If people were in this picture, who would they be, and what would they be doing? Tell a story that interprets either the seen or the unseen (or both) in this photograph, and then see how closely your story corresponds to Amanda N. Cagle's "On the Banks of the Bogue Chitto."

edges of the moon, a smooth hip bone with deep indentions as carefully hollowed out as the bowl of a pipe, and a skull nearly whole and full of black teeth with splintered roots. In these bones, we traced the lines of everything that had happened to us and everything that would.

One September Jason and I found a dog half eaten. His stomach was ballooning out like a full sail, and we ran straight to the house. A panther, our father told us. In those woods, waiting for our father to send the social worker away, the wild moan of that panther stretched taut through the dim air like a scar. 10

We entered the house that night reluctantly. Our father was sitting on the couch flipping through the phone book and writing down names and numbers. Early the next morning he went to town and did not return until nightfall. He continued to do this until he landed a job at the post office. 11

At first, he was just a temp, but he was scared and so he worked hard to convince the post office to hire him full time. After a few years, he was given his own route. He arrived at dawn and returned home too late in the evening to work the fields or check the lines on the Bogue Chitto. But, for the first time in his life, he had a steady job, which meant the state would leave his land and his children alone. 12

13   My mother constantly praised his efforts. She was happy with the steady check and the health insurance. She had grown weary of his jumps between jobs and the anxious wait and hope for food upon his return from the woods. At first, he complained about the hours and the menial task of putting letters in a box, but my mother would simply rub his shoulders and tell him to suck it up. He did just that.

14   Over the next twelve years, he stopped telling stories about how to track deer, about when to plunge the arm deep into the mounded earth to feel for potatoes, and about how to interpret the cold and thin moan of the panther. Instead, he told us about who lived in what neighborhood and about the kind of mail they received. He especially liked to talk about the residents of the Indian Hills subdivision. There were no hills, he would say, and no Indians unless you counted Mr. Gupta.

15   If he had grown restless with the job, he didn't let us know it. He had settled into the expected routine. It was not the routine of a warrior, but I, more than my brother, understood what he had to lose. Nevertheless, I, like Jason, secretly hoped that he would turn in his uniforms. We longed for the days when we relied only on the Bogue Chitto to meet all of our needs. We missed the afternoons of sitting on her banks with our father and spitting muscadine seeds into the water. Sweet potato season passed us by; we harvested a few mustard greens but not enough to sell or freeze; there was squash, but no one stopped to watch it grow heavy with hips. The fall wind blew through the bald cypress, red maple, willow oak, and loblolly pine—the fragrance of death surrounded us, but none of us detected it.

16   In fact, it was a complete surprise. It still is and probably always will be. My father was the first to find out. Two officers arrived at the post office in an unmarked car, walked in and told him Jason was found on the bank of the Bogue Chitto. They were sure because there was a wallet beside the boy's body. There was a shotgun wound, self-inflicted. These things were a matter of fact. My father was so sure the officers were mistaken that he turned down a ride with them and drove himself to the morgue to confirm that the body was not that of his son. He later had to drive back to work to tell his supervisor that he would need a little time off from work; he was not sure how much.

17   He then told mother, the rest of the children, the grandparents and the cousins, and before long the entire Jena Choctaw tribe seemed to have descended on our house. I wondered for a moment if we would perform an old ceremony. The bone pickers of my grandfather's generation knew that in every bone there was an answer, but this was a different time. My father could do little more than pick out the nicest coffin he could afford. He purchased a plot of land that none of us had ever seen before. The man who sold it to him had a big round face and tight red fingers. He drew his boot heel across the plot and shook my father's hand.

18   My father spent the days following the funeral in the pastures cutting down what remained of the butterbeans, purple hulls and Satsuma. He paced along the banks of the Bogue Chitto and stared into its water.

The large animals living in the swamp water moved now like great shadows of a larger mystery. The river mud flaked in big cracks. My father sat on the bank like a smooth stone made by the waters of many a rain-lit night.

He returned to work too soon, and whatever he did there caused 19
two more men in suits and an unmarked car to approach him. This time they came to our house, and they were not police but some type of high-ranking post office employees. They told him that he was in the midst of a nervous breakdown and that if he wanted to keep his job, he needed to check himself into the Woodland Hills Hospital for psychiatric treatment. When the men left, my cousins and I chased after them and threw small gravel rocks at their car. I didn't think for a moment that my father would go. I somehow expected him to follow behind us and to throw the furthest rock himself, but he did not. He sat inside on the couch while my mother pulled a suitcase from beneath their bed.

When I visited him at the hospital, his room was sterile and white. 20
All of the blinds were down and the only sound was that of the hum of fluorescent lights. Sitting in the corner chair, under the falseness of the lamplight, he didn't look like anyone I had ever seen.

The family was invited to sit in on a few of the therapy sessions. Once 21
the psychiatrist asked me to leave because she thought that I was interfering with my father's progress and disrupting the session. I had lashed out at him for taking the pills the psychiatrist had prescribed. I knew that neither the pills nor the stay at the white and sterile hospital would help him regain his balance. I wanted more than anything to be able to see him again as a warrior. I wanted him to leave the confines of the institution and return home to the ripening of the muscadines and the bedding of the catfish.

He did not stay long in that hospital. He returned to his job and 22
to the routines of his life. The water of the Bogue Chitto must still run through him as it does through me, but he can no longer make the walls and ceilings that surround him vanish into fields of corn and horses, grain and cows, wandering ants and squirrels. There, where we used to sit, the marsh grass dances in the wind. Missing are the marks of our feet in the soft mud on the bank of the Bogue Chitto. Missing are the small prints that should hold the form of our bodies among the ancient creases and folds.

LINDA VILLAROSA

Linda Villarosa (born 1959) is a graduate of the University of Colorado and a former executive editor of *Essence Magazine*. She currently works as a freelance journalist based in New York City and has edited or coedited several books on parenting, adolescence, and health, including *Body & Soul: The Black Woman's Guide to Physical Health and Emotional Well-Being* (2003).

How Much of the Body Is Replaceable?

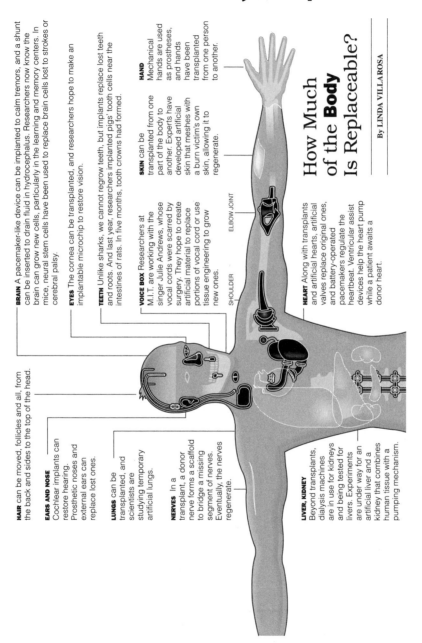

How Much of the Body Is Replaceable?

By LINDA VILLAROSA

BRAIN A pacemaker-like device can be implanted to calm tremors, and a shunt can be inserted to drain fluid in hydrocephalus. Researchers now know the brain can grow new cells, particularly in the learning and memory centers. In mice, neural stem cells have been used to replace brain cells lost to strokes or cerebral palsy.

EYES The cornea can be transplanted, and researchers hope to make an implantable microchip to restore vision.

TEETH Unlike sharks, we cannot regrow teeth, but implants replace lost teeth and roots. And last year, researchers implanted pigs' tooth cells near the intestines of rats. In five months, tooth crowns had formed.

SKIN can be transplanted from one part of the body to another. Experts have developed artificial skin that meshes with a burn victim's own skin, allowing it to regenerate.

HAND Mechanical hands are used as prostheses, and hands have been transplanted from one person to another.

VOICE BOX Researchers at M.I.T. are working with the singer Julie Andrews, whose vocal cords were scarred by surgery. They hope to create artificial material to replace portions of vocal cord or use tissue engineering to grow new ones.

SHOULDER

ELBOW JOINT

HEART Along with transplants and artificial hearts, artificial valves replace original ones, and battery-operated pacemakers regulate the heartbeat. Ventricular assist devices help the heart pump while a patient awaits a donor heart.

HAIR can be moved, follicles and all, from the back and sides to the top of the head.

EARS AND NOSE Cochlear implants can restore hearing. Prosthetic noses and external ears can replace lost ones.

LUNGS can be transplanted, and scientists are studying temporary artificial lungs.

NERVES In a transplant, a donor nerve forms a scaffold to bridge a missing segment of nerves. Eventually, the nerves regenerate.

LIVER, KIDNEY Beyond transplants, dialysis machines are in use for kidneys and being tested for livers. Experiments are under way for an artificial liver and a kidney that combines human tissue with a pumping mechanism.

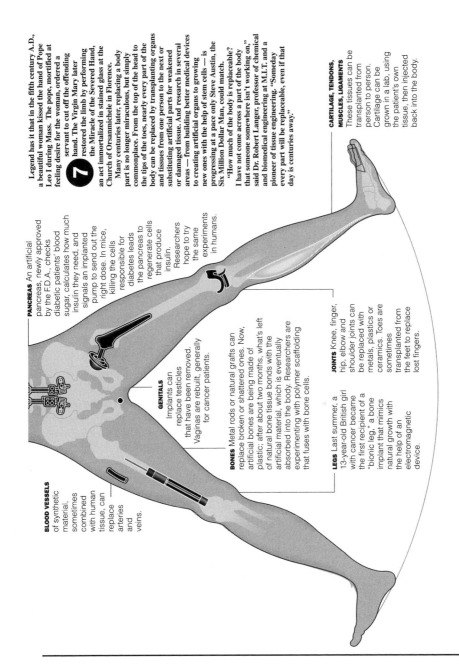

7 Legend has it that in the fifth century A.D., a beautiful woman kissed the hand of Pope Leo I during Mass. The pope, mortified at feeling desire for the woman, ordered a servant to cut off the offending hand. The Virgin Mary later restored the limb by performing the Miracle of the Severed Hand, an act immortalized in stained glass at the Church of Orsanmichele in Florence.

Many centuries later, replacing a body part is no longer miraculous, but simply commonplace. From the top of the head to the tips of the toes, nearly every part of the body can be replaced by transplanting organs and tissues from one person to the next or substituting artificial parts for weakened or damaged tissue. And research in several areas — from building better medical devices to creating artificial organs to growing new ones with the help of stem cells — is progressing at a pace only Steve Austin, the Six Million Dollar Man, could match.

"How much of the body is replaceable? I have not come across a part of the body that someone somewhere isn't working on," said Dr. Robert Langer, professor of chemical and biomedical engineering at M.I.T. and a pioneer of tissue engineering. "Someday every part will be replaceable, even if that day is centuries away."

CARTILAGE, TENDONS, MUSCLES, LIGAMENTS These tissues can be transplanted from person to person. Cartilage can be grown in a lab, using the patient's own tissue, then injected back into the body.

PANCREAS An artificial pancreas, newly approved by the F.D.A., checks diabetic patients' blood sugar, calculates how much insulin they need, and signals an implanted pump to send out the right dose. In mice, killing the cells responsible for diabetes leads the pancreas to regenerate cells that produce insulin. Researchers hope to try the same experiments in humans.

BLOOD VESSELS of synthetic material, sometimes combined with human tissue, can replace arteries and veins.

GENITALS Implants can replace testicles that have been removed. Vaginas are rebuilt, generally for cancer patients.

BONES Metal rods or natural grafts can replace broken or shattered ones. Now, artificial bones are being made of plastic; after about two months, what's left of natural bone tissue bonds with the artificial material, which is eventually absorbed into the body. Researchers are experimenting with polymer scaffolding that fuses with bone cells.

LEGS Last summer, a 13-year-old British girl with cancer became the first recipient of a "bionic leg," a bone implant that mimics natural growth with the help of an electromagnetic device.

JOINTS Knee, finger, hip, elbow and shoulder joints can be replaced with metals, plastics or ceramics. Toes are sometimes transplanted from the feet to replace lost fingers.

Content

1. Villarosa refers to "the Six Million Dollar Man," from a television show about an action hero, who, after having been severely injured, was "put back together"—better than new—using artificial parts. *The Bionic Woman* took up a similar theme. What other shows or movies use this idea, and why is it a popular subject? If you have read Mary Shelley's *Frankenstein*, discuss to what extent it belongs to this tradition.

2. Many people currently alter their body voluntarily through plastic surgery. Do you suppose that at some time in the future people will elect to replace healthy body parts with stronger, more durable artificial ones? Explore the ethical implications of this possibility. For example, if professional athletes could buy themselves better knees, arms, or legs, what would the implications of this trend be for professional sports? What about students who might want to implant computing devices into their brain to enhance math ability? (See Bill McKibben, "Designer Genes" [Chapter 11], for an extension of this discussion.)

3. Villarosa's descriptions of replaceable body parts allude to ethically complex issues such as vivisection, prolonging life with mechanical devices, restoring body parts with donated organs, and human experimentation. Are such decisions ultimately personal? Should our society regulate such choices? For example, should the demand for donated organs be left to the free market? What are the pros and cons of establishing guidelines for medical research and experimentation?

For Writing

4. *Journal Writing.* Explore how the ethical issues Villarosa raises might influence the decision to replace your own or a loved one's body part(s). What criteria would you use to decide whether to take advantage of an experimental medical advance such as a transplant or artificial implant? Is medical intervention always, to some extent, experimentation? Discuss this with a writing partner and expand your discussion into an essay. Include relevant print or online sources.

5. *Dialogues.* How do Deresiewicz's "Faux Friendship" (56–60) McKibben's "Designer Genes" (Chapter 11) suggest, like Villarosa's diagram, that technology has blurred the boundaries of human integrity?

MARK TWAIN

Mark Twain (a riverman's term for "two fathoms deep," the pen name of Samuel Clemens [1835–1910]) celebrated in his writing a lifelong love affair with the Mississippi River and with the rural life along its banks. In *The Adventures of Tom Sawyer* (1876) and *The Adventures of Huckleberry Finn* (1885), he immortalized the riverfront town of Hannibal, Missouri, where he was born and whose folkways he absorbed. A prolific writer, Twain's works grew increasingly pessimistic as he experienced grief (the death of his beloved daughter) and economic reversals later in life. Nevertheless, in his *Autobiography* (published in 1924, fourteen years after his death), Twain depicted an idyllic but comically realistic picture of a country childhood, specific in time (pre–Civil War) and place (in the country, four miles from Florida, Missouri), yet timeless and ubiquitous. The autobiography shows us two central characters, the boy Sam Clemens, who enjoyed every aspect of his Uncle John Quarles's farm, and Mark Twain, the older, wiser, and sometimes more cynical author, who writes these reminiscences after alerting readers to bear in mind that he once could "remember anything, whether it had happened or not; but my faculties are decaying, now." What he remembers now is the spirit of the farm, the people who lived there, white and black, and how they lived in abiding harmony.

Twain reinforces that spirit with an abundance of sensory details— often the mainstay of description, as they are here. Thus he evokes a rich sensory intermingling in descriptions such as the following: "I can call back the solemn twilight [*sight*] and mystery of the deep woods, the earthy smells, the faint odors of the wild flowers [*smell*], the sheen of rain-washed foliage [*sight*], the rattling clatter of drops when the wind shook the trees, the far-off hammering of woodpeckers [*sound*]. . . . I can see the blue clusters of wild grapes . . . and I remember the taste of them and the smell" [*sight, taste, smell*] (¶ 13).

Uncle John's Farm

For many years I believed that I remembered helping my grandfather drink his whiskey toddy when I was six weeks old, but I do not tell about that any more, now; I am grown old, and my memory is not as active as it used to be. When I was younger I could remember anything, whether it had happened or not; but my faculties are decaying, now, and soon I shall be so I cannot remember any but the things that [never] happened. It is sad to go to pieces like this, but we all have to do it.

My uncle, John A. Quarles, was a farmer, and his place was in the country four miles from Florida. He had eight children, and fifteen or twenty negroes, and was also fortunate in other ways. Particularly in his character. I have not come across a better man than he was. I was his guest for two or three months every year, from the fourth year after we removed to Hannibal till I was eleven or twelve years old. I have never consciously used him or his wife in a book, but his farm has come very handy to me in literature, once or twice. In *Huck Finn* and in *Tom Sawyer Detective* I moved it down to Arkansas. It was all of six hundred miles, but it was no trouble, it was not a very large farm; five hundred acres,

1

2

Title supplied

perhaps, but I could have done it if it had been twice as large. And as for the morality of it, I cared nothing for that; I would move a State if the exigencies of literature required it.

3   It was a heavenly place for a boy, that farm of my uncle John's. The house was a double log one, with a spacious floor (roofed in) connecting it with the kitchen. In the summer the table was set in the middle of that shady and breezy floor, and the sumptuous meals—well, it makes me cry to think of them. Fried chicken, roast pig, wild and tame turkeys, ducks and geese; venison just killed; squirrels, rabbits, pheasants, partridges, prairie-chickens; biscuits, hot batter cakes, hot buckwheat cakes, hot "wheat bread," hot rolls, hot corn pone; fresh corn boiled on the ear, succotash, butterbeans, string-beans, tomatoes, pease, Irish potatoes, sweet-potatoes; buttermilk, sweet milk, "clabber"; watermelons, muskmelons, cantaloupe—all fresh from the garden—apple pie, peach pie, pumpkin pie, apple dumplings, peach cobbler—I can't remember the rest. The way that the things were cooked was perhaps the main splendor—particularly a certain few of the dishes. For instance, the corn bread, the hot biscuits and wheat bread, and the fried chicken. These things have never been properly cooked in the North—in fact, no one there is able to learn the art, so far as my experience goes. The North thinks it knows how to make corn bread, but this is gross superstition. Perhaps no bread in the world is quite as good as Southern corn bread, and perhaps no bread in the world is quite so bad as the Northern imitation of it. The North seldom tries to fry chicken, and this is well; the art cannot be learned north of the line of Mason and Dixon, nor anywhere in Europe. . . .

4   It seems a pity that the world should throw away so many good things merely because they are unwholesome. I doubt if God has given us any refreshment which, taken in moderation, is unwholesome, except microbes. Yet there are people who strictly deprive themselves of each and every eatable, drinkable and smokable which has in any way acquired a shady reputation. They pay this price for health. And health is all they get for it. How strange it is; it is like paying out your whole fortune for a cow that has gone dry. . . .

5   The farmhouse stood in the middle of a very large yard, and the yard was fenced on three sides with rails and on the rear side with high palings; against these stood the smokehouse; beyond the palings was the orchard; beyond the orchard were the negro quarter and the tobacco-fields. The front yard was entered over a stile, made of sawed-off logs of graduated heights; I do not remember any gate. In a corner of the front yard were a dozen lofty hickory-trees and a dozen black-walnuts, and in the nutting season riches were to be gathered there.

6   Down a piece, abreast the house, stood a little log cabin against the rail fence; and there the woody hill fell sharply away, past the barns, the corn-crib, the stables and the tobacco-curing house, to a limpid brook which sang along over its gravelly bed and curved and frisked in and out

and here and there and yonder in the deep shade of overhanging foliage and vines—a divine place for wading, and it had swimming-pools, too, which were forbidden to us and therefore much frequented by us. For we were little Christian children, and had early been taught the value of forbidden fruit. . . .

I can see the farm yet, with perfect clearness. I can see all its belong-   7 ings, all its details; the family room of the house, with a "trundle" bed in one corner and a spinning-wheel in another, a wheel whose rising and falling wail, heard from a distance, was the mournfulest of all sounds to me, and made me homesick and low-spirited, and filled my atmosphere with the wandering spirits of the dead; the vast fireplace, piled high, on winter nights, with flaming hickory logs from whose ends a sugary sap bubbled out but did not go to waste, for we scraped it off and ate it; the lazy cat spread out on the rough hearthstones, the drowsy dogs braced against the jambs and blinking; my aunt in one chimney-corner knitting, my uncle in the other smoking his corn-cob pipe; the slick and carpet-less oak floor faintly mirroring the dancing flame-tongues and freckled with black indentations where fire-coals had popped out and died a leisurely death; half a dozen children romping in the background twilight; "split"-bottomed chairs here and there, some with rockers; a cradle—out of service, but waiting, with confidence; in the early cold mornings a snuggle of children, in shirts and chemises, occupying the hearthstone and procrastinating—they could not bear to leave that comfortable place and go out on the wind-swept floor-space between the house and kitchen where the general tin basin stood, and wash.

Along outside of the front fence ran the country road; dusty in the   8 summertime, and a good place for snakes—they liked to lie in it and sun themselves; when they were rattlesnakes or puff adders, we killed them; when they were black snakes, or racers, or belonged to the fabled "hoop" breed, we fled, without shame; when they were "house snakes" or "garters" we carried them home and put them in Aunt Patsy's work-basket for a surprise; for she was prejudiced against snakes, and always when she took the basket in her lap and they began to climb out of it it disordered her mind. She never could seem to get used to them; her opportunities went for nothing. And she was always cold toward bats, too, and could not bear them; and yet I think a bat is as friendly a bird as there is. My mother was Aunt Patsy's sister, and had the same wild super-stitions. A bat is beautifully soft and silky; I do not know any creature that is pleasanter to the touch, or is more grateful for caressings, if offered in the right spirit. I know all about these coleoptera, because our great cave, three miles below Hannibal, was multitudinously stocked with them, and often I brought them home to amuse my mother with. It was easy to man-age if it was a school day, because then I had ostensibly been to school and hadn't any bats. She was not a suspicious person, but full of trust and confidence; and when I said "There's something in my coat pocket for you," she would put her hand in. But she always took it out again, herself; I didn't have to tell her. It was remarkable, the way she couldn't learn to like private bats. . . .

9   Beyond the road where the snakes sunned themselves was a dense young thicket, and through it a dim-lighted path led a quarter of a mile; then out of the dimness one emerged abruptly upon a level great prairie which was covered with wild strawberry-plants, vividly starred with prairie pinks, and walled in on all sides by forests. The strawberries were fragrant and fine, and in the season we were generally there in the crisp freshness of the early morning, while the dew-beads still sparkled upon the grass and the woods were ringing with the first songs of the birds.

10   Down the forest slopes to the left were the swings. They were made of bark stripped from hickory saplings. When they became dry they were dangerous. They usually broke when a child was forty feet in the air, and this was why so many bones had to be mended every year. I had no ill-luck myself, but none of my cousins escaped. There were eight of them, and at one time and another they broke fourteen arms among them. But it cost next to nothing, for the doctor worked by the year—$25 for the whole family. I remember two of the Florida doctors, Chowning and Meredith. They not only tended an entire family for $25 a year, but furnished the medicines themselves. Good measures, too. Only the largest persons could hold a whole dose. Castor-oil was the principal beverage. The dose was half a dipperful, with half a dipperful of New Orleans molasses added to help it down and make it taste good, which it never did. The next standby was calomel; the next, rhubarb; and the next, jalap. Then they bled the patient, and put mustard-plasters on him. It was a dreadful system, and yet the death-rate was not heavy. The calomel was nearly sure to salivate the patient and cost him some of his teeth. There were no dentists. When teeth became touched with decay or were otherwise ailing, the doctor knew of but one thing to do: he fetched his tongs and dragged them out. If the jaw remained, it was not his fault. Doctors were not called, in cases of ordinary illness; the family's grandmother attended to those. . . .

11   The country schoolhouse was three miles from my uncle's farm. It stood in a clearing in the woods, and would hold about twenty-five boys and girls. We attended the school with more or less regularity once or twice a week, in summer, walking to it in the cool of the morning by the forest paths, and back in the gloaming at the end of the day. All the pupils brought their dinners in baskets—corn-dodger, buttermilk and other good things—and sat in the shade of the trees at noon and ate them. It is the part of my education which I look back upon with the most satisfaction. My first visit to the school was when I was seven. A strapping girl of fifteen, in the customary sunbonnet and calico dress, asked me if I "used tobacco"—meaning did I chew it. I said, no. It roused her scorn. She reported me to all the crowd, and said—

"Here is a boy seven years old who can't chaw tobacco."   12

By the looks and comments which this produced, I realized that I was   13
a degraded object; I was cruelly ashamed of myself. I determined to reform.
But I only made myself sick; I was not able to learn to chew tobacco.
I learned to smoke fairly well, but that did not conciliate anybody, and I remained a poor thing, and characterless. I longed to be respected, but I never
was able to rise. Children have but little charity for each other's defects.

As I have said, I spent some part of every year at the farm until I was   14
twelve or thirteen years old. The life which I led there with my cousins
was full of charm, and so is the memory of it yet. I can call back the solemn
twilight and mystery of the deep woods, the earthy smells, the faint odors
of the wild flowers, the sheen of rain-washed foliage, the rattling clatter
of drops when the wind shook the trees, the far-off hammering of woodpeckers and the muffled drumming of wood-pheasants in the remoteness
of the forest, the snap-shot glimpses of disturbed wild creatures skurrying
through the grass—I can call it all back and make it as real as it ever was,
and as blessed. I can call back the prairie, and its loneliness and peace,
and a vast hawk hanging motionless in the sky, with his wings spread
wide and the blue of the vault showing through the fringe of their end-
feathers. I can see the woods in their autumn dress, the oaks purple, the
hickories washed with gold, the maples and the sumacs luminous with
crimson fires, and I can hear the rustle made by the fallen leaves as we
ploughed through them. I can see the blue clusters of wild grapes hanging
amongst the foliage of the saplings, and I remember the taste of them and
the smell. I know how the wild blackberries looked, and how they tasted;
and the same with the paw-paws, the hazelnuts and the persimmons; and
I can feel the thumping rain, upon my head, of hickory-nuts and walnuts
when we were out in the frosty dawn to scramble for them with the pigs,
and the gusts of wind loosed them and sent them down. I know the stain
of blackberries, and how pretty it is; and I know the stain of walnut hulls,
and how little it minds soap and water; also what grudged experience it
had of either of them. I know the taste of maple sap, and when to gather
it, and how to arrange the troughs and the delivery tubes, and how to
boil down the juice, and how to hook the sugar after it is made; also how
much better hooked sugar tastes than any that is honestly come by, let
bigots say what they will. I know how a prize watermelon looks when it
is sunning its fat rotundity among pumpkin-vines and "simblins"; I know
how to tell when it is ripe without "plugging" it; I know how inviting
it looks when it is cooling itself in a tub of water under the bed, waiting; I know how it looks when it lies on the table in the sheltered great
floor-space between house and kitchen, and the children gathered for the
sacrifice and their mouths watering; I know the crackling sound it makes
when the carving-knife enters its end, and I can see the split fly along in
front of the blade as the knife cleaves its way to the other end; I can see its
halves fall apart and display the rich red meat and the black seeds, and

the heart standing up, a luxury fit for the elect; I know how a boy looks, behind a yard-long slice of that melon, and I know how he feels; for I have been there. I know the taste of the watermelon which has been honestly come by, and I know the taste of the watermelon which has been acquired by art. Both taste good, but the experienced know which tastes best. I know the look of green apples and peaches and pears on the trees, and I know how entertaining they are when they are inside of a person. I know how ripe ones look when they are piled in pyramids under the trees, and how pretty they are and how vivid their colors. I know how a frozen apple looks, in a barrel down cellar in the winter-time, and how hard it is to bite, and how the frost makes the teeth ache, and yet how good it is, notwith-standing. I know the disposition of elderly people to select the specked apples for the children, and I once knew ways to beat the game. I know the look of an apple that is roasting and sizzling on a hearth on a winter's evening, and I know the comfort that comes of eating it hot, along with some sugar and a drench of cream. I know the delicate art and mystery of so cracking hickory-nuts and walnuts on a flatiron with a hammer that the kernels will be delivered whole, and I know how the nuts, taken in conjunction with winter apples, cider and doughnuts, make old people's tales and old jokes sound fresh and crisp and enchanting, and juggle an evening away before you know what went with the time. I know the look of Uncle Dan'l's kitchen as it was on privileged nights when I was a child, and I can see the white and black children grouped on the hearth, with the firelight playing on their faces and the shadows flickering upon the walls, clear back toward the cavernous gloom of the rear, and I can hear Uncle Dan'l telling the immortal tales which Uncle Remus Harris was to gather into his books and charm the world with, by and by; and I can feel again the creepy joy which quivered through me when the time for the ghost-story of the "Golden Arm" was reached—and the sense of regret, too, which came over me, for it was always the last story of the evening, and there was nothing between it and the unwelcome bed.

15   I can remember the bare wooden stairway in my uncle's house, and the turn to the left above the landing, and the rafters and the slanting roof over my bed, and the squares of moonlight on the floor, and the white cold world of snow outside, seen through the curtainless window. I can remember the howling of the wind and the quaking of the house on stormy nights, and how snug and cozy one felt, under the blankets, listen-ing, and how the powdery snow used to sift in, around the sashes, and lie in little ridges on the floor, and make the place look chilly in the morning, and curb the wild desire to get up—in case there was any. I can remember how very dark that room was, in the dark of the moon, and how packed it was with ghostly stillness when one woke up by accident away in the night, and forgotten sins came flocking out of the secret chambers of the memory and wanted a hearing; and how ill chosen the time seemed for this kind of business; and how dismal was the hoo-hooing of the owl and the wailing of the wolf, sent mourning by on the night wind.

I remember the raging of the rain on that roof, summer nights, and 16
how pleasant it was to lie and listen to it, and enjoy the white splendor
of the lightning and the majestic booming and crashing of the thunder. It
was a very satisfactory room; and there was a lightning-rod which was
reachable from the window, an adorable and skittish thing to climb up
and down, summer nights, when there were duties on hand of a sort to
make privacy desirable.

I remember the 'coon and 'possum hunts, night, and the negroes, and 17
the long marches through the black gloom of the woods, and the excitement which fired everybody when the distant bay of an experienced dog
announced that the game was treed; then the wild scramblings and stum-
blings through briars and bushes and over roots to get to the spot; then the
lighting of a fire and the felling of the tree, the joyful frenzy of the dogs and
the negroes, and the weird picture it all made in the red glare—I remember
it all well, and the delight that every one got out of it, except the 'coon.

I remember the pigeon seasons, when the birds would come in mil- 18
lions, and cover the trees, and by their weight break down the branches.
They were clubbed to death with sticks; guns were not necessary, and were
not used. I remember the squirrel hunts, and the prairie-chicken hunts,
and the wild-turkey hunts, and all that; and how we turned out, mornings, while it was still dark, to go on these expeditions, and how chilly
and dismal it was, and how often I regretted that I was well enough to
go. A toot on a tin horn brought twice as many dogs as were needed, and
in their happiness they raced and scampered about, and knocked small
people down, and made no end of unnecessary noise. At the word, they
vanished away toward the woods, and we drifted silently after them in
the melancholy gloom. But presently the gray dawn stole over the world,
the birds piped up, then the sun rose and poured light and comfort all
around, everything was fresh and dewy and fragrant, and life was a boon
again. After three hours of tramping we arrived back wholesomely tired,
overladen with game, very hungry, and just in time for breakfast.

Content

1. Even though Twain's opening paragraph warns that he sometimes remembers
something, "whether it had happened or not," what he says throughout this essay
appears true and convincing. Why? Does anything seem too good to be true?
What made the farm a "heavenly place for a boy"? Do his memories of children's
broken bones (¶ 10) and his childhood shame at being unable to chew tobacco
(¶s 11–13) diminish his pleasant recollections?

Strategies/Structures/Language

2. In places Twain's description involves long lists or catalogues—of foods (¶ 3),
of the sights and sounds and activities of farm life (¶s 3–14), and of the seasons and
seasonal activities (¶s 15–18). How does he vary the lists to keep them appealing?

3. Why does Twain pack so many details into such a long paragraph (¶ 14)? If he had broken it up, where could he have done so? With what effects?

4. In this largely descriptive account, Twain provides characterizations of the local doctors (¶ 10), many interpretations ("The life was . . . full of charm," [¶ 14]), and narration of incidents—for instance, of Aunt Patsy and the snakes (¶ 8). Explain how these techniques contribute to the overall picture of life on the farm.

5. Twain uses the language of an adult to recall events from his childhood. Find a typical passage in which he enables us to see the experience as a child would but to imply or offer an adult's interpretation.

For Writing

6. *Journal Writing.* Identify a place that had considerable significance—pleasant, indifferent, unpleasant, or a mixture—for you as a child, and describe it. Use sensory details, where appropriate, to help your readers to re-create your experiences. The essays by Megan McGuire, Amanda N. Cagle, and Matt Nocton provide good examples of how to do this.

7. Pick an aspect of your childhood relationship with a parent or other adult, or a critical experience in your precollege schooling, and describe it so the reader shares your experience. Compare, if you wish, with essays by Frederick Douglass, Anne Fadiman, Ning Yu, Scott Russell Sanders, or Megan McGuire.

8. "Our three basic needs, for food and security and love, are so mixed and mingled and entwined that we cannot straightly think of one without the others," says distinguished food writer M. F. K. Fisher. Write an essay focusing on the relationship between food and people: about how food has either shown you something about yourself; shaped your relationship with an individual, family, or group; or inspired adventures, culinary, philosophical, or otherwise. Your writing can range from how-to-do-it (gardening or recipes in context) to memories of events in which food (or its absence) played a major role—evoking succulence, hospitality, seduction, stress, an entire culture conveyed in a single dish or meal. Compare, if you wish, Megan McGuire's essay "Wake-Up Call" (Chapter 8) and Lynda Barry's graphic essay "Common Scents" (Chapter 7).

9. *Dialogues.* Compare Twain's descriptions of the sights, flavors, and textures of the life on the farm and surrounding countryside with Nocton's (Chapter 6). What does each writer appear to have learned through the experiences he narrates? Compare, for example, Twain's references to "forbidden fruit" (¶ 6) and to the "fragrant and fine" "wild strawberry-plants" that grew "beyond the road where the snakes sunned themselves" (¶ 9). How do their descriptions suggest a process of internalizing the specific values of their respective cultures?

10. Twain celebrates the opulence of the South, including its cuisine (¶ 3), and disparages those who reject "good things merely because they are unwholesome" (¶ 4). What are some of the positive and negative ways that our society responds to abundance and wealth (see Charles C. Mann, "The Coming Death Shortage" [Chapter 8], and Robert Reich, "The Global Elite" [Chapter 9])? How do we glorify and also criticize extravagant lifestyles? What do these responses suggest about contemporary American culture?

MICHAEL POLLAN

Michael Pollan (born 1955) is the author of *The Omnivore's Dilemma: A Natural History of Four Meals* (2006); *In Defense of Food: An Eater's Manifesto* (2008); and *Food Rules: An Eater's Manual* (2009). He is a contributing writer to *The New York Times Magazine* and a Professor of Journalism at the University of California at Berkeley, where he directs the Knight Program in Science and Environmental Journalism. In "The Meal," excerpted from *The Omnivore's Dilemma*, Pollan examines how our relationship with the natural world has changed through the growth of industrial agriculture, the dominance of corn in the industrial food chain, and the consumption of processed food, of which corn constitutes a major part.

The Meal

The meal at the end of the industrial food chain that begins in an Iowa corn-   1
field is prepared by McDonald's and eaten in a moving car. Or at least this was the version of the industrial meal I chose to eat; it could easily have been another. The myriad streams of commodity corn, after being variously processed and turned into meat, converge in all sorts of different meals I might have eaten, at KFC or Pizza Hut or Applebee's, or prepared myself from ingredients bought at the supermarket. Industrial meals are all around us, after all; they make up the food chain from which most of us eat most of the time.

My eleven-year-old son, Isaac, was more than happy to join me at   2
McDonald's; he doesn't get there often, so it's a treat. (For most American children today, it is no longer such a treat: One in three of them eat fast food every single day.) Judith, my wife, was less enthusiastic. She's careful about what she eats, and having a fast-food lunch meant giving up a "real meal," which seemed a shame. Isaac pointed out that she could order one of McDonald's new "premium salads" with the Paul Newman dressing. I read in the business pages that these salads are a big hit, but even if they weren't, they'd probably stay on the menu strictly for their rhetorical usefulness. The marketers have a term for what a salad or veggie burger does for a fast-food chain: "denying the denier." These healthier menu items hand the child who wants to eat fast food a sharp tool with which to chip away at his parents' objections. "But Mom, you can get the salad . . ."

Which is exactly what Judith did: order the Cobb salad with Caesar   3
dressing. At $3.99, it was the most expensive item on the menu. I ordered a classic cheeseburger, large fries, and a large Coke. Large turns out to be a full 32 ounces (a quart of soda!) but, thanks to the magical economics of supersizing, it cost only 30 cents more than the 16-ounce

"small." Isaac went with the new white-meat Chicken McNuggets, a double-thick vanilla shake, and a large order of fries, followed by a new dessert treat consisting of freeze-dried pellets of ice cream. That each of us ordered something different is a hallmark of the industrial food chain, which breaks the family down into its various demographics and markets separately to each one: Together we would be eating alone together, and therefore probably eating more. The total for the three of us came to fourteen dollars, and was packed up and ready to go in four minutes. Before I left the register I picked up a densely printed handout called "A Full Serving of Nutrition Facts: Choose the Best Meal for You."

4   We could have slipped into a booth, but it was such a nice day we decided to put the top down on the convertible and eat our lunch in the car, something the food and the car have both been engineered to accommodate. These days 19 percent of American meals are eaten in the car. The car has cup holders, front seat and rear, and, except for the salad, all the food (which we could have ordered, paid for, and picked up without opening the car door) can be readily eaten with one hand. Indeed, this is the genius of the chicken nugget: It liberated chicken from the fork and plate, making it as convenient, waste-free, and automobile-friendly as the precondimented hamburger. No doubt the food scientists at McDonald's corporate headquarters in Oak Brook, Illinois, are right now hard at work on the one-handed salad.

5   But though Judith's Cobb salad did present a challenge to front-seat dining, eating it at fifty-five miles per hour seemed like the thing to do, since corn was the theme of this meal: The car was eating corn too, being fueled in part by ethanol. Even though the additive promises to *diminish* air quality in California, new federal mandates pushed by the corn processors require refineries in the state to help eat the corn surplus by diluting their gasoline with 10 percent ethanol.

6   I ate a lot of McDonald's as a kid. This was in the pre-Wallerstein era, when you still had to order a second little burger or sack of fries if you wanted more, and the chicken nugget had not yet been invented. (One memorable childhood McDonald's meal ended when our station wagon got rear-ended at a light, propelling my milk shake across the car in creamy white lariats.) I loved everything about fast food: the individual portions all wrapped up like presents (not having to share with my three sisters was a big part of the appeal; fast food was private property at its best); the familiar meaty perfume of the French fries filling the car; and the pleasingly sequenced bite into a burger—the soft, sweet roll, the crunchy pickle, the savory moistness of the meat.

7   Well-designed fast food has a fragrance and flavor all its own, a fragrance and flavor only nominally connected to hamburgers or French fries or for that matter to *any* particular food. Certainly the hamburgers and fries you make at home don't have it. And yet Chicken McNuggets do, even though they're ostensibly an entirely different food made from

a different species. Whatever it is (surely the food scientists know), for countless millions of people living now, this generic fast-food flavor is one of the unerasable smells and tastes of childhood—which makes it a kind of comfort food. Like other comfort foods, it supplies (besides nostalgia) a jolt of carbohydrates and fat, which, some scientists now believe, relieve stress and bathe the brain in chemicals that make it feel good.

Isaac announced that his white-meat McNuggets were tasty, a defi- 8 nite improvement over the old recipe. McNuggets have come in for a lot of criticism recently, which might explain the reformulation. Ruling in 2003 in a lawsuit brought against McDonald's by a group of obese teenagers, a federal judge in New York had defamed the McNugget even as he dismissed the suit. "Rather than being merely chicken fried in a pan," he wrote in his decision, McNuggets "are a McFranksteinian creation of various elements not utilized by the home cook." After cataloging the thirty-eight ingredients in a McNugget, Judge Sweet suggested that McDonald's marketing bordered on deceptive, since the dish is not what it purports to be—that is, a piece of chicken simply fried—and, contrary to what a consumer might reasonably expect, actually contains more fat and total calories than a cheeseburger. Since the lawsuit, McDonald's has reformulated the nugget with white meat, and begun handing out "A Full Serving of Nutrition Facts."* According to the flyer, a serving of six nuggets now has precisely ten fewer calories than a cheeseburger. Chalk up another achievement for food science.

When I asked Isaac if the new nuggets tasted more like chicken than 9 he old ones, he seemed baffled by the question. "No, they taste like what they are, which is nuggets," and then dropped on his dad a withering two-syllable "duh." In this consumer's mind at least, the link between a nugget and the chicken in it was never more than notional, and probably irrelevant. By now the nugget constitutes its own genre of food for American children, many of whom eat nuggets every day. For Isaac, the nugget is a distinct taste of childhood, quite apart from chicken, and no doubt a future vehicle of nostalgia—a madeleine in the making.

Isaac passed one up to the front for Judith and me to sample. 10 It looked and smelled pretty good, with a nice crust and bright white interior reminiscent of chicken breast meat. In appearance and texture a nugget certainly alludes to fried chicken, yet all I could really taste was salt, that all-purpose fast-food flavor, and, okay, maybe a note of chicken bouillon informing the salt. Overall the nugget seemed more like an abstraction than a full-fledged food, an idea of chicken waiting to be fleshed out.

The ingredients listed in the flyer suggest a lot of thought goes into 11 a nugget, that and a lot of corn. Of the thirty-eight ingredients it takes

---

* In 2005 McDonald's announced it would begin printing nutrition information on its packaging.

to make a McNugget, I counted thirteen that can be derived from corn: the corn-fed chicken itself; modified cornstarch (to bind the pulverized chicken meat); mono-, tri-, and diglycerides (emulsifiers, which keep the fats and water from separating); dextrose; lecithin (another emulsifier); chicken broth (to restore some of the flavor that processing leaches out); yellow corn flour and more modified cornstarch (for the batter); cornstarch (a filler); vegetable shortening; partially hydrogenated corn oil; and citric acid as a preservative. A couple of other plants take part in the nugget: There's some wheat in the batter, and on any given day the hydrogenated oil could come from soybeans, canola, or cotton rather than corn, depending on market price and availability.

12   According to the handout, McNuggets also contain several completely synthetic ingredients, quasiedible substances that ultimately come not from a corn or soybean field but from a petroleum refinery or chemical plant. These chemicals are what make modern processed foods possible, by keeping the organic materials in them from going bad or looking strange after months in the freezer or on the road. Listed first are the "leavening agents": sodium aluminum phosphate, monocalcium phosphate, sodium acid pyrophosphate, and calcium lactate. These are antioxidants added to keep the various animal and vegetable fats involved in a nugget from turning rancid. Then there are "antifoaming agents" like dimethylpolysiloxene, added to the cooking oil to keep the starches from binding to air molecules, so as to produce foam during the fry. The problem is evidently grave enough to warrant adding a toxic chemical to the food: According to the *Handbook of Food Additives*, dimethylpolysiloxene is a suspected carcinogen and an established mutagen, tumorigen, and reproductive effector; it's also flammable. But perhaps the most alarming ingredient in a Chicken McNugget is tertiary butylhydroquinone, or TBHQ, an antioxidant derived from petroleum that is either sprayed directly on the nugget or the inside of the box it comes in to "help preserve freshness." According to *A Consumer's Dictionary of Food Additives*, TBHQ is a form of butane (i.e., lighter fluid) the FDA allows processors to use sparingly in our food: It can comprise no more than 0.02 percent of the oil in a nugget. Which is probably just as well, considering that ingesting a single gram of TBHQ can cause "nausea, vomiting, ringing in the ears, delirium, a sense of suffocation, and collapse." Ingesting five grams of TBHQ can kill.

13   With so many exotic molecules organized into a food of such complexity, you would almost expect a chicken nugget to do something more spectacular than taste okay to a child and fill him up inexpensively. What it has done, of course, is to sell an awful lot of chicken for companies like Tyson, which invented the nugget—at McDonald's behest—in 1983. The nugget is the reason chicken has supplanted beef as the most popular meat in America.

14   Compared to Isaac's nuggets, my cheeseburger is a fairly simple construct. According to "A Full Serving of Nutrition Facts," the cheeseburger

contains a mere six ingredients, all but one of them familiar: a 100 percent beef patty, a bun, two American cheese slices, ketchup, mustard, pickles, onions, and "grill seasoning," whatever that is. It tasted pretty good, too, though on reflection what I mainly tasted were the condiments: Sampled by itself, the gray patty had hardly any flavor. And yet the whole package, especially on first bite, did manage to give off a fairly convincing burger-ish aura. I suspect, however, that owes more to the olfactory brilliance of the "grill seasoning" than to the 100 percent beef patty.

In truth, my cheeseburger's relationship to beef seemed nearly as metaphorical as the nugget's relationship to a chicken. Eating it, I had to remind myself that there was an actual cow involved in this meal—most likely a burned-out old dairy cow (the source of most fast-food beef) but possibly bits and pieces of a steer . . . as well. Part of the appeal of ham-burgers and nuggets is that their boneless abstractions allow us to forget we're eating animals. I'd been on the feedlot in Garden City only a few months earlier, yet this experience of cattle was so far removed from that one as to be taking place in a different dimension. No, I could not taste the feed corn or the petroleum or the antibiotics or the hormones—or the feed-lot manure. Yet while "A Full Serving of Nutrition Facts" did not enumer-ate these facts, they too have gone into the making of this hamburger, are part of its natural history. That perhaps is what the industrial food chain does best: obscure the histories of the foods it produces by processing them to such an extent that they appear as pure products of culture rather than nature—things made from plants and animals. Despite the blizzard of information contained in the helpful McDonald's flyer—the thousands of words and numbers specifying ingredients and portion sizes, calories and nutrients—all this food remains perfectly opaque. Where does it come from? It comes from McDonald's.

But that's not so. It comes from refrigerated trucks and from ware-houses, from slaughterhouses, from factory farms in towns like Garden City, Kansas, from ranches in Sturgis, South Dakota, from food science laboratories in Oak Brook, Illinois, from flavor companies on the New Jersey Turnpike, from petroleum refineries, from processing plants owned by ADM and Cargill, from grain elevators in towns like Jefferson, and, at the end of that long and tortuous trail, from a field of corn and soybeans farmed by George Naylor in Churdan, Iowa.

It would not be impossible to calculate exactly how much corn Judith, Isaac, and I consumed in our McDonald's meal. I figure my 4-ounce burger, for instance, represents nearly 2 pounds of corn (based on a cow's feed conversion rate of 7 pounds of corn for every 1 pound of gain, half of which is edible meat). The nuggets are a little harder to trans-late into corn, since there's no telling how much actual chicken goes into a nugget; but if 6 nuggets contain a quarter pound of meat, that would have taken a chicken half a pound of feed corn to grow. A 32-ounce soda con-tains 86 grams of high-fructose corn syrup (as does a double-thick shake), which can be refined from a third of a pound of corn; so our 3 drinks used another 1 pound. Subtotal: six pounds of corn.

18   From here the calculations become trickier because, according to the ingredients list in the flyer, corn is everywhere in our meal, but in unspecified amounts. There's more corn sweetener in my cheeseburger, of all places: The bun and the ketchup both contain HFCS. It's in the salad dressing, too, and the sauces for the nuggets, not to mention Isaac's dessert. (Of the sixty menu items listed in the handout, forty-five contain HFCS.) Then there are all the other corn ingredients in the nugget: the binders and emulsifiers and fillers. In addition to corn sweeteners, Isaac's shake contains corn syrup solids, mono- and diglycerides, and milk from corn-fed animals. Judith's Cobb salad is also stuffed with corn, even though there's not a kernel in it: Paul Newman makes his dressing with HFCS, corn syrup, corn starch, dextrin, caramel color, and xanthan gum; the salad itself contains cheese and eggs from corn-fed animals. The salad's grilled chicken breast is injected with a "flavor solution" that contains maltodextrin, dextrose, and monosodium glutamate. Sure, there are a lot of leafy greens in Judith's salad too, but the overwhelming majority of the calories in it (and there are 500 of them, when you count the dressing) ultimately come from corn. And the French fries? You would think those are mostly potatoes. Yet since half of the 540 calories in a large order of fries come from the oil they're fried in, the ultimate source of these calories is not a potato farm but a field of corn or soybeans.

19   The calculation finally defeated me, but I took it far enough to estimate that, if you include the corn in the gas tank (a whole bushel right there, to make two and a half gallons of ethanol), the amount of corn that went into producing our movable fast-food feast would easily have overflowed the car's trunk, spilling a trail of golden kernels on the blacktop behind us.

20   Some time later I found another way to calculate just how much corn we had eaten that day. I asked Todd Dawson, a biologist at Berkeley, to run a McDonald's meal through his mass spectrometer and calculate how much of the carbon in it came originally from a corn plant. It is hard to believe that the identity of the atoms in a cheeseburger or a Coke is preserved from farm field to fast-food counter, but the atomic signature of those carbon isotopes is indestructible, and still legible to the mass spectrometer. Dawson and his colleague Stefania Mambelli prepared an analysis showing roughly how much of the carbon in the various McDonald's menu items came from corn, and plotted them on a graph. The sodas came out at the top, not surprising since they consist of little else than corn sweetener, but virtually everything else we ate revealed a high proportion of corn, too. In order of diminishing corniness, this is how the laboratory measured our meal: soda (100 percent corn), milk shake (78 percent), salad dressing (65 percent), chicken nuggets (56 percent), cheeseburger (52 percent), and French fries (23 percent). What in the eyes of the omnivore looks like a meal of impressive variety turns out, when viewed through the eyes of the

mass spectrometer, to be the meal of a far more specialized kind of eater. But then, this is what the industrial eater has become: corn's koala.

So what? Why should it matter that we have become a race of corn eaters such as the world has never seen? Is this necessarily a bad thing? The answer all depends on where you stand. 21

If where you stand is in agribusiness, processing cheap corn into forty-five different McDonald's items is an impressive accomplishment. It represents a solution to the agricultural contradictions of capitalism, the challenge of increasing food industry profits faster than America can increase its population. Supersized portions of cheap corn-fixed carbon solves the problem of the fixed stomach; we may not be expanding the number of eaters in America, but we've figured out how to expand each of their appetites, which is almost as good. Judith, Isaac, and I together consumed a total of 4,510 calories at our lunch—more than half as many as we each should probably consume in a day. We had certainly done our parts in chomping through the corn surplus. (We had also consumed a lot of petroleum, and not just because we were in a car. To grow and process those 4,510 food calories took at least ten times as many calories of fossil energy, the equivalent of 1.3 gallons of oil.) 22

If where you stand is on one of the lower rungs of America's economic ladder, our cornified food chain offers real advantages: not cheap food exactly (for the consumer ultimately pays the added cost of processing), but cheap calories in a variety of attractive forms. In the long run, however, the eater pays a high price for these cheap calories: obesity, type II diabetes, heart disease. 23

If where you stand is at the lower end of the *world*'s economic ladder, however, America's corn-fed food chain looks like an unalloyed disaster. I mentioned earlier that all life on earth can be viewed as a competition for the energy captured by plants and stored in carbohydrates, energy we measure in calories. There is a limit to how many of those calories the world's arable land can produce each year, and an industrial meal of meat and processed food consumes—and wastes—an unconscionable amount of that energy. To eat corn directly (as Mexicans and many Africans do) is to consume all the energy in that corn, but when you feed that corn to a steer or a chicken, 90 percent of its energy is lost—to bones or feathers or fur, to living and metabolizing as a steer or chicken. This is why vegetarians advocate eating "low on the food chain"; every step up the chain reduces the amount of food energy by a factor of ten, which is why in any ecosystem there are only a fraction as many predators as there are prey. But processing food also burns energy. What this means is that the amount of food energy lost in the making of something like a Chicken McNugget could feed a great many more children than just mine, and that behind the 4,510 calories the three of us had for lunch stand tens of thousands of corn calories that could have fed a great many hungry people. 24

25   And how does this corn-fed food chain look if where you stand is in the middle of a field of corn? Well, it depends on whether you are the corn farmer or the plant. For the corn farmer, you might think the cornification of our food system would have redounded to his benefit, but it has not. Corn's triumph is the direct result of its overproduction, and that has been a disaster for the people who grow it. Growing corn and nothing but corn has also exacted a toll on the farmer's soil, the quality of the local water and the overall health of his community, the biodiversity of his landscape, and the health of all the creatures living on or downstream from it. And not *only* those creatures, for cheap corn has also changed, and much for the worse, the lives of several billion food animals, animals that would not be living on factory farms if not for the ocean of corn on which these animal cities float.

26   But return to that Iowa farm field for a moment and look at the matter—at us—from the standpoint of the corn plant itself. Corn, corn, corn as far as the eye can see, ten-foot stalks soldiering in perfect thirty-inch rows to the far horizon, an 80-million-acre corn lawn rolling across the continent. It's a good thing this plant can't form an impression of us, for how risible that impression would be: The farmers going broke cultivating it; the countless other species routed or immiserated by it; the humans eating and drinking it as fast as they can, some of them—like me and my family—in automobiles engineered to drink it, too. Of all the species that have figured out how to thrive in a world dominated by Homo sapiens, surely no other has succeeded more spectacularly—has colonized more acres and bodies—than *Zea mays*, the grass that domesticated its domesticator. You have to wonder why we Americans don't worship this plant as fervently as the Aztecs; like they once did, we make extraordinary sacrifices to it.

27   These, at least, were my somewhat fevered speculations, as we sped down the highway putting away our fast-food lunch. What is it about fast food? Not only is it served in a flash, but more often than not it's eaten that way too: We finished our meal in under ten minutes. Since we were in the convertible and the sun was shining, I can't blame the McDonald's ambiance. Perhaps the reason you eat this food quickly is because it doesn't bear savoring. The more you concentrate on how it tastes, the less like anything it tastes. I said before that McDonald's serves a kind of comfort food, but after a few bites I'm more inclined to think they're selling something more schematic than that—something more like a signifier of comfort food. So you eat more and eat more quickly, hoping somehow to catch up to the original idea of a cheeseburger or French fry as it retreats over the horizon. And so it goes, bite after bite, until you feel not satisfied exactly, but simply, regrettably, full.

(Study questions follow Nestle, 262.)

MARION NESTLE

Marion Nestle (born 1938) is the Paulette Goddard Professor of Nutrition, Food Studies, and Public Health at New York University. She holds a PhD in molecular biology (1968) and an M.P.H. in public health nutrition (1986) from the University of California at Berkeley. Nestle has served on the FDA Food Advisory Committee and American Cancer Society committees that issue dietary guidelines for cancer prevention. She is the author of *Food Politics: How the Food Industry Influences Nutrition and Health* (2002), *Safe Food Bacteria, Biotechnology, and Bioterrorism* (2003), and Pet Food Politics: The Chihuahua in the Coal Mine (2010). *What to Eat: An Aisle-by-Aisle Guide to Savvy Food Choices and Good Eating* (2006), which won the James Beard Foundation Book Award. In "Eating Made Simple," first published in *Scientific American* in 2007, Nestle discusses the multiple factors that influence our diet, including the activities and marketing efforts of food companies, government guidelines and regulations, and nutrition research. She provides common sense guidelines to help consumers make well-informed food choices.

Eating Made Simple

As a nutrition professor, I am constantly asked why nutrition advice seems to change so much and why experts so often disagree. Whose information, people ask, can we trust? I'm tempted to say, "Mine, of course," but I understand the problem. Yes, nutrition advice seems endlessly mired in scientific argument, the self-interest of food companies and compromises by government regulators. Nevertheless, basic dietary principles are not in dispute: eat less; move more; eat fruits, vegetables and whole grains; and avoid too much junk food.

"Eat less" means consume fewer calories, which translates into eating smaller portions and steering clear of frequent between-meal snacks. "Move more" refers to the need to balance calorie intake with physical activity. Eating fruits, vegetables and whole grains provides nutrients unavailable from other foods. Avoiding junk food means to shun "foods of minimal nutritional value"—highly processed sweets and snacks laden with salt, sugars and artificial additives. Soft drinks are the prototypical junk food; they contain sweeteners but few or no nutrients.

If you follow these precepts, other aspects of the diet matter much less. Ironically, this advice has not changed in years. The noted cardiologist Ancel Keys (who died in 2004 at the age of 100) and his wife, Margaret, suggested similar principles for preventing coronary heart disease nearly 50 years ago.

4   But I can see why dietary advice seems like a moving target. Nutrition research is so difficult to conduct that it seldom produces unambiguous results. Ambiguity requires interpretation. And interpretation is influenced by the individual's point of view, which can become thoroughly entangled with the science.

Nutrition Science Challenges

5 This scientific uncertainty is not overly surprising given that humans eat so many different foods. For any individual, the health effects of diets are modulated by genetics but also by education and income levels, job satisfaction, physical fitness, and the use of cigarettes or alcohol. To simplify this situation, researchers typically examine the effects of single dietary components one by one.

6   Studies focusing on one nutrient in isolation have worked splendidly to explain symptoms caused by deficiencies of vitamins or minerals. But this approach is less useful for chronic conditions such as coronary heart disease and diabetes that are caused by the interaction of dietary, genetic, behavioral and social factors. If nutrition science seems puzzling, it is because researchers typically examine single nutrients detached from food itself, foods separate from diets, and risk factors apart from other behaviors. This kind of research is "reductive" in that it attributes health effects to the consumption of one nutrient or food when it is the overall dietary pattern that really counts most.

7   For chronic diseases, single nutrients usually alter risk by amounts too small to measure except through large, costly population studies. As seen recently in the Women's Health Initiative, a clinical trial that examined the effects of low-fat diets on heart disease and cancer, participants were unable to stick with the restrictive dietary protocols. Because humans cannot be caged and fed measured formulas, the diets of experimental and control study groups tend to converge, making differences indistinguishable over the long run—even with fancy statistics.

It's the Calories

8 Food companies prefer studies of single nutrients because they can use the results to sell products. Add vitamins to candies, and you can market them as health foods. Health claims on the labels of junk foods distract consumers from their caloric content. This practice matters because when it comes to obesity—which dominates nutrition problems even in some of the poorest countries of the world—it is the calories that count. Obesity arises when people consume significantly more calories than they expend in physical activity.

America's obesity rates began to rise sharply in the early 1980s. Soci- 9
ologists often attribute the "calories in" side of this trend to the demands
of an overworked population for convenience foods—prepared, packaged
products and restaurant meals that usually contain more calories than
home-cooked meals.

But other social forces also promoted the calorie imbalance. The 10
arrival of the Reagan administration in 1980 increased the pace of industry deregulation, removing controls on agricultural production and
encouraging farmers to grow more food. Calories available per capita
in the national food supply (that produced by American farmers, plus
imports, less exports) rose from 3,200 a day in 1980 to 3,900 a day two
decades later.

The early 1980s also marked the advent of the "shareholder value 11
movement" on Wall Street. Stockholder demands for higher short-term
returns on investments forced food companies to expand sales in a
marketplace that already contained excessive calories. Food companies
responded by seeking new sales and marketing opportunities. They
encouraged formerly shunned practices that eventually changed social
norms, such as frequent between-meal snacking, eating in book and
clothing stores, and serving larger portions. The industry continued to
sponsor organizations and journals that focus on nutrition-related subjects and intensified its efforts to lobby government for favorable dietary
advice. Then and now food lobbies have promoted positive interpretations of scientific studies, sponsored research that can be used as a basis
for health claims, and attacked critics, myself among them, as proponents of "junk science." If anything, such activities only add to public
confusion.

Supermarkets as "Ground Zero"

No matter whom I speak to, I hear pleas for help in dealing with 12
supermarkets, considered by shoppers as "ground zero" for distinguishing health claims from scientific advice. So I spent a year visiting
supermarkets to help people think more clearly about food choices. The
result was my book *What to Eat*.

Supermarkets provide a vital public service but are not social 13
services agencies. Their job is to sell as much food as possible. Every aspect
of store design—from shelf position to background music—is based on
marketing research. Because this research shows that the more products
customers see, the more they buy, a store's objective is to expose shoppers
to the maximum number of products they will tolerate viewing.

If consumers are confused about which foods to buy, it is surely 14
because the choices require knowledge of issues that are not easily
resolved by science and are strongly swayed by social and economic
considerations. Such decisions play out every day in every store aisle.

Are Organics Healthier?

15 Organic foods are the fastest-growing segment of the industry, in part because people are willing to pay more for foods that they believe are healthier and more nutritious. The U.S. Department of Agriculture forbids producers of "Certified Organic" fruits and vegetables from using synthetic pesticides, herbicides, fertilizers, genetically modified seeds, irradiation or fertilizer derived from sewage sludge. It licenses inspectors to ensure that producers follow those rules. Although the USDA is responsible for organics, its principal mandate is to promote conventional agriculture, which explains why the department asserts that it "makes no claims that organically produced food is safer or more nutritious than conventionally produced food. Organic food differs from conventionally grown food in the way it is grown, handled and processed."

16 This statement implies that such differences are unimportant. Critics of organic foods would agree; they question the reliability of organic certification and the productivity, safety and health benefits of organic production methods. Meanwhile the organic food industry longs for research to address such criticisms, but studies are expensive and difficult to conduct. Nevertheless, existing research in this area has established that organic farms are nearly as productive as conventional farms, use less energy and leave soils in better condition. People who eat foods grown without synthetic pesticides ought to have fewer such chemicals in their bodies, and they do. Because the organic rules require pretreatment of manure and other steps to reduce the amount of pathogens in soil treatments, organic foods should be just as safe—or safer—than conventional foods.

17 Similarly, organic foods ought to be at least as nutritious as conventional foods. And proving organics to be more nutritious could help justify their higher prices. For minerals, this task is not difficult. The mineral content of plants depends on the amounts present in the soil in which they are grown. Organic foods are cultivated in richer soils, so their mineral content is higher.

18 But differences are harder to demonstrate for vitamins or antioxidants (plant substances that reduce tissue damage induced by free radicals); higher levels of these nutrients relate more to a food plant's genetic strain or protection from unfavorable conditions after harvesting than to production methods. Still, preliminary studies show benefits: organic peaches and pears contain greater quantities of vitamins C and E, and organic berries and corn contain more antioxidants.

19 Further research will likely confirm that organic foods contain higher nutrient levels, but it is unclear whether these nutrients would make a measurable improvement in health. All fruits and vegetables contain useful nutrients, albeit in different combinations and concentrations. Eating a variety of food plants is surely more important to health than

small differences in the nutrient content of any one food. Organics may be somewhat healthier to eat, but they are far less likely to damage the environment, and that is reason enough to choose them at the supermarket.

Dairy and Calcium

Scientists cannot easily resolve questions about the health effects of dairy foods. Milk has many components, and the health of people who consume milk or dairy foods is influenced by everything else they eat and do. But this area of research is especially controversial because it affects an industry that vigorously promotes dairy products as beneficial and opposes suggestions to the contrary.   20

Dairy foods contribute about 70 percent of the calcium in American diets. This necessary mineral is a principal constituent of bones, which constantly lose and regain calcium during normal metabolism. Diets must contain enough calcium to replace losses, or else bones become prone to fracture. Experts advise consumption of at least one gram of calcium a day to replace everyday losses. Only dairy foods provide this much calcium without supplementation.   21

But bones are not just made of calcium; they require the full complement of essential nutrients to maintain strength. Bones are stronger in people who are physically active and who do not smoke cigarettes or drink much alcohol. Studies examining the effects of single nutrients in dairy foods show that some nutritional factors—magnesium, potassium, vitamin D and lactose, for example—promote calcium retention in bones. Others, such as protein, phosphorus and sodium, foster calcium excretion. So bone strength depends more on overall patterns of diet and behavior than simply on calcium intake.   22

Populations that do not typically consume dairy products appear to exhibit lower rates of bone fracture despite consuming far less calcium than recommended. Why this is so is unclear. Perhaps their diets contain less protein from meat and dairy foods, less sodium from processed foods and less phosphorus from soft drinks, so they retain calcium more effectively. The fact that calcium balance depends on multiple factors could explain why rates of osteoporosis (bone density loss) are highest in countries where people eat the most dairy foods. Further research may clarify such counterintuitive observations.   23

In the meantime, dairy foods are fine to eat if you like them, but they are not a nutritional requirement. Think of cows: they do not drink milk after weaning, but their bones support bodies weighing 800 pounds or more. Cows feed on grass, and grass contains calcium in small amounts—but those amounts add up. If you eat plenty of fruits, vegetables and whole grains, you can have healthy bones without having to consume dairy foods.   24

A Meaty Debate

25   Critics point to meat as the culprit responsible for elevating blood cholesterol, along with raising risks for heart disease, cancer and other conditions.
Supporters cite the lack of compelling science to justify such allegations;
they emphasize the nutritional benefits of meat protein, vitamins and
minerals. Indeed, studies in developing countries demonstrate health improvements when growing children are fed even small amounts of meat.

26   But because bacteria in a cow's rumen attach hydrogen atoms to
unsaturated fatty acids, beef fat is highly saturated—the kind of fat that
increases the risk of coronary heart disease. All fats and oils contain some
saturated fatty acids, but animal fats, especially those from beef, have
more saturated fatty acids than vegetable fats. Nutritionists recommend
eating no more than a heaping tablespoon (20 grams) of saturated fatty
acids a day. Beef eaters easily meet or exceed this limit. The smallest
McDonald's cheeseburger contains 6 grams of saturated fatty acids, but a
Hardee's Monster Thickburger has 45 grams.

27   Why meat might boost cancer risks, however, is a matter of
speculation. Scientists began to link meat to cancer in the 1970s, but even
after decades of subsequent research they remain unsure if the relevant
factor might be fat, saturated fat, protein, carcinogens or something else
related to meat. By the late 1990s experts could conclude only that eating
beef probably increases the risk of colon and rectal cancers and possibly
enhances the odds of acquiring breast, prostate and perhaps other cancers.
Faced with this uncertainty, the American Cancer Society suggests selecting leaner cuts, smaller portions and alternatives such as chicken, fish or
beans—steps consistent with today's basic advice about what to eat.

Fish and Heart Disease

28   Fatty fish are the most important sources of long-chain omega-3 fatty
acids. In the early 1970s Danish investigators observed surprisingly
low frequencies of heart disease among indigenous populations in
Greenland that typically ate fatty fish, seals and whales. The researchers
attributed the protective effect to the foods' content of omega-3 fatty acids.
Some subsequent studies—but by no means all—confirm this idea.

29   Because large, fatty fish are likely to have accumulated methylmer-
cury and other toxins through predation, however, eating them raises
questions about the balance between benefits and risks. Understandably,
the fish industry is eager to prove that the health benefits of omega-3s
outweigh any risks from eating fish.

30   Even independent studies on omega-3 fats can be interpreted differently. In 2004 the National Oceanic and Atmospheric Administration—for
fish, the agency equivalent to the USDA—asked the Institute of Medicine
(IOM) to review studies of the benefits and risks of consuming seafood.

The ensuing review of the research on heart disease risk illustrates the challenge such work poses for interpretation.

The IOM's October 2006 report concluded that eating seafood 31 reduces the risk of heart disease but judged the studies too inconsistent to decide if omega-3 fats were responsible. In contrast, investigators from the Harvard School of Public Health published a much more positive report in the *Journal of the American Medical Association* that same month. Even modest consumption of fish omega-3s, they stated, would cut coronary deaths by 36 percent and total mortality by 17 percent, meaning that not eating fish would constitute a health risk.

Differences in interpretation explain how distinguished scientists 32 could arrive at such different conclusions after considering the same studies. The two groups, for example, had conflicting views of earlier work published in March 2006 in the *British Medical Journal*. That study found no overall effect of omega-3s on heart disease risk or mortality, although a subset of the original studies displayed a 14 percent reduction in total mortality that did not reach statistical significance. The IOM team interpreted the "nonsignificant" result as evidence for the need for caution, whereas the Harvard group saw the data as consistent with studies reporting the benefits of omega-3s. When studies present inconsistent results, both interpretations are plausible. I favor caution in such situations, but not everyone agrees.

Because findings are inconsistent, so is dietary advice about eating 33 fish. The American Heart Association recommends that adults eat fatty fish at least twice a week, but U.S. dietary guidelines say: "Limited evidence suggests an association between consumption of fatty acids in fish and reduced risks of mortality from cardiovascular disease for the general population . . . however, more research is needed." Whether or not fish uniquely protects against heart disease, seafood is a delicious source of many nutrients, and two small servings per week of the less predatory classes of fish are unlikely to cause harm.

Sodas and Obesity

Sugars and corn sweeteners account for a large fraction of the calories in 34 many supermarket foods, and virtually all the calories in drinks—soft, sports and juice—come from added sugars.

In a trend that correlates closely with rising rates of obesity, daily 35 per capita consumption of sweetened beverages has grown by about 200 calories since the early 1980s. Although common sense suggests that this increase might have something to do with weight gain, beverage makers argue that studies cannot prove that sugary drinks alone—independent of calories or other foods in the diet—boost the risk of obesity. The evidence, they say correctly, is circumstantial. But pediatricians often see obese children in their practices who consume more than 1,000 calories a day from sweetened drinks alone, and several studies indicate that children who habitually consume sugary beverages take in more calories and weigh more than those who do not.

36   Nevertheless, the effects of sweetened drinks on obesity continue to be subject to interpretation. In 2006, for example, a systematic review funded by independent sources found sweetened drinks to promote obesity in both children and adults. But a review that same year sponsored in part by a beverage trade association concluded that soft drinks have no special role in obesity. The industry-funded researchers criticized existing studies as being short-term and inconclusive, and pointed to studies finding that people lose weight when they substitute sweetened drinks for their usual meals.

37   These differences imply the need to scrutinize food industry sponsorship of research itself. Although many researchers are offended by suggestions that funding support might affect the way they design or interpret studies, systematic analyses say otherwise. In 2007 investigators classified studies of the effects of sweetened and other beverages on health according to who had sponsored them. Industry-supported studies were more likely to yield results favorable to the sponsor than those funded by independent sources. Even though scientists may not be able to prove that sweetened drinks cause obesity, it makes sense for anyone interested in losing weight to consume less of them.

38   The examples I have discussed illustrate why nutrition science seems so controversial. Without improved methods to ensure compliance with dietary regimens, research debates are likely to rage unabated. Opposing points of view and the focus of studies and food advertising on single nutrients rather than on dietary patterns continue to fuel these disputes. While we wait for investigators to find better ways to study nutrition and health, my approach—eat less, move more, eat a largely plant-based diet, and avoid eating too much junk food—makes sense and leaves you plenty of opportunity to enjoy your dinner.

Content

1. What are some of the characteristics, according to Michael Pollan in "The Meal," of "the industrial food chain" (¶s 1–7)? How, in Pollan's view, has "industrial food" changed the way we eat (¶s 2–5)?

2. Pollan estimates the amount of corn he and his family consumed in one McDonald's meal (¶ 18) and concludes that this amount "would easily have overflowed the car's trunk" (¶ 19). What are some of the economic, health, environmental, and social effects of "this corn-fed food chain" (¶s 22–27)?

3. Why, according to Marion Nestle in "Eating Made Simple," do nutritional studies differ in their conclusions about healthy eating (¶s 5–7)? Why does Nestle argue that "it is the overall dietary pattern that really counts most" (¶ 6)?

© Lee Snider/The Image Works

Excess weight around the waist, the abdominal fat that contributes to the body's "apple shape," increases the risk of a host of serious medical problems: metabolic syndrome, type 2 diabetes, heart disease, high blood pressure, stroke, some types of cancer, sleep apnea, pulmonary hypertension, and cardiac arrhythmia. These risks are well known, yet estimates are that around 65% of Americans will become moderately to severely overweight during their lifetime. Why?

Tyler Hicks/The New York Times/Redux

People are scavenging for food in a garbage dump in Port-au-Prince, Haiti, the poorest country in the Western Hemisphere, with a per capita income of $400 per year, a life expectancy of 53 years, and 80% of the people living in poverty, half of whom cannot read. Contrast this situation with Americans' lifestyle and expectancy.

FLAWED FOOD PYRAMIDS

Fats, Oils and Sweets
USE SPARINGLY

Milk, Yogurt and
Cheese Group
2–3 SERVINGS

Meat, Poultry, Fish, Dry Beans,
Eggs and Nuts Group
2–3 SERVINGS

Vegetable Group
3–5 SERVINGS

Fruit Group
2–4 SERVINGS

Bread, Cereal, Rice and
Pasta Group
6–11 SERVINGS

1992

2005

Whether you found the food pyramid created by the U.S. Department of Agriculture in 1992 beneficial or not, it was at least simple to use. The familiar triangular nutrition guide suggested how much of each food category—grains, dairy products, fruits and vegetables, meats and fats, oils and sweets—one should eat every day.

But in my opinion, the USDA's 2005 replacement, MyPyramid, is a disaster. The process the agriculture agency employed to replace the 1992 food pyramid (*left*) has been kept secret. It remains a mystery, for example, just how the department came up with a design for a new food guide that emphasizes physical activity but is devoid of food (*right*). According to the USDA staff, people should keep physically active, eat in moderation, make personalized food choices, eat a variety of foods in the recommended number of servings, and pursue gradual dietary improvement. The color and width of the vertical bands of MyPyramid are meant to denote food groups and servings, but the only way to know this in detail is to log on to a computer. Users must go to www.pyramid.gov and type in gender, age and activity level to obtain a "personalized" dietary plan at one of a dozen calorie levels.

People who seek advice from this site, and millions have, find diet plans notable for the large amounts of food they seem to recommend and for the virtual absence of appeals to "eat less" or to "avoid" certain foods. Critics, not surprisingly, discern the strong influence of food industry lobbyists here. I myself, for example, am expected to consume four cups of fruits and vegetables, six ounces of grains, five ounces of meat and, of course, three cups of milk a day, along with a couple of hundred "discretionary calories" that I can spend on junk foods. For all its flaws, the 1992 pyramid was easier to understand and use.

What MyPyramid really lacks is any notion of a hierarchical ranking of the items in a single food group in terms of nutritional desirability. The preliminary design of MyPyramid in 2004 looked much like the final version with one critical exception: it illustrated a hierarchy of desirable food choices. The grain band, for instance, placed whole-grain bread at the bottom (a positive ranking), pasta about halfway up (a middle rank) and cinnamon buns at the top ("eat less"). In the final version, the USDA eliminated all traces of hierarchy, presumably because food companies do not want federal agencies to advise eating less of their products, useful as such recommendations might be to an overweight public. —*M.N.*

Illustration by Nick Rotondo

AS FOOD CALORIES SWELL, SO DO WAISTLINES

A substantial rise in U.S. obesity rates during the past few decades was paralleled by increases in the availability of larger portion sizes, total calories, caloric sweeteners and sugary soft drinks in the food supply. The apparent dip in three of these measures (calories, sugars and sugary soft drinks) after 1998 may be explained by greater use of artificial sweeteners and the partial replacement of sugary soft drinks with beverages that are not sweetened with sugars.

U.S. OBESITY RATES ON THE RISE
Percent of total population (ages 20–74) classified as obese

1976–1980	1988–1994	1999–2000	2001–2002	2003–2004
15.1%	23.3%	31.0%	32.1%	33.9%

SUPER-SIZE PORTIONS GROW
Number of food items introduced in larger sizes by restaurants and manufacturers in the U.S.

1975–1979	1980–1984	1985–1989	1990–1994	1995–1999
6	12	36	47	63

CALORIES AVAILABLE
Per person per day in the U.S. food supply

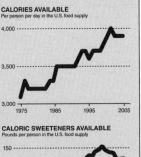

CALORIC SWEETENERS AVAILABLE
Pounds per person in the U.S. food supply

SUGARY SOFT DRINKS AVAILABLE
Gallons per person in the U.S. food supply

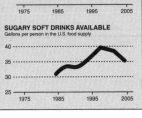

JEN CHRISTIANSEN (graphics); SOURCES: "HEALTH, UNITED STATES, 2006 WITH CHARTBOOK ON TRENDS IN THE HEALTH OF AMERICANS," NATIONAL CENTER FOR HEALTH STATISTICS, 2006 (obesity rates); "THE CONTRIBUTION OF EXPANDING PORTION SIZES TO THE U.S. OBESITY EPIDEMIC," BY L. R. YOUNG AND M. NESTLE, IN AMERICAN JOURNAL OF PUBLIC HEALTH, VOL. 92, PAGES 246–249, 2002 (portions); ECONOMIC RESEARCH SERVICE, USDA (calories, sweeteners, soft drinks). Graphic used by permission of Jen Christiansen.

4. What factors have contributed to recent increases in caloric intake (¶s 8–11)? How, according to Nestle, have food companies' marketing practices contributed to these changes in diet?

5. Explain why Nestle argues that food choices "are not easily resolved by science" (¶ 14). What are "Certified Organic" foods (¶ 15) and why might they be healthier to eat than conventionally grown crops (¶s 16–19)? Why does the consumption of dairy foods not necessarily ensure adequate consumption of calcium (¶s 21–24)? Explain why the health effects of meat consumption are in dispute (¶s 25–27) and the possible pros and cons of eating fish (¶s 28–32). Why did the Institute of Medicine and the Harvard School of Public Health differ in their conclusions about the role of omega-3 fats in the prevention of heart disease (¶s 30–32)?

Strategies/Structures/Language

6. Pollan quotes a federal judge's description of the Chicken McNugget as a "McFrankensteinian creation" (¶ 8). Find other examples of language in "The Meal" that emphasize the artificial and processed nature of industrial food. How does Pollan explain the appeal of fast food?

7. How does Pollan suggest that as industrial food becomes more removed from its source, it becomes less like "real" food and more like the language that describes it? He argues, for example, that the food McDonald's serves is "more like a signifier of comfort food" (¶ 27) than comfort food itself. Explain the connection he draws between what we eat and how we speak. Find examples in which Pollan suggests that industrial food is changing our experience of food, and our culture more generally, by changing the language we use to describe food. How do these examples explain his choice of title?

8. Nestle alludes to the different uses to which nutrition research is put, including as marketing by food companies (¶ 8) and the government's development of agricultural policies (¶s 15–16) and dietary guidelines (¶ 33). On what grounds does she question the quality of industry-supported nutrition research (¶s 8, 11, 20, 35–37)? Does she suggest that independent research is possible? Why does she "discern the strong influence of food industry lobbyists" in the development of USDA's MyPyramid ("Flawed Food Pyramids" diagram)? How might the charts in "As Food Calories Swell, So Do Waistlines" be interpreted to support the argument that the increase in "daily per capita consumption of sweetened beverages" (¶ 35) explains rising rates of obesity *and* the argument that "soft drinks have no special role in obesity" (¶ 36)?

9. In "Rising Sea Levels—An Alternative Theory" (266), Kim Warp combines two contemporary concerns, climate change and obesity, in a humorous application of fallacious reasoning. Why are the peripheral figures submerged? How do the two central figures explain the joke?

For Writing

10. *Journal Writing.* Pollan writes that hamburgers and chicken nuggets appeal to consumers in part because "their boneless abstractions allow us to forget we're eating animals" (¶ 15). Do you agree that consumers generally prefer to eat foods that are processed and packaged to distance them from their origins? Is this

preference a question of habit? What is the impact of the widespread consumption of foods that "appear as pure products of culture rather than nature" (¶ 15)?

11. ***Dialogues.*** Both Pollan and Nestle allude to the environmental consequences of industrial food production: Pollan argues that the dominance of corn in the food chain damages soil and water quality as well as "the biodiversity of [the farmer's] landscape, and the health of all the creatures living on or downstream from it" (¶ 25), while Nestle argues that organic farms "use less energy and leave soils in better condition" than conventional agriculture (¶ 16). How do Pollan and Nestle suggest that consumer and business behavior present obstacles to addressing these environmental concerns?

12. ***Second Look.*** In "The Meal," Pollan links obesity, among other conditions, to the consumption of "cheap calories" produced by the "cornified food chain" (¶ 23); in "Eating Made Simple," Nestle writes that "rising rates of obesity" represent a trend that correlates with the rise in the consumption of "sweetened beverages" (¶ 35). How does the photograph on 263 suggest that obesity is a public health issue? Explain how the anonymity, clothing, and arrangement of the two figures contribute to your reading of the photograph.

KIM WARP, *Rising Sea Levels— An Alternative Theory*

Kim Warp/The New Yorker/Cartoon Bank

Write an alternative caption for this cartoon. If you wish, consult some of the 84 million Internet entries under "Fat Rights" for ideas. Is obesity an appropriate subject for humor? Why or why not?

DAVID SEDARIS

David Sedaris was born in 1956 and graduated from the School of the Art Institute of Chicago in 1987. His national reputation as a humorist began in 1992 when he read excerpts from "The SantaLand Diaries" on National Public Radio, in a "nicely nerdy, quavering voice." These monologues, praised for their wit and deadpan delivery, anatomized various odd jobs he held after moving to New York—an elf in SantaLand at Macy's department store, an office worker, and an apartment cleaner. He explained to the *New York Times*, "I can only write when it's dark, so basically, my whole day is spent waiting for it to get dark. Cleaning apartments gives me something to do when I get up. Otherwise, I'd feel like a bum."

In *Naked* (1997) and later books—*Me Talk Pretty One Day* (2000), *Dress Your Family in Corduroy and Denim* (2004) and *When You are Engulfed in Flames* (2008)—Sedaris has drawn his most memorable material from bittersweet renderings of his family: his father, "an eccentric IBM engineer who ruins miniature golf with dissertations on wind trajectory"; his mother, a secret alcoholic ("Drinking didn't count if you followed a glass of wine with a cup of coffee") who pushed her children outside on a snow day so she could drink in secret; and his siblings, alternately attractive and pathetic. Sedaris's presentations of his relationship with his partner, Hugh, are more mellow, as in "Make That a Double," which emphasizes the illogical and irrational (to English speakers) attributions of gender in French grammar: "Because it is a female and lays eggs, a chicken is masculine . . . while the word *masculinity* is feminine."

Make That a Double

There are, I have noticed, two basic types of French spoken by   1
Americans vacationing in Paris: the Hard Kind and the Easy Kind. The Hard Kind involves the conjugation of wily verbs and the science of placing them alongside various other words in order to form such sentences as "I go him say good afternoon" and "No, not to him I no go it him say now."

The second, less complicated form of French amounts to   2
screaming English at the top of your lungs, much the same way you'd shout at a deaf person or the dog you thought you could train to stay off the sofa. Doubt and hesitation are completely unnecessary, as Easy French is rooted in the premise that, if properly packed, the rest of the world could fit within the confines of Reno, Nevada. The speaker

carries no pocket dictionary and never suffers the humiliation that inevitably comes with pointing to the menu and ordering the day of the week. With Easy French, eating out involves a simple "BRING ME A STEAK."

3   Having undertaken the study of Hard French, I'll overhear such requests and glare across the room, thinking, "That's *Mister* Steak to you, buddy." Of all the stumbling blocks inherent in learning this language, the greatest for me is the principle that each noun has a corresponding sex that affects both its articles and its adjectives. Because it is a female and lays eggs, a chicken is masculine. *Vagina* is masculine as well, while the word *masculinity* is feminine. Forced by the grammar to take a stand one way or the other, *hermaphrodite* is male and *indecisiveness* female.

4   I spent months searching for some secret code before I realized that common sense has nothing to do with it. *Hysteria, psychosis, torture, depression*: I was told that if something is unpleasant, it's probably feminine. This encouraged me, but the theory was blown by such masculine nouns as *murder, toothache*, and *Rollerblade*. I have no problem learning the words themselves, it's the sexes that trip me up and refuse to stick.

5   What's the trick to remembering that a sandwich is masculine? What qualities does it share with anyone in possession of a penis? I'll tell myself that a sandwich is masculine because if left alone for a week or two, it will eventually grow a beard. This works until it's time to order and I decide that because it sometimes loses its makeup, a sandwich is undoubtedly feminine.

6   I just can't manage to keep my stories straight. Hoping I might learn through repetition, I tried using gender in my everyday English. "Hi, guys," I'd say, opening a new box of paper clips, or "Hey, Hugh, have you seen my belt? I can't find her anywhere." I invented personalities for the objects on my dresser and set them up on blind dates. When things didn't work out with my wallet, my watch drove a wedge between my hairbrush and my lighter. The scenarios reminded me of my youth, when my sisters and I would enact epic dramas with our food. Ketchup-wigged french fries would march across our plates, engaging in brief affairs or heated disputes over carrot coins while burly chicken legs guarded the perimeter, ready to jump in should things get out of hand. Sexes were assigned at our discretion and were subject to change from one night to the next—unlike here, where the corncob and the string bean remain locked in their rigid masculine roles. Say what you like about southern social structure, but at least in North Carolina a hot dog is free to swing both ways.

7   Nothing in France is free from sexual assignment. I was leafing through the dictionary, trying to complete a homework assignment,

when I noticed the French had prescribed genders for the various land masses and natural wonders we Americans had always thought of as sexless, Niagara Falls is feminine and, against all reason, the Grand Canyon is masculine. Georgia and Florida are female, but Montana and Utah are male. New England is a she, while the vast area we call the Midwest is just one big guy. I wonder whose job it was to assign these sexes in the first place. Did he do his work right there in the sanitarium, or did they rent him a little office where he could get away from all the noise?

There are times when you can swallow the article and others when 8 it must be clearly pronounced, as the word has two different meanings, one masculine and the other feminine. It should be fairly obvious that I cooked an omelette in a frying pan rather than in a wood stove, but it bothers me to make the same mistakes over and over again. I wind up exhausting the listener before I even get to the verb.

My confidence hit a new low when my friend Adeline told me 9 that French children often make mistakes, but never with the sex of their nouns. "It's just something we grow up with," she said. "We hear the gender once, and then think of it as part of the word. There's nothing to it."

It's a pretty grim world when I can't even feel superior to a toddler. 10 Tired of embarrassing myself in front of two-year-olds, I've started referring to everything in the plural, which can get expensive but has solved a lot of my problems. In saying a *melon*, you need to use the masculine article. In saying *the melons*, you use the plural article, which does not reflect gender and is the same for both the masculine and the feminine. Ask for two or ten or three hundred melons, and the number lets you off the hook by replacing the article altogether. A masculine kilo of feminine tomatoes presents a sexual problem easily solved by asking for two kilos of tomatoes. I've started using the plural while shopping, and Hugh has started using it in our cramped kitchen, where he stands huddled in the corner, shouting, "What do we need with four pounds of tomatoes?"

I answer that I'm sure we can use them for something. The only 11 hard part is finding someplace to put them. They won't fit in the refrigerator, as I filled the last remaining shelf with the two chickens I bought from the butcher the night before, forgetting that we were still working our way through a pair of pork roasts the size of Duraflame logs. "We could put them next to the radios," I say, "or grind them for sauce in one of the blenders. Don't get so mad. Having four pounds of tomatoes is better than having no tomatoes at all, isn't it?"

Hugh tells me that the market is off-limits until my French improves. 12 He's pretty steamed, but I think he'll get over it when he sees the CD players I got him for his birthday.

Content

1. What is the underlying logic of Sedaris's premises, as a speaker of English, about the gender designations of a language? How does the French use of gender defy this logic? Grammar books don't treat this division humorously; why not? What's the difference between grammatical gender and sexual gender? Why does Sedaris find this contrast humorous?

2. Sedaris allegedly solves the problem by resorting to "referring to everything in the plural" (¶ 10), which, of course, since this is a comic piece, causes other problems. The solution is appropriate to comedy, but is it suitable for application to real-life situations? Explain.

Strategies/Structures/Language

3. Humorists often exaggerate, as Sedaris does in "Make That a Double." Find some instances of this. Why doesn't the obvious exaggeration trouble the humorist's readers or cause them to distrust the narrator?

4. What's the point of inventing "personalities for the objects" on the dresser and setting "them up on blind dates" (¶ 6) and other stratagems for learning grammatical gender? Do they work?

5. Having come to the logical conclusion of his humorous point, Sedaris stops. Is there more he could say? If so, what might that be? If not, what does this piece illustrate about why humorous writing is often short?

For Writing

6. As Sedaris does in "Make That a Double" and Britt does in "That Lean and Hungry Look" (Chapter 8), write a brief humorous essay that derives much of its humor from the system of division and classification of its subject. No topic is immune from outrageously irreverent humor; in "Possession" Sedaris, while visiting Anne Frank's secret annex, imagines how he would remodel it: "I'd get rid of the countertop and of course redo all the plumbing . . . and reclaim the fireplace. 'That's your focal point, there.'" Nevertheless, some topics are easier to work with than others; pick one you can handle comfortably, even though it might make your readers uncomfortable. Before turning it in, test it out on a classmate—on whose paper you will comment in turn.

7. *Journal Writing.* Identify some of the differences between your own culture and another one you know fairly well or have observed. If you speak the other language or dialect, explore the cultural differences the different languages suggest. Do you, like Sedaris, find some aspects of the other culture difficult to internalize?

8. *Dialogues.* Sedaris's humorous treatment of gender hints at a complex issue—the process through which we define gender socially (rather than biologically). What factors does Zora Rix in "Corporality" (557–63) identify that underpin the meanings of masculinity and femininity in American culture? If, as Sedaris claims, "Nothing in France is free from sexual assignment" (¶ 7), are behaviors in American culture similarly assigned a gender?

MATT NOCTON

Nocton (born 1975) has spent most of his life in the vicinity of his hometown, Simsbury, Connecticut, except for a year's sojourn in California—a cross-country trek that stimulated some of his best writing. He wrote the essay below as an English major at the University of Connecticut (BA 2002), and currently sells media advertising.

Nocton himself worked harvesting tobacco in Connecticut; the tobacco fields are adjacent to the state's largest airport, Bradley International Airport. "Harvest of Gold, Harvest of Shame" is the seventh revision Nocton submitted, every draft reinforcing the gulf between the bosses and the workers in the tobacco fields and sheds, every draft increasing his own awareness of the workers' exploited and powerless condition.

Harvest of Gold, Harvest of Shame

Simsbury is a small affluent town located in the heart of the Connecticut   1
River Valley. It is not a particularly exciting place and its high school students refer to it as "Simsboring." But in fact there is something unique about this quiet town. Simsbury is home to Culbro Tobacco Company's Farm No. 2. The Culbro Tobacco Company prides itself on growing the finest shade tobacco in the world. Its leaves are used to wrap expensive cigars.

Culbro employs three kinds of people: migrant workers, most of   2
whom are from Jamaica and live on the farm headquarters, inner-city people, most of whom are Hispanic and are bussed from Hartford to Simsbury at 6:15 in the morning; and finally, a few local white residents. The latter are typically the men who oversee all of the other employees. Each supervisor is referred to as the "boss man" by the less fortunate workers. When a boss man speaks to one of his subordinates, the usual response comes either in the form of Spanglish, which most of the Hispanics speak, or Patoi, which is what the Jamaicans speak.

Working in tobacco fields is demanding and repetitious and the   3
pay is minimum wage. In a typical day, a field worker is bussed to the field where he will be working with his group of roughly fifty to two hundred workers. When he gets off the bus he will find a pickup truck parked nearby full of burlap and twine. He must tie this burlap around his waist as a source of protection against the dirt and rocks that he will be dragging himself through for the next eight hours. He will then find another pick-up truck containing wooden stakes with numbers on them. There he will find the stake with his

number and stick it into the ground before the row of tobacco plants where he is about to work. A recorder or "bentkeeper" (so called because the distance between two tobacco posts is called a bent) stands under the blazing sun and monitors all the workers. He does this by looking at the numbers of each stake in each row. He flips through the pages on his clipboard until he finds the corresponding employee number. Then he checks the number of poles in the row and adds the number of "bents" in the row to a particular worker's sum total. He does this for fifty to two hundred laborers. At times when the rows are very short it is difficult to add all of the numbers fast enough to keep up with the pace of the pickers. The pickers who complete the most bents earn the most money. The bentkeeper is the only one authorized to carry the clipboard and add the bent numbers. Every so often the unshaven field boss man with the coarse black mustache and cowboy hat calls the bentkeeper. "Hey, who was working in this row? Twelve six-four-five is still staked in here. Who was working next to twelve six-four-five?" The bentkeeper nervously hands over his clipboard and the boss man takes off his sunglasses and draws on his cigarette while he examines it.

4   "What the hell is this!?! This is an eight bent row! You've been adding nine! It changed from nine to eight way the hell back there! Look at the goddamn post! Goddamn are you blind or can't you read!?! Go fix it!" He shoves the clipboard into the bentkeeper's stomach and jumps in his truck. The truck kicks up dirt and a cloud of dust as it speeds down the rocky dirt road. It comes to an abrupt halt about one hundred yards down. As the bentkeeper tries to figure out where the bents changed from nine to eight and from which numbers he must deduct points, he hears the boss man in the distance. "Hey eleven two-nine-two! Were you working next to twelve six-four-five?! You're bruising the leaves! Look at this? See this? This is from your row! We can't use these! You're going too fast. Stop bruising the goddamn leaves or I'm going to dock ten bents from your total!"

5   The humiliated bentkeeper tries not to listen as he attempts to correct his blunder while keeping pace with the pickers at the same time. A tough looking Hispanic kid breaks his concentration. "Hey bentkeeper! How many I got?" He holds up his stake so the bentkeeper can see the number.

6   The bentkeeper flips through the pages, "Uhhmm . . . sixty-eight."

7   "What!? I got more than that!"

8   "No, you've got sixty-eight."

9   "Ahh man this is bullshit. How'd you get that job anyway?" The complaining worker walks over to the water truck to get a drink.

10   In the middle of two towering tobacco plants under the white netting eleven two-nine-two mumbles slowly in a deep raspy voice with

smoke in his breath "Duh boss mon is crazy mon." He finishes his row and approaches the bentkeeper. "Hey mon, eleven two-nine-two, how many I got now?"

The bentkeeper replies "Yeah I know your number Stanley, you have 11 one-hundred and fifteen."

Stanley's smile reveals a gold front tooth with a black clover on it, 12 "Ohkay mon, yuh shades uh looking fat mon. All shades uh fat in my book mon."

After field "asparagus 1032," is finished, the nets are dropped 13 and the boss man selects two unlucky souls to spray the field. They reluctantly don cumbersome yellow suits that resemble something NASA designed for the planned mission to Mars. The only obvious difference is that the sprayers wear back packs of insecticides rather than oxygen.

Beneath the foggy mask of his suit, David's pockmarked hairy face 14 contorts into a nasty expression as he argues with his partner. Everyone hated David. He talked in the belligerent tongue of a junkyard dog. He was likened to a Neanderthal, though an allusion to something more ancient would probably suit him better. In the middle of the argument David blurts out, "I was in prison you know. . . . you know why I was there? . . . I killed a cop. . . . strangled him. . . . I'm on parole now." The significance of his comment seemed to bear no relation to the argument and his partner ignored it. He wasn't afraid of David.

All of the leaves from "asparagus 1032" are transported to the shed 15 on a trailer pulled by a big blue Ford tractor. The shed operations are run by a short stocky Hispanic man who wears a blue Hawaiian tee shirt with buttons and flowers. Working in the shed is better than working in the field. Many women work in the shed. There, by means of a giant sewing machine, they monotonously sew tobacco leaves to a stick called a "lath." Every time a worker finishes fifty laths she gets credit for one bundle. That is recorded by the bundlekeeper who patrols the shed monitoring daily progress. When a sewer calls out "bundle!" the bundlekeeper acknowledges "bundle!" and he hurries over to the end of the shed and hoists the heavy bundle from the bundle stockpile onto his shoulder. He then carries it to the idle sewer and he drops the bundle of fifty laths on top of her sewing machine. He then withdraws his hole puncher and he punches a hole in her card. Every time he punches a sewer's card he punches the master card which he wears around his neck. The master card shows how many bundles the shed completes on a daily basis. The bundlekeeper is the only one authorized to carry the hole puncher and the master card. Every so often a "boss man" will summon the bundlekeeper over and yank the master card from the bundlekeeper's neck to examine it. Then the boss man marches up and down the shed to exercise his authority. Then he stops in a thick cloud of dust to bark his favorite motivational speech "you not gonna get paid if you don't speed up!" The sewers ignore him and try to keep up with their mindless sewing machines. Those who complete the most bundles make the most money.

16   Every time a lath is completed it is racked. Then a man who has precariously positioned himself on the bottom level of rafters in the shed reaches down to the rack and picks it up. He then passes it to his partner above him on the next level who passes it up to the man above him and so on until the lath reaches the highest level that is available for another row of lath. Each lath is suspended between two rafters in the barn. They are carefully packed about a foot and a half apart across the width of the shed on every level of rafters and along the length of the barn. It normally takes about three days or a million and a half tobacco leaves to fill a shed.

17   On the dry dusty floor of the shed, the sweaty bundlekeeper looks up and admires the beautiful ceiling as it is painted with enormous green leaves with a splotch of a red shirt on one level and a yellow shirt above it and black arms with extended hands reaching to one another. For a moment he is gazing at the ceiling of the Sistine Chapel in Rome. He can imagine he is actually witnessing Michelangelo paint his masterpiece. For a moment the two men with extended hands remind the bundlekeeper of God in the heavens reaching to Adam. His imagination is suddenly snapped by a falling lath misplaced by an imperfect human being hanging from the rafters. The bundlekeeper ducks and after a loud 'thump!' he thanks God for his green hard hat.

18   As the clock rolls onto ten o'clock the boss man calls out "Coffee! Last lath!" The sewers finish sewing their last fifty leaves and the squeaky machines fall silent. The silence is invaded by the chatter of relieved sewers who have temporarily escaped the heat and dust in the shed to drink their coffee outside under the shade of a nearby tree or the side of the barn. The men in the rafters descend to retrieve their coolers to snack on bread and beer for a leisurely ten minutes.

19   Work resumes promptly at ten after ten with the boss man's "back to work!" The dissipating dust is replenished by a fresh cloud churned from the feet of a tired troop heading back to the barn. Next to the crack in the shed where a ray of sunlight illuminates floating dust particles, an old machine resumes its monotonous humming and clicking as a carefree Jamaican man whistles while feeding it leaves.

20   The boss man steps outside his dark shed for a breath of fresh air and a chance to blow his nose and spit the gritty sand from his mouth. Then he sees the next load of green leaves preceding a light brown dust cloud in field "Ketchen 918" with the new hybrid seed. Those leaves cannot be mixed. He grows red in the face because the next shed has not yet been prepared for those leaves. He stomps over to his dust colored

pickup truck to call base. After talking to the base coordinator he realizes that he will have to divide his crew into two sections with one half in one shed and another in the other shed. Now the bundlekeeper will have to run back and forth between the two sheds because of the field boss man's mistake. The stressed-out shed boss man invents another motivational speech "Hey, dees is not a carnival! dees is not the beach!" By lunch time the boss man has resumed his composure. He sneaks a peek at his watch and yells "last lath! break time! last lath!"

The shed workers rush to the water truck outside to wash their 21 hands before lunch. They sit in the weeds against the shady side of the shed and eat their lunches. The bundlekeeper and the shed boss eat in the pickup truck and listen to the Spanish radio. Out in the field the boss man calls "lunch time! Finish your rows!" The dirty and smelly pickers crawl out from underneath the nets and remove the tape from their fingers and try to wash the sticky tape, tobacco juices, and dirt from their fingertips. Then they head to the bus to find their coolers of beer and candy bars. They eat and drink for half an hour. Stanley puffs his harsh "Craven A" cigarette between mouthfuls of ham and cheese and tries not to think about tobacco.

The bentkeeper and the field boss eat in the dusty pickup and the 22 field boss lights his Marlboro and explains: "You know, when I yell at you it's nothing personal. I have to yell at you because it's my job. Man I know how it is, I was in your shoes once." The bentkeeper nods in agreement. His mind is on his lunch. It appears inedible. After growing tired of drinks and sandwiches that became warm and soggy in the hot sun for the past month, he has devised an unreliable system to solve that problem. Instead of just packing his lunch in ice, he actually freezes his entire lunch overnight. Unfortunately, when he opened his cooler on this hot day he discovered his peanut butter and jelly to be hard as a brick. Likewise his Boku juice boxes were still frozen solid.

As he sits there listening to his boss's rambling, he places his 23 sandwich on the dash and he peels away the walls of his juice box and gnaws on it as if it were some kind of primitive popsicle. No matter how he prepares his lunch he can never seem to achieve a proper balance between hot and cold. When the sun is high and it's time to eat, he discovers either a frozen block of bread and jam or a soggy something suffering heat stroke.

At half past the hour Stanley strikes his stake into the dirt with a 24 swift robotic motion. He sucks deeply on his cigarette and marches down to the end of the row. Large veins puff out of his forearm like the veins on the bottom green leaf that he snaps from the lower stalk of a thriving tobacco plant. Three more hours to go.

At the shed yet another blue tractor arrives with its precious load of 25 fresh leaves. The shed boss man orders two rafter men down to disperse the containers of tobacco among the sewers. The bundlekeeper manages to help with the heavy containers between bundle runs. He is thoroughly exhausted and his eyes are bloodshot from the irritating smoke and dust in the shed. Although three hours remain every shed laborer is anticipating the boss man's "last lath! Get on the bus!"

26   At three-thirty in the hot afternoon three buses and two Chevy pickup trucks carry exhausted tobacco workers back to farm headquarters where the workers can rest before returning to work early tomorrow in the cool morning hours.

Content

1. Which workers are Hispanics and Jamaicans? Are any white Americans? Who performs which tasks?

2. Nocton evidently doesn't expect his readers to know much about the work of harvesting tobacco. What does he expect them to learn from reading his essay? What does he expect them to do as a consequence?

3. Is Nocton himself a worker in the scene he describes? If so, can you ascertain what his job is? What are your clues? In what ways, if any, does the effectiveness of his argument depend on the authority of his personal experience?

Strategies/Structures/Language

4. Nocton's language is slow and repetitive. How does the style fit the subject?

5. Where does Nocton use dialogue? With what effects?

6. In describing the process of harvesting and drying tobacco, Nocton also portrays the structure and members of a particular community, including its gender, social, and cultural divisions. What does his portrait of this community suggest about the relationship between the worker and the product of his or her labor? Is Nocton's comparison of the shed ceiling to the Sistine Chapel (¶ 17) ironic? What does this visionary moment suggest he has learned through his work experience?

For Writing

7. Have you or any family members or close friends ever held a minimum-wage job, or do you currently hold such a job? With a partner who has had comparable job experience, analyze your respective jobs and determine their common elements. Do they have aspects in common with the jobs Nocton describes? Are there any significant differences? Either together or individually, write a satiric paper about a typical day on the job, intended to serve as a critique and to imply a plan for better working conditions or employee benefits.

8. **Mixed Modes.** Have you ever thought about how any crop that provides common raw materials—wheat, sugar, potatoes, rice, coffee, cotton—is grown and harvested? Have you or your relatives ever worked in such harvests? Find out about the production of one of these crops and compare it with the tobacco harvest that Nocton describes. On the basis of your investigation, formulate some principles of how agricultural workers should be treated and what their compensation and protection should be.

Additional Topics for Writing Description

(For strategies for writing description, see 230.)

Multiple Strategies for Writing: Description

In writing on any of the description topics below, you can employ a number of options to enable your readers to interpret the subject according to the dimensions you present—those accessible by sight, sound, touch, taste, and smell or in psychological or emotional terms:

- *Illustrations* and *examples*, to show the whole, its components, and to interpret them
- *Photographs, drawings, diagrams*, to clarify and explain
- *Symbolic* use of literal details
- A *narrative*, or *logical sequence*, to provide coherence of interrelated parts
- *Definitions, explanations, analyses* of the evidence
- *An implied or explicit argument* derived from the evidence and dependent on any of the above techniques

1. Places, for readers who haven't been there:
   a. Your dream house (or room)
   b. Your favorite spot on earth—or the place from hell
   c. A ghost town, or a dying or decaying neighborhood
   d. The site of a disaster or catastrophe, natural or man-made
   e. A foreign city or country you have visited
   f. A shopping mall or a particular store or restaurant, in use, under new management, or abandoned
   g. A factory, farm, store, or other place where you've worked
   h. The waiting room of an airport, hospital, physician's or dentist's office, or welfare office under a particular circumstance—routine or emergency
   i. A mountain, beach, lake, forest, desert, field, or other natural setting you know well
   j. Or compare and contrast two places you know well—two churches, houses, restaurants, vacation spots, schools, or any of the places identified in parts a–i, above; or a place before or after a renovation, a natural disaster, a long gap in time

See essays and poetry by O'Brien, 75–82; Yu, 161–71; Oliver, 179; Twain, 238–45; Nocton, 271–76; Cagle, 231–35.

2. People you know for readers who don't know them:
   a. A close relative or friend
   b. A friend or relative with whom you were once very close but from whom you are presently separated, physically or psychologically
   c. An antagonist

d. Someone with an occupation or skill you want to know more about—you may want to interview the person to learn what skills, training, and personal qualities the job or activity requires

e. Someone who has participated, voluntarily or involuntarily, in a significant historical event

f. A bizarre or eccentric person, a "character"

g. A high achiever, mentor or role model, in business, education, sports, the arts or sciences, politics, religion

h. A person whose reputation, public or private, has changed dramatically, for better or worse

See essays and poetry by Alexie, 83–85; Sanders, 135–42; Pelizzon, 285–86; Cagle, 231–35; Britt, 358–62; McGuire, 376–82.

3. Situations or events, for readers who weren't there:

a. A holiday, birthday, or community celebration; a high school or college party

b. A crucial job interview

c. A farmer's market, flea market, garage sale, swap meet, or auction

d. An argument, brawl, or fight

e. A performance of a play, concert, or athletic event

f. A ceremony—a graduation, wedding, christening, bar or bat mitzvah, an initiation, the swearing-in of a public official

g. A family or school reunion

h. A confrontation—between team members and referees or the coach, employee and boss, strikers and scabs, protesters and police, political rivals (local, national, or international)

See essays, poetry, fiction, cartoon, and creative nonfiction by Fadiman, 100–04; Hall, 118–21; Sedaris, 267–69; Barry, 318–28; Chast, 351; King, Jr., 399–413.

4. Experiences or feelings, for readers with analogous experiences:

a. Love—romantic, familial, patriotic, or religious (see Sanders, 135–42);

b. Isolation or rejection (see Spiegelman,93–95; Hogan, 96–99)

c. Fear (see Fadiman, 100–04)

d. Aspiration (see Douglass, 86–91)

e. Success (see McGuire, 376–82)

f. Anger (see Douglass, 86–91)

g. Peace, contentment, or happiness (see Hogan, 96–99)

h. An encounter with birth or death (see O'Brien, 75–82)

i. Coping with a handicap or disability—yours or that of someone close to you (see Hockenberry, 549–55; Sanders, 135–42)

j. Knowledge and understanding—but after the fact (Fadiman, 100–04; Sanders, 135–42)

k. Being a stranger in a strange land, as a traveler, immigrant, minority, or displaced person (Cagle, 231–35; Hockenberry, 549–55, Rix 557–63)

Definition

A definition can set limits or expand them. An objective definition may settle an argument; a subjective definition can provoke one. In either case, they answer the definer's fundamental question, What is X?

The composite photograph "Drivers Wanted" (290) offers a witty, visual definition of *square*—not cubed—for nearly everything depicted looks both flat and square except for the VW bug in the lower right-hand corner. Even objects usually conceived of as cubes—dishwasher, filing cabinet, cardboard box, house, eight-story building—look like two-dimensional squares in this rendering. Why are they shown in this way? Might their flat appearance be a pun on the meaning of *square*? Might the images be meant to convey the impression that although the VW is considered a square car, driven by square people, it is integral to life as we know it, and that life itself is composed of a superabundance of squares? If you don't "read" the ad this way, what alternatives can you offer?

The easiest way to define something is to identify it as a member of a class and then specify the characteristics that make it distinctive from all the other members of that class. "Lover" is a general term; what discriminates a particular love relationship from all others that might look like it on the surface, in posed pictures, is the subject of Scott Allison's "Picturesque" (330–332). The pictures are active, not static. They should "show him staying at her house until 11:52 PM every weekend night, knowing it takes exactly eight minutes to make it home for his midnight curfew"—a relationship constrained by deadlines, which aren't kept because the pictures "should always show him being late because he can't say goodbye to her." The relationship is romantic, dynamic: the pictures "should show them kissing, opening the door, kissing, closing the door and kissing either side of the window before finally mouthing goodbye." And the relationship is too good not to last; the pictures should show the breakup as well, "her driving away and him acting like nothing happened."

If you were writing about a relationship—sweet, sour, or indifferent—you could incorporate characters, scenes, typical actions, dialogue, memorabilia. All of these characteristics would lower the level of abstraction, usually a good idea in definition—even when talking about a general principle such as Jeffrey Wattles does in "The Golden Rule–One or Many, Gold or Glitter?" (311–17). What exactly do we mean when we say "Do to others as you want others to do to you?" And why is this particular rule "Golden"—a rule "worthy to be cherished as a rule of living or even as *the* rule of living?" Wattles answers the question by providing applications of the Rule, addressing objections to it ("the golden rule assumes that human beings are basically alike and thereby fails to do justice to the differences between people"), limitations ("The rule has been criticized as a naively idealistic standard, unsuited to a world of rugged competition") before providing a corrective; negatives first, then the positive.

Suppose you're writing an essay defining yourself as a student. A phrase or sentence will be insufficient, even if expanded to include "a computer science major" or "a business major with an accounting specialty, and a varsity diver." Although the details of that definition would separate and thereby distinguish you from, certainly, most other members of your class, they wouldn't convey the essence of what you as a person are like in your student role.

You could consider that sentence your core definition, and expand each key word into a separate paragraph to create an essay-length definition that could include "college student," "accounting major," and "varsity diver." But that still might not cover it. You could approach the subject through considering *cause-and-effect*. Why did you decide to go to college? Because you love to learn? Because you need to get specialized training for your chosen career? To get away from home? What have been the short-term effects of your decision to attend college? What are the long-term effects likely to be—on yourself, on your chosen field, perhaps on the world?

Or you might define yourself as a college student by *comparing and contrasting* your current life with that of a friend still in high school, or with someone who hasn't gone to college, or with a person you admire who has already graduated. If you work part- or full-time while attending college, you could write an *analysis* of its effect on your studying; or an *argument*, using yourself as an *extended example*, stating why it's desirable (or undesirable) for college students to work. Or, among many other possibilities, you could write a *narrative* of a typical week or semester at college. Each of these modes of writing could be an essay of definition. Each could be only partial, unless you wrote a book, for every definition is, by definition, selective. But each would serve your intended purpose. Each essay in this section represents a different common type of definition, but most use other types as well.

Definition According to Purpose.   A definition according to purpose specifies the fundamental qualities an object, principle or policy, role, or literary or artistic work has—or should have—in order to fulfill its potential. Thus, such a definition might explicitly answer such questions as, What is the purpose of X? ("A parable is a simple story designed to teach a moral truth."), What is X for? ("Horror movies exist to scare the spectators."), What does X do?, What is the role of X?

In her essay on the nature of skin, "A Supple Casing, Prone to Damage", Natalie Angier answers all of these questions in thirteen compact, fact-filled paragraphs. She explains its purpose by identifying *what it does*: "Skin keeps the outside out and offers the first line of defense against the microbial multitudes. . . . If you didn't have your skin," she explains, "you would dehydrate and die." But skin is more than a protective cover; "With its rich array of sensory receptors, skin is the bridge between private and public, wary self and beckoning other. Through the touch of its mother, a baby learns it is loved." The rest of the essay incorporates *physical description* (How much skin do humans have? How thick is it? What is it made of? What does it look like?) with *process analysis* (How skin cells grow and change over time, including how they are affected by exposure to sunlight and by aging).

Descriptive Definition.   A descriptive definition identifies the distinctive characteristics of an individual or group that set it apart from others. Thus a descriptive definition may begin by *naming* something, answering the question, What is X called? A possible answer might be Eudora Welty (unique among all other women); a walnut (as opposed to all other species of nuts); or *The Sound and the Fury* (and no other novel by William Faulkner). A descriptive definition may also *specify the relationship among the parts of a unit or group*, responding to the questions, What is the structure of X? How is X organized? How is X put together or constituted—as in the periodic table or a diagram of the body, an engine, or any other mechanical device? Lynda Barry's "Common Scents" also, through a series of cartoon panels, offers many combinations of smells, "mint, tangerines, and library books," "fried smelt, garlic, onions; 9,000 cigarettes; ½ a can of Adorne hair spray; Jade East aftershave," and more. . . . She uses these to evoke people's reactions both to the smells themselves and to the cultures and people who either denigrate or appreciate them, concluding, "Our house smelled like grease and fish and cigs, like Jade East and pork and dogs, like all the wild food my grandma boiled and fried. And if they could get *that* into a spray can, I'd buy it." The literal, descriptive definition might be, "You are what you smell like," but the connotative definition would depend not only on what the definers thought of the smells, but also on their opinions of the culture associated with that particular combination of odors.

Logical Definitions.   Logical definitions answer two related questions: Into what general category does X fall? and How does it differ from all other members of that category? ("A porpoise is a marine mammal but differs from whales, seals, dolphins, and the others in its . . .") Logical definitions are often used in scientific and philosophical writing, and indeed form the basis for the functional definition Howard Gardner presents in "Who Owns Intelligence?".

There are five key principles for writing logical definitions:

1. For economy's sake, use the most specific category to which the item to be defined belongs, rather than broader categories. Thus Gardner confines his discussion to human beings, not animals nor even all primates.
2. Any division of a class must include all members of that class. *Negative definitions* explain what is excluded from a given classification and what is not.
3. Subdivisions must be smaller than the class divided. Intelligence, says Gardner, can be divided into various functional categories: "linguistic and logical-mathematical, musical, spatial, bodily-kinesthetic, naturalist, interpersonal, and intrapersonal."
4. Categories should be mutually exclusive; they should not overlap.
5. The basis for subdividing categories must be consistent throughout each stage of subdivision. Thus, claiming that Daniel Goleman, in his "otherwise admirable *Emotional Intelligence*," confuses emotional intelligence with "certain preferred patterns of behavior," Gardner prefers the term "emotional sensitivity" because this includes both "interpersonal and intrapersonal intelligences" and therefore applies to "people who are sensitive to emotions in themselves and in others."

Essential or Existential Definition.   An essential definition might be considered a variation of a descriptive definition as it answers the question, "What is the essence, the fundamental nature of X?"—love, beauty, truth, justice, for instance. An existential definition presents the essence of its subject by answering the question, "What does it mean to be X?" or "What does it mean to live as an X" or "in a state of X?"—perhaps Chinese, supremely happy, married (or not), an AIDS victim. Thus, in "Clever and Poor," a poem of twenty-eight brief lines, Penelope Pelizzon captures the dramatic essence of the courtship of her parents, both clever, both poor, entering into marriage with a mixture of hope, ingenuity, and deception as definitions of these key concepts interlock, reinforce, sustain one another.

In the excerpt from his autobiography, *Moving Violations*, John Hockenberry offers a variety of definitions of his physical state that bleed into what—since he is paralyzed from his waist down—he is able to do, and not do, physically, emotionally, and socially (we already know that professionally he is a broadcast journalist). He offers contradictory labels—"I am a gimp, crip, physically challenged, differently abled, paralyzed"—in satiric, sardonic, in-your-face language. "Everything you think about me is right. Everything you think about me is wrong"—including assumptions about his "unlimited amounts of 'courage'" and his sexuality:

"I have massive problems with my sexuality. Actually, there is no problem with sexuality. It's just not a problem." He questions the stereotypes that the able-bodied hold of people with disabilities: "What is 'normal' but another stereotype, no different than 'angry black man,' 'Asian math genius,' 'welfare mother,' or 'gay man with a lisp'?" As he writes to dispel the stereotypes, for "as each stereotype breaks down, it reveals a pattern of wrongs," his essay implicitly urges readers to reinterpret, complicate, and thus redefine their understanding of "disability"—reinforced by the photograph of the person in the kayak, wheelchair strapped to the top.

Process Definitions.   These are concerned with how things or phenomena get to be the way they are. How is X produced? What causes X? How does it work? What does it do, or not do? With what effects? How does change affect X itself? Such questions are often the basis for scientific definitions or explanations of social or scientific phenomena. This is, in Tim O'Brien's terms, a true war story about a typical day in the life of any noncommissioned officer in the Iraq War, driving through any street, anywhere, being pelted by rocks and dirt thrown by any children at any foreigninvader. Who is the predominant influence over whom? What's the point of this—or any—invasion? Of any war?

Strategies for Writing: Definition

1. What is the purpose of the definition (or definitions) I'm writing about? Do I want to explain the subject's particular characteristics? Identify its nature? Persuade readers of my interpretation of its meaning? Entertain readers with a novel, bizarre, or highly personal meaning? How long will my essay be? (A short essay will require a restricted subject that you can cover in the limited space.)
2. For whom am I providing the definition? Why are they reading it? Do they know enough about the background of the subject to enable me to deal with it in a fairly technical way? Or must I stick to the basics—or at least begin there? If I wish to persuade or entertain my readers, can I count on them to have a pre-existing definition in mind against which I can match my own?
3. Will my entire essay be a definition, or will I incorporate definition(s) as part of a different type of essay? What proportion of my essay will be devoted to definition? Where will I include definitions? As I introduce new terms or concepts? Where else, if at all?
4. What techniques of definition will I use: naming; providing examples, brief or extended; comparing and contrasting; considering cause and effect; analysis; argument; narrative; analogy; or a mixture? Will I employ primarily positive or negative means (i.e., X is, or X is not)?
5. How much denotative (objective) definition will I use in my essay? How much connotative (subjective) definition? Will my tone be serious? Authoritative? Entertaining? Sarcastic? Or otherwise?

V. PENELOPE PELIZZON

V. Penelope Pelizzon's (born 1968) first poetry collection, *Nostos* (Ohio University Press, 2000) won the Hollis Summers Prize and the Poetry Society of America's Norma Farber First Book Award. Her new poems, nonfiction essays, and critical writings on film have recently appeared in the *Hudson Review, Field*, the *Kenyon Review*, the *New England Review, 32Poems, Fourth Genre*, the *Yale Journal of Criticism, Post Script, American Studies*, and *Narrative*. Educated at the University of Massachusetts, Boston (BA, 1992), the University of California, Irvine (MFA, 1994), and the University of Missouri (PhD, 1998). From 2002–2011 (at the University of Connecticut) she directed the Creative Writing Program.

She says, "'Clever and Poor' is one of a tiny clutch of poems that survived from my MFA days and actually made it, years later, into my first book. I think of it as the first *real* poem I ever wrote. . . . It was the first poem I wrote where the form was inevitable given the subject matter—the subject created the shaping device of the two framing adjectives. This story, an account of my parents' first meeting, was one I had tried to write, in every possible genre, for several years. The problem was that it was such a fantastically interesting series of events, this postwar precursor to match. com, rife with physical privations, social barriers, and gender taboos. Obviously, it was very emotionally loaded for me, too. Hence the challenges: how to create a portrait that was *not merely descriptive* but dramatic, what point of view to adopt that was intimate but not editorializing. Perhaps most difficult was deciding what information to leave out. So for years I struggled with this as a long narrative poem, a short story, a dialogue. Nothing worked. Then one morning I woke up early and realized—insert cartoon lightbulb over head—that I could tell the whole story quite simply using those two words as a sort of balancing gesture, almost like a game. I wrote for less than an hour, and the result was 'Clever and Poor.' The poem taught me to trust that a story will tell you its true form (which is not to say that you won't have to wrestle near to death with it until it speaks)."

Clever and Poor

She has always been clever and poor,
    especially here off the Yugoslav train
on a crowded platform of dust. Clever was
    her breakfast of nutmeg ground in water

in place of rationed tea. Poor was the cracked   5
    cup, the missing bread. Clever are the six

V. PENELOPE PELIZZON, "Clever and Poor" from NOSTOS, Ohio University Press. Reprinted with permission of Ohio University Press, Athens, Ohio. www.ohioswallow.com

handkerchiefs stitched to the size of a scarf
     and knotted at her throat. Poor is the thin coat

patched with cloth from the pockets
10   she then sewed shut. Clever is the lipstick,

Petunia Pink, she rubbed with a rag on her nails.
     Poor nails, blue with the cold. Posed

in a cape to hide her waist, her photograph
     was clever. Poor then was what she called

15   the last bills twisted in her wallet. Letter
     after letter she was clever and more

clever, for months she wrote a newspaper man
     who liked her in the picture. The poor

saved spoons of sugar, she traded them
20   for stamps. He wanted a clever wife. She was poor

so he sent a ticket: now she could come to her wedding
     by train. Poor, the baby left with the nuns.

Because she is clever, on the platform to meet him
     she thinks *Be generous with your eyes*. What is poor

25   is what she sees. Cracks stop the station clock,
     girls with candle grease to sell. Clever, poor,

clever and poor, her husband, more nervous
     than his picture, his shined shoes tied with twine.

NATALIE ANGIER

Natalie Angier (born 1958) grew up in New York City and graduated from Barnard College in 1978. After working as a magazine staff writer at *Discover* and *Time* and as an editor at *Savvy*, she became a science reporter for the *New York Times* in 1990 and won a Pulitzer Prize in the following year. Her columns were published in 1995 as *The Beauty of the Beastly: New Views on the Nature of Life*. Topics include evolutionary biology ("Mating for Life?"), DNA scorpions, and central issues of life, death (by suicide or AIDS), and creativity: *Woman: An Intimate Geography* (1999) offers a spirited and controversial celebration of "the female body—its anatomy, its chemistry, its evolution, and its laughter," including both traditional (the womb, the egg) and nontraditional elements ("the movement, strength, aggression, and fury"). Angier, who lists her hobby as "weightlifting," is also a mother; her work reflects the strengths of both. Her most recent book, *The Canon: A Whirligig Tour of the Beautiful Sciences* (2007), is an entertaining guide to science's controversies, mysteries, and beauties.

In "A Supple Casing, Prone to Damage," originally published in 2007 in the *New York Times*, Natalie Angier offers an informative primer on the composition and history of our skin while also conveying its beauty and its frailty—which makes it especially vulnerable to sun damage.

A Supple Casing, Prone to Damage

Grimly determined this past summer to enjoy myself and humor my family, I foolishly ventured outdoors during daylight hours on multiple occasions, including three pointless trips to the beach. Although I always wore sunscreen, sunglasses, a hat and as much clothing as I could get away with and not look like a homeless person, I nevertheless ended up with a few unwanted solar souvenirs. There's a kind of a praline speckling to my forearms now, reverse sandal stripes on my feet, and a bright white wristwatch outline should I ever need help accessorizing in a cave. 1

As I survey the sharp tan lines and flaking faces that surround me, I see that I am hardly alone. When it comes to how we treat our birthday suits, it seems, we are like 2-year-olds: more concerned with the wrapping and ribbons than with the present itself. We spend billions of dollars a year on makeup and skin-care products, yet we're slipshod about the one measure that dermatologists emphasize is essential for the long-term health, strength and bounce of our skin: guarding it against ultraviolet radiation. 2

That means applying full-spectrum sunscreen every day of the year, and by the gob, not the gossamer, and reapplying it later even if you're in a bad mood and don't feel like it. It also means skipping the tanning salons, forever decoupling the words "fit" and "tanned," and retreating from the fiercest light of midday, back to a shady oasis, where you can contemplate the complexity, multidexterity and deep beauty of the organ called skin. 3

That skin merits designation as an organ is not an effort to lend scientific seriousness to a body part often considered superficial compared with meaty organ kingpins like the heart, liver and brain. For one thing, as burn victims demonstrate all too tragically, you can no more survive without your skin than you can without your lungs. For another, according to Nina G. Jablonski, a professor of anthropology at Penn State University and author of "Skin: A Natural History," the definition of an organ is a set of tissues working together toward a common end and outfitted with an independent supply of blood and nerves. "Skin is like that," she said. "It has its own blood supply, its own nerve supply and its own set of commitments, which are many and wondrous." 4

5   Skin keeps the outside out and offers the first line of defense against the microbial multitudes that might otherwise make of us bed, breakfast and birthing room. Skin keeps the inside in, keeps our fluids from leaking out and allows us to carry our own piece of sea. If you didn't have your skin, according to Elaine Fuchs, who studies the biology of skin and hair at Rockefeller University, you would dehydrate and die.

6   With its rich array of sensory receptors, skin is the bridge between private and public, wary self and beckoning other. Through the touch of its mother, a baby learns it is loved.

7   By many measures, skin is the largest organ of the human body, averaging 20 square feet in surface area—roughly enough to cover the top of a twin mattress—and weighing about nine pounds. It consists of some 20 types of cells divided into two basic domains, the thin part we see and the thick understory we pinch. The top layer, or epidermis, is about the thickness of cellophane, although that thickness varies considerably across the body, from a thin point a mere five cells across on the scalp, to serious thickness of hundreds of cells on the palms of the hands and the balls of the feet. The epidermis is constantly sloughing off from above and being rebuilt from a pool of dividing stem cells at the innermost epidermal layer. Over a period of about four weeks, a newborn skin cell will detach from the starter pool and begin heading upward, gradually shedding such unnecessary cellular baggage as its nucleus, and cross-linking its primary content, the tough, stretchy protein keratin, into ever tighter bundles, and secreting a drizzle of greasy lipids that help lend skin its Saran-wrap seal.

8   By the time a fully matured epidermal cell reaches the light, Dr. Fuchs said, it's essentially a dead sack full of highly cross-linked keratin filaments. Much of the dust in your house consists of just such shed keratin sacks.

9   Also embedded in the epidermis are the melanocytes, cells that make the melanin pigments that color our skin varying shades of brown, ocher and glue. Melanin serves as the skin's primary defense against excess ultraviolet radiation, and tanning is the result of stepped-up melanin production, the body's frantic effort to protect the DNA molecules of underlying skin cells from gluttonous doses of sun.

10   In most animals, including our close kin the chimpanzee, melanocyte production centers on the hair follicles, coloring the fur while leaving the underlying skin pale. But as early humans shed their pelts, Dr. Jablonski said, the better to sweat away heat in their increasingly active hunting and gathering lives, the demand for protective melanic output moved into the skin.

11   Skin needs ultraviolet radiation to begin the synthesis of vitamin D, but dermatologists say you can probably get the necessary electromagnetic input from a mere 20 minutes of sun exposure a week, as you go about your daily affairs, sunblocked and sans beach.

12   Beneath the epidermis is the thicker dermis, the part of an animal's hide that is chemically tanned to give us leather. The dermis is a clotted

forest of blood vessels, nerves, sweat glands, hair follicles, piloerector muscles to make the product of those follicles stand on end, immune cells to battle infection, and fibroblasts, the all-important cells that synthesize collagen. More than three-quarters of skin's dry weight consists of collagen, proteins that look and act like ropes and help anchor the dermis to the restless epidermal roofline above. Interwoven with collagen are pliant twists of the protein elastin, the source of our skin's power to spring back into shape after stretching.

Our skin bends over backward and puts itself out and saves face   13
and rejuvenates and exfoliates for us, year after year, but time takes its toll. With age it gets thinner, losing collagen and elastin and the finger-like anchors that help keep our epidermis in place. The connective fibers that remain become stiffer and weaker and more chaotically cross-linked. Chronic sun exposure can hasten the breakdown by 10 years or more, which is why come next summer, I plan to go spelunking.

Content

1. Why does skin merit "designation as an organ" (¶s 4–5)? What are the differences between the epidermis and the dermis (¶s 7, 12)?

2. Why does the skin tan (¶s 9–10)? What evolutionary function do scientists believe tanning served (¶ 10)?

3. What is the function of collagen? Of elastin (¶ 12)? How does sun exposure damage skin (¶ 13)?

Strategies/Structures/Language

4. Identify some of the metaphors Angier uses to describe our skin. For example, the epidermis is constantly "being rebuilt from a pool of dividing stem cells" (¶ 7) and the dermis "is a clotted forest" (¶ 12). How do these metaphors help the reader understand the skin's characteristics and functions? How do these metaphors help persuade the reader of the "complexity, multidexterity and deep beauty" (¶ 3) of skin?

5. Is Angier's sole purpose to persuade readers to avoid damaging their skin? How does Angier suggest our attitude toward our skin reflects other social and cultural behaviors? Why, for example, does she characterize skin as "the bridge between private and public" (¶ 6) and the color of skin pigments as "brown, ocher and glue" (¶ 9)?

For Writing

6. **Journal Writing.** Does a tan body seem to imply a fit one? Explore your own perceptions of suntanned skin. Do you find tanned skin attractive despite knowing that tanned skin is also damaged skin? What factors influence you in your perception of tanning and of various shades of skin color generally?

7. **Dialogues.** How does Gawande's "On Washing Hands" offer an alternative view of skin compared to Angier's? How might these two texts complement each other?

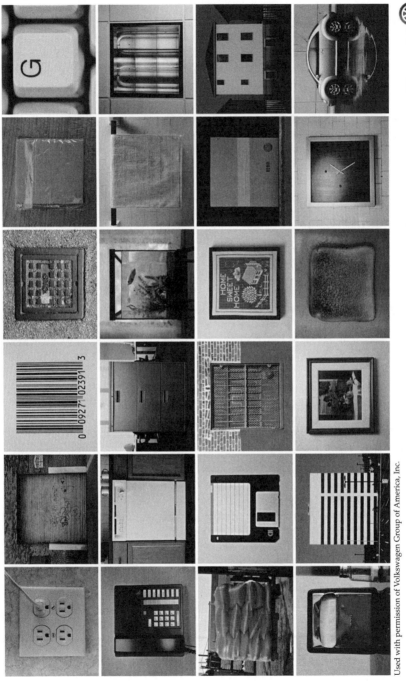

Possible ways to "read" this photograph are discussed on the first page of this chapter.

CHARLES DARWIN

Darwin (1809–1882) descended from a distinguished British scientific family; his father was a physician, and his grandfather was the renowned Erasmus Darwin, amateur naturalist. As a youth Darwin was most alert when studying natural phenomena, particularly beetles, even popping a rare specimen into his mouth to preserve it when his hands were full of other newly collected insects. So, despite his lackadaisical study of medicine at Edinburgh University (1825–1828) and equally indifferent preparation for the clergy at Cambridge (B.A., 1831), he shipped aboard the HMS *Beagle* on a scientific expedition around South America, 1831–1836. As the ship's naturalist, he recorded careful observations of plants, animals, and human behavior that were published in *The Voyage of the Beagle* (1839), and eventually led to his theories of natural selection (roughly translated as "the survival of the fittest") and evolution. The publication of the earthshaking *On the Origin of Species by Means of Natural Selection, or the Preservation of Favored Races in the Struggle for Life* (1859) was based on his painstaking observations of animals and plants, on land and sea and in the air.

"Understanding Natural Selection," a small portion of this work, contains the essence of Darwin's best-known and most revolutionary principles, that in natural selection those variations, "infinitesimally small inherited modifications," endure if they aid in survival. The claim that these modifications occur gradually, rather than being produced at a single stroke by a divine creator, is the basis for Darwin's theory of evolution, extended to humans in *The Descent of Man* (1871). Darwin's theories provoked the enormous controversy between theologians and scientists that continues to this day—as Gould's "Evolution as Fact and Theory" (401–10) makes clear.

Darwin's work continues to be read, as much for its clear and elegant literary style as for its content. Using the techniques of popular literature to explain sophisticated scientific concepts and to present mountains of detailed information, Darwin is a highly engaging writer. He uses the first person, metaphors, anecdotes, and numerous illustrations that overlap and reinforce one another—here as ways to define his subject. Because he is explaining a theory and concepts totally new to his audience, he has to ground them in the reality of numerous natural phenomena that can be seen and studied.

Understanding Natural Selection

It may be said that natural selection is daily and hourly scrutinizing, throughout the world, every variation, even the slightest; rejecting that which is bad, preserving and adding up all that is good; silently and insensibly working, whenever and wherever opportunity offers, at the improvement of each organic being in relation to its organic and inorganic conditions of life. We see nothing of these slow changes in progress, until the hand of time has marked the long lapses of ages, and then so imperfect

1

is our view into long past geological ages, that we only see that the forms of life are now different from what they formerly were.

2   Although natural selection can act only through and for the good of each being, yet characters and structures, which we are apt to consider as of very trifling importance, may thus be acted on. When we see leaf-eating insects green, and bark-feeders mottled-grey; the alpine ptarmigan white in winter, the red-grouse the color of heather, and the black-grouse that of peaty earth, we must believe that these tints are of service to these birds and insects in preserving them from danger. Grouse, if not destroyed at some period of their lives, would increase in countless numbers; they are known to suffer largely from birds of prey; and hawks are guided by eyesight to their prey—so much so, that on parts of the Continent persons are warned not to keep white pigeons, as being the most liable to destruction. Hence I can see no reason to doubt that natural selection might be most effective in giving the proper color to each kind of grouse, and in keeping that color, when once acquired, true and constant. Nor ought we to think that the occasional destruction of an animal of any particular color would produce little effect: we should remember how essential it is in a flock of white sheep to destroy every lamb with the faintest trace of black. In plants the down on the fruit and the color of the flesh are considered by botanists as characters of the most trifling importance: yet we hear from an excellent horticulturist, Downing, that in the United States smooth-skinned fruits suffer far more from a beetle, a curculio, than those with down; that purple plums suffer far more from a certain disease than yellow plums; whereas another disease attacks yellow-fleshed peaches far more than those with other colored flesh. If, with all the aids of art, these slight differences make a great difference in cultivating the several varieties, assuredly, in a state of nature, where the trees would have to struggle with other trees and with a host of enemies, such differences would effectually settle which variety, whether a smooth or downy, a yellow or purple fleshed fruit, should succeed.

3   In looking at many small points of difference between species, which, as far as our ignorance permits us to judge, seem to be quite unimportant, we must not forget that climate, food, and so on probably produce some slight and direct effect. It is, however, far more necessary to bear in mind at there are many unknown laws of correlation to growth, which, when one part of the organization is modified through variation, and the modifications are accumulated by natural selection for the good of the being, will cause other modifications, often of the most unexpected nature.

4   As we see that those variations which under domestication appear at any particular period of life, tend to reappear in the offspring of the same period; for instance, in the seeds of the many varieties of our culinary and agricultural plants; in the caterpillar and cocoon stages of the varieties of the silkworm; in the eggs of poultry, and in the color of the down of their

chickens; in the horns of our sheep and cattle when nearly adult; so in a state of nature, natural selection will be enabled to act on and modify organic beings at any age, by the accumulation of profitable variations at that age, and by their inheritance at a corresponding age. If it profit a plant to have its seeds more and more widely disseminated by the wind, I can see no greater difficulty in this being effected through natural selection, than in the cotton-planter increasing and improving by selection the down in the pods on his cotton-trees. Natural selection may modify and adapt the larva of an insect to a score of contingencies, wholly different from those which concern the mature insect. These modifications will no doubt affect, through the laws of correlation, the structure of the adult; and probably in the case of those insects which live only for a few hours, and which never feed, a large part of their structure is merely the correlated result of successive changes in the structure of their larvae. So, conversely, modifications in the adult will probably often affect the structure of the larva; but in all cases natural selection will ensure that modifications consequent on other modifications at a different period of life, shall not be in the least degree injurious: for if they became so, they would cause the extinction of the species.

Natural selection will modify the structure of the young in relation to the parent, and of the parent in relation to the young. In social animals it will adapt the structure of each individual for the benefit of the community; if each in consequence profits by the selected change. What natural selection cannot do, is to modify the structure of one species, without giving it any advantage, for the good of another species; and though statements to this effect may be found in works of natural history, I cannot find one case which will bear investigation. A structure used only once in an animal's whole life, if of high importance to it, might be modified to any extent by natural selection; for instance, the great jaws possessed by certain insects, and used exclusively for opening the cocoon—or the hard tip to the beak of nestling birds, used for breaking the egg. It has been asserted, that of the best short-beaked tumbler pigeons more perish in the egg than are able to get out of it; so that fanciers assist in the act of hatching. Now, if nature had to make the beak of a full-grown pigeon very short for the bird's own advantage, the process of modification would be very slow, and there would be simultaneously the most rigorous selection of the young birds within the egg, which had the most powerful and hardest beaks, for all with weak beaks would inevitably perish: or, more delicate and more easily broken shells might be selected, the thickness of the shell being known to vary like every other structure.

Sexual Selection

Inasmuch as peculiarities often appear under domestication in one sex and become hereditarily attached to that sex, the same fact probably occurs under nature, and if so, natural selection will be able to modify one sex in its functional relations to the other sex, or in relation to wholly different habits of life in the two sexes, as is sometimes the case with insects. And this leads me to say a few words on what I call sexual selection. This depends, not on a struggle for existence, but on a struggle between the males for possession of the females; the result is not death to the unsuccessful competitor, but few or no offspring. Sexual selection is, therefore, less rigorous than natural selection. Generally, the most vigorous males, those which are best fitted for their places in nature, will leave most progeny. But in many cases, victory will depend not on general vigor, but on having special weapons, confined to the male sex. A hornless stag or spurless cock would have a poor chance of leaving offspring. Sexual selection by always allowing the victor to breed might surely give indomitable courage, length to the spur, and strength to the wing to strike in the spurred leg, as well as the brutal cock-fighter, who knows well that he can improve his breed by careful selection of the best cocks. How low in the scale of nature this law of battle descends, I know not; male alligators have been described as fighting, bellowing, and whirling round, like Indians in a war dance, for the possession of the females; male salmons have been seen fighting all day long; male stag-beetles often bear wounds from the huge mandibles of other males. The war is, perhaps, severest between the males of polygamous animals, and these seem oftenest provided with special weapons. The males of carnivorous animals are already well armed; though to them and to others, special means of defence may be given through means of sexual selection, as the mane to the lion, the shoulder-pad to the boar, and the hooked jaw to the male salmon, for the shield may be as important for victory, as the sword or spear.

7   Amongst birds, the contest is often of a more peaceful character. All those who have attended to the subject, believe that there is the severest; rivalry between the males of many species to attract by singing the females. The rock-thrush of Guiana, birds of Paradise, and some others, congregate; and successive males display their gorgeous plumage and perform strange antics before the females, which standing by as spectators, as last choose the most attractive partner. Those who have closely attended to birds in confinement well know that they often take individual preferences and dislikes: thus Sir R. Heron has described how one pied peacock was eminently attractive to all his hen birds. It may appear childish to attribute any effect to such apparently weak means: I cannot here enter on the details necessary to support this view; but if man can in a short time give elegant carriage and beauty to his bantams, according to his standard of beauty, I can see no good reason to doubt that female birds, by selecting, during thousands of generations, the most melodious or beautiful males, according to their standard of beauty, might produce a marked effect. I strongly suspect that some well-known laws with respect to the plumage of male and female birds, in comparison with

Peter Johnson/Corbis

*What Darwinian observations or principles does this photograph
illustrate? Does each species, whose members bear a strong family
resemblance, have ways of detecting individuals that members of other
species are unaware of? How does this detection—and pairing—
contribute to their survival?*

the plumage of the young, can be explained on the view of plumage having been chiefly modified by sexual selection, acting when the birds have
come to the breeding age or during the breeding season; the modifications thus produced being inherited at corresponding ages or seasons, either by the males alone, or by the males and females; but I have not space
here to enter on this subject.

Thus it is, as I believe, that when the males and females of any animal   8
have the same general habits of life, but differ in structure, color, or orna-
ment, such differences have been mainly caused by sexual selection; that
is, individual males have had, in successive generations, some slight advantage over other males, in their weapons, means of defence, or charms;
and have transmitted these advantages to their male offspring. Yet, I would
not wish to attribute all such sexual differences to this agency: for we see
peculiarities arising and becoming attached to the male sex in our domestic animals (as the wattle in male carriers, horn-like protuberances in the
cocks of certain fowls, and so on), which we cannot believe to be either
useful to the males in battle, or attractive to the females. We see analogous
cases under nature, for instance, the tuft of hair on the breast of the turkey-
cock, which can hardly be either useful or ornamental to this bird; indeed,
had the tuft appeared under domestication, it would have been called a
monstrosity.

Illustration of the Action of Natural Selection

9 . . . Let us take the case of a wolf, which preys on various animals, securing some by craft, some by strength, and some by fleetness; and let us suppose that the fleetest prey, a deer for instance, had from any change in the country increased in numbers, or that other prey had decreased in numbers, during that season of the year when the wolf is hardest pressed for food. I can under, such circumstances see no reason to doubt that the swiftest and slimmest wolves would have the best chance of surviving, and so be preserved or selected—provided always that they retain strength to master their prey at this or at some other period of the year, when they might be compelled to prey on other animals. I can see no more reason to doubt this, than that man can improve the fleetness of his greyhounds by careful arid methodical selection, or by that unconscious selection which results from each man trying to keep the best dogs without any thought of modifying the breed.

10   Even without any change in the proportional numbers of the animals on which our wolf preyed, a cub might be born with an innate tendency to pursue certain kinds of prey. Nor can this be thought very improbable; for we often observe great differences in the natural tendencies of our domestic animals; one cat, for instance, taking to catch rats, another mice; one cat . . . bringing home winged game, another hares or rabbits, and another hunting on marshy ground and almost, nightly catching woodcocks or snipes. The tendency to catch rats rather than mice is known to be inherited. Now, if any slight innate change of habit or of structure benefited an individual wolf, it would have the best chance of surviving and of leaving offspring. Some of its young would probably inherit the same habits or structure, and by the repetition of this process, a new variety might be formed which would either supplant or coexist with the parent-form of wolf. Or, again, the wolves inhabiting a mountainous district, and those frequenting the lowlands, would naturally be forced to hunt different prey; and from the continued preservation of the individuals best fitted for the two sites, two varieties might slowly be formed. These varieties would cross and blend where they met; but to this subject of intercrossing we shall soon have to return. I may add, that . . . there are two varieties of the wolf inhabiting the Catskill Mountains in the United States, one with a light greyhoundlike form, which pursues deer, and the other more bulky, with shorter legs, which more frequently attacks the shepherd's flocks.

Content

1. What does Darwin mean by "natural selection" (¶ 1–5)? How does "natural selection" differ from "sexual selection" (¶ 6–8)?

2. Although Darwin doesn't use the term "evolution," this piece clearly illustrates that concept. Define that term, using some of Darwin's illustrations. Does

your definition anticipate creationists' objections? Should it? If you believe in creationism, how does this belief influence the way you define "evolution"?

3. Distinguish between theory, opinion, and fact in Darwin's presentation of the concepts of natural selection (¶ 1–5, 9–10).

Strategies/Structures

4. Darwin offers arguments on behalf of both natural selection and sexual selection. Which argument has the better supporting evidence? Which argument makes its case more compellingly? Why?

5. Darwin builds his case for the existence of natural selection by using numerous illustrations. Identify some. Explain how an argument can also, as in this case, be a definition.

6. What kind of authorial persona does Darwin present? In what ways is this "scientist figure" familiar today? How does this persona differ from the stereotype of the "mad scientist"?

Language

7. Is Darwin writing for an audience of other scientists? For a general readership? Or for both? What aspects of his language (choice of vocabulary, familiar or unfamiliar language, and illustrations), tone, and sentence structure reinforce your answer?

8. Are there features of Darwin's language, and sentence and paragraph structure, that indicates that this excerpt was written in the nineteenth rather than the twentieth century? Illustrate your answer.

For Writing

9. Write a definition of something (a natural phenomenon, human or animal behavior you have observed carefully over time) for an audience of nonscientists. If you are writing about the behavior of college students in a particular type of situation—for example, some aspect(s) of test-taking, dating, dressing, eating—record your observations in as objective and "scientific" a manner as you can.

HOWARD GARDNER

Howard Gardner (born 1943) studied cognitive and social psychology at Harvard (BA, 1965, PhD, 1971) and became codirector of Project Zero at the Harvard Graduate School of Education, studying the ways children and adults learn. He is currently the Hobbs Professor in Cognition and Education at Harvard and an adjunct research professor of neurology at Boston University School of Medicine. Gardner has written over twenty books and hundreds of articles, most of them focusing on creativity and intelligence. Among his most recent works are *Multiple Intelligences: New Horizons, the Development and Education of the Mind* (2006) and *Five Minds for the Future* (2009).

In his best-known book, *Frames of Mind: The Theory of Multiple Intelligences* (1983), he postulates that there are seven distinct cognitive realms in the human brain and that each governs a particular kind of intelligence. Those intelligences most commonly considered—and tested—by the American educational establishment are *linguistic*, the ability to communicate through language, and *logical-mathematical*, the ability to come up with and use abstract concepts. To these Gardner adds five other intelligences: *spatial*, the ability to perceive and reimage the physical world; *bodily-kinesthetic*, the ability to use the body in skilled or creative ways; *musical*, the ability to distinguish, remember, and manipulate tone, melody, and rhythm; *interpersonal*, the ability to understand other people; and *intrapersonal*, the ability to understand one's self and have a conscious awareness of one's emotions. A decade later Gardner added an eighth intelligence: *naturalist*, the ability to have an intuitive understanding about plants and animals. Despite criticism from people who say Gardner's multiple intelligences are really talents (something we can get along without, as opposed to traditionally defined intelligence, which is indispensable) and that they can't be easily measured, to many educators he evokes "the reverence teenagers lavish on a rock star." "Who Owns Intelligence?" first published in the *Atlantic Monthly* in February 1999, addresses these issues in attempting, once again, to pin down intelligence and who owns it—a particularly significant issue as the twenty-first century grapples with expanding concepts of intellectual property, ranging from book manuscripts, musical compositions, and mechanical inventions to websites, applications of gene therapy, and esoteric chemical and technical processes.

Who Owns Intelligence?

1 Almost a century ago Alfred Binet, a gifted psychologist, was asked by the French Ministry of Education to help determine who would experience difficulty in school. Given the influx of provincials to the capital, along with immigrants of uncertain stock, Parisian officials believed they needed to know who might not advance smoothly through the system. Proceeding in an empirical manner, Binet posed many questions to youngsters of different ages. He ascertained which questions when answered correctly predicted success in school, and which questions when answered incorrectly foretold school difficulties. The items that discriminated most clearly between the two groups became, in effect, the first test of intelligence.

2 Binet is a hero to many psychologists. He was a keen observer, a careful scholar, an inventive technologist. Perhaps even more important for his followers, he devised the instrument that is often considered psychology's

greatest success story. Millions of people who have never heard Binet's name have had aspects of their fate influenced by instrumentation that the French psychologist inspired. And thousands of psychometricians—specialists in the measurement of psychological variables—earn their living courtesy of Binet's invention.

Although it has prevailed over the long run, the psychologists' version of intelligence is now facing its biggest threat. Many scholars and observers—and even some iconoclastic psychologists—feel that intelligence is too important to be left to the psychometricians. Experts are extending the breadth of the concept—proposing many intelligences, including emotional intelligence and moral intelligence. They are experimenting with new methods of ascertaining intelligence, including some that avoid tests altogether in favor of direct measures of brain activity. They are forcing citizens everywhere to confront a number of questions: What is intelligence? How ought it to be assessed? And how do our notions of intelligence fit with what we value about human beings? In short, experts are competing for the "ownership" of intelligence in the next century.

The outline of the psychometricians' success story is well known. Binet's colleagues in England and Germany contributed to the conceptualization and instrumentation of intelligence testing—which soon became known as IQ tests. (An IQ, or intelligence quotient, designates the ratio between mental age and chronological age. Clearly we'd prefer that a child in our care have an IQ of 120, being smarter than average for his or her years, than an IQ of 80, being older than average for his or her intelligence). Like other Parisian fashions of the period, the intelligence test migrated easily to the United States. First used to determine who was "feeble-minded," it was soon used to assess "normal" children, to identify the "gifted," and to determine who was fit to serve in the Army. By the 1920s the intelligence test had become a fixture in educational practice in the United States and much of Western Europe.

Early intelligence tests were not without their critics. Many enduring concerns were first raised by the influential journalist Walter Lippmann, in a series of published debates with Lewis Terman, of Stanford University, the father of IQ testing in America. Lippmann pointed out the superficiality of the questions, their possible cultural biases, and the risks of trying to determine a person's intellectual potential with a brief oral or paper-and-pencil measure.

Perhaps surprisingly, the conceptualization of intelligence did not advance much in the decades following Binet's and Terman's pioneering contributions. Intelligence tests came to be seen, rightly or wrongly, as primarily a tool for selecting people to fill academic or vocational niches. In one of the most famous—if irritating—remarks about intelligence testing, the influential Harvard psychologist E. G. Boring declared, "Intelligence is what the tests test." So long as these tests did what they were supposed to do (that is, give some indication of school success), it did not seem necessary or prudent to probe too deeply into their meaning or to explore alternative views of the human intellect.

7   Psychologists who study intelligence have argued chiefly about three questions. The first: Is intelligence singular, or does it consist of various more or less independent intellectual faculties? The purists—ranging from the turn of-the-century English psychologist Charles Spearman to his latter-day disciples Richard J. Herrnstein and Charles Murray (of *The Bell Curve* fame)—defend the notion of a single overarching "g," or general intelligence. The pluralists—ranging from L. L. Thurstone, of the University of Chicago, who posited seven vectors of the mind, to J. P. Guilford, of the University of Southern California, who discerned 150 factors of the intellect—construe intelligence as composed of some or even many dissociable components. In his much cited *The Mismeasure of Man* (1981) the paleontologist Stephen Jay Gould argued that the conflicting conclusions reached on this issue reflect alternative assumptions about statistical procedures rather than the way the mind is. Still, psychologists continue the debate, with a majority sympathetic to the general-intelligence perspective.

8   The public is more interested in the second question: Is intelligence (or are intelligences) largely inherited? This is by and large a Western question. In the Confucian societies of East Asia individual differences in endowment are assumed to be modest, and differences in achievement are thought to be due largely to effort. In the West, however, many students of the subject sympathize with the view—defended within psychology by Lewis Terman, among others—that intelligence is inborn and one can do little to alter one's intellectual birthright.

9   Studies of identical twins reared apart provide surprisingly strong support for the "heritability" of psychometric intelligence. That is, if one wants to predict someone's score on an intelligence test, the scores of the biological parents (even if the child has not had appreciable contact with them) are more likely to prove relevant than the scores of the adoptive parents. By the same token, the IQs of identical twins are more similar than the IQs of fraternal twins. And, contrary to common sense (and political correctness), the IQs of biologically related people grow closer in the later years of life. Still, because of the intricacies of behavioral genetics and the difficulties of conducting valid experiments with human child-rearing, a few defend the proposition that intelligence is largely environmental rather than heritable, and some believe that we cannot answer the question at all.

10   Most scholars agree that even if psychometric intelligence is largely inherited, it is not possible to pinpoint the sources of differences in average IQ between groups, such as the fifteen-point difference typically observed between African-American and white populations. That is because

in our society the contemporary—let alone the historical—experiences of these two groups cannot be equated. One could ferret out the differences (if any) between black and white populations only in a society that was truly color-blind.

One other question has intrigued laypeople and psychologists: Are intelligence tests biased? Cultural assumptions are evident in early intelligence tests. Some class biases are obvious—who except the wealthy could readily answer a question about polo? Others are more subtle. Suppose the question is what one should do with money found on the street. Although ordinarily one might turn it over to the police, what if one had a hungry child? Or what if the police force were known to be hostile to members of one's ethnic group? Only the canonical response to such a question would be scored as correct.

Psychometricians have striven to remove the obviously biased items from such measures. But biases that are built into the test situation itself are far more difficult to deal with. For example, a person's background affects his or her reaction to being placed in an unfamiliar locale, being instructed by someone dressed in a certain way, and having a printed test booklet thrust into his or her hands. And as the psychologist Claude M. Steele has argued in these pages (see "Race and the Schooling of Black Americans," April, 1992), the biases prove even more acute when people know that their academic potential is being measured and that their racial or ethnic group is widely considered to be less intelligent than the dominant social group. . . .

Paradoxically, one of the clearest signs of the success of intelligence tests is that they are no longer widely administered. In the wake of legal cases about the propriety of making consequential decisions about education on the basis of IQ scores, many public school officials have become test-shy. By and large, the testing of IQ in the schools is restricted to cases involving a recognized problem (such as a learning disability) or a selection procedure (determining eligibility for a program that serves gifted children).

Despite this apparent setback, intelligence testing and the line of thinking that underlies it have actually triumphed. Many widely used scholastic measures, chief among them the SAT (renamed the Scholastic Assessment Test a few years ago), are thinly disguised intelligence tests that correlate highly with scores on standard psychometric instruments. Virtually no one raised in the developed world today has gone untouched by Binet's seemingly simple invention of a century ago.

Multiple Intelligences

The concept of intelligence has in recent years undergone its most robust challenge since the days of Walter Lippmann. Some who are informed by psychology but not bound by the assumptions of the psychometricians have invaded this formerly sacrosanct territory. They have put forth their own ideas of what intelligence is, how (and whether) it should be measured, and which values should be invoked in considerations of the human intellect. For the first time in many years the intelligence establishment is clearly on the defensive—and the new century seems likely to usher in quite different ways of thinking about intelligence.

16   One evident factor in the rethinking of intelligence is the perspective introduced by scholars who are not psychologists. Anthropologists have commented on the parochialism of the Western view of intelligence. Some cultures do not even have a concept called intelligence, and others define intelligence in terms of traits that we in the West might consider odd—obedience, good listening skills, or moral fiber, for example. Neuroscientists are skeptical that the highly differentiated and modular structure of the brain is consistent with a unitary form of intelligence. Computer scientists have devised programs deemed intelligent; these programs often go about problem-solving in ways quite different from those embraced by human beings or other animals.

17   Even within the field of psychology the natives have been getting restless. Probably the most restless is the Yale psychologist Robert J. Sternberg. A prodigious scholar, Sternberg, who is forty-nine, has written dozens of books and hundreds of articles, the majority of them focusing in one or another way on intelligence. Sternberg began with the strategic goal of understanding the actual mental processes mobilized by standard test items, such as the solving of analogies. But he soon went beyond standard intelligence testing by insisting on two hitherto neglected forms of intelligence: the "practical" ability to adapt to varying contexts (as we all must in these days of divorcing and downsizing), and the capacity to automate familiar activities so that we can deal effectively with novelty and display "creative" intelligence.

18   Sternberg has gone to greater pains than many other critics of standard intelligence testing to measure these forms of intelligence with the paper-and-pencil laboratory methods favored by the profession. And he has found that a person's ability to adapt to diverse contexts or to deal with novel information can be differentiated from success at standard IQ-test problems. . . .

19   The psychologist and journalist Daniel Goleman has achieved worldwide success with his book *Emotional Intelligence* (1995). Contending that this new concept (sometimes nicknamed EQ) may matter as much as or more than IQ, Goleman draws attention to such pivotal human abilities as controlling one's emotional reactions and "reading" the signals of others. In the view of the noted psychiatrist Robert Coles, author of *The Moral Intelligence of Children* (1997), among many other books, we should prize character over intellect. He decries the amorality of our families, hence

our children; he shows how we might cultivate human beings with a strong sense of right and wrong, who are willing to act on that sense even when it runs counter to self-interest. Other, frankly popular accounts deal with leadership intelligence (LQ), executive intelligence (EQ or ExQ), and even financial intelligence.

Like Coles's and Goleman's efforts, my work on "multiple intelli- 20 gences" eschews the psychologists' credo of operationalization and test-making. I began by asking two questions: How did the human mind and brain evolve over millions of years? and How can we account for the diversity of skills and capacities that are or have been valued in different communities around the world?

Armed with these questions and a set of eight criteria, I have con- 21 cluded that all human beings possess at least eight intelligences: linguistic and logical-mathematical (the two most prized in school and the ones central to success on standard intelligence tests), musical, spatial, bodily-kinesthetic, naturalist, interpersonal, and intrapersonal.

I make two complementary claims about intelligence. The first is 22 universal. We all possess these eight intelligences—and possibly more. Indeed, rather than seeing us as "rational animals," I offer a new definition of what it means to be a human being, cognitively speaking: *Homo sapiens sapiens* is the animal that possesses these eight forms of mental representation.

My second claim concerns individual differences. Owing to the 23 accidents of heredity, environment, and their interactions, no two of us exhibit the same intelligences in precisely the same proportions. Our "profiles of intelligence" differ from one another. This fact poses intriguing challenges and opportunities for our education system. We can ignore these differences and pretend that we are all the same; historically, that is what most education systems have done. Or we can fashion an education system that tries to exploit these differences, individualizing instruction and assessment as much as possible.

Intelligence and Morality

As the century of Binet and his successors draws to a close, we'd be wise to 24 take stock of, and to anticipate, the course of thinking about intelligence. Although my crystal ball is no clearer than anyone else's (the species may lack "future intelligence"), it seems safe to predict that interest in intelligence will not go away.

To begin with, the psychometric community has scarcely laid down 25 its arms. New versions of the standard tests continue to be created, and occasionally new tests surface as well. Researchers in the psychometric tradition churn out fresh evidence of the predictive power of their instruments and the correlations between measured intelligence and one's life chances. And some in the psychometric tradition are searching for the biological basis of intelligence: the gene or complex of genes that may affect intelligence, and neural structures that are crucial for intelligence, or telltale brain-wave patterns that distinguish the bright from the less bright.

26   Beyond various psychometric twists, interest in intelligence is likely to grow in other ways. It will be fed by the creation of machines that display intelligence and by the specific intelligence or intelligences. Moreover, observers as diverse as Richard Herrnstein and Robert B. Reich, President Clinton's first Secretary of Labor, have agreed that in coming years a large proportion of society's rewards will go to those people who are skilled symbol analysts—who can sit at a computer screen (or its technological successor), manipulate numbers and other kinds of symbols, and use the results of their operations to contrive plans, tactics, and strategies for enterprises ranging from business to science to war games. These people may well color how intelligence is conceived in decades to come—just as the need to provide good middle-level bureaucrats to run an empire served as a primary molder of intelligence tests in the early years of the century.

27   Surveying the landscape of intelligence, I discern three struggles between opposing forces. The extent to which, and the manner in which, these various struggles are resolved will influence the lives of millions of people. I believe that the three struggles are interrelated; that the first struggle provides the key to the other two; and that the ensemble of struggles can be resolved in an optimal way.

28   The first struggle concerns the breadth of our definition of intelligence. One camp consists of the purists, who believe in a single form of intelligence—one that basically predicts success in school and in school-like activities. Arrayed against the purists are the progressive pluralists, who believe that many forms of intelligence exist. Some of these pluralists would like to broaden the definition of intelligence considerably, to include the abilities to create, to lead, and to stand out in terms of emotional sensitivity or moral excellence.

29   The second struggle concerns the assessment of intelligence. Again, one readily encounters a traditional position. Once chiefly concerned with paper-and-pencil tests, the traditionally oriented practitioner is now likely to use computers to provide the same information more quickly and more accurately. But other positions abound. Purists disdain psychological tasks of any complexity, preferring to look instead at reaction time, brain waves, and other physiological measures of intellect. In contrast, simulators favor measures closely resembling the actual abilities that are prized. And skeptics warn against the continued expansion of testing. They emphasize the damage often done to individual life chances and self-esteem by a regimen of psychological testing, and call for less

technocratic, more humane methods—ranging from self-assessment to the examination of portfolios of student work to selection in the service of social equity.

The final struggle concerns the relationship between intelligence and the qualities we value in human beings. Although no one would baldly equate intellect and human worth, nuanced positions have emerged on this issue. Some (in the *Bell Curve* mold) see intelligence as closely related to a person's ethics and values; they believe that brighter people are more likely to appreciate moral complexity and to behave judiciously. Some call for a sharp distinction between the realm of intellect on the one hand, and character, morality, or ethics on the other. Society's ambivalence on this issue can be discerned in the figures that become the culture's heroes. For every Albert Einstein or Bobby Fischer who is celebrated for his intellect, there is a Forrest Gump or a Chauncey Gardiner who is celebrated for human—and humane—traits that would never be captured on any kind of intelligence test. . . . 30

The Borders of Intelligence

Writing as a scholar rather than as a layperson, I see two problems with the notion of emotional intelligence. First, unlike language or space, the emotions are not contents to be processed; rather, cognition has evolved so that we can make sense of human beings (self and others) that possess and experience emotions. Emotions are part and parcel of all cognition, though they may well prove more salient at certain times or under certain circumstances: they accompany our interactions with others, our listening to great music, our feelings when we solve—or fail to solve—a difficult mathematical problem. If one calls some intelligences emotional, one suggests that other intelligences are not—and that implication flies in the face of experience and empirical data. 31

The second problem is the conflation of emotional intelligence and a certain preferred pattern of behavior. This is the trap that Daniel Goleman sometimes falls into in his otherwise admirable *Emotional Intelligence*. Goleman singles out as emotionally intelligent those people who use their understanding of emotions to make others feel better, to solve conflicts, or to cooperate in home or work situations. No one would dispute that such people are wanted. However, people who understand emotion may not necessarily use their skills for the benefit of society. 32

For this reason I prefer the term "emotional sensitivity"—a term (encompassing my interpersonal and intrapersonal intelligences) that could apply to people who are sensitive to emotions in themselves and in others. Presumably, clinicians and salespeople excel in sensitivity to others, poets and mystics in sensitivity to themselves. And some autistic or psychopathological people seem completely insensitive to the emotional realm. I would insist, however, on a strict distinction between 33 emotional sensitivity and being a "good" or "moral" person. A person may be sensitive to the emotions of others but use that sensitivity to manipulate or to deceive them, or to create hatred.

34 I call, then, for a delineation of intelligence that includes the full range of contents to which human beings are sensitive, but at the same time designates as off limits such valued but separate human traits as creativity, morality, and emotional appropriateness. I believe that such a delineation makes scientific and epistemological sense. It reinvigorates the elastic band without stretching it to the breaking point. It helps to resolve the two remaining struggles: how to assess, and what kinds of human beings to admire.

35 Once we decide to restrict intelligence to human information-processing and product-making capacities, we can make use of the established technology of assessment. That is, we can continue to use paper-and-pencil or computer-adapted testing techniques while looking at a broader range of capacities, such as musical sensitivity and empathy with others. And we can avoid ticklish and possibly unresolvable questions about the assessment of values and morality that may well be restricted to a particular culture and that may well change over time.

36 Still, even with a limited perspective on intelligence, important questions remain about which assessment path to follow—that of the purist, the simulator, or the skeptic. Here I have strong views. I question the wisdom of searching for a "pure" intelligence—be it general intelligence, musical intelligence, or interpersonal intelligence. I do not believe that such alchemical intellectual essences actually exist; they are a product of our penchant for creating terminology rather than determinable and measurable entities. Moreover, the correlations that have thus far been found between supposedly pure measures and the skills that we actually value in the world are too modest to be useful.

37 What does exist is the use of intelligences, individually and in concert, to carry out tasks that are valued by a society. Accordingly, we should be assessing the extent to which human beings succeed in carrying out tasks of consequence that presumably involve certain intelligences. To be concrete, we should not test musical intelligence by looking at the ability to discriminate between two tones or timbres; rather, we should be teaching people to sing songs or play instruments or transform melodies and seeing how readily they master such feats. At the same time, we should abjure a search for pure emotional sensitivity—for example, a test that matches facial expressions to galvanic skin response. Rather, we should place (or observe) people in situations that call for them to be sensitive to the aspirations and motives of others. For example, we could see how they handle a situation in which they and colleagues have to break up

a fight between two teenagers, or persuade a boss to change a policy of which they do not approve.

Here powerful new simulations can be invoked. We are now in a position to draw on technologies that can deliver realistic situations or problems and also record the success of subjects in dealing with them. A student can be presented with an unfamiliar tune on a computer and asked to learn that tune, transpose it, orchestrate it, and the like. Such exercises would reveal much about the student's intelligence in musical matters. 38

Turning to the social (or human, if you prefer) realm, subjects can be presented with simulated interactions and asked to judge the shifting motivations of each actor. Or they can be asked to work in an interactive hypermedia production with unfamiliar people who are trying to accomplish some sort of goal, and to respond to their various moves and countermoves. The program can alter responses in light of the moves of the subject. Like a high-stakes poker game, such a measure should reveal much about the interpersonal or emotional sensitivity of a subject. 39

A significant increase in the breadth—the elasticity—of our concept of intelligence, then, should open the possibility for innovative forms of assessment far more realistic than the classic short-answer examinations. Why settle for an IQ or an SAT test, in which the items are at best remote proxies for the ability to design experiments, write essays, critique musical performances, and so forth? Why not instead ask people actually (or virtually) to carry out such tasks? And yet by not opening up the Pandora's box of values and subjectivity, one can continue to make judicious use of the insights and technologies achieved by those who have devoted decades to perfecting mental measurement. 40

To be sure, one can create a psychometric instrument for any conceivable human virtue, including morality, creativity, and emotional intelligence in its several senses. Indeed, since the publication of Daniel Goleman's book dozens of efforts have been made to create tests for emotional intelligence. The resulting instruments are not, however, necessarily useful. Such instruments are far more likely to satisfy the test maker's desire for reliability (a subject gets roughly the same score on two separate administrations of the test) than the need for validity (the test measures the trait that it purports to measure). 41

Such instruments-on-demand prove dubious for two reasons. First, beyond some platitudes, few can agree on what it means to be moral, ethical, a good person: consider the differing values of Jesse Helms and Jesse Jackson, Margaret Thatcher and Margaret Mead. Second, scores on such tests are much more likely to reveal test-taking savvy (skills in language and logic) than fundamental character. 42

43   In speaking about character, I turn to a final concern: the relationship between intelligence and what I will call virtue—those qualities that we admire and wish to hold up as examples for our children. No doubt the desire to expand intelligence to encompass ethics and character represents a direct response to the general feeling that our society is lacking in these dimensions; the expansionist view of intelligence reflects the hope that if we transmit the technology of intelligence to these virtues, we might in the end secure a more virtuous population.

44   I have already indicated my strong reservations about trying to make the word "intelligence" all things to all people—the psychometric equivalent of the true, the beautiful, and the good. Yet the problem remains: how, in a post-Aristotelian, post-Confucian era in which psychometrics looms large, do we think about the virtuous human being?

45   My analysis suggests one promising approach. We should recognize that intelligences, creativity, and morality—to mention just three desiderata—are separate. Each may require its own form of measurement or assessment, and some will prove far easier to assess objectively than others. Indeed, with respect to creativity and morality, we are more likely to rely on overall judgments by experts than on any putative test battery. At the same time, nothing prevents us from looking for people who combine several of these attributes—who have musical and interpersonal intelligence, who are psychometrically intelligent and creative in the arts, who combine emotional sensitivity and a high standard of moral conduct.

46   Let me introduce another analogy at this point. In college admissions much attention is paid to scholastic performance, as measured by College Board examinations and grades. However, other features are also weighed, and sometimes a person with lower test scores is admitted if he or she proves exemplary in terms of citizenship or athletics or motivation. Admissions officers do not confound these virtues (indeed, they may use different scales and issue different grades), but they recognize the attractiveness of candidates who exemplify two or more desirable traits.

47   We have left the Eden of classical times, in which various intellectual and ethical values necessarily commingled, and we are unlikely ever to re-create it. We should recognize that these virtues can be separate and will often prove to be remote from one another. When we attempt to aggregate them, through phrases like "emotional intelligence," "creative intelligence," and "moral intelligence," we should realize that we are expressing a wish rather than denoting a necessary or even a likely coupling.

48   We have an aid in converting this wish to reality: the existence of powerful examples—people who succeed in exemplifying two or more

cardinal human virtues. To name names is risky—particularly when one generation's heroes can become the subject of the next generation's pathographies. Even so, I can without apology mention Niels Bohr, George C. Marshall, Rachel Carson, Arthur Ashe, Louis Armstrong, Pablo Casals, Ella Fitzgerald.

In studying the lives of such people, we discover human possibili- 49 ties. Young human beings learn primarily from the examples of powerful adults around them—those who are admirable and also those who are simply glamorous. Sustained attention to admirable examples may well increase the future incidence of people who actually do yoke capacities that are scientifically and epistemologically separate.

In one of the most evocative phrases of the century the British nov- 50 elist E. M. Forster counseled us, "Only connect." I believe that some expansionists in the territory of intelligence, though well motivated, have prematurely asserted connections that do not exist. But I also believe that as human beings, we can help to forge connections that may be important for our physical and psychic survival.

Just how the precise borders of intelligence are drawn is a question 51 we can leave to scholars. But the imperative to broaden our definition of intelligence in a responsible way goes well beyond the academy. Who "owns" intelligence promises to be an issue even more critical in the next century than it has been in this era of the IQ test.

Content

1. What is intelligence? Compare and contrast some of the types Gardner refers to, which may be divided into two groups, the sort that "predicts success in school and in school-like activities" (¶s 4–10, 28) and all other kinds, including "the abilities to create, to lead, and to stand out in terms of emotional sensitivity or moral excellence" (¶ 28).

2. How can intelligence of a particular sort best be measured?

3. Who owns intelligence? The people who possess it? The society or social subgroup that determines what sorts of intelligence are valuable, necessary, appreciated—and those that aren't? The testers? How does Gardner's essay address this issue?

Strategies/Structures/Language

4. Find examples in Gardner's essay of the following common techniques of definition, and comment on their effectiveness in conveying one or more meanings of intelligence:

a. Illustration
b. Comparison and contrast

   c. Negation (saying what something is not)
   d. Analysis
   e. Explanation of a process (how something is measured or works)
   f. Identification of causes or effects
   g. Simile, metaphor, or analogy
   h. Reference to authority or the writer's own expertise
   i. Reference to the writer's or others' personal experience or observation

5. **Mixed Modes.** Gardner's essay is full of arguments: for his definition of intelligence, against competing definitions; for various practical ways of measuring intelligence, against particular sorts of testing. Identify some of the assertions and evidence he uses to support his claims. Are they credible?

6. Does Gardner believe it's possible to expand the definition of *intelligence* to include virtue (¶ 43), to make it encompass qualities he'd like it to have?

7. Can people change definitions of words to make them mean what they want them to mean? Or does every term have borders around it (¶ 51)? If so, who creates and enforces the boundaries?

For Writing

8. Write your own definition either of *intelligence* in general or of a specific type of intelligence such as one that Gardner discusses in his essay. You may need to define some of these yourself or consult other sources for the intelligences Gardner only touches on: a. psychometric intelligence (¶s 4–10); b. the "'practical'" ability to adapt to varying contexts (¶ 17); the "ability to deal with novel information" (¶ 18); emotional intelligence (¶s 19, 31–33); moral intelligence (¶s 19, 41–45); or creativity (¶s 41–45). Or define a form of intelligence on Gardner's personal list that includes "linguistic, logical-mathematical, musical, spatial, bodily-kinesthetic, naturalist, interpersonal, and intrapersonal." (See Gardner's book *Frames of Mind* [1983] or any other of Gardner's numerous writings on the subject.) Use one or more techniques of definition identified in question 4, and, assuming that you yourself fulfill your own definition of *intelligent*, supplement your more general definition with a specific firsthand example, and abundant illustrations, verbal and graphic.

9. Write a definition of an abstract concept for readers who may not have thought much about it—such as *love, truth, beauty, justice, greed, pride,* or *the good life*—but who have probably used it often in everyday life, something intangible that can be identified in terms of its effects, causes, manifestations, or other nonphysical properties. Use one or more techniques of definition identified above and illustrate your definition with one or two specific examples with which you are familiar. Then use the examples as a basis for making generalizations that apply to other aspects of the concept.

10. **Journal Writing.** Explore the definition of intelligence that you developed for question 8. How would you or have you used your understanding of intelligence in teaching somebody a particular skill? How might you apply your knowledge of the kinds of intelligence you excel in to your own learning processes?

ISTVAN BANYAI, *Inflation*

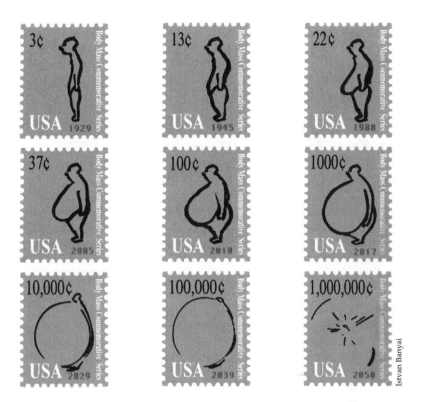

Istvan Banyai

What's the story here? What changes—in the figure and in the cost of the postage stamp—occur in the successive panels? Do they need any captions? Note the pun on "Inflation" in the title. What definitions of inflation does this cartoon provide? Could other visual images illustrate the same term? Create a different cartoon using such a concrete image to illustrate an abstract term and thereby to define it.

JEFFREY WATTLES

Jeffrey Wattles (born 1945) is a professor of philosophy at Kent State University, where his teaching and research concentrate on comparative religious thought, ethics, and ways of integrating philosophy, science, and religion. He earned a BA in philosophy from Stanford (1966), followed by a master's (1970) and doctorate (1973) from Northwestern. His work-in-progress is on *Living in Truth, Beauty, and Goodness*. "Levels of Meaning in the Golden Rule" and "Plato's Brush with the Golden Rule" preceded his book, *The Golden Rule* (1996). "The Golden Rule–One or Many, Gold or Glitter" is excerpted from the book's first chapter.

Here Wattles addresses the age old moral principle, "Do to others as you want others to do to you," and defends it against critics who argue that the Golden rule encourages an unduly simplistic moral outlook, creates a relatively low standard of morality, and does not acknowledge significant differences among people. This principle, which we begin hearing as children, is not as universal as it may seem, as its use through history comes in a variety of forms borne of a variety of contexts.

The Golden Rule—One or Many, Gold or Glitter?

1   Children are taught to respect parents and other authority figures. Adolescents are urged to control their impulses. Adults are told to conduct themselves in accord with certain moral and ethical standards. Morality, then, may seem to be just an affair of imposition, a cultural voice that says "no" in various ways to our desires. To be sure, there are times when the word "no" must be spoken and enforced. But, time and again, people have discovered something more to morality, something rooted in life itself. The "no" is but one word in the voice of life, a voice that has other words, including the golden rule: Do to others as you want others to do to you. This book is about the life in that principle.

The Unity Of the Rule

2   What could be easier to grasp intuitively than the golden rule? It has such an immediate intelligibility that it serves as a ladder that anyone can step onto without a great stretch. I know how I like to be treated; and that is how I am to treat others. The rule asks me to be considerate of others rather than indulging in self-centeredness. The study of the rule, however, leads beyond conventional interpretation, and the practice of the rule leads beyond conventional morality.

3   The rule is widely regarded as obvious and self-evident. Nearly everyone is familiar with it in some formulation or other. An angry parent uses it as a weapon: "Is that how you want others to treat you?" A defense attorney invites the members of the jury to put themselves in the shoes of his or her client. Noting that particular rules and interpretations do not cover every situation, a manual of professional ethics exhorts members

---

to treat other professionals with the same consideration and respect that they would wish for themselves. Formulated in one way or another, the rule finds its way into countless speeches, sermons, documents, and books on the assumption that it has a single, clear sense that the listener or reader grasps and approves of. In an age where differences so often occasion violence, here, it seems, is something that everyone can agree on.

Promoting the notion that the golden rule is "taught by all the   4
world's religions," advocates have collected maxims from various traditions, producing lists with entries like the following: "Hinduism: 'Let no man do to another that which would be repugnant to himself.'" "Islam: 'None of you [truly] believes until he wishes for his brother what he wishes for himself.'" The point of these lists is self-evident. Despite the differences in phrasing, all religions acknowledge the same basic, universal moral teaching. Moreover, this principle may be accepted as common ground by secular ethics as well.

Under the microscope of analysis, however, things are not so simple.   5
Different formulations have different implications, and differences in context raise the question of whether the same concept is at work in passages where the wording is nearly identical. Is the meaning of the rule constant whenever one of these phrases is mentioned? There is a persistent debate, for example, about the relative merit of the positive formulation versus the negative one, "Do not do to others what you do not want others to do to you." Nor can the full meaning of a sentence be grasped in isolation. For example, to point to "the golden rule in Confucianism" by quoting a fifteen-word sentence from the *Analects* of Confucius does not convey the historical dynamism of the rule's evolving social, ethical, and spiritual connotations. What do the words mean in their original context? How prominent is the rule within that particular tradition? Finally, how does the rule function in a given inter-action between the speaker or writer and the listener or reader? The rule may function as an authoritative reproach, a pious rehearsal of tradition, a specimen for analytic dissection, or a confession of personal commitment. Is the rule one or many? Can we even properly speak of *the* golden rule at all? Some Hindus interpret the injunction to treat others as oneself as an invitation to identify with the divine spirit within each person. Some Muslims take the golden rule to apply primarily to the brotherhood of Islam. Some Christians regard the rule as a shorthand summary of the morality of Jesus's religion. And countless people think of the rule without any religious associations at all.

Raising the question about the meanings of the golden rule in dif-   6
ferent contexts is not intended to reduce similarities to dust and ashes merely by appealing to the imponderable weight of cultural differences. Context is not the last word on meaning; the sentence expressing the golden rule contributes meaning of its own to its context. Meaning does involve context, but the fact that contexts differ does not prove that there is no commonality of meaning. Language and culture, moreover, are not

reliable clues for identifying conceptual similarity and difference, since conceptual harmony is experienced across these boundaries.

7   The golden rule, happily, has more than a single sense. It is not a static, one-dimensional proposition with a single meaning to be accepted or rejected, defended or refuted. Nor is its multiplicity chaotic. There is enough continuity of meaning in its varied uses to justify speaking of *the* golden rule. My own thesis is that the rule's unity is best comprehended not in terms of a single meaning but as a symbol of a process of growth on emotional, intellectual, and spiritual levels.

The Quality Of the Rule

8   "Gold is where you find it" runs a proverb coined by miners who found what they were seeking in unexpected places. So what sort of ore or alloy or sculpture is the teaching that, since the seventeenth century, has been called "the golden rule"? Is it gold or glitter? Certain appreciative remarks on the golden rule seem to bear witness to a discovery. "Eureka!" they seem to say. "There is a supreme principle of living! It *can* be expressed in a single statement!"

9   By contrast, theologian Paul Tillich found the rule an inferior principle. For him, the biblical commandment to love and the assurance that God *is* love "infinitely transcend" the golden rule. The problem with the rule is that it "does not tell us what we *should* wish."

10   Is the rule *golden'*? In other words, is it worthy to be cherished as a rule of living or even as *the* rule of living? The values of the rule are as much in dispute as its meanings. Most people, it seems, intuitively regard the golden rule as a good principle, and some have spoken as though there is within the rule a special kind of agency with the power to transform humankind.

11   It is understandable that the golden rule has been regarded as *the* supreme moral principle. I do not want to be murdered; therefore I should not murder another. I do not want my spouse to commit adultery, my property to be stolen, and so forth; therefore I should treat others with comparable consideration. Others have comparable interests, and the rule calls me to treat the other as someone akin to myself. Moreover, I realize that I sometimes have desires to be treated in ways that do not represent my considered best judgment, and this reflection makes it obvious that reason is required for the proper application of the golden rule. Finally, in personal relationships, I want to be loved, and, in consequence, the rule directs me to be loving. From the perspective of someone simply interested in living right rather than in the construction and critique of theories, the rule has much to recommend it.

12   Some writers have put the rule on a pedestal, giving the impression that the rule is *sufficient* for ethics in the sense that no one could ever go wrong by adhering to it or in the sense that all duties may be inferred

from it. Others have claimed that the rule is a *necessary* criterion for right action; in other words, an action must be able to pass the test of the golden rule if it is to be validated as right, and any action that fails the test is wrong. Some philosophers have hoped for an ethical theory that would be self-sufficient (depending on no controversial axioms), perfectly good (invulnerable to counterexamples), and all-powerful (enabling the derivation of every correct moral judgment, given appropriate data about the situation). They have dreamed of sculpting ethics into an independent, rational, deductive system, on the model of geometry, with a single normative axiom. However much reason may hanker for such a system, once the golden rule is taken as a candidate for such an axiom, a minor flexing of the analytic bicep is enough to humiliate it. A single counterexample suffices to defeat a pretender to this throne.

Many scholars today regard the rule as an acceptable principle for popular use but as embarrassing if taken with philosophic seriousness. Most professional ethicists rely instead on other principles, since the rule seems vulnerable to counterexamples, such as the current favorite, "What if a sadomasochist goes forth to treat others as he wants to be treated?" 13

Technically, the golden rule can defend itself from objections, since it contains within itself the seed of its own self-correction. Any easily abused interpretation may be challenged: "Would you want to be treated according to a rule construed in this way?" The recursive use of the rule—applying it to the results of its own earlier application—is a lever that extricates it from many tangles. Close examination of the counterexample of the sadomasochist... shows that to use the rule properly requires a certain degree of maturity. The counterexample does not refute the golden rule, properly understood; rather, it serves to clarify the interpretation of the rule—that the golden rule functions appropriately in a *growing* personality; indeed, the practice of the rule itself promotes the required growth. Since the rule is such a compressed statement of morality, it takes for granted at least a minimum sincerity that refuses to manipulate the rule sophistically to "justify" patently immoral conduct. Where that prerequisite cannot be assumed, problems multiply. 14

The objections that have been raised against the rule are useful to illustrate misinterpretations of the rule and to make clear assumptions that must be satisfied for the rule to function in moral theory. 15

It has been objected that the golden rule assumes that human beings are basically alike and thereby fails to do justice to the differences between people. In particular, the rule allegedly implies that what we want is what others want. As George Bernard Shaw quipped, "Don't do to others as you want them to do unto you. Their tastes may be different." The golden rule may also seem to imply that what we want for ourselves is good for ourselves and that what is good for ourselves is good for others. The positive formulation, in particular, is accused of harboring the potential for presumption; thus, the rule is suited for 16 immediate application only among those whose beliefs and needs are similar. In fact, however, the rule calls for due consideration for any relevant difference between persons—just as the agent would want such consideration from others.

17   Another criticism is that the golden rule sets too low a standard because it makes ordinary wants and desires the criterion of morality. On one interpretation, the rule asks individuals to do whatever they imagine they might wish to have done to them in a given situation; thus a judge would be obliged by the golden rule to sentence a convicted criminal with extreme leniency. As a mere principle of sympathy, therefore, it is argued, the rule is incapable of guiding judgment in cases where the necessary action is unwelcome to its immediate recipient.

18   A related problem is that the rule, taken merely as a policy of sympathy, amounts to the advice "Treat others as they want you to treat them," as in a puzzle from the opening chapter of Herman Melville's *Moby-Dick*, where Ishmael is invited by his new friend, Queequeg, to join in pagan worship. Ishmael pauses to think it over:

> But what is worship?—to do the will of God—that is worship. And what is the will of God?—to do to my fellow man what I would have my fellow man to do to me—*that* is the will of God. Now, Queequeg is my fellow man. And what do I wish that this Queequeg would do to me? Why, unite with me in my particular Presbyterian form of worship. Consequently, I must then unite with him in his; ergo, I must turn idolater.

19   If the golden rule is taken to require the agent to identify with the other in a simplistic and uncritical way, the result is a loss of the higher perspective toward which the rule moves the thoughtful practitioner.

20   The next clusters of objections have a depth that a quick, initial reply would betray, so I defer my response until later. If the rule is not to be interpreted as setting up the agent's idiosyncratic desires—or those of the recipient—as a supreme standard of goodness, then problems arise because the rule does not specify what the agent ought to desire. The rule merely requires consistency of moral judgment: one must apply the same standards to one's treatment of others that one applies to others' treatment of oneself. The lack of specificity in the rule, its merely formal or merely procedural character, allegedly renders its guidance insubstantial.

21   The rule seems to exhibit the limitations of any general moral principle: it does not carry sufficiently rich substantive implications to be helpful in the thicket of life's problems. Even though most people live with some allegiance to integrating principles, action guides, mottoes, proverbs, or commandments that serve to unify the mind, the deficiency of any principle is that it is merely a principle, merely a ginning; only the full exposition of a system of ethics can validate the place of an asserted

principle. An appeal to a general principle, moreover, can function as a retreat and a refusal to think through issues in their concreteness.

There is also criticism of a practice widely associated with the rule— 22 imagining oneself in the other person's situation. The charge is that this practice is an abstract, derivative, artificial, male, manipulative device, which can never compensate for the lack of human understanding and spontaneous goodness.

The rule has been criticized as a naively idealistic standard, un- 23 suited to a world of rugged competition. The rule may seem to require that, if I am trustworthy and want to be trusted, I must treat everyone as being equally trustworthy. Furthermore, the broad humanitarianism of the golden rule allegedly makes unrealistic psychological demands; it is unfair to family and friends to embrace the universal concerns of the golden rule.

Last, some religious issues. The golden rule has been criticized for 24 being a teaching that misleadingly lets people avoid confronting the higher teachings of religious ethics, for example, Jesus's commandment, "Love one another as I have loved you." Some find the rule of only intermediate usefulness, proposing that spiritual living moves beyond the standpoint of rules. Others have criticized the golden rule's traditional links to religion, arguing that moral intuition and moral reason can operate without reference to any religious foundation.

For responding to all these objections, there are three possible strate- 25 gies: abandon the rule, reformulate it, or retain it as commonly worded, while taking advantage of objections to clarify its proper interpretation, I take the third way.

Content

1. Wattles quotes the Golden Rule as "Do to others as you want others to do to you: (¶ 1). What other versions of this rule does he quote (see ¶ 4, 5)? In what ways do you read these principles as similar, if not identical? What differences do you find? In what ways are these variations important?

2. Wattles asserts that "the golden rule, happily, has more than a single sense. It is not a static, one-dimensional proposition with a single meaning to be accepted or rejected, defended or refuted. Nor is its multiplicity chaotic." (¶ 6). Explain this claim, which goes on to say that "There is enough continuity of meaning in its varied uses to justify speaking of the golden rule" (¶ 6).

3. "The rule may function," says Wattles, "as an authoritative reproach, a pious rehearsal of tradition, a specimen for analytic dissection, or a confession of personal commitment. Is the rule one or many?" (¶ 5). Explain your understanding of each alternative. Are these congruent? Compatible with one another?

4. On what grounds may the golden rule be "regarded as *the* supreme moral principle" (¶ 10). What principles allow Wattles to dismiss "embarrassing," "easily abused" interpretations of the golden rule, such as "What if a sadomasochist goes forth to treat others as he wants to be treated?" (¶ 13).

5. Come up with some constructive ways to address the objections Wattles identifies—such as "that the golden rule assumes that human beings are basically alike and thereby fails to do justice to the differences between people" (¶ 16)?

Strategies/Structures/Language

6. Wattles asserts, "If the golden rule is taken to require the *agent* to identify with the other in a *simplistic and uncritical way,* the result is a *loss* of the *higher perspective* toward which the rule moves the *thoughtful practitioner*" (¶ 18, italics supplied). In discussion, provide an interpretation of each of the italicized phrases.

7. If you're accustomed to having clergy interpret rules of ethical conduct for you, on what grounds can you trust your own interpretations? These are high-stakes rules that can govern your entire life; how much time and thought is it worth spending on them?

8. Wattle's discussion adds complexity to a simple-seeming rule; that is the purpose of most academic discussions, to probe beyond the too-simple, taken-for-grated aspects of a subject. Justify—or dispute—the appropriateness, the pervasiveness of this academic practice. Is this practice another name for *thinking?*

For Writing

9. "My own thesis," says Wattles, "is that the rule's unity is best comprehended not in terms of a single meaning but as a symbol of a process of growth on emotional, intellectual, and spiritual levels" (¶ 6). Closely examine your own understanding of the "Golden Rule." Set aside your automatic response to the term and look at in terms of the symbolic process of growth on emotional, intellectual, and spiritual levels" to which Wattles refers. What refinements of interpretation do you want to add?

10. **Dialogue:** Wattles, like Elie Wiesel ("Why I Write" 14–20), is concerned with transforming "No" into "Yes": "Morality, then, may seem to be jut an affair of imposition, a cultural voice that says 'no' in various ways to our desires," as in the "Thou shalt nots" of the Ten Commandments. However, "the 'No' is but one word in the voice of life, a voice that has other words, including the golden rule: Do to others as you want others to do to you" (¶ 2). Construct a set of principles that provide you with a positive, adaptable, and useful set of guidelines for moral behavior. Provide a specific example to test them against, and explain their utility—and, if possible, their beauty.

LYNDA BARRY

Lynda Barry (born 1956), daughter of a Filipino mother and an American father, grew up in an interracial neighborhood in Seattle. When she began Evergreen State College Barry "wanted to be a fine artist." "Cartoons to me were really base." Then she realized that her drawings could make her friends laugh, and shortly after she graduated, in 1978, she created

"Ernie Pook's Comeek," a wry, witty, and feminist strip now syndicated in over sixty newspapers in the United States, Canada, Russia, and Hungary. Barry's eighth comic collection is *It's So Magic* (1994); her second novel is *Cruddy* (1998). *One! Hundred! Demons!*, her autobiography in graphic novel format, was published in 2003 and followed by *What It Is* in 2008.

"Common Scents" (from *One! Hundred! Demons!*) illustrates what Barry told an interviewer, "There was always a lot of commotion in the house, mostly in the kitchen. We didn't have a set dinner or lunch or breakfast time; when we wanted to eat there was always food on the stove . . . At the time it was a little frustrating for me, because I looked to all the world like a regular little white American kid, but at home we were eating real different food and there was sometimes octopus in the refrigerator and stuff that was scary looking to my friends. . . We ate with our hands, and when you say that, people think that you're also squatting on the floor . . . but it wasn't like that. There's a whole etiquette to the way that you eat with your hands, just like you hold a fork. And it was lively and unusual, an atmosphere where I . . . could pretty much do whatever I wanted to do."

Common Scents

1

4

BUT THERE WERE BAD MYS-
TERIES TOO, LIKE THE MYSTERY
OF THE BLEACH PEOPLE WHOSE
HOUSE GAVE OFF FUMES YOU
COULD SMELL FROM THE STREET.
WE KEPT WAITING FOR THAT
HOUSE TO EXPLODE. THE BUGS
DIDN'T EVEN GO IN THEIR YARD.

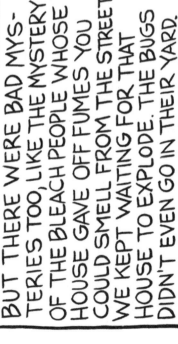

ALSO GIVING OFF BLEACH FUMES

HEYA, JANINA. HEYA.

'N I ASK YOU A PERSONAL THING?

POSSIBLY.

HOW COME YOUR HOUSE SMELLS LIKE THAT?

SMELLS LIKE WHAT?

5

SOME SMELLS WERE MYS-
TERIOUSLY WONDERFUL LIKE
AT THE PALINKI'S WHERE IT WAS
A COMBINATION OF MINT, TAN-
GERINES, AND LIBRARY BOOKS.
BUT HOW? I NEVER SAW ANY
OF THOSE THINGS THERE.

WHAT'S YOUR KIND OF AIR FRESHENER, BECAUSE THAT'S THE KIND I WANT MY MOM TO GET.

I DON'T USE AIR FRESHENER, DEAR.

WELL, THAT'S WEIRD BECAUSE YOUR HOUSE SMELLS PERFECT.

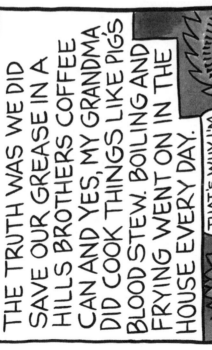

9

THE GIRL WHO SHOCKED ME WITH THE NEWS ABOUT THE SMELL OF MY HOUSE WAS THE ONE WHOSE HOUSE SMELLED LIKE THE FRESH BUS BATHROOM. HER MOTHER WAS THE MOST DISINFECTING, AIR FRESHENER SPRAYING PERSON THAT EVER LIVED.

8

THE TRUTH WAS WE DID SAVE OUR GREASE IN A HILLS BROTHERS COFFEE CAN AND YES, MY GRANDMA DID COOK THINGS LIKE PIG'S BLOOD STEW. BOILING AND FRYING WENT ON IN THE HOUSE EVERY DAY.

THAT'S WHY I'M NOT SPOSTA COME OVER, 'CAUSE THE SMELL GETS ON MY CLOTHES, MAKES MY MOM SICK.

10

SHE HAD THOSE CAR FRESHENER CHRISTMAS TREE THINGS HANGING EVERYWHERE. EVEN THE MARSHMALLOW TREATS SHE MADE HAD A FRESH PINE-SPRAY FLAVOR. SHE WAS FREE WITH HER OBSERVATIONS ABOUT THE SMELL OF OTHERS.
YOUR ORIENTALS HAVE AN ARRAY, WITH YOUR CHINESE SMELLING STRONGER THAN YOUR JAPANESE AND YOUR KOREANS FALLING SOMEWHERES IN THE MIDDLE AND DON'T GET ME STARTED ON YOUR FILIPINOS.

11

SHE DETAILED THE SMELLS OF BLACKS, MEXICANS, ITAL-IANS, SOME PEOPLE I NEVER HEARD OF CALLED "BO-HUNKS" AND THE DIFFERENCE IT MADE IF THEY WERE WET OR DRY, FAT OR SKINNY. NATURALLY I BROUGHT THIS INFORMATION HOME.
AIE N'AKO! WHITE LADIES SMELL BAD TOO, NAMAN! SHE NEVER WASH HER POOKIE! HER KILI-KILI ALWAYS SWEAT-SWEATING! THE OLD ONES SMELL LIKE E-HEE! THAT LADY IS TUNG-AH!

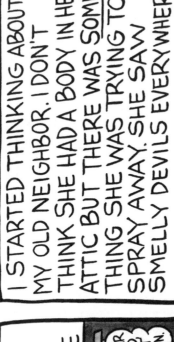

16

I'VE NEVER HEARD A SINGLE PERSON EVER SAY THEY LOVED THE SMELL OF AIR FRESHENER AND YET THERE ARE SO MANY PEOPLE WHO FILL THEIR HOMES WITH IT.

LIGHT BULB SCENT RINGS

POTPOURRI MIXES

AIR WICKS

SCENTED CANDLE NIGHTMARE

CAT PEE INCENSE

SPRAYS

POP UPS

STICK ONS

PLUG-INS

DANGLERS

17

WHEN COMBINED WITH NATURAL BUT POWER-FILLED SMELLS, THE RESULTS CAN BE TRAUMATIC.

TROPICAL PASSION AROMA THERAPY CAT BOX

PINEY WOODS PIG'S BLOOD STEW BREAKDOWN

CHERRY POP-UP FRIED LIVER

STRAWBERRY-DREAMSCAPE PLUG-IN FRIED FLOUNDER

VANILLA-SPICE DIAPER PAIL

EVEN MY GRANDMA WAS DRAWN IN BY THE PROMISES OF FRESHNESS THE ADS GAVE, ALTHOUGH NOT FOR LONG.

ONE QUICK SRRAY AND YOUR HOUSE IS SPRINGTIME FRESH!

AIE NAKO, LADY. I TRIED IT. IT SMELLS WORSE THAN THE PUET OF A VAMPIRE!

YOU'LL NEVER WORRY ABOUT FRYING FISH AGAIN!

IF I HAVE FISH, I AM NOT WORRIED! I AM THANKING GOD!

OUR HOUSE SMELLED LIKE GREASE AND FISH AND CIGS, LIKE JADE EAST AND PORK AND DOGS, LIKE ALL THE WILD FOOD MY GRANDMA BOILED AND FRIED. AND IF THEY COULD GET THAT INTO A SPRAY CAN, I'D BUY IT.

N'AKO, LYNDA! THIS DURAN FRUITS SMELLS SO BADLY BUT TASTE SO GOODLY! YOU TRY IT! GOD MADE IT! MY GOLLY! EAT! EAT!

18

19

Content

1. Good works of visual art, like good essays or stories, stand up to careful re-reading; they can't be entirely taken in or understood at a single glance. Skim "Common Scents" and then go back and review it carefully. What topics and meanings come into sharp focus on the second reading?

2. Explain the meaning of the caption of panel 7: "I probably had the strongest-smelling house in the neighborhood except for the bleach people, but I had no idea what it smelled like to others until I heard a comment about it." Can you identify some of the more exotic smells, such as "pigs blood stew" (panel 8) and duran (panel 19)?

Strategies/Structures/Language

3. None of Barry's characters look very attractive—in fact, by some criteria they'd be considered ugly. In what respects are they sympathetic or unsympathetic—just as characters are in a totally verbal story? In what ways does their appearance reinforce Barry's point?

4. What latitude does Barry have in using drawings with dialogue that she wouldn't have if the story were told entirely in writing?

For Writing/Drawing

5. If you're artistically inclined, tell a story that presents a social commentary through a series of six to eight pictures (or more, if you get carried away) with captions that reinforce the pictures and perhaps explain them. If your artistic abilities are limited, either work with a partner who can draw or use someone else's cartoons or drawings and substitute your own captions. In either case, write an analysis of what you've done, and why, to show how the illustrations and the text reinforce one another.

6. "Common Scents" obliges readers to think about smells—of people (and ethnic stereotypes of their smells), of food, of environments: "[The air freshener lady] detailed the smells of blacks, Mexicans, Italians . . . 'bo-hunks' and the difference it made if they were wet or dry, fat or skinny" (panel 11)—and to examine their prejudices concerning these smells. In fact, American culture in general may be prejudiced against most odors, given the fact that in the United States many people try to remove all odors except those of some flowers and some foods. Explain why this is so. In what ways have Barry's drawings raised your critical awareness of this practice? Would a national culture with a greater range and variety of acceptable smells be preferable?

7. **Journal Writing.** When you were growing up, how was your family different from your friends' families? Explore the ways in which you found your friends' homes and families attractive, strange, or uncomfortable. As in question 5, use your own or someone else's drawings to illustrate your memories and perceptions.

8. **Dialogues.** Write a paper in which you analyze and compare Barry's "Common Scents" or another cartoon sequence with a social point, such as Art Spiegelman's "Mein Kampf", another sequence by Spiegelman, or one of Garry Trudeau's *Doonesbury* comic strips (471).

SCOTT ALLISON

Scott Allison (born 1989) is an English and creative writing student at the University of Connecticut. He grew up in Seekonk, Massachusetts, a suburb of Providence, RI. His interest in writing developed in high school when he entered a poetry contest at the request of an English teacher. A poem about being a patriot amidst a classroom full of dissidents, his first venture into creative writing, earned him an invitation to attend the New England Young Writers Conference at Middlebury's Breadloaf campus. Despite feeling like one of the least experienced writers in attendance, envelopment in a community of creative minds left him with a dream and a passion for writing. In the summer of 2011, Allison interned at a major New York area publishing company. He is pursuing a career in writing and publishing.

In "Picturesque," Allison uses repetition to analyze the emotions felt after a long relationship. He explores the complexity of relationships by discovering what is behind the familiar joyous, picturesque photos of couples that are seen framed in people's houses and on Facebook.

Picturesque

1   Pictures of couples are deceiving. They show the couple smiling, perpetually content in each other's loving arms. They show them standing in front of the Grand Canyon and in front of Spaceship Earth at Epcot. They show them leaning on railings of cruise ships and posing in each city the ship docks. They show them at the zoo and they show them swimming in quaint New Hampshire lakes. They show them kissing with closed lips. They show them dressed to the nines and they show them doing something stupid together and laughing about it. They don't show everything they should.

2   They don't show them meeting. They should show them meeting. They should show them on their first date, which is a little awkward, especially since he hasn't planned anything special. So the pictures should just show them walking aimlessly down a street and asking each other questions. From then on the pictures should always show him feeling like he has to plan something special, but not because the first date was a failure. It wasn't.

3   They should show their first kiss. They should show him being nervous, overestimating her height, leaning down and missing her lips. They should show them laughing about it, trying again and succeeding. They should show her always bringing this up and making fun of him lightheartedly.

4   The pictures should show him writing her poetry and her not understanding it, either because he can't write poetry or because she can't read it. I'm not sure which it was. The pictures should show them misunderstanding one another. They should show her casting odd glances

---

that he doesn't see. Once in a while they should show her casting an odd glance that he does see, and vice versa. They should show him thinking he knows her, but being so so horribly mistaken. They should show him knowing exactly how she acts, being infatuated with how she acts and thinking she'll always act that way.

The pictures should show him raising his voice and her asking 5 that he stop. They should show him getting louder and her crying and running out the front door in the middle of the night. They should show him running behind with a flashlight to make sure she's okay. They should show him wishing each moment of their relationship was set to music. But I'm not talking about motion pictures, so there shouldn't be music.

The pictures should show them one thousand miles from each other. 6 But first they should show her crying uncontrollably at the airport and him trying to comfort her, though he's never had to comfort anyone before. They should show her almost missing her flight because she was hugging him for so long. They should show him saying, YOU'VE GOT TO GO, and only show him crying after driving away. They should show him visiting her after months apart and smiling and not being able to stop.

The pictures should show him wishing he could be holding some- 7 one else. The next picture should show her just thinking he's wishing this. They should show her loving him and him loving her back. They should show one entirely in love with the other and the other walking away without looking back. They should show her walking away, coming back again and again and walking away one final time, but still thinking of him and wishing she could go back. They should show him wanting her back, too, but thinking there isn't a chance to reconcile. They should show them being friends and caring for one another.

The pictures should show them on a rainy night with nothing to 8 do. They should show them driving with no destination, ending up in a parking lot and talking for several hours with their seatbelts still on. They should show him staying at her house until 11:52 PM every weekend night, knowing it takes exactly eight minutes to make it home for his midnight curfew. But they should always show him being late because he can't say goodbye to her. The pictures should show her walking him out. They should show them kissing, opening the door, kissing, closing the door and kissing either side of the window before finally mouthing goodbye. They should show him driving home and calling her when he gets into bed.

The pictures should show them waiting for her to get her period 9 and her waiting in his car when he runs into CVS to buy a pregnancy test. They should show him buying a pack of gum, too. They should show him sweating and her bawling. They should show the test coming up negative, but they should show them not being sure of the result despite the box that says it's really easy to read.

10   The pictures should show him thinking about their future together. They should show them getting married and they should show them consummating it. They paid good money for the photographer, so he should get this shot, too. It's more precious than the flower girl and the kiss at the altar combined.

11   The pictures should show him going out of his mind trying to keep up with other relationships, being dragged each of several ways and never doing what he really wants. They should show his friends criticizing him for not spending time with them anymore. They should show him talking to her about this and her taking it to mean that he doesn't want to spend time with her.

12   Maybe she influences each thought that passes through his mind, everything he touches and everything he feels. Maybe he's in love and prefers it this way, or maybe he doesn't. Maybe the relationship is nothing and none of his other relationships are much either, or maybe he just thinks this is so. The pictures should show this. They should show his thoughts.

13   Maybe they'll be together forever, or maybe they won't. Maybe they'll sleep together. Maybe one will sleep on the couch and the other will sleep in the bed. Either way, the pictures should show it. Maybe they'll sleep in the same bed for 38 years then go to Mattress Giant and get two smaller beds because her Sleep Number is much softer than his. Maybe this was just a commercial that made him laugh when they were watching TV together. She didn't laugh and that made him think that in 38 years he and she would sleep in different beds, not because their sleep numbers wouldn't match but because they wouldn't be able to relate to one another. No matter, the pictures should show this.

14   The pictures should show the couple only lasting three years. They should show her driving away and him acting like nothing happened. They should show him throwing all their posed pictures in a dumpster and keeping in his memory what mattered, the moments that weren't picturesque.

Content

1. Allison makes claims throughout the essay about what pictures of couples should really show. Identify some of these.

2. Pictures on Facebook and on the walls and mantels of homes show couples during happy times, on anniversaries, and in special places. What sorts of emotions, nuances, ties and unravelings do such pictures miss?

3. What is Allison's real focus—on the images in the pictures themselves, however ideal or real? Or is he more concerned about the complex stories that pictures can never show, the stories behind the pictures? What are some of these stories? How does he convey his focus?

4. Allison's photo images imply a story. Connect the dots, and tell the story of the relationship depicted in "Picturesque." What are its familiar elements? Its unusual ones? How well do you know these characters? Could this be the plot for a movie or TV show? Why or why not?

5. In the last sentence, what does Allison say should be kept? Why keep only "the moments that weren't picturesque" and discard all the picturesque images? Is that being fair to the relationship?

6. To love is to open yourself wholly to another person, and thus to be made vulnerable to what you can't necessarily control—as lovers, and parents, have learned throughout the centuries. First loves are particularly poignant in this respect. Bear in mind that Allison is writing shortly after the relationship ended; might he feel differently after time has passed?

Strategies/ Structures/ Language

7. Throughout the essay, Allison repeats "They should show…" Almost every sentence begins with this familiar phrase. What is the effect of this repetition? Could he have conveyed the same emotions without using this structure?

8. There are two paragraphs—13 and 14 (the conclusion) in which the author partially diverges from the repetition format. What does this shift reveal about the speaker? How are these thoughts different from the definitive "pictures" the author has already set forth?

9. "Picturesque" follows no definitive chronology. It covers the beginning and end of a relationship and various moments in between. What does this collage of "pictures," ranging from positive to negative, say about relationships? What does it say about how people think about meaningful relationships, past or present?

For Writing

10. Look at some of the most distinct "pictures" of an intense relationship in your own life, whether actual or mental images of family, friends, or a beloved. Where does the meaning reside–in the images, in your mind or imagination, or in all? Ask someone who doesn't know the people depicted to look at the photograph(s) and to tell you what he or she sees. To what extent is their interpretation congruent with yours? Why or why not? Then, reverse the procedure; look at a friend's pictures of someone you don't know and test your accuracy of interpretation.

11. Pick several images/photographs—either of people you know or of strangers—and arrange them to tell a story. Then rearrange them to tell a different story. Should the story always be true? Flattering? Where do fantasy and reality blend (you can derive some of your answers from advertising images or movie stills, or art photographs by photographers such as Edward Steichen or Robert Mapplethorpe)?

12. Scrutinize a conventional Christmas card family photograph—or a campaign poster—or a wedding picture. What does it tell you about the people (and perhaps animals) in it—their status, relationships, anything else—fill in the blanks. What's missing? Write an essay on the aims, postures, contexts of public portraiture vs "private," more intimate pictures. Is there a single "best" or right way to photograph a person, couple, or group? If so, what is it? If not, explain your own criteria for taking/making memorable pictures that tell the true story, if not the whole story.

Additional Topics for Writing Definition

(For strategies for writing definition, see 284.)

Multiple Strategies for Writing: Definition

Definition is an essential component of many kinds of writing; it is often necessary to define terms, components, or concepts as the basis for explaining something or conducting an argument. Conversely, you may employ a variety of other
strategies in writing definitions:

- *Illustrations* and *examples,* to show the meaning of the entire term or its com-
  ponents, and to interpret them
- *Photographs, drawings, diagrams, maps* as alternatives to "a thousand words"
- A *time sequence,* to show the formation or consequences of a particular
  term
- *Explanations* and *analyses* of the term
- *Comparison* and *contrast; division* and *classification,* to illustrate the parts of
  the whole
- A *narrative,* on occasion, to allow the meaning of the term to emerge gradu-
  ally as the tale unfolds
- *Negation*—what a term isn't

1. Write or draw (as Barry does,) an extended definition of one or more of the following trends, concepts, abstractions, phenomena, or institutions. Be sure to identify
your audience, limit your subject, and illustrate your essay with specific examples.

a. Peace (see "World Peace," Chapter 12)
b. War (see O'Brien, 75–82)
c. Intelligence (see Gardner, 297–309)
d. Ethics, or an ethical issue (Reich, 419–27; Singer, 481–87)
e. Personality or character
f. Physical fitness (see Nestle, 255–62; Hockenberry, 549–55; Roy-O'Reilly,
   219–23)
g. Optimism or depression (economic or psychological)
h. The nature of friendship or love (Allison, 330–32)
i. Marriage (either, the ideal marriage, or the ideal versus the reality) (see Foer,
   340–44)
j. Parenthood (see Sanders 180–91, McGuire, 376–82)
k. Education—formal or informal (see Fadiman, 100–104; Turkle, 37–43; Sedaris,
   267–69)
l. Public service (see Hoagland 489–97; Chapter 12 Nobel Peace Prize Speech)
m. A good job or profession; work; or a very bad job (see Nocton, 271–76)
n. An ecological issue (photo insert)
o. A scientific or technical phenomenon of your choice (an eclipse, the "big bang"
   theory of creation, genetic engineering, DNA, the MX missile) (see McKibben,
   515–25; Gawande, 152–59)
p. A sport, game, hobby, or recreational activity (see Verge, 105–109)

2. Explain a particular value system or belief system, such as the following:

a. Democracy, communism, socialism, or some other political theory or form of government (Universal Declaration of Human Rights, 571–76)
b. Protestantism (or a particular sect), Catholicism, Judaism (or a particular branch—Orthodox, Conservative, Reform), Buddhism (or a particular sort), Islam, or some other religion
c. A theoretical system and some of its major ramifications (feminism, Marxism, postcolonialism, Freudianism, postmodernism)

3. Prepare a dictionary of fifteen jargon or slang words used in your academic major, in your hobby, or in some other activity you enjoy, such as playing a particular sport or game, listening to a specific type of music, or working on a computer system.

Comparison and Contrast

Writers compare people, places, things, or qualities to identify their similarities, and contrast them to identify the differences. What you say about one subject usually helps to illuminate or explain the other, as we understand very well when trying to decide which college to attend, whom to hang out with (or avoid), whether (or not) to buy a car, and if so, what kind. Such explanations have the added advantage of answering questions that hinge on the similarities and differences under consideration. Your commentary can also provide the basis for judging the relative merits and demerits of the subject at hand.

For instance, comparison and contrast can help you determine whether to choose a liberal arts or technical education, and what your future will be like with whichever you select. It can help you explain the resemblances between the works of Faulkner and Hemingway, and the differences—and to justify your preference for one author over the other. Comparison and contrast can help you decide whom to vote for, what movie to see (or avoid), where to live, whether (and whom) to marry. A thoroughgoing, detailed comparison and contrast of the reasons for the quality of life with and without handguns, public transportation, or conservation of natural resources can provide a convincing argument for your choice.

But not everything will work. The subjects you select should have some obvious qualities in common to make the comparison and contrast fruitful. If you try to compare very dissimilar things, as the Mad Hatter does in *Alice in Wonderland* ("Why is a raven like a writing desk?"), you'll have to stretch for an answer ("Because they both begin with an *r* sound.") that may be either silly or irrelevant. But other comparisons by their very nature can command appropriate contrasts. Roz Chast's perceptive cartoon, "An Excerpt from Men Are from Belgium, Women Are from New Brunswick" (350–51), details major gender-related differences between the communication styles of men and women. Deborah Tannen's "Communication Styles" (344–49) is based on an extended exploration of differences in the way men and women students behave in the classroom. For instance, Tannen has found that men speak in class more often than women do. They're more at ease in the "public" classroom setting and enjoy the "debate-like form that discussion may take," while women students are "more comfortable speaking in private to a small group of people they know well" in nonconfrontational dialogue.

This intriguing contrast permits comparisons between the speakers, in addition to possible generalizations about the nature of such relationships. These questions could also be asked of the couple in Jonathan Safran Foer's "Here We Aren't, So Quickly" (340–44), whose entire lifespan the author tries to cover in a scant nineteen paragraphs. Readers, drawing on their own life experiences which they can compare and contrast with those of the characters, lightly sketched, have to fill in the blanks. And if they put in the wrong specifics, it doesn't matter, since Foer's open-endedness (paradoxically, through lists of specifics such as "We tried having dinner parties. We tried owning nothing. We left handprints in a moss garden in Kyoto. . . ." (¶ 4)) invites readers to draw on their own comparable experiences as they seek to understand, intuitively if not logically, what he means.

In writing an essay of comparison and contrast you'll need to justify your choice of subject, unless the grounds for comparison are obvious. You'll also have to limit your comparison, for no single essay—or even an entire book—can fully address the possibilities of most subjects. Suzanne Britt's "That Lean and Hungry Look" (358–61) concentrates on the temperaments, pastimes, and lifestyles of fat and thin people, rather than on the specifics of their bodies. Her generalizations—"Thin people believe in logic. Fat people see all sides. The sides fat people see are rounded blobs" (as depicted in the cartoons by both Warp and Banyai)—are intended to provide a humorous defense of the "convivial" fat, in comparison with the "oppressive" thin, whom readers will identify as general characters and personality types, rather than as specific individuals.

Megan McGuire's "Wake Up Call" (376–82) addresses the subject of her informal education. How could she grow up to be levelheaded, self-reliant, and directed toward positive goals (a college education, a military career) when reared by parents so different—from both these goals and from each other? Her father was loving but on a disability pension, and her mother was underpaid, overworked, and—at best—inattentive.

McGuire presents the information in an intentionally even-handed way, making no value judgment between her parents. She lets the readers make their own interpretations, draw their own conclusions.

The basis for the fundamental comparison and contrast in Charles C. Mann's "The Coming Death Shortage" (362–74) is readily apparent. Because U.S. life expectancy in the past century has increased from forty-seven to seventy-seven, the "orderly succession of generations," from youth to old age, is being and will continue to be overturned as people live longer and longer. This fact enables many comparisons: between the formerly old (47 is no longer old!) and the currently old (but what does that mean—65? 75? 120?). Between the genuinely young (whatever age that means) and the old (whatever age that means). Between affluent elders and impecunious youngsters. Between the wealthy who can afford whatever it costs to stay alive to be old and the less affluent who will die younger and more naturally. Between the more-healthy elderly who can hang onto high-paying jobs and the youth indefinitely suspended in "quasi-adulthood" as "parasitic singles" whose opportunities to lead mature, independent lives are on hold until the old get out of the workforce. And many more issues, susceptible to interpretations that are biological, philosophical, medical, and ethical as well as economic. Or, as Carolita Johnson's cartoon of two babes in bikinis (375) puts it, "I never thought turning eighty would be so much fun!"

Other common patterns become apparent when you examine the ways you might organize your thoughts about buying a new car. Let's say you're making lists that will be the basis of an essay to help you make decisions on type (minivan, pickup, sports car, sedan), make and model, age (new or used), cost, special features (four-wheel drive, bluetooth), and financing (buy or lease). If you've just begun to think about the subject, you could deal with each issue topic by topic, most usefully in the order listed here: type, make and model, and so on. Or you could deal with each subject as a whole before moving on to the next. If you've already decided on the particular type and price of the car—say, a small used vehicle costing between $8000 and $10,000—then you might find it more useful to devote one section, say, to the Honda Civic, another to the GEO Prizm, and a third to the Smart Car, considering all features of each car in the same order: size, handling, reliability, fuel economy, safety, sportiness, and final cost. Why the same order for each car? Because you'll confuse yourself and your readers if you follow a different organizational pattern for each car; everyone needs to know where to look in each discussion to find comparable information. Another way to organize the information would be to group all the similarities about the cars in one section and all the differences in another, arranged in order from the most important (to you) to the least. Eventually, you'll summarize your conclusion: "While I like the first car better because it's sportier and more fun to drive, and the second is great on hills and curves, I guess I'm stuck with the third because I know I can get a good deal from my great uncle, who kept it in his garage all winter and never drove it over fifty."

The pattern of comparison and contrast that emerges may depend on how long the paper is; the longer the discussion, the less easy it is for readers to remember what they need to. Try out a sample section on members of your class or writing group and see whether they can understand the points of comparison you're trying to make; if they can't, then try another method of arrangement.

Whatever pattern of comparison and contrast you use, a topic outline can help you to organize such papers, and to make sure you've covered equivalent points for each item in the comparison. However you organize the paper, you don't have to give such equal emphasis to the similarities and to the differences; some may simply be more important than others. But you do have to make your chosen points of comparison relevant. Comparison and contrast is particularly useful as a technique in explanations. You can compare something that readers don't know much about (foreign sports cars) with something that's familiar (family sedans).

As we've seen, essays of comparison and contrast may include other types of writing, particularly description, narration, and analysis. Classification and division often determine the points to be covered in such essays: my actual life versus my ideal life, country living versus city living, life on the East (or West) Coast versus life in the Midwest, middle-class life versus upper-class life. . . . And essays of comparison and contrast themselves become, at times, illustrations or arguments, direct or indirect, overt or more subtle. Long live the differences and the zest they provide.

Strategies for Writing: Comparison and Contrast

1. Will my essay focus on the similarities between two or more things (comparison) or the differences (contrast), or will I be discussing both similarities and differences? Why do I want to make the comparison or contrast? To find, explore, or deny overt or less apparent resemblances among the items? To decide which one of a pair or group is better or preferable? Or to use the comparison or contrast to argue for my preference?
2. Are my readers familiar with one or more of the objects of my comparison? If they are familiar with them all, then can I concentrate on the unique features of my analysis? (If they are familiar with only one item, start with the known before discussing the unknown. If they are unacquainted with everything, for purposes of explanation you might wish to begin with a comparison that focuses on the common elements among the items under discussion.)
3. How global or minute will my comparison be (i.e., do I want to make only a few points of comparison or contrast, or many)? Will my essay make more sense to my readers if I present each subject as a complete unit before discussing the next? Or will the comparison or contrast be more meaningful if I proceed point by point?
4. Have I ruled out trivial and irrelevant comparisons? Does each point have a counterpart that I have treated in an equivalent manner, through comparable analysis or illustration, length, and language?
5. Suppose I like or favor one item of the comparison or contrast over the others. Am I obliged to treat every item equally in language and tone, or can my tone vary to reinforce my interpretation?

JONATHAN SAFRAN FOER

Jonathan Safran Foer (born 1977) achieved a reputation as a major American novelist with the publication of his first novel, *Everything is Illuminated* in 2002, when he was twenty five; this work received a National Jewish Book Award and a Guardian First Book Award. As an undergraduate at Princeton, Foer studied creative writing with Joyce Carol Oates, and earned a B.A. in philosophy in 1999. The thesis he wrote at Princeton, profiling the life of his grandfather, a Holocaust survivor, grew into Foer's first novel and established one of the major themes of his second novel, *Extremely Loud and Incredibly Close* (2005), in which alternative narrators speak from the perspectives of terrifying international events. Among the principals is a nine-year-old child in Manhattan who inadvertently experienced the terrorist attack on the World Trade Center; and his grandparents who survived the bombing of Dresden and the Holocaust. To reinforce the unsettled, disoriented status of his characters, Foer employs various type faces, graphics, time-lapse images, blank spaces and pages. In addition to short stories, Foer has written nonfiction, *Eating Animals* (2009), a moral critique of contemporary eating habits. Foer is currently a professor in the Graduate Creative Writing Program at New York University. In 2007, he was named among *Granta's* Best of Young American Novelists.

"Here We Aren't, So Quickly" (2010) was originally published in *The New Yorker's* 20 Under 40 Fiction issue. When you view the fleeting mental snapshots that portray the love affair, marriage, and parenthood of the couple in this unconventional short story, don't try to make logical connections among the non-sequiturs in which the story is told. Just let your imagination compose the big picture like a mosaic, from the small bits that the author gives you to play with, to meditate on, to assemble and re-assemble.

Here We Aren't, So Quickly

1   I was not good at drawing faces. I was just joking most of the time. I was not decisive in changing rooms or anywhere. I was so late because I was looking for flowers. I was just going through a tunnel whenever my mother called. I was not able to make toast without the radio. I was not able to tell if compliments were backhanded. I was not as tired as I said.

2   You were not able to ignore furniture imperfections. You were too light to arm the airbag. You were not able to open most jars. You were not sure how you should wear your hair, and so, ten minutes late and halfway down the stairs, you would examine your reflection in a framed picture of dead family. You were not angry, just protecting your dignity.

I was not able to run long distances. You were so kind to my sister   3
when I didn't know how to be kind. I was just trying to remove a stain; I
made a bigger stain. You were just asking a simple question. I was almost
always at home, but I was not always at home at home. You were not
able to cope with a stack of more than three books on my bedside table,
or mixed currencies in the change dish, or plastic. I was not afraid of being alone; I just hated it. You were just admiring the progress of someone
else's garden. I was so tired of food.

We went to the Atacama. We went to Sarajevo. We went to Tobey Pond   4
every year until we didn't. We braved thirteen inches of snow to attend a
lecture in a planetarium. We tried having dinner parties. We tried owning
nothing. We left handprints in a moss garden in Kyoto, and got each other
off under a towel in Jaffa. We braved my parents' for Thanksgiving and
yours for the rest, and how did it happen that we were suddenly at my
father's side while he drowned in his own body? I lay beside him on the
bed, observed my hand reaching for his brow, said, "Despite everything—"
"What everything?" he asked, so I said, "Nothing," or nothing.

I was always destroying my passport in the wash. You were al-   5
ways awful at estimating. You were never willing to think of my habits
as charming. I was just insisting that it was already too late to master an
instrument or anything. You were never one to mention physical pain.

I couldn't explain the cycles of the moon without pen and paper,   6
or with. You didn't know where e-mails *were*. I wouldn't congratulate a
woman until she explicitly said she was pregnant. You spent a few minutes every day secretly regretting your laziness that didn't exist. I should
have forgiven you for all that wasn't your fault.

You were terrible in emergencies. You were wonderful, in "The   7
Cherry Orchard." I was always never complaining, because confrontation
was death to me, and because everything was pretty much always pretty
much O.K. with me. You were not able to approach the ocean at night.
I didn't know where my voice *was* between my phone and yours. You
were never standing by the window at parties, but you were always
by the window. I was so paranoid about kind words. I was just not
watching the news in the basement. You were just making a heroic effort
to make things look easy. I was terrible about acknowledging anyone
else's efforts. You were not green-thumbed, but you were not content
to be not content. I was always in need of just one good dress shirt, or
just one something that I never had. You were too injured by things that
happened in the distant past for anything to be effortless in the present.
I was always struggling to be natural with my hands. You were never
immune to unexpected gifts. I was mostly just joking.

I was not neurotic, just apocalyptic. You were always copying keys and   8
looking up words. I was not afraid of quiet, I just hated it. So my hand was
always in my pocket, around a phone I never answered. You were not cheap
or handy with tools, just hurt by my distance. I was never indifferent to the
children of strangers, just frustrated by my own unrelenting optimism. You

were not unsurprised when, that last night in Norfolk, I drove you to Tobey Pond, led you by the hand down the slope of brambles and across the rotting planks to the constellations in the water. Sharing our happiness diminished your happiness. I was not going to dance at our wedding, and you were not going to speak. No part of me was nervous that morning.

9   When you screamed at no one, I sang to you. When you finally fell asleep, the nurse took him to bathe him, and, still sleeping, you reached out your arms.

10   He was not a terrible sleeper. I acknowledged to no one my inability to be still with him or anyone. You were not overwhelmed but overtired. I was never afraid of rolling over onto him in my sleep, but I awoke many nights sure that he was underwater on the floor. I loved collapsing things. You loved the tiny socks. You were not depressed, but you were unhappy. Your unhappiness didn't make me defensive; I just hated it. He was never happy unless held. I loved hammering things into walls. You hated having no inner life. I secretly wondered if he was deaf. I hated the gnawing longing that accompanied having everything. We were learning to see each other's blindnesses. I Googled questions that I couldn't ask our doctor or you.

11   They encouraged us to buy insurance. We had sex to have orgasms. You loved re-upholstering. I went to the gym to go somewhere, and looked in the mirror when there was something I was hoping not to see. You hated our bed. He could stand himself up, but not get himself down. They fined us for our neighbor's garbage. We couldn't wait for the beginnings and ends of vacations. I was not able to look at a blueprint and see a renovated kitchen, so I stayed out of it. They came to our door during meals, but I talked to them and gave.

12   I counted the seconds backward until he fell asleep, and then started counting the seconds backward until he woke up. We took the same walks again and again, and again and again ate at the same easy restaurants. They said he looked like them. I was always watching movie trailers on my computer. You were always wiping surfaces. I was always hearing my father's laugh and never remembering his face. You broke everyone's heart until you suddenly couldn't. He suddenly drew, suddenly spoke, suddenly wrote, suddenly reasoned. One night I couldn't help him with his math. He got married.

13   We went to London to see a play. We tried putting aside time to do nothing but read, but we did nothing but sleep. We were always never mentioning it, because we didn't know what it was. I did nothing but look for you for twenty-seven years. I didn't even know how electricity worked. We tried spending more time not together. I was not defensive about your boredom, but my happiness had nothing to do with happiness. I loved it when people who worked for me genuinely liked me. We were always moving furniture and never making eye contact. I hated my inability to visit a foreign city without fantasizing about real estate. And then your father was dead. I often wasn't reading the book that I was holding. You were never not in someone's garden. Our mothers were dying to talk about nothing.

At a certain point you became convinced that you were always read-   14
ing yesterday's newspaper. At a certain point I stopped agonizing over being understood, and became over-reliant on my car's G.P.S. You couldn't
tolerate trace amounts of jelly in the peanut-butter jar. I couldn't tolerate
gratuitously boisterous laughter. At a certain point I could stare without
pretext or apology. Isn't it funny that if God were to reveal and explain
Himself, the majority of the world would necessarily be disappointed? At
a certain point you stopped wearing sunscreen.

How can I explain the way I shrugged off nuclear annihilation but   15
mortally feared a small fall? You couldn't tolerate people who couldn't
tolerate babies on planes. I couldn't tolerate people who insisted that
having a coffee after lunch would keep them up all night. At a certain
point I could hear my knees and felt no need to correct other people's
grammar. How can I explain why foreign cities came to mean so much to
me? At a certain point you stopped agonizing over your ambitiousness,
but at a certain point you stopped trying. I couldn't tolerate magicians
who did things that someone who actually had magical powers would
never do.

We were all doing well. I was still in love with the Olympics. The   16
smaller the matter, the more I allowed your approval to mean to me.
They kept producing new things that we didn't need that we needed.
I needed your approval more than I needed anything. My sister died at a
restaurant. My mother promised anyone who would listen that she was
fine. They changed our filters. You wanted to see the northern lights.
I wanted to learn a dead language. You were in the garden, not planting,
but standing there. You dropped two handfuls of soil.

And here we aren't, so quickly: I'm not twenty-six and you're not sixty.   17
I'm not forty-five or eighty-three, not being hoisted onto the shoulders
of anybody wading into any sea. I'm not learning chess, and you're not
losing your virginity. You're not stacking pebbles on gravestones; I'm not
being stolen from my resting mother's arms. Why didn't you lose your
virginity to me? Why didn't we enter the intersection one thousandth
of a second sooner, and die instead of die laughing? Everything else
happened—why not the things that could have?

I am not unrealistic anymore. You are not unemotional. I am not   18
interested in the news anymore, but I was never interested in the news.
What's more, I am probably ambidextrous. I was probably meant to be
effortless. You look like yourself right now. I was so slow to change, but
I changed. I was probably a natural tennis player, just like my father used
to say over and over and over.

I changed and changed, and with more time I will change more. I'm   19
not disappointed, just quiet. Not unthinking, just reckless. Not willfully
unclear, just trying to say it as it wasn't. The more I remember, the more
distant I feel. We reached the middle so quickly. After everything it's like
nothing. I have always never been here. What a shame it wasn't easy.

What a waste of what? What a joke. But come. No explaining or mending. Be beside me somewhere: on the split stools of this bar, by the edge of this cliff, in the seats of this borrowed car, at the prow of this ship, on the all-forgiving cushions of this thread bare sofa in this one-story copper-crying fixer-upper whose windows we once squinted through for hours before coming to our senses: "What would we even do with such a house?"

DEBORAH TANNEN

Deborah Tannen, born in Brooklyn in 1945, was partially deafened by a childhood illness. Her consequent interest in nonverbal communication and other aspects of conversation led ultimately to a doctorate in linguistics (University of California, Berkeley, 1979) and professorship at Georgetown University. Tannen's numerous studies of gender-related speech patterns draw on the combined perspectives of anthropology, sociology, psychology, and women's studies, as well as linguistics. Tannen brings a sensitive ear and keen analysis to communication related to gender, power, and status in the best-selling *That's Not What I Meant!: How Conversational Style Makes or Breaks Your Relations with Others* (1986), *You Just Don't Understand: Women and Men in Conversation* (1990), *Talking from 9 to 5* (1994), *I Only Say This Because I Love You* (2001), *Conversational Style: Analyzing Talk Among Friends* (2005), *You're Wearing That?: Understanding Mothers and Daughters in Conversation* (2006), and You Were Always Mom's Favorite!: Sisters in Conversation Throughout Their Lives (2009).

Much of Deborah Tannen's research, like her writing, is based on comparative analyses of the contrasting behavior of men and women in a variety of situations. "Communication Styles" was originally published as "Teachers' Classroom Strategies Should Recognize that Men and Women Use Language Differently" in the *Chronicle of Higher Education* (June 19, 1991). Here Tannen explores differences in the ways that men and women students interact, and how the size, informality, and composition of the group influences who speaks up and who remains silent.

Communication Styles

1   When I researched and wrote my book, *You Just Don't Understand: Women and Men in Conversation*, the furthest thing from my mind was reevaluating my teaching strategies. But that has been one of the direct benefits of having written the book.

The primary focus of my linguistic research always has been the lan- 2
guage of everyday conversation. One facet of this is conversational style:
how different regional, ethnic, and class backgrounds, as well as age and
gender, result in different ways of using language to communicate. *You
Just Don't Understand* is about the conversational styles of women and
men. As I gained more insight into typically male and female ways of using language, I began to suspect some of the causes of the troubling facts
that women who go to single-sex schools do better in later life, and that
when young women sit next to young men in classrooms, the males talk
more. This is not to say that all men talk in class, nor that no women do.
It is simply that a greater percentage of discussion time is taken by men's
voices.

The research of sociologists and anthropologists such as Janet Lever, 3
Marjorie Harness Goodwin, and Donna Eder has shown that girls and
boys learn to use language differently in their sex-separate peer groups.
Typically, a girl has a best friend with whom she sits and talks, frequently
telling secrets. It's the telling of secrets, the fact and the way that they talk
to each other, that makes them best friends. For boys, activities are central:
Their best friends are the ones they do things with. Boys also tend to play
in larger groups that are hierarchical. High-status boys give orders and
push low-status boys around. So boys are expected to use language to
seize center stage: by exhibiting their skills, displaying their knowledge,
and challenging and resisting challenges.

These patterns have stunning implications for classroom interac- 4
tion. Most faculty members assume that participating in class discussion
is a necessary part of successful performance. Yet speaking in a classroom
is more congenial to boys' language experience than to girls', since it en-
tails putting oneself forward in front of a large group of people, many of
whom are strangers and at least one of whom is sure to judge speakers'
knowledge and intelligence by their verbal display.

Another aspect of many classrooms that makes them more hospita- 5
ble to most men than to most women is the use of debate-like formats as a
learning tool. Our educational system, as Walter Ong argues persuasively
in his book *Fighting for Life* (Cornell University Press, 1981), is fundamentally male in that the pursuit of knowledge is believed to be achieved by
ritual opposition: public display followed by argument and challenge.
Father Ong demonstrates that ritual opposition—what he calls "adversa-
tiveness" or "agonism"—is fundamental to the way most males approach
almost any activity. (Consider, for example, the little boy who shows he
likes a little girl by pulling her braids and shoving her.) But ritual opposition is antithetical to the way most females learn and like to interact. It is
not that females don't fight, but that they don't fight for fun. They don't
ritualize opposition.

Anthropologists working in widely disparate parts of the world have 6
found contrasting verbal rituals for women and men. Women in

completely unrelated cultures (for example, Greece and Bali) engage in ritual laments: spontaneously produced rhyming couplets that express their pain, for example, over the loss of loved ones. Men do not take part in laments. They have their own, very different verbal ritual: a contest, a war of words in which they vie with each other to devise clever insults.

7   When discussing these phenomena with a colleague, I commented that I see these two styles in American conversation: Many women bond by talking about troubles, and many men bond by exchanging playful insults and put-downs, and other sorts of verbal sparring. He exclaimed: "I never thought of this, but that's the way I teach: I have students read an article, and then I invite them to tear it apart. After we've torn it to shreds, we talk about how to build a better model."

8   This contrasts sharply with the way I teach: I open the discussion of readings by asking, "What did you find useful in this? What can we use in our own theory building and our own methods?" I note what I see as weaknesses in the author's approach, but I also point out that the writer's discipline and purposes might be different from ours. Finally, I offer personal anecdotes illustrating the phenomena under discussion and praise students' anecdotes as well as their critical acumen.

9   These different teaching styles must make our classrooms wildly different places and hospitable to different students. Male students are more likely to be comfortable attacking the readings and might find the inclusion of personal anecdotes irrelevant and "soft." Women are more likely to resist discussion they perceive as hostile, and, indeed, it is women in my classes who are most likely to offer personal anecdotes.

10   A colleague who read my book commented that he had always taken for granted that the best way to deal with students' comments is to challenge them; this, he felt it was self-evident, sharpens their minds and helps them develop debating skills. But he had noticed that women were relatively silent in his classes, so he decided to try beginning discussion with relatively open-ended questions and letting comments go unchallenged. He found, to his amazement and satisfaction, that more women began to speak up.

11   Though some women in his class clearly liked this better, perhaps some of the men liked it less. One young man in my class wrote in a questionnaire about a history professor who gave students questions to think about and called on people to answer them: "He would then play devil's advocate . . . *i.e.*, he debated us. . . . That class *really* sharpened me intellectually. . . . We as students do need to know how to defend ourselves." This young man valued the experience of being attacked and challenged publicly. Many, if not most, women would shrink from such "challenge," experiencing it as public humiliation.

12   A professor at Hamilton College told me of a young man who was upset because he felt his class presentation had been a failure. The

professor was puzzled because he had observed that class members had listened attentively and agreed with the student's observations. It turned out that it was this very agreement that the student interpreted as failure: Since no one had engaged his ideas by arguing with him, he felt they had found them unworthy of attention.

So one reason men speak in class more than women is that many 13 of them find the "public" classroom setting more conducive to speaking, whereas most women are more comfortable speaking in private to a small group of people they know well. A second reason is that men are more likely to be comfortable with the debate-like form that discussion may take. Yet another reason is the different attitudes toward speaking in class that typify women and men.

Students who speak frequently in class, many of whom are men, as- 14 sume that it is their job to think of contributions and try to get the floor to express them. But many women monitor their participation not only to get the floor but to avoid getting it. Women students in my class tell me that if they have spoken up once or twice, they hold back for the rest of the class because they don't want to dominate. If they have spoken a lot one week, they will remain silent the next. These different ethics of participation are, of course, unstated, so those who speak freely assume that those who remain silent have nothing to say, and those who are reining themselves in assume that the big talkers are selfish and hoggish.

When I looked around my classes, I could see these differing eth- 15 ics and habits at work. For example, my graduate class in analyzing conversation had 20 students, 11 women and 9 men. Of the men, four were foreign students: two Japanese, one Chinese, and one Syrian. With the exception of the three Asian men, all the men spoke in class at least occasionally. The biggest talker in the class was a woman, but there were also five women who never spoke at all, only one of whom was Japanese. I decided to try something different.

I broke the class into small groups to discuss the issues raised in the 16 readings and to analyze their own conversational transcripts. I devised three ways of dividing the students into groups: one by the degree program they were in, one by gender, and one by conversational style, as closely as I could guess it. This meant that when the class was grouped according to conversational style, I put Asian students together, fast talkers together, and quiet students together. The class split into groups six times during the semester, so they met in each grouping twice. I told students to regard the groups as examples of interactional data and to note the different ways they participated in different groups. Toward the end of the term, I gave them a questionnaire asking about their class and group participation.

I could see plainly from my observation of the groups at work that 17 women who never opened their mouths in class were talking away in the small groups. In fact, the Japanese woman commented that she found it particularly hard to contribute to the all-woman group she was in because "I was overwhelmed by how talkative the female students were in the female-only group." This is particularly revealing because it highlights that the same person who can be "oppressed" into silence in one context can become the talkative "oppressor" in another. No one's conversational style is absolute; everyone's style changes in response to the context and others' styles.

18 Some of the students (seven) said that they preferred the same-gender groups; others preferred the same-style groups. In answer to the question "Would you have liked to speak in class more than you did?" six of the seven who said Yes were women; the one man was Japanese. Most startlingly, this response did not come only from quiet women; it came from women who had indicated they had spoken in class never, rarely, sometimes, and often. Of the 11 students who said the amount they had spoken was fine, 7 were men. Of the four women who checked "fine," two added qualifications indicating it wasn't completely fine: One wrote in "maybe more," and one wrote, "I have an urge to participate but often feel I should have something more interesting/relevant/wonderful/intelligent to say!!"

19 I counted my experiment a success. Everyone in the class found the small groups interesting, and no one indicated he or she would have preferred that the class not break into groups. Perhaps most instructive, however, was the fact that the experience of breaking into groups, and of talking about participation in class, raised everyone's awareness about classroom participation. After we had talked about it, some of the quietest women in the class made a few voluntary contributions, though sometimes I had to insure their participation by interrupting the students who were exuberantly speaking out.

20 Americans are often proud that they discount the significance of cultural differences: "We are all individuals," many people boast. Ignoring such issues as gender and ethnicity becomes a source of pride: "I treat everyone the same." But treating people the same is not equal treatment if they are not the same.

21 The classroom is a different environment for those who feel comfortable putting themselves forward in a group than it is for those who find the prospect of doing so chastening, or even terrifying. When a professor asks, "Are there any questions?," students who can formulate statements the fastest have the greatest opportunity to respond. Those who need significant time to do so have not really been given a chance at all, since by the time they are ready to speak, someone else has the floor.

22 In a class where some students speak out without raising hands, those who feel they must raise their hands and wait to be recognized do not have equal opportunity to speak. Telling them to feel free to jump in will not make them feel free; one's sense of timing, of one's rights and

obligations in a classroom, are automatic, learned over years of interaction. They may be changed over time, with motivation and effort, but they cannot be changed on the spot. And everyone assumes his or her own way is best. When I asked my students how the class could be changed to make it easier for them to speak more, the most talkative woman said she would prefer it if no one had to raise hands, and a foreign student said he wished people would raise their hands and wait to be recognized.

My experience in this class has convinced me that small-group interaction should be part of any class that is not a small seminar. I also am convinced that having the students become observers of their own interaction is a crucial part of their education. Talking about ways of talking in class makes students aware that their ways of talking affect other students, that the motivations they impute to others may not truly reflect others' motives, and that the behaviors they assume to be self-evidently right are not universal norms. 23

The goal of complete equal opportunity in class may not be attainable, but realizing that one monolithic classroom-participation structure is not equal opportunity is itself a powerful motivation to find more-diverse methods to serve diverse students—and every classroom is diverse. 24

Content

1. In your experience, are boys (more often than girls) "expected to use language to seize center stage: by exhibiting their skills, displaying their knowledge, and challenging and resisting challenges" (¶ 3)? How does this translate into classroom performance (¶s 4, 7)? In your experience, is Ong's claim true that "ritual opposition . . . is fundamental to the way most males approach almost any activity" (¶ 5)?

2. "Treating people the same is not equal treatment if they are not the same" (¶ 20). Explain how this idea applies in a classroom.

3. Does Tannen argue that the differences between men's and women's communication styles are biologically or culturally determined? Does she equate student talkativeness in class with an inquiring mind? With intelligent preparation? Or does she base her equation exclusively on gender? Explain your answers.

Strategies/Structures/Language

4. Tannen's article follows the format of physical and social science research: statement of the problem, review of the literature, identification of research methodology, explanation of the research procedure, interpretation of the research findings, and generalizations to other situations or recommendations for either further research or practical applications or both. Show where each stage occurs in this article.

5. "No one's conversational style is absolute; everyone's style changes in response to the context and others' styles" (¶ 17). Explain, with reference to your own experience and other students' behavior in your classes—and out.

For Writing

6. *Journal Writing.* Do some primary investigation to replicate Tannen's observation that "when young women sit next to [presumably she means *share the same classroom*, not necessarily *sit in immediate proximity to*] young men in classrooms, the males talk more" (¶ 2). Is this true in any or all of your classes? Typically, do men speak more than women in classes taught by men? Do women speak more or less than men in classes taught by women? Do the ages and life experiences of men and women influence the extent of their class participation? Generalize from your findings and interpret them with regard to Tannen's findings. Do you think the men and women students at your school are typical of students at all American colleges or only at colleges of the type that yours represents (private or public community college, four-year undergraduate school, research university)?

7. Do you agree with Tannen's conclusion that "small-group interaction should be part of any class that is not a small seminar" (¶ 23)? If so, why? If not, why not? What demands does this format place on the students? What does this format imply about the way we learn?

8. Write an essay about any of the Content questions. Base your essay on your own experience, and reinforce it with three interviews—one with a student of a different gender from yours, another with a student of a different racial background, another with a student from a different socio-economic class. (To control for teaching style and content, all the students should be enrolled in the same course at the same time.) To what extent are your conclusions influenced by your informants' class and ethnicity, in comparison with their gender?

9. *Dialogues.* Do men and women use electronic communication differently? While Tannen argues in "Communication Styles" that "women . . . resist [classroom] discussion they perceive as hostile" (¶ 9), she does not distinguish between men's and women's use of technologically enhanced communication. Does electronic communication diminish differences in the ways men and women communicate? How does electronic communication change behaviors traditionally associated with gender? Write an essay that extends Tannen's analysis of gender differences in communicating to the world of electronic communication.

ROZ CHAST

Roz Chast (born in 1954 in Brooklyn) has published nine collections of her work, most recently *Theories of Everything* (2006), in which "An Excerpt from Men Are from Belgium, Women Are from New Brunswick" was published. She received a BFA in 1977 from Rhode Island School of Design. Chast began publishing in the *New Yorker* in 1979 and has continued to do so ever since. She has also provided cartoons and editorial illustrations for many other magazines, among them *Vogue, National Lampoon, Scientific American, Time,* and *Mother Jones.* She has illustrated children's books, including *The Alphabet from A to Y with Bonus Letter Z!* (2007), and contributed to various *New Yorker* collections of cartoons. "Men Are from Belgium, Women Are from New Brunswick" decodes gender-specific ways of communicating in everyday life and illustrates the multitude of conflicting emotions that can simmer beneath the surface of apparently straightforward and banal language. (Note that the title below applies to the entire cartoon; it is not an excerpt.)

An Excerpt from Men Are from Belgium, Women Are from New Brunswick

Roz Chast/The New Yorker/Cartoon Bank.

Content

1. Does Chast's depiction of communication between the sexes correspond to your experience? Does Chast's graphic illustration of the process of communication challenge gender stereotypes? Why or why not? How would the verbal and nonverbal responses change if the "guy" rather than the "gal" in the cartoon had cooked the meatloaf? What clues, if any, indicate that this cartoon narrative was created by a "gal"? Would a "guy's" work have been the same? If not, in what significant ways would it have been different?

2. How do the columned format and the images in this cartoon work together to convey both a humorous and serious side of this subject? Is there a resolution to the conflict between the two characters? What does the image of the licensed professional (therapist? marriage counselor?) contribute to the reader's understanding of this mini-narrative?

Strategies/Structures/Language

3. How does Chast extract humor from the situation by small shifts in language and emphasis?

4. What can you deduce about the character's personalities from their language and from the artist's use of punctuation, underlining, and capitalization? What is the effect of hand-written, as opposed to typed, text?

For Writing

5. **Journal Writing.** In what types of situations do people avoid stating what they mean? How do intonation, word choice, gestures, and facial expressions contribute to the complexities of such communications? Are mixed signals an inherent part of communication? Include in your response a specific situation in which you felt that you could not say what you felt. Were you able to convey your views nevertheless? Why or why not?

6. **Dialogues.** Compare Chast's depiction of what women and men "actually mean" with Art Spiegelman's understated treatment of the Holocaust in "Mein Kampf" (93–5). For example, what do the artist's references to the Holocaust suggest about his feelings toward his family's history? What does his reassurance to his son that "King Kong" is "only a story" imply about his attitude toward the Holocaust? In comparison, what unstated messages do Chast's characters' statements and thoughts suggest about their relationship with one another?

7. Deborah Tannen argues in "Communication Styles" in this chapter that many men and women have different styles of learning that are based on their preferred ways of communicating. Using Chast's comic as a starting point, present an argument that explains some of the differences in communication styles between men and women (or two other groups such as parents/children; children of particular ages/stages in life; teachers/students; doctors/patients . . .). What are the social and psychological factors that explain these differences? Support your argument with specific, convincing details.

NATALIE ANGIER

For biographical information, see page 286.

Angier's writing is characteristically clear, precise, and witty. She explains the unfamiliar in terms of the familiar, giving research a memorably human perspective. Thus, in "Why Men Don't Last," first published in the *New York Times* (Feb. 17, 1999), Angier examines significant differences between the biology of men and women, translating statistical and psychological research (on risk taking, compulsive gambling, suicidal behavior, masculinity) into language and concepts general readers can readily understand—without oversimplifying the subject or demeaning the audience.

Why Men Don't Last: Self-Destruction as a Way of Life

My father had great habits. Long before ficus trees met weight machines, he was a dogged exerciser. He did push-ups and isometrics. He climbed rocks. He went for long, vigorous walks. He ate sparingly and avoided sweets and grease. He took such good care of his teeth that they looked fake.

My father had terrible habits. He was chronically angry. He threw things around the house and broke them. He didn't drink often, but when he did, he turned more violent than usual. He didn't go to doctors, even when we begged him to. He let a big, ugly mole on his back grow bigger and bigger, and so he died of malignant melanoma, a curable cancer, at 51.

My father was a real man—so good and so bad. He was also Everyman.

Men by some measures take better care of themselves than women do and are in better health. They are less likely to be fat, for example; they exercise more, and suffer from fewer chronic diseases like diabetes, osteoporosis and arthritis.

By standard measures, men have less than half the rate of depression seen in women. When men do feel depressed, they tend to seek distraction in an activity, which, many psychologists say, can be a more effective technique for dispelling the mood than is a depressed woman's tendency to turn inward and ruminate. In the United States and many other industrialized nations, women are about three times more likely than men to express suicidal thoughts or to attempt to kill themselves.

6   And yet . . . men don't last. They die off in greater numbers than women do at every stage of life, and thus their average life span is seven years shorter. Women may attempt suicide relatively more often, but in the United States, four times more men than women die from the act each year.

7   Men are also far more likely than women to die behind the wheel or to kill others as a result of their driving. From 1977 to 1995, three and a half times more male drivers than female drivers were involved in fatal car crashes. Death by homicide also favors men; among those under 30, the male-to-female ratio is 8 to 1.

8   Yes, men can be impressive in their tendency to self-destruct, explosively or gradually. They are at least twice as likely as women to be alcoholics and three times more likely to be drug addicts. They have an eightfold greater chance than women do of ending up in prison. Boys are much more likely than girls to be thrown out of school for a conduct or antisocial personality disorder, or to drop out on their own surly initiative. Men gamble themselves into a devastating economic and emotional pit two to three times more often than women do.

9   "Between boys' suicide rates, dropout rates and homicide rates, and men's self-destructive behaviors generally, we have a real crisis in America," said William S. Pollack, a psychologist at Harvard Medical School and co-director of the Center for Men at McLean Hospital in Belmont, Mass. "Until recently, the crisis has gone unheralded."

10   It is one thing to herald a presumed crisis, though, and to cite a ream of gloomy statistics. It is quite another to understand the crisis, or to figure out where it comes from or what to do about it. As those who study the various forms of men's self-destructive behaviors realize, there is not a single, glib, overarching explanation for the sex-specific patterns they see.

11   A crude evolutionary hypothesis would have it that men are natural risk-takers, given to showy displays of bravado, aggression and daring all for the sake of attracting a harem of mates. By this premise, most of men's self-destructive, violent tendencies are a manifestation of their need to take big chances for the sake of passing their genes into the river of tomorrow.

12   Some of the data on men's bad habits fit the risk-taker model. For example, those who study compulsive gambling have observed that men and women tend to display very different methods and preferences for throwing away big sums of money.

13   "Men get enamored of the action in gambling," said Linda Chamberlain, a psychologist at Regis University in Denver who specializes in treating gambling disorders. "They describe an overwhelming rush of feelings and excitement associated with the process of gambling. They like the feeling of being a player, and taking on a struggle with the house to show that they can overcome the odds and beat the system. They tend to prefer the table games, where they can feel powerful and omnipotent while everybody watches them."

14   Dr. Chamberlain noted that many male gamblers engage in other risk-taking behaviors, like auto racing or hang gliding. By contrast, she said, "Women tend to use gambling more as a sedative, to numb themselves

and escape from daily responsibilities, or feelings of depression or alien-
ation. Women tend to prefer the solitary forms of gambling, the slot machines or video poker, where there isn't as much social scrutiny."

Yet the risk-taking theory does not account for why men outnumber   15
women in the consumption of licit and illicit anodynes. Alcohol, heroin
and marijuana can be at least as numbing and sedating as repetitively
pulling the arm of a slot machine. And some studies have found that
men use drugs and alcohol for the same reasons that women often over-
eat: as an attempt to self-medicate when they are feeling anxious or in
despair.

   "We can speculate all we want, but we really don't know why men   16
drink more than women," said Enoch Gordis, the head of the National Institute on Alcohol Abuse and Alcoholism. Nor does men's comparatively
higher rate of suicide appear linked to the risk-taking profile. To the contrary, Paul Duberstein, an assistant professor of psychiatry and oncology
at the University of Rochester School of Medicine, has found that people
who complete a suicidal act are often low in a personality trait referred
to as "openness to experience," tending to be rigid and inflexible in their
behaviors. By comparison, those who express suicidal thoughts tend to
score relatively high on the openness-to-experience scale.

   Given that men commit suicide more often than women, and women   17
talk about it more, his research suggests that, in a sense, women are the
greater risk-takers and novelty seekers, while the men are likelier to feel
trapped and helpless in the face of changing circumstances.

   Silvia Cara Canetto, an associate professor of psychology at Colo-   18
rado State University in Fort Collins, has extensively studied the role of
gender in suicidal behaviors. Dr. Canetto has found that cultural narratives may determine why women attempt suicide more often while men
kill themselves more often. She proposes that in Western countries, to talk
about suicide or to survive a suicidal act is often considered "feminine,"
hysterical, irrational and weak. To actually die by one's own hand may be
viewed as "masculine," decisive, strong. Even the language conveys the
polarized, weak-strong imagery: a "failed" suicide attempt as opposed to
a "successful" one.

   "There is indirect evidence that there is negative stigma toward men   19
who survive suicide," Dr. Canetto said. "Men don't want to 'fail,' even
though failing in this case means surviving." If the "suicidal script" that
identifies completing the acts as "rational, courageous and masculine"
can be "undermined and torn to pieces," she said, we might have a new
approach to prevention.

   Dr. Pollack of the Center for Men also blames many of men's   20
self-destructive ways on the persistent image of the dispassionate, resilient, action-oriented male—the Marlboro Man who never even gasps for
breath. For all the talk of the sensitive "new man," he argues, men have yet
to catch up with women in expanding their range of acceptable emotions

and behaviors. Men in our culture, Dr. Pollack says, are pretty much limited to a menu of three strong feelings: rage, triumph, lust. "Anything else and you risk being seen as a sissy," he said.

21   In a number of books, most recently "Real Boys: Rescuing Our Sons From the Myths of Boyhood," he proposes that boys "lose their voice, a whole half of their emotional selves," beginning at age 4 or 5. "Their vulnerable, sad feelings and sense of need are suppressed or shamed out of them," he said—by their peers, parents, the great wide televised fist in their face.

22   He added: "If you keep hammering it into a kid that he has to look tough and stop being a crybaby and a mama's boy, the boy will start creating a mask of bravado."

23   That boys and young men continue to feel confused over the proper harmonics of modern masculinity was revealed in a study that Dr. Pollack conducted of 200 eighth-grade boys. Through questionnaires, he determined their scores on two scales, one measuring their "egalitarianism"—the degree to which they think men and women are equal, that men should change a baby's diapers, that mothers should work and the like—and the other gauging their "traditionalism" as determined by their responses to conventional notions, like the premise that men must "stand on their own two feet" and must "always be willing to have sex if someone asks."

24   On average, the boys scored high on both scales. "They are split on what it means to be a man," said Dr. Pollack.

25   The cult of masculinity can beckon like a siren song in baritone. Dr. Franklin L. Nelson, a clinical psychologist at the Fairbanks Community Mental Health Center in Alaska, sees many men who get into trouble by adhering to sentimental notions of manhood. "A lot of men come up here hoping to get away from a wimpy world and live like pioneers by old-fashioned masculine principles of individualism, strength and ruggedness," he said. They learn that nothing is simple; even Alaska is part of a wider, interdependent world and they really do need friends, warmth and electricity.

26   "Right now, it's 35 degrees below zero outside," he said during a January interview. "If you're not prepared, it doesn't take long at that temperature to freeze to death."

Content

1. Angier uses several categories of division in this piece: the "so good and so bad" habits of "Everyman" (¶ 3); the self-destructive habits and rates of men versus women (throughout); the division between the rugged individual versus the egalitarian help meet roles today's men are expected to play (¶s 23–25). Why do such divisions enable readers to clearly recognize similarities as well as differences?

2. Angier's explanations for these divisions are equally divided. What evidence does she offer to support the "crude evolutionary hypothesis" that "men are

natural risk-takers, given to showy display of bravado, aggression and daring all for the sake of attracting a harem of mates" (¶ 11)? What evidence does she offer to contradict this hypothesis?

3. What might be some reasons why women talk about committing suicide more than men do, but that men actually have a higher rate of suicide than women do (¶s 16–19)?

Strategies/Structures/Language

4. What are the dangers and difficulties of categorizing behavior by gender? Why aren't the divisions and classifications Angier uses more clear-cut? Is this a phenomenon of the research she cites, of her writing, of the way things are in real life, or of some combination of the three?

5. Angier is writing as a reporter of other people's research. Do we know where she stands on the subject—which hypothesis for men's risk-taking behavior she believes? Is her essay slanted in favor of one opinion or another, either in terms of her examples or her language?

6. Should a reporter be neutral? Isn't the selection of evidence in itself a form of tipping the scale in favor of one side or another?

For Writing

7. *Journal Writing.* In what ways does American culture encourage men to develop a "mask of bravado" (¶ 22)? In your experience, are men punished when expressing their emotional needs? What aspects of the sex roles that you experienced as part of your childhood have you consciously changed or might want to change in raising your own children?

8. Have you ever done anything risky or dangerous to avoid looking like a wimp or to avoid falling into one or another stereotypical role for either men or women? Write a paper for an audience different from yourself; for instance, if you're a risk-taking man, write for a more prudent audience of women or men (if it makes a difference to your argument, specify which gender), and have such a reader critique your paper before you revise it.

9. *Mixed Modes.* Angier, like other science writers, has the difficult job of translating scientific research into language that newspaper readers can understand. From the following list of authors she cites on the role of gender in suicidal behaviors, choose one source and identify, with illustrations, the principles by which Angier works. Consider aspects such as document format, uses of evidence, presentation of data (via graphs, charts, statistics), technicality of language, definitions of scientific terms, citation of supporting research. Use illustrations, graphic as well as written, to clarify.

Canetto, Silvia Sara, and David Lester. "Gender, Culture, and Suicidal Behavior." *Transcultural Psychiatry* 35.2 (1998): 163–90.

Canetto, Silvia Sara, and Isaac Sakinofsky. "The Gender Paradox in Suicide." *Suicide and Life-Threatening Behavior* 28.1 (Spring 1998): 1–23.

Chamberlain, Linda, Michael R. Ruetz, and William G. McCown. *Strange Attractors: Chaos, Complexity, and the Art of Family Therapy.* New York: Wiley, 1997.

Duberstein, Paul R., Yeates Conwell, and Christopher Cox. "Suicide in Widowed Persons." *American Journal of Geriatric Psychiatry* 6.4 (Fall 1998): 328–34.

Gordis, Enoch. "Alcohol Problems in Public Health Policy." *Journal of the American Medical Association* (Dec. 1997): 1781–87.

Pollack, William S. *Real Boys: Rescuing Our Sons from the Myths of Boyhood.* New York: Random, 1998.

Pollack, William S., and Ronald F. Levant, eds. *New Psychotherapy for Men.* New York: Wiley, 1998.

10. **Dialogues.** Angier argues that there is not one "overarching explanation for the sex-specific patterns" scientists who study self-destructive behaviors observe (¶ 10). Does Deborah Tannen's argument, in "Communication Styles" (344–49), that boys learn to "use language to seize center stage" (¶ 3) and are more comfortable demonstrating "verbal display" in the classroom (¶ 4) represent an overarching explanation for the sex-specific patterns she observes in the classroom? Does Tannen's argument represent an application of what Angier calls "the risk-taker model" (¶ 12)? Might what Angier calls the "cult of masculinity" (¶ 25) explain classroom behavior?

11. **Second look.** What does the photo on p. 186 suggest about the reasons people engage in risky behaviors such as alcohol abuse? Are risky behaviors simply a part of growing up? Are such rites of passage different for men and women?

SUZANNE BRITT

Suzanne Britt was born in 1946 in Winston-Salem, North Carolina, and educated at Salem College and Washington University. Britt, who teaches English at Meredith College, describes herself as "stately, plump," and says, "I talk, eat, drink, walk around the block, read, have a stream of company, and sit on the grass outside. I try not to preach, do handicrafts, camp, bowl, argue, visit relatives, or serve on committees." "That Lean and Hungry Look," first published in *Newsweek*, is a contemporary example of a classical mode of literature—the "character"—a common form of description in which the stereotypical features of a character type ("the angry man") or role ("the schoolboy," "the housewife") are identified and often satirized.

Britt's humorous defense of fat people was first published in 1978, before obesity became a national epidemic. At that time, it would have been read as a lighthearted reinforcement of people's right to indulge in hot fudge sundaes and "two doughnuts and a big orange drink anytime they wanted it," augmented by double fudge brownies. But three decades later, obesity is considered a national epidemic. Sixty-seven percent of American adults—129.6 million—are estimated to be overweight, and 32 percent of those are categorized as "obese" (having more than 30 percent body fat). These figures do not include the 19 percent of overweight school-age children. By 2015, 75% of adult Americans are predicted to be overweight, with obesity rising to 40% of the total (25% of children). Complications from obesity, including strokes, heart disease, high blood pressure, diabetes, some cancers, and kidney and gallbladder disorders, contribute to 300,000 deaths a year, lowering life expectancy and dramatically increasing health care costs—currently by over $100 billion a year. How do these sobering statistics affect the reading of "That Lean and Hungry Look" today?

That Lean and Hungry Look

Caesar was right. Thin people need watching. I've been watching them 1 for most of my adult life, and I don't like what I see. When these narrow fellows spring at me, I quiver to my toes. Thin people come in all personalities, most of them menacing. You've got your "together" thin person, your mechanical thin person, your condescending thin person, your tsk-tsk thin person, your efficiency expert thin person. All of them are dangerous.

In the first place, thin people aren't fun. They don't know how to goof 2 off, at least in the best, fat sense of the word. They've always got to be a doing. Give them a coffee break, and they'll jog around the block. Supply them with a quiet evening at home, and they'll fix the screen door and lick S&H green stamps. They say things like "there aren't enough hours in the day." Fat people never say that. Fat people think the day is too damn long already.

Thin people make me tired. They've got speedy little metabolisms 3 that cause them to bustle briskly. They're forever rubbing their bony hands together and eying new problems to "tackle." I like to surround myself with sluggish, inert, easygoing fat people, the kind who believe that if you clean it up today, it'll just get dirty again tomorrow.

Some people say the business about the jolly fat person is a myth, 4 that all of us chubbies are neurotic, sick, sad people. I disagree. Fat people may not be chortling all day long, but they're a hell of a lot *nicer* than the wizened and shriveled. Thin people turn surly, mean and hard at a young age because they never learn the value of a hot-fudge sundae for easing tension. Thin people don't like gooey soft things because they themselves are neither gooey nor soft. They are crunchy and dull, like carrots. They go straight to the heart of the matter while fat people let things stay all blurry and hazy and vague, the way things actually are. Thin people want to face the truth. Fat people know there is no truth. One of my thin friends is always staring at complex, unsolvable problems and saying, "The key thing is . . ." Fat people never say that. They know there isn't any such thing as the key thing about anything.

Thin people believe in logic. Fat people see all sides. The sides fat 5 people see are rounded blobs, usually gray, always nebulous and truly

SUZANNE BRITT, "That Lean and Hungry Look," NEWSWEEK 1978. Reprinted by permission of the author.

not worth worrying about. But the thin persons persists. "If you consume more calories than you burn," says one of my thin friends, "you will gain weight. It's that simple." Fat people always grin when they hear statements like that. They know better.

6   Fat people realize that life is illogical and unfair. They know very well that God is not in his heaven and all is not right with the world. If God was up there, fat people could have two doughnuts and a big orange drink anytime they wanted it.

7   Thin people have a long list of logical things they are always spouting off to me. They hold up one finger at a time as they reel off these things, so I won't lose track. They speak slowly as if to a young child. The list is long and full of holes. It contains tidbits like "get a grip on yourself," "cigarettes kill," "cholesterol clogs," "fit as a fiddle," "ducks in a row," "organize" and "sound fiscal management." Phrases like that.

8   They think these 2,000-point plans lead to happiness. Fat people know happiness is elusive at best and even if they could get the kind thin people talk about, they wouldn't want it. Wisely, fat people see that such programs are too dull, too hard, too off the mark. They are never better than a whole cheesecake.

9   Fat people know all about the mystery of life. They are the ones acquainted with the night, with luck, with fate, with playing it by ear. One thin person I know once suggested that we arrange all the parts of a jigsaw puzzle into groups according to size, shape and color. He figured this would cut the time needed to complete the puzzle by at least 50 per cent. I said I wouldn't do it. One, I like to muddle through. Two, what good would it do to finish early? Three, the jigsaw puzzle isn't the important thing. The important thing is the fun of four people (one thin person included) sitting around a card table, working a jigsaw puzzle. My thin friend had no use for my list. Instead of joining us, he went outside and mulched the boxwoods. The three remaining fat people finished the puzzle and made chocolate, double-fudge brownies to celebrate.

10   The main problem with thin people is they oppress. Their good intentions, bony torsos, tight ships, neat corners, cerebral machinations and pat solutions loom like dark clouds over the loose, comfortable, spread-out, soft world of the fat. Long after fat people have removed their coats and shoes and put their feet up on the coffee table, thin people are still sitting on the edge of the sofa, looking neat as a pin, discussing rutabagas. Fat people are heavily into fits of laughter, slapping their thighs and whooping it up, while thin people are still politely waiting for the punch line.

11   Thin people are downers. They like math and morality and reasoned evaluating of the limitations of human beings. They have their skinny little acts together. They expound, prognose, probe and prick.

12   Fat people are convivial. They will like you even if you're irregular and have acne. They will come up with a good reason why you never

wrote the great American novel. They will cry in your beer with you. They will put your name in the pot. They will let you off the hook. Fat people will gab, giggle, guffaw, gallumph, gyrate and gossip. They are generous, giving and gallant. They are gluttonous and goodly and great. What you want when you're down is soft and jiggly, not muscled and stable. Fat people know this. Fat people have plenty of room. Fat people will take you in.

Content

1. Britt is describing two categories of people, thin and fat. Does she stereotype them? If so, what does she gain from stereotyping? If not, how does she individualize each category? Is her depiction accurate? Why or why not?

2. Why has she chosen to overlook characteristics typical of either group—for instance, the effects on one's health of being either too fat or too thin? Does she treat thin people fairly? Does she intend to do so?

3. For the purpose of contrast, Britt has concentrated on the differences between fat and thin people. What similarities, if any, do they have? Are these related to their weight?

Strategies/Structures/Language

4. Throughout, Britt makes blanket generalizations about both thin and fat people. Does she support these? Is her evidence appropriate? Is it sufficiently comprehensive to make her case?

5. At what point in the essay do you realize that Britt is being humorous? Does her humor reinforce or undermine her point? Explain your answer.

6. Britt's language is conversational, sometimes slangy: "Thin people are downers. . . . They have their skinny little acts together" (¶ 11). In what ways does the language reinforce what Britt says about fat people?

For Writing

7. *Journal Writing.* Keep a food journal for a week and comment on your consumption patterns and moods in a serious and a satirical mode. Do your dietary patterns appear to affect your mood or vice versa? How does your relationship to food reflect your general outlook on life? Does observing your dietary habits inspire you to make any changes in your life?

8. ***Mixed Modes.*** Write a humorous essay in which you divide a larger category (such as students, parents, Southerners, Easterners, Californians) into subcategories as Britt does in the first paragraph, and then characterize each subcategory through comparing and contrasting its parts (working students, athletes, nerds, partiers). Writing collaboratively, each partner could describe one category or subcategory. If you like, borrow some of Britt's techniques, including her use of informal language ("too damn long already" ¶ 2); exaggeration ("always staring at complex, unsolvable problems" ¶ 4); alliteration ("bustle briskly" ¶ 3); and clichés ("God is not in his heaven" ¶ 6). Photographs, drawings, or cartoons can enhance the descriptions.

9. By yourself or with a partner, select one major cause of obesity in America today, research its causes, and provide a workable solution to the problem.

10. ***Second Look.*** Consider how the photograph of people scavenging for food in Haiti (p. 262) challenges us to think about beautiful bodies, material well-being, and environmental costs of our standard of living. In what ways does our society face conflicting messages about the health aspects and aesthetics of thinness? Why, for example, do we associate thinness with glamour? Does our obsession with dieting and exercise blind us to starvation in our own and neighboring countries?

CHARLES C. MANN

Charles C. Mann's journalistic writing and books focus on the fascinating and complex interconnections among science, technology, and commerce. He is an award-winning correspondent for *Science, Wired*, and *The Atlantic Monthly*; his work has been published in many newspapers and magazines, nationally and internationally, including the *Boston Globe, Fortune, Geo* (Germany), the *New York Times, Paris-Match* (France), *Quark* (Japan), *Smithsonian, Der Stern* (Germany), *Technology Review* (MIT), *Vanity Fair*, and the *Washington Post*. His most recent book, *1491: New Revelations of the Americas Before Columbus* (2005), won the U.S. National Academy of Sciences' Keck award for best book of the year. "Forever Young," which first appeared in *The Atlantic Monthly* in 2005 titled "The Coming Death Shortage," explores "the social conflicts that will ensue as the interests of increasingly long-lived older generations diverge from those of their heirs." Mann argues that the "intergenerational warfare" that increased longevity will instigate unprecedented change since "almost every aspect of society is based on the orderly succession of generations."

The Coming Death Shortage

1   ANNA NICOLE SMITH'S role as a harbinger of the future is not widely acknowledged. Born Vickie Lynn Hogan, Smith first came to the attention of the American public in 1993, when she earned the title Playmate of the Year. In 1994 she married J. Howard Marshall, a Houston oil magnate said to be worth more than half a billion dollars. He was eighty-nine and wheelchair-bound; she was twenty-six and quiveringly mobile. Fourteen months later Marshall died. At his funeral the widow appeared in a white dress with a vertical neckline. She also claimed that Marshall had

promised half his fortune to her. The inevitable litigation sprawled from Texas to California and occupied batteries of lawyers, consultants, and public relations specialists for more than seven years.

Even before Smith appeared, Marshall had disinherited his older son. And he had infuriated his younger son by lavishing millions on a mistress, an exotic dancer, who then died in a bizarre face-lift accident. To block Marshall senior from squandering on Smith money that Marshall junior regarded as rightfully his, the son seized control of his father's assets by means that the trial judge later said were so "egregious," "malicious," and "fraudulent" that he regretted being unable to fine the younger Marshall more than $44 million in punitive damages.[1]

In its epic tawdriness the Marshall affair was natural fodder for the tabloid media. Yet one aspect of it may soon seem less a freak show than a cliche. If an increasingly influential group of researchers is correct, the lurid spectacle of intergenerational warfare will become a typical social malady.

The scientists' argument is circuitous but not complex. In the past century U.S. life expectancy has climbed from forty-seven to seventy-seven, increasing by nearly two thirds. Similar rises happened in almost every country. And this process shows no sign of stopping: according to the United Nations, by 2050 global life expectancy will have increased by another ten years. Note, however, that this tremendous increase has been in *average* life expectancy—that is, the number of years that most people live. There has been next to no increase in the *maximum* lifespan, the number of years that one can possibly walk the earth—now thought to be about 120. In the scientists' projections, the ongoing increase in average lifespan is about to be joined by something never before seen in human history: a rise in the maximum possible age at death.

Stem-cell banks, telomerase amplifiers, somatic gene therapy—the list of potential longevity treatments incubating in laboratories is startling. Three years ago a multi-institutional scientific team led by Aubrey de Grey, a theoretical geneticist at Cambridge University, argued in a widely noted paper that the first steps toward "engineered negligible senescence"—a rough-and-ready version of immortality—would have "a good chance of success in mice within ten years." The same techniques, De Grey says, should be ready for human beings a decade or so later.

---

[1] After this article was submitted, a federal appellate court ruled that the Anna Nicole Smith case properly should have been decided not by the federal court in California that awarded her $88 million but by the Texas probate court that had previously ruled wholly against her. Smith appealed to the U.S. Supreme Court, joined by the Bush administration, which wished to preserve federal jurisdiction over state probate proceedings. The court ruled 9–0 for Smith in May 2006, sending the case back to appellate court. No matter who finally wins this *Bleak House* legal battle, though, the case remains emblematic of the social conflicts that will ensue as the interests of increasingly long-lived older generations diverge from those of their heirs. [*Atlantic* editors' footnote.] Smith herself died in 2007, age thirty-nine, legal issues unresolved.

"In ten years we'll have a pill that will give you twenty years," says Leonard Guarente, a professor of biology at Massachusetts Institute of Technology. "And then there'll be another pill after that. The first hundred-and-fifty-year-old may have already been born."

6   Critics regard such claims as wildly premature. In March ten respected researchers predicted in the *New England Journal of Medicine* that "the steady rise in life expectancy during the past two centuries may soon come to an end," because rising levels of obesity are making people sicker. The research team leader, S. Jay Olshansky, of the University of Illinois School of Public Health, also worries about the "potential impact of infectious disease." Believing that medicine can and will overcome these problems, his "cautious and I think defensibly optimistic estimate" is that the average lifespan will reach eighty-five or ninety—in 2100. Even this relatively slow rate of increase, he says, will radically alter the underpinnings of human existence. "Pushing the outer limits of lifespan" will force the world to confront a situation no society has ever faced before: an acute shortage of dead people.

7   The twentieth-century jump in life expectancy transformed society. Fifty years ago senior citizens were not a force in electoral politics. Now the AARP is widely said to be the most powerful organization in Washington. Medicare, Social Security, retirement, Alzheimer's, snowbird economies, the population boom, the golfing boom, the cosmetic-surgery boom, the nostalgia boom, the recreational-vehicle boom, Viagra—increasing longevity is entangled in every one. Momentous as these changes have been, though, they will pale before what is coming next.

8   From religion to real estate, from pensions to parent-child dynamics, almost every aspect of society is based on the orderly succession of generations. Every quarter century or so, children take over from their parents—a transition as fundamental to human existence as the rotation of the planet about its axis. In tomorrow's world, if the optimists are correct, grandparents will have living grandparents; children born decades from now will ignore advice from people who watched the Beatles on *The Ed Sullivan Show*. Intergenerational warfare—the Anna Nicole Smith syndrome—will be but one consequence. Trying to envision such a world, sober social scientists find themselves discussing pregnant seventy-year-olds, offshore organ farms, protracted adolescence, and lifestyles policed by insurance companies. Indeed, if the biologists are right, the coming army of centenarians will be marching into a future so unutterably different that they may well feel nostalgia for the long-ago days of three score and ten.

9   The oldest in vitro fertilization clinic in China is located on the sixth floor of a no-star hotel in Changsha, a gritty flyover city in the south-central portion of the country. It is here that the clinic's founder and director, Lu Guangxiu, pursues her research into embryonic stem cells.

Most cells *don't* divide, in spite of what elementary school stu- 10
dents learn—they just get old and die. The body subcontracts out the job
of replacing them to a special class of cells called stem cells. Embryonic
stem cells—those in an early-stage embryo—can grow into any kind of
cell: spleen, nerve, bone, whatever. Rather than having to wait for a heart
transplant, medical researchers believe, a patient could use stem cells to
grow a new heart: organ transplant without an organ donor.

The process of extracting stem cells destroys an early-stage embryo, 11
which has led the Bush administration to place so many strictures on
stem-cell research that scientists complain it has been effectively banned
in this country. A visit to Lu's clinic not long ago suggested that ultimately
Bush's rules won't stop anything. Capitalism won't let them.

During a conversation Lu accidentally brushed some papers to the 12
floor. They were faxes from venture capitalists in San Francisco, Hong
Kong, and Stuttgart. "I get those all the time," she said. Her operation
was short of money—a chronic problem for scientists in poor countries.
But it had something of value: thousands of frozen embryos, an inevitable
byproduct of in vitro fertilizations. After obtaining permission from patients, Lu uses the embryos in her work. It is possible that she has access
to more embryonic stem cells than all U.S. researchers combined.

Sooner or later, in one nation or another, someone like Lu will cut a 13
deal: frozen embryos for financial backing. Few are the stemcell researchers who believe that their work will not lead to tissue-and-organ farms
and that these will not have a dramatic impact on the human lifespan. If
Organs Us is banned in the United States, Americans will seek out longevity centers elsewhere. As Stephen S. Hall wrote in *Merchants of Immortality*,
biotechnology increasingly resembles the software industry. Dependence
on venture capital, loathing of regulation, pathological secretiveness, penchant for hype, willingness to work overseas—they're all there. Already
the U.S. Patent Office has issued four hundred patents concerning human
stem cells.

Longevity treatments will almost certainly drive up medical costs, 14
says Dana Goldman, the director of health economics at the RAND Corporation, and some might drive them up significantly. Implanted de-
fibrillators, for example, could constantly monitor people's hearts for
signs of trouble, electrically regulating the organs when they miss a beat.
Researchers believe that the devices would reduce heart-disease deaths
significantly. At the same time, Goldman says, they would by themselves drive up the nation's health-care costs by "many billions of dollars" (Goldman and his colleagues are working on nailing down how
much), and they would be only one of many new medical interventions.
In developed nations antiretroviral drugs for AIDS typically cost about
$15,000 a year. According to James Lubitz, the acting chief of the aging
and chronic-disease statistics branch of the Centers for Disease Control's
National Center for Health Statistics, there is no a priori reason to suppose

that lifespan extension will be cheaper, that the treatments will have to be administered less frequently, or that their inventors will agree to be less well compensated. To be sure, as Ramez Naam points out in *More Than Human*, which surveys the prospects for "biological enhancement," drugs inevitably fall in price as their patents expire. But the same does not necessarily hold true for medical procedures: heart bypass operations are still costly, decades after their invention. And in any case there will invariably be newer, more effective, and more costly drugs. Simple arithmetic shows that if 80 million U.S. senior citizens were to receive $15,000 worth of treatment every year, the annual cost to the nation would be $1.2 trillion—"the kind of number," Lubitz says, "that gets people's attention."

15   The potential costs are enormous, but the United States is a rich nation. As a share of gross domestic product, the cost of U.S. health care roughly doubled from 1980 to the present, explains David M. Cutler, a health-care economists at Harvard. Yet unlike many cost increases, this one signifies that people are better off. "Would you rather have a heart attack with 1980 medicine at the 1980 price?" Clutler asks. "We get more and better treatments now, and we pay more for the additional services. I don't look at that and see an obvious disaster."

16   The critical issue, in Goldman's view, will be not the costs per se but determining who will pay them. "We're going to have a very public debate about whether this will be covered by insurance," he says. "My sense is that it won't. It'll be like cosmetic surgery—you pay out of pocket." Necessarily, a pay-as-you-go policy would limit access to longevity treatments. If high-level antiaging therapy were expensive enough, it could become a perk for movie stars, politicians, and CEOs. One can envision Michael Moore fifty years from now, still denouncing the rich in political tracts delivered through the next generation's version of the Internet— neural implants, perhaps. Donald Trump, a 108-year-old multibillionaire in 2054, will be firing the children of the apprentices he fired in 2004. Meanwhile, the maids, chauffeurs, and gofers of the rich will stare mortality in the face.

17   Short of overtly confiscating rich people's assets, it would be hard to avoid this divide. Yet as Goldman says, there will be "furious" political pressure to avert the worst inequities. For instance, government might mandate that insurance cover longevity treatments. In fact, it is hard to imagine any democratic government foolhardy enough *not* to guarantee access to those treatments, especially when the old are increasing in number and political clout. But forcing insurers to cover longevity treatments would only change the shape of the social problem. "Most everyone will want to take [the treatment]," Goldman says. "So that jacks up the price of insurance, which leads to more people uninsured. Either way, we may be bifurcating society."

18   Ultimately, Goldman suggests, the government would probably end up paying outright for longevity treatments—an enormous new

entitlement program. How could it be otherwise? Older voters would want it because it is in their interest; younger ones would want it because they, too, will age. "At the same time," he says, "nobody likes paying taxes, so there would be constant pressure to contain costs."

To control spending, the program might give priority to people with 19 healthy habits; no point in retooling the genomes of smokers, risk takers, and addicts of all kinds. A kind of reverse eugenics might occur, in which governments would freely allow the birth of people with "bad" genes but would let nature take its course on them as they aged. Having shed the baggage of depression, addiction, mental retardation, and chemical-sensitivity syndrome, tomorrow's legions of perduring old would be healthier than the young. In this scenario moralists and reformers would have a field day.

Meanwhile, the gerontocratic elite will have a supreme weapon 20 against the young: compound interest. According to a 2004 study by three researchers at the London Business School, historically the average rate of real return on stock markets worldwide has been about 5 percent. Thus a twenty-year-old who puts $10,000 in the market in 2010 should expect by 2030 to have about $27,000 in real terms—a tidy increase. But that happy forty-year-old will be in the same world as septuagenarians and octogenarians who began investing their money during the Carter administration. If someone who turned seventy in 2010 had invested $10,000 when he was twenty, he would have about $115,000. In the same twenty-year period during which the young person's account would grew from $10,000 to $27,000, the old person's account would grow from $115,000 to $305,000. Inexorably, the gap between them will widen.

The result would be a tripartite society: the very old and very rich 21 on top, beta-testing each new treatment on themselves; a mass of the ordinary old, forced by insurance into supremely healthy habits, kept alive by medical entitlement; and the diminishingly influential young. In his novel *Holy Fire* (1996) the science fiction writer and futurist Bruce Sterling conjured up a version of this dictator-ship-by-actuary: a society in which the cautions, careful centenarian rules, supremely fit and disproportionately affluent, if a little frail, look down with ennui and mild contempt on their juniors. Marxist class warfare, upgraded to the biotech era!

In the past, twenty-and thirty-year-olds had the chance of sud- 22 den windfalls in the form of inheritances. Some economists believe that bequests from previous generations have provided as much as a quarter of the start-up capital for each new one—money for college tuitions, new houses, new businesses. But the image of an ingenue's getting a leg up through a sudden bequest from Aunt Tilly will soon be a relic of late-millennium romances.

Instead of helping their juniors begin careers and families, tomor- 23 row's rich oldsters will be expending their disposable income to enhance their memories, senses, and immune systems. Refashioning their flesh to ever higher levels of performance, they will adjust their metabolisms on computers, install artificial organs that synthesize smart drugs, and swallow genetically tailored bacteria and viruses that clean out arteries, fine-tune neurons, and repair broken genes. Should one be reminded of H. G. Wells's *The Time Machine*, in which humankind is divided into two species, the ethereal Eloi and the brutish, underground-dwelling Morlocks? "As I recall," Goldman told me recently, "in that book it didn't work out very well for the Eloi."

24   When lifespans extend indefinitely, the effects are felt throughout the life cycle, but the biggest social impact may be on the young. According to Joshua Goldstein, a demographer at Princeton, adolescence will in the future evolve into a period of experimentation and education that will last from the teenage years into the midthirties. In a kind of *wanderjahr* prolonged for decades, young people will try out jobs on a temporary basis, float in and out of their parents' homes, hit the Europass-and-hostel circuit, pick up extra courses and degrees, and live with different people in different places. In the past the transition from youth to adulthood usually followed an orderly sequence: education, entry into the labor force, marriage, and parenthood. For tomorrow's thirtysomethings, suspended in what Goldstein calls "quasi-adulthood," these steps may occur in any order.

25   From our short-life-expectancy point of view, quasi-adulthood may seem like a period of socially mandated fecklessness—what Leon Kass, the chair of the President's Council on Bioethics, has decried as the coming culture of "protracted youthfulness, hedonism, and sexual license." In Japan, ever in the demographic forefront, as many as one out of three young adults is either unemployed or working part-time, and many are living rent-free with their parents. Masahiro Yamada, a sociologist at Tokyo Gakugei University, has sarcastically dubbed them *parasaito shinguru*, or "parasite singles." Adult offspring who live with their parents are common in aging Europe, too. In 2003 a report from the British Prudential finacial-services group awarded the 6.8 million British in this category the mocking name of "kippers"—"kids in parents' pockets eroding retirement savings."

26   To Kass, the main cause of this stasis is "the successful pursuit of longer life and better health." Kass's fulminations easily lend themselves to ridicule. Nonetheless, he is in many ways correct. According to Yuji Genda, an economist at Tokyo University, the drifty lives of parasite singles are indeed a byproduct of increased longevity, mainly because longer-lived seniors are holding on to their jobs. Japan, with the world's oldest population, has the highest percentage of working senior citizens of any developed nation: one out of three men over sixty-five is still on the job. Everyone in the nation, Genda says, is "tacitly aware" that the old are "blocking the door."

In a world of two-hundred-year-olds "the rate of rise in income and status perhaps for the first hundred years of life will be almost negligible," the crusty maverick economist Kenneth Boulding argued in a prescient article from 1965. "It is the propensity of the old, rich, and powerful to die that gives the young, poor, and powerless hope." (Boulding died in 1993, opening up a position for another crusty maverick economist.)

Kass believes that "human beings, once they have attained the burdensome knowledge of good and bad, should not have access to the tree of life." Accordingly, he has proposed a straightforward way to prevent the problems of youth in a society dominated by the old: "Resist the siren song of the conquest of aging and death." Senior citizens, in other words, should let nature take its course once humankind's biblical seventy-year lifespan is up. Unfortunately, this solution is self-canceling, since everyone who agrees with it is eventually eliminated. Opponents, meanwhile, live on and on. Kass, who is sixty-six, has another four years to make his case.

Increased longevity may add to marital strains. The historian Lawrence Stone was among the first to note that divorce was rare in previous centuries partly because people died so young that bad unions were often dissolved by early funerals. As people lived longer, Stone argued, divorce became "a functional substitute for death." Indeed, marriages dissolved at about the same rate in 1860 as in 1960, except that in the nineteenth century the dissolution was more often due to the death of a partner, and in the twentieth century to divorce. The corollary that children were as likely to live in households without both biological parents in 1860 as in 1960 is also true. Longer lifespans are far from the only reason for today's higher divorce rates, but the evidence seems clear that they play a role. The prospect of spending another twenty years sitting across the breakfast table from a spouse whose charm has faded must have already driven millions to divorce lawyers. Adding an extra decade or two can only exacerbate the strain.

Worse, child-rearing, a primary marital activity, will be even more difficult than it is now. For the past three decades, according to Ben J. Wattenberg, a senior fellow at the American Enterprise Institute, birth rates around the world have fallen sharply as women have taken advantage of increased opportunities for education and work outside the home. "More education, more work, lower fertility," he says. The title of Wattenberg's latest book, published in October 2004, sums up his view of tomorrow's demographic prospects: *Fewer*. In his analysis, women's continuing movement outside the home will lead to a devastating population crash—the mirror image of the population boom that shaped so much of the past century. Increased longevity will only add to the downward pressure on birth rates, by making childbearing even more difficult. During their twenties, as Goldstein's quasi-adults, men and women will be unmarried and relatively poor. In their thirties and forties they will finally grow old enough to begin meaningful careers—the worst time to have children. Waiting still longer will mean entering the maelstrom of reproductive technology, which seems likely to remain expensive, alienating, and prone to complications. Thus the parental paradox: increased longevity means *less* time for pregnancy and child-rearing, not more.

31   Even when women manage to fit pregnancy into their careers, they will spend a smaller fraction of their lives raising children than ever before. In the mid-nineteenth century, white women in the United States had a life expectancy of about forty years and typically bore five or six children. (I specify Caucasians because records were not kept for African Americans.) These women literally spent more than half their lives caring for offspring. Today U.S. white women have a life expectancy of nearly eighty and bear an average of 1.9 children—below replacement level. If a woman spaces two births close together, she may spend only a quarter of her days in the company of offspring under the age of eighteen. Children will become ever briefer parentheses in long, crowded adult existences. It seems inevitable that the bonds between generations will fray.

32   Purely from a financial standpoint, parenthood has always been a terrible deal. Mom and Dad fed, clothed, housed, and educated the kids but received little in the way of tangible return. Ever since humankind began acquiring property, wealth has flowed from older generations to younger ones. Even in those societies where children herded cattle and tilled the land for their aged progenitors, the older generation consumed so little and died off so quickly that the net movement of assets and services was always downward. "Of all the misconceptions that should be banished from discussions of aging," F. Landis MacKellar, an economist at the International Institute for Applied Systems Analysis, in Austria, wrote in the journal *Population and Development Review* in 2001, "the most persistent and egregious is that in some simpler and more virtuous age children supported their parents."

33   This ancient pattern changed at the beginning of the twentieth century, when government pension and social security schemes spread across Europe and into the Americas. Within the family parents still gave much more than they received, according to MacKellar, but under the new state plans the children in effect banded together outside the family and collectively reimbursed the parents. In the United States workers pay less to Social Security than they eventually receive; retirees are subsidized by the contributions of younger workers. But on the broadest level financial support from the young is still offset by the movement of assets within families—a point rarely noted by critics of "greedy geezers."

34   Increased longevity will break up this relatively equitable arrangement. Here concerns focus less on the super-rich than on middle-class senior citizens, those who aren't surfing the crest of compound interest. These people will face a Hobson's choice. On the one hand, they will be unable to retire at sixty-five, because the young would end up bankrupting themselves to support them—a reason why many would-be reformers

propose raising the retirement age. On the other hand, it will not be feasible for most of tomorrow's nonagenarians and centenarians to stay at their desks, no matter how fit and healthy they are.

The case against early retirement is well known. In economic jargon 35 the ratio of retirees to workers is known as the "dependency ratio," because through pension and Social Security payments people who are now in the work force funnel money to people who have left it. A widely cited analysis by three economists at the Organization for Economic Cooperation and Development estimated that in 2000 the overall dependency ratio in the United States was 21.7 retirees for every 100 workers, meaning (roughly speaking) that everyone older than sixty-five had five younger workers contributing to his pension. By 2050 the dependency ratio will have almost doubled, to 38 per 100; that is, each retiree will be supported by slightly more than two current workers. If old-age benefits stay the same, in other words, the burden on younger workers, usually in the form of taxes, will more than double.

This may be an underestimate. The OECD analysis did not assume 36 any dramatic increase in longevity or the creation of any entitlement program to pay for longevity care. If both occur, as gerontological optimists predict, the number of old will skyrocket, as will the cost of maintaining them. To adjust to these "very bad fiscal effects," says the OECD economist Pablo Antolin, one of the report's coauthors, societies have only two choices: "raising the retirement age or cutting the benefits." He continues, "This is arithmetic—it can't be avoided." The recent passage of a huge new prescription-drug program by an administration and Congress dominated by the "party of small government" suggests that benefits will not be cut. Raising the age of retirement might be more feasible politically, but it would lead to a host of new problems—see today's Japan.

In the classic job pattern, salaries rise steadily with seniority. Com- 37 panies underpay younger workers and overpay older workers as a means of rewarding employees who stay at their jobs. But as people have become more likely to shift firms and careers, the pay increases have become powerful disincentives for companies to retain employees in their fifties and sixties. Employers already worried about the affordability of older workers are not likely to welcome calls to raise the retirement age; the last thing they need is to keep middle managers around for another twenty or thirty years. "There will presumably be an elite group of super-rich who would be immune to all these pressures," Ronald Lee, an economic demographer at the University of California at Berkeley, says. "Nobody will kick Bill Gates out of Microsoft as long as he owns it. But there will be a lot of pressure on the average old person to get out."

In Lee's view, the financial downsizing need not be inhumane. One 38 model is the university, which shifted older professors to emeritus status, reducing their workload in exchange for reduced pay. Or, rather, the university *could* be a model: age-discrimination litigation and professors' unwillingness to give up their perks, Lee says, have largely torpedoed the system. "It's hard to reduce someone's salary when they are older," he says. "For the person, it's viewed as a kind of disgrace. As a culture we need to get rid of that idea."

39   The Pentagon has released few statistics about the hundreds or thousands of insurgents captured in Afghanistan and Iraq, but one can be almost certain that they are disproportionately young. Young people have ever been in the forefront of political movements of all stripes. University students protested Vietnam, took over the U.S. embassy in Tehran, filled Tiananmen Square, served as the political vanguard for the Taliban. "When we are forty," the young writer Filippo Marinetti promised in the 1909 *Futurist Manifesto*, "other younger and stronger men will probably throw us in the wastebasket like useless manuscripts—we want it to happen!"

40   The same holds true in business and science. Steve Jobs and Stephen Wozniak founded Apple in their twenties; Albert Einstein dreamed up special relativity at about the same age. For better and worse, young people in developed nations will have less chance to shake things up in tomorrow's world. Poorer countries, where the old have less access to longevity treatments, will provide more opportunity, political and financial. As a result, according to Fred C. Iklé, an analyst with the Center for Strategic and International Studies, "it is not fanciful to imagine a new cleavage opening up in the world order." On one side would be the " 'bioengineered' nations," societies dominated by the "becalmed temperament" of old people. On the other side would be the legions of youth—"the protagonists," as the political theorist Samuel Huntington has described them, "of protest, instability, reform, and revolution."

41   Because poorer countries would be less likely to be dominated by a gerontocracy, tomorrow's divide between old and young would mirror the contemporary division between rich northern nations and their poorer southern neighbors. But the consequences might be different—unpredictably so. One assumes, for instance, that the dictators who hold sway in Africa and the Middle East would not hesitate to avail themselves of longevity treatments, even if few others in their societies could afford them. Autocratic figures like Arafat, Franco, Perón, and Stalin often leave the scene only when they die. If the human lifespan lengthens greatly, the dictator in Gabriel García Márquez's *The Autumn of the Patriarch*, who is "an indefinite age somewhere between 107 and 232 years," may no longer be regarded as a product of magical realism.

42   Bioengineered nations, top-heavy with the old, will need to replenish their labor forces. Here immigration is the economist's traditional solution. In abstract terms, the idea of importing young workers from poor regions of the world seems like a win-win solution: the young get jobs, the old get cheap service. In practice, though, host nations have found that the foreigners in their midst are stubbornly . . . foreign. European nations are wondering whether they really should have let in so many Muslims. In the United States, traditionally hospitable to migrants, bilingual

education is under attack and the southern border is increasingly locked down. Japan, preoccupied by *Nihonjinron* (theories of "Japaneseness"), has always viewed immigrants with suspicion if not hostility. Facing potential demographic calamity, the Japanese government has spent millions trying to develop a novel substitute for immigrants: robots smart and deft enough to take care of the aged.

According to Ronald Lee, the Berkeley demographer, rises in 43 life expectancy have in the past stimulated economic growth. Because they arose mainly from reductions in infant and child mortality, these rises produced more healthy young workers, which in turn led to more-productive societies. Believing they would live a long time, those young workers saved more for retirement than their forebears, increasing society's stock of capital—another engine of growth. But these positive effects are offset when increases in longevity come from old people's neglecting to die. Older workers are usually less productive than younger ones, earning less and consuming more. Worse, the soaring expenses of entitlement programs for the old are likely, Lee believes, "to squeeze out government expenditures on the next generation," such as education and childhood public-health programs. "I think there's evidence that something like this is already happening among the industrial countries," he says. The combination will force a slowdown in economic growth: the economic pie won't grow as fast. But there's a bright side, at least potentially. If the fall in birth rates is sufficiently vertiginous, the number of people sharing that relatively smaller pie may shrink fast enough to let everyone have a bigger piece. One effect of the longevity-induced "birth dearth" that Wattenburg fears, in other words, may be higher per capita incomes.

For the past thirty years the United States has financed its budget 44 deficits by persuading foreigners to buy U.S. Treasury bonds. In the nature of things, most of these foreigners have lived in other wealthy nations, especially Japan and China. Unfortunately for the United States, those other countries are marching toward longevity crises of their own. They, too, will have fewer young, productive workers. They, too, will be paying for longevity treatments for the old. They, too, will be facing a grinding economic slowdown. For all these reasons they may be less willing to finance our government. If so, Uncle Sam will have to raise interest rates to attract investors, which will further depress growth—a vicious circle.

Longevity-induced slowdowns could make young nations more 45 attractive as investment targets, especially for the cash-strapped pension-and-insurance plans in aging countries. The youthful and ambitious may well follow the money to where the action is. If Mexicans and Guatemalans have fewer rich old people blocking their paths, the river of migration may begin to flow in the other direction. In a reverse brain drain, the Chinese coast guard might discover half-starved American postgraduates stuffed into the holds of smugglers' ships. Highways out of Tijuana or Nogales might bear road signs telling drivers to watch out for *norteamericano* families running across the blacktop, the children's Hello Kitty backpacks silhouetted against a yellow warning background.

46   Given that today nobody knows precisely how to engineer major increases in the human lifespan, contemplating these issues may seem premature. Yet so many scientists believe that some of the new research will pay off, and that lifespans will stretch like taffy, that it would be shortsighted not to consider the consequences. And the potential changes are so enormous and hard to grasp that they can't be understood and planned for at the last minute. "By definition," says Aubrey de Grey, the Cambridge geneticist, "you live with longevity for a very long time."

Content

1. Why does Mann begin his essay with the court case over J. Howard Marshall's estate? What's at the heart of "intergenerational warfare" (¶ 3)?

2. Mann reports that average life expectancy is predicted to reach the late 80s or early 90s by the end of this century (¶s 4, 6). According to Mann, what are some of the issues associated with increases in average life expectancy (¶s 7–8)? Which of these issues are primarily socioeconomic (Social Security), personal or behavioral (Viagra), or ethical ("pregnant seventy year-olds")? Which seem the most serious? Which seem to call for public policy decisions? Discuss Carolita Johnson's cartoon ("I never thought turning eighty would be so much fun," 375) in respect to the ethical and social policy issues it raises.

3. Why are embryonic stem cells in demand? According to Mann, why are attempts to restrict stem-cell research futile (¶s 10–13)?

4. Why are medical procedures that expand longevity likely to drive up health care costs (¶ 14)? What issues does Mann raise in his discussion of who will pay for these longevity treatments (¶s 16–19)? Why does Mann argue that "it would be hard to avoid this divide" between those who can access these treatments and those who can't (¶ 17)? What forces might increase general access to longevity treatments and what pressures might restrict such access (¶s 17–18)?

5. Why, according to Mann, does the prospect of a longer average life expectancy suggest the development of "a tripartite society" (¶ 21)? What assumptions does he make about voting behavior (¶ 18), public policy (¶s 18–19), savings rates (¶ 20), and spending habits (¶ 23) in predicting this outcome?

6. How does Mann believe longer life spans will affect the young (¶s 24–27)? Marriage and the family (¶s 29–31)? The intergenerational flow of wealth (¶s 32–34)? The structure of the labor market (¶s 35–37)? The divide between the developed and undeveloped countries (¶s 40–42)? Economic growth (¶s 43–45)?

Strategies/Structures/Language

7. Mann argues that longevity treatments might lead to a "kind of reverse eugenics" (¶ 19). Explain the steps in his line of reasoning. What assumptions does he make? Do you detect any flaws in his argument? Find other examples of claims Mann makes that depend on debatable assumptions. For example, examine his claim that "tomorrow's rich oldsters will be expending their disposable income to

enhance their memories, senses, and immune systems" (¶ 23) and that "increased longevity means *less* time for pregnancy and child-rearing, not more" (¶ 30). Can you make a counterargument to these claims based on the evidence and logic Mann provides?

For Writing

8. ***Journal Writing.*** Many films and books explore the human desire to prolong life indefinitely through science, black magic, or a vampire's bite. Explore the fascination with such narratives, perhaps by analyzing in detail a film or novel that you particularly like. How does the narrative resolve the quest for immortality? How does it characterize death?

9. ***Dialogues.*** Mann argues that capitalism will invariably lead to the development of "longevity centers" (¶s 11–13) whose treatments will be in near-universal demand (¶ 17). Bill McKibben, in "Designer Genes" (515–25), similarly argues that market forces dictate that in our consumerist culture germline genetic engineering, once introduced, "will accelerate endlessly and unstoppably into the future" (¶ 38). How does each author depict social forces opposing such developments? Write an essay based on the evidence and arguments in "The Coming Death Shortage" and "Designer Genes" in which you argue that social and community structures will work to restrict market forces in the allocation of medical advances such as longevity treatments and genetic engineering. Do you expect your current position to change as you yourself grow older? As you deal with—and make decisions for and about—aging parents or grandparents?

"I never thought turning eighty would be so much fun!"

10. **Mixed Modes.** Mann includes several terms in his description of the social conflicts that might arise with increasing life expectancy, including *"maximum lifespan"* (¶ 4), "engineered negligible senescence" (¶ 5), "embryonic stem cells" (¶ 10), "kippers" (¶ 25), "the dependency ratio" (¶ 35), "gerontocracy" (¶ 41), and *"Nihonjinron"* (¶ 42). How are the definitions of these terms—and others—critical to his argument? How does he introduce each definition? Where in the paragraph does the definition appear? What is the pattern of these definitions? Why is it effective?

MEGAN McGUIRE

Megan McGuire was born in 1983, grew up in Connecticut, and earned a BA in English and political science from the University of Connecticut in 2005. A member of the Army National Guard in college, she was commissioned as a Second Lieutenant soon after graduation. But this just scratches the surface.

Of her essay, she writes, "I generally do not reflect that often on my life growing up or how I got to where I am. I'm satisfied with what I've accomplished, who I am, and where I'm headed. I count myself lucky to have lived in two very different kinds of environments while growing up, one of which that was filled with love and support and fulfilled all the stereotypical ideas of childhood. I played outside until the streetlights came on and spent my summers at my grandparents' lake house. The other portion of my late childhood and adolescence was somewhat of a culture shock. Its forced independence created self-sufficiency and responsibility that, although acquired in a less than favorable way, have just as adequately contributed to my general successes in life as the more cushioned existence I experienced earlier. I never intended to record any portions of my life, but as a class assignment I began to do so and was surprised at the flooding of memories that I had almost forgotten. I was also surprised at how liberating it was to put parts of my life on paper. I felt as if I had inadvertently explained myself and who I am, answering some questions I didn't even know I had and revealing even more—a fulfilling experience that I plan to pursue further."

Wake Up Call

1   *It was morning. My father just left my room. He had come in, as he came in every morning Monday through Friday, to inform me that it was no longer time for dreaming, the time had come to wake up and prepare for another monotonous day at school. Even at the age of ten the ability to wake up early eluded me. I gradually forced my eyes open, first briefly, then for a period of*

thirty seconds. Each time I opened my eyes I would stay awake a little longer. I did this every morning, partially denying that I had to leave the comfort of my warm bed, waiting for my second warning yell from down the hall that I was going to be late if I didn't wake up soon. I stared up at the canopy that covered my bed. I had begged for a canopy bed for years and one summer my father found one at a tag sale for a price we could afford. I loved that bed. It had a white frame and a royal blue canopy, with a miniature floral print. There were many times that I greatly desired something, and although I may have had to wait, I almost always got what I asked for if I wanted it long enough. Everyone has fleeting wants, but if the need was persistent, my father always came through.

Along with the bed, I had always wanted a typewriter. As far back as I can   2 remember I loved books. I don't remember learning to read, but I remember sitting on my father's lap while he read one of his big books, following along to the sound of his voice. We made constant trips to the local library; just being around books was exciting. I don't remember struggling to read but I remember the first book I ever read, an early learning book, a "Spot, the Dog" book, and I read it cover to cover. I became an insatiable reader and decided very young that I wanted to be a writer. For my birthday one year I was given an old typewriter, an antique. The keys were the traditional punch keys and I spent a good week figuring out how to insert the paper and not have my words type diagonally across the page. I soon learned that being a writer was not an easy task. First I actually needed to have something to write about and second, it was very time consuming. I decided, therefore, to enjoy my love of books and revisit the profession of writing at a later date, when I had something of significance to say.

School allowed an outlet for my desire to write by providing me topics to   3 write about so I didn't have to think them up on my own. I enjoyed school but could never figure out why it required being up so early in the morning. It was a struggle, to be sure. This particular morning was no different. I eventually rolled out of bed. My clothes were still in a laundry basket by the door to my room. Dad was great, but he never seemed to get the hang of putting clothes away. I sifted through until I found something to wear. I chose a pair of jeans with a patch across the knee that my grandmother had sewn on for me and a black t-shirt decorated by yours truly using crafty puff paint, a trend at the time and very cool. I managed to find a pair of somewhat matching socks and donned them as well. I learned to do my own hair very early on. Dad never seemed to master anything beyond a lopsided ponytail and my older sister was far too busy being thirteen to help me, so I quickly braided my long blond hair and stepped off toward the kitchen, wishing I knew how to French-braid so I could have a nice hair-do like my girly classmates. Instead I looked as if I couldn't decide whether or not I wanted to be Barbie or Ken.

Breakfast consisted of a bowl of cereal which I inhaled quickly. My brother   4 was still in bed. It might have been difficult waking me up for school, but it was impossible to wake up my brother. There was actually a time when he was dragged physically to school by my father and upon arriving he jumped out of the car, ran *away, was chased down, caught and physically dragged into the building, kicking and screaming, by not only my father but the principal as well. It was disconcerting at the time and is now merely comical. I kissed Dad goodbye and hurried out of our apartment to the bus stop. My Dad was home when I left for school and I knew he would be home waiting for me at 3:20 when I stepped through the door. We were on state, I wasn't sure at the time what that meant, but I knew it meant Dad didn't have to work and at the grocery store we paid for food with colorful stamps that looked like my play money but apparently had more value. It also meant that during the holidays we went to the town hall and were given presents that were labeled "Girl 8–10" and "Boy 11–12" and we got to meet Santa. I knew we didn't have a lot of money, certainly not like my friend Lauren who lived in a big old colonial house, had a playroom in addition to her own room, but I had a canopy bed, a typewriter, and I knew my Dad was always home if I needed him. There was never a day when I wasn't hugged or kissed or told I was loved. I was happy.*

5   It is morning. My alarm clock is blaring in my ear from across the room for the second time. Snooze is a wonderful thing. I'm lucky this morning, my alarm clock actually works. It is possibly the oldest alarm clock, most certainly older then I am even at ten. The digital numbers sometimes fade on and off, but if I am lucky, it will burst to life at the appointed time in the morning and emit the most horrendous static sound, eventually forcing me awake. Rolling out of bed is easy, my bed consists of a mattress on the floor, the box spring adds some elevation to the mattress and acts as a substitute for a real frame. I sort through a large brown plastic garbage bag filled with clothes and find something suitable to wear. I put on a pair of stretchy elastic pants that were purchased at Ames as part of my back to school shopping and an oversized t-shirt that belonged to my mother. I can't seem to find a pair of socks. I vaguely remember leaving my laundry in the washing machine overnight. I walk into my older sister's room quietly and softly open her top drawer and steal a clean pair of socks. I stealthily exit the room and return to my own.

6   I share my room with my younger sister. I don't think our room was designed as a bedroom. The stairs lead directly to our room from the bottom floor and the two actual bedrooms and bathroom branch off our room that is something akin to a loft. My brother has one of the bedrooms and my older sister has the other. I hop into the bathroom, hairspray my hair into some wavelike fashion statement that epitomizes coolness and head downstairs. I spend a good twenty minutes leashing our four dogs up outside and as a result leave myself no time for breakfast. I head into the kitchen to see if there is anything quick I can grab and take with me. I try to be quiet, only a curtain separates my mother's room from the kitchen and I don't want to wake her up. She must have made it home late last night, I don't remember hearing her come in. I open the fridge, no milk. I grab a couple of pieces of bread and head out to the bus.

On the way down the dirt driveway I drag one of the large garbage 7 barrels from the back of the house, Monday, trash day. It tips over when I snag it on a rock and all the contents spill out into the drive. Fabulous. I pick up what I can, trying not to get dirty. I stain my shirt. I don't have time to change and I don't think I have anything else clean to wear. My brother follows me outside, along with my younger sister. We wait outside the house for the bus. Our house is an old colonial that was moved from one side of town to its current location at some point in its history. It was placed on an unstable rocky foundation and as a result has settled nicely so that all the floors are bowed in one way or another. The paint is a yellowish color and is excessively chipped, giving the surface a textured appearance. The house is blocked from sight on one side by large bushes and from the front by a large tree. I am ashamed of our house. It looks dilapidated and old, nothing like the nicely vinyl sided homes on the rest of our street. I am happy there are bushes and trees hiding it from sight.

I sit in the back corner of the class. In my other school it was cool to 8 sit in the back, but apparently here the cool kids sit in front. Bad move. Everyone here wears jeans. If I had bought jeans I would have only been allowed to pick one outfit at Ames, so I bought stretch pants so I could have two outfits when school started. I still haven't determined how I am going to alternate what I wear. If I interchange tops with bottoms I still only have four outfits. There are five days in a school week, so I will have to repeat at least once. The other kids will remember what I wear. I want a pair of dark blue jeans like the pretty girl in the front row. She has dark hair in a French-braid, blue jeans and a pretty clean white shirt with ruffles on the collar. Her name is Kate. I know the answers to all the questions the teacher asks but I don't raise my hand. Smart kids are not cool. In my other school they called me Webster. I was like a dictionary. I get put in a remedial math level due to my less than enthusiastic effort but wish I had tried harder, all the cool kids were in advanced math. Tricky, tricky.

It is morning. I am freezing. I could swear the cold breeze outside 9 comes right through the drafty closed window of my room. What time is it? My alarm clock didn't go off. I look across the room and the digital numbers are not there. No one is up. If I don't get up, no one gets up. My brother doesn't bother if I don't force him and my little sister relies on the same clock that we share in our room. My older sister doesn't need to get up. Her boyfriend and she sleep until he has to go to work at noon. She feels better now; the morning sickness isn't so bad anymore. I climb out of bed; the floor feels like a sheet of ice against my bare feet. I grab the oversized robe on the floor and put it over my already layered clothing. I flick the light switch and nothing happens. Was there a storm? How come there isn't any power?

10   The bathroom has a little more light; the window is on the one side of the house not smothered by vegetation. I glance in the mirror and notice that there is a black substance crusted under my nose and on my eyelashes. My little sister has it on her nose too. I wash my face off and head downstairs. The kerosene heater is covered in the black substance too; it must be some kind of soot. The TV won't turn on. I still have no idea what time it is. The thermostat is turned all the way down. We must be out of oil again. The living room houses the kerosene heater and is the warmest room in the house. Mom isn't home; she must have left for work already. On the dining room table is my permission slip that is due today. She forgot to sign it. I grab a pen and sign her name as authoritatively as I can, and I realize it doesn't matter since I missed the bus anyway. I go to the bathroom downstairs, the ceramic on the toilet is ice cold so I try to hover over it in the same manner as I would a public bathroom. I try to flush, the water goes down but nothing replenishes the bowl, this seems somewhat odd. I crank the handle on the sink and the faucet responds with a funny noise and no water comes out.

11   I pick up the phone and dial Mom at work. At least something works. I'm on hold for about five minutes and she finally picks up. I get yelled at for not being in school. How could I have missed the bus? Does she have to be home to do everything? I'm ten years old, I should be able to wake up and get to school without her holding my hand. Where is Amber? Mom, we have no electricity and no water for some reason and the kerosene heater is broken and we need to go to the store when you get home, there isn't anything to eat. There's plenty to eat, make something, I'll be home around seven.

12   The fridge has milk and eggs and various condiments. It feels warm and the light doesn't turn on when I open the door. I go into the mudroom to look for something to make. The shelves are lined with jars filled with tomatoes, green beans and mixed vegetables. I remember the Saturday during the summer when Mom showed me how to jar the vegetables from the garden to preserve them. It was fun. I had never jarred vegetables before. Now they were the only things that looked back at me, the jars of vegetables and a box of brownie mix. At ten years old vegetables are still the less appetizing of the two, so I grab the box of brownie mix and head to the kitchen. I forget we have an electric stove. I take a couple of pieces of bread and head to the living room, still no TV.

13   I put on some clothes and take four dollars of change out of the change jar in my Mom's room. I walk the two miles to Cumberland Farms and buy some cookies and a couple of Airheads, my favorite kind of candy. I pass the library on the way back, situated in the old center of town, next to the police station and the old town hall. No TV, might as well get a book. I take out *The Witch of Blackbird Pond*. I love this book because it mentions the meadows near my house, the

great expanse of fields that stretch from Rocky Hill to Wethersfield and through Glastonbury. I love going there when I want to feel alone and put my life into perspective. In the summer I lie in the field and watch the clouds float by.

When I get home everyone is up. I hear Amber yelling. She needs to get out of this place, this is bullshit, she can't wait to move out. She doesn't go to school right now, she'd be a freshman this year. I can't wait until high school. I spend my afternoon reading my book. Mom gets home at about 8:30. She's carrying a Styrofoam to-go container. She stopped at Angellino's for dinner on the way home with a girlfriend from work. The house is dark. I was able to find a candle and it was flickering on the dining room table. She smiles and takes three oil lamps out of a paper bag and sets them on the table. Late one month and they just shut you off. I have a feeling we were late more than just one month but I don't say it. I learn that if you fill the toilet bowl with enough snow it will flush automatically. The pipes must have froze, when the hell is he going to come and fix that damn furnace, I pay way too much for this place. She says this, but I know I haven't seen the oil truck here in weeks. I use a towel and a bowl of water from a bottle to wash up by the light of the oil lamp. Amber and Mom are fighting. How can you go out for dinner? We have no food here, no electricity, no water. The argument continues until Mom slaps her. Amber leaves. I go downstairs and Mom shows me the jeans she bought. I think about the pair I've been industriously saving for every week by cleaning an old lady's house: four floors for $13.50. I wonder how much hers cost.

After a certain length of time if a family is without heat or running water the town lets you stay in a hotel for free. The four of us share a room at the Suisse Chalet. I don't know where Amber is. I call it the Sleazy Chalet and everybody laughs. It's nice to watch TV. I haven't seen the Simpsons in four weeks. We stay at the Chalet for a week. Sometimes Mom would work really early and we wouldn't have a ride to school. It is a nice vacation. When we get home on Friday there is a pink notice on our back door. On Monday we are at the Howard Johnson's and our household goods are in storage. It is a much better motel. Bickford's is right at the bottom of the hill so I can walk and get pancakes if I'm hungry. Mike works there and now Amber does too, so I don't have to pay. I start at my new school next week. It's cool because it's the same town my Dad grew up in. He said some of his old teachers are still there. I'll be happy to get back to school. I've missed a lot.

It is afternoon. I just walked home from school. There's a pink note on our door. Looks like I'm not graduating here, good thing I didn't order a class ring. I've seen four pink notes since eighth grade, this is nothing new. I'm an expert packer. It's just like Tetris, everything will fit if you do it right. I make sure I leave out everything that I'll need, clothes and schoolbooks. I also throw anything with sentimental value into a bag. So much gets lost.

17   Three weeks I have been living in New Britain. I can't stand it here. I don't like this guy, Mom's friend or not. I'm sleeping on the floor living out of my duffel bag. Amber should be here any minute. She moved back to Connecticut from North Carolina just this week. What a relief. Should I leave a note for Mom? I wonder how long it will take her to notice I'm gone? I'm a coward. I have every reason to leave but I can't force myself to tell her I'm going. I need to get back to school or I won't graduate. What if she cries? What if she tries to make me feel guilty, like I'm abandoning her? She always "tries" so hard for us but it's not enough. I know I can do better on my own. No matter how hard I have to work, I will give myself stability.

18   I missed three weeks of school. Fortunately my new school doesn't know this so I'm still on track to graduate. Mom hasn't called yet. I got a job. Maybe I'll have enough money to buy a car soon. Getting to work is difficult having no transportation other than my own two feet. Location severely limits my job options. My apartment is nice. My job has time and a half on Sunday so if I work every Sunday and at least five nights I'm hoping I'll be able to save a little. I wake up, go to school, go to work and study into the waning hours of the night. I'm always exhausted, only one more year until college. My grandmother always said that if I wanted to go to college I would have to work hard. Your mother won't help you and your father can't help you so you better study hard and get a scholarship. I study hard. I'm graduating in the top ten of my class but I haven't gotten any scholarships.

19   It's late. I just got home from work. My feet hurt. I'm 21 years old. I am a full-time student. I have two jobs and I am in the Army National Guard. I've lived on my own since I was 17. I'm always tired and always busy. My apartment is always warm, even if it means working more hours and there is food in my house. Sometimes I sit in my apartment and wonder what my life would be like if Dad hadn't gotten sick and I never moved in with my mother. We didn't have money, but I had a lot. I moved away and learned what it meant to work, what it meant to be hungry and cold, and what the world is really like. I saw what selfishness and bad habits could do. I learned about everything I didn't want to be. Maybe it was the combination of the two worlds. The beginning of my life was filled with love and support and I truly believed I could be anything I wanted to be as long as I worked hard. The latter portion of my adolescence taught me how to work hard. If I was never truly in want of anything would I be as motivated to be so much more than what I came from? I don't resent any part of my life. Everything that was has made me what I am. I'm lucky.

Content

1. McGuire presents examples of good and poor parenting. What are the components of each? Can you infer from her essay the factors that contribute to each parent's "style" of parenting? From the details McGuire presents, is it possible for readers to construct a more sympathetic interpretation of her mother than might initially meet the eye?

2. What kind of personality and character does McGuire have? Is this consistent throughout her childhood? How would you account for her strength of character and purpose?

3. Megan and her older sister appear to be turning out very differently during adolescence. To what extent can this be attributed to the parenting they have experienced? By the end of the narrative, McGuire is clearly headed for professional success and personal happiness. Has she overridden her upbringing, benefited from it, or both?

Strategies/Structures/Language

4. What is the tone of this piece? Is it consistent throughout? Self-pity and self-congratulation generally turn off readers; do you detect any shred of either in this piece? If so, where? If not, why not?

5. Throughout the essay, material objects assume symbolic value: how are readers expected to interpret the canopy bed (¶ 1), the "colorful stamps" (¶ 4), "presents labeled 'Girl 8–10'" (¶ 4), the various items of Megan's clothing (¶s 3, 4, 5, 8) and her mother's new jeans (¶ 8), the "dilapidated" old colonial house (¶ 7), the "pink notice" (¶s 15, 16)?

For Writing

6. **Journal Writing.** When and where did you feel safe as a child? Identify the external and psychological circumstances that contributed to that sense of security. Did you or do you associate that security with particular material objects or with specific activities?

7. **Mixed Modes.** This essay implies an ideal of parenting. With a partner, construct the definition of an ideal parent (or father or mother) whose good parenting would produce an ideal child. Identify and explain several characteristics of the ideal, both parent and child.

8. How can people emerge from disastrous upbringing as strong, capable, and powerful adults? Explain, analyzing the example of your own life or that of someone you know, or the life of a public figure including writers represented in *The Essay Connection* such as Frederick Douglass (86–91) or Martin Luther King, Jr. (399–413). You may wish to consult some of the writings on resilience, or positive psychology, by authors such as Martin Seligman and Mihaly Csikszentmihalyi (see, for example, *The American Psychologist*, January 2000 and March 2001 issues).

Additional Topics for Writing Comparison and Contrast

(For strategies for writing comparison and contrast, p. 339)

Multiple Strategies for Writing: Comparison and Contrast

In writing on any of the comparison and contrast topics below, you can employ assorted strategies to make the comparisons more meaningful and the contrasts sharp and distinctive, and to interpret their significance.

- *Definitions* of essential terms, component parts
- *Verbal illustrations* and *examples*, to show the meaning or significance of the comparison and contrast
- *Photographs, drawings, diagrams, maps*, to reinforce the verbal illustrations
- *Explanations* and *analyses* of the similarities and differences
- *Division* and *classification*, to illustrate the parts of the whole
- A *narrative*, on occasion, to allow the meaning of the term to emerge gradually as the tale unfolds
- *Negation*, to show why one part is unlike the other

1. Write an essay, full of examples, that compares and contrasts any of the following pairs:

a. Two people with a number of relevant characteristics in common (two of your teachers, roommates, friends, lovers, employers, clergy, relatives playing the same role—that is, two of your siblings, two of your grandparents, a father or mother and a step-parent)

b. Two cities or regions of the country you know well, or two neighborhoods you have lived in

c. Two comparable historical figures with similar positions, such as two presidents, two senators, two generals, two explorers, two immigrants from the same home country

d. Two religions or two sects or churches within the same religion

e. Two utopian communities (real or imaginary)

f. Two explanations or interpretations of the same scientific, economic, religious, psychological, or political phenomenon (for instance, creationism versus Darwinism; Freudian versus Skinnerian theory of behavior)

g. The cuisine of two different countries or two or more parts of a country (Greek versus French cooking; Szechuan, Cantonese, and Peking Chinese food)

2. Write a balanced essay involving a comparison and contrast of one of the subjects below that justifies your preference for one over the other. Write for a reader who is likely to debate your choice.

a. An American-made versus foreign-made product (specify the country, the manufacturers, and the make/model or other distinguishing characteristics)

b. The styles of two performers—musicians, actors or actresses, dancers, athletes participating in the same sport, comedians

c. The work of two writers, painters, theater or film directors; or two (or three) works by the same writer or painter

d. Two political parties, candidates for the same office, campaigns, or machines, past or present

e. Two colleges or universities (or programs or sports teams within them) that you know well

f. Two styles of friendship, courtship, marriage, or family (both may be contemporary, or you may compare and contrast past and present styles)

g. Two academic majors, professions, or careers

h. Life in the mainstream or on the margin (specify of which group, community, or society)

3. Write an essay, by yourself or with a partner, for an audience of fellow students, comparing the reality with the ideal of one of the following:

a. Dating or courtship styles

b. Your current job and the most satisfying job you could have

c. Your current accomplishment in a particular area (sports, a performing art, a skill, or a level of knowledge) with what you hope to attain

d. Friendship

e. Parenthood

f. Your present dwelling and your dream house

g. The way you currently spend your leisure time, or money, the way you'd like to spend it, and the way you think you *ought* to spend it

h. The present state of affairs versus the future prospects of some issue of social significance, such as world population, ecology, the control of nuclear arms, the activities and treatment of international terrorists, an appropriate climate for world peace. These are huge topics; you will need to refine them further to discuss in a single paper.

Appealing to Reason: Deductive and Inductive Arguments

When you write persuasively you're trying to move your readers to either belief or action or both, as the "Declaration of Independence" (393–97) reveals. You can do this through appealing to their reasons, their emotions, or their sense of ethics, as you know if you've ever tried to prove a point on an exam or change an attitude in a letter to the editor. Photographer Gordon Parks's "American Gothic" 1942 (395) that accompanies The Declaration is an homage to Grant Wood's famous "American Gothic" 1929 painting, in which two motionless, iconic figures in front of a plain white wooden farmhouse stare impassively at the viewer, the balding farmer, in overalls and a black suit jacket, holding erect a three-pronged pitchfork as if to protect himself and his aproned wife. By posing the African-American cleaning woman, flanked by an erect broom and mop whose volume nearly equals hers, in front of an American flag, Parks combines title and image to comment on the inequalities of opportunity, ownership, and citizenship in the land of the free, and to argue for change. Other pictures, cartoons, and visual images can also make their points with eloquent succinctness. Evan Eisenberg's satiric commentary, "Dialogue Boxes You Should Have Read More Carefully" (415–16) critiques Microsoft's near-monopoly, while the allegorical cartoon, "The Road to Success," although first published a century ago, maps out that road in value-laden terms still relevant today (417). In Chapter 10 we discuss appeals to emotion and ethics; here we'll concentrate on argumentation.

An argument, as we're using the term here, does not mean a knock-down confrontation over an issue: "Philadelphia is the most wonderful place in the world to live!" "No, it's not. Social snobbery has ruined the City of Brotherly Love." Nor is an argument hard-sell brainwashing that admits of no alternatives: "America—love it or leave it!" When you write an argument, however, as a reasonable writer you'll present a reasonable proposition that states what you believe. ("In the twenty-first century, the United States will continue to remain the best country in the world for freedom, democracy, and the opportunity to succeed.") You'll need to offer logic, evidence, and perhaps emotional appeals, to try to convince your readers of the merits of what you say. Sometimes, but not always, you'll also argue that they should adopt a particular course of action.

Tim Berners-Lee, inventor of the World Wide Web, presents such an argument in "Long Live the Web: A Call for Continued Open Standards and Neutrality" (429–38). Here he argues for the preservation of its fundamental, "profound concept," "that any person could share information with anyone else, anywhere"—free of charge. Vigilance must protect and preserve "Open standards," which "drive innovation" and enable "linked data" that enable a free exchange of "knowledge about how to cure diseases, foster business value and govern our world more effectively" (¶ 37)–thereby enabling the Web to fulfill its goal, "to serve humanity" (¶ 42). Through expert evidence, statements of principle, and analogies (the Web "brings principles established in the U.S. Constitution, the British Magna Carta . . . into the network age: freedom from being snooped on, filtered, censored and disconnected" (¶ 5), he makes his point.

Unless you're writing an indirect argument that makes its point through satire, irony, an imagined character whose actions or life story illustrate a point (see Jonathan Swift, "A Modest Proposal," [461–68]), or some other oblique means, you'll probably want to identify the issue at hand and justify its significance early in the essay: "Mandatory drug testing is essential for public officials with access to classified information." If it's a touchy subject, you may wish at this point to demonstrate good will toward readers likely to disagree with you by showing the basis for your common concern: "Most people would agree that it's important to protect children and adolescents from harmful influences." You could follow this by acknowledging the merits of their valid points: "And it's also true that drug abuse is currently a national crisis, and deserves immediate remedy." You'll need to follow this with an explanation of why, nevertheless, your position is better than theirs: "But mandatory drug testing for everyone would be a violation of their civil liberties, incredibly costly, and subject to abuse through misuse of the data."

There are a number of suitable ways to organize the body of your argument. If your audience is inclined to agree with much of what you say, you might want to put your strongest point first and provide the most evidence for that, before proceeding to the lesser points, arranged in order of descending importance:

1. Mandatory drug testing for everyone is unconstitutional.
       (three paragraphs)
2. Mandatory drug testing would be extremely costly, an expense grossly disproportionate to the results.
       (two paragraphs)

3. The results of mandatory drug testing would be easy to abuse—to falsify, to misreport, to misinterpret.

    (one paragraph)

4. Consequently, mandatory drug testing for everyone would cause more problems than it would solve.

    (conclusion—one paragraph)

For an antagonistic audience you could do the reverse, beginning with the points easiest to accept or agree with and concluding with the most difficult. Or you could work from the most familiar to the least familiar parts.

No matter what organizational pattern you choose, you'll need to provide supporting evidence—through specific examples, facts and figures, the opinions of experts, case histories, narratives, analogies, considerations of cause and effect. Any or all of these techniques can be employed in either *inductive* or *deductive* reasoning. Chances are that most of your arguments will proceed by induction. You might use an individual example intended as representative of the whole, as Scott Russell Sanders does in "Under the Influence: Paying the Price of My Father's Booze" (180–91), anatomizing his father's alcoholism to illustrate the alcoholic's characteristic behavior.

Or you might use a larger number of examples and apply inductive reasoning to prove a general proposition. Research scientists and detectives work this way, as do some social commentators and political theorists. Robert Reich identifies the characteristics of "The Global Elite" (419–27) and uses them both to counteract the myths that the United States is a benevolent, egalitarian society and to argue against the separatism—moral and economic secession—that upper-income Americans currently practice to dissociate themselves from responsibilities toward the rest of society.

An essay of deductive reasoning proceeds from a general proposition to a specific conclusion. The model for a deductive argument is the syllogism, a three-part sequence that begins with a major premise, is followed by a minor premise, and leads to a conclusion. Aristotle's classic example of this basic logical pattern is

> Major premise: All men are mortal.
> Minor premise: Socrates is a man.
> Conclusion: Therefore, Socrates is mortal.

Sometimes an essay will identify all parts of the syllogism; sometimes one or more parts will be implied. In "The Declaration of Independence" (393–97), Thomas Jefferson and his coauthors explore the consequences of the explicitly stated propositions that "all men are created equal" and that, as a consequence, their "unalienable Rights" cannot be denied.

In his classic essay, "Letter from Birmingham Jail" (399–413), Martin Luther King, Jr.—shown in a 1966 photograph on p. 401 escorting black children to a newly integrated school—argues for the proposition that "one has a moral responsibility to disobey unjust laws" and uses a vast range of resources to demonstrate his point. He uses biblical and historical examples to explain the situation in Birmingham; illustrations from his own life and from the lives of his own children and other victims of racial segregation; and more generalized incidents of brutal treatment of "unarmed, nonviolent Negroes."

He identifies the process of nonviolent resistance: "collection of the facts to determine whether injustices exist; negotiation; self-purification; and direct action" (¶ 6). In the course of making his main argument, Dr. King addresses a host of lesser arguments: "Why direct action? . . . Isn't negotiation a better path?" (¶ 10); Why not give local politicians time to act? (¶ 12); Wait! What's the rush? (¶s 13, 23–25); "How can you advocate breaking some laws and obeying others?" (¶ 15), with a related consideration, What is the difference between a just and an unjust law? (¶s 16 ff); "I would agree with St. Augustine that 'an unjust law is no law at all'" (¶ 15). Isn't your nonviolent approach "extremist" (¶s 31 ff)? Why not let the white church handle this (¶s 32–35)? All of Dr. King's illustrations and answers lead to one conclusion: "We will reach the goal of freedom in Birmingham and all over the nation, because the goal of America is freedom. Abused and scorned though we may be, our destiny is tied up with America's destiny" (¶ 44).

No matter what your argumentative strategy, you will want to avoid *logical fallacies*, errors of reasoning that can lead you to the wrong conclusion. The most common logical fallacies to be aware of are the following:

- *Arguing from analogy*: Comparing only similarities between things, concepts, or situations while overlooking significant differences that might weaken the argument. "Having a standing army is just like having a loaded gun in the house. If it's around, people will want to use it."
- *Argumentation ad hominem* (from Latin, "argument to the man"): Attacking a person's ideas or opinions by discrediting him or her as a person. "Napoleon was too short to be a distinguished general." "She was seen at the Kit Kat Lounge three nights last week; she can't possibly be a good mother."
- *Argument from doubtful or unidentified authority*: Treating an unqualified, unreliable, or unidentified source as an expert on the subject at hand. "They say you can't get pregnant the first time." "'History is bunk!' said Henry Ford."
- *Begging the question*: Regarding as true from the start what you set out to prove; asserting that what is true is true. "Rapists and murderers awaiting trial shouldn't be let out on bail" assumes that the suspects have already been proven guilty, which is the point of the impending trial.

- *Arguing in a circle*: Demonstrating a premise by a conclusion and a conclusion by a premise. "People should give 10 percent of their income to charity because that is the right thing to do. Giving 10 percent of one's income to charity is the right thing to do because it is expected."
- *Either/or reasoning*: Restricting the complex aspects of a difficult problem or issue to only one of two possible solutions. "You're not getting any younger. Marry me or you'll end up single forever."
- *Hasty generalization*: Erroneously applying information or knowledge of one or a limited number of representative instances to an entire, much larger category. "Poor people on welfare cheat. Why, just yesterday I saw an SUV parked in front of the tenement at 9th and Main."
- *Non sequitur* (from the Latin, "it does not follow"): Asserting as a conclusion something that doesn't follow from the first premise or premises. "The Senator must be in cahoots with that shyster developer, Landphill. After all, they were college fraternity brothers."
- *Oversimplification*: Providing simplistic answers to complex problems. "Ban handguns and stop murderous assaults in public schools."
- *Post hoc ergo propter hoc* (from Latin, "after this, therefore because of this"): Confusing a cause with an effect and vice versa. "Bicyclists are terribly unsafe riders. They're always getting into accidents with cars." Or confusing causality with proximity: just because two events occur in sequence doesn't necessarily mean that the first caused the second. Does war cause famine, or is famine sometimes the cause of war?

After you've written a logical argument, have someone who disagrees with you read it critically to look for loopholes. Your critic's guidelines could be the same questions you might ask yourself while writing the paper, as indicated in the process strategies below. If you can satisfy yourself and a critic, you can take on the world. Or is that a logical fallacy?

Strategies for Writing: Appealing to Reason: Deductive and Inductive Arguments

1. Do I want to convince my audience of the truth of a particular matter? Do I want essentially to raise their consciousness of an issue? Do I want to promote a belief or refute a theory? Or do I want to move my readers to action? If action, what kind? To change their minds, attitudes, or behavior? To right a wrong, or alter a situation?
2. At the outset, do I expect my audience to agree with my ideas? To be neutral about the issues at hand? Or to be opposed to my views? Can I build into my essay responses to my readers' anticipated reactions, such as rebuttals to their possible objections? Do I know enough about my subject to be able to do this?

3. What is my strongest (and presumably most controversial) point, and where should I put it? At the beginning, if my audience agrees with my views? At the end, after a gradual buildup, for an antagonistic audience? How much development (and consequent emphasis) should each point have? Will a deductive or inductive format best express my thesis?
4. What will be my best sources of evidence? My own experience? The experiences of people I know? Common sense or common knowledge? Opinion from experts in a relevant field? Scientific evidence? Historic records? Economic, anthropological, or statistical data?
5. What tone will best reinforce my evidence? Will my audience also find this tone appealing? Convincing? Would an appropriate tone be sincere? Straightforward? Objective? Reassuring? Confident? Placating? What language can I use to most appropriately convey this tone?

MARILYN NELSON

Marilyn Nelson, daughter of an Air Force pilot and a teacher, was born in Cleveland in 1946. Brought up on different military bases, Nelson started writing while still in elementary school. Her college degrees are from the University of California, Davis (BA, 1968), the University of Pennsylvania (MA, 1970), and the University of Minnesota (PhD, 1979). She is a widely published poet (as Marilyn Waniek before 1995) whose academic career has been primarily at the University of Connecticut. Recipient of numerous honors and fellowships (including a Guggenheim), in 2002 she was chosen as Connecticut Poet Laureate. *The Homeplace* (1990) honors her family, from Rufus Atwood (slave name "Pomp"), c. 1845–1915, to her father and his dashing, heroic group of black World War II aviators, the Tuskegee Airmen.

> Suddenly when I hear airplanes overhead—
> big, silver ones
> whose muscles fill the sky—
> I listen: That sounds like
> someone I know.
> And the sky looks much closer.

Nelson's numerous award-winning books include *The Fields of Praise*, which was a National Book Award finalist and recipient of the 1999 Poets' Prize, and *Carver: A Life in Poems*, which was both a Newbery Honor Book and a Coretta Scott King Honor book. Her work ranges widely, from a rendition of Euripides' play *Hecuba* to several books for children, including *A Wreath for Emmett Till* (2005) and *Sweethearts of Rhythm: The Story of the Greatest All Girl Swing Band in the World* (2009). Between 2004 and 2010 she generously offered her home, Soul Mountain, as a writers' retreat. "When I have time and energy, I make quilts," she says.

Carver: A Life in Poems (2001), from which "Friends in the Klan" is reprinted, consists of fifty-nine vignettes that tell the story of George Washington Carver, pioneering African-American educator and scientist. In "Friends in the Klan" Nelson employs natural, straightforward language with a subtle manipulation of poetic form to create a portrait of grace and disgrace at a historical juncture where the personal and the political collide.

Friends in the Klan (1923)

Black veterans of WWI experienced
such discrimination in veterans' hospitals
that the Veterans' Administration, to save face,

MARILYN NELSON, "Friends in the Klan." From CARVER: A LIFE IN POEMS by Marilyn Nelson. Copyright © 2001 by Marilyn Nelson. Published by Front Street, an imprint of Boyds Mills Press, Inc. Reprinted with permission.

opened in Tuskegee a brand-new hospital,
for Negroes only. Under white control. 5
(White nurses, who were legally excused
from touching blacks, stood holding their elbows
and ordering colored maids around, white shoes
tapping impatiently.)
                    The Professor joined 10
the protest. When the first black doctor arrived
to jubilation, the KKK uncoiled
its length and hissed. *If you want to stay alive*
be away Tuesday. Unsigned. But a familiar hand.
The Professor stayed. And he prayed for his friend in the Klan. 15

Marilyn Nelson chose this 1922 photograph, "Parade of the KKK," to accompany the
publication of her poem, "Friends in the Klan." Why did the Ku Klux Klan wear white
robes and hoods while employing terrorism, violence, and lynching to promote white
supremacy? How would their costumes have been seen by Klan members? By potential
victims—not only African American, but Catholic or Jewish? How could "The Professor,"
George Washington Carver, possibly have a "friend in the Klan"? And pray for him?

THOMAS JEFFERSON

Politician, philosopher, architect, inventor, and writer, Thomas Jefferson
(1743–1826) was born near Charlottesville, Virginia, and was educated at
the College of William and Mary. He served as a delegate to the Continental Congress in 1775, as governor of the Commonwealth of Virginia,

and as third president of the United States. With help from Benjamin Franklin and John Adams, he wrote "The Declaration of Independence" in mid-June 1776, and after further revision by the Continental Congress in Philadelphia, it was signed on July 4. Frequently called "an expression of the American mind," Jefferson's Declaration is based on his acceptance of democracy as the ideal form of government, a belief also evidenced in his refusal to sign the Constitution until the Bill of Rights was added. Jefferson died at Monticello, his home in Charlottesville, on July 4, 1826, the fiftieth anniversary of the signing of the Declaration.

The Declaration is based on a deductive argument, with the fundamental premises stated in the first sentence of the second paragraph, "We hold these truths to be self-evident. . . ." The rest of the argument follows logically—patriots among the Colonists who read this might say inevitably—from the premises of this emphatic, plainspoken document. What evidence is there in the Declaration that the British might react to it as a hot-headed manifesto, perhaps even a declaration of war? Can a cluster of colonies simply secede by fiat?

The Declaration of Independence

1   When in the course of human events, it becomes necessary for one people to dissolve the political bands which have connected them with another, and to assume among the Powers of the earth, the separate and equal station to which the Laws of Nature and of Nature's God entitle them, a decent respect to the opinions of mankind requires that they should declare the causes which impel them to the separation.

2   We hold these truths to be self-evident, that all men are created equal, that they are endowed by their Creator with certain unalienable Rights, that among these are Life, Liberty and the pursuit of Happiness. That to secure these rights, Governments are instituted among Men deriving their just powers from the consent of the governed. That whenever any Form of Government becomes destructive of these ends, it is the Right of People to alter or to abolish it, and to institute new Government, laying its foundation on such principles and organizing its powers in such form, as to them shall seem most likely to affect their Safety and Happiness. Prudence, indeed, will dictate that Governments long established should not be changed for light and transient causes; and accordingly all experience hath shown, that mankind are more disposed to suffer, while evils are sufferable, than to right themselves by abolishing the forms to which they are accustomed. But when a long train of abuses and usurpations pursuing invariably the same Object evinces a design to reduce them under absolute Despotism, it is their right, it is their duty, to throw off such government, and to provide new Guards for their future security. Such has been the patient

In 1942, as a photographer for the Farm Security Administration, a Depression Era government agency, Gordon Parks took this after-hours picture of Ella Watson, a cleaning woman who worked in his office building. As a fellow African-American, he had experienced virulent bigotry and discrimination in the nation's capital, and understood that Ms. Watson's own "disastrous life" could be used to symbolize this version of "American Gothic," the title of the picture. How do you interpret this combination of a slight figure with a very large broom and mop in front of a huge American flag? In what ways does this picture comment on "The Declaration of Independence" (393–97), Martin Luther King, Jr.'s "Letter from Birmingham Jail" (399–413), and Sojourner Truth's "Ain't I a Woman?" (458–59)?

sufferance of these Colonies; and such is now the necessity which constrains them to alter their former Systems of Government. The history of the present King of Great Britain is a history of repeated injuries and usurpations, all having in direct object the establishment of an absolute Tyranny over these States. To prove this, let Facts be submitted to a candid world.

He has refused his Assent to Laws, the most wholesome and necessary for the public good. 3

He had forbidden his Governors to pass Laws of immediate and pressing importance, unless suspended in their operation till his Assent should be obtained; and when so suspended, he has utterly neglected to attend them. 4

He has refused to pass other Laws for the accommodation of large districts of people, unless those people would relinquish the right of 5

Representation in the Legislature, a right inestimable to them and formidable to tyrants only.

6   He has called together legislative bodies at places unusual, uncomfortable, and distant from the depository of their Public Records, for the sole purpose of fatiguing them into compliance with his measures.

7   He has dissolved Representative Houses repeatedly, for opposing with manly firmness his invasions on the rights of the people.

8   He has refused for a long time, after such dissolutions, to cause others to be elected; whereby the Legislative Powers, incapable of Annihilation, have returned to the People at large for their exercise; the State remaining in the mean time exposed to all the dangers of invasion from without, and convulsions within.

9   He has endeavoured to prevent the population of these States; for that purpose obstructing the Laws of Naturalization of Foreigners; refusing to pass others to encourage their migration hither, and raising the conditions of new Appropriations of Lands.

10   He has obstructed the Administration of Justice, by refusing his Assent to Laws for establishing Judiciary Powers.

11   He has made Judges dependent on his Will alone, for the tenure of their offices, and the amount and payment of their salaries.

12   He has erected a multitude of New Offices, and sent hither swarms of Officers to harass our People, and eat out their substance.

13   He has kept among us, in time of peace, Standing Armies without the Consent of our Legislature.

14   He has affected to render the Military independent of and superior to the Civil Power.

15   He has combined with others to subject us to jurisdictions foreign to our constitution, and unacknowledged by our laws; giving his Assent to their acts of pretended Legislation:

16   For quartering large bodies of armed troops among us:

17   For protecting them, by a mock Trial, from Punishment for any Murders which they should commit on the Inhabitants of these States:

18   For cutting off our Trade with all parts of the world:

19   For imposing Taxes on us without our Consent:

20   For depriving us in many cases, of the benefits of Trial by Jury:

21   For transporting us beyond Seas to be tried for pretended offenses:

22   For abolishing the free System of English Laws in a Neighbouring Province, establishing therein an Arbitrary government, and enlarging its boundaries so as to render it at once an example and fit instrument for introducing the same absolute rule into these Colonies:

23   For taking away our Charters, abolishing our most valuable Laws, and altering fundamentally the Forms of our Governments:

24   For suspending our own Legislatures, and declaring themselves invested with Power to legislate for us in all cases whatsoever.

He has abdicated Government here, by declaring us out of his Pro-   25
tection and waging War against us.

He has plundered our seas, ravaged our Coasts, burnt our towns   26
and destroyed the Lives of our people.

He is at this time transporting large Armies of foreign Mercenaries   27
to compleat works of death, desolation and tyranny, already begun with
circumstances of Cruelty & perfidy scarcely paralleled in the most barbarous ages, and totally unworthy the Head of a civilized nation.

He has constrained our fellow Citizens taken Captive on the high   28
Seas to bear Arms against their Country, to become the executioners of
their friends and Brethren, or to fall themselves by their Hands.

He has excited domestic insurrections amongst us, and has endea-   29
voured to bring on the inhabitants of our frontiers, the merciless Indian
Savages, whose known rule of warfare, is an undistinguished destruction
of all ages, sexes and conditions.

In every stage of these Oppressions We Have Petitioned for Redress   30
in the most humble terms: Our repeated petitions have been answered
only by repeated injury. A Prince, whose character is thus marked by every act which may define a Tyrant, is unfit to be the ruler of a free People.

Not have We been wanting in attention to our British brethren. We   31
have warned them from time to time of attempts by their legislature to
extend an unwarrantable jurisdiction over us. We have reminded them
of the circumstances of our emigration and settlement here. We have ap-
pealed to their native justice and magnanimity and we have conjured
them by the ties of our common kindred to disavow these usurpations,
which would inevitably interrupt our connections and correspondence.
They too have been deaf to the voice of justice and of consanguinity.
We must, therefore acquiesce in the necessity, which denounces our Separation, and hold them, as we hold the rest of mankind, Enemies in War, in
Peace Friends.

We, therefore, the Representatives of the United States of America,   32
in General Congress, Assembled, appealing to the Supreme Judge of the
world for the rectitude of our intentions, do, in the Name, and by Authority of the good People of these Colonies, solemnly publish and declare,
That these United Colonies are, and of Right ought to be Free and Independent States; that they are Absolved from all Allegiance to the British
Crown and that all political connection between them and the State of
Great Britain, is and ought to be totally dissolved; and that as Free and
Independent States, they have full power to levy War, conclude Peace,
contract Alliances, establish Commerce, and to do all other Acts and
Things which Independent States may of right do. And for the support
of this Declaration, with a firm reliance on the protection of Divine Providence, we mutually pledge to each other our lives, our Fortunes and our
sacred Honor.

Content

1. What are "the Laws of Nature and of Nature's God" to which Jefferson refers in paragraph 1? Why doesn't he specify what they are? Is a brief allusion to them in the first paragraph sufficient support for the fundamental premise of the second paragraph?

2. What is Jefferson's fundamental premise (¶ 2)? Does he ever prove it? Does he need to?

3. In paragraphs 3–31 the Declaration states a series of the American colonists' grievances against the British King, George III. What are some of these grievances? Can they be grouped into categories related to the "unalienable rights" Jefferson has specified at the outset, the rights to "Life, Liberty and the pursuit of Happiness"?

4. From the nature of the grievances Jefferson identifies, what ideal of government does he have in mind? Can such a government exist among colonial peoples, or only in an independent nation?

Strategies/Structures/Language

5. Could the American colonists have expected the British simply to agree that separation had become necessary? Or is "The Declaration of Independence" in effect a declaration of war? How does the conclusion (¶ 32) appear to be the inevitable consequence of the reasoning that precedes it? Are there any feasible alternatives? How do Jefferson's choice of words (semantics) and sentence structure (syntax) imply that separation is the inevitable effect of the king's actions?

6. Why has Jefferson listed the grievances in the order in which they appear?

7. Is "The Declaration of Independence" written primarily for an audience of the British King and his advisors? Who else would be likely to be vitally involved?

8. What is the tone of this document? How would Jefferson have expected this tone to have affected King George III and associates? How might the same tone have affected the American patriots of 1776?

For Writing

9. *Journal Writing.* Are the ideals celebrated in the "Declaration of Independence" relevant today? Or, does the wording of the *Declaration* seem specific to the historical context in which it was written? What passages do you find particularly relevant or obsolete with respect to contemporary society? Which of Jefferson's grievances can be translated into and applied to contemporary issues?

10. Use your journal (question 9) to write an essay in which you discuss the extent to which the federal government of the United States exhibits one or more of the ideals of government that Jefferson promoted in "The Declaration of Independence."

11. Write your own "declaration of independence," in which you justify setting yourself (or yourself as a member of a particular social, occupational, economic, ethnic, or cultural group) free from an oppressor or oppressive group.

12. *Dialogues.* While Jefferson structures the "Declaration" around the legitimacy of the colonies' political separation from the British Crown, Martin Luther King, Jr. (below) stresses the fundamental unity of all Americans, including those who try

to hinder racial justice: "We are caught in an inescapable network of mutuality, tied in a single garment of destiny" (¶ 4). How does King convince his reader that racial justice necessitates an end to segregation, rather than promoting autonomy, as the *Declaration* argues of political justice? Where does King's logic depart from Jefferson's in crucial ways?

13. ***Second Look.*** Equality and the enjoyment of "certain unalienable Rights" (¶ 2) were, in 1776, concepts restricted to men of European descent. How does Gordon Parks's photograph of the African-American woman (395) juxtapose class, gender, and race with the ideals of "Life, Liberty, and the pursuit of Happiness" (¶ 2)? How does the photograph's focus and the arrangement of the flag (off-center, blurred), the sharp quality of the woman's dotted dress and broom, and the tilt of her head and shadowed features all work together to elicit a particular interpretation?

MARTIN LUTHER KING, JR.

"Letter from Birmingham Jail," a literary and humanitarian masterpiece, reveals why Martin Luther King, Jr. was the most influential leader of the American civil rights movement in the 1950s and 1960s, and, why, with Mahatma Gandhi, he was one of this century's most influential advocates for human rights. King was born in Atlanta in 1929, the son of a well-known Baptist clergyman, educated at Morehouse College, and ordained in his father's denomination.

A forceful and charismatic leader, Dr. King became at twenty-six a national spokesperson for the civil rights movement when in 1955 he led a successful boycott of the segregated bus system of Montgomery, Alabama. Dr. King became president of the Southern Christian Leadership Conference and led the sit-ins and demonstrations—including the 1964 march on Washington, D.C., which climaxed with his famous "I Have a Dream" speech—that helped to ensure passage of the 1964 Civil Rights Act and the Voting Rights Act of 1965. He received the Nobel Peace Prize in 1964, its youngest winner. Toward the end of his life, cut short by assassination in 1968, Dr. King was increasingly concerned with improving the rights and the lives of the nation's poor, irrespective of race, and with ending the war in Vietnam. His birthday became a national holiday in 1986.

In 1963 King wrote the letter reprinted below while imprisoned for "parading without a permit." Though ostensibly replying to eight clergymen—Protestant, Catholic, and Jewish—who feared violence in the Birmingham desegregation demonstrations, King actually intended his letter for the worldwide audience his civil rights activities commanded. Warning that America had more to fear from passive moderates ("the appalling silence of good people") than from extremists, King defended his policy of "nonviolent direct action" and explained why he was compelled to disobey "unjust laws"—supporting his argument with references to Protestant, Catholic, and Jewish examples ("Was not Jesus an extremist for love. . . ."), as well as to the painful examples of segregation in his own life.

Letter from Birmingham Jail

April 16, 1963

1   *My Dear Fellow Clergymen:*
     While confined here in the Birmingham city jail, I came across your recent statement calling my present activities "unwise and untimely." Seldom do I pause to answer criticism of my work and ideas. If I sought to answer all the criticisms that cross my desk, my secretaries would have little time for anything other than such correspondence in the course of the day, and I would have no time for constructive work. But since I feel that you are men of genuine good will and that your criticisms are sincerely set forth, I want to try to answer your statement in what I hope will be patient and reasonable terms.

2   I think I should indicate why I am here in Birmingham, since you have been influenced by the view which argues against "outsiders coming in." I have the honor of serving as president of the Southern Christian Leadership Conference, an organization operating in every southern state, with headquarters in Atlanta, Georgia. We have some eighty-five affiliated organizations across the South, and one of them is the Alabama Christian Movement for Human Rights. Frequently we share staff, educational and financial resources with our affiliates. Several months ago the affiliate here in Birmingham asked us to be on call to engage in a nonviolent direct-action program if such were deemed necessary. We readily consented, and when the hour came we lived up to our promise. So I, along with several members of my staff, am here because I was invited here. I am here because I have organizational ties here.

3   But more basically, I am in Birmingham because injustice is here. Just as the prophets of the eighth century B.C. left their villages and carried their "thus saith the Lord" far beyond the boundaries of their home towns, and, just as the Apostle Paul left his village of Tarsus and carried the gospel of Jesus Christ to the far corners of the Greco-Roman world, so am I compelled to carry the gospel of freedom beyond my own home town. Like Paul, I must constantly respond to the Macedonian call for aid.

AUTHOR'S NOTE: This response to a published statement by eight fellow clergymen from Alabama (Bishop C. C. J. Carpenter, Bishop Joseph A. Durick, Rabbi Hilton L. Grafman, Bishop Paul Hardin, Bishop Holan B. Harmon, the Reverend George M. Murray, the Reverend Edward V. Ramage and the Reverend Earl Stallings) was composed under somewhat constricting circumstances. Begun on the margins of the newspaper in which the statement appeared while I was in jail, the letter was continued on scraps of writing paper supplied by a friendly Negro trusty, and concluded on a pad my attorneys were eventually permitted to leave me. Although the text remains in substance unaltered, I have indulged in the author's prerogative of polishing it for publication.

© Bettmann / Corbis

Dr. Martin Luther King, Jr., and other notable figures in the 60s Civil Rights movement—Andy Young (left), Joan Baez, and Hosea Williams (next to Baez)—are escorting black children into a newly integrated school in Grenada, Mississippi, on September 20,1966. What arguments are embedded in this picture? What is the point of having such a high profile delegation of escorts? Where would this picture have first been published? Reprinted? Who would be expected to view it? With what reaction(s)? What has happened since this picture was taken to make this a telling scene in American history rather than a typical first-day-of-school picture today?

Moreover, I am cognizant of the interrelatedness of all commu-   4
nities and states. I cannot sit idly by in Atlanta and not be concerned
about what happens in Birmingham. Injustice anywhere is a threat to
justice everywhere. We are caught in an inescapable network of mutuality, tied in a single garment of destiny. Whatever affects one directly,
affects all indirectly. Never again can we afford to live with the narrow, provincial "outside agitator" idea. Anyone who lives inside the
United States can never be considered an outsider anywhere within its
bounds.

You deplore the demonstrations taking place in Birmingham. But   5
your statement, I am sorry to say, fails to express a similar concern for
the conditions that brought about the demonstrations. I am sure that
none of you would want to rest content with the superficial kind of
social analysis that deals merely with effects and does not grapple with
underlying causes. It is unfortunate that demonstrations are taking place
in Birmingham, but it is even more unfortunate that the city's white
power structure left the Negro community with no alternative.

6   In any nonviolent campaign there are four basic steps: collection of the facts to determine whether injustices exist; negotiation; self-purification; and direct action. We have gone through all these steps in Birmingham. There can be no gainsaying the fact that racial injustice engulfs this community. Birmingham is probably the most thoroughly segregated city in the United States. An ugly record of brutality is widely known. Negroes have experienced grossly unjust treatment in the courts. There have been more unsolved bombings of Negro homes and churches in Birmingham than in any other city in the nation. These are the hard brutal facts of the case. On the basis of these conditions, Negro leaders sought to negotiate with the city fathers. But the latter consistently refused to engage in good-faith negotiation.

7   Then, last September, came the opportunity to talk with leaders of Birmingham's economic community. In the course of the negotiations, certain promises were made by the merchants—for example, to remove the stores' humiliating racial signs. On the basis of these promises, the Reverend Fred Shuttlesworth and the leaders of the Alabama Christian Movement for Human Rights agreed to a moratorium on all demonstrations. As the weeks and months went by, we realized that we were the victims of a broken promise. A few signs, briefly removed, returned; the others remained.

8   As in so many past experiences, our hopes had been blasted, and the shadow of deep disappointment settled upon us. We had no alternative except to prepare for direct action, whereby we would present our very bodies as a means of laying our case before the conscience of the local and the national community. Mindful of the difficulties involved, we decided to undertake a process of self-purification. We began a series of workshops on nonviolence, and we repeatedly asked ourselves: "Are you able to accept blows without retaliating?" "Are you able to endure the ordeal of jail?" We decided to schedule our direct-action program for the Easter season, realizing that except for Christmas, this is the main shopping period of the year. Knowing that a strong economic-withdrawal program would be the by-product of direct action, we felt that this would be the best time to bring pressure to bear on the merchants for the needed change.

9   Then it occurred to us that Birmingham's mayoralty election was coming up in March, and we speedily decided to postpone action until after election day. When we discovered that the Commissioner of Public Safety, Eugene "Bull" Connor, had piled up enough votes to be in the run-off, we decided again to postpone action until the day after the run-off so that the demonstrations could not be used to cloud the issues. Like many others, we waited to see Mr. Connor defeated, and to this end we endured postponement after postponement. Having aided in this community need, we felt that our direct-action program could be delayed no longer.

You may well ask: "Why direct action? Why sit-ins, marches and [10] so forth? Isn't negotiation a better path?" You are quite right in calling for negotiation. Indeed this is the very purpose of direct action. Nonviolent direct action seeks to create such a crisis and foster such a tension that a community which has constantly refused to negotiate is forced to confront the issue. It seeks so to dramatize the issue that it can no longer be ignored. My citing the creation of tension as part of the work of the nonviolent-resister may sound rather shocking. But I must confess that I am not afraid of the word "tension." I have earnestly opposed violent tension, but there is a type of nonviolent tension which is necessary for growth. Just as Socrates felt that it was necessary to create a tension in the mind so that individuals could rise from the bondage of myths and half-truths to the unfettered realm of creative analysis and objective appraisal, so must we see the need for nonviolent gadflies to create the kind of tension in society that will help men rise from the dark depths of prejudice and racism to the majestic heights of understanding and brotherhood.

The purpose of our direct-action program is to create a situation so [11] crisis-packed that it will inevitably open the door to negotiation. I therefore concur with you in your call for negotiation. Too long has our beloved Southland been bogged down in a tragic effort to live in monologue rather than dialogue.

One of the basic points in your statement is that the action that [12] I and my associates have taken in Birmingham is untimely. Some have asked: "Why didn't you give the new city administration time to act?" The only answer that I can give to this query is that the new Birmingham administration must be prodded about as much as the outgoing one, before it will act. We are sadly mistaken if we feel that the election of Albert Boutwell as mayor will bring the millennium to Birmingham. While Mr. Boutwell is a much more gentle person than Mr. Connor, they are both segregationists, dedicated to maintenance of the status quo. I have hope that Mr. Boutwell will be reasonable enough to see the futility of massive resistance to desegregation. But he will not see this without pressure from devotees of civil rights. My friends, I must say to you that we have not made a single gain in civil rights without determined legal and nonviolent pressure. Lamentably, it is an historical fact that privileged groups seldom give up their privileges voluntarily. Individuals may see the moral light and voluntarily give up their unjust posture; but, as Reinhold Niebuhr has reminded us, groups tend to be more immoral than individuals.

We know through painful experience that freedom is never [13] voluntarily given by the oppressor; it must be demanded by the oppressed. Frankly, I have yet to engage in a direct-action campaign that was "well-timed" in the view of those who have not suffered unduly from the disease of segregation. For years now I have heard the word

"Wait!" It rings in the ear of every Negro with piercing familiarity. This "Wait" has almost always meant "Never." We must come to see, with one of our distinguished jurists, that "justice too long delayed is justice denied."

14   We have waited for more than 340 years for our constitutional and Godgiven rights. The nations of Asia and Africa are moving with jet-like speed toward gaining political independence, but we still creep at horse-and-buggy pace toward gaining a cup of coffee at a lunch counter. Perhaps it is easy for those who have never felt the stinging darts of seg-regation to say, "Wait." But when you have seen vicious mobs lynch your mothers and fathers at will and drown your sisters and brothers at whim; when you have seen hate-filled policemen curse, kick and even kill your black brothers and sisters; when you see the vast majority of your twenty million Negro brothers smothering in an airtight cage of poverty in the midst of an affluent society; when you suddenly find your tongue twisted and your speech stammering as you seek to explain to your six-year-old daughter why she can't go to the public amusement park that has just been advertised on television, and see tears welling up in her eyes when she is told that Funtown is closed to colored children, and see ominous clouds of inferiority beginning to form in her little mental sky, and see her beginning to distort her personality by developing an unconscious bitter-ness toward white people; when you have to concoct an answer for a five-year-old son who is asking: "Daddy, why do white people treat colored people so mean?"; when you take a cross-country drive and find it neces-sary to sleep night after night in the uncomfortable corners of your auto-mobile because no motel will accept you; when you are humiliated day in and day out by nagging signs reading "white" and "colored"; when your first name becomes "nigger," your middle name becomes "boy" (how-ever old you are) and your last name becomes "John," and your wife and mother are never given the respected title "Mrs."; when you are harried by day and haunted by night by the fact that you are a Negro, living con-stantly at tiptoe stance, never quite knowing what to expect next, and are plagued with inner fears and outer resentments; when you are forever fighting a degenerating sense of "nobodiness"—then you will under-stand why we find it difficult to wait. There comes a time when the cup of endurance runs over, and men are no longer willing to be plunged into the abyss of despair. I hope, sirs, you can understand our legitimate and unavoidable impatience.

15   You express a great deal of anxiety over our willingness to break laws. This is certainly a legitimate concern. Since we so diligently urge people to obey the Supreme Court's decision of 1954 outlawing segregation in the public schools, at first glance it may seem rather para-doxical for us consciously to break laws. One may well ask: "How can you advocate breaking some laws and obeying others?" The answer lies in the fact that there are two types of laws: just and unjust. I would be the

first to advocate obeying just laws. One has not only a legal but a moral responsibility to obey just laws. Conversely, one has a moral responsibility to disobey unjust laws. I would agree with St. Augustine that "an unjust law is no law at all."

Now, what is the difference between the two? How does one determine whether a law is just or unjust? A just law is a man-made code that squares with the moral law or the law of God. An unjust law is a code that is out of harmony with the moral law. To put it in the terms of St. Thomas Aquinas: An unjust law is a human law that is not rooted in eternal law and natural law. Any law that uplifts human personality is just. Any law that degrades human personality is unjust. All segregation statutes are unjust because segregation distorts the soul and damages the personality. It gives the segregator a false sense of superiority and the segregated a false sense of inferiority. Segregation, to use the terminology of the Jewish philosopher Martin Buber, substitutes an "I-it" relationship for an "I-thou" relationship and ends up relegating persons to the status of things. Hence segregation is not only politically, economically and sociologically unsound, it is morally wrong and sinful. Paul Tillich has said that sin is separation. Is not segregation an existential expression of man's tragic separation, his awful estrangement, his terrible sinfulness? Thus it is that I can urge men to obey the 1954 decision of the Supreme Court, for it is morally right; and I can urge them to disobey segregation ordinances, for they are morally wrong.

Let us consider a more concrete example of just and unjust laws. An unjust law is a code that a numerical or power majority group compels a minority group to obey but does not make binding on itself. This is *difference* made legal. By the same token, a just law is a code that a majority compels a minority to follow and that it is willing to follow itself. This is *sameness* made legal.

Let me give another explanation. A law is unjust if it is inflicted on a minority that, as a result of being denied the right to vote, had no part in enacting or devising the law. Who can say that the legislature of Alabama which set up that state's segregation laws was democratically elected? Throughout Alabama all sorts of devious methods are used to prevent Negroes from becoming registered voters, and there are some counties in which even though Negroes constitute a majority of the population, not a single Negro is registered. Can any law enacted under such circumstances be considered democratically structured?

Sometimes a law is just on its face and unjust in its application. For instance, I have been arrested on a charge of parading without a permit. Now, there is nothing wrong in having an ordinance which requires a permit for a parade. But such an ordinance becomes unjust when it is used to maintain segregation and to deny citizens the First-Amendment privilege of peaceful assembly and protest.

20   I hope you are able to see the distinction I am trying to point out. In no sense do I advocate evading or defying the law, as would the rabid segregationist. That would lead to anarchy. One who breaks an unjust law must do so openly, lovingly, and with a willingness to accept the penalty. I submit that an individual who breaks a law that conscience tells him is unjust, and who willingly accepts the penalty of imprisonment in order to arouse the conscience of the community over its injustice, is in reality expressing the highest respect for the law.

21   Of course, there is nothing new about this kind of civil disobedience. It was evidenced sublimely in the refusal of Shadrach, Meshach and Abednego to obey the laws of Nebuchadnezzar, on the ground that a higher moral law was at stake. It was practiced superbly by the early Christians, who were willing to face hungry lions and the excruciating pain of chopping blocks rather than submit to certain unjust laws of the Roman Empire. To a degree, academic freedom is a reality today because Socrates practiced civil disobedience. In our own nation, the Boston Tea Party represented a massive act of civil disobedience.

22   We should never forget that everything Adolf Hitler did in Germany was "legal" and everything the Hungarian freedom fighters did in Hungary was "illegal." It was "illegal" to aid and comfort a Jew in Hitler's Germany. Even so, I am sure that, had I lived in Germany at the time, I would have aided and comforted my Jewish brothers. If today I lived in a Communist country where certain principles dear to the Christian faith are suppressed, I would openly advocate disobeying that country's anti-religious laws.

23   I must make two honest confessions to you, my Christian and Jewish brothers. First, I must confess that over the past few years I have been gravely disappointed with the white moderate. I have almost reached the regrettable conclusion that the Negro's great stumbling block in his stride toward freedom is not the White Citizen's Counciler or the Ku Klux Klanner, but the white moderate, who is more devoted to "order" than to justice; who prefers a negative peace which is the absence of tension to a positive peace which is the presence of justice; who constantly says: "I agree with you in the goal you seek, but I cannot agree with your methods of direct action"; who paternalistically believes he can set the timetable for another man's freedom; who lives by a mythical concept of time and who constantly advises the Negro to wait for a "more convenient season." Shallow understanding from people of good will is more frustrating than absolute misunderstanding from people of ill will. Lukewarm acceptance is much more bewildering than outright rejection.

24   I had hoped that the white moderate would understand that law and order exist for the purpose of establishing justice and that when they fail in this purpose they become the dangerously structured dams that block the flow of social progress. I had hoped that the white moderate would

understand that the present tension in the South is a necessary phase of the transition from an obnoxious negative peace, in which the Negro passively accepted his unjust plight, to a substantive and positive peace, in which all men will respect the dignity and worth of human personality. Actually, we who engage in non-violent direct action are not the creators of tension. We merely bring to the surface the hidden tension that is already alive. We bring it out in the open, where it can be seen and dealt with. Like a boil that can never be cured so long as it is covered up but must be opened with all its ugliness to the natural medicines of air and light, injustice must be exposed, with all the tension its exposure creates, to the light of human conscience and the air of national opinion before it can be cured.

In your statement you assert that our actions, even though peaceful, 25 must be condemned because they precipitate violence. But is this a logical assertion? Isn't this like condemning a robbed man because his possession of money precipitated the evil act of robbery? Isn't this like condemning Socrates because his unswerving commitment to truth and his philosophical inquiries precipitated the act by the misguided populace in which they made him drink hemlock? Isn't this like condemning Jesus because his unique God-consciousness and never-ceasing devotion to God's will precipitated the evil act of crucifixion? We must come to see that, as the federal courts have consistently affirmed, it is wrong to urge an individual to cease his efforts to gain his basic constitutional rights because the quest may precipitate violence. Society must protect the robbed and punish the robber.

I had also hoped that the white moderate would reject the myth 26 concerning time in relation to the struggle for freedom. I have just received a letter from a white brother in Texas. He writes: "All Christians know that the colored people will receive equal rights eventually, but it is possible that you are in too great a religious hurry. It has taken Christianity almost two thousand years to accomplish what it has. The teachings of Christ take time to come to earth." Such an attitude stems from a tragic misconception of time, from the strangely irrational notion that there is something in the very flow of time that will inevitably cure all ills. Actually, time itself is neutral; it can be used either destructively or constructively. More and more I feel that the people of ill will have used time much more effectively than have the people of good will. We will have to repent in this generation not merely for the hateful words and actions of the bad people but for the appalling silence of the good people. Human progress never rolls in on wheels of inevitability; it comes through the tireless efforts of men willing to be coworkers with God, and without this hard work, time itself becomes an ally of the forces of social stagnation. We must use time creatively, in the knowledge that the time is always ripe to do right. Now is the time to make real the promise of democracy and transform our pending national elegy into a creative psalm of brotherhood. Now is the time to lift our national policy from the quicksand of racial injustice to the solid rock of human dignity.

27   You speak of our activity in Birmingham as extreme. At first I was rather disappointed that fellow clergymen would see my nonviolent efforts as those of an extremist. I began thinking about the fact that I stand in the middle of two opposing forces in the Negro community. One is a force of complacency, made up in part of Negroes who, as a result of long years of oppression, are so drained of self-respect and a sense of "somebodiness" that they have adjusted to segregation; and in part of a few middle-class Negroes who, because of a degree of academic and economic security and because in some ways they profit by segregation, have become insensitive to the problems of the masses. The other force is one of bitterness and hatred, and it comes perilously close to advocating violence. It is expressed in the various black nationalist groups that are springing up across the nation, the largest and best-known being Elijah Muhammad's Muslim movement. Nourished by the Negro's frustration over the continued existence of racial discrimination, this movement is made up of people who have lost faith in America, who have absolutely repudiated Christianity, and who have concluded that the white man is an incorrigible "devil."

28   I have tried to stand between these two forces, saying that we need emulate neither the "do-nothingism" of the complacent nor the hatred and despair of the black nationalist. For there is the more excellent way of love and nonviolent protest. I am grateful to God that, through the influence of the Negro church, the way of nonviolence became an integral part of our struggle.

29   If this philosophy had not emerged, by now many streets of the South would, I am convinced, be flowing with blood. And I am further convinced that if our white brothers dismiss as "rabble-rousers" and "outside agitators" those of us who employ nonviolent direct action, and if they refuse to support our non-violent efforts, millions of Negroes will, out of frustration and despair, seek solace and security in black-nationalist ideologies—a development that would inevitably lead to a frightening racial nightmare.

30   Oppressed people cannot remain oppressed forever. The yearning for freedom eventually manifests itself, and that is what has happened to the American Negro. Something within has reminded him of his birthright of freedom, and something without has reminded him that it can be gained. Consciously or unconsciously, he has been caught up by the *Zeitgeist*, and with his black brothers of Africa and his brown and yellow brothers of Asia, South America and the Caribbean, the United States Negro is moving with a sense of great urgency toward the promised land of racial justice. If one recognizes this vital urge that has engulfed the Negro community, one should readily understand why public demonstrations are taking place. The Negro has many pent-up resentments and latent frustrations, and he must release them. So let him march; let him make prayer pilgrimages to the city hall; let him go on freedom rides—and try to understand why he must do so. If his repressed emotions are not released in nonviolent ways, they will seek expression through violence; this is not a threat but a fact of history. So I have not said to my people: "Get rid of

THE ENVIRONMENT: SAVE IT OR LOSE IT

Corbis

Photograph 1: Grand Teton reflected in Jackson Lake, Grand Teton National Park, Wyoming

Although in the twenty-first century we Americans tend to take the existence of our national parks for granted, many of them have a contentious history, including Grand Teton National Park. The Teton Range is a stretch of the Rocky Mountains, 40 miles long and 7–9 miles wide, adjacent to Yellowstone National Park. Grand Teton, pictured here, is 13,770 feet high; eight other peaks are over 12,000 feet above sea level. The area was used for twelve thousand years by Native American hunters, with Jackson Hole (named after fur trapper David Jackson) a crossroads for trade and travel; the Lewis and Clark expedition and other explorers and surveyors mapped the area in the nineteenth century. In the early twentieth century, a proposal to make the site an extension of Yellowstone National Park aroused the wrath of various groups. Sheep and cattle ranchers (themselves enemies) wanted to continue grazing their herds; others lobbied for traditional hunting, grazing, and ranching activities. In 1927, philanthropist John D. Rockefeller, Jr. and others secretly bought the land and held it in trust for the National Park Service, but because of harassment and opposition from both local residents and the U.S. Senate, Grand Teton National Park was not signed into existence until 1950—requiring support and intervention from presidents Calvin Coolidge, Franklin Roosevelt, and Harry Truman.

CONSIDERING THE IMAGE

1. What makes this a picture-perfect photograph? What mood does it convey? What messages about the environment does it send? Does it disclose any of the disputes, bitterness, skullduggery, secrecy, and threats that comprise the history of the area up until 1950, and that bleed beyond even this border? To what extent might it be possible to generalize about the public image and history of other national parks, either existing or proposed?
2. This is a beautiful sight: the blue sky is full of puffy white clouds; the snowy mountains appear pristine, as does the clear lake that mirrors them. The evergreens in the foreground appear healthy, the surrounding snow white and untouched by human beings, the water pure. To what extent do these images reflect reality? Are there any people or animals in this picture? To your knowledge, is this environment threatened in any way? Check the accuracy of your evidence, concerning this or any other national park of your choice.
3. What do people mean by "Save our nationals parks"? Identify some of the ways this can be done.

1

© Rob Crandall/The Image Work

Photograph 2: Bison herd crossing road in Yellowstone National Park, August 2004 *Yellowstone National Park, mostly in Wyoming, is known for its geothermal activity—geysers, boiling springs (and consequently earthquakes)—and for its mountains, waterfalls, petrified wood, and varied terrain. Outside of Alaska, it is the largest surviving stretch of pristine land in the United States and the focal point of the 31,250 square-mile Greater Yellowstone ecosystem that includes Grand Teton National Park and the adjacent national forests and wilderness areas: home to 1,700 species of trees and 60 species of mammals. In addition to black bears, elk, moose, pronghorn and bighorn sheep, and mountain lions, endangered species—gray wolves and grizzly bears—have been reintroduced after years of deliberate slaughter and are thriving.*

Yet all is not tranquil in Eden. The area is subject to 35 natural fires per year, 29 an inevitable consequence of lightning, and 6 caused by humans. Before 1970, when the impact of fires on natural ecosystems was finally recognized, all fires were suppressed, leaving large areas of underbrush and dying forests ready for uncontrollable conflagration. Current policy allows natural fires to burn unless they endanger lives and property. Today's population of 3,000 bison has recently shrunk from nearly twice that due to slaughter at the urging of cattle ranchers who claimed that brucellosis would decimate their herds (although the disease could have been controlled through vaccinations). But the greatest damage to the park's environment is caused by humans. The number of visitors in 2010 (3.6 million) was seven times greater than the pre-World War II annual average. The park's users make enormous demands on water and sanitation: they drive polluting snowmobiles through wilderness areas, break off limestone structures, steal petrified wood, throw trash into the geysers—and yes, they feed the bears.

CONSIDERING THE IMAGE

1. Who has the right of way in this picture? Does it remind you of any other street scenes? Is this the ideal way for people to view wildlife—from their cars, in transit? What effect does proximity to people have on wildlife species that were accustomed to living in isolation?

2. Research and comment on one or another of the changes in wildlife, fire, and land management in Yellowstone National Park during the past hundred (or even fifty) years. What influences policy decisions on whether to reintroduce wild species that were once native (such as grizzlies and wolves), whether to declare them endangered, and what the optimum population of a given species is? To what extent should human visitors be restricted: in numbers, behavior, use of machinery (such as snowmobiles) and weapons? Who should make these decisions? Who should monitor them?

Photograph 3: Computer composite image of North America, August 10, 2001 *We have become accustomed to the beautiful, iconic photograph of Earth (the "Blue Marble") taken during the Apollo 17 space mission (1972) that shows large patches of snow in the Arctic, green in Greenland and the Eastern seaboard, deep blue oceans, and white clouds swirling over portions of South America and the Antarctic. All looks serene, and—from that vast distance of 125,000 miles—immortal, unassailable, clean.*

Compare the image shown here, a composite of multiple, Earth-observing satellite images taken on the night of August 10, 2001, during the annual Perseids, an awesome meteor shower—as many as sixty an hour visible from the Northern Hemisphere. But the lights here are not from meteors but from the brightest spots of human habitation: the greater the congestion, the brighter the lights. You can view comparable images, but closer, via Google Earth.

CONSIDERING THE IMAGE

1. Consider the levels of luminescence, the brightest spots illuminating both coasts of North America and the entire eastern seaboard. What is most striking about this picture? In what ways can you "read" it—visually? Intellectually? Ecologically? Compare and contrast this image with the image of Grand Teton National Park (Photograph 1).
2. What might the continent have looked like a hundred years ago? Fifty years ago? What would you predict seeing fifty years from now? With what consequences?

Photograph 4: "Seven Million Londoners" *proclaim the banners streaming from the lampposts marching along Oxford Street in October 2005. Crowds throng this major shopping street, their turbans, hats, and beards representing people from all over the world—so many, packed so closely together, that they dwarf the cars and even the double-decker bus attempting to make its way along the congested thoroughfare.*

Might we interpret this as evidence of too many people? The crowds here could be replicated in many places in the world—subways and sidewalks bursting with commuters in New York, Beijing, and Tokyo, many wearing masks to filter polluted air; open-air markets seething with seas of shoppers in Lagos; traffic jams in Bangkok—and on the Long Island Expressway, "the world's longest parking lot"; jerry-built favelas *(slums) in Rio; pilgrims bathing, sari blending into sari, in the Gänges—simultaneously sacred and polluted; vacationers too close together while skiing, swimming, camping, hiking—you name it—in what was once wilderness.*

In Hot, Flat, and Crowded: Why We Need a Green Revolution—and How It Can Renew America *(2008), Thomas Friedman cites the 2007 United Nations Population Division report estimating that the world's population will increase 40% or more, from 6.7 billion in 2007 to 9.2 billion in 2050, mostly in the "less developed regions" ill equipped to provide people's basic needs: "food, housing, education, employment." In 1800, London—population 1 million—was the world's largest city. By 1960, there were*

AP Photo/Michael Stephens/PA

111 cities with more than a million; today that number has nearly tripled. There will be 26 "megacities" by 2015, with populations of over 10 million. Five key problems, says Friedman ("energy supply and demand, petropolitics, climate change, energy poverty, and biodiversity loss"), have been building for years, but the tipping point in destruction of quality of life occurred on January 1, 2000 (47). More than half the 2008 population lives in cities, the sites of particular congestion and stress on the infrastructure, including "loss of arable land, deforestation, overfishing, water shortages, and air and water pollution" (29–30). Although the developed regions' population is expected to remain static, at around 1.2 billion, these people use a disproportionate percentage of resources. Each of the United States' 312 million inhabitants, for example, consumes as much in a year as do 32 Kenyans. Since the U.S. population is ten times greater, the U.S. resource use is 320 times as large as in Kenya (65).

Considering the Image

1. Look closely at the individuals in this crowd. Do they look purposeful, peaceful? Is the group orderly? What are they doing? Where are they going? Do they give any indication that they are bothered or inconvenienced by such large numbers—either in their immediate vicinity, or in the knowledge that there are "Seven Million Londoners"? Why or why not?
2. What, if anything, should cities do to make their inhabitants aware of their impact on the world's diminishing resources? Research the optimum city size and come up with some solutions on how city size might be related to conservation efforts in a specific area of the world.

Photograph 5: Car wrecks in Bærum, Norway, Summer 1997 *We could view this photograph as a work of art: Colorful ribbons of a crumpled substance, full of irregularities and indentations. The colors range from blue and white, deep red, maroon, orange, yellow, and lime green; all are bright, as is the blue sky above. But we also recognize what we're looking at—wrecked cars—each of which may have been further compressed for more compact waste disposal. The story behind each wreck may tell of human loss—of judgment, of health and strength, of life. There is economic loss as well—not only in the medical costs of the accident, but of the car itself, which has little or no value if it is totaled. Or one car may simply have been considered obsolete or old and junked: how many years, how much mileage does it take to make a car old? Each replacement vehicle, of course, requires more raw materials, just as each junked car requires (in addition to money) either space to store the refuse, or energy to strip out the reusable parts and to recycle the steel.*

The same commentary could be made about all sorts of other manufactured items, large and small—refrigerators, air conditioners, computer monitors, cell phones, rechargers, batteries, dirty diapers, plastic bags, and bottles, to name only a few of millions. Add to this the accumulation of waste—industrial, human, and animal—all of which grows in proportion to the humans whose own population explosion affects every aspect of the problem. As Al Gore's An Inconvenient Truth *explains, "It took more than 10,000 generations for the human population to reach 2 billion. Then it began to rocket upward from 2 billion to 9 billion in the course of a single lifetime: ours" (216), each and every person generating waste from the moment of their birth until their last breath.*

CONSIDERING THE IMAGE

1. What are the costs of the accumulation of junk, detritus, refuse, and waste of all kinds—to a single municipality, state, nation? Who pays for the land, labor, and energy to dump this refuse? To what other uses might the space, money, and energy currently tied up in waste disposal be put? Are there any benefits to the generation of junk and garbage, or are there only costs? Explain.
2. Visit a local business or institution (such as a hospital of school, or your college residence or dining hall) and determine what sorts of waste are generated on a daily, weekly, and/or annual basis. What is done with it? At what cost? What would be the best ways to reduce or eliminate some of this waste?
3. Develop a plan by which you can conduct your daily life in a more environmentally friendly manner. What resources—electricity, water, heat, gasoline, paper, other—can you conserve? Identify three to four of these, explain your conservation plan, and identify its costs (including expenditures of time and effort) and benefits.

James p. Bair/National Geographic/Getty Images

Photograph 6: Border of Haiti and the Dominican Republic (south of Dajabon, Dominican Republic), 2001 *This photograph illustrates the effect of the environmental management policies of two different governments, those of Haiti (pop. 8,700,000) and the Dominican Republic (pop. 10,000,000). In the nineteenth century these two nations, occupying the Caribbean island of Hispaniola, 600 miles off the Florida coast, were blessed, as Jared Diamond observes, in Collapse, with an "exuberance . . . of forests, full of trees and valuable wood." Haiti differed from the Dominican Republic in its higher population density, lower rainfall, and a colonial slave-plantation culture in which the "French ships that brought slaves to Haiti returned to Europe with cargoes of Haitian timber." By mid-nineteenth century, the land was largely stripped of trees. Haiti's ruthless "Papa Doc" and "Baby Doc" Duvalier followed an unstable series of presidents; none protected the environment, leaving only 1% of Haiti forested today. As Diamond points out, wherever deforestation occurs, its consequences "include loss of timber and other forest building materials, soil erosion, loss of soil fertility, sediment loads in the rivers, loss of watershed protection and hence of potential hydroelectric power, and decreased rainfall" (330).*

Diamond continues, in contrast is the Dominican Republic, with 28% forested land, rigorously and ruthlessly maintained. In the 1860s and 1870s the Dominican Republic appeared to be on the Haitian road to environmental ruin. People were clearing the forests for sugar plantations and burning trees to make charcoal for cooking fuel; as the twentieth century began, rapid urbanization and deforestation were occurring. However, in contrast to Haitian neglect, citizens in the Dominican Republic launched bottom-up conservation efforts, executed with rigor by that country's own ruthless, evil dictators, Trujillo and Balaguer. Although they maintained extensive logging operation, their management included natural reforestation and use of the army to expel squatters and rogue loggers. Among numerous environmental safeguards, they preserved "forested watersheds" in order to provide adequate hydroelectric power and water for the Republic's burgeoning industries and growing population (343); imported and subsidized gas as the preferred cooking fuel (over charcoal); and established 74 large national parks, in contrast to two threatened ones in Haiti. Whereas outsiders rule the roost in Haiti and think small, in the Dominican Republic, citizens' groups and NGOs promote environmental efforts on a large scale.

CONSIDERING THE IMAGE

1. Use the above information to interpret what you see in this photograph.
2. Propose an environmental policy—one feasible in a democracy rather than in a strong-arm dictatorship—that will both sustain natural resources and accommodate human needs.

Photograph 7: Fire caused by Brazilian farmers burning out of control in the Amazon state of Rondonia, Brazil, October 1998 *Subsistence farmers, often squatters—estimated to be between 200 and 500 million people worldwide—employ slash-and-burn agriculture, clearing forests to plant crops. Rainforest soil is a "wet desert" with a few nutrients that it becomes depleted within four years and is thereby made unfit for use, forever. The farmers, can move on to other parts of the forest where they continue this destructive cycle.*

The Amazon rainforest, sometimes called "the lungs of our planet," produces 20% of the world's oxygen and contains the largest diversity of plant and animal species in the world. Over 438,000 species of plants of economic and social interest have been registered, and many more are uncatalogued; one in five of the world's birds live there. Even a single hectare (2.47 acres) includes more than 750 types of trees and 1,500 other plants. Yet these are vanishing before our eyes. Although Brazil has one-third of the world's remaining rainforests, more than 2.7 million acres are burned or logged every year. Twenty percent of the Amazon rainforest has already been destroyed as the land is cleared there in the same enterprises for which the North American forests (and those in Haiti—see commentary on Photograph 6) were demolished: timber, ranching, grazing, hydroelectric power, subsistence, and more extensive agriculture.

Within forty years the entire Amazon rainforest could disappear entirely, and with it the last 200,000 indigenous tribespeople—a population decimated from the estimated ten million who lived there five centuries ago—in addition to a massive loss of biodiversity as plants and animals become extinct. Other profound, ugly consequences include less rain, less oxygen, and more carbon dioxide in the atmosphere; air and water pollution; soil erosion; the spread of malaria; and increased global warming. What would it take to save the rain forest: United Nations action? A strong-arm dictator (like the Dominican Republic's Balaguer) with an enlightened public policy? Scientists' reports, reinforced by local advocates? Subsidies to the subsistence farmers and squatters? Who will pay the costs? And where will the money come from?

Source: Leslie Taylor, The Healing Power of Rainforest Herbs (Garden City: Square One Publishers, Inc., 2004).

CONSIDERING THE IMAGE

1. How does knowledge of the above commentary influence your reading of this photograph? Could you imagine this forest burning occurring in other places in the world? With what consequences?
2. The rainforest's natural products—nuts, fruits, oil-producing and medicinal plants—could be harvested at a profit for the individual farmers. But would that be sufficient to bring about the massive changes in public policy, conservation practices, and individual attitudes necessary to save the rainforest? What can individuals do, anywhere, to conserve and preserve the environment—at home, and elsewhere in the world? What can private groups do? Will it take the concerted efforts of governments worldwide and international agencies, such as the UN, to effect long-term changes?

Photograph 8: Water streaming from a melting iceberg carved from Kangerlua Glacier (Jakobshavn Icefjord) in Disko Bay, Ililussant, Greenland, July 31, 2006 *Melting glaciers of the Antarctic, and Greenland ice sheets, are a beautiful but ominous sight. Accompanied by booms and crashes, huge chunks of snow and ice—compacted for as long as 150,000 years—break off and fall into the warming Arctic Ocean. The world's temperature is expected to rise 3–8 degrees in the twenty-first century, largely due to greenhouse gases such as carbon dioxide and methane from smokestacks, vehicles, and burning forests. Glaciers are melting worldwide, from the Andes to the Alps to the snows of Kilimanjaro; many are expected to vanish entirely within thirty or forty years, and the oceans to rise several feet, according to the Intergovernmental Panel on Climate Change, representing a consensus of 2,000 scientists.*

But these aspects of global warming are truly only the tip of the iceberg. As the natural habitat of polar bears and other arctic animals shrinks, they will be forced to cling to icebergs in the open sea and to swim between increasingly distant ice floes to search for food; their population in the Hudson Bay south of Churchill has declined 20% in seventeen years. The impact may be felt far from the Arctic, too. Rising water levels in the oceans cause floods from Bangladesh to New Zealand to Cape Cod. Houses, whole villages, wash away, the process exacerbated by severe hurricanes that lash coastal areas. The result? Lost lives, billions of dollars of damage, destruction of coral reefs and marine habitats, salinated water unfit for humans or agriculture, and increases in malaria and other diseases. As the snow melts, the air temperatures rise and contribute to greater aridity worldwide, forcing indigenous peoples from the Andes to Africa to compete for ever-scarcer water. These are but a few of the numerous interrelated and devastating effects of global warming.

CONSIDERING THE IMAGE

1. How could melting glaciers have such worldwide effects? How could they produce such seemingly contradictory consequences, producing both flooding and drought?

2. In *An Inconvenient Truth*, Al Gore proposes several arguments to refute those who deny that global warming exists and that something needs to be done about it. These include challenging the "misconception that the scientific community is in a state of disagreement about whether global warming is real" (261); presenting evidence that changes are not happening gradually, as some people claim, but rather are accelerating to a crisis point at lightning speed (254–55); countering "the false belief that we have to choose between a healthy economy and a healthy environment" (270–71); and emphasizing that global warming is *not* too large a problem to reverse, as some argue, though this will require judicious intervention and extensive international cooperation (278). Pick one of Gore's positions, discuss it with a partner or with your class, and write a response, amplifying the points Gore makes.

Source: Al Gore, *An Inconvenient Truth: The Planetary Emergency of Global Warming and What We Can Do About It.* Emmaus, PA: Rodale, 2006.

your discontent." Rather, I have tried to say that this normal and healthy discontent can be channeled into the creative outlet of nonviolent direct action. And now this approach is being termed extremist.

But though I was initially disappointed at being categorized as an extremist, as I continued to think about the matter I gradually gained a measure of satisfaction from the label. Was not Jesus an extremist for love: "Love your enemies, bless them that curse you, do good to them that hate you, and pray for them which despitefully use you, and persecute you." Was not Amos an extremist for justice: "Let justice roll down like waters and righteousness like an ever-flowing stream." Was not Paul an extremist for the Christian gospel: "I bear in my body the marks of the Lord Jesus." Was not Martin Luther an extremist: "Here I stand; I cannot do otherwise, so help me God." And John Bunyan: "I will stay in jail to the end of my days before I make a butchery of my conscience." And Abraham Lincoln: "This nation cannot survive half slave and half free." And Thomas Jefferson: "We hold these truths to be self-evident, that all men are created equal. . . ." So the question is not whether we will be extremists, but what kind of extremists we will be. Will we be extremists for hate or for love? Will we be extremists for the preservation of injustice or for the extension of justice? In that dramatic scene on Calvary's hill three men were crucified. We must never forget that all three were crucified for the same crime—the crime of extremism. Two were extremists for immorality, and thus fell below their environment. The other, Jesus Christ, was an extremist for love, truth and goodness, and thereby rose above his environment. Perhaps the South, the nation and the world are in dire need of creative extremists.

I had hoped that the white moderate would see this need. Perhaps I was too optimistic; perhaps I expected too much. I suppose I should have realized that few members of the oppressor race can understand the deep groans and passionate yearnings of the oppressed race, and still fewer have the vision to see that injustice must be rooted out by strong, persistent and determined action. I am thankful, however, that some of our white brothers in the South have grasped the meaning of this social revolution and committed themselves to it. They are still all too few in quantity, but they are big in quality. Some—such as Ralph McGill, Lillian Smith, Harry Golden, James McBride Dabbs, Ann Braden and Sarah Patton Boyle—have written about our struggle in eloquent and prophetic terms. Others have marched with us down nameless streets of the South. They have languished in filthy, roach-infested jails, suffering the abuse and brutality of policemen who view them as "dirty nigger-lovers." Unlike so many of their moderate brothers and sisters, they have recognized the urgency of the moment and sensed the need for powerful "action" antidotes to combat the disease of segregation.

Let me take note of my other major disappointment. I have been so greatly disappointed with the white church and its leadership. Of course, there are some notable exceptions. I am not unmindful of the fact that each of you has taken some significant stands on this issue. I commend you, Reverend Stallings, for your Christian stand on this past Sunday, in welcoming Negroes to your worship service on a non-segregated basis. I commend the Catholic leaders of this state for integrating Spring Hill College several years ago.

34   But despite these notable exceptions, I must honestly reiterate that I have been disappointed with the church. I do not say this as one of those negative critics who can always find something wrong with the church. I say this as a minister of the gospel, who loves the church; who was nurtured in its bosom; who has been sustained by its spiritual blessings and who will remain true to it as long as the cord of life shall lengthen.

35   When I was suddenly catapulted into the leadership of the bus protest in Montgomery, Alabama, a few years ago, I felt we would be supported by the white church. I felt that the white ministers, priests and rabbis of the South would be among our strongest allies. Instead, some have been outright opponents, refusing to understand the freedom movement and misrepresenting its leaders; all too many others have been more cautious than courageous and have remained silent behind the anesthetizing security of stained-glass windows.

36   In spite of my shattered dreams, I came to Birmingham with the hope that the white religious leadership of this community would see the justice of our cause and, with deep moral concern, would serve as the channel through which our just grievances could reach the power structure. I had hoped that each of you would understand. But again I have been disappointed.

37   I have heard numerous southern religious leaders admonish their worshipers to comply with a desegregation decision because it is the law, but I have longed to hear white ministers declare: "Follow this decree because integration is morally right and because the Negro is your brother." In the midst of blatant injustices inflicted upon the Negro, I have watched white churchmen stand on the sideline and mouth pious irrelevancies and sanctimonious trivialities. In the midst of a mighty struggle to rid our nation of racial and economic injustice, I have heard many ministers say: "Those are social issues, with which the gospel has no real concern." And I have watched many churches commit themselves to completely otherworldly religion which makes a strange, un-Biblical distinction between body and soul, between the sacred and the secular.

38   I have traveled the length and breadth of Alabama, Mississippi and all the other southern states. On sweltering summer days and crisp autumn mornings I have looked at the South's beautiful churches with their lofty spires pointing heavenward. I have beheld the impressive outlines of her massive religious-education buildings. Over and over I have found myself asking: "What kind of people worship here? Who is their God? Where were their voices when the lips of Governor Barnett dripped with words of interposition and nullification? Where were they when Governor Wallace gave a clarion call for defiance and hatred? Where were their voices of support when bruised and weary Negro men and women decided to rise from the dark dungeons of complacency to the bright hills of creative protest?"

Yes, these questions are still in my mind. In deep disappointment 39
I have wept over the laxity of the church. But be assured that my tears
have been tears of love. There can be no deep disappointment where
there is not deep love. Yes, I love the church. How could I do otherwise?
I am in the rather unique position of being the son, the grandson and the
great-grandson of preachers. Yes, I see the church as the body of Christ.
But, oh! How we have blemished and scarred that body through social
neglect and through fear of being nonconformists.

There was a time when the church was very powerful—in the time 40
when the early Christians rejoiced at being deemed worthy to suffer for
what they believed. In those days the church was not merely a thermometer
that recorded the ideas and principles of popular opinion; it was a thermostat that transformed the mores of society. Whenever the early Christians
entered a town, the people in power became disturbed and immediately
sought to convict the Christians for being "disturbers of the peace" and
"outside agitators." But the Christians pressed on, in the conviction that
they were "a colony of heaven," called to obey God rather than man. Small
in number, they were big in commitment. They were too God-intoxicated to
be "astronomically intimidated." By their effort and example they brought
an end to such ancient evils as infanticide and gladiatorial contests.

Things are different now. So often the contemporary church is a 41
weak, ineffectual voice with an uncertain sound. So often it is an archde-
fender of the status quo. Far from being disturbed by the presence of the
church, the power structure of the average community is consoled by the
church's silent—and often even vocal—sanction of things as they are.

But the judgment of God is upon the church as never before. If to- 42
day's church does not recapture the sacrificial spirit of the early church, it
will lose its authenticity, forfeit the loyalty of millions, and be dismissed
as an irrelevant social club with no meaning for the twentieth century. Every day I meet young people whose disappointment with the church has
turned into outright disgust.

Perhaps I have once again been too optimistic. Is organized religion 43
too inextricably bound to the status quo to save our nation and the world?
Perhaps I must turn my faith to the inner spiritual church, the church
within the church, as the true *ekklesia* and the hope of the world. But again
I am thankful to God that some noble souls from the ranks of organized
religion have broken loose from the paralyzing chains of conformity and
joined us as active partners in the struggle for freedom. They have left their
secure congregations and walked the streets of Albany, Georgia, with us.
They have gone down the highways of the South on tortuous rides for freedom. Yes, they have gone to jail with us. Some have been dismissed from
their churches, have lost the support of their bishops and fellow ministers.
But they have acted in the faith that right defeated is stronger than evil
triumphant. Their witness has been the spiritual salt that has preserved
the true meaning of the gospel in these troubled times. They have carved a
tunnel of hope through the dark mountain of disappointment.

44   I hope the church as a whole will meet the challenge of this decisive hour. But even if the church does not come to the aid of justice, I have no despair about the future. I have no fear about the outcome of our struggle in Birmingham, even if our motives are at present misunderstood. We will reach the goal of freedom in Birmingham and all over the nation, because the goal of America is freedom. Abused and scorned though we may be, our destiny is tied up with America's destiny. Before the pilgrims landed at Plymouth, we were here. Before the pen of Jefferson etched the majestic words of the Declaration of Independence across the pages of history, we were here. For more than two centuries our forebears labored in this country without wages; they made cotton king; they built the homes of their masters while suffering gross injustice and shameful humiliation— and yet out of a bottomless vitality they continued to thrive and develop. If the inexpressible cruelties of slavery could not stop us, the opposition we now face will surely fail. We will win our freedom because the sacred heritage of our nation and the eternal will of God are embodied in our echoing demands.

45   Before closing I feel impelled to mention one other point in your statement that has troubled me profoundly. You warmly commended the Birmingham police force for keeping "order" and "preventing violence." I doubt that you would have so warmly commended the police force if you had seen its dogs sinking their teeth into unarmed, nonviolent Negroes. I doubt that you would so quickly commend the policemen if you were to observe their ugly and inhumane treatment of Negroes here in the city jail; if you were to watch them push and curse old Negro women and young Negro girls; if you were to see them slap and kick old Negro men and young boys; if you were to observe them as they did on two occasions, refuse to give us food because we wanted to sing our grace together. I cannot join you in your praise of the Birmingham police department.

46   It is true that the police have exercised a degree of discipline in handling the demonstrators. In this sense they have conducted themselves rather "nonviolently" in public. But for what purpose? To preserve the evil system of segregation. Over the past few years I have consistently preached that nonviolence demands that the means we use must be as pure as the ends we seek. I have tried to make clear that it is wrong to use immoral means to attain moral ends. But now I must affirm that it is just as wrong, or perhaps even more so, to use moral means to preserve immoral ends. Perhaps Mr. Connor and his policemen have been rather nonviolent in public, as was Chief Pritchett in Albany, Georgia, but they have used the moral means of nonviolence to maintain the immoral end of racial injustice. As T. S. Eliot has said: "The last temptation is the greatest treason: To do the right deed for the wrong reason."

47   I wish you had commended the Negro sit-inners and demonstrators of Birmingham for their sublime courage, their willingness to suffer and

their amazing discipline in the midst of great provocation. One day the South will recognize its real heroes. They will be the James Merediths, with the noble sense of purpose that enables them to face jeering and hostile mobs, and with the agonizing loneliness that characterizes the life of the pioneer. They will be old, oppressed, battered Negro women, symbolized in a seventy-two-year-old woman in Montgomery, Alabama, who rose up with a sense of dignity and with her people decided not to ride segregated buses, and who responded with ungrammatical profundity to one who inquired about her weariness: "My feet is tired, but my soul is at rest." They will be the young high school and college students, the young ministers of the gospel and a host of their elders, courageously and nonviolently sitting in at lunch counters and willingly going to jail for conscience' sake. One day the South will know that when these disinherited children of God sat down at lunch counters, they were in reality standing up for what is best in the American dream and for the most sacred values in our Judaeo-Christian heritage, thereby bringing our nation back to those great wells of democracy which were dug deep by the founding fathers in their formulation of the Constitution and the Declaration of Independence.

Never before have I written so long a letter. I'm afraid it is much too long to take your precious time. I can assure you that it would have been much shorter if I had been writing from a comfortable desk, but what else can one do when he is alone in a narrow jail cell, other than write long letters, think long thoughts and pray long prayers? 48

If I have said anything in this letter that overstates the truth and indicates an unreasonable impatience, I beg you to forgive me. If I have said anything that understates the truth and indicates my having a patience that allows me to settle for anything less than brotherhood, I beg God to forgive me. 49

I hope this letter finds you strong in faith. I also hope that circumstances will soon make it possible for me to meet each of you, not as an integrationist or a civil-rights leader but as a fellow clergyman and a Christian brother. Let us all hope that the dark clouds of racial prejudice will soon pass away and the deep fog of misunderstanding will be lifted from our fear-drenched communities, and in some not too distant tomorrow the radiant stars of love and brotherhood will shine over our great nation with all their scintillating beauty. 50

Yours for the cause of Peace and Brotherhood,
Martin Luther King, Jr.

Content

1. In paragraph 4 King makes several assertions on which he bases the rest of his argument. What are they? Does he ever prove them, or does he assume that readers will take them for granted?

2. In paragraph 5 King asserts that Birmingham's "white power structure left the Negro community with no alternative" but to commit civil disobedience. Does he ever prove this? Does he need to? Is it a debatable statement?

3. What, according to King, are the "four basic steps" in "any nonviolent campaign" (¶ 6)? What is the goal of "nonviolent direct action" (¶ 10)? What is the constructive, "nonviolent tension" (¶ 10) King favors?

4. Why has King been disappointed by white moderates (¶s 23–32)? By the white church (¶s 33–44)? What does he want white moderates to do? What does he claim that the church should do?

5. How does King deal with the argument that civil rights activists are too impatient, that they should go slow because "it has taken Christianity almost two thousand years to accomplish what it has" (¶ 26)? How does he refute the argument that he is an extremist (¶ 27)?

Strategies/Structures/Language

6. How does King establish, in the salutation and first paragraph, his reasons for writing? The setting in which he writes? His intended audience? In what ways does he demonstrate a sensitive, reasonable tone?

7. King's letter ostensibly replies to that of the eight clergymen. Find passages in which he addresses them, and analyze the voice he uses. In what relation to the clergymen does King see himself? He also has a secondary audience; who are its members? Locate passages that seem especially directed to this second audience. In what relation to this audience does King see himself?

8. Why does King cite the theologians Aquinas (a Catholic), Buber (a Jew), and Tillich (a Protestant) in paragraph 16? What similarities link the three?

9. After defending his actions against the criticisms of the clergymen, King takes the offensive in paragraphs 23–44. How does he signal this change?

10. Which parts of King's letter appeal chiefly to reason? To emotion? How are the two types of appeals interrelated?

11. King uses large numbers of rhetorical questions throughout this essay (see ¶s 18, 25, 31, 38, 39). Why? With what effects?

12. How does King define a "just law" (¶s 16, 17)? An "unjust law" (¶s 16, 17)? Why are these definitions crucial to the argument that follows?

For Writing

13. With a partner, write a position paper identifying the circumstances, if any, under which breaking the law is justifiable. If you use Dr. King's definition of just and unjust law (¶s 15–20) or make any distinction, say, between moral law and civil law, be sure to explain what you mean. You may, if you wish, use examples with which you are personally familiar. Or you may elaborate on some of the examples King uses (¶ 22) or on examples from King's own civil rights activities, such as the boycotts in the early 1950s of the legally segregated Montgomery bus system (¶ 35).

14. If you are a member of a church, or attend a church regularly, address members of the congregation on what, if any, commitment you think your church should make to better the lives of other groups who do not attend that church. Does this commitment extend to civil disobedience?

15. Would you ever be willing to go to jail for a cause? What cause or types of causes? Under what circumstances? If you knew that a prison record might bar you from some privileges in some states (such as practicing law or medicine), would you still be willing to take such a risk?

16. *Journal Writing.* Write a narrative about a historical event that occurred during your lifetime, perhaps the election of Barack Obama as the forty-fourth President of the United States. To what extent were you aware that you were living through a moment of history-in-the-making? Did you fully realize how the event would change the world or your life? Did you go back to the event and retell it to yourself to make sense of it?

17. *Dialogues.* Given King's characterization of the church as "the body of Christ" (¶ 39), how might he interpret the fight Frederick Douglass recounts in "Resurrection" (86–91)? When and under what circumstances might he consider violence justifiable? How might he interpret Douglass's fight as a metaphorical struggle for what calls "somebodiness" (¶ 27)?

18. *Second Look.* How does the photograph in this essay of Dr. King and other civil rights figures escorting children to school illustrate King's belief in the efficacy of nonviolent direct action? Why are the mothers of the children absent from the photograph? How does the arrangement of the people photographed affect your interpretation of this historical moment? For example, the only woman pictured, Joan Baez, who is white and a celebrity, stands in the center of the group, while each child is sheltered by the male adults. What kinds of assumptions about race and gender does this photograph challenge?

CARTOON ARGUMENTS

EVAN EISENBERG

Evan Eisenberg (born 1955) studied philosophy and classics at Harvard and Princeton and biology at the University of Massachusetts, Amherst, preparatory to becoming a journalist specializing in nature, culture, music, and technology. In addition to two books, *The Recording Angel: Explorations in Phonography* (1987, 2005) and *The Ecology of Eden* (1988), offering a model of how to prevent environmental disaster, Eisenberg's serious works have appeared in *The Atlantic, The New Republic, The New York Times, Natural History,* and other periodicals. His humorous pieces have been featured in *The New Yorker* (where "Dialogue Boxes" first appeared, in 2005), *Esquire, Slate, Salon,* and elsewhere. This piece provides a strong critique of Microsoft in a concise form, readily accessible to any computer user. As you read, note not only the text in the dialogue boxes, but the icons and the—very limited—options for response.

Dialogue Boxes You Should Have Read More Carefully

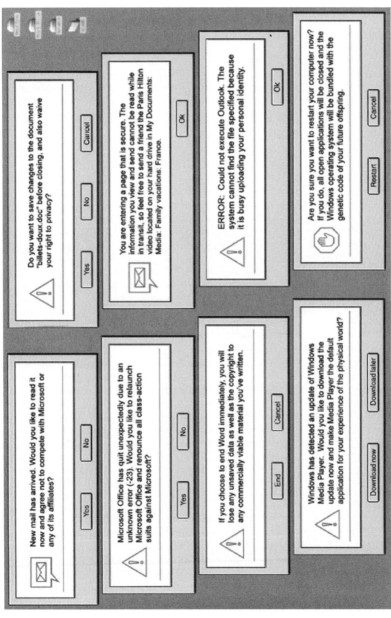

Evan Eisenberg, "Dialogue Boxes You Should Have Read More Carefully." Copyright © 2004 by Evan Eisenberg. Reprinted by permission of the author. This selection first appeared in The *New York Times*.

THE ROAD TO SUCCESS

Allegorical representations of the road to virtue, or to heaven, have been common in Western culture since the Middle Ages. Consider the Hell-Earth-Paradise structure of Dante's *Divine Comedy*; and the journeys of Everyman, and of Christian Pilgrim in *Pilgrim's Progress*. "The Road to Success" was first used by the National Cash Register Company as a visual, allegorical representation of the way to success in the business world. In 1913 it was published in *The Etude*, a magazine for music teachers, students, and professionals. This guide to success reflects the magazine's motto "Music Exalts Life!" That its advice remains as current today as it did a century ago is reflected in the popularity of this cartoon on posters and on T-shirts, intended (as the website says) for "young people starting out, new businesses, and anyone seeking success." As you examine "the road to success," what deterrents do you discover on the road? Which of the aids to success represent individual qualities, and which result from a functioning social and educational system? Have any qualities become irrelevant in the past century?

The National Cash Register Co.

Content

1. Each of Eisenberg's dialogue boxes embeds an argument about Microsoft. Identify the argument of each and the specific charge against Microsoft's relation to those who use its operating system.

2. Now consider all the arguments together. What's their point?

3. The artist expects that readers will share the values represented in this cartoon. Identify some of the salient values depicted on the Road to Success, both positive ("True Knowledge"—why is this a tunnel?) and negative ("Vices" as a hand grabbing people). (If you need to enlarge the picture, it's easy to do so on the "Road to Success" website.) Do you, as a 21st Century reader, in fact, share these values? Why or why not?

4. If you know of any computer games that have a comparable structure to "The Road to Success," explain what these are and why they are similar.

Strategies/Structures/Language

5. In Eisenberg's dialogue boxes, what's missing from some of the limited choices in the actions the computer user can take? Identify these, and explain what will happen if the user chooses one or another of the permissible alternatives.

6. Eisenberg conducts his argument by letting readers do most of the work and come to all of the conclusions. How can he be sure they'll read the boxes the way he wants them to and arrive at the same conclusions that he does?

7. How closely has Eisenberg imitated Microsoft's language?

8. Although readers are looking at "The Road to Success" in two dimensions, the cartoon is more meaningful if it is interpreted in three dimensions. Explain this map by reading in the contours, the highs and lows, hills and valleys, steep and gradual gradations. How do the labels (such as "Failure," "Oblivion," "Short Cuts"), as well as the contours of the Road itself, reinforce the moral geography of the cartoon?

9. Where are people running in "The Road to Success"? Why are they lounging in the areas labeled "Bohemianism" and "Always Right Club"? Why can they ultimately ascend by train during the last part of the journey?

For Writing

10. Find cartoons that make arguments, and analyze several to show how they do it—either through only visual means or through a combination of words and images. Editorial or political cartoons are a good source. If you work with a partner, you can check your interpretations against each other's.

11. Present your own version of "The Road to Success" or another argument in cartoon format, using either a single or multiple panel. If you can't draw, you can provide your own captions for existing cartoons. See, for instance, *The New Yorker's* website, http://www.cartoonbank.com.

12. **Dialogues.** Compare "The Road to Success" op-art comic and Lynda Barry's graphic narrative "Common Scents" (318–328). In what ways is each a traditional story with a beginning, middle, and end, with a climax and resolution? How does each narrative challenge an unstated assumption or belief and so act as an "anti-story," or one that undermines an existing story? Who, or what, is the

protagonist in each narrative? What stake does each narrator have in the outcome of the story she tells? Would you characterize the narrators as observers, supporting actors, stand-ins for the reader, victims, or heroes? How does the relationship between the narrator and reader differ in each narrative? How does each artist challenge your ideas about what stories—and comics—are supposed to do? If you wish, expand your analysis to address the same issues in Art Spiegelman's "Mein Kampf (My Struggle)" (93–95).

ROBERT REICH

Robert Reich (born 1946), earned a BA at Dartmouth College (1968) and a JD degree from Yale Law School (1973), was a Rhodes scholar at Oxford, and taught at Harvard's John F. Kennedy School of Government, and at Brandeis University before moving in 2005 to a professorship at the University of California, Berkeley's Goldman School of Public Policy. In 2003 he received the Václav Havel Prize for his "contributions to social thought." Active in politics since his student days, Reich interned for Senator Robert Kennedy, coordinated Eugene McCarthy's 1968 presidential campaign, and was secretary of labor during Clinton's first term as president (1993–1996). *Locked in the Cabinet* (1997) discusses his experiences.

Many of Reich's books on economics are intended for a general audience, including *Tales of a New America: The Anxious Liberal's Guide to the Future* (1988); and *Aftershock: The Next Economy and America's Future* (2010). *The Next American Frontier* (1983) provided a rationale for the Democratic Party's economic policy, explaining that "government intervention sets the boundaries, decides what's going to be marketed, sets the rules of the game through procurement policies, tax credits, depreciation allowances, loans and loan guarantees." *Tales of a New America* defines four economic myths: "Mob at the Gate" labels foreigners as adversaries to American citizens; "The Triumphant Individual" reinforces the myth of the American Dream; "The Benevolent Community" claims that Americans act out of social responsibility to one another; and "The Rot at the Top" accuses the elite class of corruption and abuse of their power. "The Global Elite," first published in the *New York Times Magazine* (1991) provides factual information to counteract the myths of a benevolent, egalitarian society and implicitly argues for a more equitable—and democratic—distribution of our country's wealth.

The Global Elite

The idea of "community" has always held a special attraction for   1
Americans. In a 1984 speech, President Ronald Reagan celebrated America's "bedrock"—"its communities where neighbors help one another, where families bring up kids together, where American values

are born." Governor Mario M. Cuomo of New York, with a very different political leaning, has been almost as lyrical. "Community . . . is the reality on which our national life has been founded," he said in 1987.

2   There is only one problem with this picture. Most Americans no longer live in traditional communities. They live in suburban subdivisions bordered by highways and sprinkled with shopping malls, or in tony condominiums and residential clusters, or in ramshackle apartment buildings and housing projects. Most of them commute to work and socialize on some basis other than geographic proximity. And most people pick up and move to a different neighborhood every five years or so.

3   But Americans generally have one thing in common with their neighbors: They have similar incomes. And that simple fact lies at the heart of the new community. This means that their educational backgrounds are likely to be similar, that they pay roughly the same in taxes, and that they indulge in the same consumer impulses. "Tell me someone's ZIP code," the founder of a direct-mail company once bragged, "and I can predict what they eat, drink, drive—even think."

4   Americans who own their homes usually share one political cause with their neighbors: a near obsessive concern with maintaining or upgrading property values. And this common interest is responsible for much of what has brought neighbors together in recent years. Complete strangers, although they may live on the same street or in the same condominium complex, suddenly feel intense solidarity when it is rumored that low-income housing will be constructed in their midst or that a poorer school district will be consolidated with their own.

5   The renewed emphasis on "community" in American life has justified and legitimized these economic enclaves. If generosity and solidarity end at the border of similarly valued properties, then the most fortunate can be virtuous citizens at little cost. Since most people in one neighborhood or town are equally well off, there is no cause for a guilty conscience. If inhabitants of another area are poorer, let them look to one another. Why should *we* pay for *their* schools?

6   So the argument goes, without acknowledging that the critical assumption has already been made: "We" and "they" belong to fundamentally different communities. Through such reasoning, it has become possible to maintain a self-image of generosity toward, and solidarity with, one's "community" without bearing any responsibility to "them"—the other "community."

7   America's high earners—the fortunate top fifth—thus feel increasingly justified in paying only what is necessary to insure that everyone in their community is sufficiently well educated and has access to the public services they need to succeed.

8 Last year, the top fifth of working Americans took home more money than the other four-fifths put together—the highest portion in postwar history. These high earners will relinquish somewhat more of their income to the Federal Government this year than in 1990 as a result of

last fall's tax changes, although considerably less than in the late 1970s, when the tax code was more progressive. But the continuing debate over whether the wealthy are paying their fair share of taxes obscures a larger issue, with more profound implications for America: The fortunate fifth is quietly seceding from the rest of the nation.

This is occurring gradually, without much awareness by members of the top group—or, for that matter, by anyone else. And the Government is speeding this process as Washington shifts responsibility for many public services to state and local governments.

The secession is taking several forms. In many cities and towns, the wealthy have in effect withdrawn their dollars from the support of public spaces and institutions shared by all and dedicated the savings to their own private services. As public parks and playgrounds deteriorate, there is a proliferation of private health clubs, golf clubs, tennis clubs, skating clubs, and every other type of recreational association in which costs are shared among members. Condominiums and the omnipresent residential communities dun their members to undertake work that financially strapped local governments can no longer afford to do well—maintaining roads, mending sidewalks, pruning trees, repairing street lights, cleaning swimming pools, paying for lifeguards, and, notably, hiring security guards to protect life and property. (The number of private security guards in the United States now exceeds the number of public police officers.)

Of course, wealthier Americans have been withdrawing into their own neighborhoods and clubs for generations. But the new secession is more dramatic because the highest earners now inhabit a different economy from other Americans. The new elite is linked by jet, modem, fax, satellite, and fiber-optic cable to the great commercial and recreational centers of the world, but it is not particularly connected to the rest of the nation.

That is because the work this group does is becoming less tied to the activities of other Americans. Most of their jobs consist of analyzing and manipulating symbols—words, numbers, or visual images. Among the most prominent of these "symbolic analysts" are management consultants, lawyers, software and design engineers, research scientists, corporate executives, financial advisors, strategic planners, advertising executives, television and movie producers, and other workers whose job titles include terms like "strategy," "planning," "consultant," "policy," "resources," or "engineer."

These workers typically spend long hours in meetings or on the telephone and even longer hours in planes or hotels—advising, making presentations, giving briefings, and making deals. Periodically, they issue reports, plans, designs, drafts, briefs, blueprints, analyses, memorandums, layouts, renderings, scripts, or projections. In contrast with people whose jobs tend to be tedious and repetitive, symbolic analysts find their work varied and intellectually challenging. In fact, the work is often enjoyable.

These symbolic analysts are in ever greater demand in a world market that places an increasing value on identifying and solving problems. Requests for their software designs, financial advice, or engineering blueprints come from all parts of the globe. This largely explains why most (but by no means all) symbolic analysts have become wealthier, even as the ever-growing worldwide supply of unskilled labor continues to depress the wages of other Americans.

15　Successful Americans have not completely disengaged themselves from the lives of their less fortunate compatriots. Some devote substantial resources and energies to helping the rest of society, not through their tax payments, but through voluntary efforts. "Generosity is a reflection of what one does with his or her resources—and not what he or she advocates the government do with everyone's money," Ronald Reagan said in 1984.

16　The argument is fair enough. Government is not the only device for redistributing wealth. In his speech accepting the Presidential nomination at the Republican National Convention in 1988, George Bush said that the real magnanimity of America was to be found in a "brilliant diversity" of private charities, "spread like stars, like a thousand points of light in a broad and peaceful sky."

17　No nation congratulates itself more enthusiastically on its charitable acts than America; none engages in a greater number of charity balls, bake sales, benefit auctions, and border-to-border hand holdings for good causes. Much of this is sincerely motivated and admirable.

18　But close examination reveals that many of these acts of benevolence do not help the needy. Particularly suspect is the private givings of those in the top income-tax bracket. Studies have revealed that their largess does not flow mainly to social services for the poor—to better schools, health clinics, or recreational centers. Instead, most voluntary contributions of wealthy Americans go to the places and institutions that entertain, inspire, cure, or educate wealthy Americans—art museums, opera houses, theaters, orchestras, ballet companies, private hospitals, and elite universities.

19　And even these charitable contributions are relatively skimpy. Last year, American households with incomes of less than $10,000 gave an average of 5.5 percent of their earnings to charity or to a religious organization; those making more than $100,000 a year gave only 2.9 percent. After the 1986 tax-code overhaul reduced the benefits of charitable giving, the very rich became even stingier. According to Internal Revenue Service data, taxpayers earning $500,000 or more slashed their average donations to $16,062 in 1988 from $47,432 in 1980.

20　Corporate philanthropy is following the same general pattern. In recent years, the largest American corporations have been sounding the alarm about the nation's fast deteriorating primary and secondary schools. Few are more eloquent and impassioned about the need for better schools than American executives. "How well we educate all of our children will determine our competitiveness globally, and our economic health domestically, and our communities' character and vitality," said a report of The Business Roundtable, a New York–based association of top executives.

Accordingly, there are numerous "partnerships" between corpora- 21 tions and public schools: scholarships for poor children qualified to attend college, and programs in which businesses adopt individual schools by making conspicuous donations of computers, books, and, on occasion, even money. That such activities are loudly touted by public relations staffs should not detract from the good they do.

Despite the hoopla, business donations to education and charitable 22 causes actually tapered off markedly in the 1980s, even as the economy boomed. In the 1970s, corporate giving to education jumped an average of 15 percent a year. In 1990, however, giving was only 5 percent over that in 1989; and in 1989 it was 3 percent over 1988. Moreover, most of this money goes to colleges and universities—in particular, to the alma maters of symbolic analysts, who expect their children and grandchildren to follow in their footsteps. Only 1.5 percent of corporate giving in the late 1980s was to public primary and secondary schools.

Notably, these contributions have been smaller than the amounts 23 corporations are receiving from states and communities in the form of subsidies or tax breaks. Companies are quietly procuring such deals by threatening to move their operations—and jobs—to places around the world with a more congenial tax climate. The paradoxical result has been even less corporate revenue to spend on schools and other community services than before. The executives of General Motors, for example, who have been among the loudest to proclaim the need for better schools, have also been among the most relentless in pursuing local tax abatements and in challenging their tax assessments. G.M.'s successful efforts to reduce its taxes in North Tarrytown, N.Y., where the company has had a factory since 1914, cut local revenues by $1 million in 1990, part of a larger shortfall that forced the town to lay off scores of teachers.

The secession of the fortunate fifth has been apparent in how and where 24 they have chosen to work and live. In effect, most of America's large urban centers have splintered into two separate cities. One is composed of those whose symbolic and analytic services are linked to the world economy. The other consists of local service workers—custodians, security guards, taxi drivers, clerical aides, parking attendants, salespeople, restaurant employees—whose jobs are dependent on the symbolic analysts. Few blue-collar manufacturing workers remain in American cities. Between 1953 and 1984, for example, New York City lost 600,000 factory jobs; in the same interval, it added about 700,000 jobs for symbolic analysts and service workers.

The separation of symbolic analysts from local service workers within 25 cities has been reinforced in several ways. Most large cities now possess two school systems—a private one for the children of the top-earning group and a public one for the children of service workers, the remaining blue-collar workers, and the unemployed. Symbolic analysts spend considerable time and energy insuring that their children gain entrance to good private schools, and then small fortunes keeping them there—dollars that under a more progressive tax code might finance better public education.

26   People with high incomes live, shop, and work within areas of cities that, if not beautiful, are at least esthetically tolerable and reasonably safe; precincts not meeting these minimum standards of charm and security have been left to the less fortunate.

27   Here again, symbolic analysts have pooled their resources to the exclusive benefit of themselves. Public funds have been spent in earnest on downtown "revitalization" projects, entailing the construction of clusters of post-modern office buildings (complete with fiber-optic cables, private branch exchanges, satellite dishes, and other communications equipment linking them to the rest of the world), multilevel parking garages, hotels with glass enclosed atriums, upscale shopping plazas and galleries, theaters, convention centers, and luxury condominiums.

28   Ideally, these complexes are entirely self-contained, with air-conditioned walkways linking residences, businesses, and recreational space. The lucky resident is able to shop, work, and attend the theater without risking direct contact with the outside world—that is, the other city.

29   When not living in urban enclaves, symbolic analysts are increasingly congregating in suburbs and exurbs where corporate headquarters have been relocated, research parks have been created, and where bucolic universities have spawned entrepreneurial ventures. Among the most desirable of such locations are Princeton, N.J.; northern Westchester and Putnam Counties in New York; Palo Alto, Calif.; Austin, Tex.; Bethesda, Md.; and Raleigh-Durham, N.C.

30   Engineers and strategists of American auto companies, for example, do not live in Flint or Saginaw, Mich., where the blue-collar workers reside; they cluster in their own towns of Troy, Warren, and Auburn Hills. Likewise, the vast majority of financial specialists, lawyers, and executives working for the insurance companies of Hartford would never consider living there; after all, Hartford is the nation's fourth-poorest city. Instead, they flock to Windsor, Middlebury, West Hartford, and other towns that are among the wealthiest in the country.

31   This trend, too, has been growing for decades. But technology has accelerated it. Today's symbolic analysts linked directly to the rest of the globe can choose to live and work in the most pastoral of settings.

32   The secession has been encouraged by the Federal Government. For the last decade, Washington has in effect shifted responsibility for many public services to local governments. At their peak, Federal grants made up 25 percent of state and local spending in the late 1970s. Today, the Federal share has dwindled to 17 percent. Direct aid to local governments, in the form of programs introduced in the Johnson and Nixon

Administrations, has been the hardest hit by budget cuts. In the 1980s, Federal dollars for clean water, job training and transfers, low-income housing, sewage treatment, and garbage disposal shrank by some $50 billion a year, and Washington's share of spending on local transit declined by 50 percent. (The Bush Administration has proposed that states and localities take on even more of the costs of building and maintaining roads, and wants to cut Federal aid for mass transit.) In 1990, New York City received only 9.6 percent of all its revenue from the Federal Government, compared with 16 percent in 1981.

States have quickly transferred many of these new expenses to fis- 33
cally strapped cities and towns, with a result that by the start of the 1990s, localities were bearing more than half the costs of water and sewage, roads, parks, welfare, and public schools. In New York State, the local communities' share has risen to about 75 percent of these costs.

Cities and towns with affluent inhabitants can bear these burdens 34
relatively easily. Poorer ones, faced with the twin problem of lower incomes and greater demand for social services, have had far more difficulty. And as the gap between the richest and poorest communities has widened, the shift in responsibility for public services to cities and towns has functioned as another means of relieving wealthier Americans of the cost of aiding less fortunate citizens.

The result has been a growing inequality in basic social and com- 35
munity services. While the city tax rate in Philadelphia, for example, is about triple that of communities around it, the suburbs enjoy far better schools, hospitals, recreation, and police protection. Eighty-five percent of the richest families in the greater Philadelphia area live outside the city limits, and 80 percent of the region's poorest live inside. The quality of a city's infrastructure—roads, bridges, sewage, water treatment—is likewise related to the average income of its inhabitants.

The growing inequality in government services has been most ap- 36
parent in the public schools. The Federal Government's share of the costs of primary and secondary education has dwindled to about 6 percent. The bulk of the cost is divided about equally between the states and local school districts. States with a higher concentration of wealthy residents can afford to spend more on their schools than other states. In 1989, the average public-school teacher in Arkansas, for example, received $21,700; in Connecticut, $37,300.

Even among adjoining suburban towns in the same state the differ- 37
ences can be quite large. Consider three Boston-area communities located within minutes of one another. All are predominantly white, and most residents within each town earn about the same as their neighbors. But the disparity of incomes between towns is substantial.

Belmont, northwest of Boston, is inhabited mainly by symbolic ana- 38
lysts and their families. In 1988, the average teacher in its public schools earned $36,100. Only 3 percent of Belmont's eighteen-year-olds dropped

out of high school, and more than 80 percent of graduating seniors chose to go on to a four-year college.

39   Just east of Belmont is Somerville, most of whose residents are low-wage service workers. In 1988, the average Somerville teacher earned $29,400. A third of the town's eighteen-year-olds did not finish high school, and fewer than a third planned to attend college.

40   Chelsea, across the Mystic River from Somerville, is the poorest of the three towns. Most of its inhabitants are unskilled, and many are unemployed or only employed part time. The average teacher in Chelsea, facing tougher educational challenges than his or her counterparts in Belmont, earned $26,200 in 1988, almost a third less than the average teacher in the more affluent town just a few miles away. More than half of Chelsea's eighteen-year-olds did not graduate from high school, and only 10 percent planned to attend college.

41   Similar disparities can be found all over the nation. Students at Highland Park High School in a wealthy suburb of Dallas, for example, enjoy a campus with a planetarium, indoor swimming pool, closed-circuit television studio and state-of-the-art science laboratory. Highland Park spends about $6,000 a year to educate each student. This is almost twice that spent per pupil by the towns of Wilmer and Hutchins in southern Dallas County. According to Texas education officials, the richest school district in the state spends $19,300 a year per pupil; its poorest, $2,100 a year.

42   The courts have become involved in trying to repair such imbalances, but the issues are not open to easy judicial remedy.

43   The four-fifths of Americans left in the wake of the secession of the fortunate fifth include many poor blacks, but racial exclusion is neither the primary motive for the separation nor a necessary consequence. Lower-income whites are similarly excluded, and high-income black symbolic analysts are often welcomed. The segregation is economic rather than racial, although economically motivated separation often results in *de facto* racial segregation. Where courts have found a pattern of racially motivated segregation, it usually has involved lower-income white communities bordering on lower-income black neighborhoods.

44   In states where courts have ordered equalized state spending in school districts, the vast differences in a town's property values—and thus local tax revenues—continue to result in substantial inequities. Where courts or state governments have tried to impose limits on what affluent communities can pay their teachers, not a few parents in upscale towns have simply removed their children from the public schools and applied the money they might otherwise have willingly paid in higher taxes to private school tuitions instead. And, of course, even if statewide expenditures were better equalized, poorer states would continue to be at a substantial disadvantage.

45   In all these ways, the gap between America's symbolic analysts and everyone else is widening into a chasm. Their secession from the rest of

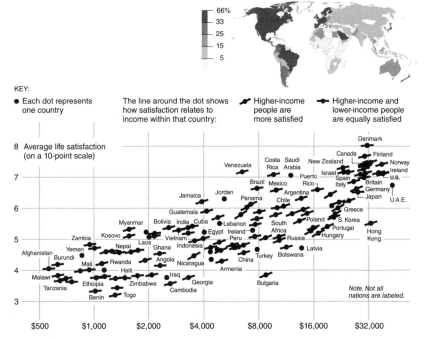

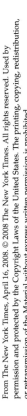

KEY:

● Each dot represents one country

The line around the dot shows how satisfaction relates to income within that country:

➤ Higher-income people are more satisfied

➤◄ Higher-income and lower-income people are equally satisfied

8 Average life satisfaction (on a 10-point scale)

G.D.P. per capita, converted to dollars at prices that equalize purchasing power. [Note the relationship between income and amount of individual satisfaction. Compare this diagram with the two maps on 482. To what degree do the "Political Trouble Spots of the Modern World" and the "Environmental Trouble Spots of the Modern World" indicated on these maps correspond to the diagram of individual satisfaction above? Explain this correspondence. For additional commentary see 499, question 12.]

the population raises fundamental questions about the future of American society. In the new global economy—in which money, technologies, and corporations cross borders effortlessly—a citizen's standard of living depends more and more on skills and insights, and on the infrastructure needed to link these abilities to the rest of the world. But the most skilled and insightful Americans, who are already positioned to thrive in the world market, are now able to slip the bonds of national allegiance, and by so doing disengage themselves from their less-favored fellows. The stark political challenge in the decades ahead will be to reaffirm that, even though America is no longer a separate and distinct economy, it is still a society whose members have abiding obligations to one another.

Content

1. Does Reich prove convincingly that "the fortunate fifth [those Americans with the highest income] is quietly seceding from the rest of the nation" (¶ 8)? To what extent does your receptivity to his argument depend on whether or not you consider yourself or your family a member of the "fortunate fifth"?

2. Who are "symbolic analysts" (¶s 12–14, 25–31)? Does Reich demonstrate that these persons comprise a significant portion of the "fortunate fifth"? Why does he identify their job titles (¶ 12), activities (¶ 13), lifestyles (¶s 25–28), and places of work and residence (¶s 28–30) in long lists? In what ways does he expect his readers to interpret these lists?

3. Reich illustrates many of the points of his argument with reference to the public schools in rich and poor districts (¶s 36–44, for example). Why does he focus on schools?

4. If Reich has convinced you of his premise (see question 1 above), has he also convinced you of his conclusion that "the most skilled and insightful Americans . . . are now able to slip the bonds of national allegiance, and by so doing disengage themselves from their less-favored fellows. The stark political challenge . . . will be to reaffirm that . . . [America] is still a society whose members have abiding obligations to one another" (¶ 45)? If he has convinced you, what does he want you to do as a consequence? If he hasn't convinced you, why hasn't he?

Strategies/Structures/Language

5. The specific statistical information and other figures in Reich's 1991 article change annually, if not more often. Is their alteration within the next decade likely to affect either Reich's argument or your receptivity to it? Since numbers are always in flux, why use them in an argument?

6. Reich's sentences are fairly long, but his paragraphs are short, usually from one to three sentences. (The longest paragraph, ¶ 32, has eight sentences.) This is because the article was originally published in a newspaper, the *New York Times Magazine*; newspapers provide paragraph breaks not to indicate where the material logically breaks or changes course but to rest readers' eyes as they roam the page. What is the effect, if any, of such a large number of short paragraphs in a serious article?

7. Which side does Reich favor? At what point in the argument does he expect his readers to realize this?

8. Does Reich's division of workers into "symbolic and analytic services" and "local service workers" cover most people in cities? Where do "blue-collar manufacturing workers" live (see ¶ 24)? Are such labels necessary or helpful in constructing the argument Reich makes?

For Writing

9. Argue, by yourself or with a team, as Reich does but using your own examples (and some of his factual information, among other sources) that, as Reich concludes, "even though America is no longer a separate and distinct economy, it is still a society whose members have abiding obligations to one another" (¶ 45). One way to address the subject is to consider the implications of a particular public policy issue (such as school busing, property taxation, equalization of school funding across rich and poor districts, gated residential communities with private security guards, privatization of Social Security). See, for example, Martin Luther King, Jr.'s, "Letter from Birmingham Jail" (399–413), and the essays by Matt Nocton (271–76) and Peter Singer (481–87).

10. **Journal Writing.** What factors, other than income, bring people together in a geographical community, whether a suburban or urban neighborhood, a small

town within a metropolitan area, or a rural town? In your experience, does ethnicity, religion, or a particular interest, perhaps recreational activities, play a major role in defining a community? To what extent do these factors correlate with income levels? Is income level the defining factor in your community's character?

11. ***Dialogues.*** Is it socially desirable for the upper fifth in income to "secede" from "the rest of the nation," as Reich asserts in paragraph 8 and challenges thereafter? How might American attitudes toward wealth that Reich describes foster the emergence of a separate, elite workforce? Do Americans consider poverty a form of failure or disgrace, as Singer's "The Singer Solution to World Poverty" (481–87) implies? Expand your answer by incorporating part of Martin Luther King, Jr.'s analysis of systemic discrimination against African-Americans. Does such a social structure encourage or discourage excellence?

12. What does the chart on 4 suggest about the relationship between economic growth and the well-being of a nation's citizens? Speculate why the citizens of countries at lower levels of GDP per capita tend to report equal levels of satisfaction regardless of income differences. Why might the lower-income citizens of some countries with high levels of GDP per capita report less satisfaction with their lives relative to higher-income citizens? Which countries represent the outliers (the data points on the margins of the dominant statistical relationship)? What factors might be responsible for their position relative to other countries?

13. ***Second Look.*** Consider Reich's argument with respect to the photograph of the cleaning woman in front of the American flag (395). How do these images suggest that exclusion defines what is American? Does the "new elite" as Reich defines it (¶ 11) grow out of a history rooted in the disenfranchisement or forced assimilation of specific ethnic groups? Is the idea of a unified American culture a pretense that conceals social inequity? In what ways do Lange's photograph of the "Migrant Mother" (483) expand or complicate your answers?

TIM BERNERS-LEE

Tim Berners-Lee (born 1955 in London) is a British computer scientist credited with inventing the World Wide Web. Berners-Lee earned a degree in physics from Queen's College, Oxford in 1976. In 1980, he began working at CERN, the European Particle Physics Laboratory. In 1989, while at CERN, he proposed linking hypertext with the Internet. A year later, this became the Web. Berners-Lee is the founder of the WWW Foundation, director of the WWW Consortium, and in 2009, he was elected a member of the United States National Academy of Sciences. He currently holds the 3Com Founders Chair at the MIT Computer Science and Artificial Intelligence Laboratory. In 1999, *Time* named him one of the 100 Most Important People of the twentieth century. He was also named the Greatest Briton of 2004 and in 2007 he was knighted and awarded the Order of Merit by Queen Elizabeth II.

In "Long Live the Web: A Call for Continued Open Standards and Neutrality," originally published in *Scientific American* (2010), Berners-Lee argues for changes in the way we use the Web in favor of "a single, universal information space." He warns of the threats posed by social networking sites that could potentially break the Web into "fragmented islands." Twenty years after creating the Web, he urges us to preserve its founding principles.

Long Live the Web: A Call for Continued Open Standards and Neutrality

1   The world wide web went live, on my physical desktop in Geneva, Switzerland, in December 1990. It consisted of one Web site and one browser, which happened to be on the same computer. The simple setup demonstrated a profound concept: that any person could share information with anyone else, anywhere. In this spirit, the Web spread quickly from the grassroots up. Today, at its 20th anniversary, the Web is thoroughly integrated into our daily lives. We take it for granted, expecting it to "be there" at any instant, like electricity.

2   The Web evolved into a powerful, ubiquitous tool because it was built on egalitarian principles and because thousands of individuals, universities and companies have worked, both independently and together as part of the World Wide Web Consortium, to expand its capabilities based on those principles.

3   The Web as we know it, however, is being threatened in different ways. Some of its most successful inhabitants have begun to chip away at its principles. Large social-networking sites are walling off information posted by their users from the rest of the Web. Wireless Internet providers are being tempted to slow traffic to sites with which they have not made deals. Governments—totalitarian and democratic alike—are monitoring people's online habits, endangering important human rights.

4   If we, the Web's users, allow these and other trends to proceed unchecked, the Web could be broken into fragmented islands. We could lose the freedom to connect with whichever Web sites we want. The ill effects could extend to smartphones and pads, which are also portals to the extensive information that the Web provides.

5   Why should you care? Because the Web is yours. It is a public resource on which you, your business, your community and your government depend. The Web is also vital to democracy, a communications channel that makes possible a continuous worldwide conversation. The Web is now more critical to free speech than any other medium. It brings principles established in the U.S. Constitution, the British Magna Carta and other important documents into the network age: freedom from being snooped on, filtered, censored and disconnected.

6   Yet people seem to think the Web is some sort of piece of nature, and if it starts to wither, well, that's just one of those unfortunate things we can't help. Not so. We create the Web, by designing computer protocols

and software; this process is completely under our control. We choose what properties we want it to have and not have. It is by no means finished (and it's certainly not dead). If we want to track what government is doing, see what companies are doing, understand the true state of the planet, find a cure for Alzheimer's disease, not to mention easily share our photos with our friends, we the public, the scientific community and the press must make sure the Web's principles remain intact—not just to preserve what we have gained but to benefit from the great advances that are still to come.

Universality Is the Foundation

Several principles are key to assuring that the Web becomes ever more valuable. The primary design principle underlying the Web's usefulness and growth is universality. When you make a link, you can link to anything. That means people must be able to put anything on the Web, no matter what computer they have, software they use or human language they speak and regardless of whether they have a wired or wireless Internet connection. The Web should be usable by people with disabilities. It must work with any form of information, be it a document or a point of data, and information of any quality—from a silly tweet to a scholarly paper. And it should be accessible from any kind of hardware that can connect to the Internet: stationary or mobile, small screen or large. 7

These characteristics can seem obvious, self-maintaining or just unimportant, but they are why the next blockbuster Web site or the new homepage for your kid's local soccer team will just appear on the Web without any difficulty. Universality is a big demand, for any system. 8

Decentralization is another important design feature. You do not have to get approval from any central authority to add a page or make a link. All you have to do is use three simple, standard protocols: write a page in the HTML (hypertext markup language) format, name it with the URI naming convention, and serve it up on the Internet using HTTP (hypertext transfer protocol). Decentralization has made widespread innovation possible and will continue to do so in the future. 9

The URI is the key to universality. (I originally called the naming scheme URI, for universal resource identifier; it has come to be known as URL, for uniform resource locator.) The URI allows you to follow any link, regardless of the content it leads to or who publishes that content. Links turn the Web's content into something of greater value: an interconnected information space. 10

Several threats to the Web's universality have arisen recently. Cable television companies that sell Internet connectivity are considering whether to limit their Internet users to downloading only the company's mix of entertainment. Social-networking sites present a different kind of problem. Facebook, LinkedIn, Friendster and others typically provide 11 value by capturing information as you enter it: your birthday, your e-mail address, your likes, and links indicating who is friends with whom and who is in which photograph. The sites assemble these bits of data into brilliant databases and reuse the information to provide value-added service—but only within their sites. Once you enter your data into one of these services, you cannot easily use them on another site. Each site is a silo, walled off from the others. Yes, your site's pages are on the Web, but your data are not. You can access a Web page about a list of people you have created in one site, but you cannot send that list, or items from it, to another site.

12   The isolation occurs because each piece of information does not have a URI. Connections among data exist only within a site. So the more you enter, the more you become locked in. Your social-networking site becomes a central platform—a closed silo of content, and one that does not give you full control over your information in it. The more this kind of architecture gains widespread use, the more the Web becomes fragmented, and the less we enjoy a single, universal information space.

13   A related danger is that one social-networking site—or one search engine or one browser—gets so big that it becomes a monopoly, which tends to limit innovation. As has been the case since the Web began, continued grassroots innovation may be the best check and balance against any one company or government that tries to undermine universality. GnuSocial and Diaspora are projects on the Web that allow anyone to create their own social network from their own server, connecting to anyone on any other site. The Status.net project, which runs sites such as identi.ca, allows you to operate your own Twitter-like network without the Twitter-like centralization.

Open Standards Drive Innovation

14   Allowing any site to link to any other site is necessary but not sufficient for a robust Web. The basic Web technologies that individuals and companies need to develop powerful services must be available for free, with no royalties. Amazon.com, for example, grew into a huge online bookstore, then music store, then store for all kinds of goods because it had open, free access to the technical standards on which the Web operates. Amazon, like any other Web user, could use HTML, URI and HTTP without asking anyone's permission and without having to pay. It could also use improvements to those standards developed by the World Wide Web Consortium, allowing customers to fill out a virtual order form, pay online, rate the goods they had purchased, and so on.

15   By "open standards" I mean standards that can have any committed expert involved in the design, that have been widely reviewed as acceptable, that are available for free on the Web, and that are royalty-free (no need to pay) for developers and users. Open, royalty-free standards

that are easy to use create the diverse richness of Web sites, from the big names such as Amazon, Craigslist and Wikipedia to obscure blogs written by adult hobbyists and to homegrown videos posted by teenagers.

Openness also means you can build your own Web site or company 16 without anyone's approval. When the Web began, I did not have to obtain permission or pay royalties to use the Internet's own open standards, such as the well-known transmission control protocol (TCP) and Internet protocol (IP). Similarly, the Web Consortium's royalty-free patent policy says that the companies, universities and individuals who contribute to the development of a standard must agree they will not charge royalties to anyone who may use the standard.

Open, royalty-free standards do not mean that a company or indi- 17 vidual cannot devise a blog or photo-sharing program and charge you to use it. They can. And you might want to pay for it if you think it is "better" than others. The point is that open standards allow for many options, free and not.

Indeed, many companies spend money to develop extraordinary ap- 18 plications precisely because they are confident the applications will work for anyone, regardless of the computer hardware, operating system or Internet service provider (ISP) they are using—all made possible by the Web's open standards. The same confidence encourages scientists to spend thousands of hours devising incredible databases that can share information about proteins, say, in hopes of curing disease. The confidence encourages governments such as those of the U.S. and the U.K. to put more and more data online so citizens can inspect them, making government increasingly transparent. Open standards also foster serendipitous creation: someone may use them in ways no one imagined. We discover that on the Web every day.

In contrast, not using open standards creates closed worlds. Apple's 19 iTunes system, for example, identifies songs and videos using URIs that are open. But instead of "http:" the addresses begin with "itunes:," which is proprietary. You can access an "itunes:" link only using Apple's proprietary iTunes program. You can't make a link to any information in the iTunes world—a song or information about a band. You can't send that link to someone else to see. You are no longer on the Web. The iTunes world is centralized and walled off. You are trapped in a single store, rather than being on the open marketplace. For all the store's wonderful features, its evolution is limited to what one company thinks up.

Other companies are also creating closed worlds. The tendency for 20 magazines, for example, to produce smartphone "apps" rather than Web apps is disturbing, because that material is off the Web. You can't bookmark it or e-mail a link to a page within it. You can't tweet it. It is better to build a Web app that will also run on smartphone browsers, and the techniques for doing so are getting better all the time.

Some people may think that closed worlds are just fine. The worlds 21 are easy to use and may seem to give those people what they want. But as we saw in the 1990s with the America Online dial-up information system that gave you a restricted subset of the Web, these closed, "walled gardens," no matter how pleasing, can never compete in diversity, richness and innovation with the mad, throbbing Web market outside their gates. If a walled garden has too tight a hold on a market, however, it can delay that outside growth.

Keep the Web separate from the Internet

22 Keeping the web universal and keeping its standards open help people invent new services. But a third principle—the separation of layers—partitions the design of the Web from that of the Internet.

23 This separation is fundamental. The Web is an application that runs on the Internet, which is an electronic network that transmits packets of information among millions of computers according to a few open protocols. An analogy is that the Web is like a household appliance that runs on the electricity network. A refrigerator or printer can function as long as it uses a few standard protocols—in the U.S., things like operating at 120 volts and 60 hertz. Similarly, any application—among them the Web, e-mail or instant messaging—can run on the Internet as long as it uses a few standard Internet protocols, such as TCP and IP.

24 Manufacturers can improve refrigerators and printers without altering how electricity functions, and utility companies can improve the electrical network without altering how appliances function. The two layers of technology work together but can advance independently. The same is true for the Web and the Internet. The separation of layers is crucial for innovation. In 1990 the Web rolled out over the Internet without any changes to the Internet itself, as have all improvements since. And in that time, Internet connections have sped up from 300 bits per second to 300 million bits per second (Mbps) without the Web having to be redesigned to take advantage of the upgrades.

Electronic Human Rights

25 Although internet and web designs are separate, a Web user is also an Internet user and therefore relies on an Internet that is free from interference. In the early Web days it was too technically difficult for a company or country to manipulate the Internet to interfere with an individual Web user. Technology for interference has become more powerful, however. In 2007 BitTorrent, a company whose "peer-to-peer" network protocol allows people to share music, video and other files directly over the Internet, complained to the Federal Communications Commission that the ISP giant Comcast was blocking or slowing traffic to subscribers who were using the BitTorrent application. The FCC told Comcast to stop the practice, but in April 2010 a federal court ruled the FCC could not require Comcast

to do so. A good ISP will often manage traffic so that when bandwidth is short, less crucial traffic is dropped, in a transparent way, so users are aware of it. An important line exists between that action and using the same power to discriminate.

This distinction highlights the principle of net neutrality. Net neu-   26
trality maintains that if I have paid for an Internet connection at a certain quality, say, 300 Mbps, and you have paid for that quality, then our communications should take place at that quality. Protecting this concept would prevent a big ISP from sending you video from a media company it may own at 300 Mbps but sending video from a competing media company at a slower rate. That amounts to commercial discrimination. Other complications could arise. What if your ISP made it easier for you to connect to a particular online shoe store and harder to reach others? That would be powerful control. What if the ISP made it difficult for you to go to Web sites about certain political parties, or religions, or sites about evolution?

Unfortunately, in August, Google and Verizon for some reason sug-   27
gested that net neutrality should not apply to mobile phone–based connections. Many people in rural areas from Utah to Uganda have access to the Internet only via mobile phones; exempting wireless from net neutrality would leave these users open to discrimination of service. It is also bizarre to imagine that my fundamental right to access the information source of my choice should apply when I am on my WiFi-connected computer at home but not when I use my cell phone.

A neutral communications medium is the basis of a fair, competitive   28
market economy, of democracy, and of science. Debate has risen again in the past year about whether government legislation is needed to protect net neutrality. It is. Although the Internet and Web generally thrive on lack of regulation, some basic values have to be legally preserved.

No Snooping

Other threats to the web result from meddling with the Internet, including   29
snooping. In 2008 one company, Phorm, devised a way for an ISP to peek inside the packets of information it was sending. The ISP could determine every URI that any customer was browsing. The ISP could then create a profile of the sites the user went to in order to produce targeted advertising.

Accessing the information within an Internet packet is equivalent   30
to wiretapping a phone or opening postal mail. The URIs that people use reveal a good deal about them. A company that bought URI profiles of job applicants could use them to discriminate in hiring people with certain political views, for example. Life insurance companies could discriminate against people who have looked up cardiac symptoms on the Web. Predators could use the profiles to stalk individuals. We would all use the Web very differently if we knew that our clicks can be monitored and the data shared with third parties.

31   Free speech should be protected, too. The Web should be like a white sheet of paper: ready to be written on, with no control over what is written. Earlier this year Google accused the Chinese government of hacking into its databases to retrieve the e-mails of dissidents. The alleged break-ins occurred after Google resisted the government's demand that the company censor certain documents on its Chinese-language search engine.

32   Totalitarian governments aren't the only ones violating the network rights of their citizens. In France a law created in 2009, named Hadopi, allowed a new agency by the same name to disconnect a household from the Internet for a year if someone in the household was *alleged* by a media company to have ripped off music or video. After much opposition, in October the Constitutional Council of France required a judge to review a case before access was revoked, but if approved, the household could be disconnected without due process. In the U.K., the Digital Economy Act, hastily passed in April, allows the government to order an ISP to terminate the Internet connection of anyone who appears on a list of individuals suspected of copyright infringement. In September the U.S. Senate introduced the Combating Online Infringement and Counterfeits Act, which would allow the government to create a blacklist of Web sites—hosted on or off U.S. soil—that are accused of infringement and to pressure or require all ISPs to block access to those sites.

33   In these cases, no due process of law protects people before they are disconnected or their sites are blocked. Given the many ways the Web is crucial to our lives and our work, disconnection is a form of deprivation of liberty. Looking back to the Magna Carta, we should perhaps now affirm: "No person or organization shall be deprived of the ability to connect to others without due process of law and the presumption of innocence."

34   When your network rights are violated, public outcry is crucial. Citizens worldwide objected to China's demands on Google, so much so that Secretary of State Hillary Clinton said the U.S. government supported Google's defiance and that Internet freedom—and with it, Web freedom—should become a formal plank in American foreign policy. In October, Finland made broadband access, at 1 Mbps, a legal right for all its citizens.

Linking to the Future

35 As long as the web's basic principles are upheld, its ongoing evolution is not in the hands of any one person or organization—neither mine nor anyone else's. If we can preserve the principles, the Web promises some fantastic future capabilities.

36   For example, the latest version of HTML, called HTML5, is not just a markup language but a computing platform that will make Web apps even more powerful than they are now. The proliferation of smartphones

will make the Web even more central to our lives. Wireless access will be a particular boon to developing countries, where many people do not have connectivity by wire or cable but do have it wirelessly. Much more needs to be done, of course, including accessibility for people with disabilities and devising pages that work well on all screens, from huge 3-D displays that cover a wall to wristwatch-size windows.

A great example of future promise, which leverages the strengths of all the principles, is linked data. Today's Web is quite effective at helping people publish and discover documents, but our computer programs cannot read or manipulate the actual data within those documents. As this problem is solved, the Web will become much more useful, because data about nearly every aspect of our lives are being created at an astonishing rate. Locked within all these data is knowledge about how to cure diseases, foster business value and govern our world more effectively.

Scientists are actually at the forefront of some of the largest efforts to put linked data on the Web. Researchers, for example, are realizing that in many cases no single lab or online data repository is sufficient to discover new drugs. The information necessary to understand the complex interactions between diseases, biological processes in the human body, and the vast array of chemical agents is spread across the world in a myriad of databases, spreadsheets and documents.

One success relates to drug discovery to combat Alzheimer's disease. A number of corporate and government research labs dropped their usual refusal to open their data and created the Alzheimer's Disease Neuroimaging Initiative. They posted a massive amount of patient information and brain scans as linked data, which they have dipped into many times to advance their research. In a demonstration I witnessed, a scientist asked the question, "What proteins are involved in signal transduction and are related to pyramidal neurons?" When put into Google, the question got 233,000 hits—and not one single answer. Put into the linked databases world, however, it returned a small number of specific proteins that have those properties.

The investment and finance sectors can benefit from linked data, too. Profit is generated, in large part, from finding patterns in an increasingly diverse set of information sources. Data are all over our personal lives as well. When you go onto your social-networking site and indicate that a newcomer is your friend, that establishes a relationship. And that relationship is data.

Linked data raise certain issues that we will have to confront. For example, new data-integration capabilities could pose privacy challenges that are hardly addressed by today's privacy laws. We should examine legal, cultural and technical options that will preserve privacy without stifling beneficial data-sharing capabilities.

Now is an exciting time. Web developers, companies, governments and citizens should work together openly and cooperatively, as we have done thus far, to preserve the Web's fundamental principles, as well as those of the Internet, ensuring that the technological protocols and social conventions we set up respect basic human values. The goal of the Web is to serve humanity. We build it now so that those who come to it later will be able to create things that we cannot ourselves imagine.

Content

1. Berners-Lee, inventor of the world wide web, identifies its "profound concept," "that any person could share information with anyone else, anywhere" (¶ 1). Explain the spirit and some of the implications of these "egalitarian principles" (¶ 2).

2. Why is the Web "vital to democracy"(¶ 5)? Why is it "now more critical to free speech than any other medium" (¶ 5)? What are the implications of having one's communication "snooped on, filtered, censored and disconnected" (¶ 5), as indeed occurs in some countries (recently, China, Egypt) when citizens do something the government doesn't like?

3. What does it mean to interpret the Web as a "public resource"? How might matters have been different if Berners-Lee had decided, at the outset of his invention, to privatize the Web? In what ways have you as a student, and society more generally, benefitted from its freedoms—of access, of communication?

4. What does Berners-Lee predict will be the consequences to open communication if its universality is threatened? What evidence does he offer concerning such threats?

5. Definitions are crucial to Berners-Lee's argument. What does he mean by "universality"—"When you make a link, you can link to anything" (¶ 7)? How does he define "open standards" (¶ 13–15)? Why is it important for someone to be able to "build your own Web site or company without anyone's approval" (¶ 16)?

6. Explain Berners-Lee's assertion, "not using open standards creates closed worlds" (¶ 19). What are the arguments for and against this concept (¶ 18–21)?

7. Why should the Web be kept separate from the Internet (¶ 22–24)?

Strategies/Structures/Language

8. Berners-Lee is the inventor of the Web. Should the extra authority that this gives him mean that readers should be convinced at the outset of the truth of his claims? Why or why not?

9. Berners-Lee uses a metaphor to explain, "People seem to think the Web is some sort of piece of nature, and if it starts to wither, well, that's just one of those unfortunate things we can't help. Not so," he counters (¶ 6). Why is this metaphor effective?

10. Examine Berners-Lee's analogy, "Electronic Human Rights" (¶ 25). What are these electronic human rights? How are they related to "net neutrality" (¶ 26–28)?

11. In a similar fashion, Berners-Lee claims, "Accessing the information within an Internet packet is equivalent to wiretapping a phone or opening postal mail" (¶ 30), and he is as adamant about violations of this sort as he is about maintaining related freedoms (¶ 31–34). In what ways do such analogies help readers understand Berners-Lee's more abstract concepts? Win hearts and minds?

For Writing

11. *Journal writing.* Keep a record of your use of the Internet for 24 hours. Categorize the uses and tally them. If these uses had a price tag, how much would you be willing to spend to maintain these services? What would you miss if you couldn't afford it?

12. **Dialogues.** It is clear that the universality of the Internet, as well as of social-networking capability, creates a host of ethical issues. Pick one or more ethical issues discussed by Berners-Lee, and by Nicholas Carr ("Is Google Making Us Stupid?" 45–54), William Deresiewicz, "Faux Friendship" (56–60), or Tim Stobierski (66–68). Discuss this with a colleague, and either individually or together write an essay in which you discuss the implications. You should propose a solution that addresses some of the problems Berners-Lee raises.

13. Write a position paper or op-ed article on why the Internet is "now more critical to free speech than any other medium" (¶ 5)? And why it is vital to democracy?

MATTHEW ALLEN

Matthew Allen (born 1980) earned a BA at Brigham Young University (2005) and is currently pursuing graduate studies in English Language and Linguistics at Purdue University. After brief stints in law and government, Allen taught high school English and ESL in Massachusetts. Allen spent a few years in Europe and daydreams about returning.

In several ways, Allen says, "'The Rhetorical Situation of the Scientific Paper' is the culmination of my undergraduate studies. First, I drew on the different disciplines I had studied, including biology, psychology, and English language and linguistics, as I researched and wrote this paper. Second, the countless revisions I went through for this paper showed me how much I had matured as a writer. For years, I dreaded criticism so much that I refused to proofread or redraft my work. After becoming an editor and writing tutor [at BYU's Writing Center], I finally realized the value of feedback and revision." Allen says his paper went through more than six major revisions before it was published in *Young Scholars in Writing: Undergraduate Research in Writing and Rhetoric* (2004). In it, Allen argues that the "experimental report, like all written accounts, is an interpretation, subject to creativity, convention, form, and style" (¶ 26).

The Rhetorical Situation of the Scientific Paper and the "Appearance" of Objectivity

1   Mention the words *rhetoric* and *science* together, and many people see an intrinsic contradiction. After all, two hallmarks of modern science are objectivity and empirical method, whereas rhetoric bears the marks of a long and sometimes sordid history of sophistic oratory and biased argumentation. Gerald Holton describes this distinction: Rhetoric is often perceived as the art of persuasion, while science is generally seen as the art of demonstration (173). This idea implies, to use a figure of speech, that rhetoric and science should not be seen together in public. The distinction between the two, however, is probably more fabricated than genuine. Scholars, especially during the last several decades, have argued that scientific practice and discourse do have rhetorical and persuasive elements.

2   Published scientific papers bridge the gap between a scientist's work and the public's knowledge of that work. Research that goes unpublished, to use an image from Robert Day, is like a tree falling in a forest when no one is around—there is no "sound" without an audience (1). In order for this knowledge to be received and accepted by the intended audience, generally the scientific community, the research or experimental report must follow certain conventions, not the least of which are methodological validity and pertinence to the existing body of scientific knowledge. The authors of scientific papers must demonstrate the validity and objectivity of their findings and make them seem interesting and relevant to already-established conclusions. In effect, this is a rhetorical situation: a speaker (the author) communicates knowledge about a particular subject to an audience via the scientific paper, intending, on some level, to persuade that audience.

3   What is most interesting about the rhetorical situation of the scientific paper is that the writer persuades his or her audience largely through the *appearance of* objectivity. Many people, as Charles Bazerman points out, think that writing based on scientific premises is not really writing at all (14), that it is an unbiased vessel for transmitting truth. But in this essay, I analyze Renske Wassenberg, Jeffrey E. Max, Scott D. Lindgren, and Amy Schatz's article, "Sustained Attention in Children and Adolescents after Traumatic Brain Injury: Relation to Severity of Injury, Adaptive Functioning, ADHD and Social Background" (herein referred to as "Sustained Attention in Children and Adolescents"), recently published in *Brain Injury*, to illustrate that the writer of an experimental report in effect creates an exigence and then addresses it through rhetorical strategies that contribute to the appearance of objectivity.

Scientific Inquiry and Objectivity

It would seem that the objective nature of modern science precludes any   4
possibility of rhetoric's entering into scientific writing. The assumption
is that writing is interpretive and science is not. This notion results from
an apparently sound connection: scientific writing is scientific; science is
objective; therefore, scientific writing is objective. Objectivity certainly is
one of the key goals and primary assumptions of scientific practice and
writing. Nevertheless, it is inaccurate to think that the subjective human
element can be completely eliminated through even the most objective
scientific method. As Peter Medawar suggests, "There is no such thing
as unprejudiced observation. Every act of observation we make is biased.
What we see or otherwise sense is a function of what we have seen or
sensed in the past" (230).

While the historic public face of science may exude objectivity, there   5
is a pervasive, if less openly discussed, subjective side. Even if scientists
were able to collect data in a purely objective way, Brent Slife and Richard
Williams contend that "we cannot ignore the necessity of *interpreting* the
data yielded by scientific method" (5, emphasis in original). Although
computer programs may seem to be doing unbiased interpreting in some
cases, human beings must ultimately give meaning to data, however
raw they may or may not be. For example, an experiment that measured
the brain waves of laboratory rats under certain conditions might yield
a group of numbers, a data set. That data set would be virtually meaningless (i.e., it would not tell the researchers what they had found) until
it was organized in some coherent way. But what kind of organization
would be most coherent? A graph, a table, perhaps a qualitative description? Each organizational approach might produce different findings, but
many approaches will be equally valid. The choice of methods and organization of data will ultimately depend on the point of view of the person
doing the interpreting and the scientific needs of the project. A computer
might flawlessly organize data a particular way, but that computer was
programmed by someone. The point is that ideas outside of the actual
data set must be projected onto the data set before it means anything. As
Slife and Williams explain, "in this sense, data can never be facts until
they have been given an interpretation that is dependent on ideas that do
not appear in the data themselves" (6).

This type of evidence leads to Bazerman's assertion that the "popu-   6
lar belief of this past century that scientific language is simply a transparent transmitter of natural facts is . . . of course wrong" (14). Medawar goes
even further, declaring that the scientific paper gives "a totally misleading
narrative of the processes of thought that go into the making of scientific
discoveries" (233). One of his points is that there is a creative side to science, a side often sacrificed to an assumed objectivity. Creativity is more
subjective than objective, and so alternative interpretations exist.

Experimental Papers and Persuasive Argument

7   Despite attempts to influence the reader, the type of rhetoric involved in scientific writing does not, as Kristine Hansen emphasizes, involve "bombast, flowery phrases, or appeals to emotion, all aimed at deceiving" (xvi). Rather, contend John Schuster and Richard Yeo, "scientific argumentation is essentially persuasive argument and therefore is rightly termed *rhetorical* in the sense defined by students of 'the new rhetoric,' where 'rhetoric' denotes the entire field of discursive structures and strategies used to render arguments persuasive in given situations" (xii). As scientists write reports of original research, all the while conforming to certain accepted structures and styles, such as logic, clarity, and empiricism, they still give a rhetorical shape to their writing. Gerald Holton describes this process as a "proactive rhetoric of assertion"—when a scientist becomes convinced of something, he or she hopes to persuade others about that same idea or phenomenon when the work is published (176).

8   There are practical motivations beyond contributing to scientific knowledge for using scientific rhetoric to emphasize the importance of publishable research. Scientists, according to Day, are primarily measured by and known for their publications (ix). In the competitive world of academics and research, scientists need to publish to gain prestige and promotions. Poorly written, nonstandard, or unconvincing papers are naturally less likely to be chosen for publication.

The Rhetorical Situation and Its Exigence

9   According to Lloyd Bitzer, rhetoric is always situational; it is a pragmatic response "to a situation of a certain kind," functioning "ultimately to produce action or change in the world" (3). The rhetorical situation, according to Bitzer, has several key features, but my primary concern is with exigence, which is central to understanding scientific rhetoric. An exigence, as defined by Bitzer, is "an imperfection marked by urgency; it is a defect, an obstacle, something waiting to be done, a thing which is other than it should be" (6). An exigence such as winter or death that cannot be altered through rhetoric or through any other means is not a rhetorical exigence (6). This understanding of exigence is further elucidated by Bitzer's definition of rhetoric:

> In short, rhetoric is a mode of altering reality, not by direct application of energy to objects, but by the creation of discourse which changes reality through the mediation of thought and action. The rhetor alters reality by bringing into existence a discourse of such a character that the audience, in thought and action, is so engaged that it becomes mediator of change. In this sense rhetoric is always persuasive. (3)

10   This concept of rhetoric and exigence is exemplified in many of the speeches and writings of Martin Luther King, Jr. King believed that the

racially inequitable social conditions around him could be altered through speech and subsequent action. King helped to change the reality of racial inequality through rhetoric, including his famous "I Have a Dream" speech. His discourse engaged, and continued to engage, his audience, often prompting people to action. King did not himself rewrite legislation or policies, but his rhetoric contributed to the actions of those who did.

In a scientific paper, the reality being altered is the accumulating knowledge of the scientific community. The rhetorical exigence is, in Lawrence Prelli's words, the "gap in the collective body of knowledge" (23). Simply put, a scientist performs an experiment to better understand a law, principle, or phenomenon and then creates and publishes a scientific paper to communicate the results to the scientific community. In a sense, the scientist is "fixing" a problem—he or she has come to a better understanding of something than anyone else and is therefore able to fill in that "gap" in knowledge. As Prelli suggests, "[a] scientific orientation inclines one to define rhetorical situations in terms of the presence or absence of objectively verifiable information and the consonance of new evidence with already-accepted knowledge" (23).

Prelli seems to imply, justifiably, that scientific rhetoric is secondary to scientific knowledge and practice. If the new knowledge cannot be scientifically verified and reconciled with traditional knowledge, the rhetorical aspects of the paper alone, the strategies used to make the new knowledge seem like an answer, are useless. The scientist must first have identified a problem in order to propose the answer he or she has found. Experimental reports, Bazerman says, are special in this way because they describe "an event created so that it might be told" (59). Scientists formulated problems, according to their methodologies, in order to solve them—in essence, they create more than discover the rhetorical situation because they construct an exigence.

In "Sustained Attention in Children and Adolescents," the authors express their exigence when they state the study's primary objective: "To examine the relationship of child and family psychological variables and traumatic brain injury (TBI) severity as it relates to sustained attention" (751). The driving question is clear: What, if any, is the relationship between psychosocial variables and TBI? This question certainly is compelling and worthwhile, but was it discovered or created? The authors imply a creative process of arriving at their exigence:

> Attention problems are commonly reported after TBI in children. There is little known about the effects of TBI on specific attentional components: orienting to sensory stimuli, executive functions and maintaining the alert state. The focus of this study is on sustained attention (i.e. the capacity to maintain arousal and alertness over time). According to Dennis et al., sustained attention is a regulator of cognitive activities needed for academic tasks, adaptive

functioning and social interactions. A deficiency in sustained attention may, therefore, have a significant impact on the child's development in the acute and chronic stages of TBI. (752)

14   As this paragraph from the introduction illustrates, the authors created an exigence by building upon previous research and their own insights and by constructing a logical hypothesis (eventually an entire study) to address that exigence. In essence, they arrived at their research question through inference. The exigence, however valid, was essentially created through a careful, thoughtful, and creative process. The authors' review of the literature did not inevitably lead to their hypothesis. They creatively took two factors (pre-TBI psychological variables and post-TBI sustained attention) and postulated a relationship between them. Yet, the connection is scientifically valid: many of their ideas have been discussed or established in previous research, and they can test their new ideas empirically.

Rhetorical Strategies Used to Shape the Persuasive Paper

15   In effect, the authors of experimental papers address the exigence of the rhetorical situation through a carefully crafted rhetoric. The writing, as Bazerman says, "appears to hide itself" (14). This subtle approach is a specific rhetorical strategy: there seems to be no style—hence, no rhetoric—when in fact there is one. The writing style in most experimental reports intentionally deemphasizes creativity and human voice. The general choice is to use rhetoric that is persuasive through emphasizing logic and objectivity over creativity. Such rhetorical aspects of scientific writing tend to be subsumed or hidden by the larger goal of conveying meaning clearly and impartially.

16   For example, the passive voice, whereby the writer can easily omit the agent (the "doer" in the clause), is more prevalent in scientific writing than in most other genres. The editors of *Merriam Webster's Dictionary of English Usage* point out that while the active voice is generally preferable, "a few [usage] commentators find the passive useful in scientific writing (one even believes it to be necessary) because of the tone of detachment and impersonality that it helps establish" (721).

17   The authors of "Sustained Attention in Children and Adolescents" definitely agree with this remark about the importance of the passive voice. An analysis of the first 118 or so lines of the article (the introduction and part of the method section) attests to the author's careful choice of language: over one-third of the verb constructions are passives (about 26 of 70). For most non-scientific published writing, passive constructions tend to be around 10 to 15 percent, a ratio that the article noticeably surpasses (*Merriam Webster's* 720) The significance of this frequent use of passives is that actions and findings (i.e., non-human elements) are

emphasized over human elements. The agent is noticeably missing in the following passive sentences from the article:

- The Paediatric Assessment of Cognitive Efficiency (PACE) was used in this study to test two types of deficits, inattention and impulsiveness. (752)
- Inattention and impulsiveness were not further elucidated because the two error measures, omission and commission errors, were not independently analyzed. (752)
- It was hypothesized that children with severe TBI will produce significantly more errors on the PACE than children with mild/moderate TBI. (753)
- No differences were found between the Mild/Moderate and Severe TBI group in regards to demographic characteristics. (754)

For each of these actions, there must have been an agent, someone   18
using the assessment, choosing not to further elucidate certain factors, hypothesizing, and failing to find differences. The authors' use of the passive voice to emphasize the action and deemphasize the agent (the authors omit the agent in nearly every passive construction in the first 118 lines) certainly does create a "tone of detachment and impersonality," even one of objectivity.[1]

The standard organization of scientific papers is another way to   19
emphasize the factual and objective over the interpretive and subjective. The organization helps portray the paper's information logically and persuasively. The modern research paper, as Day explains, has the basic universal form of IMRAD—Introduction, Methods, Results, and Discussion— because this form is "so eminently logical" (11). Holton dubs this rationale the "well-tested machinery of logic and analysis, the direct evidence of the phenomena" (174). Plainly stated, the scientific paper is structured according to a scientific ideal: the method is set forth, and the results are reported, analyzed, and discussed. The organization by sequential sections is logical; the analysis is scientific because the discussion (the possibly non-scientific human element) is kept separate from the results. This type of organization, Medawar argues, implies an inductive process of unbiased observation leading to generalization (229). While the accuracy of this method may be questioned, it is logically convincing because, as Louis Pasteur purportedly told his students, it makes the results seem inevitable (Holton 174).

"Sustained Attention in Children and Adolescents" strictly adheres   20
to the IMRAD method of organization. The report contains an introduction; a methods section, which is further broken down into six subsections; a results section; and a discussion. The authors could have chosen another method of organization, but doing so would probably have reduced the likelihood of their getting the article published, and had it been published in a novel format, frequent readers of research reports would likely have been put off to some degree. As it stands, readers of "Sustained

Attention in Children and Adolescents" waste no time getting to the crux of the study—it's right there in the introduction and discussion—but all the technical evidence is still available. One interesting aspect of this particular study is that it is essentially part of a "soft" or social science. The variables in the study are all centered on human beings, studied according to various psychological tests. The patently scientific organization of the paper, however, seems to leave no question that this study was done according to "hard" science principles.

21   The same type of logical persuasion exemplified in the IMRAD organization is common in the introductions of many papers, a part of the report designed to emphasize the relevance and necessity of the particular findings to preexisting scientific evidence. John Swales found that scientists tend to use a very specific rhetorical strategy, what he termed the Create a Research Space (CARS) communication move schema (Golebiowski 1). After analyzing dozens of research paper introductions from various fields (e.g., physics, biology and medicine, and social sciences), Swales and subsequent researchers found that nearly every one of them contained three to six rhetorical organization "moves" aimed at making the paper seem important and relevant.

22   Swales' CARS model consists of three principle communicative moves: Move 1—establish centrality within the research; Move 2—establish a niche within the research; and Move 3—occupy the niche with the present research (Golebiowski 1–2). These moves help the author clearly state the exigence (the lack of knowledge) and the proposed solution (the present research). Scientists can use the introduction of the scientific paper to relate their research to others and to show how important the present findings are to the corpus of scientific knowledge. Findings that are relevant and timely should indeed be welcomed and accepted by the larger community, and so carefully introducing one's topic makes all the more sense.

23   These principal CARS communicative moves are central to the introduction of "Sustained Attention in Children and Adolescents." The authors establish centrality within their research area, Move 1, by briefly discussing traumatic brain injury (TBI) in children and adolescents and by stating that "childhood TBI [is] a significant public health problem" because it "is the leading cause of child deaths in the US and one of the most frequent causes of interruption to normal child development" (751). The authors also discuss previous research, eventually building up to their own research, and thereby establish their study's relevance through the implication that they share the same central assumptions and information base.

24   The authors establish a niche within the research, Move 2, primarily by indicating a gap in the research and by claiming that they will build upon the research of a previous study. After reviewing the general topic of TBI, the authors claim, "There is little known about the effects of TBI on specific attentional components: orienting to sensory stimuli, executive functions and maintaining the alert state" (752). They immediately move to occupy this niche, Move 3, by stating. "The focus of this study is

on sustained attention (i.e. the capacity to maintain arousal and alertness over time)" (752). After identifying sustained attention as their primary area of interest, the authors continue moving from general to specific and from Move 2 to Move 3. They review the literature dealing with sustained attention and then, in the last paragraph of the introduction, identify one study in particular from which they will proceed: "The present study aims to extend the findings of Taylor et al. in several ways" (753). The authors' intention seems clear: find something new without radically departing from what other researchers have already established.

Conclusion

Indubitably, scientific reports further our understanding of the world and the phenomena around us. James Watson and Francis Crick's famous paper that established the double helix structure of DNA, for example, radically altered biological studies (and in many ways, society at large). In "Sustained Attention in Children and Adolescents," the researchers found that people treating children with traumatic brain injury need to "consider pre-injury child and family psychosocial characteristics in addition to severity of injury" (751). While not as revolutionary as Watson and Crick's paper, the authors point out that their study helps fill a dearth of medical knowledge. Their findings are probably very important to those affected by TBI and those treating them. 25

It is important, however, to recognize that just as all scientific data are interpreted, this experimental report, like all written accounts, is an interpretation, subject to creativity, convention, form, and style. For example, the very tests used in the research and the results of those tests may not really show what the authors understood them to show. The authors inferred a connection between the tests and the test results and their eventual interpretations. The tests themselves are fundamentally based on theories, as are all scientific methods, but are essentially treated by the authors as being objective (at least if they are administered under ideal circumstances). A "soft" science experiment, this study is reported in "hard" science fashion. 26

Writing experimental reports is an especially provocative practice because through these studies today's hypotheses and theories become tomorrow's scientific facts and laws. In Sundar Sarukkai's words, "The writing of science is not only a representation of the ideas of science; it is also integral to the creation of new meaning and truth claims" (1). In one sense, the "creation of new meaning and truth claims" implies a rhetorical situation, where the writing is meant to persuade. Certainly, scientists and researchers should be aware of embedded rhetorical strategies. But given the profound and pervasive influence of science in Western culture, we should all—scientist or not—be attentive to how our knowledge is shaped. 27

I would like to thank Beth Hedengren and Kristine Hansen for generously sharing their time and knowledge to help me develop this article. 28

Notes

1. By way of comparison, James Watson and Francis Crick's famous article in *Nature* proposing the structure of DNA contains about 24 percent passive constructions, markedly fewer than "Sustained Attention in Children and Adolescents'" approximately 37 percent. Subtract the passive constructions in Watson and Crick's article that include the agent and the number drops to around 17 percent. The comparison between the two articles is useful because it shows that using the passive voice is a choice—a strategy to create a certain ethos, in this case, one of objectivity.

Works Cited

Bazerman, Charles. *Shaping Written Knowledge: The Genre and Activity of the Experimental Article in Science.* Madison: U of Wisconsin P, 1988.

Bitzer, Lloyd F. "The Rhetorical Situation." *Philosophy and Rhetoric* 1 (1968): 1–14.

Day, Robert A. *How to Write and Publish a Scientific Paper.* 4th ed. Phoenix: Oryx, 1994.

Golebiowski, Zosia. "Application of Swales' Model in the Analysis of Research Papers by Polish Authors." *International Review of Applied Linguistics in Language Teaching* 37.3 (1999). Online. *Academic Search Elite.* 14 Mar. 2003.

Hansen, Kristine. *A Rhetoric for the Social Sciences: A Guide to Academic and Professional Communications.* Upper Saddle River, NJ: Prentice Hall, 1998.

Holton, Gerald. "Quanta, Relativity, and Rhetoric." *Persuading Science: The Art of Scientific Rhetoric.* Ed. Marcello Pera and William R. Shea. Canton, MA: Science History, 1991. 173–203.

Medawar, Peter. "Is the Scientific Paper a Fraud?" *BBC Third Programme, Listener.* BBC. London, UK. 1963. Rpt. in *The Threat and the Glory: Reflections on Sciences and Scientists.* Ed. David Pyke. New York: HarperCollins, 1990. 228–33.

Merriam-Webster's Dictionary of English Usage. Springfield: Merriam-Webster, 1994.

Prelli, Lawrence J. *A Rhetoric of Science: Inventing Scientific Discourse.* Columbia: U of South Carolina P, 1989.

Sarukkai, Sundar. *Translating the World: Science and Language.* Lanham: Washington, D.C., 2002.

Schuster, John A., and Richard R. Yeo. Introduction. *The Politics and Rhetoric of Scientific Method: Historical Studies.* Boston: D. Reidel, 1986. ix–xxxvii.

Slife, Brent D., and Richard N. Williams. *What's Behind the Research: Discovering Hidden Assumptions in the Behavioral Sciences.* Thousand Oaks: Sage, 1995.

Wassenberg, Renske, Jeffrey E. Max, Scott D. Lindgren, and Amy Schatz. "Sustained Attention in Children and Adolescents after Traumatic Brain Injury: Relation to Severity of Injury, Adaptive Functioning, ADHD and Social Background." *Brain Injury* 18 (2004): 751–64.

Watson, J. D., and F. H. C. Crick, "Molecular Structure of Nucleic Acids: A Structure for Deoxyribose Nucleic Acid." *Nature* 4356 (1953): 737–38.

Content

1. What evidence does Allen provide to corroborate Peter Medawar's observation that "there is no such thing as unprejudiced observation. Every act of observation we make is biased" (¶ 4)? If this is so, why does scientific writing have the reputation for being objective and unbiased?

2. Is data meaningless without interpretation (¶ 4)? Is objective interpretation—of anything—impossible? What rhetorical strategies do scientists use to present their evidence convincingly?

3. Explain Allen's conclusion that "scientists formulate problems, according to their methodologies, in order to solve them—in essence, they create more than discover the rhetorical situation because they construct an exigence" (¶ 12). What does he mean by "rhetorical situation"? By "exigence"?

4. In what ways has Allen demonstrated his conclusion, that "this experimental report ["Sustained Attention"], like all written accounts, is an interpretation, subject to creativity, convention, form, and style" (¶ 26)?

Strategies/Structures/Language

5. Allen has undertaken the difficult task of trying to summarize a thirteen-page scientific paper and analyze its rhetorical strategies in ten paragraphs (¶s 15–24). Although he has done an exemplary job, this section of the paper is nevertheless difficult to understand. Why?

6. Might some of the difficulties in understanding this paper be due to the specialized vocabularies of (a) rhetorical analysis or (b) the language of "Sustained Attention?" Does Allen define new rhetorical concepts the first time he uses a new word or term?

For Writing

7. Either independently or with a partner, analyze a published scientific or social scientific paper in your field, or one of the scientific or social science essays in *The Essay Connection* (such as those by Gawande, "On Washing Hands" (153–59); Angier, "Why Men Don't Last" (353–56); Tim Berners-Lee, "Long Live the Web" (429–38); Mann, "The Coming Death Shortage" (362–74) to show why, where, and how they are interpretive (and therefore not objective). *Note*: This does *not* mean these essays are unreliable; indeed, they are all of high quality, though not without controversy.

Additional Topics for Writing
Appealing to Reason: Deductive and
Inductive Arguments

(For strategies for appealing to reason, see 390–91.)

Multiple Strategies for Writing: Arguments

Arguments commonly employ assorted strategies to make their points as compelling as possible and to interpret their significance. Among these are the following:

- *Definitions* of essential terms, component parts. These may be objective or favorable to the writer's point of view.
- *Illustrations* and *examples*, to show the meaning or significance of the key issues
- *Explanations* and *analyses* of the salient points
- *Comparison* and *contrast* of the pro and con positions
- *Division* and *classification* of the relevant subtopics and side issues
- A *narrative*, on occasion, either at the beginning to humanize the abstract or theoretical issue under consideration or at the end to Allow the full import of the argument to make a final impact
- *Cause* and *effect*, to show the beneficial consequences of the arguer's point of view and the detrimental consequences of the opposition's stance

1. By yourself or with a partner, write a logical, clearly reasoned, well-supported argument appropriate to the subject in organization, language, and tone and appealing to your designated audience. Be sure you have in mind a particular reader or group of readers who you know (or suspect) are likely to be receptive or hostile to your position, or uncommitted people whose opinion you're trying to influence.

   a. Tackling a particular ecological issue—you pick the controversy—is (or is not) worth the effort and expense.
   b. Smoking, drinking, or using "recreational" drugs is (is not) worth the risks.
   c. Economic prosperity is (is not) more important to our country than conservation and preservation of our country's resources.
   d. The Social Security system should (should not) be preserved in its present form for current and future generations.
   e. Everyone should (should not) be entitled to comprehensive medical care (supply one: from the cradle to the grave; in early childhood; while a student; in old age; if they're unable to pay for it).
   f. Drunk drivers should (should not) be jailed, even for a first offense.
   g. Cell phone use should (should not) be prohibited for drivers of motor vehicles when in use or in other venues (public transportation; elevators; restaurants; locker rooms)
   h. Companies manufacturing products that may affect consumers' health or safety (such as food, drugs, liquor, automobiles, pesticides) should (should not) have consumer representatives on their boards of directors.

i. The civil rights, women's liberation, gay liberation, or some comparable movement has (has not) accomplished major and long-lasting benefits for the group it represents.
j. Intercollegiate athletic teams that are big business should (should not) hire their players; intercollegiate athletes should (should not) have professional status.
k. Strong labor unions should (should not) be preserved.
l. The costs of America's space program are worth (far exceed) the benefits.
m. The federal government should (should not) take over the nation's health care system.
n. The Patriot Act should (should not) be repealed.
o. The possibility of identity theft is (is not) a reasonable tradeoff for ease of Internet usage.

2. Write a letter to your campus, city, or area newspaper in which you take a stand on an issue, defending or attacking it. You could write on one of the topics in Additional Topics 1 above or differ with a recent column or editorial. Hot button issues are fine if you have appropriate support for your argument. Send in your letter (keep a copy for yourself), and see if it is published. If so, what kind of response did it attract?

3. Write to your state or federal legislator, urging the passage or defeat of a particular piece of legislation currently being considered. (You will probably find at least one side of the issue being reported in the newspapers or a newsmagazine.) An extra: If you receive a reply, analyze it to see whether it addresses the specific points you raise. In what fashion? Does it sound like an individual response or a form letter?

Appealing to Emotion and Ethics

The essence of an emotional appeal is passion. You write from passion, and you expect your readers to respond with equal fervor. "I have a dream." "The only thing we have to fear is fear itself." "We have nothing to offer but blood, toil, tears, and sweat." "The West wasn't won with a loaded gun!" You'll be making your case, combining appeals to reason, emotion, and ethics in specific, concrete, memorable ways that you expect to have an unusually powerful impact on your readers. So your writing will probably be more colorful than it might be in less emotional circumstances, with a high proportion of vivid examples, narratives, anecdotes, character sketches, analogies ("Will Iran or Egypt or X be another Vietnam?"), and figures of speech, including metaphors ("a knee-jerk liberal"), and similes ("The Southern Senator had a face like an old Virginia ham and a personality to match.").

You can't incite your readers, either to agree with you or to take action on behalf of the cause you favor, by simply bleeding all over the page. The process of writing and rewriting and revising again will act to cool your red-hot emotion and will enable you to modulate in subsequent drafts what you might have written the first time just to get it out of your system: "Hell, no! We won't go!" As the essays in this section and elsewhere reveal, writers who appeal most effectively to their readers' emotions themselves exercise considerable control over the organization and examples they use to make their points.

They also keep particularly tight rein over their own emotions, as revealed in the tone and connotations of their language, crucial in an emotional appeal. Tone, the prevailing mood of the work, like a tone of voice conveys your attitude toward your subject and toward the evidence you present in support of your point.

The tone of Joyce Mirikitani's "Recipe" for "Round Eyes" seems objective, a matter-of-fact presentation of a process, "For best results, powder entire face, including eyelids"—until the last line, "Do not cry"—slaps readers in the face as they acknowledge the speaker's capitulation to racism.

In "About Suffering" (498–503), Sheryl R. Kennedy describes a visit to a soldier, Luke, at Walter Reed Army Medical Center. Luke lost his leg in the Iraq war, and his world has changed, changed utterly. Kennedy's sympathetic but unsentimental examination of his condition, and of human suffering generally, leads to her implicit question, "How much of this suffering—if any—was warranted?" Her answer is implied in the soldier's bitterness, her own fear of visiting "traumatically brain injured patients," of seeing "the vacant eyes and 'persistent vegetative states,'" her grief at "thinking of Luke's once beautiful leg" cremated, "history repeating itself by another young man just doing his job."

To establish a climate that encourages readers to sympathize emotionally, you as a writer can present telling facts and allow the readers to interpret them, rather than continually nudging the audience with verbal reminders to see the subject your way.

If you are appealing to your readers' emotions through irony, the tone of your words, their music, is likely to be at variance with their overt message—and to intentionally undermine it. Thus the narrator of Swift's "A Modest Proposal" (461–68) can, with an impassive face, advocate that year-old children of the poor Irish peasants be sold for "a most delicious, nourishing, and wholesome food, whether stewed, roasted, baked, or broiled"; and, in an additional inhumane observation, "I make no doubt that it will equally serve in a fricassee or a ragout."

The connotations, overtones of the language, are equally significant in emotional appeals, as they subtly (or not so subtly) reinforce the overt, literal meanings of the words. Lincoln, arriving at Gettysburg in 1863 to deliver the speech that would rank among the most memorable in American history, deliberately uses biblical language ("Fourscore" instead of "eighty"), biblical phrasing, biblical cadences to reinforce the solemnity of the occasion—dedication of the graveyard at Gettysburg. This language also underscores the seriousness of the Civil War, then in progress, and its profound consequences. In contrast to the majesty of Lincoln's language, Swift's narrator depersonalizes human beings, always calling the children *it*, with an impersonal connotation, and never employing the humanizing terms of *he, she,* or *baby*. The *it* emphasizes the animalistic connotations of the narrator's references to a newborn as "a child just dropped from its dam," further dehumanizing both mother and child.

Language, tone, and message often combine to present an *ethical appeal*—a way of impressing your readers that you as the author (and perhaps as a character in your own essay) are a knowledgeable person of good moral character, good will, and good sense. Consequently, you are a person of integrity, and to be believed as a credible, reasonable advocate of the position you take in your essay.

Thus Peter Singer, in "The Singer Solution to World Poverty" (481–87), employs straightforward language, logic, and clear-cut examples to open his readers' eyes to ethical issues that many people who consider themselves ethical either ignore or disregard. In a matter-of-fact way, Singer, an ethicist who is considered controversial because of the logical extent (some would say extremes) his principles lead to, identifies a simple principle for supporting the world's poor: "Whatever money you're spending on luxuries, not necessities, should be given away."

The brief appeal of Sojourner Truth's charismatic oratory, "Ain't I a Woman?" (458–59), makes the feminist argument for gender (and racial) equality to the 1851 Ohio Women's Rights Convention; alas, this is still alive and valid over a century and a half after she delivered it. As with Singer's solution to world poverty, Truth's statements are brief and require the audience to do much of the work, filling in the evidence and the logic behind the refrain "Ain't I a woman?"

Although ethical appeals usually tap our most profound moral values, they can be made in humorous ways, often by satire, as implied even in the title of Sherman Alexie's "What Sacagawea Means to Me" (83–85). Alexie uses language common in academic writing (one type of "establishment") to criticize the establishment's treatment of minorities (Native Americans). When Open design studio published the satiric op-art column "Introducing **new** GoValue!™ service" (470) in May, 2006—with the slogan "Your money is important to us"—there were many problems with airline travel that were easy to satirize: issues of space, luggage delays, bad (or nonexistent) food. Since then, the difficulties of air travel have multiplied—making it easy for frustrated readers (and passengers) to add many more "forbidden" boxes to this cartoon.

Ed Dante's "The Shadow Scholar" (472–79) raises troubling ethical issues about the pervasive cheating in academia, as hired ghostwriters can game the system by writing letters of application, course and term papers, lesson plans, online courses, legal briefs, lab reports, theses, dissertations. "Say what you want about me, but I am not the reason your students cheat," says Dante (not his real name)—YOU (the teacher who doesn't care, doesn't pay attention to your students' work) are, he implies (¶ 52).

Social satire—as we can see from these writings as well as from Swift's "A Modest Proposal"—always implies the need for reform. Self-satire, however, as Jason Verge presents his Montreal Canadien fanhood in "The Habs" (105–09) may just be poking fun at one's human fallibilities.

Because they usually make their point indirectly, fables, parables, and other stories with subtle moral points are often used to appeal to readers' emotions and ethical sense. The photographs of winsome (never repulsive, never ugly!) waifs often grace fundraising advertisements for famine relief, amplified by biographies of their pitiful lives; only our contributions can save them. One of the dangers in using such poster-child appeals is the possibility that you'll include too many emotional signals or ultraheavy emotional language and thereby write a paper that repels your readers by either excessive sentimentality or overkill.

Works by student writers in this book, such as Amanda Cagle's "On the Banks of the Bogue Chitto" (231–35) and Megan McGuire's "Wake Up Call" (376–82), deal directly with the impact of very difficult issues (poverty, instability, divorce, disability, suicide) on their families, particularly as they affected the authors as children growing up—resilient, resourceful, creative. Their language and examples, precise but unsentimental, are more appealing to readers—and ultimately more moving—than any "alas, poor me" approach would be. All embed powerful ethical issues.

Indeed, appeals to emotion and ethics are often intertwined. Such appeals are everywhere—for example, in the connotations of descriptions and definitions. Furthermore, if your readers like and trust you, they're more likely to believe what you say and to be moved to agree with your point of view. The evidence in a scientific report, however strong in itself, is buttressed by the credibility of the researcher. The sense of realism, the truth of a narrative, is enhanced by the credibility of the narrator. We believe Lincoln and Sheryl Kennedy and we trust the spirit of satirist Swift, even if we believe he is exaggerating, if not downright inventing, the substance of his narrative. Hearts, common sense, sensibility, and sympathy compel agreement where minds hesitate. Don't hesitate to make ethical use of this understanding.

Strategies for Writing: Appealing to Emotion and Ethics

1. Do I want to appeal primarily to my readers' emotions (and which emotions) or to their ethical sense of how people ought to behave? (Remember that in either case the appeals are intertwined with reason—see Chapter 9, "Appealing to Reason: Deductive and Inductive Arguments.")
2. To what kinds of readers am I making these appeals? What ethical or other personal qualities should I as an author exhibit? How can I lead my readers to believe that I am a person of sound character and good judgment?
3. What evidence can I choose to reinforce my appeals and my authorial image? Examples from my own life? The experiences of others? References to literature or scientific research? What order of arrangement would be most convincing? From the least emotionally moving or involving to the most? Or vice versa?
4. How can I interpret my evidence to move my readers to accept it? Should I explain very elaborately, or should I let the examples speak for themselves? If you decide on the latter, try out your essay on someone unfamiliar with the examples to see if they are in fact self-evident.
5. Do I want my audience to react with sympathy? Pity? Anger? Fear? Horror? To accomplish this, should I use much emotional language? Should my appeal be overt, direct? Or would indirection, understatement, be more effective? Would irony—saying the opposite of what I really mean (as Swift does)—be more appropriate than a direct approach? Could I make my point more effectively with a fable, parable, comic tale, or invented persona than with a straightforward analysis and overt commentary?

JANICE MIRIKITANI

Janice Mirikitani, poet and community activist, was born in Stockton, California (1941) as a third-generation Japanese-American. She and her family were interned throughout World War II in Arkansas. After the war they moved to Chicago to avoid West Coast racism, but after her parents' divorce and mother's remarriage she moved again to California, where she has lived most of her life. She earned a BA from UCLA in 1962 and teaching credentials from UC-Berkeley in 1963. Since 1966 she has worked at the Glide Church/Urban Center in San Francisco, initially as program director and since 1983 as president, directing rape and abuse recovery programs for women, and overseeing meal, housing, and computer literacy projects for the poor and homeless.

Her three books of poetry include *Awake in the River* (1978), *Shedding Silence* (1987), and *We, the Dangerous: New and Selected Poems* (1995). "I found that my wounds begin to heal"—she herself is an incest victim—"when the voices of those endangered by silence are given power." Her numerous awards include being named Poet Laureate of San Francisco in 2000.

Using the template of a food recipe, "Recipe for Round Eyes" deals with the physical and emotional pains of being an outsider, in this case, being an Asian in America.

Recipe

Round Eyes

Ingredients: scissors, Scotch magic transparent tape,
                eyeliner-water based, black.
                Optional: false eyelashes.

Cleanse face thoroughly.

For best results, powder entire face, including eyelids,
    (lighter shades suited to total effect desired)

With scissors, cut magic tape 1/16" wide, 3/4"-1/2" long–
depending on length of eyelid.

Stick firmly onto mid-upper eyelid area
    (looking down into handmirror facilitates finding
    adequate surface)

If using false eyelashes, affix first on lid, folding any
excess over the base of eyelash with glue.

Paint black eyeliner on tape and entire lid.

Do not cry.

ABRAHAM LINCOLN

Abraham Lincoln (1809–1865) was a self-made, self-taught son of Kentucky pioneers. He served four terms in the Illinois state legislature before being elected to Congress in 1847. As sixteenth president of the United States (1861–1865), Lincoln's supreme efforts were devoted to trying to secure the passage of the Thirteenth Amendment to outlaw slavery and to preserve the still young United States of America from the forces expressed through and beyond the bloody Civil War that threatened to destroy its young men, its economy, and the very government itself.

The Gettysburg Address

Four score and seven years ago our fathers brought forth on this conti- 1
nent, a new nation, conceived in liberty, and dedicated to the proposition that all men are created equal.

Now we are engaged in a great civil war, testing whether that 2
nation, or any nation so conceived and so dedicated, can long endure. We are met on a great battlefield of that war. We have come to dedicate a portion of that field, as a final resting place for those who here gave their lives that the nation might live. It is altogether fitting and proper that we should do this.

But, in a larger sense, we cannot dedicate—we cannot consecrate—we 3
cannot hallow—this ground. The brave men, living and dead, who struggled here, have consecrated it, far above our poor power to add or detract. The world will little note, nor long remember what we say here, but it can never forget what they did here. It is for us the living, rather, to be dedicated here to the unfinished work which they who fought here have thus far so nobly advanced. It is rather for us to be here dedicated to the great task remaining before us—that from these honored dead we take increased devotion—that we here highly resolve that these dead shall not have died in vain—that this nation, under God, shall have a new birth of freedom—and that government of the people, by the people, for the people, shall not perish from the earth.

Content

1. What principles of the founding of the United States does Lincoln emphasize in the first sentence? Why are these so important to the occasion of his address? To the theme of this address?

2. What does Lincoln imply and assert is the relation of life and death? Birth and rebirth?

Strategies/Structures/Language

3. Why would Lincoln, knowing that his audience expected longer orations, deliberately have decided to make his speech so short? Lincoln's speech commemorated a solemn occasion: the dedication of a major battlefield of the ongoing Civil War. Wouldn't such a short speech have undermined the significance of the event?

4. Identify the language and metaphors of birth that Lincoln uses throughout this address. For what purpose? With what effect?

5. Why did Lincoln use biblical language and phrasing conspicuously at the beginning and end of the address, such as "four score and seven years ago" instead of the more common "eighty-seven"?

6. Lincoln uses many *antitheses*—oppositions, contrasts. Identify some and show how they reinforce the meaning.

7. Another important rhetorical device is the *tricolon*, "the division of an idea into three harmonious parts, usually of increasing power,"—for example, "government of the people, by the people, for the people . . ." Find others and show why they are so memorable.

For Writing

8. Write a short, dignified speech for a solemn occasion, real or imaginary. Let the majesty of your language and the conspicuous rhetorical patterns of your sentences and paragraphs (through such devices as antithesis and parallelism) reinforce your point.

9. Rewrite the "Gettysburg Address" as it might have been spoken by a more recent president or other politician, using language, paragraphing, and sentence structures characteristic of the speaker and the times. One such speech, a parody, is William Safire's "Carter's Gettysburg Address," which begins: "Exactly two hundred and one years, five months and one day ago, our forefathers—and our foremothers, too, as my wife, the First Lady, reminds me—our highly competent Founding Persons brought forth on this land mass a new nation, or entity, dreamed up in liberty and dedicated to the comprehensive program of insuring that all of us are created with the same basic human rights."

SOJOURNER TRUTH

Sojourner Truth (1797–1883) was born Isabella Baumfree to a family of slaves on an estate in Ulster County, New York. She was sold several times, enduring the hardships of slavery with the help of her religious faith. She fled her owners in 1827, was taken in by the Van Wagener family, whose name she assumed for a time, and became an inspirational evangelical preacher. In 1843, a spiritual calling led her to change her name to Sojourner Truth and set out as a traveling preacher, living on the kindness of strangers, and eventually joining an abolitionist cooperative community in Massachusetts. After the breakup of the community, she dictated her memoirs to one of its members, Olive Gilbert, which William Lloyd Garrison published as *The Narrative of Sojourner Truth* (1850). Her book provided her with an income and gave her more opportunities to speak out against slavery and in support of women's rights. During the Civil War, she worked with freed slaves at a government refugee camp in Virginia and was employed by the National Freedman's Relief Association in Washington, DC. She met President Abraham Lincoln in 1864. Truth delivered her most famous speech at the 1851 Ohio Women's Rights Convention. While some historians have suggested that the speech was embellished afterward and prior to publication—perhaps by adding repetitions of the phrase "ain't I a woman?"—it nevertheless stands as a model of persuasive and inspirational oratory.

Ain't I a Woman?

1 Well, children, where there is so much racket there must be something out of kilter. I think that 'twixt the negroes of the South and the women at the North, all talking about rights, the white men will be in a fix pretty soon. But what's all this here talking about?

2 That man over there says women need to be helped into carriages, and lifted over ditches, and to have the best place everywhere. Nobody ever helps me into carriages, or over mud-puddles, or gives me any best place! And ain't I a woman? Look at me! Look at my arm! I have ploughed and planted, and gathered into barns, and no man could head me! And ain't I a woman? I could work as much and eat as much as a man—when I could get it—and bear the lash as well! And ain't I a woman? I have borne thirteen children, and seen them most all sold off to slavery, and when I cried out with my mother's grief, none but Jesus heard me! And ain't I a woman?

3 Then they talk about this thing in the head; what's this they call it? [Intellect, someone whispers.] That's it, honey. What's that got to do with women's rights or negro's rights? If my cup won't hold but a pint, and yours holds a quart, wouldn't you be mean not to let me have my little half-measure full?

4 Then that little man in black there, he says women can't have as much rights as men, 'cause Christ wasn't a woman! Where did your Christ come from? Where did your Christ come from? From God and a woman! Man had nothing to do with Him.

5 If the first woman God ever made was strong enough to turn the world upside down all alone, these women together ought to be able to turn it back, and get it right side up again! And now they is asking to do it, the men better let them.

6 Obliged to you for hearing me, and now old Sojourner ain't got nothing more to say.

Content

1. Identify the arguments Truth makes in support of gender equality. Does she suggest that female equality will diminish or enhance the position of white men? Why does she comment that "the white men will be in a fix pretty soon" (¶ 1)?

2. What evidence does Truth offer her audience to back up her arguments? Why is she a credible witness?

3. Some historians have presented evidence that Truth's audience at the 1851 Ohio Women's Rights Convention received her warmly and favorably rather than, as this version of the speech implies, in the face of some hostility. Why might she or other women's rights activists have changed the speech prior to publication? Does this ambiguity about the authenticity of a historical event change your interpretation of her speech? If so, how?

Strategies/Structures/Language

4. How does the phrase "ain't I a woman?" underscore Truth's argument? Why do repetitions of this key phrase move the reader?

5. Truth was a dedicated political activist (see 458). Why does she claim to be unfamiliar with the word "intellect" (¶ 3)?

6. Why does Truth begin by referring to her audience as "children" (¶ 1)? How does her question "But what's all this here talking about" build on this foundation (¶ 1)?

7. What does the metaphor "my cup" refer to (¶ 3)? How does this metaphor introduce Sojourner's argument that Christ was born of "God and a woman" (¶ 4)?

For Writing

8. *Journal Writing.* Explore the memory of an inspirational experience, whether spiritual (e.g., during prayer or a sermon), intellectual (e.g., in the classroom), or aesthetic (e.g., through experiencing or creating a work of art). How important was language to this experience? Did the experience transcend language? How might you recreate such an experience or communicate it to others?

9. *Dialogues.* Compare Truth's relationship to her own body with Zara Rix's in "Corporality" (557–63). Consider Rix's experience of her body as "a strange, alien thing" (¶ 33) and as the repository of "others' stories" (¶ 1). How does Truth's voice marginalize and yet draw attention to her body? What does her use of her body as evidence suggest about her relationship to her personal history and that of her fellow African-Americans?

10. *Second Look.* Dorothea Lange's photograph of Florence Owens Thompson and her children (483) has become known as "Migrant Mother." How might you read this photograph as a portrait of feminine weakness? and/or strength? How does it suggest, as Sojourner Truth argues, that "women together ought to be able to turn [the world] . . . right side up again" (¶ 5)? How does the arrangement of the three children influence your interpretation of the photograph? Does learning that Florence Owens Thompson was Native American and a labor activist influence your interpretation of her portrait?

JONATHAN SWIFT

Jonathan Swift, author of *Gulliver's Travels* (1726) and other satiric essays, poems, and tracts, was well acquainted with irony. Born in Dublin in 1667, the son of impoverished English Anglicans, he obtained a degree from Trinity College, Dublin, in 1685 only by "special grace." When James II arrived in Ireland in 1688, he initiated pro-Catholic, anti-Protestant policies that remained in force until the ascendancy of William III. Swift, along with many Anglo-Irish, was forced to flee to England, was eventually ordained as an Anglican priest, and rose prominently in London literary and political circles until 1713. Although he had hoped for a church appointment in England, his desertion of the Whig Party for the Tories was ironically rewarded with an appointment as dean of St. Patrick's (Anglican) Cathedral in Dublin, which he regarded as virtual exile. Nevertheless, despite his religious differences with the Irish people, Swift became a beloved leader in the Irish resistance to English oppression, motivated less by partisan emotions than by his own "savage indignation" against injustice. He died in 1745.

Tischler Fotografen/Peter Arnold/Getty Images

A well-dressed Chinese schoolgirl in uniform stands and waits amidst rubble in an urban slum neighborhood in Shengen, beyond which gleam the modern high-rise buildings that signal renewal and hope of a way up and out. This photograph, like the "We shall overcome" photograph of Dr. Martin Luther King, Jr., Joan Baez, and others escorting African-American schoolchildren to a newly integrated school in 1966 (401), makes direct and indirect arguments about children, human rights, and society. What are some of these arguments? What evidence does each photograph provide for your interpretation? What do you have to supply from your knowledge of history or culture?

Swift wrote "A Modest Proposal" in the summer of 1729, after three years of drought and crop failure had forced over 35,000 peasants to leave their homes and wander the countryside looking for work, food, and shelter for their starving families, ignored by the insensitive absentee landowners. The "Proposal" carries the English landowners' treatment of the Irish to its logical—but repugnant—extreme: if they are going to devour any hope the Irish have of living decently, why don't they literally eat the Irish children? The persona Swift creates is logical, consistent, seemingly rational—and utterly inhumane, an advocate of infanticide and cannibalism. Yet nowhere in the "Proposal" does the satirist condemn the speaker; he relies on the readers' sense of morality for that. This tactic can be dangerous, for a reader who misses the irony may take the "Proposal" at face value. But Swift's intended readers, English (landlords included) as well as Irish who could act to alleviate the people's suffering, understood very well what he meant. The victims themselves, largely illiterate, would probably have been unaware of this forceful plea on their behalf.

A Modest Proposal

1   It is a melancholy object to those who walk through this great town or travel in the country, when they see the streets, the roads, and cabin doors, crowded with beggars of the female sex, followed by three, four, or six children, all in rags and importuning every passenger for an alms. These mothers, instead of being able to work for their honest livelihood, are forced to employ all their time in strolling to beg sustenance for their helpless infants: who as they grow up either turn thieves for want of work, or leave their dear native country to fight for the pretender in Spain, or sell themselves to the Barbadoes.

2   I think it is agreed by all parties that this prodigious number of children in the arms, or on the backs, or at the heels of their mothers, and frequently of their fathers, is in the present deplorable state of the kingdom a very great additional grievance; and, therefore, whoever could find out a fair, cheap, and easy method of making these children sound, useful members of the commonwealth, would deserve so well of the public as to have his statue set up for a preserver of the nation.

3   But my intention is very far from being confined to provide only for the children of professed beggars; it is of a much greater extent, and shall take in the whole number of infants at a certain age who are born of parents in effect as little able to support them as those who demand our charity in the streets.

4   As to my own part, having turned my thoughts for many years upon this important subject, and maturely weighed the several schemes of our projectors, I have always found them grossly mistaken in their computation. It is true, a child just dropped from its dam may be supported by her

milk for a solar year, with little other nourishment; at most not above the value of two shillings, which the mother may certainly get, or the value in scraps, by her lawful occupation of begging; and it is exactly at one year old that I propose to provide for them in such a manner as instead of being a charge upon their parents or the parish, or wanting food and raiment for the rest of their lives, they shall on the contrary contribute to the feeding, and partly to the clothing, of many thousands.

There is likewise another great advantage in my scheme, that it will 5 prevent those voluntary abortions, and that horrid practice of women murdering their bastard children, alas! too frequent among us! sacrificing the poor innocent babes I doubt more to avoid the expense than the shame, which would move tears and pity in the most savage and inhuman breast.

The number of souls in this kingdom being usually reckoned one 6 million and half, of these I calculate there may be about two hundred thousand couple whose wives are breeders; from which number I subtract thirty thousand couple who are able to maintain their own children (although I apprehend there cannot be so many, under the present distress of the kingdom); but this being granted, there will remain an hundred and seventy thousand breeders. I again subtract fifty thousand for those women who miscarry, or whose children die by accident or disease within the year. There only remain an hundred and twenty thousand children of poor parents annually born. The question therefore is, how this number shall be reared and provided for? which, as I have already said, under the present situation of affairs, is utterly impossible by all the methods hitherto proposed. For we can neither employ them in handicraft or agriculture; we neither build houses (I mean in the country) nor cultivate land; they can very seldom pick up a livelihood by stealing, till they arrive at six years old, except where they are of towardly parts; although I confess they learn the rudiments much earlier; during which time they can, however, be properly looked upon only as probationers; as I have been informed by a principal gentleman in the country of Cavan, who protested to me that he never knew above one or two instances under the age of six, even in a part of the kingdom so renowned for the quickest proficiency in that art.

I am assured by our merchants, that a boy or a girl before twelve 7 years old is no saleable commodity; and even when they come to this age they will not yield above three pounds, or three pounds and a half a crown at most on the Exchange; which cannot turn to account either to the parents or kingdom, the charge of nutriment and rags having been at least four times that value.

I shall now therefore humbly propose my own thoughts, which 8 I hope will not be liable to the least objection.

I have been assured by a very knowing American of my acquain- 9 tance in London, that a young healthy child well nursed is at a year old the most delicious, nourishing, and wholesome food, whether stewed, roasted, baked, or broiled; and I make no doubt that it will equally serve in a fricassee or a ragout.

10   I do therefore humbly offer it to public consideration that of the hundred and twenty thousand children already computed, twenty thousand may be reserved for breed, whereof only one fourth part to be males; which is more than we allow to sheep, black cattle, or swine; and my reason is, that these children are seldom the fruits of marriage, a circumstance not much regarded by our savages; therefore, one male will be sufficient to serve four females. That the remaining hundred thousand may, at a year old, be offered in sale to the persons of quality and fortune through the kingdom; always advising the mother to let them suck plentifully in the last month, so as to render them plump and fat for a good table. A child will make two dishes at an entertainment for friends; and when the family dines alone, the fore or hind quarter will make a reasonable dish, and seasoned with a little pepper or salt will be very good boiled on the fourth day, especially in winter.

11   I have reckoned upon a medium that a child just born will weigh twelve pounds, and in a solar year, if tolerably nursed, will increase to twenty-eight pounds.

12   I grant this food will be somewhat dear, and therefore very proper for landlords, who, as they have already devoured most of the parents, seem to have the best title to the children.

13   Infant's flesh will be in season throughout the year, but more plentiful in March, and a little before and after: for we are told by a grave author, an eminent French physician, that fish being a prolific diet, there are more children born in Roman Catholic countries about nine months after Lent than at any other season; therefore, reckoning a year after Lent, the markets will be more glutted than usual, because the number of popish infants is at least three to one in this kingdom: and therefore it will have one other collateral advantage, by lessening the number of papists among us.

14   I have already computed the charge of nursing a beggar's child (in which list I reckon all cottagers, laborers, and four-fifths of the farmers) to be about two shillings per annum, rags included; and I believe no gentleman would repine to give ten shillings for the carcass of a good fat child, which, as I have said, will make four dishes of excellent nutritive meat, when he has only some particular friend or his own family to dine with him. Thus the squire will learn to be a good landlord, and grow popular among the tenants; the mother will have eight shillings net profit, and be fit for work till she produces another child.

15   Those who are more thrifty (as I must confess the times require) may flay the carcass; the skin of which artificially dressed will make admirable gloves for ladies, and summer boots for fine gentlemen.

16   As to our city of Dublin, shambles may be appointed for this purpose in the most convenient parts of it, and butchers we may be assured

will not be wanting: although I rather recommend buying the children alive, and dressing them hot from the knife as we do roasting pigs.

A very worthy person, a true lover of his country, and whose virtues I highly esteem, was lately pleased in discoursing on this matter to offer a refinement upon my scheme. He said that many gentlemen of this kingdom, having of late destroyed their deer, he conceived that the want of venison might be well supplied by the bodies of young lads and maidens, not exceeding fourteen years of age nor under twelve; so great a number of both sexes in every country being now ready to starve for want of work and service; and these to be disposed of by their parents, if alive, or otherwise by their nearest relations. But with due deference to so excellent a friend and so deserving a patriot, I cannot be altogether in his sentiments; for as to the males, my American acquaintance assured me from frequent experience that their flesh was generally tough and lean, like that of our schoolboys by continual exercise, and their taste disagreeable; and to fatten them would not answer the charge. Then as to the females, it would, I think, with humble submission be a loss to the public, because they soon would become breeders themselves: and besides, it is not improbable that some scrupulous people might be apt to censure such a practice (although indeed very unjustly), as a little bordering upon cruelty; which, I confess, has always been with me the strongest objection against any project, how well soever intended. 17

But in order to justify my friend, he confessed that this expedient was put into his head by the famous Psalmanazar, a native of the island Formosa, who came from thence to London about twenty years ago: and in conversation told my friend, that in his country when any young person happened to be put to death, the executioner sold the carcass to persons of quality as a prime dainty; and that in his time the body of a plump girl of fifteen, who was crucified for an attempt to poison the emperor, was sold to his imperial majesty's prime minister of state, and other great mandarins of the court, in joints from the gibbet, at four hundred crowns. Neither indeed can I deny, that if the same use were made of several plump young girls in this town, who without one single groat to their fortunes cannot stir abroad without a chair, and appear at the playhouse and assemblies in foreign fineries which they never will pay for, the kingdom would not be the worse. 18

Some persons of a desponding spirit are in great concern about that vast number of poor people, who are aged, diseased, or maimed, and I have been desired to employ my thoughts what course may be taken to ease the nation of so grievous an encumbrance. But I am not in the least pain upon that matter, because it is very well known that they are every day dying and rotting by cold and famine, and filth and vermin, as fast as can be reasonably expected. And as to the young laborers, they are now in as hopeful a condition: they cannot get work, and consequently pine 19 away for want of nourishment, to a degree that if at any time they are accidentally hired to common labor, they have not strength to perform it; and thus the country and themselves are happily delivered from the evils to come.

20   I have too long digressed, and therefore shall return to my subject. I think the advantages by the proposal which I have made are obvious and many, as well as of the highest importance.

21   For first, as I have already observed, it would greatly lessen the number of papists, with whom we are yearly overrun, being the principal breeders of the nation as well as our most dangerous enemies; and who stay at home on purpose to deliver the kingdom to the Pretender, hoping to take their advantage by the absence of so many good Protestants, who have chosen rather to leave their country than stay at home and pay tithes against their conscience to an Episcopal curate.

22   Secondly, The poor tenants will have something valuable of their own, which by law may be made liable to distress and help to pay their landlord's rent, their corn and cattle being already seized, and money a thing unknown.

23   Thirdly, Whereas the maintenance of a hundred thousand children from two years old and upward, cannot be computed at less than ten shillings a piece per annum, the nation's stock will be thereby increased fifty thousand pounds per annum, beside the profit of a new dish introduced to the tables of all gentlemen of fortune in the kingdom who have any refinement in taste. And the money will circulate among ourselves, the goods being entirely of our own growth and manufacture.

24   Fourthly, The constant breeders beside the gain of eight shillings sterling per annum by the sale of their children, will be rid of the charge of maintaining them after the first year.

25   Fifthly, This food would likewise bring great custom to taverns, where the vintners will certainly be so prudent as to procure the best receipts for dressing it to perfection, and consequently have their houses frequented by all the fine gentlemen, who justly value themselves upon their knowledge in good eating; and a skillful cook who understands how to oblige his guests, will contrive to make it as expensive as they please.

26   Sixthly, This would be a great inducement to marriage, which all wise nations have either encouraged by rewards or enforced by laws and penalties. It would increase the care and tenderness of mothers toward their children, when they were sure of a settlement for life to the poor babes, provided in some sort by the public, to their annual profit instead of expense. We should see an honest emulation among the married women, which of them would bring the fattest child to the market. Men would become as fond of their wives during the time of their pregnancy as they are now of their mares in foal, their cows in calf, their sows when

they are ready to farrow; nor offer to beat or kick them (as is too frequent a practice) for fear of a miscarriage.

Many other advantages might be enumerated. For instance, the addition of some thousand carcasses in our exportation of barreled beef, the propagation of swine's flesh, and improvement in the art of making good bacon, so much wanted among us by the great destruction of pigs, too frequent at our table; which are no way comparable in taste or magnificence to a well-grown, fat, yearling child, which roasted whole will make a considerable figure at a lord mayor's feast or any other public entertainment. But this and many others I omit, being studious of brevity.

Supposing that one thousand families in this city would be constant customers for infants' flesh, besides others who might have it at merry-meetings, particularly at weddings and christenings, I compute that Dublin would take off annually about twenty thousand carcasses; and the rest of the kingdom (where probably they will be sold somewhat cheaper) the remaining eighty thousand.

I can think of no one objection that will possibly be raised against this proposal, unless it should be urged that the number of people will be thereby much lessened in the kingdom. This I freely own, and it was indeed one principal design in offering it to the world. I desire the reader will observe, that I calculate my remedy for this one individual kingdom of Ireland and for no other that ever was, is, or I think ever can be upon earth. Therefore let no man talk to me of other expedients; of taxing our absentees at five shillings a pound: of using neither clothes nor household furniture except what is of our own growth and manufacture: of utterly rejecting the materials and instruments that promote foreign luxury: of curing the expensiveness of pride, vanity, idleness, and gaming in our women: of introducing a vein of parsimony, prudence, and temperance: of learning to love our country, in the want of which we differ even from Laplanders and the inhabitants of Topinamboo: of quitting our animosities and factions, nor acting any longer like the Jews, who were murdering one another at the very moment their city was taken: of being a little cautious not to sell our country and conscience for nothing: of teaching landlords to have at least one degree of mercy toward their tenants; lastly, of putting a spirit of honesty, industry, and skill into our shopkeepers; who, if a resolution could now be taken to buy only our native goods, would immediately unite to cheat and exact upon us in the price, the measure, and the goodness, nor could ever yet be brought to make one fair proposal of just dealing, though often and earnestly invited to it.

Therefore I repeat, let no man talk to me of these and the like expedients, till he has at least some glimpse of hope that there will be ever some hearty and sincere attempts to put them in practice.

But as to myself, having been wearied out for many years with offering vain, idle, visionary thoughts, and at length utterly despairing of success, I fortunately fell upon this proposal; which, as it is wholly new, so it has something solid and real, of no expense and little trouble, full in our own power, and whereby we can incur no danger in disobliging England. For this kind of commodity will not bear exportation, the flesh being of too tender a consistence to admit a long continuance in salt, although perhaps I could name a country which would be glad to eat up our whole nation without it.

32   After all, I am not so violently bent upon my own opinion as to reject any offer proposed by wise men, which shall be found equally innocent, cheap, easy, and effectual. But before something of that kind shall be advanced in contradiction to my scheme, and offering a better, I desire the author or authors will be pleased maturely to consider two points. First, as things now stand, how they will be able to find food and raiment for a hundred thousand useless mouths and backs. And secondly, there being a round million of creatures in human figure throughout this kingdom, whose subsistence put into a common stock would leave them in debt two millions of pounds sterling, adding those who are beggars by profession to the bulk of farmers, cottagers, and laborers, with the wives and children who are beggars in effect; I desire those politicians who dislike my overture, and may perhaps be so bold as to attempt an answer, that they will first ask the parents of these mortals, whether they would not at this day think it a great happiness to have been sold for food at a year old in the manner I prescribe, and thereby have avoided such a perpetual scene of misfortunes as they have since gone through by the oppression of landlords, the impossibility of paying rent without money or trade, the want of common sustenance, with neither house nor clothes to cover them from the inclemencies of the weather, and the most inevitable prospect of entailing the like or greater miseries upon their breed for ever.

33   I profess, in the sincerity of my heart, that I have not the least personal interest in endeavoring to promote this necessary work, having no other motive than the public good of my country, by advancing our trade, providing for infants, relieving the poor, and giving some pleasure to the rich. I have no children by which I can propose to get a single penny; the youngest being nine years old, and my wife past childbearing.

Content

1. What is the overt thesis of Swift's essay? What is its implied (and real) thesis? In what ways do these theses differ?

2. What are the primary aims and values of the narrator of the essay? Identify the economic advantages of his proposal that he offers in paragraphs 9–16. How do the narrator's alleged aims and values differ from the aims and values of Swift as the essay's author?

3. What do the advantages that the narrator offers for his proposal (¶s 21–26) reveal about the social and economic conditions of Ireland when Swift was writing?

4. Why is it a "very knowing *American*" (emphasis added) who has assured the narrator of the suitability of year-old infants for food (¶ 9)?

5. Swift as the author of the essay expects his readers to respond to the narrator's cold economic arguments on a humane, moral level. What might such an appropriate response be?

Strategies/Structures/Language

6. What persona (a created character) does the speaker of Swift's essay have? How are readers to know that this character is not Swift himself?

7. Why does the narrator use so many mathematical computations throughout? How do they reinforce his economic argument? How do they enhance the image of his cold-bloodedness?

8. Why did Swift choose to present his argument indirectly rather than overtly? What advantages does this indirect, consistently ironic technique provide? What disadvantages does it have (for instance, do you think Swift's readers are likely to believe he really advocated eating babies)?

9. What is the prevailing tone of the essay? How does it undermine what the narrator says? How does the tone reinforce Swift's implied meaning?

10. Why does Swift say "a child just dropped from its dam" (¶ 4) instead of "just born from his mother"? What other language reinforces the animalistic associations (see, for instance, "breeders" in ¶ 17)?

For Writing

11. **Journal Writing.** Why do satire and parody often score more political points than straightforward reportage and editorial writing? Explore a memorable television show or Internet site that uses satire and parody to make a political statement. When does the humor work and when does it miss the mark? Does the humor ever cut too close to the bone? What's the purpose of political satire in our culture?

12. **Dialogues.** Either individually or as part of a team, write a Modest Proposal of your own. Pick some problem that you think needs to be solved, and propose, for a critical audience, a radical solution—a dramatic way to preserve endangered species, use genetic engineering, or eliminate identity theft or addiction, for example. You may draw on McKibben's "Designer Genes" (515–25); Fallows's "Tinfoil Underwear" (192–98); or DiFranza's "Hooked from the First Cigarette" (122–31).

13. Write an essay in which a created character, a narrative persona, speaks ironically (as Swift's narrator does) about your subject. The character's values should be at variance with the values you and your audience share. For instance, if you want to propose stiff penalties for drunk driving, your narrator could be a firm advocate of drinking, and of driving without restraint, and could be shown driving unsafely while under the influence of alcohol, indifferent to the dangers.

ETHICAL ARGUMENTS: VISUAL VERSIONS

OPEN

Open is an edgy design studio in New York City. The name suggests "Come on in, we're OPEN."

Introducing new GoValue!™ service

1   It was reported recently that Airbus was considering standing-room-only "seats" for its planes. Passengers would be strapped to padded back-boards, allowing airlines to squeeze in more people. Sounds like a great idea. But why stop there?

Introducing

new

**GoValue!™
service**

Now available*
on all domestic
and international
flights. Enjoy!

*You have no choice

BeHassleFree™
Do flight attendants bug
you during a flight?
Well, we got rid of them.
Now you can have some
peace and quiet!

TravelExtraLite™
We've eliminated all
cargo compartments
and overhead storage
bins. No more lugging all
those heavy bags!

PrivacyPlusXT™
Since we've removed
the lavatories from our
planes, you can use the
restroom in the comfort
of your own home.

StandingRoom™
Everybody knows airline
seats are uncomfortable.
Now we're doing
something about it!

FlexTravelTime™
Go with the flow! Your
flight might get there
up to 48 hours after its
scheduled arrival time.
Relax! What's the rush?

HealthYesNow™
Everybody knows
snacks and soft drinks
are bad for you. So
we don't serve them!
Or any other food.

EcoFastUltra™
Our new windowless
planes are more aero-
dynamic, increasing
fuel efficiency by .001%.
Happy Earth Day!

Your money is important to us. ValueFunAir

Courtesy OPEN

GARRY TRUDEAU

Garry Trudeau (born in New York City in 1948) launched his comic strip, *Doonesbury*, in 1970 just as he graduated from Yale. The strip was an instant hit; for forty years the characters of Zonker, Boopsie, Lacey, Duke, and Joanie Caucus have remained American icons, participating in consistent satire of contemporary events, politics, personalities, and lifestyles— whether privileged or counterculture. Indeed, many of the 1400 newspapers nationally and internationally in which the strip appears print it on their editorial pages rather than with the rest of the comics. In 1975 Trudeau won a Pulitzer Prize for editorial cartooning; he was a Pulitzer Prize finalist in 1989, 2004, and 2005. His work has been collected in over 60 editions and has appeared in film and on Broadway. "Satire is an ungentlemanly art," says Trudeau. "It's lacking in balance. It's unfair"—and thus keeps the complacent on razor's edge. No one is immune, even the greatest fans—such as college students satirized in the following strip.

Doonesbury

Content

1. The strategy of Open's satire, like that of many satires, is to take an idea that was initially presented as a straightforward proposal and then derive a number of ridiculous analogies to reveal the weaknesses and flaws of the original. So, what's wrong with Airbus's idea of having "standing-room-only" seats on its planes, in which passengers would be strapped to padded backboards, allowing up to 200 more passengers per planeload?

2. The standing-room information, originally published in *The New York Times*, April 25, 2006, was incorrect; the satire was published in the *Times* on May 1, 2006. A retraction published May 3, 2006, in *Plane News* and elsewhere says that although Airbus had "researched that idea in 2003, it has since abandoned" the plan; moreover, because the Airbus A 380 superjumbo jet could "accommodate 853 passengers in regular seats, standing-room positions would not be needed." Does knowledge of the truth diminish the point of the satire?

3. If your college culture decreed that partying started on Thursday night, rather than Wednesday as depicted in the Doonesbury strip, would that fact change the point of the strip? Your reaction to it?

Strategies/Structures/Language

4. The purpose of satire is often to right a wrong (see Swift's "A Modest Proposal" 461–68) or to reform ill-conceived plans. Since standing-room seats never took off, what's the point of paying attention to this satire now?

5. Satire often works through exaggeration of actual facts. What's exaggerated in the "**new** GoValue!™ Service"? In the *Doonesbury* strip? What's not?

6. Show how both satires, through clever graphics combined with ironic language, cause readers—including those in the target populations—to laugh. At whom or what are readers laughing?

For Writing

7. In the few years since the "**new** GoValue!™ Service" was published, airlines have continued to cut costs and to expect more money and/or more sacrifices from passengers. Have any of the proposals in this op-art editorial come to pass? Does the existence of these—or their equivalents—lend credibility to the satire? With a partner, (if you wish), preferably a frequent flyer, write your own "Modest Proposal" concerning current airline travel, or a Passengers' Bill of Rights, straightforward or satiric.

8. Present the ideas you generated in question 7 in the form of icons, avatars, or cartoons.

ED DANTE

Ed Dante is the pseudonym of an East Coast author who dare not tell his name. For the past ten years he has made his living ($66,000 in 2010) by writing papers-to-order for students who cheat–on admissions essays, undergraduate papers, masters' theses, and doctoral dissertations. He boasts that he can write forty pages a day, 5000 pages a year, "for courses in history, cinema, labor relations, pharmacology, theology, sports management, maritime security, airline services, sustainability, municipal budgeting, marketing, philosophy, ethics. . . ."

The essay was published in *The Chronicle of Higher Education*, November 16, 2010—where it generated "more than 640 comments, the most on any article published by the *Chronicle*" ("Something Is Rotten in Academe," *The Chronicle Review* 14 Jan 2011 B 16-17). Although Dante admits to his academic audience "I am vulnerable to ethical scrutiny. . . . I am not the reason your students cheat," he largely ignores the ethical issues of cheating that he argues are pervasive in academia. Contending that "61% of undergraduates have admitted to some form of cheating on assignments and exams," Dante says "there is little discussion about custom papers and how they differ from more detectable forms of plagiarism, or about why students cheat in the first place. It is my hope that this essay will initiate such a conversation." Let the discussion begin; Dante himself is "planning to retire," tired of helping teachers "make your students look competent."

The Shadow Scholar

The request came in by e-mail around 2 in the afternoon. It was from a previous customer, and she had urgent business. I quote her message here verbatim (if I had to put up with it, so should you): "You did me business ethics propsal for me I need propsal got approved pls can you will write me paper?"   1

I've gotten pretty good at interpreting this kind of correspondence. The client had attached a document from her professor with details about the paper. She needed the first section in a week. Seventy-five pages.   2

I told her no problem.   3

It truly was no problem. In the past year, I've written roughly 5,000 pages of scholarly literature, most on very tight deadlines. But you won't find my name on a single paper.   4

I've written toward a master's degree in cognitive psychology, a Ph.D. in sociology, and a handful of postgraduate credits in international diplomacy. I've worked on bachelor's degrees in hospitality, business administration, and accounting. I've written for courses in history, cinema, labor relations, pharmacology, theology, sports management, maritime security, airline services, sustainability, municipal budgeting, marketing, philosophy, ethics, Eastern religion, postmodern architecture, anthropology, literature, and public administration. I've attended three dozen online universities. I've completed 12 graduate theses of 50 pages or more. All for someone else.   5

You've never heard of me, but there's a good chance that you've read some of my work. I'm a hired gun, a doctor of everything, an academic mercenary. My customers are your students. I promise you that. Somebody in your classroom uses a service that you can't detect, that you can't defend against, that you may not even know exists.   6

I work at an online company that generates tens of thousands of dollars a month by creating original essays based on specific instructions provided by cheating students. I've worked there full time since 2004. On any day of the academic year, I am working on upward of 20 assignments.   7

In the midst of this great recession, business is booming. At busy times, during midterms and finals, my company's staff of roughly 50   8

Ed Dante, [pseud], "The Shadow Scholar." Chronicle Review, Chronicle of Higher Education Nov.12, 2010 B 6-9. Reprinted by permission of the Chronicle Review, Chronicle of Higher Education, Nov. 12, 2010.

writers is not large enough to satisfy the demands of students who will pay for our work and claim it as their own.

9   You would be amazed by the incompetence of your students' writing. I have seen the word "desperate" misspelled every way you can imagine. And these students truly are desperate. They couldn't write a convincing grocery list, yet they are in graduate school. They really need help. They need help learning and, separately, they need help passing their courses. But they aren't getting it.

10   For those of you who have ever mentored a student through the writing of a dissertation, served on a thesis-review committee, or guided a graduate student through a formal research process, I have a question: Do you ever wonder how a student who struggles to formulate complete sentences in conversation manages to produce marginally competent research? How does that student get by you?

11   I live well on the desperation, misery, and incompetence that your educational system has created. Granted, as a writer, I could earn more; certainly there are ways to earn less. But I never struggle to find work. And as my peers trudge through thankless office jobs that seem more intolerable with every passing month of our sustained recession, I am on pace for my best year yet. I will make roughly $66,000 this year. Not a king's ransom, but higher than what many actual educators are paid.

12   Of course, I know you are aware that cheating occurs. But you have no idea how deeply this kind of cheating penetrates the academic system, much less how to stop it. Last summer *The New York Times* reported that 61 percent of undergraduates have admitted to some form of cheating on assignments and exams. Yet there is little discussion about custom papers and how they differ from more-detectable forms of plagiarism, or about why students cheat in the first place.

13   It is my hope that this essay will initiate such a conversation. As for me, I'm planning to retire. I'm tired of helping you make your students look competent.

14   It is late in the semester when the business student contacts me, a time when I typically juggle deadlines and push out 20 to 40 pages a day. I had written a short research proposal for her a few weeks before, suggesting a project that connected a surge of unethical business practices to the patterns of trade liberalization. The proposal was approved, and now I had six days to complete the assignment. This was not quite a rush order, which we get top dollar to write. This assignment would be priced at a standard $2,000, half of which goes in my pocket.

15   A few hours after I had agreed to write the paper, I received the following e-mail: "sending sorces for ur to use thanx."

16   I did not reply immediately. One hour later, I received another message:

17   "did u get the sorce I send
18   please where you are now?

Desprit to pass spring projict"   19

Not only was this student going to be a constant thorn in my side,   20
but she also communicated in haiku, each less decipherable than the one
before it. I let her know that I was giving her work the utmost attention,
that I had received her sources, and that I would be in touch if I had any
questions. Then I put it aside.

From my experience, three demographic groups seek out my ser-   21
vices: the English-as-second-language student; the hopelessly deficient
student; and the lazy rich kid.

For the last, colleges are a perfect launching ground—they are built   22
to reward the rich and to forgive them their laziness. Let's be honest:
The successful among us are not always the best and the brightest, and
certainly not the most ethical. My favorite customers are those with an
unlimited supply of money and no shortage of instructions on how they
would like to see their work executed. While the deficient student will
generally not know how to ask for what he wants until he doesn't get it,
the lazy rich student will know exactly what he wants. He is poised for a
life of paying others and telling them what to do. Indeed, he is acquiring
all the skills he needs to stay on top.

As for the first two types of students—the ESL and the hope-   23
lessly deficient—colleges are utterly failing them. Students who come to
American universities from other countries find that their efforts to learn a
new language are confounded not only by cultural difficulties but also by
the pressures of grading. The focus on evaluation rather than education
means that those who haven't mastered English must do so quickly or
suffer the consequences. My service provides a particularly quick way to
"master" English. And those who are hopelessly deficient—a euphemism,
I admit—struggle with communication in general.

Two days had passed since I last heard from the business student.   24
Overnight I had received 14 e-mails from her. She had additional instructions for the assignment, such as "but more again please make sure they
are a good link between the leticture review and all the chapter and the
benfet of my paper finally do you think the level of this work? how match
i can get it?"

I'll admit, I didn't fully understand that one.   25

It was followed by some clarification: "where u are can you get my   26
messages? Please I pay a lot and dont have ao to faile I strated to get very
worry."

Her messages had arrived between 2 A.M. and 6 A.M. Again I as-   27
sured her I had the matter under control.

It was true. At this point, there are few academic challenges that I   28
find intimidating. You name it, I've been paid to write about it.

Customers' orders are endlessly different yet strangely all the same.   29
No matter what the subject, clients want to be assured that their assignment is in capable hands. It would be terrible to think that your Ivy

League graduate thesis was riding on the work ethic and perspicacity of a public-university slacker. So part of my job is to be whatever my clients want me to be. I say yes when I am asked if I have a Ph.D. in sociology. I say yes when I am asked if I have professional training in industrial/organizational psychology. I say yes when asked if I have ever designed a perpetual-motion-powered time machine and documented my efforts in a peer-reviewed journal.

30   The subject matter, the grade level, the college, the course—these things are irrelevant to me. Prices are determined per page and are based on how long I have to complete the assignment. As long as it doesn't require me to do any math or video-documented animal husbandry, I will write anything.

31   I have completed countless online courses. Students provide me with passwords and user names so I can access key documents and online exams. In some instances, I have even contributed to weekly online discussions with other students in the class.

32   I have become a master of the admissions essay. I have written these for undergraduate, master's, and doctoral programs, some at elite universities. I can explain exactly why you're Brown material, why the Wharton M.B.A. program would benefit from your presence, how certain life experiences have prepared you for the rigors of your chosen course of study. I do not mean to be insensitive, but I can't tell you how many times I've been paid to write about somebody helping a loved one battle cancer. I've written essays that could be adapted into Meryl Streep movies.

33   I do a lot of work for seminary students. I like seminary students. They seem so blissfully unaware of the inherent contradiction in paying somebody to help them cheat in courses that are largely about walking in the light of God and providing an ethical model for others to follow. I have been commissioned to write many a passionate condemnation of America's moral decay as exemplified by abortion, gay marriage, or the teaching of evolution. All in all, we may presume that clerical authorities see these as a greater threat than the plagiarism committed by the future frocked.

34   With respect to America's nurses, fear not. Our lives are in capable hands—just hands that can't write a lick. Nursing students account for one of my company's biggest customer bases. I've written case-management plans, reports on nursing ethics, and essays on why nurse practitioners are lighting the way to the future of medicine. I've even written pharmaceutical-treatment courses, for patients who I hope were hypothetical.

35   I, who have no name, no opinions, and no style, have written so many papers at this point, including legal briefs, military-strategy assessments, poems, lab reports, and, yes, even papers on academic integrity, that it's hard to determine which course of study is most infested with cheating. But I'd say education is the worst. I've written papers for students in elementary-education programs, special-education majors, and ESL-training courses. I've written lesson plans for aspiring high-school

teachers, and I've synthesized reports from notes that customers have taken during classroom observations. I've written essays for those studying to become school administrators, and I've completed theses for those on course to become principals. In the enormous conspiracy that is student cheating, the frontline intelligence community is infiltrated by double agents. (Future educators of America, I know who you are.)

As the deadline for the business-ethics paper approaches, I think 36 about what's ahead of me. Whenever I take on an assignment this large, I get a certain physical sensation. My body says: Are you sure you want to do this again? You know how much it hurt the last time. You know this student will be with you for a long time. You know you will become her emergency contact, her guidance counselor and life raft. You know that for the 48 hours that you dedicate to writing this paper, you will cease all human functions but typing, you will Google until the term has lost all meaning, and you will drink enough coffee to fuel a revolution in a small Central American country.

But then there's the money, the sense that I must capitalize on op- 37 portunity, and even a bit of a thrill in seeing whether I can do it.

And I can. It's not implausible to write a 75-page paper in two days. 38 It's just miserable. I don't need much sleep, and when I get cranking, I can churn out four or five pages an hour. First I lay out the sections of an assignment—introduction, problem statement, methodology, literature review, findings, conclusion—whatever the instructions call for. Then I start Googling.

I haven't been to a library once since I started doing this job. 39 Amazon is quite generous about free samples. If I can find a single page from a particular text, I can cobble that into a report, deducing what I don't know from customer reviews and publisher blurbs. Google Scholar is a great source for material, providing the abstract of nearly any journal article. And of course, there's Wikipedia, which is often my first stop when dealing with unfamiliar subjects. Naturally one must verify such material elsewhere, but I've taken hundreds of crash courses this way.

After I've gathered my sources, I pull out usable quotes, cite them, 40 and distribute them among the sections of the assignment. Over the years, I've refined ways of stretching papers. I can write a four-word sentence in 40 words. Just give me one phrase of quotable text, and I'll produce two pages of ponderous explanation. I can say in 10 pages what most normal people could say in a paragraph.

I've also got a mental library of stock academic phrases: "A close 41 consideration of the events which occurred in____during the____demonstrate that____had entered into a phase of widespread cultural, social, and economic change that would define____for decades to come." Fill in the blanks using words provided by the professor in the assignment's instructions.

42   How good is the product created by this process? That depends—on the day, my mood, how many other assignments I am working on. It also depends on the customer, his or her expectations, and the degree to which the completed work exceeds his or her abilities. I don't ever edit my assignments. That way I get fewer customer requests to "dumb it down." So some of my work is great. Some of it is not so great. Most of my clients do not have the wherewithal to tell the difference, which probably means that in most cases the work is better than what the student would have produced on his or her own. I've actually had customers thank me for being clever enough to insert typos. "Nice touch," they'll say.

43   I've read enough academic material to know that I'm not the only bullshit artist out there. I think about how Dickens got paid per word and how, as a result, *Bleak House* is . . . well, let's be diplomatic and say exhaustive. Dickens is a role model for me.

44   So how does someone become a custom-paper writer? The story of how I got into this job may be instructive. It is mostly about the tremendous disappointment that awaited me in college.

45   My distaste for the early hours and regimented nature of high school was tempered by the promise of the educational community ahead, with its free exchange of ideas and access to great minds. How dispiriting to find out that college was just another place where grades were grubbed, competition overshadowed personal growth, and the threat of failure was used to encourage learning.

46   Although my university experience did not live up to its vaunted reputation, it did lead me to where I am today. I was raised in an upper-middle-class family, but I went to college in a poor neighborhood. I fit in really well: After paying my tuition, I didn't have a cent to my name. I had nothing but a meal plan and my roommate's computer. But I was determined to write for a living, and, moreover, to spend these extremely expensive years learning how to do so. When I completed my first novel, in the summer between sophomore and junior years, I contacted the English department about creating an independent study around editing and publishing it. I was received like a mental patient. I was told, "There's nothing like that here." I was told that I could go back to my classes, sit in my lectures, and fill out Scantron tests until I graduated.

47   I didn't much care for my classes, though. I slept late and spent the afternoons working on my own material. Then a funny thing happened. Here I was, begging anybody in authority to take my work seriously. But my classmates did. They saw my abilities and my abundance of free time. They saw a value that the university did not.

48   It turned out that my lazy, Xanax-snorting, Miller-swilling classmates were thrilled to pay me to write their papers. And I was thrilled to take their money. Imagine you are crumbling under the weight of university-issued parking tickets and self-doubt when a frat boy offers you cash to write about Plato. Doing that job was a no-brainer. Word of my services spread

quickly, especially through the fraternities. Soon I was receiving calls from strangers who wanted to commission my work. I was a writer!

Nearly a decade later, students, not publishers, still come from everywhere to find me.

I work hard for a living. I'm nice to people. But I understand that in simple terms, I'm the bad guy. I see where I'm vulnerable to ethical scrutiny.

But pointing the finger at me is too easy. Why does my business thrive? Why do so many students prefer to cheat rather than do their own work?

Say what you want about me, but I am not the reason your students cheat.

You know what's never happened? I've never had a client complain that he'd been expelled from school, that the originality of his work had been questioned, that some disciplinary action had been taken. As far as I know, not one of my customers has ever been caught.

With just two days to go, I was finally ready to throw myself into the business assignment. I turned off my phone, caged myself in my office, and went through the purgatory of cramming the summation of a student's alleged education into a weekend. Try it sometime. After the 20th hour on a single subject, you have an almost-out-of-body experience.

My client was thrilled with my work. She told me that she would present the chapter to her mentor and get back to me with our next steps. Two weeks passed, by which time the assignment was but a distant memory, obscured by the several hundred pages I had written since. On a Wednesday evening, I received the following e-mail:

"Thanx u so much for the chapter is going very good the porfesser likes it but wants the folloing suggestions please what do you thing?:

'"The hypothesis is interesting but I'd like to see it a bit more focused. Choose a specific connection and try to prove it.'

"What shoud we say?"

This happens a lot. I get paid per assignment. But with longer papers, the student starts to think of me as a personal educational counselor. She paid me to write a one-page response to her professor, and then she paid me to revise her paper. I completed each of these assignments, sustaining the voice that the student had established and maintaining the front of competence from some invisible location far beneath the ivory tower.

The 75-page paper on business ethics ultimately expanded into a 160-page graduate thesis, every word of which was written by me. I can't remember the name of my client, but it's her name on my work. We collaborated for months. As with so many other topics I tackle, the connection between unethical business practices and trade liberalization became a subtext to my everyday life.

So, of course, you can imagine my excitement when I received the good news:

"thanx so much for u help I can going to graduate to now".

Content

1. Why do colleges value writing (even if the students don't)? What should they do to ensure that students know how to write well, and in useful and meaningful ways?

2. "I work at an online company [of fifty writers] that generates tens of thousands of dollars a month by creating original essays based on specific instructions provided by cheating students. . . . Business is booming" (¶ 7). Why is business so good? Why do students cheat on their written work? Your answer should include explanations from student, faculty, and administrative perspectives (for additional information, see the replies to Dante, "Something Is Rotten in Academe," *The Chronicle Review* 14 Jan 2011 B 16–17).

3. Why are the following "demographic groups" most likely to seek out Dante's services" "the English-as-second-language student; the hopelessly deficient student; and the lazy rich kid" (¶ 21)? What problems does each group have? Do they have any problems in common?

4. Dante says he can write on anything except math "or video-documented animal husbandry" (¶ 30): "I have become a master of the admissions essay. I have written these for undergraduate, master's, and doctoral programs, some at elite universities. I can explain exactly why you're Brown material, why the Wharton M.B.A. program would benefit from your presence, how certain life experiences have prepared you for the rigors of your chosen course of study. . . . I can't tell you how many times I've been paid to write about somebody helping a loved one battle cancer" (¶ 32) . Should colleges admit prospective students who cheat on their admissions essays? Suppose the cheating is discovered after the student has been admitted; should he or she be expelled?

5. "Although plagiarism is rampant across all fields, education is the worst. I've written papers for students in elementary-education programs, special-education majors, and ESL-training courses. . . . those studying to become school administrators . . . theses for those on course to become principals" (¶ 35). Why is there so much cheating among actual and prospective teachers? What does this say about their own ethical standards and practices? Should America's children be studying in classrooms and schools run by cheaters?

6. Why do colleges value writing (even if the students don't)? What can be done to prevent students from buying admissions essays and papers-to-order? Again, your answer should include explanations from student, faculty, and administrative perspectives (for additional information, see the replies to Dante, "Something Is Rotten in Academe," *The Chronicle Review* 14 Jan 2011 B 16–17).

Strategies/Structures/Language

7. Why has Dante written this essay under a pseudonym? Why did he choose the name "Dante"?

8. Judging from the writing in this essay, is Dante himself a good writer? Why or why not?

9. Dante says has "refined ways of stretching papers. I can write a four-word sentence in 40 words. . . . I can say in 10 pages what most normal people could say in a paragraph" (¶ 40). Why does he do this? Does the writing in "The Shadow Scholar" seem inflated? Why or why not?

10. How relevant is Dante's stock academic formula to papers you've tried to write:

11. "'A close consideration of the events which occurred in ___ during the ____ demonstrate that ____ had entered into a phase of widespread cultural, social, and economic change that would define ____ for decades to come" (¶ 41).

For Writing

12. Why do colleges value writing (even if the students don't)? What should they do to ensure that students know how to write well, and in useful and meaningful ways? Address this issue from student, faculty, and administrative perspectives.

13. Have you ever cheated by buying a paper or hiring someone else to write it? (If so, you may need to write this paper, as Dante has done, under a pseudonym.)

PETER SINGER

Designated in 2005 by *Time* magazine as one of the "world's most influential people," philosopher Peter Singer is known for challenging conventional notions of ethical correctness. Born in Melbourne, Australia, in 1946 to a family decimated by the Nazi holocaust, Singer was educated at the University of Melbourne (BA, 1967; MA, 1969) and Oxford University (B Phil, 1971). After teaching at Oxford and New York University, he served as Chair of the Philosophy Department at Monash University in Australia and led the Centre for Human Bioethics there (1983–1998). Currently, he is a professor of Bioethics at Princeton University. Singer first gained attention as a protector of animal rights with *Animal Liberation* (1975), in which he criticized "speciesism"—the valuing of human rights above those of other species. He continued to explore the ethics of human–animal relations with *In Defense of Animals* (1985), *Animal Factories* (1990), and *The Great Ape Project* (1994). In *Making Babies* (1985), *Should the Baby Live?* (1985), and *Rethinking Life and Death* (1995), he addressed problems of science, technology, conception, and human life. Singer's views on end-of-life issues are consistent with his utilitarian approach to wealth advocated in "The Singer Solution to World Poverty"—that what is the greatest good for the greatest number should prevail. Their application, to animals, infants, and the elderly has aroused considerable controversy. More recent books include, *How Ethical is Australia?* (2005), *The Way We Eat: Why Our Food Choices Matter* (2006), *The Moral of the Story: An Authology of Ethics through Literature* (2005), and *The Life You Can Save: Acting Now to End World Poverty* (2009).

"The Singer Solution to World Poverty" is a wake-up call for ethical responsibility—a reminder that serious questions of right and wrong behavior lie just beyond the horizon of middle-class awareness. Singer starkly presents the death and degradation that come with child poverty, creates the "Bugatti senario" to test the reader's ethical commitments (to saving an expensive car or a child's life), and even provides an 800 number for immediate action.

The Singer Solution to World Poverty

1   In the Brazilian film *Central Station*, Dora is a retired schoolteacher who makes ends meet by sitting at the station writing letters for illiterate people. Suddenly she has an opportunity to pocket a thousand dollars. All she has to do is persuade a homeless nine-year-old-boy to follow her to an address she has been given. (She is told he will be adopted by wealthy foreigners.) She delivers the boy, gets the money, spends some of it on a television set, and settles down to enjoy her new acquisition. Her neighbor spoils the fun, however, by telling her that the boy was too old to be adopted—he will be killed and his organs sold for transplantation. Perhaps Dora knew this all along, but after her neighbor's plain speaking, she spends a troubled night. In the morning Dora resolves to take the boy back.

2   Suppose Dora had told her neighbor that it is a tough world, other people have nice new TVs too, and if selling the kid is the only way she can get one, well, he was only a street kid. She would then have become, in the eyes of the audience, a monster. She redeems herself only by being prepared to bear considerable risks to save the boy.

3   At the end of the movie, in cinemas in the affluent nations of the world, people who would have been quick to condemn Dora if she had not rescued the boy go home to places far more comfortable than her apartment. In fact, the average family in the United States spends almost one third of its income on things that are no more necessary to them than Dora's new TV was to her. Going out to nice restaurants, buying new clothes because the old ones are no longer stylish, vacationing at beach resorts—so much of our income is spent on things not essential to the preservation of our lives and health. Donated to one of a number of charitable agencies, that money could mean the difference between life and death for children in need.

4   All of which raises a question: in the end, what is the ethical distinction between a Brazilian who sells a homeless child to organ peddlers and an American who already has a TV and upgrades to a better one, knowing that the money could be donated to an organization that would use it to save the lives of kids in need?

PETER SINGER, "The Singer Solution to Poverty," THE NEW YORK TIMES MAGAZINE, September 5, 1999. Reprinted by permission of the author.

Library of Congress Prints and Photographs Division Washington DC, LC-USF34-T01-009058-C

This photo, titled "Migrant Mother," is Dorothea Lange's best-known picture. What stories does it tell? How do these stories relate to Sojourner Truth's "Ain't I a Woman?" (458–59), Jonathan Swift's "Modest Proposal" (461–68), and Peter Singer's "Solution to World Poverty" (481–87)? When poverty and maternity are the common denominator, does it matter that the woman, in real life Florence Owens Thompson, an Oklahoma Cherokee, is neither African-American nor Irish? Does it matter that the photograph enabled Lange to attain professional reputation and reward, while the subject remained impoverished and unknown?

Of course, there are several differences between the two situations that could support different moral judgments about them. For one thing, to be able to consign a child to death when he is standing right in front of you takes a chilling kind of heartlessness; it is much easier to ignore an appeal for money to help children you will never meet. Yet for a utilitarian philosopher like myself—that is, one who judges whether acts are right or wrong by their consequences—if the upshot of the American's failure to donate the money is that one more kid dies on the streets of a Brazilian city, then it is in some sense just as bad as selling the kid to the organ peddlers. But one doesn't need to embrace my utilitarian ethic to see that at the very least, there is a troubling incongruity in being so quick to condemn Dora for taking the child to the organ peddlers while at the same time not regarding the American consumer's behavior as raising a serious moral issue.

6   In his 1996 book, *Living High and Letting Die*, the New York University philosopher Peter Unger presented an ingenious series of imaginary examples designed to probe our intuitions about whether it is wrong to live well without giving substantial amounts of money to help people who are hungry, malnourished, or dying from easily treatable illnesses like diarrhea. Here's my paraphrase of one of these examples:

7   Bob is close to retirement. He has invested most of his savings in a very rare and valuable old car, a Bugatti, which he has not been able to insure. The Bugatti is his pride and joy. In addition to the pleasure he gets from driving and caring for his car, Bob knows that its rising market value means that he will always be able to sell it and live comfortably after retirement. One day when Bob is out for a drive, he parks the Bugatti near the end of a railway siding and goes for a walk up the track. As he does so, he sees that a runaway train, with no one aboard, is running down the railway track. Looking farther down the track, he sees the small figure of a child very likely to be killed by the runaway train. He can't stop the train and the child is too far away to warn of the danger, but he can throw a switch that will divert the train down the siding where his Bugatti is parked. Then nobody will be killed—but the train will destroy his Bugatti. Thinking of his joy in owning the car and the financial security it represents, Bob decides not to throw the switch. The child is killed. For many years to come, Bob enjoys owning his Bugatti and the financial security it represents.

8   Bob's conduct, most of us will immediately respond, was gravely wrong. Unger agrees. But then he reminds us that we too have opportunities to save the lives of children. We can give to organizations like UNICEF or Oxfam America. How much would we have to give one of these organizations to have a high probability of saving the life of a child threatened by easily preventable diseases? (I do not believe that children are more worth saving than adults, but since no one can argue that children have brought their poverty on themselves, focusing on them simplifies the issues.) Unger called up some experts and used the information they provided to offer some plausible estimates that include the cost of raising money, administrative expenses, and the cost of delivering aid where it is most needed. By his calculation, $200 in donations would help a sickly two-year-old transform into a healthy six-year-old—offering safe passage through childhood's most dangerous years. To show how practical philosophical argument can be, Unger even tells his readers that they can easily donate funds by using their credit card and calling one of these toll-free numbers: (800) 367-5437 for UNICEF; (800) 693-2687 for Oxfam America.

9   Now you too have the information you need to save a child's life. How should you judge yourself if you don't do it? Think again about Bob and his Bugatti. Unlike Dora, Bob did not have to look into the eyes of the child he was sacrificing for his own material comfort. The child was

a complete stranger to him and too far away to relate to in an intimate, personal way. Unlike Dora too, he did not mislead the child or initiate the chain of events imperiling him. In all these respects, Bob's situation resembles that of people able but unwilling to donate to overseas aid and differs from Dora's situation.

If you still think that it was very wrong of Bob not to throw the 10 switch that would have diverted the train and saved the child's life, then it is hard to see how you could deny that it is also very wrong not to send money to one of the organizations listed above. Unless, that is, there is some morally important difference between the two situations that I have overlooked.

Is it the practical uncertainties about whether aid will really reach 11 the people who need it? Nobody who knows the world of overseas aid can doubt that such uncertainties exist. But Unger's figure of $200 to save a child's life was reached after he had made conservative assumptions about the proportion of the money donated that will actually reach its target.

One genuine difference between Bob and those who can afford to 12 donate to overseas aid organizations but don't is that only Bob can save the child on the tracks, whereas there are hundreds of millions of people who can give $200 to overseas aid organizations. The problem is that most of them aren't doing it. Does this mean that it is all right for you not to do it?

Suppose that there were more owners of priceless vintage cars— 13 Carol, Dave, Emma, Fred, and so on, down to Ziggy—all in exactly the same situation as Bob, with their own siding and their own switch, all sacrificing the child in order to preserve their own cherished car. Would that make it all right for Bob to do the same? To answer this question affirmatively is to endorse follow-the-crowd ethics—the kind of ethics that led many Germans to look away when the Nazi atrocities were being committed. We do not excuse them because others were behaving no better.

We seem to lack a sound basis for drawing a clear moral line between 14 Bob's situation and that of any reader of this article with $200 to spare who does not donate it to an overseas aid agency. These readers seem to be acting at least as badly as Bob was acting when he chose to let the runaway train hurtle toward the unsuspecting child. In the light of this conclusion, I trust that many readers will reach for the phone and donate that $200. Perhaps you should do it before reading further.

Now that you have distinguished yourself morally from people who put 15 their vintage cars ahead of a child's life, how about treating yourself and your partner to dinner at your favorite restaurant? But wait. The money you will spend at the restaurant could also help save the lives of children overseas! True, you weren't planning to blow $200 tonight, but if you were to give up dining out just for one month, you would easily save that amount. And what is one month's dining out compared to a child's life? There's the rub. Since there are a lot of desperately needy children in the world, there will always be another child whose life you could save for another $200. Are you therefore obliged to keep giving until you have nothing left? At what point can you stop?

16   Hypothetical examples can easily become farcical. Consider Bob. How far past losing the Bugatti should he go? Imagine that Bob had got his foot stuck in the track of the siding, and if he diverted the train, then before it rammed the car it would also amputate his big toe. Should he still throw the switch? What if it would amputate his foot? His entire leg?

17   As absurd as the Bugatti scenario gets when pushed to extremes, the point it raises is a serious one: only when the sacrifices become very significant indeed would most people be prepared to say that Bob does nothing wrong when he decides not to throw the switch. Of course, most people could be wrong; we can't decide moral issues by taking opinion polls. But consider for yourself the level of sacrifice that you would de-mand of Bob, and then think about how much money you would have to give away in order to make a sacrifice that is roughly equal to that. It's almost certainly much, much more than $200. For most middle-class Americans, it could easily be more like $200,000.

18   Isn't it counterproductive to ask people to do so much? Don't we run the risk that many will shrug their shoulders and say that morality, so con-ceived, is fine for saints but not for them? I accept that we are unlikely to see, in the near or even medium-term future, a world in which it is nor-mal for wealthy Americans to give the bulk of their wealth to strangers. When it comes to praising or blaming people for what they do, we tend to use a standard that is relative to some conception of normal behav-ior. Comfortably off Americans who give, say, 10 percent of their income to overseas aid organizations are so far ahead of most of their equally comfortable fellow citizens that I wouldn't go out of my way to chastise them for not doing more. Nevertheless, they should be doing much more, and they are in no position to criticize Bob for failing to make the much greater sacrifice of his Bugatti.

19   At this point various objections may crop up. Someone may say, "If every citizen living in the affluent nations contributed his or her share, I wouldn't have to make such a drastic sacrifice, because long before such levels were reached the resources would have been there to save the lives of all those children dying from lack of food or medical care. So why should I give more than my fair share?" Another, related objection is that the government ought to increase its overseas aid allocations, since that would spread the burden more equitably across all taxpayers.

20   Yet the question of how much we ought to give is a matter to be de-cided in the real world—and that, sadly, is a world in which we know that most people do not, and in the immediate future will not, give substantial

amounts to overseas aid agencies. We know too that at least in the next year, the United States government is not going to meet even the very modest United Nations–recommended target of 0.7 percent of gross national product; at the moment it lags far below that, at 0.09 percent, not even half of Japan's 0.22 percent or a tenth of Denmark's 0.97 percent. Thus, we know that the money we can give beyond that theoretical "fair share" is still going to save lives that would otherwise be lost. While the idea that no one need do more than his or her fair share is a powerful one, should it prevail if we know that others are not doing their fair share and that children will die preventable deaths unless we do more than our fair share? That would be taking fairness too far.

Thus, this ground for limiting how much we ought to give also fails. 21 In the world as it is now, I can see no escape from the conclusion that each one of us with wealth surplus to his or her essential needs should be giving most of it to help people suffering from poverty so dire as to be life-threatening. That's right: I'm saying that you shouldn't buy that new car, take that cruise, redecorate the house, or get that pricy new suit. After all, a thousand-dollar suit could save five children's lives.

So how does my philosophy break down in dollars and cents? An 22 American household with an income of $50,000 spends around $30,000 annually on necessities, according to the Conference Board, a nonprofit economic research organization. Therefore, for a household bringing in $50,000 a year, donations to help the world's poor should be as close as possible to $20,000. The $30,000 required for necessities holds for higher incomes as well. So a household making $100,000 could cut a yearly check for $70,000. Again, the formula is simple: whatever money you're spending on luxuries, not necessities, should be given away.

Now, evolutionary psychologists tell us that human nature just isn't 23 sufficiently altruistic to make it plausible that many people will sacrifice so much for strangers. On the facts of human nature, they might be right, but they would be wrong to draw a moral conclusion from those facts. If it is the case that we ought to do things that, predictably, most of us won't do, then let's face that fact head-on. Then, if we value the life of a child more than going to fancy restaurants, the next time we dine out we will know that we could have done something better with our money. If that makes living a morally decent life extremely arduous, well, then that is the way things are. If we don't do it, then we should at least know that we are failing to live a morally decent life—not because it is good to wallow in guilt but because knowing where we should be going is the first step toward heading in that direction.

When Bob first grasped the dilemma that faced him as he stood by 24 that railway switch, he must have thought how extraordinarily unlucky he was to be placed in a situation in which he must choose between the life of an innocent child and the sacrifice of most of his savings. But he was not unlucky at all. We are all in that situation.

Content

1. What was your reaction to the "Bugatti scenario," which Singer describes as a "hypothetical example" designed to test the reader's ethics? Do you agree that Bob's conduct was "gravely wrong" (¶ 8)? What about the incremental version of the scenario—how much is the child's life worth? A toe, a foot, a leg? (¶ 16).

2. Singer describes his philosophical stance as utilitarian; he "judges whether acts are right or wrong by their consequences" (¶ 5). How does the utilitarian point of view inform "The Singer Solution"? What actions and what consequences is the article concerned with? Where does Singer stress consequences as a criterion for decision making?

Strategies/Structures/Language

3. Emotion can lead to motion: Authors can move readers to action by arousing intense feelings and then providing an outlet for them. Singer appeals to emotion with the *Central Station* example and the idea of children starving to death. However, he expects the reader to rationally test their ethics in the "Bugatti scenario" and the call for overseas aid donations. Did your emotional reactions to the portrayals of poverty help you make up your mind, or did they get in the way of your ethical deliberations?

4. Consider to what extent Singer uses visual images in his argument. What are some scenes or pictures that remained in your mind after you read the article? Why does Singer rely on imagery? Do you think his use of imagery is effective?

For Writing

5. Do you think that Singer presents a highly effective solution to world poverty? Should his ideas perhaps replace current methods of poverty relief? Write an argument explaining why you agree with Singer's program, or explain how you disapprove of the "Singer Solution" and why.

6. ***Journal Writing.*** Is there an ethical situation to which you feel that a utilitarian point of view does *not* apply? When are considerations of efficiency and expediency relevant to ethical situations? Does a utilitarian approach require a moral or ethical framework?

7. ***Dialogues.*** Do you agree with Singer's utilitarian argument that "only when the sacrifices become very significant indeed would most people be prepared to say that Bob does nothing wrong when he decides not to throw the switch" (¶ 17)? (See question 1.) Compare Singer's assumptions with those Swift's narrator makes in advancing a utilitarian solution to mass starvation in "A Modest Proposal" (461–68). Why does Singer's utilitarian stance lead to a dramatically different conclusion than Swift's?

8. With a classmate, develop an ethical test to help readers confront an issue that you feel is important. Using Singer's methods, construct a hypothetical example that offers the readers choices and helps them come to a decision about a difficult moral problem. Test it out on several classmates, and write a paper reporting and interpreting your findings. What values do these allocations represent? Do you share these? Why or why not?

EDWARD HOAGLAND

Edward Hoagland (born 1932), best known as a nature and travel writer, has a distinct style marked by close observation and attention to detail in mostly remote settings. Hoagland grew up in New York City, spending a great deal of time in rural Connecticut as well. Hoagland's stammer, which has persisted his entire life, has greatly influenced his writing. He says: "Words are spoken at considerable cost to me, so a great value is placed on each one. That has had some effect on me as a writer. As a child, since I couldn't talk to people, I became close to animals. I became an observer, and in all my books, even the novels, witnessing things is what counts." In the summers of 1951 and 1952, Hoagland joined the Ringling Bros. and Barnum & Bailey Circus. This experience resulted in his first novel, *Cat Man* (1955). In 1954–55, Hoagland served two years in the Army before publishing his second novel, *The Circle Home* in 1960. Hoagland has taught at Sarah Lawrence, CUNY, the University of Iowa, Columbia, Brown, and Bennington. His travels in Africa, the Alaskan wilderness, British Columbia, and Antarctica provide the settings for his prolific nature writing, which is chronicled in an extensive collection of essays, stories, novels, and nonfiction books. Of his twenty-one books, the most recent are *Compass Points* (2001), *Early in the Season* (2008), and *Sex and the River Styx* (2011). "Children Are Diamonds ," first published in *Portland Magazine* (2007), was chosen as Best American Essay of 2008, a judgment affirmed by fellow essayist John Updike, who called him "the best essayist of my generation."

As you read, think about the meaning of the title, whose brilliant words do not appear until the last paragraph.

Children Are Diamonds

In Africa, Everything Is An Emergency. Your radiator blows out, and as you solder a repair job, kids emerge from the bush, belonging to a village that you'll never see and reachable by a path you hadn't noticed. Though one of them has a Kalashnikov, they aren't threatening, only hungry. Eight or ten of them, aged eight or ten, they don't expect to be fed by you or any other strange adult. Although you know some Swahili, you can't converse, not knowing Lango, but because there is plenty of water in the streams roundabout, they are fascinated that you choose to drink instead from bottles you have brought. Gradually growing bold enough to peer into the open windows of your truck, they don't attempt to fiddle with the door or reach inside, seeing no food or curious mechanical delectables. The boxes packed there white-man-style are cryptically uninformative. Meningitis

---

Edward Hoagland, "Children Are Diamonds" from Portland Magazine. Reprinted with permission of the author.

and polio vaccines, malaria meds, deworming pills, folic acid, vitamin A, and similar famine fighters. However, the kids will remain as long as you do, and you don't dare leave because this fabric of politesse would tear if you did, as it would have already if they were five years older. You wish you could ask them if mines have been laid in the road recently by either the rebels or the government forces. Their fathers, the men of the village, haven't emerged because they're probably off with the guerrillas, and the women would not show themselves in time of war anyway. It's a balance you must maintain here: friendliness and mystery.

2   The city splits at the seams with squatter camps, swollen by an enormous flux of displaced refugees from within hungry Kenya itself, not to mention all the illegals from the civil wars afire in the countries that surround it: Somalia, Sudan, Ethiopia, Congo, Rwanda. Look on a map: dire suffering. Need I say more?

3   The joke, if you can call it that, among whites here is if you feel a hand grope for your wallet, the second thing to do is try to save the life of the pickpocket. This is a city veering into calamity, where transient whites like me still dribble in because it's a hub for aid groups, and yet it's a traditional wash-up spot for Anglo ne'er-do-wells who try to define themselves by where they have been. With the AIDS pandemic, it will soon be too late for a number of things.

4   I help out in a place where we feed street kids and treat them with skin ointments, antibiotics, inoculations, minerals, vitamins, whatever we happen to have. Powdered milk, powdered eggs, surplus soups or porridges that another nongovernmental organization may have given us. We have a basketball hoop up, and soccer balls, board games, playing cards, a tent fly hooked to the back wall in the courtyard with cots arranged underneath it as a shelter where the children can feel some safety in numbers at least. What makes you burn out are the ones dying visibly of AIDS. Yet you don't want to banish them again to the furnace of the streets or, on the other hand, specialize merely as a hospice, where salvageable kids aren't going to want to come. Many of them wish to go to school but have no home to go to school from or money for the fees. So I scrounged a blackboard and teach addition, subtraction, geography, the English alphabet, when I have a break from refereeing a gritty soccer game or supervising the dishwashing or triaging kids with fevers or contusions who ought to go to the hospital (not that that Dickensian trip is often in their best interest). We had artful dodgers eating our fruits and sandwiches between excursions into robbery, drugs, peddling—but also earnest tykes, plenty of them, whom your heart absolutely goes out to. Yet triage is frustrating.

5   You don't have to be a doctor to help people who have no aspirin or disinfectant or pills for malaria, tuberculosis, dysentery, or epilepsy, no splints or bandaging, and no other near by facility to walk to in the bush. No Kaopectate, cough suppressants, malnutrition supplements, antibiotics for bilharziasis or sleeping sickness or yaws. If you were a

nurse, patients would be brought to you with these diseases or hepatitis or broken limbs. The old stone and concrete ruins of a Catholic chapel that has been forgotten since the colonial powers left could be reoccupied if you chased the leopards and the cobras out, because joy is what is partly needed, especially at first, and joy, I think, is, like photosynthesis for plants, an evidence of God. But joy, like beauty, is a continuum too, and in temperate climates it waxes with the sun somewhat as plants do.

I can do the basic mechanics if we break down on the road, and I know when to speed up or—equally important—slow down, when figures with guns appear to block our passage. (If it's soldiers, you never speed up, but the decision is not that easy because every male can look like a soldier in a war zone, and the soldiers look like civilians.) The big groups, such as Doctors Without Borders, CARE, Oxfam, Save the Children, have salaried international staff they can fly in from Honduras, Bangkok, or New Delhi to plug a momentary defection or a flip-out—dedicated career people, like the UN's ladies and gentlemen, with New York, Geneva, London, Paris, Rome behind them, who've been vetted: not much fooling around. But there are various smaller outfits, whose fliers you don't receive in the mail back home, that will hire "the spiritual drifter," as my friend Al put it to me, to haul pallets of plywood, bags of cement, first-aid kits in bulk, and bags of potatoes, bayou rice, cases of your basic tins, like corned beef, tuna, salmon, peas, what-have-you, and trunks of medicine to provision the solo picayune apostle out doing Christ's appalling work in the hinterlands. 6

You draw up lists of refugees so no one gets double their ration by coming through the corn queue twice. Use ink stamped on the wrists if you have to—if their names are always Mohammed or Josephine. And you census the children as well and weigh a sampling of them in a sling scale, plus measure their upper-arm fat, if they have any, with calipers to compile the ratio of malnutrition in the populace, severe versus moderate, and so on. I've helped inject against measles, tetanus, typhoid, when not enough licensed people were there, having been a vet's assistant at one point in my teens. I've powwowed with the traditional clan chiefs and tribal healers, the leopard-skin priests and village shamans and elders, or young militia commanders, and delivered babies when nobody competent was around. I've squeezed the rehydration salts into babies' mouths when they're at death's door, or mixed the fortified formula that you spoon into them, and chalked the rows of little white squares in the dirt where you have all the children sit individually at their feeding hours so that every individual gets the same amount of protein, the same units of vitamins A, C, E, B, calcium, iron, phosphorus, out of the 55-gallon steel drum you're stewing the emergency preparation in. *Hundreds* of passive, dying children sitting cross-legged in the little squares, waiting for you to reach each of them. You don't think that breaks your heart? Chalk is never gonna look the same. 7

8   You meet many travelers: businessmen with attaché cases full of bank notes to persuade the bureaucrats in Government House to sign on to a certain project scheme; ecologists on a mission to save the chimpanzees; trust-fund hippies doing this route overland, now that you can't go from Istanbul into Afghanistan; specialists from one of the UN's many agencies studying a development proposal or transiting to the more difficult terrain of Rwanda, Zimbabwe, Somalia, then resting for a spell on the way back. The taxi stand is busy from sunrise to pitch dark, and the pool on the roof is patronized by African middle-class parents, some of whom are teaching their kids how to swim, as well as the KLM airline pilots and Swissair stewardesses, the Danish or USAID water-project administrators waiting for permanent housing, or bustling missionaries passing through.

9   Food is so central that you can't exaggerate the issue. My waitress, for example, was hungry for protein even though she worked in an expatriates' hotel. There was a pot of gruel in the kitchen for the help, but it wasn't nourishing enough for a lactating mother, and the chicken parts and fresh fruit, meat, and vegetables the guests ate were exactly inventoried each night to compare what remained in the refrigerator with the restaurant's orders. Nor did she eat leftovers from people's plates, because she'd heard that AIDS can be spread by saliva. And, although she wouldn't be robbed at night once she reached her bus station, she said that to get to it she needed to use her tips to take a taxi because men with clubs waited next to a corner between here and there.

10   The fabled "Cape to Cairo" artery from South Africa toward Khartoum and Egypt is no more—a jaunt that was throttled first by Idi Amin and is now choked off again by the war in southern Sudan. Beyond the city's suburbs, indeed, signs of human occupancy almost disappear in the elephant grass and regrown jungle, because for the next eighty or a hundred miles all of this has been a triangle of death, incinerated in Uganda's own civil wars: Amin's eight years of butcheries and then, when he was overthrown, Obote who in an ostensibly saner manner killed just as many until Museveni upended him. So many clanking tanks, halftracks, and fearsome assault platoons crawled up this road, mowing down anything that moved, that even *in* the peace Museveni established, nobody wanted to take the chance of living anywhere that might be visible in the forest. Bower birds, sunbirds, bee-eaters, secretary birds, reedbucks, dik-diks, spitting cobras, and black mambas were about, but the people who had somehow survived on site or returned afterward were not going to trust the neighborhood of the road, except for bicycling quickly along the asphalt. And then the trick was to vanish imperceptibly when you reached your destination, with no path to a hidden village that soldiers rumbling by in a grisly truck would notice. Settlements had been scorched, torched, eviscerated horribly, the skulls piled up from the massacres. And women still sometimes flinched—broke into a run for the woods—at the sound of my motor.

In the sixties, after Uganda's independence from the British, it had   11
been mainly these local forest tribes, such as the Baris and Acholis, who
logically should have been part of Uganda to begin with anyway, fighting the Muslim government. Then in the seventies a new president of
Sudan had made peace with them, with regional freedom of religion
and cultural autonomy, until the eighties, when a new fundamental-
ist Sharia swing reignited the war, led now by the big plains tribes,
Nuer and Dinka, pastoralists living between these mountains and
forests and the vast Sahel of the Arabs. It was a more serious insurrec-
tion, with the southern black army officers defecting to command the
rebels, and, on the government side, the Baggara Arab tribes armed
for lethal, devastating cattle raids against their neighbors the Dinkas.
The United States was allied with Khartoum for strategic reasons at
the time—to harass Muammar al-Qaddafi on Libya's flank—and dis-
couraged even food aid reaching the southerners. So a quarter for a
million people starved.

One morning in Sudan I woke to a lovely morning sun and boundless   12
rolling perspectives after I climbed to a viewpoint behind the church that
overlooked the modest gorge of the Bahr el Jebel, the "Mountain Nile." It
flows under the Imatong Range, Sudan's highest, its ridges behind me, all
downstream from the Victoria and Albert sections of the Nile in Uganda's
lake country. Near Malakal it is joined by the Bahr el Ghazal, the "Gazelle
River," from the west, and the Sobat, from the east, to form the White
Nile. Then at Khartoum, the Blue Nile, from Ethiopia, joins the White
to constitute the famous Nile that flows to Shendi, Atbara, Wadi Haifa,
Aswan, Luxor, Cairo, and the delta close to Alexandria: nowhere, though,
is it more beautiful than around here. Beyond the gorge sit endless savanna grasslands, woodlands, parkland, in tropical, light-filled yellows
and greens, where, although the hartebeests, kobs, buffalo, and reedbucks may already have been eaten and the rhinos and elephants shot
for their horns or tusks to buy guns, the vistas remain primeval because
for decades civil war has prevented any other kind of development, like
logging, tourism, or mining. I had a spear-length stick in hand to defend
myself afoot or keep the wildlife at bay and, more appropriately, remind
myself of how the Dinkas, as a cattle people from time immemorial, had
been able to protect their herds and pasturage from the Baggara Arab
tribes whose homelands adjoined theirs, even though the Baggara domesticated horses as well as cattle and rode into battle, instead of merely running. A Dinka, who could run for twenty miles with six spears in his free
hand, attacking from the reeds and rushes of every river crossing, every
hyacinth swamp, was not a foe whose cattle could be rustled and women
stolen with impunity. But the equilibrium of spear versus spear had been
skewed when Khartoum gave the Baggara guns and sent its army in motor vehicles and helicopter gunships to mow down the lumbering cattle
who escaped the horses, driving the surviving herdsmen off their beloved
prairies, steppes, swamps, and plains.

13   We were inoculating babies against measles before the dry ice that kept the vaccine fresh was gone. But an elephantiasis sufferer was in the line. How could she have survived this long? We gave her Cephalexin, for whatever that might be worth. The queue was checkered with people with rag-fashioned bandaging, wearing blue robes for one particular clan, red for another, with body paint, headcloths, loincloths, tribal scarifications on the forehead. One man had what was possibly a giraffe's scrotum as a carryall on a rawhide strap from his shoulder, yet he was wearing a garage-sale apron from Peoria.

14   As we drove north, the people walking were sparse, and mostly from the local Madi or Bari tribes, a foot shorter than the Dinkas and thicker-set, scrambling along like forest-and-mountain folk, not striding like cattle herders, plainsmen. As food got shorter again the next week, they would disappear into the woods, and gaunt Dinkas would take over the roads, famished stalking something to eat. We saw a burly man with a bushbuck that he had snared slung over his shoulder, who started to run when he heard the motor, till he realized we were aid workers and not about to steal his meat, as guys in a Sudan People's Liberation Army vehicle would have. Another man, two miles on, was squatting on his heels, quietly collecting wood doves one by one every few minutes, when they fluttered down to drink at a roadside puddle he had poisoned with the juice of a certain plant that grew nearby. He too was frightened that this clutch of birds he had already caught might be snatched away, until white faces in the window proved we weren't hungry. He showed us the deadly root, and how pretty his half-dozen unplucked pigeons were, as well as a pumpkin he wanted to sell.

15   Close to the rope ferry from Kerripi to Kajo Kaja, we passed several Dinkas with fishing nets and spears tall enough to fend off a crocodile or disable a hippo—which was what they were good at when not embedded in the intimacies of their cattle culture, with five hundred lowing beasts, and perhaps a lion outside the kraal to reason with; the rituals of manhood to observe; the myriad color configurations and hieroglyphic markings of each man's or boy's special display ox or bull, for him to honor, celebrate, and sing to; and the sinuous, cultivated, choreographic eloquence of its individual horns, which he tied bells and tassels to. The colors were named after the fish eagle, ibis, bustard, leopard, brindled crocodile, mongoose, monitor lizard, goshawk, baboon, elephant ivory, and so on. Like the Nuer, who were so similar, the Dinka had been famous among anthropologists but were now shattered by the war. Adventure, marriage, contentment, art, and beauty had been marked and sculpted by the visual or intuitive impact of cattle, singly and in their wise and milling, rhythmic herds, as bride wealth and the principal currency, but also the coloring registering like impressionistic altarpieces, the scaffolding of clan relations and religion. A scorched-earth policy by the Arab army and militias needed only to wipe out their cattle to

disorient and dishearten the Dinka. We stopped, and people emerged from the bush. One man was burdened by a goiter the size of a bagpipe's bladder; another, by a hernia bulging like an overnight bag. They were Madi, Bari, the so-called Juba peoples, displaced by the war and siege. We had palliatives like vitamins, acetaminophen, valium, cotrimoxazole, even some iodine pills for the goiter man, although, like the hernia character, he needed surgery.

There were patients with cataracts, VD, bronchitis, scabies, nosebleeds, 16 chest pains, Parkinson's, thrush, cellulitis, breast tumors, colon troubles, a dislocated elbow, plus the usual heartbreaking woman whose urinary tract, injured in childbirth, dripped continuously, turning her into a pariah, although it would have been as easy as the hernia for a surgeon to fix. My friend could do the elbow, with my help, and knock back an infection temporarily, but not immunize the babies or anybody because our vaccines had had no refrigeration for so long. She bestowed her smile. The line that formed, the fact that she was going to finger and eyeball everybody, was reassuring.

One night in the sunset's afterglow a man with broken eyeglasses 17 led us to the straw church he had built, quoting Isaiah, chapter 18, and Matthew, chapter 24: "For nation will go to war against nation, kingdom against kingdom; there will be famines." Ladoku was his name, and it's no exaggeration to say that his church was constructed mainly of straw or that any big drugstore would have had ten-dollar glasses that would have helped him a lot.

On the river herons, egrets, ibises, buzzards, guinea fowl, whale- 18 headed storks flapped every which way over the dugouts of lanky men wielding fishing tridents. They stopped at hamlets of huts only a yard above the water to let people off or leave freight, with cattle browsing in the shallows, their left horn sometimes trained a certain way by the gradual application of weights. A herder, proudly dusted with ceremonial dung-ash, was poised upon one leg, the toes of the other hooking that knee so as to jut out quite jauntily as he leaned on the point of his fighting spear, with his fishing spear dandled in his free hand. Whether Nuer or Dinka, these were people of sufficient numbers that they hadn't needed to bother learning a common language like Arabic or English to speak with other tribes, and they stared with more interest at the cargo of goodies on the deck than at the foreign or inferior strangers. The captain, although he was ethnically an Arab, had been born to shopkeepers in Malakal and had gone onto the river as a boy with his uncle, who was a pilot during the British era, and then married a daughter of the king of the Shilluk. The Shilluk were a river tribe located just northward of the Nuer and Dinka, sharing Malakal with the others as a hub. Though less numerous, they were knit rather tighter as warriors, if only because they *had* a king, so that their tough neighbors seldom messed with them.

19   The lions here have lost their sense of propriety. They are rattled, eating human carrion like hyenas and hauling down live individual human beings, as if there hadn't been a truce in force between the local people and the local lions for eons. Before the war, lions always knew and taught their young where they would be trespassing—what domestic beasts they shouldn't kill unless they anticipated retaliation—and people, as well, knew where it was asking for trouble for them to go. Deliberately hunting a big black-maned male might be a manhood ritual, but it was never casually undertaken with a Kalashnikov, never meaningless. Neither species was a stranger to the other or its customary habitat— whereas many of these poor refugees had been on their last legs, eating lizards, drinking from muddy puddles, wandering displaced hundreds of miles from their home ground, where they belonged. And so, on the one hand, young lionesses grew up stalking staggering people, and, on the other, soldiers in jeeps were shooting lions that they ran across with Tommy guns, for fun. No rite of passage, no conversation or negotiation was involved: no spear in the teeth, which then became a cherished necklace worn at dances.

20   Back in Uganda I was back in the world of AIDS. Sudan's war had kept most infected people out of the zone we'd been in, but within a few minutes I noticed that several youngsters clustered around were not healthy. They weren't wasted from starvation or fascinated by a motor vehicle, like the crowds of kids where we'd come from. I couldn't tell whether they were orphans or belonged to someone, but their stumbling, discolored emaciation meant they were dying of AIDS.

21   Flying over Juba we saw muzzle flashes, burning huts, and a blackish tank askew on a roadway as we banked. Inside that broken circle of machine-gun sniping and mortar explosions nobody was moving as in a normal provincial city, just scurrying for bare essentials. From the air, you could spot the positions that were crumbling and who, hunkered there, was doomed.

22   I ran into a couple of gaunt, drained Maryknoll nuns recuperating on a two-week Christmas holiday from their current post at Chukudum, in the Didinga Hills of borderline Sudan, where a pretty waterfall burbles down the rock bluff behind the garden of the priory, and Khartoum's Antonov bomber plane wheels over every morning looking for a target of opportunity. These nursing sisters are seasoned heroes. They're deep-dyed. You meet them on the hairiest road, coming or going from a posting, and they don't wilt. *They* don't believe that God is dead. They are wary but unflappable.

23   I load a truck with the standard fortified nutritional preparations and spare stethoscopes, blood-pressure cuffs, tourniquets, penlights, tongue depressors, tendon hammers, antimalarial amodiaquine, paracetamol, antibiotics such as amoxicillin, cotrimoxazole, ciprofloxacin, and doxycycline, mebendazole for worms, water purifiers, tetracycline eye

ointment, ibuprofen, bandages in quantity and tape and nylon strapping, syringes and needles, scalpels, antiseptic for sterilizing, insecticide-
treated mosquito netting for many people besides ourselves, IV cannulas,
stitching needles and thread, umbrellas and tenting for the sun and rain,
white coats for each of us to wear to give us an air of authority, and as
much plastic sheeting as I have room for to shelter families in the coming
rainy season. My friend Al says that children are diamonds, and knew so
from the front lines, having witnessed the successive Ethiopian and Somali famines and the Sahel droughts of the Kababish country in northern
Sudan, knew that you can be nearer my God to thee without sectarianism. One Christ, many proxies.

Content

1. Hoagland's opening statement, "In Africa, Everything Is An Emergency,"
is the operative concept for the whole essay. What emergencies does Hoagland
identify? In whose opinions are these *emergencies?*

2. Given the pervasive level of need and the minimal resources, the large number of emergencies, and the fact that they can't all be dealt with at once, how do
people administering aid sort them out? Prioritize them? What sorts of supplies,
sanitation, physical conditions, and nutrition do Americans take for granted that
are in short supply in Kenya?

3. What ethical principles govern the behavior of those administering medical aid
and providing food? Identify some of the sections of the UN "Universal Declaration
of Human Rights" (571–76) that are most applicable to emergencies such as these?

4. Hoagland concludes (¶ 23) with his friend Al's observation that "children are
like diamonds." What does he mean by this? Explain your answer in terms of the
entire essay, with particular emphasis on the two concluding sentences: " . . . he
knew so from the front lines, having witnessed the successive Ethiopian and
Somali famines and the Sahel droughts of the Kababish country in northern
Sudan, knew that you can be nearer my God to thee without sectarianism. One
Christ, many proxies."

Strategies/Structures/Language

5. Hoagland is in Kenya and is talking about that country. Would his commentary be any different if he were in "any of the countries that surround it: Somalia, Sudan, Ethiopia, Congo, Rwanda?" Explain his comment as a generalization,
"Look on a map: dire suffering. Need I say more?" (¶ 2).

6. Bear in mind that Hoagland is writing from the perspective of an American
aid volunteer in Kenya, a "hub for aid groups," but that it's also "a traditional
wash-up spot for Anglo ne'er-do-wells" (¶ 3), and that there are many sorts of
people to be served, as well. How can Hoagland discuss the administration of aid
without either descending into pity, condescension, or smugness? What are the
appropriate ethical positions to take with regard to this difficult subject matter?

7. Nearly every paragraph contains one or more lists. What's in these lists ?
Why does Hoagland use so many?

8. Nevertheless, in spite of the lists the essay is full of stories embedded in a larger story, and moves briskly along. What is the main story? What are these smaller stories about? Who are the main characters? Are there heroes? Villains—in terms of either people or circumstances?

For Writing

9. Pick an aspect of nutrition or medical care whose treatment/solution you would take for granted in the United States, but which is a matter of life, death, disfigurement, or dysfunctioning in Kenya. Explain what it is, why you can take it for granted in the United States, and then propose a solution that is realistic and practical (don't be content with "just throw money at it"). Consult Internet sources as necessary for additional information.

10. ***Dialogue.*** Compare the author's ethical stance and ethical issues discussed in Swift's "Modest Proposal" (461–68), a classic essay on poverty and some solutions; and Peter Singer's "The Singer Solution to World Poverty" (481–87), a modern classic. Is Hoagland dealing with the same issues? Is poverty the same worldwide (compare with the minimum wage workers Ehrenreich discusses in "Serving in Florida" [143–51]), or is it a concept relative to the particular society in which one lives. Is Singer's solution applicable to the problems of poverty in Kenya as Hoagland describes them?

SHERYL KENNEDY

Sheryl Kennedy (born 1951) writes, "In January of 1969, I left college after one semester, ready to experience first-hand the tumult of the sixties: I hopped on a Greyhound bus and hit the streets of Boston ready to join the revolution. I thought I didn't need the classroom experience to get an education—I was wrong." Thirty-eight years later she returned to the University of Connecticut, experiencing, in Lawrence Ferlinghetti's words, "a new rebirth of wonder," for which she thanks professors Gerry and Charles Van Doren.

Her essay, "About Suffering," which won second prize in the university-wide creative nonfiction contest, was written in a freshman writing class in response to an assigned poem, W. H. Auden's "Musee des Beaux Arts." Kennedy explains, "My friend Staff Sergeant Luke Murphy had just gotten his leg blown off in Iraq. I was devastated for him and confused by the apathy concerning those wounded in the war. The middle section, *The Ploughman Speaks*, was written first. I really did feel his voice come through me!" Kennedy updated her commentary in June, 2008: Today, two years later, "the number of wounded is officially over 30,000, not counting the many thousands suffering mental and emotional trauma (PTSD). Toe and finger losses are not counted as amputations (I'm not sure about eyes), and a patient sustaining multiple amputations is only counted as one injured person, so the figures can be deceiving. I continue to comb many related sites, including the Department of Defense, for information about the wounded, traumatized and the 'non-combat related' deaths, of which many are suicides. However, since there is no way to put an exact number on the amputations, I wonder if we should say 'phantoms of countless limbs,' instead of an estimated number."

About Suffering

S ometime after Luke's tragedy, I began listening to W. H. Auden read-   1
  ing his poetry on tape. Driving the back roads of Connecticut, with
the sound of his nasal voice and Oxford accent becoming increasingly
familiar as he read, I was deeply moved by one poem, *Musee des Beaux
Arts*, Auden's poetic reaction to an exhibit of Brueghel paintings in the
Brussels museum. I listened to the poem over and over again. For days, it
played in a continuous loop and became the soundtrack that marked the
beginning of my understanding of what had happened. Every word was
important to me because of Luke.

It begins: About suffering they were never wrong,   2
             The old Masters . . .

The old masters knew that people's suffering always takes place   3
while we are busy doing other things, Auden writes—"eating, or opening
a window, or just walking dully along." The poem goes on to describe
The Fall of Icarus, painted in the 17th century by Pieter Brueghel the Elder,
which shows an industrious scenario: a farmer busily plowing his field
near a shepherd and his flock, all overlooking a sunlit bay where a portly
friar casts a fishing line and glorious ships are setting sail for the open
sea. But there is more in the picture: Icarus is falling out of the sky into the
water—and as Auden tells us, "the sun shone As it had to on the white
legs disappearing into the green . . ." Why has no one noticed? Why does
the ploughman turn his back? Doesn't he hear the splash or the boy's cry?
Why is the ship, laden with its riches, just sailing calmly on its way?
I traveled with Auden's voice a companion on my daily rounds. His   4
poem, a powerful testament to indifference written in the early days of
World War II, played again and again on my aging tape deck until one
day the sound quality began to disintegrate, Auden's voice fading in and
out with a crackling sound like static on a radio. I thought the tape had
finally worn out, and reached over to remove it when I became alarmed
by a bizarre disturbance in the air. I was scarcely able to drive as an otherworldly echo, dim at first then louder and louder, a new voice, sharp and
insistent, heavily accented, finally overtook Auden's . . .

Part One: The Ploughman Speaks

5   Forgive me Mr. Auden, but I am a poor farmer who has waited three hundred and eighty years to tell my story. Your poem is an interesting one, but I feel I must enlighten you concerning the part that I played in the painting you describe. I remember the morning that Pieter Brueghel the Elder came to the edge of my miserable plot of rocky soil to watch me struggle through the mud with my rude plow. As I regarded him out of the corner of my eye, he cleaned and sorted his expensive brushes and leisurely set up his easel in the morning sunlight, took out his paints and began to dabble about. He never greeted me nor asked about my family. He loves to paint us, the "peasantry" (we are so colorful and quaint!), but his interest is not in us as people, but rather in his own high-minded ideas. For all these years I have carried the burden of representing those who turn away from the suffering of others when it was Brueghel who turned away!

6   Mr. Auden, let me tell you what suffering I left at home that morning. After burying our youngest child only two days before, I had stayed up all the previous night helping my wife nurse our daughter through the very same fever that had taken our son. Marta is numb with grief and still she must wash the clothes, tend the garden, milk the cow, scrub the floors on her hands and knees, prepare food for me and our children. I closed the door that morning upon the cries of my children so that I might go to my fields to coax some good hay and a few carrots, leeks and turnips out of the sand and rocks. Did Brueghel care to know any of this? Did he, with his keen artistic eye, notice my hollow red-rimmed eyes, my gnarled hands, the sad stoop of my weary back?

7   Does Brueghel, the great master, truly understand suffering? Can he see what is right in front of his eyes? Mr. Brueghel sees only what he wants to see: a lone man plowing in a picturesque field overlooking the sea, a ship in full sail, Brother Halleck trying for a fish, my own young brother tending his flock. A pretty picture on the surface I will grant you, except for the white legs slipping into the water. A picture that many must have seen and exclaimed, "Look at that farmer, how he turns away! What kind of man is he?"

8   From what am I turning away? A foolish young criminal who seeks to escape his fate by flying like a bird? A boy who wastes his time in dreaming and expects hard working people to be torn away from their enterprise to come to his rescue? I did not turn away, but rather continued in the direction of my plow, completely unaware of the boy and his white legs. We did not see him, Mr. Auden! We did not see nor hear him in his plight, or we certainly would have left our work and clambered down the rocks to his rescue. I was too far away, and Brother Halleck is as blind as a bat. My own young brother Iain was counting his sheep . . . and of course the shipmates navigating their glorious craft laden with riches— all of their eyes were cast toward the open sea. You are an intelligent man,

you know who saw the boy—it was Brueghel, of course. But he was too busy painting the interesting tragedy to cry out!

So there it is, the truth at last. I am blameless! I will sleep tonight,   9 even in my own suffering and grief, knowing that I have told my story, which is the story of an innocent man.

Part Two: An Important Failure

On April 24 [2006] the phone rang just after breakfast while I was opening   10 the kitchen window to the fresh spring air. It was Sally Murphy, who has been my friend since we were in our twenties, calling from Florida. "It's Luke," she choked, "he's had an accident." She went on to explain the circumstances of the tragedy. Her son's Humvee in Iraq had come under fire, and Luke was struck violently by flying shrapnel from an improvised explosive device and was now clinging to life in an army field hospital near Baghdad. She told me that his left leg had been blown off, that doctors were struggling to save his right leg, severely mangled, large chunks of muscle gone, tendons and nerves ripped and burned. She explained how Luke, with these grievous injuries, had dragged himself from the burning vehicle, taken a head count of his men, calmed them down, radioed for help. What remained of his left leg had been amputated by medics in the back of a truck on the way to the field hospital in an attempt to save him from bleeding to death.

Sally told me that her first reaction to the early morning phone call   11 from the Army was dismissive. "No, I'm sorry, you must have the wrong number, it is not my son you are talking about . . ." Her blonde Luke, second of three sons, an extraordinarily handsome man of twenty-four years with piercing blue eyes and an impish smile. A friendly kid who loved a good laugh and a good argument and had been dubbed "Luke the Lawyer" in junior high.

I was stunned into silence; I didn't know what to say to my friend.   12 How does one receive this gruesome news on a bright spring day, standing in a sunny kitchen, drying the last blue flowered dish, the smell of coffee and toast still strong in the air? What sense could I make of this day, what could I do or say now that would be of any importance? I felt guilty and ashamed that I had not done enough to prevent Luke from going to war. We had failed Luke, I had failed Luke. I felt nausea, revulsion at my comfort, my health, my life. And I felt anger; murderous rage at the powers that had sent Luke ten thousand miles away but did not protect him.

In August I made my first trip to Ward 57 of Walter Reed Army   13 Medical Center to visit Luke. I was told by those who had been there before me that visiting the huge army hospital would be a powerful experience, but difficult to see, difficult to know what to say or do. It would be uncomfortable. I thought I was ready, but nothing could have prepared me for what I witnessed as I walked onto the enormous ward, brilliantly lit, room after room full of men just like Luke, missing arms, legs, hands, eyes. The empty beds made up immaculately with white sheets, starched and bleached, purposefully left empty in readiness for those who would be coming in tonight, tomorrow, next week. To walk down the hallway of the ward might invite a near collision with a patient rounding a corner on two prosthetic legs, one arm missing, or a grief-stricken family just arriving to see their wounded child for the first time.

14   I found Luke in good spirits and feeling strong, and later noticed his arm muscles rippling as he wheeled down the long halls, showing me around and joking with the nurses. He casually pointed out his old rooms, rooms where he had lain during the first months in agonizing pain from multiple surgeries, experiencing recurring unexplained high fevers, drugged and sick, his one leg immobilized with countless titanium pins attached to a heavy external fixator.

15   We took an elevator to the cafeteria, had lunch, and I listened to Luke, the young Staff Sergeant. He recounted the whole story of that day in April, still a harrowing tale after many retellings. He told other stories, of the men he'd lost in previous roadside bombings, and of having to give orders to the youngest members of his unit, the stunned eighteen year olds, to scrape up the leftover flesh and other human tissue that remained

On Memorial Day 2005, Veterans for Peace constructed this "Arlington West" memorial on the beach at Santa Monica, California, to commemorate their comrades killed in the Iraq War. Compare and contrast told by the Images In the foreground—the kneeling soldier amidst the crosses on the sand, however temporary—with the beachgoers at the water's edge, intent on their recreation, indifferent to the drama at their backs. In what ways does this photograph comment on "About Suffering"?

after the bodies had been removed, and place the material in plastic bags. Graphic descriptions of the dead bodies of Iraqis left by the roadside, their heads swollen in the blazing sun to the size of basketballs. I listened to every story, and began to understand the meaning of the phrase "to bear witness."

I asked Luke what I should tell people when I went home, if he 16 had any message. He said to say that he had not felt physically protected while he was in Iraq. He also said that he felt duped into going to Iraq for a second deployment under a program that our government calls, ironically, "Stop/Loss," a term lifted from stock market jargon. The program is, in effect, a draft foisted upon those military personnel who are about to finish their service but who receive orders for redeployment in the months or weeks before their expected release date. He also wanted me to make sure that people knew that he is one of roughly twenty thousand men and women maimed by the war thus far. That Ward 57 is haunted by the phantoms of perhaps thirty thousand missing limbs.

On the way back to Luke's room after lunch we passed the entrance 17 to Ward 58 marked by a sign that read "Neuroscience Unit." I hesitated at the double doors, ready for the rest of my "tour." I glanced at Luke. "NO-o-o-o, you don't want to go in there . . .," he said with eyebrows raised. I was about to say that I did want to go in, but I turned away from the doors, and followed the wheelchair down the hall. I could only imagine what he was preventing me from witnessing: the traumatically brain injured patients, their pain different from the amputees; the vacant eyes and "persistent vegetative states"; the families of those men and women. Why did I not insist upon going in? Why, after seeing all that I had seen did I turn away in fear at those who lie in the twilight between life and death?

Part Three: The Torturer's Horse

On the drive home from Walter Reed, tired and emotionally drained, 18 I wondered what had happened to Luke's amputated leg. A leg that I remembered as being muscular and tan, leg hair bleached white-blonde from the Florida sun. What had happened to the limbs of all those twenty thousand amputees? Was there some hapless soldier given the job of cremating young body parts? What had happened to the ashes? I imagined them being loaded into a plane, sprinkled over the White House lawn and dug into the rich soil of every suburban lawn in America.

It was at that moment that grief hit me. Thinking of Luke's once 19 beautiful leg, unrecognizable, being placed into a faraway crematorium with no one there to mourn, history repeating itself by another young man just doing his job.

Content

1. It's possible to understand this essay without reading W. H. Auden's poem, "Musee des Beaux Arts," on which it is based, since some of the poem's essential meaning—that, as Kennedy says, "people's suffering always takes place while we [ordinary people] are busy doing other things" (¶ 3), the ordinary activities of ordinary lives. It's also possible to understand the essay without looking at "The Fall of Icarus," the seventeenth century painting by Pieter Brueghel the Elder on which the poem is based, which Kennedy describes in ¶ 3—no one—not the farmer plowing his field, the shepherd tending his flock, nor the friar fishing—notices Icarus falling from the sky, his—as Auden says—"white legs disappearing into the green." Explain the introduction as you understand it (exclusively from Kennedy's essay).

2. **Second Look**. Now, read the Auden poem and view the Brueghel painting, both readily available through print and Internet sources. Then re-read the essay through this doubly new lens of poem and painting. "Musee des Beaux Arts," for instance, was written in 1938, when Hitler's invasion of Europe was in process, leading to World War II; what is the relevance of this? What meanings come into focus that weren't apparent from your initial reading of Kennedy's essay? How do these specific works, juxtaposed with the example of the wounded soldier, concretize an abstraction—suffering?

3. Why does Kennedy devote a major section—Part One—of this essay to a monologue by the farmer in the painting, defending himself against Auden's charge of indifference to suffering? On what grounds does the farmer base his self-defense? Is his argument credible? Ethical? Does he become a sympathetic character in the course of his speech?

4. How do the introduction (Auden's poem and Brueghel's painting) and Part One (the farmer's monologue) prepare readers for Part Two: Luke's loss of his leg in the Iraq War? Why does Kennedy title this section "An Important Failure"?

5. What is the ultimate meaning of "About Suffering"? What are the underlying ethical issues in this essay?

Strategies/Structures/Language

6. This is a creative nonfiction essay, yet Part One, the monologue by the farmer in the painting, is clearly fictional. Justify the mixture of fact and fiction to make an ethical point, using both Kennedy's essay and Swift's "A Modest Proposal" (461–68) as examples.

7. Does Kennedy's creation of a fictitious example to discuss suffering interfere with or undercut the true example of suffering she presents in her visit to Luke in the Walter Reed Army Medical Center? Luke, as she presents him, actually seems to be making an excellent recovery: "I found Luke in good spirits and feeling strong" (¶ 14). In what ways, then, does his example reinforce her point? Would her argument have been more effective if her subject had appeared more devastated, more miserable?

8. The imagery of Luke's lost leg, "once beautiful," now "unrecognizable," dominates the conclusion—and makes what points? Given this, why title this section "The Torturer's Horse," a quotation from "Musee des Beaux Arts"—"Where the

dogs go on with their doggy life and the torturer's horse/Scratches its innocent behind on a tree." Why use this quotation here, this literary allusion, instead of Auden's reference to "the white legs disappearing into the green/water" or another reference in Auden to the "boy falling out of the sky"?

For Writing

9. Write an essay about an abstract concept ("good," "evil," "war," "peace," "love," "hate," among innumerable possibilities), using a poem as well as a personal example to provide a specific illustration of or commentary on your position.

10. Use an example of someone who has been a victim to make an ethical point about a larger issue. Avoid sentimentality, clichés, excessive emotion—and don't preach. Let the example speak for itself, as do the examples in this essay by Kennedy, Hockenberry's from "Moving Violations" (549–55), Hoagland's "Children Are Diamonds" (489–97), and Swift's "A Modest Proposal" (461–68).

Additional Topics for Writing Appealing to Emotion and Ethics

(For strategies for appealing to emotion and ethics, see 455.)

Multiple Strategies for Writing: Appealing to Emotion and Ethics

Implied arguments, appeals to emotion and ethics, commonly employ assorted strategies to make their points as compelling as possible, and to interpret their significance. Among these are the following:

- *Definitions* of essential terms, component parts. These are likely to be subjective and favorable to the writer's point of view.
- A *narrative*, which may comprise the entire argument or an interrelated series of narrative examples. The *narrator* is likely to be the author, using characters or events to make the point, *dialogue, a time sequence*, evocative *setting(s)*, and *symbolism* to reinforce the implied point.
- *Definitions, illustrations*, and *examples*, to show the meaning or significance of the key issues
- *Process analysis*, to show either how the subject at hand arose and why it needs to be addressed or to show the process by which a remedy or solution can be effected
- *Comparison* and *contrast* of the pro and con positions
- *Division* and *classification* of the relevant subtopics and side issues
- *Cause* and *effect*, to show the beneficial consequences of the arguer's point of view and the detrimental consequences of the opposition's stance

1. Write an essay that attempts to persuade one of the following audiences through a combination of appeals to reason, emotion, and ethics.

   a. To someone you'd like for a friend, lover, or spouse, or an enemy with whom you'd like a reconciliation: Love me.
   b. To an athlete, or to an athletic coach: Play according to the rules, even when the referee (umpire, or other judge) isn't looking.
   c. To a prospective employer: I'm the best person for the job. Hire me.
   d. To a police officer: I shouldn't receive this traffic ticket. Or, to a judge or jury: I am innocent of the crime of which I'm accused.
   e. To the voters: Vote for me (or for a candidate of my choice).
   f. To admissions officers of a particular college, university, or of a program within that institution (such as medical or law school, graduate program, or a division with a special undergraduate degree): Let me in.
   g. To the prospective buyer of something you want to sell or service you can perform: Buy this. Trust me.
   h. To an audience prejudiced against a particular group or simply to a majority audience: It is wrong to discriminate against X. (X may be a minority, female, a member of a particular national or religious group, gay, disabled, elderly . . .)
   i. To an antagonist on any issue: As Joan Didion says, *"Listen to me, see it my way, change your mind."*

j. To people engaging in behavior that threatens their lives or their health: Stop doing X (or stop doing X to excess)—smoking, drinking, overeating, undereating, or using drugs. Or: Start doing X—exercising regularly, using bike helmets or seatbelts, planning for the future by getting an education, a stable job, free of debt, an investment plan, a retirement plan . . .

2. Pick a work of fiction or nonfiction whose content intrigues you and whose style you admire, and write a brief parody (probably involving considerable exaggeration) of it to show your understanding of the content and your appreciation of the style.

3. Write a satire to argue implicity for a point, as Swift does in "A Modest Proposal" (461–68). Use whatever techniques seem appropriate, such as creating a character who does the talking for you; setting a scene (such as of pathos or misery) that helps make your point; using a tone involving understatement, irony, or exaggeration. Be sure to supply enough clues to enable your readers to understand what you really mean.

4. Write a humorous paper primarily for enjoyment—your own and your audience's—on a familiar topic that either shows its pleasant aspects to advantage (Twain, "Uncle John's Farm" 238–45) or parodies its subject (Verge, "The Habs" 105–109; Britt, "That Lean and Hungry Look" 358–61).

5. Write a worst-case scenario designed to frighten readers into accepting your argument on any of the above topics or those in Chapter 9 (386–451).

PART V: *CONTROVERSY IN CONTEXT: WHO ARE WE?*

Identity

Issues of identity permeate *The Essay Connection*, as they do throughout life. "Who am I?" we want to know, from childhood onward. "Where do I belong?" arrives early and remains throughout our lifetimes as we develop an understanding of family, friends, peers, nation, and wider world. What we initially take for granted—"I am an American"—or Hispanic American, African-American, Asian-American, or—fill in the blanks—becomes progressively more complicated as we understand more about our history, our heritage, our expectations. Changing the representations of one's identity, on *MySpace, Facebook, craigslist*, blogs, or other easily mutable locations is for some a daily, even an hourly, pastime. Responding to these requires a keen eye, a nimble imagination, an ability to improvise and reinvent oneself, as well as a sense of skepticism—do we really believe what we're reading or viewing? What we might have been inclined to trust in the days of cold print today becomes unstable in the twinkling of an eye. Reader, viewer, beware!

Some aspects of identity are highly conspicuous, such as one's name, skin color, body size and shape, or speech. Some are less visible, more ambiguous: one's ethnicity or nationality, physical or mental state, native intelligence or degree of education, or economic status. Other aspects of identity are more unobtrusive unless the individual—or society— chooses to emphasize them: individual beliefs and values, relationships with others, one's DNA, or the results of medical alteration. Some aspects of identity we consider intrinsic to our heritage: the "inalienable rights" addressed in "The Declaration of Independence"—"Life, Liberty, and the Pursuit of Happiness" (393–97) and a healthful environment of clean air and abundant water (though many, such as Hoagland in "Children Are Diamonds" [489–97], demonstrate why we can no longer take the latter for granted). Other aspects of identity we choose deliberately: whether or not to attend college, where to live after graduation, what friends to have, whom to marry, whether or not to have children. Yet because life is never static, whatever is incorporated into relationships, like whatever is embedded in society and in the natural world, is subject to change. The authors, in this chapter on identity and throughout the book, attempt to capture the transient as well as the more permanent aspects of identity and to interpret and analyze the causes and consequences of what makes us who we are. We can interpret identity, as well as other topics, from the following perspectives:

- Political
- Economic
- Religious
- Social
- Intellectual
- Aesthetic

(an easy way to remember these is that they spell P-E-R-S-I-A), though feel free to add other aspects as well.

It is possible to read every chapter of this book, every topic—growing up, family relationships, heritage, the natural world, science and technology, education, human and civil rights—through the lens of identity. But this chapter specifically focuses on two significant aspects of identity that affect everyone on this earth: national identity and physical identity.

National Identity   E. B. White's two-paragraph definition of "Democracy" was published in *The New Yorker*'s Fourth-of-July issue six months after the United States had entered World War II—on the side of democracy and in opposition of fascism. "Democracy is the line that forms on the right. It is the don't in don't shove. . . . Democracy is the recurrent suspicion that more than half of the people are right more than half of the time." White's definition provides low-key, familiar illustrations of many of the principles addressed in the Bill of Rights: freedom of speech, press, religion, assembly, and the right to petition, granted to ordinary citizens. These citizens are, in White's encomium, people who, even in wartime, resent stuffed shirts and high hats; people who can appreciate baseball, the national pastime, and the hope for victory that exists (even) "at the beginning of the ninth"; people who can enjoy the small pleasures of life, "the mustard on the hotdog and the cream in the rationed coffee." Yet critics have pointed out the "whiteness" of the culture this definition represents. For in 1943 racial segregation persisted not only throughout the South, but in our nation's capital. In the South, many African-Americans were not allowed to vote or to use the public libraries; how could they ever experience "the feeling of privacy in the voting booths, the feeling of communion in the libraries"? In 1943 major league baseball was lily-white; Jackie Robinson, the first African-American player, would not be hired until 1947; the notion of "national pastime" needed to expand, and has done so, dramatically, over time.

New Yorker readers, themselves predominantly white in 1943, might not have noticed the whiteness of the world that White (no pun intended) depicted. Twenty years later the Civil Rights movement profoundly challenged this orientation, as articulated in Martin Luther King, Jr.'s eloquent "Letter from Birmingham Jail" (399–413), where he was confined after being arrested in a nonviolent civil rights protest. His rallying cry, "Injustice anywhere is a threat to justice everywhere. We are caught in an inescapable network of mutuality. . . . Whatever affects one directly, affects all indirectly" finds current resonance "Universal Declaration of Human Rights" (571–76).

A strong element of his Civil Rights campaign was Dr. King's sense of "mutuality," his concern for as Barack Obama said in a 2008 speech, "To Form a Move Perfect Union," the "future of black children and white children and Asian children and Hispanic children and Native American children." Both leaders reject the claim that "those kids who don't look like us are somebody else's problem," as Obama says. "The children of America are not those kids, they are our kids, and we will not let them fall. . . ." In this spirit, student Zara Rix, herself the child of Italian-Australian parents, addresses the positive consequences and the complexities of growing up in multi-ethnic America in "Corporality" (557–63).

The Essay Connection is, in fact, a testament to the wide spectrum of Americans of the diverse identities who have not failed; people who have been highly successful as human beings in a variety of fields and activities and who have written about these topics. These include African-Americans (Toni Morrison, Frederick Douglass, and Dr. King), Native Americans (Sherman Alexie and Linda Hogan), Asian-Americans (Lynda Barry and Janice Mirikitani), and survivors or children of survivors of the Holocaust (Elie Wiesel and Art Spiegelman). The American Dream is compressed into the expectation that regardless of one's origin, everyone in America has the "shining, golden opportunity" for self-fulfillment: "work hard and you'll succeed." That the American Dream may be a national myth, an overly simplistic vision of national identity, is posited by Sherman Alexie's satiric "What Sacagawea Means to Me" (83–85), and by the ethical questions raised by Robert Reich's "The Global Elite" (419–27), and Peter Singer's "The Singer Solution to World Poverty" (481–87).

Genetic Identity   "Who am I," a question as old as the Greek philosophers, used to involve—on a physical and perhaps social level—more clear-cut answers than it does today. That biology is destiny (i.e., that women and African-Americans, for example, have their lifelong fate predetermined from birth) has been challenged in a number of significant ways in the past century. With these challenges come the provocations, potential benefits and problems, ethical issues, and myriad of unforeseen consequences that are predicted to multiply in future years. No longer do large numbers of Americans accept what used to be considered inevitable: that gender, strength, intelligence, physical ability or disability, propensity for (or existence of) disease is determined at birth or through later injury and is essentially unchangeable throughout life. These stereotypes, however, provide the basis for much contemporary humor, including Roz Chast's "Men Are from Belgium, Women Are from New Brunswick" (350–51) and the Botox babes cartoon, "I never thought turning eighty would be so much fun!" (375).

Charles C. Mann's "The Coming Death Shortage" (362–74)—confronts the problems likely to occur when rich people cease to die according to their natural biological span of years. Fulfillment of the American Dream, says Mann, depends on old people dying on schedule so the young can take their places. This natural progression is altered when elderly people have enough money to buy costly medical procedures that can extend their lives indefinitely; if they beat the biological endgame young people won't have a chance.

Bill McKibben's "Designer Genes" (515–25) explores the ethical dimensions of human biological engineering, of modifying the genetic identity of human beings—as is currently being done with plants and animals—"to make them *better* in some way; to delete, modify, or add genes in developing embryos . . . [to] make them taller and more muscular, or smarter and less aggressive, maybe handsome and possibly straight." Even as early as 1993, 43 percent of Americans polled by the March of Dimes would willingly "engage in genetic engineering 'simply to enhance their children's looks or intelligence.'" Among families today dealing with—or trying to prevent—deafness, Down's syndrome, or Lou Gehrig's disease, powerful arguments erupt over whether prevention or eradication of these problems in future generations would diminish the resources given to current sufferers. Should tomorrow's children be improved if today's are neglected? Among more "normal" families—and what is "normal" in these days of in vitro fertilization, embryo transplants, and more—what would happen if genetic engineering could create new and improved models of superior children at, say, ten year intervals? Would this lead to a "biological arms race" in which each new generation would be superior to homegrown babies with natural, unmodified DNA, as well as to its genetically engineered predecessors? If parents could add "thirty points to their child's IQ," would failure to "soup up" the embryos amount to child abuse? If we disallow the opportunistic notions that those with the most money or the easiest access to the treatment should get what they want, what principles should be operative?

Beauty   That genetic engineering raises innumerable ethical questions and offers few if any clear-cut answers is echoed in Virginia Postrel's "The Truth About Beauty" (539–43). She argues that, "we know beauty when we see it, and our reactions are remarkably consistent" to "the centuries-old bust of Neferititi, the Venus de Milo, and the exquisite faces painted by Leonardo and Botticelli." Her comments hold true even though the Cupid's bow faces of the "It" girls of the silent movies gave way to the beach-blanket bimbos of the 1950s, who a half-century later gave way to the looks of Britney Spears and Paris Hilton and the ever self-inventing Madonna, adaptive to time and taste. Contrary to the new Dove ads, Postrel claims that "beauty is not just a social construct, and not every girl is beautiful just the way she is."

In response to physical beauty we could propose—as many have done throughout *The Essay Connection*, and elsewhere—additional dimensions of human identity:

- *Intelligence*, in all its infinite varieties: familial, social, political, physical, aesthetic, mechanical, and more (see Scott Russell Sanders, "The Inheritance of Tools" [135–42]; Howard Gardner, "Who Owns Intelligence?" [297–309]).
- *Temperament*, whether inborn or cultivated, that may include where one ranks on a continuum of extremes that range, for instance, from being highly goal-oriented to vague; being aggressive to laid-back; or being either tolerant or intolerant of risk, change, ambiguity, or uncertainty (see Natalie Angier, "Why Men Don't Last: Self-Destruction as a Way of Life" [353–56]; Deborah Tannen, "Communication Styles" [344–49].
- *Holder/conveyor of a belief system or set of values*, formal or informal: religious, ethical, philosophical, political, aesthetic (see Elie Wiesel, "Why I Write: Making No Become Yes" [14–20]; Edward Hoagland, "Children are Diamonds," [489–97]).
- *Occupation or avocation or consuming passion*, initially defined in terms of one's parents' social or economic status, then by one's education, and eventually by one's type of job and one's stature therein (see Tim Berners-Lee, "Long Live the Web" [429–38]).

Identity Creation, Identity Theft   That there are innumerable aspects of identity and innumerable possibilities for self-creation, re-creation, and interpretation is apparent, in part from James Fallows's "Tinfoil Underwear" (192–98), which explores a topic that, on its face (oops), seems so obvious to today's generation of students that it scarcely needs discussion. Nevertheless, what may seem to be an innocent posting of photographs—candid or manipulated, serious or in jest—and information about oneself is fraught with possibilities for manipulation, fraud, theft, and other forms of abuse. Who reads what is broadcast to the wide world, or even to a restricted segment thereof? Where does this material reside—not only photographs but other vital personal information, such as Social Security number, medical history, credit record? Who owns these manifestations of oneself? Who can store them, alter them, transmit them, comment on them, buy and sell them? Use them for other transactions licit and illicit? These are questions that, before the ubiquitous presence of the Internet, might not have been asked or would certainly have been answered differently than they are today, as discussed in essays by: Sherry Turkle, "How Computers Change the Way are Think" (37–43); Nicholas Carr, "Is Google Making Us Stupid? What the Internet Is Doing to Our Brains" (45–54); and William Deresiewicz, "Faux Friendship" (56–60).

Indeed, all of the issues addressed in this chapter raise questions that may have different answers tomorrow than they do today. Identity, like life itself, is never static. Who we are, what we make of ourselves, what we become and may yet become again raises new questions, and in turn new answers. Welcome to the wide, wonderful world of knowledge and self-knowledge—at times full of roadblocks and fear, but nevertheless, as long as there is hope for the world (to be addressed in Chapter 12), full of challenge and inspiration as well.

JI LEE

Ji Lee, born in Seoul, Korea, raised in Sao Paulo, Brazil, earned a BFA from Parsons in 1996. Lee is a designer whose prestigious employers include Saatchi and Saatchi, Google, and Facebook. In addition to satiric New York Times op-ed cartoons, he has published "Talk Back: The Bubble Project," with space for readers to supply their own words for photographic dialogue bubbles.

Li's website, pleaseenjoy.com, shows fifteen cupids in the original illustration, of which twelve were published in the New York Times. Which were deleted? What editorial decisions might have influenced which images stayed and which were cut? What information do the different arrows convey? The cupids' body shapes? Wing size? Clothing? Modes of transportation?

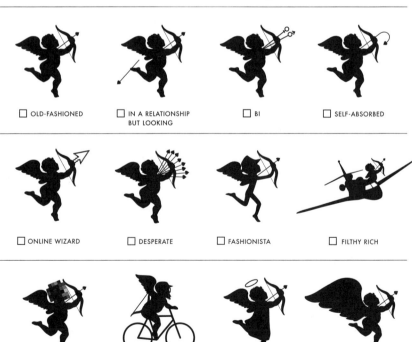

Pick Your Cupid

☐ OLD-FASHIONED ☐ IN A RELATIONSHIP BUT LOOKING ☐ BI ☐ SELF-ABSORBED

☐ ONLINE WIZARD ☐ DESPERATE ☐ FASHIONISTA ☐ FILTHY RICH

☐ NO-STRINGS-ATTACHED ☐ HIPSTER ☐ CHRISTIAN ☐ OVERACHIEVER

Ji Lee

BILL McKIBBEN

After graduating from Harvard in 1982, Bill McKibben (born 1960) started at the top, becoming a staff writer, and later an editor, for *The New Yorker*. Five years later he turned to writing full time, married, moved to upstate New York, and had a child. His books, such as *The End of Nature* (1989); *Hope, Human and Wild: True Stories of Living Lightly on the Earth* (1995); and *Maybe One: A Case for Smaller Families* (1998), concentrate on "the effects of rampant consumerism on the future of the global ecosystem." All of his books, says commentator Michael Coffey, "pursue the same theme . . . what do we consume, why do we consume it, and what are the consequences?" Answering his own question, McKibben replies, "What I've learned so far is that what is sound and elegant and civilized and respectful of community is also environmentally benign."

Enough: Staying Human in an Engineered Age (2003) is about the moral ramifications of biological engineering—the topic of "Designer Genes," as well. This essay, first published in *Orion* in 2003, was reprinted in the book *The Best American Spiritual Writing* in 2004. Here McKibben offers a chilling, clearheaded analysis of what could happen if aspiring (and wealthy) parents resort to genetic engineering to create new and ever-newer models of superior children, a "biological arms race." Each new model might seem better than its predecessor in intelligence, say, or appearance or strength, and every one might appear superior to the homegrown babies who receive their DNA naturally. Be careful what you wish for, warns McKibben. "'Suppose parents could add thirty points to their child's IQ? Wouldn't you want to do it?' . . . Deciding not to soup them up . . . well, it could come to seem like child abuse".

Designer Genes

I grew up in a household where we were very suspicious of dented cans. Dented cans were, according to my mother, a well-established gateway to botulism, and botulism was a bad thing, worse than swimming immediately after lunch. It was one of those bad things measured in extinctions, as in "three tablespoons of botulism toxin could theoretically kill every human on Earth." Or something like that.

So I refused to believe the early reports, a few years back, that socialites had begun injecting dilute strains of the toxin into their brows in an effort to temporarily remove the vertical furrow that appears between one's eyes as one ages. It sounded like a Monty Python routine, some clinic where they daubed your soles with plague germs to combat athlete's foot. But I was wrong to doubt. As the world now knows, Botox has become, in a few short years, a staple weapon in the cosmetic arsenal—so prevalent that, in the words of one writer, "it is now rare in certain social enclaves to see a woman over the age of thirty-five with the ability to look angry." With their facial muscles essentially paralyzed, actresses are having trouble acting; since the treatment requires periodic booster shots, doctors "warn that you could marry a woman (or a man) with a flawlessly even face and wind up with someone who four months later looks like a Shar-Pei." But never mind—now you can get Botoxed in strip mall storefronts and at cocktail parties.

3   People, in other words, will do fairly far out things for less than pressing causes. And more so all the time: public approval of "aesthetic surgery" has grown 50 percent in the United States in the last decade. But why stop there? Once you accept the idea that our bodies are essentially plastic and that it's okay to manipulate that plastic, there's no reason to think that consumers would balk because "genes" were involved instead of, say, "toxins." Especially since genetic engineering would not promote your own vanity, but instead be sold as a boon to your child.

4   The vision of genetic engineers is to do to humans what we have already done to salmon and wheat, pine trees and tomatoes. That is, to make them *better* in some way; to delete, modify, or add genes in developing embryos so that the cells of the resulting person will produce proteins that make them taller and more muscular, or smarter and less aggressive, maybe handsome and possibly straight. Even happy. As early as 1993, a March of Dimes poll found that 43 percent of Americans would engage in genetic engineering "simply to enhance their children's looks or intelligence."

5   Ethical guidelines promulgated by the scientific oversight boards so far prohibit actual attempts at human genetic engineering, but researchers have walked right to the line, maybe even stuck their toes a trifle over. In the spring of 2001, for instance, a fertility clinic in New Jersey impregnated fifteen women with embryos fashioned from their own eggs, their partner's sperm, and a small portion of an egg donated by a second woman. The procedure was designed to work around defects in the would-be mother's egg—but in at least two of the cases, tests showed the resulting babies carried genetic material from all three "parents."

6   And so the genetic modification of humans is not only possible, it's coming fast; a mix of technical progress and shifting mood means it could easily happen in the next few years. Consider what happened with plants. A decade ago, university research farms were growing small plots of genetically modified grain and vegetables. Sometimes activists who didn't like what they were doing would come and rip the plants up, one by one. Then, all of a sudden in the mid-1990s, before anyone had paid any real attention, farmers had planted half the corn and soybean fields in America with transgenic seed.

7   Every time you turn your back this technology creeps a little closer. Gallops, actually, growing and spreading as fast as the internet. One moment you've sort of heard of it; the next moment it's everywhere. But we haven't done it yet. For the moment we remain, if barely, a fully human species. And so we have time yet to consider, to decide, to act. This is arguably the biggest decision humans will ever make.

Right up until this decade, the genes that humans carried in their bod- 8
ies were exclusively the result of chance—of how the genes of the sperm
and the egg, the father and the mother, combined. The only way you could
intervene in the process was by choosing who you would mate with—
and that was as much wishful thinking as anything else, as generation
upon generation of surprised parents have discovered.

But that is changing. We now know two different methods to 9
change human genes. The first, and less controversial, is called somatic
gene therapy. Somatic gene therapy begins with an existing individual—
someone with, say, cystic fibrosis. Researchers try to deliver new, modified
genes to some of her cells, usually by putting the genes aboard viruses
they inject into the patient, hoping that the viruses will infect the cells
and thereby transmit the genes. Somatic gene therapy is, in other words,
much like medicine. You take an existing patient with an existing condition, and you in essence try and convince her cells to manufacture the
medicine she needs.

Germline genetic engineering, on the other hand, is something 10
very novel indeed. "Germ" here refers not to microbes, but to the egg
and sperm cells, the germ cells of the human being. Scientists intent
on genetic engineering would probably start with a fertilized embryo
a week or so old. They would tease apart the cells of that embryo, and
then, selecting one, they would add to, delete, or modify some of its
genes. They could also insert artificial chromosomes containing pre-
designed genes. They would then take the cell, place it inside an egg
whose nucleus had been removed, and implant the resulting new embryo inside a woman. The embryo would, if all went according to plan,
grow into a genetically engineered child. His genes would be pushing
out proteins to meet the particular choices made by his parents and
by the companies and clinicians they were buying the genes from. Instead of coming solely from the combination of his parents, and thus
the combination of their parents, and so on back through time, those
genes could come from any other person, or any other plant or animal,
or out of the thin blue sky. And once implanted, they will pass to his
children and on into time.

But all this work will require one large change in our current way of 11
doing business. Instead of making babies by making love, we will have
to move conception to the laboratory. You need to have the embryo out
there where you can work on it—to make the necessary copies, try to
add or delete genes, and then implant the one that seems likely to turn
out best. Gregory Stock, a researcher at the University of California and
an apostle of the new genetic technologies, says that "the union of egg
and sperm from two individuals . . . would be too unpredictable with
intercourse." And once you've got the embryo out on the lab bench,
gravity disappears altogether. "Ultimately, says Michael West, CEO of
Advanced Cell Technology, the firm furthest out on the cutting edge
of these technologies, "the dream of biologists is to have the sequence

of DNA, the programming code of life, and to be able to edit it the way you can a document on a word processor."

12   Does it sound far-fetched? We began doing it with animals (mice) in 1978, and we've managed the trick with most of the obvious mammals, except one. Some of the first germline interventions might be semimedical. You might, say some advocates, start by improving "visual and auditory acuity," first to eliminate nearsightedness or prevent deafness, then to "improve artistic potential." But why stop there? "If something has evolved elsewhere, then it is possible for us to determine its genetic basis and transfer it into the human genome," says Princeton geneticist Lee Silver—just as we have stuck flounder genes into strawberries to keep them from freezing, and jellyfish genes into rabbits and monkeys to make them glow in the dark.

13   But would we actually do this? Is there any real need to raise these questions as more than curiosities, or will the schemes simply fade away on their own, ignored by the parents who are their necessary consumers?

14   Anyone who has entered a baby supply store in the last few years knows that even the soberest parents can be counted on to spend virtually unlimited sums in pursuit of successful offspring. What if the "Baby Einstein" video series, which immerses "learning-enabled" babies in English, Spanish, Japanese, Hebrew, German, Russian, and French, could be bolstered with a little gene tweaking to improve memory? What if the Wombsongs prenatal music system, piping in Brahms to your waiting fetus, could be supplemented with an auditory upgrade? One sociologist told the *New York Times* we'd crossed the line from parenting to "product development," and even if that remark is truer in Manhattan than elsewhere, it's not hard to imagine what such attitudes will mean across the affluent world.

15   Here's one small example. In the 1980s, two drug companies were awarded patents to market human growth hormone to the few thousand American children suffering from dwarfism. The PDA thought the market would be very small, so HGH was given "orphan drug status," a series of special market advantages designed to reward the manufacturers for taking on such an unattractive business. But within a few years, HGH had become one of the largest selling drugs in the country, with half a billion dollars in sales. This was not because there'd been a sharp increase in the number of dwarves, but because there'd been a sharp increase in the number of parents who wanted to make their slightly short children taller. Before long the drug companies were arguing that the children in the bottom 5 percent of their normal height range were in fact in need of three to five shots a week of HGH. Take eleven-year-old Marco Oriti. At four foot one, he was about four inches shorter than average, and projected to eventually top out at five foot four. This was enough to convince his parents to start on a six-day-a-week HGH regimen, which will cost them $150,000 over the next four years. "You want to give your child the edge no matter what," said his mother.

A few of the would-be parents out on the current cutting edge of   16
the reproduction revolution—those who need to obtain sperm or eggs for
in vitro fertilization—exhibit similar zeal. Ads started appearing in Ivy
League college newspapers a few years ago: couples were willing to pay
$50,000 for an egg, provided the donor was at least five feet, ten inches
tall, white, and had scored 1400 on her SATs. There is, in other words,
a market just waiting for the first clinic with a catalogue of germline
modifications, a market that two California artists proved when they
opened a small boutique, Gene Genies Worldwide, in a trendy part of
Pasadena. Tran Kim-Trang and Karl Mihail wanted to get people thinking
more deeply about these emerging technologies, so they outfitted their
store with petri dishes and models of the double helix and printed up
brochures highlighting traits with genetic links: creativity, extroversion,
thrill-seeking criminality. When they opened the doors, they found people
ready to shell out for designer families (one man insisted he wanted the
survival ability of a cockroach). The "store" was meant to be ironic, but
the irony was lost on a culture so deeply consumeristic that this land of
manipulation seems like the obvious next step. "Generally, people refused
to believe this store was an art project," says Tran. And why not? The next
store in the mall could easily have been a Botox salon.

But say you're not ready. Say you're perfectly happy with the prospect   17
of a child who shares the unmodified genes of you and your partner. Say
you think that manipulating the DNA of your child might be dangerous,
or presumptuous, or icky? How long will you be able to hold that line if
the procedure begins to spread among your neighbors? Maybe not so long
as you think. If germline manipulation actually does begin, it seems likely
to set off a kind of biological arms race. "Suppose parents could add thirty
points to their child's IQ?" asks MIT economist Lester Thurow. "Wouldn't
you want to do it? And if you don't, your child will be the stupidest in the
neighborhood." That's precisely what it might feel like to be the parent
facing the choice. Individual competition more or less defines the society
we've built, and in that context love can almost be defined as giving your
kids what they need to make their way in the world. Deciding not to soup
them up . . . well, it could come to seem like child abuse.

Of course, the problem about arms races is that you never really get   18
anywhere. If everyone's adding thirty IQ points, then having an IQ of one
hundred fifty won't get you any closer to Stanford than you were at the
outset. The very first athlete engineered to use twice as much oxygen as
the next guy will be unbeatable in the Tour de France—but in no time
he'll merely be the new standard. You'll have to do what he did to be
in the race, but your upgrades won't put you ahead, merely back on a
level playing field. You might be able to argue that society as a whole
was helped, because there was more total brainpower at work, but your
kid won't be any closer to the top of the pack. All you'll be able to do is
guarantee she won't be left hopelessly far behind.

19   In fact, the arms race problem has an extra ironic twist when it comes to genetic manipulation. The United States and the Soviet Union could, and did, keep adding new weapons to their arsenals over the decades. But with germline manipulation, you get only one shot; the extra chromosome you stick in your kid when he's born is the one he carries throughout his life. So let's say baby Sophie has a state-of-the-art gene job: her parents paid for the proteins discovered by, say, 2005 that on average yield ten extra IQ points. By the time Sophie is five, though, scientists will doubtless have discovered ten more genes linked to intelligence. Now anyone with a platinum card can get twenty IQ points, not to mention a memory boost and a permanent wrinkle-free brow. So by the time Sophie is twenty-five and in the job market, she's already more or less obsolete—the kids coming out of college plainly just have better hardware.

20   "For all his billions, Bill Gates could not have purchased a single genetic enhancement for his son Rory John," writes Gregory Stock at the University of California. "And you can bet that any enhancements a billion dollars can buy Rory's child in 2030 will seem crude alongside those available for modest sums in 2060." It's not, he adds, "so different from upgraded software. You'll want the new release."

21   The vision of one's child as a nearly useless copy of Windows 95 should make parents fight like hell to make sure we never get started down this path. But the vision gets lost easily in the gushing excitement about "improving" the opportunities for our kids.

22   Beginning the hour my daughter came home from the hospital, I spent part of every day with her in the woods out back, showing her trees and ferns and chipmunks and frogs. One of her very first words was "birch," and you couldn't have asked for a prouder papa. She got her middle name from the mountain we see out the window; for her fifth birthday she got her own child-sized canoe; her school wardrobe may not be relentlessly up-to-date, but she's never lacked for hiking boots. As I write these words, she's spending her first summer at sleepaway camp, one we chose because the kids sleep in tents and spend days in the mountains. All of which is to say that I have done everything in my power to try to mold her into a lover of the natural world. That is where my deepest satisfactions lie, and I want the same for her. It seems benign enough, but it has its drawbacks; it means less time and money and energy for trips to the city and music lessons and so forth. As time goes on and she develops stronger opinions of her own, I yield more and more, but I keep trying to stack the deck, to nudge her in the direction that's meant something to me. On a Saturday morning, when the question comes up of what to do, the very first words out of my mouth always involve yet another hike. I can't help myself.

23   In other words, we already "engineer" our offspring in some sense of the word: we do our best, and often our worst, to steer them in particular directions. And our worst can be pretty bad. We all know people whose lives were blighted trying to meet the expectations of their parents. We've

all seen the crazed devotion to getting kids into the right schools, the right professions, the right income brackets. Parents try to pass down their prejudices, their politics, their attitude toward the world ("we've got to toughen that kid up—he's going to get walked all over"). There are fathers who start teaching the curveball at the age of four, and sons made to feel worthless if they don't make the Little League traveling team. People move house so that their kids can grow up with the right band of schoolmates. They threaten to disown them for marrying African Americans, or for not marrying African Americans. No dictator anywhere has ever tried to rule his subjects with as much attention to detail as the average modern parent.

Why not take this just one small step further? Why not engineer 24 children to up the odds that all that nudging will stick? In the words of Lee Silver, a Princeton geneticist, "Why not seize this power? Why not control what has been left to chance in the past? Indeed, we control all other aspects of our children's lives and identities through powerful social and environmental influences. . . . On what basis can we reject positive genetic influences on a person's essence when we accept the rights of parents to benefit their children in every other way?" If you can buy your kid three years at Deerfield, four at Harvard, and three more at Harvard Law, why shouldn't you be able to turbocharge his IQ a bit?

But most likely the answer has already occurred to you as well. Be- 25 cause you know plenty of people who managed to rebel successfully against whatever agenda their parents laid out for them, or who took that agenda and bent it to fit their own particular personality. In our society that's often what growing up is all about—the sometimes excruciatingly difficult, frequently liberating break with the expectations of your parents. The decision to join the Peace Corps (or, the decision to leave the commune where you grew up and go to business school). The discovery that you were happiest davening in an Orthodox shul three hours a day, much to the consternation of your good suburban parents who almost always made it to Yom Kippur services; the decision that, much as you respected the Southern Baptist piety of your parents, the Bible won't be your watchword.

Without the grounding offered by tradition, the search for the 26 "authentic you" can be hard; our generations contain the first people who routinely shop religions, for instance. But the sometimes poignant difficulty of finding yourself merely underscores how essential it is. Silver says the costs of germline engineering and a college education might be roughly comparable; in both cases, he goes on, the point is to "increase the chances the child will become wiser in some way, and better able to achieve success and happiness." But that's half the story, at best. College is where you go to be exposed to a thousand new influences, ideas that should be able to take you in almost any direction. It's where you go to get out from under your parents' thumb, to find out that you actually don't have to go to law school if you don't want to. As often as not, the harder parents try to wrench their kids in one direction, the harder those

© Daniel Lee

Twins, particularly identical twins, are special, capable of having a unique relationship and intimate understanding not shared with others who lack this common genetic heritage. Explain some of the advantages—and possible disadvantages—of such a relationship. If such twins were conceived as the result of into in vitro fertilization or another method of artificial reproduction, does the method of conception affect your answer? What differences—ethical and relational—exist between natural-born twins and human clones? Now, look again at this picture, very closely. What do the twins resemble? If you sense a resemblance to animals, you are "reading" this photo accurately, for it is composed of manipulated animal images. Does this knowledge affect your answers to any of the above questions? What statement does the manipulated photo make about the subject, which is no longer twins, but cloning?

kids eventually fight to determine their own destiny. I am as prepared as I can be for the possibility—the probability—that Sophie will decide she wants to live her life in the concrete heart of Manhattan. It's her life (and perhaps her kids will have a secret desire to come wander in the woods with me).

27   We try to shape the lives of our kids—to "improve" their lives, as we would measure improvement—but our gravity is usually weak enough that kids can break out of it if and when they need to. (When it isn't, when parents manage to bend their children to the point of breaking, we think of them as monstrous.) "Many of the most creative and valuable human lives are the result of particularly difficult struggles" against expectation and influence, writes the legal scholar Martha Nussbaum.

28   That's not how a genetic engineer thinks of his product. He works to ensure absolute success. Last spring an Israeli researcher announced

that he had managed to produce a featherless chicken. This constituted an improvement, to his mind, because "it will be cheaper to produce since its lack of feathers means there is no need to pluck it before it hits the shelves." Also, poultry farmers would no longer have to ventilate their vast barns to keep their birds from overheating. "Feathers are a waste," the scientist explained. "The chickens are using feed to produce something that has to be dumped, and the farmers have to waste electricity to overcome that fact." Now, that engineer was not trying to influence his chickens to shed their feathers because they'd be happier and the farmer would be happier and everyone would be happier. He was inserting a gene that created a protein that made good and certain they would not be producing feathers. Just substitute, say, an even temperament for feathers, and you'll know what the human engineers envision.

"With reprogenetics," writes Lee Silver, "parents can gain *complete*   29
control [emphasis mine] over their destiny, with the ability to guide and enhance the characteristics of their children, and their children's children as well." Such parents would not be calling their children on the phone at annoying frequent intervals to suggest that it's time to get a real job; instead, just like the chicken guy, they would be inserting genes that produced proteins that would make their child behave in certain ways throughout his life. You cannot rebel against the production of that protein. Perhaps you can still do everything in your power to defeat the wishes of your parents, but that protein will nonetheless be pumped out relentlessly into your system, defining who you are. You won't grow feathers, no matter how much you want them. And maybe they can engineer your mood enough that your lack of plumage won't even cross your mind.

Such children will, in effect, be assigned a goal by their program-   30
mers: "intelligence," "even temper," "athleticism." (As with chickens, the market will doubtless lean in the direction of efficiency. It may be hard to find genes for, say, dreaminess.) Now two possibilities arise. Perhaps the programming doesn't work very well, and your lad spells poorly, or turns moody, or can't hit the inside fastball. In the present world, you just tell yourself that that's who he is. But in the coming world, he'll be, in essence, a defective product. Do you still accept *him* unconditionally? Why? If your new Jetta got thirty miles to the gallon instead of the forty it was designed to get, you'd take it back. You'd call it a lemon. If necessary, you'd sue.

Or what if the engineering worked pretty well, but you decided,   31
too late, that you'd picked the wrong package, hadn't gotten the best features? Would you feel buyer's remorse if the kid next door had a better ear, a stronger arm?

Say the gene work went a little awry and left you with a kid who   32
had some serious problems; what kind of guilt would that leave you with? Remember, this is not a child created by the random interaction of your genes with those of your partner, this is a child created with specific intent. Does *Consumer Reports* start rating the various biotech offerings?

33   What if you had a second child five years after the first, and by that time the upgrades were undeniably improved: how would you feel about the first kid? How would he feel about his new brother, the latest model?

34   The other outcome—that the genetic engineering works just as you had hoped—seems at least as bad. Now your child is a product. You can take precisely as much pride in her achievements as you take in the achievements of your dishwashing detergent. It was designed to produce streak-free glassware, and she was designed to be sweet-tempered, social, and smart. And what can she take pride in? Her good grades? She may have worked hard, but she'll always know that she was spec'ed for good grades. Her kindness to others? Well, yes, it's good to be kind—but perhaps it's not much of an accomplishment once the various genes with some link to sociability have been catalogued and manipulated. I have no doubt that these qualms would be one of the powerful psychological afflictions of the future—at least until someone figures out a fix that keeps the next generations from having such bad thoughts.

35   Britain's chief rabbi, Jonathan Sacks, was asked a few years ago about the announcement that Italian doctors were trying to clone humans. "If there is a mystery at the heart of human condition, it is otherness: the otherness of man and woman, parent and child. It is the space we make for otherness that makes love something other than narcissism." I remember so well the feeling of walking into the maternity ward with Sue, and walking out with Sue and Sophie: where there had been two there were now, somehow, three, each of us our own person, but now commanded to make a family, a place where we all could thrive. She was so mysterious, that Sophie, and in many ways she still is. There are times when, like every parent, I see myself reflected in her, and times when I wonder if she's even related. She's ours to nurture and protect, but she is who *she is*. That's the mystery and the glory of any child.

36   Mystery, however, is not one of the words that thrills engineers. They try to deliver solid bridges, unyielding dams, reliable cars. We wouldn't want it any other way. The only question is if their product line should be expanded to include children.

37 Right now both the genes, and the limits that they set on us, connect us with every human that came before. Human beings can look at rock art carved into African cliffs and French caves thirty thousand years ago and feel an electric, immediate kinship. We've gone from digging sticks to combines, and from drum circles to symphony orchestras (and back again to drum circles), but we still hear in the same range and see in the same spectrum, still produce adrenaline and dopamine in the same ways, still think in many of the same patterns. We are, by and large, the same people, more closely genetically related to one another than we may be to our engineered grandchildren.

These new technologies show us that human meaning dangles by a far thinner thread than we had thought. If germline genetic engineering ever starts, it will accelerate endlessly and unstoppably into the future, as individuals make the calculation that they have no choice but to equip their kids for the world that's being made. The first child whose genes come in part from some corporate lab, the first child who has been "enhanced" from what came before—that's the first child who will glance back over his shoulder and see a gap between himself and human history.

These would be mere consumer decisions—but that also means that they would benefit the rich far more than the poor. They would take the gap in power, wealth, and education that currently divides both our society and the world at large, and write that division into our very biology. A sixth of the American population lacks health insurance of any kind—they can't afford to go to the doctor for a *check-up*. And much of the rest of the world is far worse off. If we can't afford the fifty cents per person it would take to buy bed nets to protect most of Africa from malaria, it is unlikely we will extend to anyone but the top tax bracket these latest forms of genetic technology. The injustice is so obvious that even the strongest proponents of genetic engineering make little attempt to deny it. "Anyone who accepts the right of affluent parents to provide their children with an expensive private school education cannot use 'unfairness' as a reason for rejecting the use of reprogenetic technologies," says Lee Silver.

These new technologies, however, are not yet inevitable. Unlike global warming, this genie is not yet out of the bottle. But if germline genetic engineering is going to be stopped, it will have to happen now, before it's quite begun. It will have to be a political choice, that is—one we make not as parents but as citizens, not as individuals but as a whole, thinking not only about our own offspring but about everyone.

So far the discussion has been confined to a few scientists, a few philosophers, a few ideologues. It needs to spread widely, and quickly, and loudly. The stakes are absurdly high, nothing less than the meaning of being human. And given the seductions that we've seen—the intuitively and culturally delicious prospect of a *better* child—the arguments against must be not only powerful but also deep. They'll need to resonate on the same intuitive and cultural level. We'll need to feel in our gut the reasons why, this time, we should tell Prometheus thanks, but no thanks.

Content

1. This essay is an excellent example of inductive reasoning that makes its major points in the conclusion (¶s 40–41), after presenting an escalating series of examples. What's the thesis? Is it ever explicitly stated? Explain, with examples, how it can be inferred from virtually every paragraph.

2. How close are humans to achieving "germline genetic engineering" that would enable scientists, or physicians, to construct DNA sequences, "the programming code of life," and "to be able to edit [them] the way you can a document on a word processor" (¶ 11)?

3. What does McKibben speculate the consequences might be of a "biological arms race" devoted to continually enhancing infants' IQ, physical strength, beauty, or other desirable features (¶s 17–20)? What evidence does he offer that people are already receptive to such genetic enhancements (consider, for instance, the current market for egg donors with specific characteristics of height, color, and SAT scores [¶ 16])?

4. Why is genetic engineering inherently unfair, and why would attempts to level the playing field at the high end inevitably have negative social consequences for the poor (¶s 39–41)?

Strategies/Structures/Language

5. Why does McKibben begin his essay with botulism toxin ("three tablespoons [of which] could theoretically kill every human on Earth") and quickly segue to Botox—a dilute strain of the same toxin and a "staple weapon in the cosmetic arsenal" (¶s 1–2)? What language in these first two paragraphs lets readers know where he stands on the issue?

6. Why does McKibben compare the consequences of germline genetic engineering to upgrading computer software: "The vision of one's child as a nearly useless copy of Windows 95 should make parents fight like hell to make sure we never get started down this path" (¶ 21)? Does McKibben's example of a genetically engineered "featherless chicken" (¶ 28) reinforce his argument? Explain.

For Writing

7. With a partner—preferably one who disagrees with you—explore the question, "On what basis can we reject positive genetic influences on a person's essence when we accept the rights of parents to benefit their children in every other way" (¶ 24)? Do you agree with McKibben that in our competitive and affluent society genetic engineering could lead to a "biological arms race" (¶ 17) among parents devoted to continually enhancing infants' IQ, physical strength, beauty, or other desirable features (¶s 17–20)? Together, write an essay on the social and cultural factors that influence parents in the "pursuit of successful offspring" (¶ 14). Present your positions on the topic of whether genetic enhancements should be left up to parents by analyzing how and why such a choice might be politically curtailed.

8. *Journal Writing.* Have you (or someone you know well) experienced a conflict between your family's and community's expectations and perceptions of you and your own quest for self-determination? How do you balance the need to develop your own intellect and character with your need to respect and be accepted within your family and community? Do you agree that rebelling is essential in the development of an "authentic" self (¶s 25–26)?

9. On the basis of your journal writing (see question 8), write an essay on whether we are defined by our genetic inheritance. If, as McKibben suggests, we could not "rebel against . . . that protein [which] will nonetheless be pumped out relentlessly into your system, defining who you are" (¶ 29), do we exert any free will over who we are?

10. ***Dialogues.*** What does Joyce Mirikitani's poem "Recipe" (456) suggest about the relationship between identity and gender? How much freedom do we have to decide who we are, given the genetic and social influences on our development as gendered beings? Or simply as human beings, given the range of potential genetic options that McKibben raises? What does Mirikitani's poem imply about Western culture's definitions of woman, man, intellect, tragedy, pride, change, and choice?

JONAH LEHRER

Jonah Lehrer (born 1981) is an American author and essayist. Lehrer earned a degree in neuroscience from Columbia, where he studied and worked as a research assistant under renowned neuroscientist Eric Kandel. Lehrer also studied pyschology, philosophy, and physiology at Oxford as a Rhodes Scholar. He has written two books, *Proust Was a Neuroscientist* (2007) and *How We Decide* (2010), and is a contributing editor at *Wired, Scientific American Mind,* and National Public Radio's *Radiolab.* He has also written for publications such as *Nature, The Boston Globe* and *The New Yorker,* in which "Don't" was first published in 2009—and subsequently named a "Best American Science Essay."

In "Don't," Lehrer discusses the issues of personality and self-control and their link to success in life, namely in academics. He blends genres, covering his topic from a scientific standpoint with in-depth reporting on experiments, while reaching a personal level, as well, profiling both the subjects and scientists involved.

Don't!

IN THE LATE NINETEEN SIXTIES, Carolyn Weisz, a four-year-old with long brown hair, was invited into a "game room" at the Bing Nursery School, on the campus of Stanford University. The room was little more than a large closet containing a desk and a chair. Carolyn was asked to sit down in the chair and pick a treat from a tray of marshmallows, cookies, and pretzel sticks. Carolyn chose the marshmallow. (Although she's now forty-four, Carolyn still has a weakness for those air-puffed balls of corn syrup and gelatin. "I know I shouldn't like them," she says. "But they're just so delicious!") A researcher then made Carolyn an offer: she could either eat one marshmallow right away or, if she was willing to wait while he stepped out for a few minutes, she could have two marshmallows   1

Jonah Lehrer. "Don't." New Yorker May 18, 2009 Best Am Science 2010. Used by permission of the author.

when he returned. He said that if she rang a bell on the desk while he was away, he would come running back, and she could eat one marshmallow but would forfeit the second. Then he left the room.

2   Although Carolyn has no direct memory of the experiment, and the scientists would not release any information about the subjects, she strongly suspects that she was able to delay gratification. "I've always been really good at waiting," Carolyn told me. "If you give me a challenge or a task, then I'm going to find a way to do it, even if it means not eating my favorite food." Her mother, Karen Sortino, is still more certain: "Even as a young kid, Carolyn was very patient. I'm sure she would have waited." But her brother Craig, who also took part in the experiment, displayed less fortitude. Craig, a year older than Carolyn, still remembers the torment of trying to wait. "At a certain point, it must have occurred to me that I was all by myself," he recalls. "And so I just started taking all the candy." According to Craig, he was also tested with little plastic toys—he could have a second one if he held out—and he broke into the desk, where he figured there would be additional toys. "I took everything I could," he says. "I cleaned them out. After that, I noticed the teachers encouraged me to not go into the experiment room anymore."

3   Footage of these experiments, which were conducted over several years, is poignant, as the kids struggle to delay gratification for just a little bit longer. Some cover their eyes with their hands or turn around so that they can't see the tray. Others start kicking the desk, or tug on their pigtails, or stroke the marshmallow as if it were a tiny stuffed animal. One child, a boy with neatly parted hair, looks carefully around the room to make sure that nobody can see him. Then he picks up an Oreo, delicately twists it apart, and licks off the white cream filling before returning the cookie to the tray, a satisfied look on his face.

4   Most of the children were like Craig. They struggled to resist the treat and held out for an average of less than three minutes. "A few kids ate the marshmallow right away," Walter Mischel, the Stanford professor of psychology in charge of the experiment, remembers. "They didn't even bother ringing the bell. Other kids would stare directly at the marshmallow and then ring the bell thirty seconds later." About 30 percent of the children, however, were like Carolyn. They successfully delayed gratification until the researcher returned, some fifteen minutes later. These kids wrestled with temptation but found a way to resist.

5   The initial goal of the experiment was to identify the mental processes that allowed some people to delay gratification while others simply surrendered. After publishing a few papers on the Bing studies in the early seventies, Mischel moved on to other areas of personality research. "There are only so many things you can do with kids trying not to eat marshmallows."

6   But occasionally Mischel would ask his three daughters, all of whom attended the Bing, about their friends from nursery school. "It was really just idle dinnertime conversation," he says. "I'd ask them, 'How's Jane?

How's Eric? How are they doing in school?' " Mischel began to notice a link between the children's academic performance as teenagers and their ability to wait for the second marshmallow. He asked his daughters to assess their friends academically on a scale of zero to five. Comparing these ratings with the original data set, he saw a correlation. "That's when I realized I had to do this seriously," he says. Starting in 1981, Mischel sent out a questionnaire to all the reachable parents, teachers, and academic advisers of the 653 subjects who had participated in the marshmallow task, who were by then in high school. He asked about every trait he could think of, from their capacity to plan and think ahead to their ability to "cope well with problems" and get along with their peers. He also requested their SAT scores.

Once Mischel began analyzing the results, he noticed that low 7 delayers, the children who rang the bell quickly, seemed more likely to have behavioral problems, both in school and at home. They got lower SAT scores. They struggled in stressful situations, often had trouble paying attention, and found it difficult to maintain friendships. The child who could wait fifteen minutes had an SAT score that was, on average, 210 points higher than that of the kid who could wait only thirty seconds.

Carolyn Weisz is a textbook example of a high delayer. She attended 8 Stanford as an undergraduate, and got her Ph.D. in social psychology at Princeton. She's now an associate psychology professor at the University of Puget Sound. Craig, meanwhile, moved to Los Angeles and has spent his career doing "all kinds of things" in the entertainment industry, mostly in production. He's currently helping to write and produce a film. "Sure, I wish I had been a more patient person," Craig says. "Looking back, there are definitely moments when it would have helped me make better career choices and stuff."

Mischel and his colleagues continued to track the subjects into their 9 late thirties. Ozlem Ayduk, an assistant professor of psychology at the University of California at Berkeley, found that low-delaying adults have a significantly higher body-mass index and are more likely to have had problems with drugs—but it was frustrating to have to rely on self-reports. "There's often a gap between what people are willing to tell you and how they behave in the real world," he explains. And so last year Mischel, who is now a professor at Columbia, and a team of collaborators began asking the original Bing subjects to travel to Stanford for a few days of experiments in an fMRI machine. Carolyn says she will be participating in the scanning experiments later this summer; Craig completed a survey several years ago but has yet to be invited to Palo Alto. The scientists are hoping to identify the particular brain regions that allow some people to delay gratification and control their temper. They're also conducting a variety of genetic tests, as they search for the hereditary characteristics that influence the ability to wait for a second marshmallow.

If Mischel and his team succeed, they will have outlined the neural 10 circuitry of self-control. For decades, psychologists have focused on raw intelligence as the most important variable when it comes to predicting success in life. Mischel argues that intelligence is largely at the mercy of self-control: even the smartest kids still need to do their homework. "What we're really measuring with the marshmallows isn't will power or self-control," Mischel says. "It's much more important than that. This task forces kids to find a way to make the situation work for them. They want the second marshmallow, but how can they get it? We can't control the world, but we can control how we think about it."

11   Walter Mischel is a slight, elegant man with a shaved head and a face of deep creases. He talks with a Brooklyn bluster, and he tends to act out his sentences, so that when he describes the marshmallow task he takes on the body language of an impatient four-year-old. "If you want to know why some kids can wait and others can't, then you've got to think like they think," Mischel says.

12   Mischel was born in Vienna in 1930. His father was a modestly successful businessman with a fondness for cafe society and Esperanto, while his mother spent many of her days lying on the couch with an ice pack on her forehead, trying to soothe her frail nerves. The family considered itself fully assimilated, but after the Nazi annexation of Austria in 1938, Mischel remembers being taunted in school by the Hitler Youth and watching as his father, hobbled by childhood polio, was forced to limp through the streets in his pajamas. A few weeks after the takeover, while the family was burning evidence of their Jewish ancestry in the fireplace, Walter found a long-forgotten certificate of U.S. citizenship issued to his maternal grandfather decades earlier, thus saving his family.

13   The family settled in Brooklyn, where Mischel's parents opened up a five-and-dime. Mischel attended New York University, studying poetry under Delmore Schwartz and Allen Tale, and taking studio-art classes with Philip Guston. He also became fascinated by psychoanalysis and new measures of personality, such as the Rorschach test. "At the time, it seemed like a mental X-ray machine," he says. "You could solve a person by showing them a picture." Although he was pressured to join his uncle's umbrella business, he ended up pursuing a Ph.D. in clinical psychology at Ohio State.

14   But Mischel noticed that academic theories had limited applica-tion, and he was, struck by the futility of most personality science. He still flinches at the naiveté of graduate students who based their diagnoses on a battery of meaningless tests. In 1955 Mischel was offered an opportunity to study the "spirit possession" ceremonies of the Orisha faith in Trinidad, and he leapt at the chance. Although his research was supposed to involve the use of Rorschach tests to explore the connections between the unconscious and the behavior of people when possessed, Mischel soon grew interested in a different project. He lived in a part of the island that was evenly split between people of East Indian and of African descent; he noticed that each

group defined the other in broad stereotypes. "The East Indians would describe the Africans as impulsive hedonists who were always living for the moment and never thought about the future," he says. "The Africans, meanwhile, would say that the East Indians didn't know how to live and would stuff money in their mattress and never enjoy themselves."

Mischel took young children from both ethnic groups and offered 15 them a simple choice: they could have a miniature chocolate bar right away or, if they waited a few days, they could get a much bigger chocolate bar. Mischel's results failed to justify the stereo-types—other variables, such as whether or not the children lived with their father, turned out to be much more important—but they did get him interested in the question of delayed gratification. Why did some children wait and not others? What made waiting possible? Unlike the broad traits supposedly assessed by personality tests, self-control struck Mischel as potentially measurable.

In 1958 Mischel became an assistant professor in the Department of 16 Social Relations at Harvard. One of his first tasks was to develop a survey course on "personality assessment," but Mischel quickly concluded that while prevailing theories held personality traits to be broadly consistent, the available data didn't back up this assumption. Personality, at least as it was then conceived, couldn't be reliably assessed at all. A few years later, he was hired as a consultant on a personality assessment initiated by the Peace Corps. Early Peace Corps volunteers had sparked several embarrass-ing international incidents—one mailed a postcard on which she expressed disgust at the sanitary habits of her host country—so the Kennedy adminis-tration wanted a screening process to eliminate people unsuited for foreign assignments. Volunteers were tested for standard personality traits, and Mischel compared the results with ratings of how well the volunteers per-formed in the field. He found no correlation; the time-consuming tests pre-dicted nothing. At this point, Mischel realized that the problem wasn't the tests—it was their premise. Psychologists had spent decades searching for traits that exist independently of circumstance, but what if personality can't be separated from context? "It went against the way we'd been thinking about personality since the four humors and the ancient Greeks," he says.

While Mischel was beginning to dismantle the methods of his field, 17 the Harvard psychology department was in tumult. In 1960 the personality psychologist Timothy Leary helped start the Harvard Psilocybin Project, which consisted mostly of self-experimentation. Mischel remembers graduate students' desks giving way to mattresses, and large packages from Ciba chemicals, in Switzerland, arriving in the mail. Mischel had nothing against hippies, but he wanted modern psychology to be rigorous and empirical. And so, in 1962, Walter Mischel moved to Palo Alto and went to work at Stanford.

There is something deeply contradictory about Walter Mischel—a 18 psychologist who spent decades critiquing the validity of personality tests—inventing the marshmallow task, a simple test with impressive predictive power. Mischel, however, insists there is no contradiction. "I've always believed there are consistencies in a person that can be looked at," he says. "We just have to look in the right way." One of Mischel's classic studies documented the aggressive behavior of children in a variety of situations at a summer camp in New Hampshire. Most psychologists assumed that aggression was a stable trait, but Mischel found that children's responses depended on the details of the interaction. The same child might consistently lash out when teased by a peer but readily submit to adult punishment. Another might react badly to a warning from a counselor but play well with his bunkmates. Aggression was best assessed in terms of what Mischel called "if-then patterns." If a certain child was teased by a peer, then he would be aggressive.

19   One of Mischel's favorite metaphors for this model of personality, known as interactionism, concerns a car making a screeching noise. How does a mechanic solve the problem? He begins by trying to identify the specific conditions that trigger the noise. Is there a screech when the car is accelerating, or when it's shifting gears, or turning at slow speeds? Unless the mechanic can give the screech a context, he'll never find the broken part. Mischel wanted psychologists to think like mechanics and look at people's responses under particular conditions. The challenge was devising a test that accurately simulated something relevant to the behavior being predicted. The search for a meaningful test of personality led Mischel to revisit, in 1968, the protocol he'd used on young children in Trinidad nearly a decade earlier. The experiment seemed especially relevant now that he had three young daughters of his own. "Young kids are pure id," Mischel says. "They start off unable to wait for anything—whatever they want they need. But then, as I watched my own kids, I marveled at how they gradually learned how to delay and how that made so many other things possible."

20   A few years earlier, in 1966, the Stanford psychology department had established the Bing Nursery School. The classrooms were designed as working laboratories, with large one-way mirrors that allowed researchers to observe the children. This past February, Jennifer Winters, the assistant director of the school, showed me around the building. While the Bing is still an active center of research—the children quickly learn to ignore the students scribbling in notebooks—Winters isn't sure that Mischel's marshmallow task could be replicated today. "We recently tried to do a version of it, and the kids were very excited about having food in the game room," she says. "There are so many allergies and peculiar diets today that we don't do many things with food."

21   Mischel perfected his protocol by testing his daughters at the kitchen table. "When you're investigating will power in a four-year-old, little things make a big difference," he says. "How big should the marshmallows be? What kind of cookies work best?" After several months of patient tinkering, Mischel came up with an experimental design that closely simulated

the difficulty of delayed gratification. In the spring of 1968, he conducted the first trials of his experiment at the Bing. "I knew we'd designed it well when a few kids wanted to quit as soon as we explained the conditions to them," he says. "They knew this was going to be very difficult."

At the time, psychologists assumed that children's ability to wait depended 22 on how badly they wanted the marshmallow. But it soon became obvious that every child craved the extra treat. What, then, determined self-control? Mischel's conclusion, based on hundreds of hours of observation, was that the crucial skill was the "strategic allocation of attention." Instead of getting obsessed with the marshmallow—the "hot stimulus"—the patient children distracted themselves by covering their eyes, pretending to play hide-and-seek underneath the desk, or singing songs from *Sesame Street*. Their desire wasn't defeated—it was merely forgotten. "If you're thinking about the marshmallow and how delicious it is, then you're going to eat it," Mischel says. "The key is to avoid thinking about it in the first place."

In adults, this skill is often referred to as metacognition, or 23 thinking about thinking, and it's what allows people to outsmart their shortcomings. (When Odysseus had himself tied to the ship's mast, he was using some of the skills of metacognition: knowing he wouldn't be able to resist the Sirens' song, he made it impossible to give in.) Mischel's large data set from various studies allowed him to see that children with a more accurate understanding of the workings of self-control were better able to delay gratification. "What's interesting about four-year-olds is that they're just figuring out the rules of thinking," Mischel says. "The kids who couldn't delay would often have the rules backward. They would think that the best way to resist the marshmallow is to stare right at it, to keep a close eye on the goal. But that's a terrible idea. If you do that, you're going to ring the bell before I leave the room."

According to Mischel, this view of will power also helps explain 24 why the marshmallow task is such a powerfully predictive test. "If you can deal with hot emotions, then you can study for the SAT instead of watching television," Mischel says. "And you can save more money for retirement. It's not just about marshmallows."

Subsequent work by Mischel and his colleagues found that these 25 differences were observable in subjects as young as nineteen months. Looking at how toddlers responded when briefly separated from their mothers, they found that some immediately burst into tears or clung to the door, but others were able to overcome their anxiety by distracting themselves, often by playing with toys. When the scientists set the same children the marshmallow task at the age of five, they found that the kids who had cried also struggled to resist the tempting treat.

The early appearance of the ability to delay suggests that it has a 26 genetic origin, an example of personality at its most predetermined, Mischel resists such an easy conclusion. "In general, trying to separate nature and nurture makes about as much sense as trying to separate personality and situation," he says. "The two influences are completely interrelated." For instance, when Mischel gave delay-of-gratification tasks to children from low-income families in the Bronx, he noticed that their ability to delay was below average, at least compared with that of children in Palo Alto. "When you grow up poor, you might not practice delay as much," he says. "And if you don't practice, then you'll never figure out how to distract yourself. You won't develop the best delay strategies, and those strategies won't become second nature." In other words, people learn how to use their mind just as they learn how to use a computer: through trial and error.

27   But Mischel has found a shortcut. When he and his colleagues taught children a simple set of mental tricks—such as pretending that the candy is only a picture, surrounded by an imaginary frame—he dramatically improved their self-control. The kids who hadn't been able to wait sixty seconds could now wait fifteen minutes. "All I've done is given them some tips from their mental user manual," Mischel says. "Once you realize that will power is just a matter of learning how to control your attention and thoughts, you can really begin to increase it."

28   Marc Berman, a lanky graduate student with an easy grin, speaks about his research with the infectious enthusiasm of a freshman taking his first philosophy class. Berman works in the lab of John Jonides, a psychologist and neuroscientist at the University of Michigan, who is in charge of the brain-scanning experiments on the original Bing subjects. He knows that testing forty-year-olds for self-control isn't a straightforward proposition. "We can't give these people marshmallows," Berman says. "They know they're part of a long-term study that looks at delay of gratification, so if you give them an obvious delay task they'll do their best to resist. You'll get a bunch of people who refuse to touch their marshmallow."

29   This meant that Jonides and his team had to find a way to measure will power indirectly. Operating on the premise that the ability to delay eating the marshmallow had depended on a child's ability to banish thoughts of it, they decided on a series of tasks that measure the ability of subjects to control the contents of working memory—the relatively limited amount of information we're able to consciously consider at any given moment. According to Jonides, this is how self-control "cashes out" in the real world: as an ability to direct the spotlight of attention so that our decisions aren't determined by the wrong thoughts.

30   Last summer the scientists chose fifty-five subjects, equally split between high delayers and low delayers, and sent each one a laptop computer loaded with working-memory experiments. Two of the experiments were of particular interest. The first is a straightforward exercise known as the "suppression task." Subjects are given four random words, two printed in blue and two in red. After reading the words, they're told to forget the blue words and remember the red words. Then the scientists

provide a stream of "probe words" and ask the subjects whether the probes are the words they were asked to remember. Though the task doesn't seem to involve delayed gratification, it tests the same basic mechanism. Interestingly, the scientists found that high delayers were significantly better at the suppression task: they were less likely to think that a word they'd been asked to forget was something they should remember.

In the second, known as the Go/No Go task, subjects are flashed a set of faces with various expressions. At first, they are told to press the space bar whenever they see a smile. This takes little effort, since smiling faces automatically trigger what's known as "approach behavior." After a few minutes, however, subjects are told to press the space bar when they see frowning faces. They are now being forced to act against an impulse. Results show that high delayers are more successful at not pressing the button in response to a smiling face.

When I first started talking to the scientists about these tasks last summer, they were clearly worried that they wouldn't find any behavioral differences between high and low delayers. It wasn't until early January that they had enough data to begin their analysis (not surprisingly, it took much longer to get the laptops back from the low delayers), but it soon became obvious that there were provocative differences between the two groups. A graph of the data shows that as the delay time of the four-year-olds decreases, the number of mistakes made by the adults sharply rises.

The big remaining question for the scientists is whether these behavioral differences are detectable in an fMRI machine. Although the scanning has just begun—Jonides and his team are still working out the kinks—the scientists sound confident. "These tasks have been studied so many times that we pretty much know where to look and what we're going to find," Jonides says. He rattles off a short list of relevant brain regions, which his lab has already identified as being responsible for working-memory exercises. For the most part, the regions are in the frontal cortex—the overhang of brain behind the eyes—and include the dorsolateral prefrontal cortex, the anterior prefrontal cortex, the anterior cingulate, and the right and left inferior frontal gyri. While these cortical folds have long been associated with self-control, they're also essential for working memory and directed attention. According to the scientists, that's not an accident. "These are powerful instincts telling us to reach for the marshmallow or press the space bar," Jonides says. "The only way to defeat them is to avoid them, and that means paying attention to something else. We call that will power, but it's got nothing to do with the will."

The behavioral and genetic aspects of the project are overseen by Yuichi Shoda, a professor of psychology at the University of Washington, who was one of Mischel's graduate students. He's been following these "marshmallow subjects" for more than thirty years: he knows everything about them, from their academic records and their social graces to their ability to deal with frustration and stress. The prognosis for the genetic research remains uncertain. Although many studies have searched for the underpinnings of personality since the completion of the Human Genome Project in 2003, many of the relevant genes remain in question. "We're incredibly complicated creatures," Shoda says. "Even the simplest aspects of personality are driven by dozens and dozens of different genes." The scientists have decided to focus on genes in the dopamine pathways, since those neurotransmitters are believed to regulate both motivation and attention. However, even if minor coding differences influence delay ability—and that's a likely possibility—Shoda doesn't expect to discover these differences: the sample size is simply too small.

35   In recent years, researchers have begun making house visits to many of the original subjects, including Carolyn Weisz, as they try to better understand the familial contexts that shape self-control. "They turned my kitchen into a lab," Carolyn told me. "They set up a little tent where they tested my oldest daughter on the delay task with some cookies. I remember thinking, I really hope she can wait."

36   While Mischel closely follows the steady accumulation of data from the laptops and the brain scans, he's most excited by what comes next. "I'm not interested in looking at the brain just so we can use a fancy machine," he says. "The real question is what can we do with this fMRI data that we couldn't do before?" Mischel is applying for an NIH grant to investigate various mental illnesses, like obsessive-compulsive disorder and attention-deficit disorder, in terms of the ability to control and direct attention. Mischel and his team hope to identify crucial neural circuits that cut across a wide variety of ailments. If there is such a circuit, then the same cognitive tricks that increase delay time in a four-year-old might help adults deal with their symptoms. Mischel is particularly excited by the example of the substantial subset of people who failed the marshmallow task as four-year-olds but ended up becoming high-delaying adults. "This is the group I'm most interested in," he says. "They have substantially improved their lives."

37   Mischel is also preparing a large-scale study involving hundreds of schoolchildren in Philadelphia, Seattle, and New York City to see if self-control skills can be taught. Although he previously showed that children did much better on the marshmallow task after being taught a few simple "mental transformations," such as pretending; the marshmallow was a cloud, it remains unclear if these new skills persist over the long term. In other words, do the tricks work only during the experiment or do the children learn to apply them at home, when deciding between homework and television?

38   Angela Lee Duckworth, an assistant professor of psychology at the University of Pennsylvania, is leading the program. She first grew interested in the subject after working as a high school math teacher. "For the most part, it was an incredibly frustrating experience," she says. "I gradually became convinced that trying to teach a teenager algebra when they don't have self-control is a pretty futile exercise." And so, at the age

of thirty-two, Duckworth decided to become a psychologist. One of her main research projects looked at the relationship between self-control and grade point average. She found that the ability to delay gratification—eighth-graders were given a choice between a dollar right away or two dollars the following week—was a far better predictor of academic performance than IQ. She said that her study shows that "intelligence is really important, but it's still not as important as self-control."

Last year, Duckworth and Mischel were approached by David Levin, 39 the cofounder of KIPP, an organization of sixty-six public charter schools across the country. KIPP schools are known for their long workday—students are in class from 7:25 A.M. to 5 P.M.—and for dramatic improvement of inner-city students' test scores. (More than 80 percent of eighth-graders at the KIPP academy in the South Bronx scored at or above grade level in reading and math, which was nearly twice the New York City average.) "The core feature of the KIPP approach is that character matters for success," Levin says. "Educators like to talk about character skills when kids are in kindergarten—we send young kids home with a report card about 'working well with others' or 'not talking out of turn.' But then, just when these skills start to matter, we stop trying to improve them. We just throw up our hands and complain."

Self-control is one of the fundamental "character strengths" 40 emphasized by KIPP—the KIPP academy in Philadelphia, for instance, gives its students a shirt emblazoned with the slogan "Don't Eat the Marshmallow." Levin, however, remained unsure about how well the program was working—"We know how to teach math skills, but it's harder to measure character strengths," he says—so he contacted Duckworth and Mischel, promising them unfettered access to KIPP students. Levin also helped bring together additional schools willing to take part in the experiment, including Riverdale Country School, a private school in the Bronx; the Evergreen School for gifted children, in Shoreline, Washington; and the Mastery Charter Schools, in Philadelphia.

For the past few months, the researchers have been conducting pilot 41 studies in the classroom as they try to figure out the most effective way to introduce complex psychological concepts to young children. Because the study will focus on students between the ages of four and eight, the classroom lessons will rely heavily on peer modeling, such as showing kindergarteners a video of a child successfully distracting herself during the marshmallow task. The scientists have some encouraging preliminary results—after just a few sessions, students show significant improvements in the ability to deal with hot emotional states—but they are cautious about predicting the outcome of the long-term study. "When you do these large-scale educational studies, there are ninety-nine uninteresting reasons the study could fail," Duckworth says. "Maybe a teacher doesn't show the video, or maybe there's a field trip on the day of the testing. This is what keeps me up at night."

Mischel's main worry is that even if his lesson plan proves to be 42 effective, it might still be overwhelmed by variables the scientists can't control, such as the home environment. He knows that it's not enough just to teach kids mental tricks—the real challenge is turning those tricks into habits, and that requires years of diligent practice. "This is where your parents are important," Mischel says. "Have they established rituals that force you to delay on a daily basis? Do they encourage you to wait? And do they make waiting worthwhile?" According to Mischel, even the most mundane routines of childhood—such as not snacking before dinner, or saving up your allowance, or holding out until Christmas morning—are really sly exercises in cognitive training: we're teaching ourselves how to think so that we can outsmart our desires. But Mischel isn't satisfied with such an informal approach. "We should give marshmallows to every kindergartner," he says. "We should say, 'You see this marshmallow? You don't have to eat it. You can wait. Here's how.'"

Content

1. Briefly summarize the "marshmallow experiment." How is it possible for researchers to make generalizations on the basis of such a simple experiment with four-year-old children that account for personality traits and success when they're much older? Do you find the evidence convincing?

2. Why did it take the researcher, Walter Mischel, a Stanford psychologist, more than a decade for the implications of his research to dawn on him (See ¶s 5–6)?

3. "For decades, psychologists have focused on raw intelligence as the most important variable when it comes to predicting success in life. Mischel argues that intelligence is largely at the mercy of self-control: even the smartest kids still need to do their homework" (¶ 10). If true, how can self-control and delayed gratification be encouraged, by parents and teachers, without thoroughly frustrating children and interfering with their natural spontaneity?

4. Why to Mischel is the most interesting group "the subset of people who failed the marshmallow task as four-year-olds but ended up becoming high-delaying adults . . . They have substantially improved their lives" (¶36)? This research is still in progress; the results aren't in. What factors might have influenced this significant change of behavior? Can people will themselves to change their basic personality traits?

5. On the down side, if children aren't trained for "self-control" as very young people, can they learn this later on? Are people lacking in self-control as it is described throughout this essay doomed to failure later in life? How important is this particular single factor in a person's identity? Is Mischel over-rating its importance?

Strategies/Structures/Language

6. " 'If you can deal with hot emotions, then you can study for the SAT instead of watching television,' Mischel says, 'And you can save more money for retirement. It's not just about marshmallows." To what extent does Mischel's research depend on analogy? Are these analogies convincing? Why or why not?

7. The language of Lehrer's essay is simple, easy to read. Does this mean that the ideas it conveys are also simple? If so, why weren't they immediately apparent to researchers? Is there any predictable pace of scientific research, allowing for differences within or across fields?

For Writing

8. Test out for yourself the premises of the delayed gratification experiment. Try delaying your gratification three times, under different circumstances. Whether the stakes are low (an extra marshmallow) or higher, what does your informal research tell you about yourself? Are you a high delayer? Or a low delayer? Does your life pattern to date corroborate Mischel's personality assessment?

9. *Dialogue.* With a partner who has also tried this out, write up the results of your investigation in a conventional scientific format: research question; literature review–optional; research method; results; interpretation; generalization, if possible. Do your conclusions confirm Mischel's? Why or why not?

10. *Second look.* Why, in your experience, do some people of any age delay gratification and others don't? Do the reasons Mischel offers corroborate your own understanding of the issue? To what extent can you attribute your successes/failures in life to this or any other single personality characteristic?

11. If you don't like this aspect of your behavior/personality, are you willing to change it? Come up with a proposal for a plan of action. Would it be as simple as Mischel's "We parents and psychologists 'should give marshmallows to every kindergartner. We should say, 'You see this marshmallow? You don't have to eat it. You can wait. Here's how'" (¶ 42).

VIRGINIA POSTREL

Virginia Postrel (born 1960) graduated from Princeton (1982) with a degree in English. A writer on cultural and economic topics for many publications, including the *Wall Street Journal*, she was an economics columnist for *The New York Times* (2000–2006) and is currently a contributing editor for the *Atlantic Monthly* and a columnist for *Forbes*. She has been a media fellow at the Hoover Institution at Stanford University and is the author of *The Future and Its Enemies: The Growing Conflict Over Creativity, Enterprise, and Progress* (1998) and *The Substance of Style: How the Rise of Aesthetic Value is Remaking Commerce, Culture, and Consciousness* (2004). In "The Truth About Beauty," first published in the *Atlantic Monthly* in 2007, Postrel argues that by selling the idea that all women are beautiful, Dove's "Campaign for Real Beauty" actually reinforces our culture's perception of beauty as the source and measure of a woman's value.

The Truth About Beauty

Cosmetics makers have always sold "hope in a jar"—creams and 1 potions that promise youth, beauty, sex appeal, and even love for the women who use them. Over the last few years, the marketers at

Dove have added some new-and-improved enticements. They're now promising self-esteem and cultural transformation. Dove's "Campaign for Real Beauty," declares a press release, is "a global effort that is intended to serve as a starting point for societal change and act as a catalyst for widening the definition and discussion of beauty." Along with its thigh-firming creams, self-tanners, and hair conditioners, Dove is peddling the crowd-pleasing notions that beauty is a media creation, that recognizing plural forms of beauty is the same as declaring every woman beautiful, and that self-esteem means ignoring imperfections.

2   Dove won widespread acclaim in June 2005 when it rolled out its thigh-firming cream with billboards of attractive but variously sized "real women" frolicking in their underwear. It advertised its hair-care products by showing hundreds of women in identical platinum-blonde wigs—described as "the kind of hair found in magazines"—tossing off those artificial manes and celebrating their real (perfectly styled, colored, and conditioned) hair. It ran print ads that featured atypical models, including a plump brunette and a ninety-five-year-old, and invited readers to choose between pejorative and complimentary adjectives: "Wrinkled or wonderful?" "Oversized or outstanding?" The public and press got the point, and Dove got attention. Oprah covered the story, and so did the *Today* show. Dove's campaign, wrote *Advertising Age*, "undermines the basic proposition of decades of beauty-care advertising by telling women—and young girls—they're beautiful just the way they are."

3   Last fall, Dove extended its image building with a successful bit of viral marketing: a seventy-five-second online video called *Evolution*. Created by Ogilvy & Mather, the video is a close-up of a seemingly ordinary woman, shot in harsh lighting that calls attention to her uneven skin tone, slightly lopsided eyes, and dull, flat hair. In twenty seconds of time-lapse video, makeup artists and hair stylists turn her into a wide-eyed, big-haired beauty with sculpted cheeks and perfect skin. It's *Extreme Makeover* without the surgical gore.

4   But that's only the beginning. Next comes the digital transformation, as a designer points-and-clicks on the model's photo, giving her a longer, slimmer neck, a slightly narrower upper face, fuller lips, bigger eyes, and more space between her eyebrows and eyes. The perfected image rises to fill a billboard advertising a fictitious line of makeup. Fade to black, with the message "No wonder our perception of beauty is distorted." The video has attracted more than 3 million YouTube views. It also appears on Dove's campaignforrealbeauty.com Web site, where it concludes, "Every girl deserves to feel beautiful just the way she is."

5   Every girl certainly wants to, which explains the popularity of Dove's campaign. There's only one problem: Beauty exists, and it's unevenly distributed. Our eyes and brains pretty consistently like some human forms better than others. Shown photos of strangers, even babies look longer at the faces adults rank the best-looking. Whether you prefer Nicole Kidman to Angelina Jolie, Jennifer Lopez to Halle Berry, or Queen Latifah to Kate Moss may be a matter of taste, but rare is the beholder

who would declare Holly Hunter or Whoopi Goldberg—neither of whom is homely—more beautiful than any of these women.

For similar reasons, we still thrill to the centuries-old bust of Nefertiti, the Venus de Milo, and the exquisite faces painted by Leonardo and Botticelli. Greta Garbo's acting style seems stilted today, but her face transcends time. We know beauty when we see it, and our reactions are remarkably consistent. Beauty is not just a social construct, and not every girl is beautiful just the way she is.

Take Dove's *Evolution* video. The digital transformation is fascinating because it magically makes a beautiful woman more striking. Her face's new geometry triggers an immediate, visceral response—and the video's storytelling impact is dependent on that predictable reaction. The video makes its point about artifice only because most people find the manipulated face more beautiful than the natural one.

In *Survival of the Prettiest: The Science of Beauty*, Nancy Etcoff, a psychologist at Harvard Medical School, reported on experiments that

Courtesy of Unilever

In this composite of stills from Dove's viral-marketing video, the left half depicts the "evolution" of the face represented from the right half of the original photograph. What changes have been made: in eye; nose; lips—upper and lower; skin—color, texture, highlights; length of neck: hair—style, volume, highlights: clothing—color, design, exposure of shoulder and bone structure? What apples does the altered half of the photograph contain that are absent from the original? Is beauty, and perhaps sexiness or other types of appeal, in the mind of the subject, the photo-manipulator/ad designer, the viewer, or all of these?

let people rate faces and digitally "breed" ever-more-attractive composite generations. The results for female faces look a lot like the finished product in the Dove video: "thinner jaws, larger eyes relative to the size of their faces, and shorter distances between their mouths and chins" in one case, and "fuller lips, a less robust jaw, a smaller nose and smaller chin than the population average" in another. These features, wrote Etcoff, "exaggerate the ways that adult female faces differ from adult male faces. They also exaggerate the youthfulness of the face." More than youth, the full lips and small jaws of beautiful women reflect relatively high levels of female hormones and low levels of male hormones—indicating greater fertility—according to psychologist Victor Johnston, who did some of these experiments.

9   More generally, evolutionary psychologists suggest that the features we see as beautiful—including indicators of good health like smooth skin and symmetry—have been rewarded through countless generations of competition for mates. The same evolutionary pressures, this research suggests, have biologically programmed human minds to perceive these features as beautiful. "Some scientists believe that our beauty detectors are really detectors for the combination of youth and femininity," wrote Etcoff. Whether the beauty we detect arises from nature or artifice doesn't change that visceral reflex.

10   Perhaps surprisingly, Etcoff herself advised Dove on several rounds of survey research and helped the company create workshops for girls. Dove touts her involvement (and her doctorate and Harvard affiliation) in its publicity materials. She sees the campaign as a useful corrective. Media images, Etcoff notes in an e-mail, are often so rarefied that "they change our ideas about what people look like and what normal looks like . . . Our brains did not evolve with media, and many people see more media images of women than actual women. The contrast effect makes even the most beautiful non-model look less attractive; it produces a new 'normal.'"

11   Dove began its campaign by recognizing the diverse manifestations of universally beautiful patterns. The "real women" pictured in the thigh-cream billboards may not have looked like super-models, but they were all young, with symmetrical faces, feminine features, great skin, white teeth, and hourglass shapes. Even the most zaftig had relatively flat stomachs and clearly defined waists. These pretty women were not a random sample of the population. Dove diversified the portrait of beauty without abandoning the concept altogether.

12   But the campaign didn't stop there. Dove is defining itself as the brand that loves regular women—and regular women, by definition, are not extraordinarily beautiful. The company can't afford a precise definition of *real beauty* that might exclude half the population—not a good strategy for selling mass-market consumer products. So the campaign leaves *real beauty* ambiguous, enabling the viewers to fill in the concept with their own desires. Some take *real beauty* to mean "nature unretouched" and interpret the *Evolution* video as suggesting that uncannily beautiful faces are not merely rare but nonexistent. Others emphasize the importance of

character and personality: Real beauty comes from the inside, not physical appearance. And *Advertising Age*'s interpretation is common: that Dove is reminding women that "they're beautiful just the way they are."

Another Dove ad, focusing on girls' insecurities about their looks, 13 concludes, "Every girl deserves to feel good about herself and see how beautiful she really is." Here, Dove is encouraging the myth that physical beauty is a false concept, and, at the same time, falsely equating beauty with goodness and self-worth. If you don't see perfection in the mirror, it suggests, you've been duped by the media and suffer from low self-esteem.

But adult women have a more realistic view. "Only two percent 14 of women describe themselves as beautiful" trumpets the headline of Dove's press release. Contrary to what the company wants readers to believe, however, that statistic doesn't necessarily represent a crisis of confidence; it may simply reflect the power of the word *beautiful*. Dove's surveys don't ask women if they think they're unattractive or ugly, so it's hard to differentiate between knowing you have flaws, believing you're acceptably but unimpressively plain, and feeling worthlessly hideous. In another Dove survey, 88 percent of the American women polled said they're at least somewhat satisfied with their face, while 76 percent said they're at least somewhat satisfied with their body. But dissatisfaction is not the same as unhappiness or insecurity.

Like the rest of the genetic lottery, beauty is unfair. Everyone falls short 15 of perfection, but some are luckier than others. Real confidence requires self-knowledge, which includes recognizing one's shortcomings as well as one's strengths. At a recent conference on biological manipulations, I heard a philosopher declare during lunch that she'd never have plastic surgery or even dye her hair. But, she confessed, she'd pay just about anything for fifteen more IQ points. This woman is not insecure about her intelligence, which is far above average; she'd just like to be smarter. Asking women to say they're beautiful is like asking intellectuals to say they're geniuses. Most know they simply don't qualify.

Content

1. What is Postrel's thesis? Why does she consider a marketing campaign based on the idea that "beauty is a media creation" (¶ 1), an appealing, if disingenuous ploy? What evidence does she provide in support of the idea that "beauty exists" (¶ 5)? If beauty does exist, why, according to Postrel, is Dove's message so appealing? Why does she suggest that Dove's professed goal of "widening the definition" of beauty (¶ 1) "falsely [equates] beauty with goodness and self-worth" (¶ 13)?

2. Postrel argues that "recognizing plural forms of beauty" is *not* the same "as declaring every woman beautiful" (¶ 1). How do the Dove advertisements Postrel describes in paragraph 2 make such an association? Why does Postel consider these ads misleading? Does her argument imply that beauty *doesn't* exist in plural forms?

Strategies/Structures/Language

3. Postrel's list of beauties in paragraphs 5 and 6 consists of film stars, singers, models, the Egyptian queen Nefertiti, an ancient Greek marble sculpture, and the creations of two Renaissance artists (Leonardo da Vinci and Sandro Botticelli). What do these beauties have in common? When Postrel writes that "our eyes and brains pretty consistently like some human forms better than others" (¶ 5), who does the plural pronoun "our" include? How has Postrel constructed her list to support her overall argument?

4. According to Postrel, what does the preference for one face over another indicate? Must the reader agree that Queen Latifah and Jennifer Lopez are more beautiful than Holly Hunter and Whoopi Goldberg (¶ 5) to agree with Postrel's argument? Might you find these women beautiful in different ways and still find Postrel's argument persuasive?

5. Postrel argues that beauty is rewarded "through countless generations of competition for mates" (¶ 9) and is an evolutionary device that signals "greater fertility" (¶ 8). Do you see a contradiction between this assertion and her observation that "regular women, by definition, are not extraordinarily beautiful" (¶ 12)? Explain.

For Writing

6. *Journal Writing.* Do you agree with Postrel that self-esteem does *not* come from "ignoring imperfections" (¶ 1), but rather, from "recognizing one's shortcomings as well as one's strengths" (¶ 15)? How do you define "shortcomings"? Is physical attractiveness, like the development of one's intelligence or talents, a matter of "the genetic lottery" (¶ 15), or a question of lifestyle, appropriate choices, attitude, and discipline? Must beauty necessarily be related to one's physical appearance?

7. *Dialogues.* "Introducing **new** GoValue!™ Service" (470) satirically redefines concepts such as freedom, convenience, and privacy. How, according to Postrel, does Dove redefine beauty? How would you create a cosmetic company's advertisement similar to "GoValue!™ Service"? For example, the ad copy might read "Overweight? Don't worry! Fat is the new thin!" or "Crows feet got you down? Remember, age is just a number—and we've got the anti-wrinkle cream to keep that number at bay." Alternatively, you might create a satiric narrative that explores concepts of beauty and self-esteem in the vein of Lynda Barry's "Common Scents" (318–28) or Suzanne Britt's "That Lean and Hungry Look" (358–61). Experiment with a variety of devices such as self-deprecation, exaggeration, irreverence, and slang to examine cultural ideas about beauty, age, race, and body type.

GELAREH ASAYESH

"When a natural disaster hits, people talk for years about . . . the power of the earth tremor that remade the landscape of their lives. But the emotional disasters in our lives go largely unacknowledged, their repercussions unclaimed," says Gelareh Asayesh, in *Saffron Sky*, of her parents' decision in 1977 to move the family from Tehran, Iran (where she was born in 1961), to Chapel Hill, North Carolina. In Iran they lived in material comfort but in political opposition to the repressive Shah.

In Chapel Hill, as graduate students, they became outsiders, "wrenched from all that was loved and familiar" in Iran, "faced with an unspoken choice: to be alienated from the world around us or from our innermost selves." Although Asayesh was educated at the University of North Carolina-Chapel Hill and went on to become a journalist working for the *Boston Globe,* the *Miami Herald,* and the *Baltimore Sun,* the appeals and tensions of these contradictory cultures have never been fully resolved.

In *Saffron Sky: A Life Between Iran and America* (1999), Asayesh explores the contrasts between these two ways of life, her ambivalent attitude toward her homeland intensified by her marriage to an American and her own parenthood. Returning to Iran in October 1990, just before the Persian Gulf war, Asayesh is newly aware of the world of "rigidity and restriction"—rules against wearing lipstick, or too sheer stockings, or letting the hair show—enforced by the intrusive gender police. Yet, as "Shrouded in Contradiction," published in the *New York Times Magazine* (November 2001), reveals, "To wear *hijab* is to invite contradiction. Sometimes I hate it. Sometimes I value it"—as a covering of both restriction and freedom.

Shrouded in Contradiction

I grew up wearing the miniskirt to school, the veil to the mosque. In the Tehran of my childhood, women in bright sundresses shared the sidewalk with women swathed in black. The tension between the two ways of life was palpable. As a schoolgirl, I often cringed when my bare legs got leering or contemptuous glances. Yet, at times, I long for the days when I could walk the streets of my country with the wind in my hair. When clothes were clothes. In today's Iran, whatever I wear sends a message. If it's a chador, it embarrasses my Westernized relatives. If it's a skimpy scarf, I risk being accused of stepping on the blood of the martyrs who died in the war with Iraq. Each time I return to Tehran, I wait until the last possible moment, when my plane lands on the tarmac, to don the scarf and long jacket that many Iranian women wear in lieu of a veil. To wear hijab—Islamic covering—is to invite contradiction. Sometimes I hate it. Sometimes I value it. 1

Most of the time, I don't even notice it. It's annoying, but so is wearing pantyhose to work. It ruins my hair, but so does the humidity in Florida, where I live. For many women, the veil is neither a symbol nor a statement. It's simply what they wear, as their mothers did before them. Something to dry your face with after your ablutions before prayer. A place for a toddler to hide when he's feeling shy. Even for a woman like me, who wears it with a hint of rebellion, *hijab* is just not that big a deal. 2

Except when it is. 3

Reuters/Corbis Wire/Corbis

In what ways does the clothing depicted in this photograph signal the identity of each figure? According to the dimensions of gender, nationality/ethnicity, age? What gender is the child? How can you tell? What are the men doing? The women? In what ways do their postures, the direction of their gazes indicate their relationships? What political statements does this photograph make?

4   "Sister, what kind of get-up is this?" a woman in black, one of a pair, asks me one summer day on the Caspian shore. I am standing in line to ride a gondola up a mountain, where I'll savor some ice cream along with vistas of sea and forest. Women in chadors stand wilting in the heat, faces gleaming with sweat. Women in makeup and clunky heels wear knee-length jackets with pants, their hair daringly exposed beneath sheer scarves.

5   None have been more daring than I. I've wound my scarf into a turban, leaving my neck bare to the breeze. The woman in black is a government employee paid to police public morals. "Fix your scarf at once!" she snaps.

6   "But I'm hot," I say.

7   "You're hot?" she exclaims. "Don't you think we all are?"

8   I start unwinding my makeshift turban. "The men aren't hot," I mutter.

9   Her companion looks at me in shocked reproach. "Sister, this isn't about men and women," she says, shaking her head. "This is about Islam."

10   I want to argue. I feel like a child. Defiant, but powerless. Burning with injustice, but also with a hint of shame. I do as I am told, feeling

acutely conscious of the bare skin I am covering. In policing my sexuality, these women have made me more aware of it.

The veil masks erotic freedom, but its advocates believe *hijab* 11 transcends the erotic—or expands it. In the West, we think of passion as a fever of the body, not the soul. In the East, Sufi poets used earthly passion as a metaphor; the beloved they celebrated was God. Where I come from people are more likely to find delirious passion in the mosque than in the bedroom.

There are times when I feel a hint of this passion. A few years after 12 my encounter on the Caspian, I go to the wake of a family friend. Sitting in a mosque in Mashhad, I grip a slippery black veil with one hand and a prayer book with the other. In the center of the hall, there's a stack of Koranic texts decorated with green-and-black calligraphy, a vase of white gladioluses and a large photograph of the dearly departed. Along the walls, women wait quietly.

From the men's side of the mosque, the mullah's voice rises in 13 lament. His voice is deep and plaintive, oddly compelling. I bow my head, sequestered in my veil while at my side a community of women pray and weep with increasing abandon. I remember from girlhood this sense of being exquisitely alone in the company of others. Sometimes I have cried as well, free to weep without having to offer an explanation. Perhaps they are right, those mystics who believe that physical love is an obstacle to spiritual love; those architects of mosques who abstained from images of earthly life, decorating their work with geometric shapes that they believed freed the soul to slip from its worldly moorings. I do not aspire to such lofty sentiments. All I know is that such moments of passionate abandon, within the circle of invisibility created by the veil, offer an emotional catharsis every bit as potent as any sexual release.

Outside, the rain pours from a sullen sky. I make my farewells and 14 walk toward the car, where my driver waits. My veil is wicking muddy water from the sidewalk. I gather up the wet and grimy folds with distaste, longing to be home, where I can cast off this curtain of cloth that gives with one hand, takes away with the other.

Content

1. For what purpose or purposes is the *hijab* (or *hejaab*) worn? Why does Asayesh write, "In today's Iran, whatever I wear sends a message" (¶ 1)? To what viewers in Iran? Would the message be the same to viewers in America?

2. Asayesh has ambivalent feelings about wearing the *hijab,* the veil-like covering for women mandated in Islamic countries. What are these?

3. The author is bicultural: Asayesh is Iranian-American. Are her conflicts related to the fact that she lives in dual cultures? Or would these same conflicts exist if she lived in or held the values of a single culture?

Strategies/Structures/Language

4. Asayesh introduces her subject with a reference to wearing both miniskirts and veils. How does this reference help to convey the forms of division and classification she will pursue in her discussion? How does her conclusion help to tie her essay together?

5. Asayeshs essay contains several contradictions. Identify them and explain how they contribute to the project of division and classification she undertakes in her essay.

6. Is Asayesh's definition of *hijab* adequate? Do some research on *hijab* and explain why the definition each provides is either adequate or inadequate for the purposes of her essay.

7. In Asayesh's essay, who is "paid to police public morals" (¶ 5)? What does the policing of public morals entail? Compare and contrast, in discussion or in writing, the differences in the scrutiny of individual women's dress (and behavior) in the culture depicted in this essay and in other writings on the subject.

For Writing

8. Choose a particular article of clothing, describe it in detail (fabric, cost, quality, style), and trace the history of the changed messages it (as worn by a particular individual or group) has sent over time. You might consider the original purpose of the article (for example, a baseball cap, a fur coat, blue jeans, a military uniform) and then examine how and why the connotations of wearing this have changed—over time and when worn by different types of people. What message—cultural, economic, political, aesthetic, and/or other—is sent by each type of wearing?

9. Writing as an individual or with a partner, address the subject of what clothes your fellow students wear. Use the essay by Asayesh as a point of reference. Analyze the clothing of a typical man and woman. In what respects are they similar? Different? Do any articles of clothing predominate? What "messages" do they send to particular audiences in particular contexts? What dictates this dress? Custom? Individual preference? Group behavior? Other factors?

10. Write an essay that addresses Asayesh's topic. How can those not familiar with the history of the *hejaab* "help but think of [Asayesh, or any woman who wears a *hejaab*] as a victim"? How can these and other women who choose to wear a *hejaab* for the reasons these authors identify avoid being seen as "an accomplice in the savagery of the Muslim world for wear.

11. **Dialogues.** Asayesh alludes to different cultural conceptions of femininity. How does Minikitani poem, "Recipe" (456) imply a particular conception of gender difference? How might this poem's central contradiction explain why Asayesh feels "like a child. Defiant, but powerless" (¶ 10) Or, examine the same topic with reference to Angier's "Why Men Don't Last" (353–56), Tannen's "Communication Styles" (344–49), or Mann's "The Coming Death Shortage" (362–74).

12. **Mixed Modes.** Asayesh includes two narratives in her essay, one about her visit to the Caspian shore on a hot day, and the other about a wake in a mosque. How do these strategies illustrate her themes?

13. **Second Look.** How might the photograph on 546 illustrate Asayesh's "sense of being exquisitely alone in the company of others" while wearing the *hijab* (¶ 13)? How might the photograph explain her ambivalence toward the veil?

JOHN HOCKENBERRY

John Hockenberry (born in 1956 in Dayton, Ohio) is an award-winning journalist who has written for many publications, including *The New York Times, The New Yorker, Wired,* and the *Washington Post.* Formerly a correspondent for NBC (1996–2005), he has worked as a Middle East correspondent for National Public Radio, where he anchored "The DNA Files" (1998–2003). He has published a novel, *A River Out of Eden* (2001), and written a one-man show, *Spoke Man* (1996), that appeared off-Broadway. His memoir, *Moving Violations: War Zones, Wheelchairs and Declarations of Independence* (1995), from which this excerpt is taken, recounts the 1976 car accident that left him a paraplegic. In this excerpt Hockenberry describes the stereotypes attached to the physically disabled individual. Using confrontational and conversational language, as well as biting humor, Hockenberry critiques the ways in which contemporary American culture, particularly through the medium of television, thrives on the perpetuation of stereotypes, including those focused on race and the disabled.

from *Moving Violations*

People often ask me what I would prefer to be called. Do they think   1
I have an answer?

I'm a crip for life. I cannot walk. I have "lost the use of my legs." I am   2
paralyzed from the waist down. I use a wheelchair. I am wheelchair-bound.
I am confined to a wheelchair. I am a paraplegic. I require "special assistance for boarding." I am a gimp, crip, physically challenged, differently
abled, paralyzed. I am a T-5 para. I am sick. I am well. I have a T4–6 in-
complete dural lesion, a spinal cord injury, a broken back, "broken legs"
to Indian cabbies in New York who always ask, "What happened to your
legs, Mister?"

I have a spastic bladder, pneumatic tires, air in all four of my   3
tires. Solid wheelchair tires are for hospitals and weenies. No self-
respecting crip would be caught dead in one. I use a catheter to take a
whiz. I require no leg bag. That's for the really disabled. I have no van
with a wheelchair lift anymore. Those are for the really disabled, and
thank God I'm not one of them. I need no motor on my wheelchair.
Those are for the really disabled, and I am definitely not one of those.
From mid-chest down I have no sensation. I am numb all the way to
my toes.

Anyone. Anywhere. Anytime.

"WI helped break down my belief that I will be sitting in my chair, watching others do what I no longer can do. I was afraid before the trip, that I was going to be the "disabled" needing lots of help. No one on this trip ever made me feel anything like that." —Nancy D., 50

If you have a disability and you want to go on a trip where disability is not the focus, you've come to the right place. Since 1978 WI has conducted integrated wilderness trips involving people with disabilities as well as people who do not have disabilities - as equals and peers. Our mission is to provide real outdoor adventures for everyone.

www.wildernessinquiry.org
800-728-0719 · 808 14th Ave SE, Minneapolis, MN 55414-1546

Wilderness Inquiry

Wilderness Inquiry

Wilderness Inquiry sponsors a variety of national and international trips that involve camping, hiking, kayaking, canoeing, and other outdoor experiences on land, sea, and rivers—in wilderness, national parks, and game preserves. Their trips accommodate people of all ages and abilities. Given the language of the ad, how would you expect this kayaker, his wheelchair strapped to the top of his kayak, to be treated on this trip?

I know what they're all thinking. My dick doesn't work. The truth?   4
My dick works sometimes. My dick works without fail. I have two dicks.
I have totally accepted my sexuality. I have massive problems with my
sexuality. Actually, there is no problem with sexuality. It's just not a problem. I think we can just drop this subject of sexuality because it's not an
issue. Not at all. The truth? I had a little problem there in the beginning,
then I learned how to compensate. Now everything is fine. It's actually
better than fine. To be perfectly honest, I am the sexual version of crack.
There are whole clinics set up for people who became addicted to sleeping with me. All right, the truth? Not so fast.

You do not have to feel guilty for causing my situation even though   5
your great-great-grandparents may have been slave owners. You do have
to feel guilty and fawning and contrite if I ever catch you using a wheelchair stall in an airport men's room or parking in a disabled space. I feel
as though I caused my situation and deserve to be cast from society, on
which I am a burden. I am a poster boy demanding a handout. I am the
800 number you didn't call to donate money. I am the drum major in Sally
Struther's parade of wretches. I watch the muscular dystrophy telethon
every year without fail. I would like to have Jerry Lewis sliced thinly and
packed away in Jeffrey Dahmer's freezer. I am not responsible for my situation and roll around with a chip on my shoulder ready to lash out at
and assault any person making my life difficult, preferably with a deadly
weapon.

I have unlimited amounts of "courage," which is evident to everyone   6
but myself and other crips. I get around in a wheelchair. I am a wheelchair
"racer." I am just rolling to work. I am in denial. I have accepted my disability and have discovered within myself a sublime reservoir of truth.
I can't accept my disability, and the only truth I am aware of is that my
life is shit and that everyone is making it worse. I am a former food stamp
recipient. I am in the 35 percent tax bracket. I am part of the disability
rights movement. I am a sell-out wannabe TV star media scumbag who
has turned his broken back on other crips.

I am grateful for the Americans with Disabilities Act, which has   7
heralded a new era of civil rights in this country. I think the Americans
with Disabilities Act is the most useless, empty, unenforceable law of the
last quarter-century. It ranks up there as one of the most pansy-assed ex-
cuses for a White House news conference in U.S. history. I think that the
disabled community is a tough, uncompromising coalition of activists.
I think the disabled community is a back-biting assembly of noisy, mutually suspicious clowns who would eagerly sell out any revolution just to
appear on a telethon, or in the White House Rose Garden, or in a Levis'
commercial.

I cannot reach the cornflakes in my cupboard. I cannot do a   8
handstand. I cannot use most revolving doors. I cannot rollerblade.
Bowling is more of a waste of time than it used to be. (One of the chief

advantages of being in a wheelchair is always having an excuse not to go bowling, even though I do miss the shoes.) I'm telling you these things because I want us to share, and for you to understand my experiences and then, together, bridge the gulf between us. I want you all to leave me alone.

9   I'm a guy in a chair, crip for life. Everything you think about me is right. Everything you think is wrong.

10   What is "normal" but another stereotype, no different than "angry black man," "Asian math genius," "welfare mother," or "gay man with a lisp"? Each stereotype thrives in direct proportion to the distance from each class of persons it claims to describe. Get close to the real people and these pretend images begin to break up, but they don't go easily. As each stereotype breaks down, it reveals a pattern of wrongs. Losing a stereotype is about being wrong retroactively. For a person to confront such assumptions they must admit an open-ended wrong for as long as those assumptions have lived inside them. There is the temptation to hold on to why you believed in stereotypes. "I was told gays were like that as a child." "I never knew many blacks, and that's what my parents believed about them." "I was once frightened and disgusted by a person in a wheelchair." To relinquish a stereotype is to lose face by giving up a mask.

11   We trade in masks in America. Especially in politics. Politicians love to talk about the "American people" and what they allegedly want or don't want. But who are they, really? The America evoked most often today by politicians and pundits is a closet full of masks denoting race, nationality, and a host of other characteristics. America's definitive social unit of measurement is no longer the family, nor is it the extended family. On the other end of the scale, it is not the village or hamlet, neighborhood or block, city, state, or region. I grew up in America at a time when its logo was the racially balanced commercial image of four or five children, one black, white, Asian, female, and disabled (optional) romping in an idyllic, utopian, and quite nonexistent playground.

12   You can still occasionally see this image in the children's fashion supplement to *The New York Times Magazine*. These are happy measuring sticks of a demographic formula, perfect faces of social equilibrium to distract from the fact that each child is usually clad in the designer fabric hard currency equivalent of the GNP of Guyana or Cameroon. In the eighties the fashion chain Benetton crossed the old American emblem with the UN General Assembly and produced its own utopian logo of a meticulously integrated, multiracial youth army, no disabled (not optional).

13   We once portrayed these idealized young people as seeds of a racially harmonious society we dreamed would come. Now those children shout

down the long narrow lenses of music video cameras, or gun each other down on the streets. Our communities have become multiracial, just as the dream foretold. But they are not utopias. Integration is no guarantee of harmony. It is what most of the world has known since the end of World War Two. It is this nation's last, cruel lesson of the twentieth century.

Today, if one measures America at all, it is in audience units. 14 America is the union of all the multiracial groups of ostensibly "normal" people, ranging from submissive and polite to angry and aggressive, who can be seated in a television studio in front of a talk-show host. There they stare at, and react to, the famous hosts, the famous guests, or anyone else on stage. Mad people, older people, teenagers, victims, predators, all of the species in America's great political aviary pass in front of the audience. America turns its thumbs up or down, then goes to a commercial break. There is no verdict. There is just the din of many verdicts. As the camera scans the audience, the people who can be anticipated to have a distinct opinion, or more likely, an outrage, are handed the microphone. "Why don't you just leave him if he beats you?" "It's people like you skinheads who spread hate in this country." America punctuates each of these outraged questions and challenges with applause, jeers, and shouts.

I caught the delivery of verdicts from one such clump of Americana 15 between commercial breaks on the "Oprah Winfrey" show some time after my accident. I had always thought of myself as a face in the audience. On this show I saw myself on the stage with a group of four married couples, each with a disabled partner. Three of the couples contained a partner in a wheelchair; the other was a blind woman and her sighted husband. The theme of the show that day was something like "One of them is fine and the other one is defective. How do they manage?" The audience applauded with an enthusiasm they reserved for First Ladies, and Oprah herself had that deep, breathy voice that television talk-show hosts reserve for the inspirational subjects—the serious themes that justify all of those celebrity interviews and fluff. Here, "Crips and Their Spouses" was gripping television.

The couples represented an odd composite of the crip popula- 16 tion. This was Oprah's idea of the crips next door, and that next door, in this case, was not necessarily the state institution. Just your average run-of-the-mill crip and spouse combo package. There were no Vietnam vets on this panel, no wheelchair jocks, no quadriplegics, no gunshot ghetto homies with their stripped-down Quickie ultra-lights, and, of course, they had neglected to call me.

Three of the couples might as well have had lamp shades on their 17 heads. They were nonthreatening, overweight, jolly, well-adjusted types with a hint of acne, all wearing loud, baggy shirts. These are the people the audience was used to giving a wide berth on the bus and then ignoring. One of the women was in a dented, ill-fitting wheelchair with gray hospital wheels. They said things like, "Hey, Oprah, it just takes more planning. It's no big deal." They laughed a lot. The audience imagined working near one of these people; it did not have to imagine being one.

18   One of the couples was different; a thin guy in a wheelchair and his pretty, young, unparalyzed wife. They had dated in college before his "accident." They were nearly dressed and clearly held the most fascination for the audience members. "How difficult was it for you after his accident?" Oprah addressed herself to the young woman when she wanted to know some detail. No, she had never thought of breaking up with him after the accident. "It's no different than anything else that might make a relationship difficult." The audience began to applaud while Oprah nodded. On their faces was a kind of sentimental approval. The audience wanted her to know that she could have left him . . . she would have had the perfect excuse . . . no jury would have convicted, certainly not in that audience. She seemed slightly sensitive about this point because she insisted again that she had not thought of breaking up the relationship, and that it really was just another thing, like a joint checking account, for a couple to deal with.

19   The joint checking account line really got them. "I just want to say that I think you are such an inspiration to us all," an audience member addressed the panel. It didn't really matter what the panelists said, especially the young couple. It only mattered what the audience thought about the young man's plight and his courageous girlfriend. It was far more important to assume that he was broken, that she was tied to him now selflessly, and that they would make the best of things. "Yes, Oprah; we manage just fine," she said in her small voice with her husband's nodding assent. Oprah addressed the young man once. "You must be so happy to have someone like Amy," or whatever her name was.

20   I was rooting for these folks to hold their own. Though I was just a little older, I could tell that I had logged lots more wheelchair time than the young guy on TV. I could feel what was coming, I saw the audience greedily looking them up and down. I saw what we were supposed to think about them. He: strong, brave, and struck down in his youth. She: stronger and braver for spending her youth with him. On their faces you could see that the conditions of this public execution were just beginning to dawn on them.

21   But it was just Oprah. It was all in good fun. I was making too much of a television talk show. They weren't forced to go out onto that stage. A voice inside said, "If you weren't so angry and dysfunctional, John, maybe you would be invited to go on 'Oprah' too."

It didn't take long for Oprah to deliver. "So there's one thing I want 22 to know." She looks directly at the young girl as the hungry crowd buzzes with anticipation. Oh, my god, she's going to ask. Like a car accident in the movies, the world slows down at this point. I can see the smile freeze on the face of the young woman. The crowd goes wild. The camera cuts away to Oprah.

"What I want to know is . . ." 23

She pauses for sincerity. The crowd is totally with her. The woman 24 must know what's about to happen. She must have been asked a million times. I wondered if the guy knew. The guy probably had no idea. Or maybe it was a condition for going on the show. I'm screaming at the TV now: "Tell her it's none of her damn business. We're counting on you out here. Tell Oprah to stuff it!"

Oprah delivers. 25

"Amy, can he do it?" 26

Loud gasp from the crowd. I imagine that it must have sounded this 27 way when Sydney Carton's head was lopped off in *A Tale of Two Cities*. The camera immediately cuts to the woman's face, which has blushed a deep red. She tries something of a laugh, glances at her husband, who is out of the shot. Eventually, when the noise dies down, she says, "Yes, he can, Oprah." She giggles.

The camera pulls wide, and the two onstage seem very small. He 28 takes her hand for comfort. The crowd bursts into applause. Even the other crips on stage are applauding. He withdraws his hand, as though it had been placed in hot oil. The camera cuts back to Oprah, who is nodding to the crowd half-heartedly, trying to get them to stop clapping. She looks somewhere between a very satisfied Perry Mason and a champion mud wrestler. Now we know what the show was really about. It wasn't just Oprah; the whole crowd seemed to care only about this. The oddest thing was that after the question and the embarrassed answer the audience seemed to think they now knew how "it" was done. What did they know? They knew that they had the guts to ask this question; they didn't really care about the answer.

Oprah, here's something I have always wanted to know. Do black 29 guys really have giant dicks? The angry voice yelled at the television and then turned it off. Is that what people think when they stare? What constitutes "doing it"? There was no answer for them. There was no answer for me. Questions like these were the weapon. They need no real answer and apparently are always loaded in the chambers of people's curiosity. Stereotypes bring forth righteous anger and deep humiliation. At the same time, they are completely understandable, like an old piece of furniture you have walked by every day of your life. . . .

Content

1. What criteria does Hockenberry suggest determines who is "really disabled" (¶ 3)? Why does he insist that he's "not one of those" (¶ 3)?

2. According to Hockenberry, what presumptions do the nondisabled make about the disabled (¶s 4–5)? Why does he represent these presumptions as extreme and opposing? Why does Hockenberry tell the reader, "Everything you think about me is right. Everything you think is wrong" (¶ 9)?

3. Hockenberry writes that "Each stereotype thrives in direct proportion to the distance from each class of persons it claims to describe" (¶ 10). Why are stereotypes difficult to give up? What are the benefits of "giving up a mask" (¶ 10)?

4. Hockenberry writes, "Our communities have become multiracial, just as the dream foretold. But they are not utopias." Why, according to him, hasn't America become "a racially harmonious society" (¶ 13)?

5. As Hockenberry describes his reaction to the *Oprah* episode, he slows his pace, carefully describing the different characters and the angles of the camera, and recounting his own speech as well as that of the people on camera (¶s 15–28). What is the effect of this careful pacing? How does this strategy build on Hockenberry's earlier discussion of stereotypes? Why does he compare Oprah's intrusive question with an equally intrusive and obnoxious question about black men in the final paragraph (¶ 29)?

Strategies/Structures/Language

6. How does Hockenberry's language suggest that television has increasingly come to dominate and define American culture? Find examples such as "your average run-of-the-mill crip and spouse combo package" (¶ 16) and explain how such phrases support Hockenberry's cultural critique.

7. Why does Hockenberry compare this *Oprah Winfrey* show with an execution (¶s 20, 27) and a trial by jury (¶ 17)? How does he prepare the reader for this narrative (¶ 14)?

8. How does Hockenberry use clichés such as "I am in denial" (¶ 6) and "a new era of civil rights in this country" (¶ 7)? What do these clichés suggest about his view of stereotypes and his characterization of American culture as "a closet full of masks" (¶ 11)?

For Writing

9. What is the impact of television shows in which participants reveal their personal lives? Under what circumstances might you be persuaded to participate in such a show? Is Hockenberry being ironic when he writes, "A voice inside said, 'If you weren't so angry and dysfunctional, John, maybe you would be invited to go on "Oprah" too' " (¶ 21)? Write an essay that examines our culture's attitudes toward television shows that encourage self-exposure.

10. **Second Look.** The photograph for adventure vacations on 365 features a wheelchair-bound man kayaking. Does this advertisement speak to the disabled or the nondisabled? What does Hockenberry's analysis suggest about his views of representing the disabled in nontraditional ways? Might he disparage the implication that a wheelchair-bound kayaker has "unlimited amounts of 'courage'" (¶ 6)?

ZARA RIX

Zara Rix (born 1982) is a graduate student in English at the University of Connecticut. She is the oldest of four children from an Australian-Italian marriage; her mother moved to the United States with her family at 13, and her father stopped in the United States on his way back to Australia from Europe at 25. "He never intended to stay in the U.S.," says Rix, "and my mother was willing to move to Australia with him, but the timing (in the form of work, children, my maternal grandparents) never worked out. My mother says the marriage probably succeeded because they were in the U.S., on nobody's cultural home ground, when they began married life."

She wrote this essay when studying *corporalité* in a contemporary Francophone literature class. "It was an experiment, a game," she explains. "I wanted to see what I would read if I treated my body like a book. The results surprised me. Almost all my memories of significant events attached to my body involve other people, other nations, or both. For example, the scar on my right knee is from a car accident when I was two, the first time my father brought me to meet his family in Australia. Examples like that continued to crop up as I wrote. My body's story incorporated the stories of my family, my friends, places I've lived, and in the midst of those stories, places, and people, I tried to find me. If so much of my self is defined in contrast or in relation to others, then where am I? This isn't an abstract philosophical question; I cannot even talk about my body—my present, corporeal self—without referencing others. So it was both a surprise and not a surprise when the essay began circling around identity and issues of race and being a second-generation American, issues that interest me although I have no clear-cut answers to the questions they pose.

"As much as this essay deals with individual identity," she continues, "I was comforted by the corporate aspect of my *corporalité*. I focused a lot of the essay on my friends because we are similar more because of our differences than despite them. And while I know that for the most part my experience deals with a very specific social and educational class of people, I think that's all right. Questions regarding identity, race, and 'Americanness' occur across a spectrum of people, and so I can see my story as one part of that corporate search."

Corporality

I use my body to map who I am. Perhaps "map" is the wrong word, since I know I'm more than the external SWF. Running my eyes down my body, I read stories upon each part of me. *Corporalité*, the French call it: reading the body in a text, reading the body as though it were a text. I like their word. *Corps* is the word for "body," but in English it sounds like "core." Reading me, I read my core, and I'm surprised how much of my *corps* is corporate; others' stories flow through me until parts of them are included in my body. All these stories, I realize, are layered. More than a map, I need a deep-water chart in order to navigate.

2   I (the SWF) am 5' 4". I range between 110 and 120 pounds, and I look like my friend Aliya. Not on the face, perhaps (she's Taiwanese), but our bodies are almost mirror images. We can share clothes and shoes, and we both look good in red. She prefers a maroon shade but I like the bright red that brings out the color in my face: celebratory red, in Chinese.

3   Aliya and I started school together at the age of five. Both of our parents moved to the Lexington suburbs for the school system and both of our parents (ambitious) enrolled us in first grade, skipping kindergarten. It didn't work. We got held back.

4   "My English wasn't good enough," Aliya says. She came from Taiwan two years earlier.

5   Aliya went to special English classes, but I don't remember ever having trouble understanding her. I consistently beat her at spelling, but that was only satisfying until she forbade me from drawing humans during free time. Aliya said she had a special magic where if she drew someone, she could tell if the person was good or evil by the number of lines in their hair. I tried to do the same thing, but she said I couldn't because I didn't have the special magic; I could only draw animals and objects.

6   I'm not sure when we became friends. I think I started thinking of her as a friend by fifth grade, and by seventh grade the rest of our friends moved out of state or overseas. Aliya and I remained. Midway through middle school, Aliya described us as best friends and, once I adjusted to the idea, I realized it was true. We'd grown into a friendship.

7   Outwardly, I sometimes think we've also grown into each other, although supposedly genetics governs that. Our Asian/Caucasian differences remain, but they're irrelevant to what's inside. I know her metabolism (Aliya needs to eat within two hours of a set mealtime or she'll grow cranky), and Aliya understands what I'm saying even with my mouth full. When we visit each other's homes, we translate our grandmothers' greetings: Chinese or Italian into English. Aliya calls me by my home name, Zarita, and I can almost pronounce "Xian-Yu." We travel together. She visited me at boarding school in Australia, and I visited her when she attended Oxford.

8   Two summers ago, after I finished working in France and after she finished an internship in a hospital in Dehradun, we met up in India. We stayed with my college roommate and her family, and they arranged for us to tour northern India in a taxi. Aliya insisted on visiting McLeod Ganj;

---

* From *Image.*

she wanted to bring her father a gift from the Dalai Lama's temple. While there, displaced Tibetans stopped to talk to us along the street. Aliya wore a red salwar (a bridal color in India) and they asked her if she was Tibetan. They asked me for money.

Driving home in the taxi, I watched out the window for tea 9 plantations, elephants, and eucalyptus trees. Aliya listened to music.

"Hey," I asked, "you know how we've spent so much time 10 overseas—do you think that's made you different?"

She looked at me. 11

I repeated the question, in case she hadn't heard. "Do you think it's 12 made you different? You know, as though you don't fit in anywhere?"

"No," she said, shortly, replacing her earpiece. "I always felt 13 different. I looked different."

I was confused. Honestly, I don't remember ever thinking Aliya 14 looked different. My memory of the Lexington school system is of lots of Asians. Or at least, most of our friends were Asians, I thought. Now, as I look at a photo of our group of friends from junior prom, I count 10 Asian-skinned people (if I include the dark-skinned Armenians, who are technically European) and 11 whites (if I include the Israelis, who look white but are technically Asian). If I undo my arbitrary skin-color count, sorting us into European vs. Asian ancestry, the numbers remain the same. But that only represented our group of friends. The populations of Lexington and wider New England as a whole are predominantly white, something I didn't notice until Aliya pointed it out to me.

At times like this, when Aliya forwards me "You Know You're 15 Asian If . . ." emails or sits on my bed reading my brother's copy of *American Born Chinese*, I feel the difference between us. It lies like a jagged crack down the center of our friendship, marking the boundary of our individualities. It doesn't hurt, but it reminds me that no matter how similar we are, there are aspects of Aliya's experience that I will never comprehend.

I am white. Clearly, unmistakably white. Veins show blue 16 through my skin. I can trace them like a roadmap over my feet, down my arms and into my hands, up my neck until they meet the blue of my eyes.

"So blue!" 17

Javier adored putting his hand under my chin, tilting my face as he 18 examined my eyes. I dated him briefly while living in France, where we both taught English. He was Mexican, but there wasn't much call for a Spanish teacher.

I was captivated by his smooth hair, held back in a band, and his 19 *conquistador* nose, but he made me uncomfortable when he exclaimed over my eyes and traced his fingers over my pale skin. He asked me to tell him frankly, what stereotypes of Mexicans are in the US. I said I didn't know because in my town there are more Asians than Mexicans. That in itself was an answer, I suppose, if he knew how to translate the social undercurrents of Massachusetts' suburbs.

20   Shortly after Javier and I stopped seeing each other, he moved in with a different blue-eyed girl. My roommate Beatriz, annoyed that he never returned the DVDs she brought with her from Mexico, snorted. "You were his first pick," she told me. "You have blonde hair *and* blue eyes."

21   I don't have blonde hair.

22   My hair is brown, neither dark nor light. It's nothing remarkable, and so I pay for blonde highlights. Sometimes, carried away by "adding summer warmth" or the fun of being blond(er), I make my hair very light. After Javier, I dyed it back to brown. The dye sat on top of the blonde, making it orange when it faded. I dyed it again.

23   In New York, a few months after our trip to India, Aliya complimented my hair. "It looks good," she said. "And it's so curly now you cut it."

24   It took Fahaad, the friend we were visiting, a full day to realize my hair was brown again. He looked at me, frowned, and then looked closer. "Hey!" he said. "Why'd you dye it? It looked good!"

25   Fahaad is sort-of Indian. He joined Lexington High School right before I moved back from Australia. Both of us were in eleventh grade, lost, and trying to understand how we fit in (or, in my case, re-fit in) to SATs, AP classes, and burgeoning life (read: college) decisions.

26   "I thought you were going to be another Indian Muslim," he told me years later. "They kept talking about you moving back, and the only other Zaras I know are Muslim."

27   It took us a long time to figure out where Fahaad came from. His family moved to Lexington from Malaysia, but he didn't look Malaysian and when we asked where he came from, he said, "I'm American." He is, too. He was born in California; more American than Aliya, if birthplace is a marker.

28   "I'm American, too," Aliya told him. "Naturalized. But we speak Chinese at home and you sure weren't speaking English when your mom called."

29   Fahaad's family is from the northeast of India, closer to China than the Ganges. "That's why I'm chinky-eyed," he explained.

30   Once, either at the end of high school or the beginning of college, Aliya didn't talk to him for a week. "You know what he said?" Her voice over the phone was tight. "He said, 'Light matters to dark people.' And I don't care if—well, okay, it's true—but he shouldn't *say* it!"

31   Back in Lexington one summer after high school, Fahaad put his arm beside mine. "I'm too dark," he said, "and you're too light." His nose wrinkled. I was shocked. My skin had been flippantly dismissed. I was used to being the only blue-eyed one in our group of friends, the only one

who sunburned and got teased, but I'd never felt an aesthetic judgment on the color of my skin. "If we had kids," he added, "they'd be the right color."

It felt odd to look down at our arms, to look at my white-and-red 32 splotched hands and the brown into beige of his palms, and think he was right.

As a child, I once woke up and didn't recognize my arm. It lay 33 beside my face on the bed, but my arm had fallen asleep during the night and I couldn't feel it. I ordered the fingers to move and watched them wriggle without feeling the scratch of my sheets. It looked like a strange, alien thing.

That happened to me again, another time when my arm lay beside 34 Fahaad's. I woke early, when dawn was just starting to lighten the day, leaving the world visible but colorless. Fahaad's warmth was behind me, and in front of me I saw two arms. I knew one of my arms was beneath me and that therefore only one of those two was mine, but the arms were so close, so entangled, I couldn't tell which belonged to me and which belonged to him.

This isn't that hard, I told myself. *He's a guy; his arm is bigger and it's* 35 *got to be hairier.*

I studied our arm hairs, and as I did so, I realized that I hadn't 36 thought of color. A thrill of excitement ran through me: I hadn't thought to look for color. It was as though, for the first time I could recall, skin and all it symbolized didn't matter.

If I told you I didn't sleep with Fahaad, would you still believe his 37 body is written on mine?

Because what I read doesn't stop there. My delight at looking for the 38 difference of sex and not of race made me wonder. If I felt that Javier dated my whiteness more than he dated me, if I sometimes suspected Fahaad enjoyed my blondeness more than I wanted him to, how was I different? I didn't think I was drawn to them because they were "exotic"—Javier spoke English while I was still floundering in French, and I'd known Fahaad for enough years to have no illusions—but perhaps I did have something to prove. If my joy at not thinking about color felt like a release, then—no less than them—wasn't I trapped by belonging to a family that was on the wrong side of colonization?

I think of it as my ugly underbelly: white and pasty, like something 39 that emerges after you've poked at rotting wood.

Despite Australia's heat, the only time I saw my belly while at 40 boarding school was over exeats. Exeat weekends shut down the boarding house, and I spent that time with my grandparents. That, after all, was the main purpose of my being in Australia: so that I could get to know my father's family.

41   For me, those were comfortable weekends, filled with sleeping in, reading the funnies, and feeling as though I belonged someplace. I could come out to breakfast whenever I liked, tucking my T-shirt up so my navel was bare and not having to worry about whether my shorts were in style.

42   Grandpa sat at the head of the kitchen table each morning, his back to the sliding doors so that the light fell on his newspaper. "All the troubles in the world," he told me, "were caused by colonization. My Godfather! The French, the Dutch, and the Portuguese—every one of them—and the British had to go in and sort it all out."

43   I sat next to him, eating my cornflakes. Grandpa didn't keep the air conditioner on in the morning, so the doors were open and warm Australian air, smelling of Grandpa's garden and sunshine, breezed across my bare legs.

44   When Grandpa was finished with the world, he usually turned to the family. "Your cousin," he told me, "By Gor, she dates all of them. Black, brown, red, speckled, spotted, striped."

45   The real trouble, of course, started with his children. They didn't listen to him. They married Dagos, Polacks, Dutch, and had the nerve to be happy.

46   My mother was the Dago. Her feet waggle at me from the end of my legs. Humiliatingly, I was born with bunions. I imagine the knobby bones being like the warped trunks of vineyards along the hills of Gorizia.

47   The first time my mother brought me to Italy, I was eleven and my ears played tricks on me. I sat by the side of the luggage claim and watched the Carabinieri. They looked like something out of a story book, with the red stripes down their trousers and gleaming badges on their caps. They were talking about lunch, or some other entirely mundane detail, and I frowned at them. Story book characters have no right to do commonplace things like eat lunch or lounge by the sliding doors.

48   "Are you understanding anything?" My mother looked concerned, and it took me a moment to realize she'd addressed me in English. When I concentrated harder, I realized that the Carabinieri were speaking Italian. It hadn't sounded like either English or Italian to me; it had just been words about lunch. Many years later, after I'd lived and worked in France a while, I found the same thing occurring. If I didn't think about it, I couldn't tell whether I was hearing English or French. I thought in both languages, and could only remember which language a conversation occurred in by recalling who I'd been speaking to at the time.

49   It's always my tongue that exposes me.

50   "Ma non è italiana?" The waiter looked startled. Small wonder. I look north Italian and speak simple sentences with my mother's accent.

Anything more complex than "Yes, thank you," however, gives me away: I make the grammatical mistakes of a child.

"Se mettre à parler est plus difficile que de comprendre," my French teacher told me. To put one's self to speaking is harder than to understand. 51

I want to understand, though, and I want to speak and be understood. I see this, even now, back in the US again. I hear others talking and strain to understand what they're saying: the Spanish-speaking maintenance people, the Korean Bible study, Aliya's Taiwanese grandmother. My body leans forward, as though absorbing the words into me will erase the barrier, or as though if I correctly interpret facial expressions and posture, the words won't matter. This method hasn't worked yet, so I suppose I'll have to work to learn the language and understand the customs. 52

Trying to make myself understood is almost as hard. Here I am: a SWF body that blends in. When I'm asked where I'm from, I say, "Boston." It's true. Thus far most years of my life have been spent in and around the Boston area. I'm a US citizen and consider myself American. 53

If I say "Boston," though, very few question me further. Unlike Fahaad or Aliya—or even my parents, with their accented English—no one expects me to elaborate. And often, that's okay. For day-to-day affairs, my story is as irrelevant as everyone else's, and for less usual situations, I'm saved a lot of trouble. I'm selfishly okay with that, too. In Chinese (or Italian) restaurants, no one expects me to place the orders. And unlike Fahaad, who faces airport security guards as a brown Muslim, I don't need to "dress like I expect to keep living." 54

"Boston" isn't my story, though. Neither is Lexington. They're parts of my story, parts of me, but so are Australia and Italy, France and India, Aliya and Fahaad. 55

So is Ghana. I studied at the university in Legon during college, and whenever I went to the market, vendors and children cried out, "Obruni!" It was entirely without malice, and they laughed if I answered, "Obibini." 56

"Obruni doesn't mean 'white person,'" a professor told me. "It just means 'foreigner.' Even people from North Africa, they are obruni." 57

The year after I was in Ghana, another group of American exchange students came back and had a T-shirt made. OBRUNI, it said. If the word hadn't been printed white on a black background, I may have asked for one. I could wear it over my body and advertise: 58

This is my country, but it's also not. 59

This is my home, but it's also not. 60

I'm not a foreigner, but I'm also not . . . Not quite locatable on a map. 61

Content

1. Explain why Rix views her body as "corporate" (¶ 1). Why does she need "a deep-water chart" to read her body (¶ 1)? How does she distinguish between "core" and a "corporate" *corps* (¶ 1)?

2. Rix writes that the "Asian/Caucasian" differences between herself and her friend Aliya are "irrelevant to what's inside" (¶ 7). Nevertheless, at times she senses the difference as "a jagged crack down the center of our friendship" (¶ 15). Explain this contradiction, if it is one. Considering their similarities and differences (¶s 2–5), their translations of their grandmothers' greetings, and their use of each other's ethnic names (¶ 7), are the girls' ethnic differences a source of their individuality or a metaphor for it—or both?

3. How does the girls' visit to northern India (¶s 8–13) change their relationship? Why hasn't Rix asked Aliya before their travels abroad whether she feels as if she doesn't "fit in" (¶s 12, 14)?

4. What does Rix's attitude toward her hair and her changes of color suggest about her feelings toward her ethnicity and identity? How do her relationships with Javier (¶s 17–22) and Fahaad (¶s 24–37) illustrate her feelings about her ethnic and national identity and *"corporalité"* (¶ 1)? What does she have to "prove" by dating Fahaad (¶ 38)?

5. As you get to know Rix through her narrative, why does "SWF" fail to describe her? Why is she "Not quite locatable on a map" (¶ 61)?

Strategies/Structures/Language

6. Trace the geographical "map" that Rix's narrative describes. How does she structure her narrative around her travels? What does she learn in each location? Does the "map" of the world she describes correspond to the "map" of her body? How does the "map" of her story organize its themes?

7. What role do foreign languages play in Rix's narrative? How does language expand and hinder her understanding of herself and others? Do language differences represent for Rix impenetrable cultural differences?

For Writing

8. **Journal Writing.** How do you define yourself? Make a list of defining characteristics such as age, ethnicity, gender, political affiliation, religious faith, sexual orientation, socioeconomic background, family (or other) values, and personality. Do these classifications fully express who you are? Does the identity you project to the world differ from who you *really* are?

9. Using your journal writing (question 8) and Rix's narrative, write an essay about how an individual constructs his or her own identity in the contemporary world. How does your definition of identity compare to Rix's? Does identity depend on time and place? What cultural norms play a major role in shaping our identities? How much individuality can a person express within one's peer group, family, or community?

10. **Dialogues.** Why does Rix feel that her body is "corporate"? What elements of her identity does she experience as intrinsic and which does she. . . . experience as the result of the social and intellectual maturation that occurred over time? How does the author live through her cultural history and ethnicity? How does she experience cultural displacement as an opportunity to gain self-knowledge?

11. Write a paper defining yourself according to the four or five most significant dimensions of personality, mind, character, body, interests, commitments, or passions that you'd like your readers to know about you. You may use photographs, drawings, icons, significant objects (clothing, your residence, car, favorite books) to augment your definition. In what ways does this definition resemble your *Facebook* self-portrait, if you have one? If you intend this to be for a specific readership—for instance, a prospective employer or scholarship donor—indicate the audience and show how you're shaping your self-presentation to this reader.

Additional Topics for Discussion and Writing

1. If you or people you know well, perhaps family members or good friends, are from another country, discuss with them their understanding of what national identity means to them. Take notes and write a paper on your findings. In what ways do the countries you're discussing resemble one another? In what ways do they differ? You can approach the topic from one or more of the perspectives below.

- *Political level.* What are some conspicuous aspects of national politics, the relation of the government to the citizens? (For example, is the government totalitarian? Democratic? Communist? Socialist? Who holds power and how do they exercise it?)
- *Individual level.* What does "the American Dream" mean to you? How likely are you or your family to fulfill it? Is going to college related to this fulfillment? Does the other country have an equivalent? If so, what is this? If not, according to what criteria do people feel contented, satisfied? If goals are limited in either culture, why is this so? What can an individual do to address, accommodate, or overcome these limitations?

2. Either in relation to question 1 or independent of it, write a paper on the nature of your own identity, with respect to "the good life." What, for you, is a "good life," and how would living such a life affect your identity? Either through reading about or in dialogue with someone whose life might serve as a role model, identify define, and analyze three or four components of the good life. You will need to explain the reasons for the choices you expect to make during the life you're anticipating. Possible dimensions might be:

- *Philosophical, spiritual, ethical.* According to what principles (the Golden Rule, for example) do I want to make decisions? Treat other people? (see the "Universal Declaration of Human Rights" 571–76)
- *Educational.* What do I want to gain from my formal education? What have I already learned, informally, that I expect to remain of value throughout life? What am I not interested in learning? Why?
- *Relational.* How close do I expect to remain to my parents, grandparents, siblings? Do I want or need a lot of good friends? Do I expect to marry or to live for a long period with a significant other? Do I intend to have children? If so, how many? How will I integrate these relationships with the rest of my life?
- *Material.* What material goods do I currently need to function happily and well? In the future? Consider significant aspects of clothing, food, shelter, transportation, intellectual or artistic life, recreation, or whatever else is important to you.
- *Ecological.* How "green" will my future be? How big a "footprint" do I expect to leave on this earth? (For example, what means of transportation do I expect to use the most heavily?)

3. Research and write a paper on a changing identity, either a national or internationally known figure (you might get some ideas from Noble Prize-winners in various areas—see Chapter 12 or consult the Nobelprize.org website) or someone you know well, perhaps even yourself. What changes—physical, lifestyle, job, geographic, anything else—were or will be made? For what reasons? (Consider, for instance, Frederick Douglass's life change from slave to freedman ["Resurrection" 86–91]). To provide desired physical or intellectual changes, would you use cosmetic surgery, chemicals, genetic engineering on yourself or loved ones? Under what circumstances? With what limitations?

4. To what extent is beauty and/or an attractive physique integral to your self-definition? To whether or not you find others appealing?

5. Define identity theft according to the experiences you or someone you know have had with it, consult prevention guidelines (see James Fallows's, "Tinfoil Underwear" 192–98), and write a paper on how to prevent identity theft. You may wish to consider the four categories of the Identity Theft Resource Center's definition:

- Financial (using another's identity to obtain goods and services)
- Criminal (posing as another when apprehended for a crime)
- Business/commercial (using another's business name to obtain credit)
- Identity cloning (using another's information to assume that identity in daily life)

Human Rights and World Peace: Universal Declaration of Human Rights, and Nobel Peace Prize Speeches

In this final chapter, it is fitting to focus on world peace and on the significant contributions of individuals and organizations to the sustenance and survival of large numbers of people, animals, and the planet itself. To focus only on the negative (consider, for example, the reports of William Collins and colleagues on global warming, 199–211; see also the photo insert on environmental issues) would be to ignore the best that is represented by the Universal Declaration of Human Rights (571–76) and recipients of the Nobel Prize, whose acceptance speeches comprise this chapter.

The Universal Declaration of Human Rights, a statement of ethical principles for the right conduct of society, has precedents in the U.S. Constitution's Bill of Rights, and the French "Declaration of the Rights of Man and of the Citizen" (1789), but it is more comprehensive than its predecessors and endeavors to encompass every nation in the world. This Declaration was issued in 1948, three years after the United Nations was formed to promote "a world in which human beings shall enjoy freedom of speech and belief and freedom from fear and want." Eleanor Roosevelt, the first chairperson of the United Nations Commission on Human Rights, which drafted the Declaration, said, "It is not a treaty. . . . It may well become the international Magna Carta. . . ." The Declaration guarantees what its drafters considered significant and fundamental human rights such as freedom of speech, press, assembly, religion, and the rule of law; the right be part of a family, to have a sustainable standard of living and health care, to obtain an education, to work, to participate in government, and to travel beyond the borders of one's country. Importantly, the Declaration asserts that everyone shall be free from gender inequality, racial discrimination, slavery, and exploitation. The Declaration has been the foundation for numerous subsequent international conferences, such as the 1979 Convention on the Elimination of All Forms of Discrimination against Women, the 1984 Convention against Torture and Other Cruel, Inhuman and Degrading Treatment and Punishment, and the 1989 Convention on the Rights of the Child. Widely cited by scholars, lawyers, and constitutional courts, the Declaration has provided the framework for developing the European Union's standards for human rights legislation, and its language has been incorporated into the constitutions of various countries. Goodness, selflessness, and adherence to high moral principles, as the lives and works of the Nobel Prize winners reveal, can emerge even in times of trauma—often, in responses to the challenges of trauma itself. Their talks, like their works, are beacons of faith, hope, and good will. If, as Franklin Roosevelt said, "the only thing we have to fear is fear itself," we need to reinforce a value system that will enable us to lead lives governed by principles and values that bring out the best rather than the worst of our common humanity. This is the message, implied and stated overtly, by every one of these Nobel Prize winners.

These Nobel winners form an international spectrum of the brave, the bold, the morally beautiful. Some of these Nobelists are people of high visibility and power—United Nations Secretary General Kofi Annan (Egypt); national leaders Al Gore (U.S.A.) and Frederik Willem de Klerk (South Africa); and organizational movers and shapers such as Wangari Maathai (Kenya), founder of the Green Belt Movement. Others are religious and political leaders who have suffered extensive privations for living their beliefs: the 14th Dalai Lama (Tibet), sentenced by the Chinese to lifetime exile as the embodiment of the Tibetan Buddhist nation; and Aung San Suu Kyi (Myanmar), Burmese pro-democracy leader confined by the military junta to house arrest for over seventeen years. Still others include Guatemalan champion of indigenous rights and culture, Mayan Rigoberta Menchú Tum. Activist humanitarian organizations are represented by the U.N.'s Intergovernmental Panel on Climate Change, which shared the 2007 award with Al Gore and Médecins sans Frontiéres (Doctors Without Borders), represented by James Orbinski.

All of these Nobel recipients, and others (like Martin Luther King, Jr.), are "witnesses to the truth of injustice," as Dr. James Orbinski, president of Médecins Sans Frontières (1998–2000) when the organization (Doctors Without Borders) received the 1999 Nobel Peace Prize, says, willing to lay their lives on the line—and to lose them, as Dr. King and others have done—for a moral cause. Each of these awards is enmeshed in a complex web of political, moral, and ethical issues in flux, which the prefatory notes attempt to address. (More detailed discussions may be found on the Nobel Prize website [http://nobelprize.org]—a good place to begin a long trail of investigation and analysis.) Like the lives of these inspiring leaders, the words in these stimulating speeches can guide us to some answers.

How we as individuals, family members, friends, and citizens can do our best not only to lead the good life but to make that life better for humankind is one of the aims of a liberal education and of this book. Following the readings in this chapter you will find suggestions for discussion and writing. The individual speeches presented here may be read in connection with or opposition to one another and in relation to other works throughout the book. Among others these include Collins's and Havel's essays on climate change (199–211 and 211–14); Pollan's (247–54) and Nestle's (255–62) analyses of the politics of food production; and essays on human rights and reconciliation: "The Declaration of Independence" (393–97), Martin Luther King Jr.'s "Letter From Birmingham Jail" (399–413), Lincoln's "The Gettysburg Address" (457), and Sojourner Truth's "Ain't I a Woman?" (458–59).

UNITED NATIONS

After World War II ended, in 1945, the United Nations was established to advance international peace and cooperation. Its mandate was to address not only the immediate aftermath of war but ongoing social, economic, legal and humanitarian issues. Initially composed of 51 member nations, the UN General Assembly has increased today to 192 members, the most recent being Switzerland, Timor-Leste, and Montenegro. In addition to the General Assembly, its major administrative bodies consist of the Economic and Social Council, the Security Council, the Secretariat, and the International Court of Justice. Like the rest of international politics, the UN has been fraught with disagreement and dissension throughout its history, though its members remain committed to prevent a repetition of the atrocities and genocide of World War II, "barbarous acts which have outraged the conscience of mankind" (*Preamble*). To reinforce these aims, led by Eleanor Roosevelt as the first chairperson of the Commission on Human Rights, the General Assembly adopted the Universal Declaration of Human Rights on December 10, 1948. She considered it "the international Magna Carta."

The Universal Declaration of Human Rights affirmed the UN principles to promote "a world in which human beings shall enjoy freedom of speech and belief and freedom from fear and want," and advocates such important human rights as freedom of speech, press, assembly, religion, and the rule of law, and a number of rights: to receive an education, to participate in government, to work, and to a decent standard of living and health care. Although member nations are not legally compelled to honor it, this document—reprinted here in full—is a simple, eloquent statement of the ideal principles of human rights and human relations which undergird life for individuals, families, and society more generally, intended to transcend time, culture, and nationality. Unfortunately, subsequent international events have not borne out its affirms that everyone will be free from slavery, gender inequality, racial discrimination, and exploitation.

The Universal Declaration of Human Rights

Preamble

Whereas recognition of the inherent dignity and of the equal and inalienable rights of all members of the human family is the foundation of freedom, justice and peace in the world,

Whereas disregard and contempt for human rights have resulted in barbarous acts which have outraged the conscience of mankind, and the advent of a world in which human beings shall enjoy freedom of speech and belief and freedom from fear and want has been proclaimed as the highest aspiration of the common people,

Whereas it is essential, if man is not to be compelled to have recourse, as a last resort, to rebellion against tyranny and oppression, that human rights should be protected by the rule of law,

Whereas it is essential to promote the development of friendly relations between nations,

Whereas the peoples of the United Nations have in the Charter reaffirmed their faith in fundamental human rights, in the dignity and worth of the human person and in the equal rights of men and women and have determined to promote social progress and better standards of life in larger freedom,

Whereas Member States have pledged themselves to achieve, in cooperation with the United Nations, the promotion of universal respect for and observance of human rights and fundamental freedoms,

Whereas a common understanding of these rights and freedoms is of the greatest importance for the full realization of this pledge,

Now, Therefore THE GENERAL ASSEMBLY proclaims THIS UNIVERSAL DECLARATION OF HUMAN RIGHTS as a common standard of achievement for all peoples and all nations, to the end that every individual and every organ of society, keeping this Declaration constantly in mind, shall strive by teaching and education to promote respect for these rights and freedoms and by progressive measures, national and international, to secure their universal and effective recognition and observance, both among the peoples of Member States themselves and among the peoples of territories under their jurisdiction.

Article 1

All human beings are born free and equal in dignity and rights. They are endowed with reason and conscience and should act towards one another in a spirit of brotherhood.

Article 2

Everyone is entitled to all the rights and freedoms set forth in this Declaration, without distinction of any kind, such as race, colour, sex, language, religion, political or other opinion, national or social origin, property, birth or other status. Furthermore, no distinction shall be made on the basis of the political, jurisdictional or international status of the country or territory to which a person belongs, whether it be independent, trust, non-self-governing or under any other limitation of sovereignty.

Article 3

Everyone has the right to life, liberty and security of person.

Article 4

No one shall be held in slavery or servitude; slavery and the slave trade shall be prohibited in all their forms.

Article 5

No one shall be subjected to torture or to cruel, inhuman or degrading treatment or punishment.

Article 6

Everyone has the right to recognition everywhere as a person before the law.

Article 7

All are equal before the law and are entitled without any discrimination to equal protection of the law. All are entitled to equal protection against any discrimination in violation of this Declaration and against any incitement to such discrimination.

Article 8

Everyone has the right to an effective remedy by the competent national tribunals for acts violating the fundamental rights granted him by the constitution or by law.

Article 9

No one shall be subjected to arbitrary arrest, detention or exile.

Article 10

Everyone is entitled in full equality to a fair and public hearing by an independent and impartial tribunal, in the determination of his rights and obligations and of any criminal charge against him.

Article 11

(1) Everyone charged with a penal offence has the right to be presumed innocent until proved guilty according to law in a public trial at which he has had all the guarantees necessary for his defence.
(2) No one shall be held guilty of any penal offence on account of any act or omission which did not constitute a penal offence, under national or international law, at the time when it was committed. Nor shall a heavier penalty be imposed than the one that was applicable at the time the penal offence was committed.

Article 12

No one shall be subjected to arbitrary interference with his privacy, family, home or correspondence, nor to attacks upon his honour and reputation. Everyone has the right to the protection of the law against such interference or attacks.

Article 13

(1) Everyone has the right to freedom of movement and residence within the borders of each state.
(2) Everyone has the right to leave any country, including his own, and to return to his country.

Article 14

(1) Everyone has the right to seek and to enjoy in other countries asylum from persecution.
(2) This right may not be invoked in the case of prosecutions genuinely arising from non-political crimes or from acts contrary to the purposes and principles of the United Nations.

Article 15

(1) Everyone has the right to a nationality.
(2) No one shall be arbitrarily deprived of his nationality nor denied the right to change his nationality.

Article 16

(1) Men and women of full age, without any limitation due to race, nationality or religion, have the right to marry and to found a family. They are entitled to equal rights as to marriage, during marriage and at its dissolution.
(2) Marriage shall be entered into only with the free and full consent of the intending spouses.
(3) The family is the natural and fundamental group unit of society and is entitled to protection by society and the State.

Article 17

(1) Everyone has the right to own property alone as well as in association with others.
(2) No one shall be arbitrarily deprived of his property.

Article 18

Everyone has the right to freedom of thought, conscience and religion; this right includes freedom to change his religion or belief, and freedom, either alone or in community with others and in public or private, to manifest his religion or belief in teaching, practice, worship and observance.

Article 19

Everyone has the right to freedom of opinion and expression; this right includes freedom to hold opinions without interference and to seek, receive and impart information and ideas through any media and regardless of frontiers.

Article 20

(1) Everyone has the right to freedom of peaceful assembly and association.
(2) No one may be compelled to belong to an association.

Article 21

(1) Everyone has the right to take part in the government of his country, directly or through freely chosen representatives.
(2) Everyone has the right of equal access to public service in his country.
(3) The will of the people shall be the basis of the authority of government; this will shall be expressed in periodic and genuine elections which shall be by universal and equal suffrage and shall be held by secret vote or by equivalent free voting procedures.

Article 22

Everyone, as a member of society, has the right to social security and is entitled to realization, through national effort and international co-operation and in accordance with the organization and resources of each State, of the economic, social and cultural rights indispensable for his dignity and the free development of his personality.

Article 23

(1) Everyone has the right to work, to free choice of employment, to just and favourable conditions of work and to protection against unemployment.
(2) Everyone, without any discrimination, has the right to equal pay for equal work.
(3) Everyone who works has the right to just and favourable remuneration ensuring for himself and his family an existence worthy of human dignity, and supplemented, if necessary, by other means of social protection.
(4) Everyone has the right to form and to join trade unions for the protection of his interests.

Article 24

Everyone has the right to rest and leisure, including reasonable limitation of working hours and periodic holidays with pay.

Article 25

(1) Everyone has the right to a standard of living adequate for the health and well-being of himself and of his family, including food, clothing, housing and medical care and necessary social services, and the right to security in the event of unemployment, sickness, disability, widowhood, old age or other lack of livelihood in circumstances beyond his control.
(2) Motherhood and childhood are entitled to special care and assistance. All children, whether born in or out of wedlock, shall enjoy the same social protection.

Article 26

(1) Everyone has the right to education. Education shall be free, at least in the elementary and fundamental stages. Elementary education shall be compulsory. Technical and professional education shall be made generally available and higher education shall be equally accessible to all on the basis of merit.
(2) Education shall be directed to the full development of the human personality and to the strengthening of respect for human rights and fundamental freedoms. It shall promote understanding, tolerance and friendship among all nations, racial or religious groups, and shall further the activities of the United Nations for the maintenance of peace.
(3) Parents have a prior right to choose the kind of education that shall be given to their children.

Article 27

(1) Everyone has the right freely to participate in the cultural life of the community, to enjoy the arts and to share in scientific advancement and its benefits.
(2) Everyone has the right to the protection of the moral and material interests resulting from any scientific, literary or artistic production of which he is the author.

Article 28

Everyone is entitled to a social and international order in which the rights and freedoms set forth in this Declaration can be fully realized.

Article 29

(1) Everyone has duties to the community in which alone the free and full development of his personality is possible.
(2) In the exercise of his rights and freedoms, everyone shall be subject only to such limitations as are determined by law solely for the purpose of securing due recognition and respect for the rights and freedoms of others and of meeting the just requirements of morality, public order and the general welfare in a democratic society.
(3) These rights and freedoms may in no case be exercised contrary to the purposes and principles of the United Nations.

Article 30

Nothing in this Declaration may be interpreted as implying for any State, group or person any right to engage in any activity or to perform any act aimed at the destruction of any of the rights and freedoms set forth herein.

AL GORE

Albert Arnold "Al" Gore, Jr. (born 1948) shared the Nobel Peace Prize for 2007 with the Intergovernmental Panel on Climate Change (IPCC) for their efforts to inform the world about "man-made climate change" and their work to establish measures needed to counteract such change. Gore, says the Nobel press release, "is probably the single individual who has done most to create greater worldwide understanding of the measures that need to be adopted" to strengthen "the struggle against climate change." Representing Tennessee, Gore was elected to the U.S. House of Representatives in 1976–84 and to the U.S. Senate, 1985–93. Among Gore's notable contributions was the legislation developed to create a national information infrastructure, "The Information Superhighway." He then served eight years as Bill Clinton's Vice President. He won the popular vote for the presidency in 2000, but as a consequence of a Supreme Court decision lost the Florida election recount, and ultimately the presidency, to George W. Bush. His books on ecology have been bestsellers: *Earth in the Balance: Ecology and the Human Spirit* (1992); *An Inconvenient Truth: The Planetary Emergency of Global Warming and What We Can Do About It* (2006), the movie based on this book won an Oscar for Best Documentary; and *Our Choice: A Plan to Solve the Climate Crisis* (2009). Gore's mission is to warn people of the rapid climate changes that have thrown the world into crisis, to cause them to acknowledge these harsh environmental truths and acknowledge "a moral imperative to act." The following Nobel lecture was delivered in Oslo, Norway, on December 10, 2007.

A Planetary Emergency (2007)

Nobel Lecture, Oslo, 10 December 2007.   1

We, the human species, are confronting a planetary emergency—a   2 threat to the survival of our civilization that is gathering ominous and destructive potential even as we gather here. But there is hopeful news as well: we have the ability to solve this crisis and avoid the worst—though not all—of its consequences, if we act boldly, decisively and quickly.

However, despite a growing number of honorable exceptions, too   3 many of the world's leaders are still best described in the words Winston Churchill applied to those who ignored Adolf Hitler's threat: "They go on in strange paradox, decided only to be undecided, resolved to be irresolute, adamant for drift, solid for fluidity, all powerful to be impotent."

So today, we dumped another 70 million tons of global-warming pollu-   4 tion into the thin shell of atmosphere surrounding our planet, as if it were an open sewer. And tomorrow, we will dump a slightly larger amount, with the cumulative concentrations now trapping more and more heat from the sun.

As a result, the earth has a fever. And the fever is rising. The experts   5 have told us it is not a passing affliction that will heal by itself. We asked for a second opinion. And a third. And a fourth. And the consistent conclusion, restated with increasing alarm, is that something basic is wrong.

6   We are what is wrong, and we must make it right.

7   Last September 21, as the Northern Hemisphere tilted away from the sun, scientists reported with unprecedented distress that the North Polar ice cap is "falling off a cliff." One study estimated that it could be completely gone during summer in less than 22 years. Another new study, to be presented by U.S. Navy researchers later this week, warns it could happen in as little as 7 years.

8   Seven years from now.

9   In the last few months, it has been harder and harder to misinterpret the signs that our world is spinning out of kilter. Major cities in North and South America, Asia and Australia are nearly out of water due to massive droughts and melting glaciers. Desperate farmers are losing their livelihoods. Peoples in the frozen Arctic and on low-lying Pacific islands are planning evacuations of places they have long called home. Unprecedented wildfires have forced a half million people from their homes in one country and caused a national emergency that almost brought down the government in another. Climate refugees have migrated into areas already inhabited by people with different cultures, religions, and traditions, increasing the potential for conflict. Stronger storms in the Pacific and Atlantic have threatened whole cities. Millions have been displaced by massive flooding in South Asia, Mexico, and 18 countries in Africa. As temperature extremes have increased, tens of thousands have lost their lives. We are recklessly burning and clearing our forests and driving more and more species into extinction. The very web of life on which we depend is being ripped and frayed.

10   We never intended to cause all this destruction. . . .

11   But unlike most other forms of pollution, CO_2 is invisible, tasteless, and odorless—which has helped keep the truth about what it is doing to our climate out of sight and out of mind. Moreover, the catastrophe now threatening us is unprecedented—and we often confuse the unprecedented with the improbable.

12   We also find it hard to imagine making the massive changes that are now necessary to solve the crisis. And when large truths are genuinely inconvenient, whole societies can, at least for a time, ignore them. Yet as George Orwell reminds us: "Sooner or later a false belief bumps up against solid reality, usually on a battlefield."

13   In the years since this prize was first awarded, the entire relationship between humankind and the earth has been radically transformed. And still, we have remained largely oblivious to the impact of our cumulative actions.

14   Indeed, without realizing it, we have begun to wage war on the earth itself. Now, we and the earth's climate are locked in a relationship familiar to war planners: "Mutually assured destruction."

More than two decades ago, scientists calculated that nuclear war 15 could throw so much debris and smoke into the air that it would block life-giving sunlight from our atmosphere, causing a "nuclear winter." Their eloquent warnings here in Oslo helped galvanize the world's resolve to halt the nuclear arms race.

Now science is warning us that if we do not quickly reduce the 16 global warming pollution that is trapping so much of the heat our planet normally radiates back out of the atmosphere, we are in danger of creating a permanent "carbon summer."

As the American poet Robert Frost wrote, "Some say the world will 17 end in fire; some say in ice." Either, he notes, "would suffice."

But neither need be our fate. It is time to make peace with the 18 planet. . . .

We must understand the connections between the climate crisis and 19 the afflictions of poverty, hunger, HIV-AIDS and other pandemics. As these problems are linked, so too must be their solutions. We must begin by making the common rescue of the global environment the central organizing principle of the world community. . . .

The world needs an alliance—especially of those nations that weigh 20 heaviest in the scales where earth is in the balance. I salute Europe and Japan for the steps they've taken in recent years to meet the challenge, and the new government in Australia, which has made solving the climate crisis its first priority.

But the outcome will be decisively influenced by two nations that 21 are now failing to do enough: the United States and China. While India is also growing fast in importance, it should be absolutely clear that it is the two largest CO_2 emitters—most of all, my own country—that will need to make the boldest moves, or stand accountable before history for their failure to act.

Both countries should stop using the other's behavior as an excuse 22 for stalemate and instead develop an agenda for mutual survival in a shared global environment. . . .

We have to expand the boundaries of what is possible. In the words 23 of the Spanish poet, Antonio Machado, "Pathwalker, there is no path. You must make the path as you walk."

WANGARI MAATHAI

Wangari Maathai was born in Nyeri, Kenya (Africa) in 1940, earned a BS in biology from Mount St. Scholastica College in Atchison, Kansas (1964), a MS from University of Pittsburgh (1966), and after studying in Germany, obtained a PhD from the University of Nairobi. There she chaired the Department of Veterinary Anatomy. During this time, while serving in the National Council of Women of Kenya, she introduced the idea of planting

Wangari Maathai receiving the Nobel Peace Prize, December 10, 2004.

trees on farms and in school and church compounds. Trees would refor-
est the mountains and create an environment conducive to clean drinking
water; they would provide firewood; fruit trees would help alleviate malnutrition. Over 30 million were planted in Kenya through the Green Belt
Movement; this eventually developed into the Pan African Green Belt Network serving Tanzania, Uganda, Malawi, Lesotho, Ethiopia, Zimbabwe,
and other countries. As a co-chair of the Jubilee 2000 Africa Campaign, she
promoted cancellation of the unpayable backlog debts of the poor countries in Africa by the year 2000 and led a campaign against land grabbing
and rapacious allocation of forest land. Beaten, harassed, and jailed for her
efforts by Daniel arap Moi, Kenya's strongman president, she was elected
to parliament in 2002 in Kenya's first free elections in a generation and
soon thereafter was appointed Kenya's Assistant Minister of Environment,
Natural Resources, and Wildlife. She has received innumerable awards,
worldwide, for her visionary efforts. Maathai's latest book, *The Challenge
for Africa* (2009), calls for the betterment of the continent on a cultural and
moral basis. Maathai died on September 25, 2011.

The Green Belt Movement (2004)

. . . In this year's prize, the Norwegian Nobel Committee has placed the critical issue of environment and its linkage to democracy and peace before the world. For their visionary action, I am profoundly grateful. Recognizing that sustainable development, democracy and peace are indivisible is an idea whose time has come. Our work over the past 30 years has always appreciated and engaged these linkages. 1

My inspiration partly comes from my childhood experiences and observations of Nature in rural Kenya. It has been influenced and nurtured by the formal education I was privileged to receive in Kenya, the United States and Germany. As I was growing up, I witnessed forests being cleared and replaced by commercial plantations, which destroyed local biodiversity and the capacity of the forests to conserve water. 2

Excellencies, ladies and gentlemen, 3

In 1977, when we started the Green Belt Movement, I was partly responding to needs identified by rural women, namely lack of firewood, clean drinking water, balanced diets, shelter and income. 4

Throughout Africa, women are the primary caretakers, holding significant responsibility for tilling the land and feeding their families. As a result, they are often the first to become aware of environmental damage as resources become scarce and incapable of sustaining their families. 5

The women we worked with recounted that unlike in the past, they were unable to meet their basic needs. This was due to the degradation of their immediate environment as well as the introduction of commercial farming, which replaced the growing of household food crops. But international trade controlled the price of the exports from these small-scale farmers and a reasonable and just income could not be guaranteed. I came to understand that when the environment is destroyed, plundered or mismanaged, we undermine our quality of life and that of future generations. 6

Tree planting became a natural choice to address some of the initial basic needs identified by women. Also, tree planting is simple, attainable and guarantees quick, successful results within a reasonable amount time. This sustains interest and commitment. 7

So, together, we have planted over 30 million trees that provide fuel, food, shelter, and income to support their children's education and household needs. The activity also creates employment and improves soils and watersheds. Through their involvement, women gain some degree of power over their lives, especially their social and economic position and relevance in the family. This work continues. 8

Initially, the work was difficult because historically our people have been persuaded to believe that because they are poor, they lack not 9

---

only capital, but also knowledge and skills to address their challenges. Instead they are conditioned to believe that solutions to their problems must come from 'outside.' Further, women did not realize that meeting their needs depended on their environment being healthy and well managed. They were also unaware that a degraded environment leads to a scramble for scarce resources and may culminate in poverty and even conflict. They were also unaware of the injustices of international economic arrangements.

10   In order to assist communities to understand these linkages, we developed a citizen education program, during which people identify their problems, the causes and possible solutions. They then make connections between their own personal actions and the problems they witness in the environment and in society. They learn that our world is confronted with a litany of woes: corruption, violence against women and children, disruption and breakdown of families, and disintegration of cultures and communities. They also identify the abuse of drugs and chemical substances, especially among young people. There are also devastating diseases that are defying cures or occurring in epidemic proportions. Of particular concern are HIV/AIDS, malaria and diseases associated with malnutrition.

11   On the environment front, they are exposed to many human activities that are devastating to the environment and societies. These include widespread destruction of ecosystems, especially through deforestation, climatic instability, and contamination in the soils and waters that all contribute to excruciating poverty.

12   In the process, the participants discover that they must be part of the solutions. They realize their hidden potential and are empowered to overcome inertia and take action. They come to recognize that they are the primary custodians and beneficiaries of the environment that sustains them.

13   Entire communities also come to understand that while it is necessary to hold their governments accountable, it is equally important that in their own relationships with each other, they exemplify the leadership values they wish to see in their own leaders, namely justice, integrity and trust.

14   Although initially the Green Belt Movement's tree planting activities did not address issues of democracy and peace, it soon became clear that responsible governance of the environment was impossible without democratic space. Therefore, the tree became a symbol for the democratic struggle in Kenya. Citizens were mobilised to challenge widespread abuses of power, corruption and environmental mismanagement. In Nairobi's Uhuru Park, at Freedom Corner, and in many parts of the country, trees of peace were planted to demand the release of prisoners of conscience and a peaceful transition to democracy.

Through the Green Belt Movement, thousands of ordinary citizens 15 were mobilized and empowered to take action and effect change. They learned to overcome fear and a sense of helplessness and moved to defend democratic rights.

In time, the tree also became a symbol for peace and conflict reso- 16 lution, especially during ethnic conflicts in Kenya when the Green Belt Movement used peace trees to reconcile disputing communities. During the ongoing re-writing of the Kenyan constitution, similar trees of peace were planted in many parts of the country to promote a culture of peace. Using trees as a symbol of peace is in keeping with a widespread African tradition. For example, the elders of the Kikuyu carried a staff from the thigi tree that, when placed between two disputing sides, caused them to stop fighting and seek reconciliation. Many communities in Africa have these traditions.

Such practises are part of an extensive cultural heritage, which con- 17 tributes both to the conservation of habitats and to cultures of peace. With the destruction of these cultures and the introduction of new values, local biodiversity is no longer valued or protected and as a result, it is quickly degraded and disappears. For this reason, The Green Belt Movement explores the concept of cultural biodiversity, especially with respect to indigenous seeds and medicinal plants.

As we progressively understood the cause of environmental degra- 18 dation, we saw the need for good governance. Indeed, the state of any country's environment is a reflection of the kind of governance in place, and without good governance there can be no peace. Many countries, which have poor governance systems, are also likely to have conflicts and poor laws protecting the environment.

In 2002, the courage, resilience, patience and commitment of mem- 19 bers of the Green Belt Movement, other civil society organizations, and the Kenyan public culminated in the peaceful transition to a democratic government and laid the foundation for a more stable society.

Excellencies, friends, ladies and gentlemen, 20

It is 30 years since we started this work. Activities that devastate the 21 environment and societies continue unabated. Today we are faced with a challenge that calls for a shift in our thinking, so that humanity stops threatening its life-support system. We are called to assist the Earth to heal her wounds and in the process heal our own—indeed, to embrace the whole creation in all its diversity, beauty and wonder. This will happen if we see the need to revive our sense of belonging to a larger family of life, with which we have shared our evolutionary process.

In the course of history, there comes a time when humanity is called 22 to shift to a new level of consciousness, to reach a higher moral ground. A time when we have to shed our fear and give hope to each other.

That time is now. 23

KOFI ANNAN

Kofi Annan spent his entire career in the United Nations. Born in 1938 in Kumasi, Ghana, Annan completed an undergraduate degree in economics at Macalester College in St. Paul, Minnesota, in 1961 and studied economics in Geneva from 1961 to 1962 before beginning work at the UN as a budget officer with the World Health Organization in Geneva. As a Sloan Fellow (1971–1972) he earned an MS in management from M.I.T. He later served with the UN Economic Commission for Africa in Addis Ababa; the UN Emergency Force in Ismailia; and the Office of the UN High Commissioner for Refugees in Geneva. At the UN in New York he held a variety of posts, including that of under secretary-general during a period of unprecedented growth in UN peacekeeping operations around the world (including Kuwait, Iraq, Bosnia, and Herzegovina) to, in 1995, 70,000 military and civilian personnel from seventy-seven countries. He was chosen as the seventh secretary-general of the UN in January of 1997 and served until his retirement in 2006. The 2001 Nobel Peace Prize was awarded to both the United Nations and to Kofi Annan for "their work for a better organized and more peaceful world. For one hundred years," says the citation, "the Norwegian Nobel Committee has sought to strengthen organized cooperation between states. The end of the cold war has at last made it possible for the UN to perform more fully the part it was originally intended to play. Today the organization is at the forefront of efforts to achieve peace and security in the world," and of international efforts to meet the world's economic, social, and environmental challenges. These include significant action on human rights and providing humanitarian aid to countries experiencing famine, drought, and medical epidemics such as HIV/AIDS.

Kofi Annan was United Nations Secretary General 1997–2006.

Doug Kanter/AFP/Getty Images

The United Nations in the 21st Century (2001)

We have entered the third millennium through a gate of fire. If today, after the horror of 11 September, we see better, and we see further— we will realize that humanity is indivisible. New threats make no distinction between races, nations or regions. A new insecurity has entered every mind, regardless of wealth or status. A deeper awareness of the bonds that bind us all—in pain as in prosperity—has gripped young and old. 1

In the early beginnings of the 21st century—a century already violently disabused of any hopes that progress towards global peace and prosperity is inevitable—this new reality can no longer be ignored. It must be confronted. 2

The 20th century was perhaps the deadliest in human history, devastated by innumerable conflicts, untold suffering, and unimaginable crimes. Time after time, a group or a nation inflicted extreme violence on another, often driven by irrational hatred and suspicion, or unbounded arrogance and thirst for power and resources. In response to these cataclysms, the leaders of the world came together at mid-century to unite the nations as never before. 3

A forum was created—the United Nations—where all nations could join forces to affirm the dignity and worth of every person, and to secure peace and development for all peoples. Here States could unite to strengthen the rule of law, recognize and address the needs of the poor, restrain man's brutality and greed, conserve the resources and beauty of nature, sustain the equal rights of men *and* women, and provide for the safety of future generations. 4

We thus inherit from the 20th century the political, as well as the scientific and technological power, which—if only we have the will to use them—give us the chance to vanquish poverty, ignorance and disease. 5

In the 21st century I believe the mission of the United Nations will be defined by a new, more profound, awareness of the sanctity and dignity of every human life, regardless of race or religion. This will require us to look beyond the framework of States, and beneath the surface of nations or communities. We must focus, as never before, on improving the conditions of the individual men and women who give the state or nation its richness and character. We must begin with the young Afghan girl [born in poverty], recognizing that saving that one life is to save humanity itself. 6

Over the past five years, I have often recalled that the United Nations' Charter begins with the words: "We the peoples." What is not always recognized is that "we the peoples" are made up of individuals whose claims to the most fundamental rights have too often been sacrificed in the supposed interests of the state or the nation. 7

8   A genocide begins with the killing of one man—not for what he has done, but because of who he is. A campaign of "ethnic cleansing" begins with one neighbour turning on another. Poverty begins when even one child is denied his or her fundamental right to education. What begins with the failure to uphold the dignity of one life, all too often ends with a calamity for entire nations.

9   In this new century, we must start from the understanding that peace belongs not only to states or peoples, but to each and every member of those communities. The sovereignty of States must no longer be used as a shield for gross violations of human rights. Peace must be made real and tangible in the daily existence of every individual in need. Peace must be sought, above all, because it is the condition for every member of the human family to live a life of dignity and security.

10   The rights of the individual are of no less importance to immigrants and minorities in Europe and the Americas than to women in Afghanistan or children in Africa. They are as fundamental to the poor as to the rich; they are as necessary to the security of the developed world as to that of the developing world.

11   From this vision of the role of the United Nations in the next century flow three key priorities for the future: eradicating poverty, preventing conflict, and promoting democracy. Only in a world that is rid of poverty can all men and women make the most of their abilities. Only where individual rights are respected can differences be channelled politically and resolved peacefully. Only in a democratic environment, based on respect for diversity and dialogue, can individual self-expression and self-government be secured, and freedom of association be upheld. . . .

12   The idea that there is one people in possession of the truth, one answer to the world's ills, or one solution to humanity's needs, has done untold harm throughout history—especially in the last century. Today, however, even amidst continuing ethnic conflict around the world, there is a growing understanding that human diversity is both the reality that makes dialogue necessary, and the very basis for that dialogue.

13   We understand, as never before, that each of us is fully worthy of the respect and dignity essential to our common humanity. We recognize that we are the products of many cultures, traditions and memories; that mutual respect allows us to study and learn from other cultures; and that we gain strength by combining the foreign with the familiar.

14   In every great faith and tradition one can find the values of tolerance and mutual understanding. The Qur'an, for example, tells us that "We created you from a single pair of male and female and made you into nations and tribes, that you may know each other." Confucius urged his followers: "when the good way prevails in the state, speak boldly and act boldly. When the state has lost the way, act boldly and speak softly." In the Jewish tradition, the injunction to "love thy neighbour as thyself," is considered to be the very essence of the Torah.

This thought is reflected in the Christian Gospel, which also teaches 15
us to love our enemies and pray for those who wish to persecute us. Hindus are taught that "truth is one, the sages give it various names." And in the Buddhist tradition, individuals are urged to act with compassion in every facet of life.

Each of us has the right to take pride in our particular faith or heri- 16
tage. But the notion that what is ours is necessarily in conflict with what is theirs is both false and dangerous. It has resulted in endless enmity and conflict, leading men to commit the greatest of crimes in the name of a higher power.

It need not be so. People of different religions and cultures live side 17
by side in almost every part of the world, and most of us have overlapping identities which unite us with very different groups. We *can* love what we are, without hating what—and who—we are *not*. We can thrive in our own tradition, even as we learn from others, and come to respect their teachings.

This will not be possible, however, without freedom of religion, of 18
expression, of assembly, and basic equality under the law. Indeed, the lesson of the past century has been that where the dignity of the individual has been trampled or threatened—where citizens have not enjoyed the basic right to choose their government, or the right to change it regularly— conflict has too often followed, with innocent civilians paying the price, in lives cut short and communities destroyed.

The obstacles to democracy have little to do with culture or religion, 19
and much more to do with the desire of those in power to maintain their position at any cost. This is neither a new phenomenon nor one confined to any particular part of the world. People of all cultures value their freedom of choice, and feel the need to have a say in decisions affecting their lives.

The United Nations, whose membership comprises almost all the 20
States in the world, is founded on the principle of the equal worth of every human being. It is the nearest thing we have to a representative institution that can address the interests of all states, and all peoples. Through this universal, indispensable instrument of human progress, States can serve the interests of their citizens by recognizing common interests and pursuing them in unity. No doubt, that is why the Nobel Committee says that it "wishes, in its centenary year, to proclaim that the only negotiable route to global peace and cooperation goes by way of the United Nations."

I believe the Committee also recognized that this era of global chal- 21
lenges leaves no choice but cooperation at the global level. When States undermine the rule of law and violate the rights of their individual citizens, they become a menace not only to their own people, but also to their neighbours, and indeed the world. What we need today is better governance—legitimate, democratic governance that allows each individual to flourish, and each State to thrive.

MÉDECINS SANS FRONTIÈRES

22   "Médecins Sans Frontières" ("Doctors Without Borders") received the Nobel Peace Prize in 1999 for "pioneering humanitarian work on several continents." The Nobel citation explains, "Since its foundation in the early 1970s, Médecins Sans Frontières has adhered to the fundamental principle that all disaster victims, whether the disaster is natural or human in origin, have a right to professional assistance, delivered as quickly and efficiently as possible. National boundaries and political circumstances or sympathies must have no influence on who is to receive humanitarian help." MSF has remained independent. It moves into hostile and dangerous situations rapidly, and in the process of treating victims of crisis, pinpoints the causes of such catastrophes and helps to influence public opinion to warring parties. "At the same time, each fearless and self-sacrificing" helper— doctor, nurse, aide—"shows each victim a human face, stands for respect for that person's dignity, and is a source of hope for peace and reconciliation."

23   James Orbinski, president of MSF from 1998 to 2000, accepted the award on behalf of the organization. Born in the United Kingdom in 1960, Orbinski moved to Montreal in 1968. He earned bachelor's degree from Trent College in 1984 and an MD from McMaster Medical School in 1990. After spending his final year of medical school in Rwanda doing pediatric AIDS research, he formed MSF Canada in 1990 and worked with MSF during the Somalian civil war (1992), in Afghanistan during the civil war (1993), in Rwanda during the genocide (1994), in Zaire during the early stages of the civil war (1996), and on the National Immunization program. Orbinski has been awarded the Order of Canada and the Meritorious Service Cross. Orbinski is also Chair of the Board of Directors of Dignitas International, a humanitarian organization aimed at treating and preventing HIV/AIDS. He is currently an associate professor of medicine and the Chair of Global Health at the Dalla Lana School of Public Health at the University of Toronto.

Humanitarianism (1999)

1   The honor you give us today could so easily go to so many organizations, or worthy individuals, who struggle in their own society. But clearly, you have made a choice to recognize MSF. We began formally in 1971 as a group of French doctors and journalists who decided to make themselves available to assist. This meant sometimes a rejection of the practices of states that directly assault the dignity of people. Silence has long been confused with neutrality, and has been presented as a necessary condition for humanitarian action.

From its beginning, MSF was created in opposition to this assumption. We are not sure that words can always save lives, but we know that silence can certainly kill. Over our 28 years we have been—and are today—firmly and irrevocably committed to this ethic of refusal. This is the proud genesis of our identity, and today we struggle as an imperfect movement, but strong in thousands of volunteers and national staff, and with millions of donors who support both financially and morally, the project that is MSF. This honor is shared with all who in one way or another, have struggled and do struggle every day to make live the fragile reality that is MSF.

Humanitarianism occurs where the political has failed or is in crisis.   2
We act not to assume political responsibility, but firstly to relieve the inhuman suffering of failure. The act must be free of political influence, and the political must recognize its responsibility to ensure that the humanitarian can exist. Humanitarian action requires a framework in which to act.

In conflict, this framework is international humanitarian law. It es-   3
tablishes rights for victims and humanitarian organisations and fixes the responsibility of states to ensure respect of these rights and to sanction their violation as war crimes. Today this framework is clearly dysfunctional. Access to victims of conflict is often refused. Humanitarian assistance is even used as a tool of war by belligerents. And more seriously, we are seeing the militarisation of humanitarian action by the international community.

In this dysfunction, we will speak-out to push the political to as-   4
sume its inescapable responsibility. Humanitarianism is not a tool to end war or to create peace. It is a citizen's response to political failure. It is an immediate, short term act that cannot erase the long term necessity of political responsibility.

And ours is an ethic of refusal. It will not allow any moral political   5
failure or injustice to be sanitized or cleansed of its meaning. The 1992 crimes against humanity in Bosnia-Herzegovina. The 1994 genocide in Rwanda. The 1997 massacres in Zaire. The 1999 actual attacks on civilians in Chechnya. These cannot be masked by terms like "Complex Humanitarian Emergency," or "Internal Security Crisis." Or by any other such euphemism—as though they are some random, politically undetermined event. Language is determinant. It frames the problem and defines response, rights and therefore responsibilities. It defines whether a medical or humanitarian response is adequate. And it defines whether a political response is inadequate. No one calls a rape a complex gynecologic emergency. A rape is a rape, just as a genocide is a genocide. And both are a crime. For MSF, this is the humanitarian act: to seek to relieve suffering, to seek to restore autonomy, to witness to the truth of injustice, and to insist on political responsibility.

The work that MSF chooses does not occur in a vacuum, but in a   6
social order that both includes and excludes, that both affirms and denies, and that both protects and attacks. Our daily work is a struggle, and it is intensely medical, and it is intensely personal. MSF is not a formal

institution, and with any luck at all, it never will be. It is a civil society organization, and today civil society has a new global role, a new informal legitimacy that is rooted in its action and in its support from public opinion. It is also rooted in the maturity of its intent, in for example the human rights, the environmental and the humanitarian movements, and of course, the movement for equitable trade. Conflict and violence are not the only subjects of concern. We, as members of civil society, will maintain our role and our power if we remain lucid in our intent and independence.

7   As civil society we exist relative to the state, to its institutions and its power. We also exist relative to other non-state actors such as the private sector. Ours is not to displace the responsibility of the state. Ours is not to allow a humanitarian alibi to mask the state responsibility to ensure justice and security. And ours is not to be co-managers of misery with the state. If civil society identifies a problem, it is not theirs to provide a solution, but it is theirs to expect that states will translate this into concrete and just solutions. Only the state has the legitimacy and power to do this. Today, a growing injustice confronts us. More than 90% of all death and suffering from infectious diseases occurs in the developing world. Some of the reasons that people die from diseases like AIDS, TB, Sleeping Sickness and other tropical diseases is that life saving essential medicines are either too expensive, are not available because they are not seen as financially viable, or because there is virtually no new research and development for priority tropical diseases. This market failure is our next challenge. The challenge however, is not ours alone. It is also for governments, International Government Institutions, the Pharmaceutical Industry and other NGOs to confront this injustice. What we as a civil society movement demand is change, not charity.

8   We affirm the independence of the humanitarian from the political, but this is not to polarize the "good" NGO against "bad" governments, or the "virtue" of civil society against the "vice" of political power. Such a polemic is false and dangerous. As with slavery and welfare rights, history has shown that humanitarian preoccupations born in civil society have gained influence until they reach the political agenda. But these convergences should not mask the distinctions that exist between the political and the humanitarian. Humanitarian action takes place in the short term, for limited groups and for limited objectives. This is at the same time both its strength and its limitation. The political can only be conceived in the long term, which itself is the movement of societies. Humanitarian action is by definition universal, or it is not. Humanitarian responsibility has no frontiers. Wherever in the world there is manifest distress, the humanitarian by vocation must respond. By contrast, the political knows borders, and where crisis occurs, political response will vary because historical relations, balance of power, and the interests of one or the other must be considered. The time and space of the humanitarian are not those of the

political. These vary in opposing ways, and this is another way to locate the founding principles of humanitarian action: the refusal of all forms of problem solving through sacrifice of the weak and vulnerable. No victim can be intentionally discriminated against, OR neglected to the advantage of another. One life today cannot be measured by its value tomorrow: and the relief of suffering "here," cannot legitimize the abandoning of relief "over there." The limitation of means naturally must mean the making of choice, but the context and the constraints of action do not alter the fundamentals of this humanitarian vision. It is a vision that by definition must ignore political choices.

RIGOBERTA MENCHÚ TUM

Rigoberta Menchú Tum received the 1992 Nobel Peace Prize "in recognition of her work for social justice and ethno-cultural reconciliation based on respect for the rights of indigenous peoples." In the 1970s and 1980s Guatemala, like many other countries in South and Central America, was filled with tremendous tension between descendants of European immigrants and the native Indian peoples, who were brutally suppressed and persecuted. Menchú Tum, a social and political activist, said the Nobel committee, "stands out as a vivid symbol of peace and reconciliation across ethnic, cultural and social dividing lines," nationwide and worldwide.

Rigoberta Menchú Tum was born in 1959 to a poor Indian peasant family in Guatemala and raised in the Quiche branch of the Mayan culture. As a teenager she became involved in social reform activities through the Catholic Church, including becoming an advocate for women's rights—efforts that aroused opposition of those in power. The Menchú family was accused of guerilla activities; her father was imprisoned and tortured for allegedly having participated in the execution of a local plantation owner. After his release he became a member of the Committee of the Peasant Union (CUC), which Menchú Tum joined in 1979—the year her brother was tortured and killed by the army. The following year her father was killed by security forces, and her mother died after being arrested, raped, and tortured. In 1981 Menchú Tum's activities in educating the Indian peasant population to re-sist military oppression forced her to go into hiding in Guatemala and then flee to Mexico. She helped to found an opposition body, the United Representation of the Guatemalan Opposition (RUOG). In a week of recorded interviews with anthropologist Elisabeth Burgos-Debray, she told her life story. The book, *I, Rigoberta Menchú,* was published in 1983, translated into a dozen languages, and soon acquired incendiary international fame as the embodiment of the atrocities committed by the Guatemalan army in peasant villages during the civil war.

In 1999 David Stoll, though fully supportive of her Nobel Prize, published a critique of the book—*Menchú and the Story of All Poor Guatemalans*

(1999)—demonstrating that parts of her own and her family history are in error, even when she speaks as an eyewitness. Stoll, an anthropologist who studied Mayan peasants, feels that "by inaccurately portraying the events in her own village as representative of what happened in all such indigenous villages in Guatemala, she gives a misleading interpretation of the relationship of the Mayan peasants to the revolutionary movement." The Nobel Prize committee defended its decision to award the prize to Menchú Tum, saying that this "was not based exclusively or primarily on the autobiography," and dismissed any suggestion that the Committee should consider revoking the prize. *The Rigoberta Menchú Controversy* (2002) is a superb collection of "primary documents—newspaper articles, interviews, and official statements" complemented by assessments by distinguished international scholars of the political, historical, and cultural implications of this debate.

Five Hundred Years of Mayan Oppression (1992)

1   Please allow me, ladies and gentlemen, to say some words about my country and the Civilization of the Mayas. The Maya people developed and spread geographically through some 300,000 square km; they occupied parts of the South of Mexico, Belize, Guatemala, as well as Honduras and El Salvador; they developed a very rich civilization in the area of political organization, as well as in social and economic fields; they were great scientists in the fields of mathematics, astronomy, agriculture, architecture and engineering; they were great artists in the fields of sculpture, painting, weaving and carving. . . .

2   Who can predict what other great scientific conquests and developments these people could have achieved, if they had not been conquered in blood and fire, and subjected to an ethnocide that affected nearly 50 million people in the course of 500 years.

3   I would describe the meaning of this Nobel Prize, in the first place as a tribute to the indian people who have been sacrificed and have disappeared because they aimed at a more dignified and just life with fraternity and understanding among the human beings. To those who are no longer alive to keep up the hope for a change in the situation in respect of poverty and marginalization of the indians, of those who have been banished, of the helpless in Guatemala as well as in the entire American Continent.

4   This growing concern is comforting, even though it comes 500 years later, to the suffering, the discrimination, the oppression and the exploitation that our people has been exposed to, but who, thanks to their own

cosmovision—and concept of life, have managed to withstand and finally see some promising prospects. How those roots, that were to be eradicated, now begin to grow with strength, hopes and visions for the future!

It also represents a sign of the growing international interest for, and 5 understanding of the original Rights of the People, of the future of more than 60 million indians that live in our America, and their uproar because of the 500 years of oppression that they have endured. For the genocides beyond comparison that they have had to suffer all this time, and from which other countries and the elite of the Americas have profited and taken advantage.

Let there be freedom for the indians, wherever they may be in the 6 American Continent or else in the world, because while they are alive, a glow of hope will be alive as well as the real concept of life.

The expressions of great happiness by the Indian Organizations in 7 the entire Continent and the worldwide congratulations received for the award of the Nobel Peace Prize, clearly indicate the great importance of this decision. It is the recognition of the European debt to the American indigenous people; it is an appeal to the conscience of Humanity so that those conditions of marginalization that condemned them to colonialism and exploitation may be eradicated; it is a cry for life, peace, justice, equality and fraternity between human beings.

The peculiarities of the vision of the indian people are expressed 8 according to the way in which they relate. First of all, between human being[s], through communication. Second, with the earth, as with our mother, because she gives us our lives and is not a mere merchandise. Third, with nature, because we are integral parts of it, and not its owners.

To us mother earth is not only a source of economic riches that give 9 us the maize, which is our life, but she also provides so many other things that the privileged ones of today strive after. The earth is the root and the source of our culture. She keeps our memories, she receives our ancestors and she therefore demands that we honour her and return to her, with tenderness and respect, those goods that she gives us. We have to take care of her and look after mother earth so that our children and grandchildren may continue to benefit from her. If the world does not learn now to show respect to nature, what kind of future will the new generations have?

From these basic features derive behaviour, rights and obligations 10 in the American Continent, for indians as well as for non-indians, whether they be racially mixed, blacks, whites or Asian. The whole society has the obligation to show mutual respect, to learn from each other and to share material and scientific achievements, in the most convenient way. The indians have never had, and they do not have, the place that they should have occupied in the progress and benefits of science and technology, although they have represented an important basis.

11   If the indian civilizations and the European civilizations could have made exchanges in a peaceful and harmonious manner, without destruction, exploitation, discrimination and poverty, they could, no doubt, have achieved greater and more valuable conquests for Humanity.

12   Let us not forget that when the Europeans came to America, there were flourishing and strong civilizations there. One cannot talk about a discovery of America, because one discovers that which one does not know about, or that which is hidden. But America and its native civilizations had discovered themselves long before the fall of the Roman Empire and the Medieval Europe. The significance of its cultures form part of the heritage of humanity and continue to astonish the learned ones. . . .

13   We the indians are willing to combine tradition with modernism, but not at all costs. We will not tolerate nor permit that our future be planned as possible guardians of ethno-touristic projects at continental level.

14   At a time when the commemoration of the Fifth Centenary of the arrival of Columbus in America has repercussions all over the world, the revival of hopes for the indian people claims that we reassert to the world our existence and the value of our cultural identity. It demands that we endeavour to actively participate in the decisions that concern our destiny, in the building-up of our countries/nations. Should we, in spite of all, not be taken into consideration, there are factors that guarantee our future: struggle and endurance; courage; the decision to maintain our traditions that have been exposed to so many perils and sufferings; solidarity towards our struggle on the part of numerous countries, governments, organizations and citizens of the world.

15   That is why I dream of the day when the relationship between the indigenous people and other people is strengthened; when they can join their potentialities and their capabilities and contribute to make life on this planet less unequal.

AUNG SAN SUU KYI

Aung San Suu Kyi, the daughter of Burma's liberation leader Aung San, was born in Rangoon, then Burma, now Myanmar, in 1945. In 1991 she was awarded the Nobel Peace Prize, which her sons accepted on her behalf because she was under house arrest. Her father, General Aung San, then commander of the Burma Independence Army, was assassinated when Suu Kyi was two years old. Her mother, Daw Khin Kyi, continued to champion the cause, attaining prominence in social planning and social policy, and it was partly through her efforts that the Independent Union of Burma was established in 1948. In 1960 Daw Khin Kyi was appointed Burma's ambassador to India. Suu Kyi, who accompanied her mother, attended preparatory

David Van Der Veen/AFP/Getty Images

"Read" the speech that Aung San Suu Kyi is making. Who is her audience? What does she want to happen as a consequence of her speaking? How do her physical attractiveness, gender, and dress reinforce—or contradict—your interpretation?

school in New Delhi, followed by a BA in philosophy, politics, and economics at Oxford. Her background, marriage to Michael Aris, a scholar of Tibetan civilization, and friendships with high-ranking officials in England, the United States, Bhutan, Japan, and India, led to work at the UN, study at Oxford, and international visibility as she assumed leadership of the opposition party, the National League for Democracy, in Burma as her mother was dying in 1988.

Harassment of Suu Kyi and her nonviolent party began immediately, with brutal arrests and killings. After facing down troops with rifles aimed at her in April 1989, she was placed under house arrest in July 1989. Her heroic actions had already made her an important symbol in the struggle against oppression. In May 1990, despite Suu Kyi's continued detention, her party won 82 percent of the seats in parliament, but the military state voided the results. It was in this climate that the Nobel Prize committee awarded her the Peace Prize, "to honor her nonviolent struggle for democracy and human rights" and to show "support for the many people throughout the world who are striving to attain democracy, human rights, and ethnic conciliation by peaceful means." As of 2010, Aung San Suu Kyi had spent a total of eighteen years under house arrest, refusing offers of freedom and reunion with her husband (who died in 1999 without being allowed to visit her) and sons if she would leave the country and withdraw from politics. Like Nelson Mandela, she chose separation from her family as one of the personal sacrifices she had to make in order to work for a larger, more humanitarian cause—in this case, a free Burma.

The Revolution of Spirit (1991)

1 . . . I stand before you here today to accept on behalf of my mother, Aung San Suu Kyi, this greatest of prizes, the Nobel Prize for Peace. Because circumstances do not permit my mother to be here in person, I will do my best to convey the sentiments I believe she would express.

2 Firstly, I know that she would begin by saying that she accepts the Nobel Prize for Peace not in her own name but in the name of all the people of Burma. She would say that this prize belongs not to her but to all those men, women and children who, even as I speak, continue to sacrifice their well being, their freedom and their lives in pursuit of a democratic Burma. Theirs is the prize and theirs will be the eventual victory in Burma's long struggle for peace, freedom and democracy.

3 Speaking as her son, however, I would add that I personally believe that by her own dedication and personal sacrifice she has come to be a worthy symbol through whom the plight of all the people of Burma may be recognized.

4 And no one must underestimate that plight. The plight of those in the countryside and towns, living in poverty and destitution, those in prison, battered and tortured; the plight of the young people, the hope of Burma, dying of malaria in the jungles to which they have fled; that of the Buddhist monks, beaten and dishonoured. Nor should we forget the many senior and highly respected leaders besides my mother who are all incarcerated.

5 It is on their behalf that I thank you, from my heart, for this supreme honour. The Burmese people can today hold their heads a little higher in the knowledge that in this far distant land their suffering has been heard and heeded.

6 We must also remember that the lonely struggle taking place in a heavily guarded compound in Rangoon is part of the much larger struggle, worldwide, for the emancipation of the human spirit from political tyranny and psychological subjection. The Prize, I feel sure, is also intended to honour all those engaged in this struggle wherever they may be. It is not without reason that today's events in Oslo fall on the International Human Rights Day, celebrated throughout the world.

7 Mr Chairman, the whole international community has applauded the choice of your Committee. Just a few days ago, the United Nations passed a unanimous and historic resolution welcoming Secretary-General Javier Pérez de Cuéllar's statement on the significance of this award and endorsing his repeated appeals for my mother's early release from detention. Universal concern at the grave human rights situation in Burma was clearly expressed. Alone and isolated among the entire nations of the world a single dissenting voice was heard, from the military junta in Rangoon, too late and too weak.

This regime has through almost thirty years of misrule reduced the 8
once prosperous "Golden Land" of Burma to one of the world's most economically destitute nations. In their heart of hearts even those in power
now in Rangoon must know that their eventual fate will be that of all
totalitarian regimes who seek to impose their authority through fear, repression, and hatred. When the present Burmese struggle for democracy
erupted onto the streets in 1988 it was the first of what became an international tidal wave of such movements throughout Eastern Europe, Asia
and Africa. Today, in 1991, Burma stands conspicuous in its continued suffering at the hands of a repressive, intransigent junta, the State Law and
Order Restoration Council. However, the example of those nations which
have successfully achieved democracy holds out an important message
to the Burmese people: that, in the last resort, through the sheer economic
unworkability of totalitarianism this present regime will be swept away.
And today in the face of rising inflation, a mismanaged economy and
near worthless Kyat, the Burmese Government is undoubtedly reaping
as it has sown.

However, it is my deepest hope that it will not be in the face of com- 9
plete economic collapse that the regime will fall, but that the ruling junta
may yet heed such appeals to basic humanity as that which the Nobel
Committee has expressed in its award of this year's Prize. I know that
within the military government there *are* those to whom the present policies of fear and repression are abhorrent, violating as they do the most
sacred principles of Burma's Buddhist heritage. This is no empty wishful
thinking but a conviction my mother reached in the course of her dealings
with those in positions of authority, illustrated by the election victories of
her party in constituencies comprised almost exclusively of military personnel and their families. It is my profoundest wish that these elements
for moderation and reconciliation among those now in authority may
make their sentiments felt in Burma's hour of deepest need.

I know that if she were free today my mother would in thanking you 10
also ask you to pray that the oppressors and the oppressed should throw
down their weapons and join together to build a nation founded on humanity in the spirit of peace.

Although my mother is often described as a political dissident who 11
strives by peaceful means for democratic change, we should remember
that her quest is basically spiritual. As she has said, "The quintessential
revolution is that of the spirit," and she has written of the "essential spiritual aims" of the struggle. The realization of this depends solely on human responsibility. At the root of that responsibility lies, and I quote, "the
concept of perfection, the urge to achieve it, the intelligence to find a path
towards it, and the will to follow that path if not to the end, at least the
distance needed to rise above individual limitation. . . ." "To live the full
life," she says, "one must have the courage to bear the responsibility of
the needs of others . . . one must *want* to bear this responsibility." And she

links this firmly to her faith when she writes, " . . . Buddhism, the foundation of traditional Burmese culture, places the greatest value on man, who alone of all beings can achieve the supreme state of Buddhahood. Each man has in him the potential to realize the truth through his own will and endeavour and to help others to realize it." Finally she says, "The quest for democracy in Burma is the struggle of a people to live whole, meaningful lives as free and equal members of the world community. It is part of the unceasing human endeavour to prove that the spirit of man can transcend the flaws of his nature."

12   It only remains for me to thank you all from the bottom of my heart. Let us hope and pray that from today the wounds start to heal and that in the years to come the 1991 Nobel Prize for Peace will be seen as a historic step towards the achievement of true peace in Burma. The lessons of the past will not be forgotten, but it is our hope for the future that we celebrate today.

THE 14TH DALAI LAMA, TENZIN GYATSO

The 14th Dalai Lama, Tenzin Gyatso, born to a peasant family in Takster, Tibet, in 1935, was recognized at the age of two as the reincarnation of his predecessor, the 13th Dalai Lama. In the Buddhist faith, Dalai Lamas (the name means "Oceans of Wisdom") are believed to be manifestations of the Bodhisattva of Compassion, who chose to reincarnate to serve the people. His monastic education began at six and culminated in a Doctorate of Buddhist Philosophy awarded when he was twenty-five. His political education took place concurrently, for in 1950 he assumed full power as Head of State and Government when Tibet's autonomy was threatened by Communist China. His meetings with Mao Tse-Tung and Chou En-Lai were in vain, for in 1959 he was forced into exile in India by the Chinese military occupation of Tibet—events depicted in the popular film *Kundun* (meaning "The Presence").

Since then the Dalai Lama has conducted the Tibetan government-in-exile from Dharamsala, India, and—unlike many of his predecessors—traveled worldwide on diplomatic missions, in part aiming to preserve the integrity of the Tibetan national identity and cultural heritage. He proposed to the Congressional Human Rights Caucus in 1987 a Five-Point Peace Plan designed to ensure the integrity of Tibet: (1) designate Tibet as a zone of peace, (2) end the massive transfer of ethnic Chinese into Tibet, (3) restore to Tibet fundamental human rights and democratic freedoms, (4) abandon China's use of Tibet to produce nuclear weapons and as a dumping ground for nuclear waste, and (5) create a self-governing Tibet, in association with the People's Republic of China. The Tibetan people themselves, insists His Holiness, "must be the ultimate deciding authority." It was because of these "constructive and forward-looking proposals for the solution of international conflicts, human rights issues, and global

Tenzin Gyatso, the 14th Dalai Lama, speaking in Seattle in April 2008, in advance of the Beijing Olympics, on peoples' right to peaceful demonstration.

environmental problems" that the 14th Dalai Lama was awarded the Nobel Peace Prize for 1989. Although none of these proposals has come to pass, the Dalai Lama remains a revered spiritual leader, internationally respected except by the government of the People's Republic of China.

Inner Peace and Human Rights (1989)

Peace, in the sense of the absence of war, is of little value to someone who is dying of hunger or cold. It will not remove the pain of torture inflicted on a prisoner of conscience. It does not comfort those who have lost their loved ones in floods caused by senseless deforestation in a neighbouring country. Peace can only last where human rights are respected, where the people are fed, and where individuals and nations are free. True peace with oneself and with the world around us can only be achieved through the development of mental peace. The other phenomena mentioned above are similarly interrelated. Thus, for example, we see that a clean environment, wealth or democracy mean little in the face of war, especially nuclear war, and that material development is not sufficient to ensure human happiness. 1

Material progress is of course important for human advancement. In Tibet, we paid much too little attention to technological and economic development, and today we realise that this was a mistake. At the same 2 time, material development without spiritual development can also cause serious problems. In some countries too much attention is paid to external things and very little importance is given to inner development. I believe both are important and must be developed side by side so as to achieve a good balance between them. Tibetans are always described by foreign visitors as being a happy, jovial people. This is part of our national character, formed by cultural and religious values that stress the importance of mental peace through the generation of love and kindness to all other living sentient beings, both human and animal. Inner peace is the key: if you have inner peace, the external problems do not affect your deep sense of peace and tranquility. In that state of mind you can deal with situations with calmness and reason, while keeping your inner happiness. That is very important. Without this inner peace, no matter how comfortable your life is materially, you may still be worried, disturbed or unhappy because of circumstances.

3   Clearly, it is of great importance, therefore, to understand the interrelationship among these and other phenomena, and to approach and attempt to solve problems in a balanced way that takes these different aspects into consideration. Of course it is not easy. But it is of little benefit to try to solve one problem if doing so creates an equally serious new one. So really we have no alternative: we must develop a sense of universal responsibility not only in the geographic sense, but also in respect to the different issues that confront our planet.

4   Responsibility does not only lie with the leaders of our countries or with those who have been appointed or elected to do a particular job. It lies with each one of us individually. Peace, for example, starts with each one of us. When we have inner peace, we can be at peace with those around us. When our community is in a state of peace, it can share that peace with neighbouring communities, and so on. When we feel love and kindness towards others, it not only makes others feel loved and cared for, but it helps us also to develop inner happiness and peace. And there are ways in which we can consciously work to develop feelings of love and kindness. For some of us, the most effective way to do so is through religious practice. For others it may be non-religious practices. What is important is that we each make a sincere effort to take our responsibility for each other and for the natural environment we live in seriously.

5   I am very encouraged by the developments which are taking place around us. After the young people of many countries, particularly in northern Europe, have repeatedly called for an end to the dangerous destruction of the environment which was being conducted in the name of economic development, the world's political leaders are now starting to take meaningful steps to address this problem. The report to the United Nations Secretary-General by the World Commission on the Environment and Development (the Brundtland Report) was an important step in educating governments on the urgency of the issue. Serious efforts to bring peace to war-torn zones and to implement the right to self-determination

of some people have resulted in the withdrawal of Soviet troops from Afghanistan and the establishment of independent Namibia. Through persistent nonviolent popular efforts dramatic changes, bringing many countries closer to real democracy, have occurred in many places, from Manila in the Philippines to Berlin in East Germany. With the Cold War era apparently drawing to a close, people everywhere live with renewed hope. Sadly, the courageous efforts of the Chinese people to bring similar change to their country was brutally crushed last June. But their efforts too are a source of hope. The military might has not extinguished the desire for freedom and the determination of the Chinese people to achieve it. I particularly admire the fact that these young people who have been taught that "power grows from the barrel of the gun," chose, instead, to use nonviolence as their weapon.

What these positive changes indicate, is that reason, courage, deter- 6 mination, and the inextinguishable desire for freedom can ultimately win. In the struggle between forces of war, violence and oppression on the one hand, and peace, reason and freedom on the other, the latter are gaining the upper hand. This realisation fills us Tibetans with hope that some day we too will once again be free.

The awarding of the Nobel Prize to me, a simple monk from far- 7 away Tibet, here in Norway, also fills us Tibetans with hope. It means, despite the fact that we have not drawn attention to our plight by means of violence, we have not been forgotten. It also means that the values we cherish, in particular our respect for all forms of life and the belief in the power of truth, are today recognised and encouraged. It is also a tribute to my mentor, Mahatma Gandhi, whose example is an inspiration to so many of us. This year's award is an indication that this sense of universal responsibility is developing. I am deeply touched by the sincere concern shown by so many people in this part of the world for the suffering of the people of Tibet. That is a source of hope not only for us Tibetans, but for all oppressed people.

As you know, Tibet has, for forty years, been under foreign occu- 8 pation. Today, more than a quarter of a million Chinese troops are stationed in Tibet. Some sources estimate the occupation army to be twice this strength. During this time, Tibetans have been deprived of their most basic human rights, including the right to life, movement, speech, worship, only to mention a few. More than one sixth of Tibet's population of six million died as a direct result of the Chinese invasion and occupation. Even before the Cultural Revolution started, many of Tibet's monasteries, temples and historic buildings were destroyed. Almost everything that remained was destroyed during the Cultural Revolution. I do not wish to dwell on this point, which is well documented. What is important to realise, however, is that despite the limited freedom granted after 1979, to rebuild parts of some monasteries and other such tokens of liberalisation, the fundamental human rights of the Tibetan people are still today being systematically violated. In recent months this bad situation has become even worse.

9   If it were not for our community in exile, so generously sheltered and supported by the government and people of India and helped by organisations and individuals from many parts of the world, our nation would today be little more than a shattered remnant of a people. Our culture, religion and national identity would have been effectively eliminated. As it is, we have built schools and monasteries in exile and have created democratic institutions to serve our people and preserve the seeds of our civilisation. With this experience, we intend to implement full democracy in a future free Tibet. Thus, as we develop our community in exile on modern lines, we also cherish and preserve our own identity and culture and bring hope to millions of our countrymen and -women in Tibet.

10   The issue of most urgent concern at this time, is the massive influx of Chinese settlers into Tibet. Although in the first decades of occupation a considerable number of Chinese were transferred into the eastern parts of Tibet—in the Tibetan provinces of Amdo (Chinghai) and Kham (most of which has been annexed by neighboring Chinese provinces)—since 1983 an unprecedented number of Chinese have been encouraged by their government to migrate to all parts of Tibet, including central and western Tibet (which the People's Republic of China refers to as the so-called Tibet Autonomous Region). Tibetans are rapidly being reduced to an insignificant minority in their own country. This development, which threatens the very survival of the Tibetan nation, its culture and spiritual heritage, can still be stopped and reversed. But this must be done now, before it is too late.

For Discussion and Writing

Each of the issues identified below is complicated, for matters of war and peace are never simple, never static, particularly when negotiated in an international arena. Most can be seen not just from two points of view, but from many perspectives embedded in the political, economic, religious, ethical, and cultural values of a great variety of individuals, cultures, and countries. In discussing any of the topics identified below, or others stimulated by your reading and thinking, you will find it helpful to talk with your instructor, peers, and to consult reliable outside sources (determined, in part, according to the principles presented in How to Search . . . accessible at the companion website for this text). You will be aiming to write papers informed by accurate information, terms clearly defined, that avoid blanket generalizations and simplistic conclusions.

Rather than trying to cover the gigantic issues embedded in the overall subject, pick a small enough segment of the topic to handle in a well-developed paper. The complex nature of the issues embedded in these subjects—war, peace, maintenance of a healthful productive ecology and environment, national culture, economic survival, values, justice, security, civil liberties, social action, leadership, among others—lends itself to group projects. Each participant could be assigned to research a specific segment of a larger issue and the results could be combined in a co-authored paper. It is advisable, even when discussing issues on which you feel strongly, to avoid either/or thinking, stereotyping, and incendiary language. It is appropriate, however, to build your case on accurate information, principle, and passion—the principles of communication and of life—that have guided the Nobel Prize winners and established exemplary models for nations as well as individual citizens.

Because the events related to human rights, world peace, and world survival occur in political, economic, and natural milieus that are constantly changing, you will need to update your information before discussing any of the topics or their implications or consequences. Be aware that all of them, like any other source of information on any subject—particularly those as incendiary as ethnic, tribal, religious, or national identity; ecology; global warming—contain opinions and other interpretations of fact that support the author's point of view, just as your own writing does. As every reading in *The Essay Connection* illustrates, every author who writes expresses biases; reliable authors also honor the obligation to be fair.

1. Examine the "Universal Declaration of Human Rights." Given the enormous variability of human life, worldwide, how is it possible to encompass human rights in 29 articles? Are there rights treated generally which you think should be broken into more specific components? If so, which ones? Why?

2. After discussing the concepts with a partner, explain in your own words Article 1, "All human beings are born free and equal in dignity and rights. They are endowed with reason and conscience and should act towards one another in a spirit of brotherhood." What do each of these key words mean, "born free and equal," "dignity and rights," "reason and conscience"? What does the "spirit of brotherhood mean"? Is that a right or an obligation?

3. Article 3 says "Everyone has the right to life, liberty and security of person." Has this Right been honored? Always? Everywhere? Frame your answer by

explaining the background of the political events that led to the work of one of the Nobel Peace Prize recipients—Al Gore, Aung San Suu Kyi, Rigoberta Menchú Tum, or the 14th Dalai Lama.

4. Pick any other Right in this Declaration and, using the Internet, find and interpret five instances how it has been honored or violated worldwide in the twenty-first century.

Ways to Think and Write about the Readings

1. Provide an extended definition of *peace*, using examples from the speeches or lives of two or three of the Nobel Peace Prize recipients and supplemented by your own understanding of the term. Is *peace* a constant term, or one that changes with changing interpretations of current events and past history? Why do war, imprisonment, torture, genocide, segregation, and other forms of evil figure so prominently in the struggle to find and maintain peace?

2. Should our first priority be survival of the planet? What can we do, as individuals, as nations, as international alliances, to promote a return to global health? Your discussion will need to acknowledge highly variable standards of living (and availability of resources) around the world, and competing priorities and agendas for allocations of effort, action, money, and other resources.

3. Is world peace possible? Is long-term prosperity possible without peace? Will our quest involve nation with (or against) nation; culture with (or against) culture; technology, economy, or ideology with (or against) its counterpart?

4. What are—or should be—the highest priorities for our private life in the United States? Security? Freedom? Peace and prosperity? A healthful environment? Truly equal opportunity for all (remember, for instance, that as of 2008 there are 2.3 million Americans in prison)? How do—or should—these coincide with our national priorities?

5. There are infinite possibilities for natural disasters (floods, fires, tornadoes, snowstorms) and terrorist attacks in the future. What changes, specific or vague, will these events make in the ways we live our lives, plan for our futures, look at our environment, our neighbors, our friends—and our enemies?

6. What civil liberties are indispensable to life as guaranteed by the Constitution of the United States? How do these compare with rights in "The Universal Declaration of Human Rights" (571–76)? What can we, as individuals and as a nation, do to balance the free and open nature of our hospitable society against needs for protection and security?

7. Is it possible for our country to act unilaterally in attaining any of its aims? To what extent do we live in a world in which the interests of all countries are intimately intertwined? Is it even possible for our country to consider autonomy, in light of its global business interests, dependence on foreign oil, and a host of other products? You might pick a single area—medicine, oil or other natural resources, automobiles, the Internet—and focus your answer on that area.

8. How can we avoid suspicion and paranoia, dividing the world into "us" against "them," and nevertheless be on our guard? Against what must we be on guard?

9. What qualities does it take to become a nationally or internationally distinguished leader? What can the rest of us learn from the experiences of the Nobel Peace Prize winners?

10. What would you personally be willing to sacrifice your time and freedom to attain? Would you lay down your life for a cause? If so, what is that cause and why is it worth this degree of commitment?

Index